Species	mph	km/h	Species
Ostrich (*Struthio camelus*)	16	25·6 (l)	Flying frog (*Hyla venulosa*)
Brown hare (*Lepus europaeus*)	16	25·6	Asiatic elephant (*Elephas maximus*)
Bluefin tuna (*Thunnus thynnus*)	13·3	21·28	Hornet (*Vespa crabro*)
Race horse (*Equus caballus*)	11·8	18·88 (m)	Crabeater seal (*Lobodon carcinophagus*)
Red deer (*Cervus elaphus*)	11	17·6	Bumble bee (*Bombus terrestris*)
Greyhound (*Canis familiaris*)	10–11	16–17·6	Black mamba (*Dendroaspis polylepsis*)
Red fox (*Vulpes vulpes*)	10	16	North American porcupine (*Erithizon dorsatum*)
Bonefish (*Albula vulpes*)	9·3	14·8	Dace (*Leuciscus leuciscus*)
Eastern grey kangaroo (*Macropus giganteus*)	8·7	13·92	Bluebottle fly (*Calliphora* sp)
Emu (*Dromaius novaehollandiae*)	7·5	12	European eel (*Anguilla anguilla*)
Jackdaw (*Corvus monedula*)	7·26	11·61	Honey-bee (*Apis mellifera*)
Mountain zebra (*Equus zebra*)	6	9·6	House rat (*Rattus rattus*)
Swordfish (*Xiphias gladius*)	5·81	9·29	Peacock butterfly (*Nymphalis io*)
American free-tailed bat (*Tadarida brasiliensis*)	5·12	8·19	House fly (*Musca domestica*)
Blue wildebeest (*Connochaetes taurinus*)	4·5	7·2 (n)	Human flea (*Pulex irritans*)
Dragonfly (*Austrophlebia costalis*)	3·6	5·75	Red racer snake (*Coluber flagellum*)
Whippet (*Canis familiaris*)	2·5	4	Common shrew (*Sorex araneus*)
Coyote (*Canis latrans*)	2·46	3·93	Mole (*Talpa europaea*)
Deer botfly (*Cephenemyia pratti*)	2·24	3·58	Yellow-bellied sea snake (*Pelamis platurus*)
Flying fish (*Exocoetus volitans*)	1·17	1·87	House spider (*Tegenaria attrica*)
Killer whale (*Orcinus orca*)	1·12	1·79	Centipede (*Scutiger coleoptrata*)
Hawk-moth (*Sphingidae*)	1·07	1·71 (n)	Millipede (*Diopsiulus regressus*)
Giraffe (*Giraffa camelopardalis*)	0·9	1·44	Mosquito (*Aedes aegypti*)
Black rhinoceros (*Diceros bicornis*)	0·3	0·48	Scorpion (*Scolopendra* sp)
Horse-fly (*Tabanus bovinus*)	0·25	0·4	Shrimp (*Crangon vulgaris*)
Mako shark (*Isurus oxyrinchus*)	0·23	0·36	Giant tortoise (*Geochelone gigantea*)
Fritillary (*Prepona* sp)	0·22	0·35	Rosy boa (*Lichanura roseofusca*)
Sei whale (*Balaenoptera borealis*)	0·098	0·15 (o)	Three-toed sloth (*Bradypus tridactylus*)
Domestic cat (*Felis catus*)	0·031	0·049	Common garden snail (*Helix aspersa*)
Minke whale (*Balaenoptera acutorostrata*)	0·02	0·032	Army ants (*Eciton* sp)
Man (*Homo sapiens*)	0·00039	0·00062 (p)	Neptune crab (*Neptunus pelagines*)
Common dolphin (*Delphinus delphis*)			
Short-finned pilot whale (*Globicephala macrorhynchus*)			
Californian sea lion (*Zalophus californianus*)			
African elephant (*Loxodonta africana*)			
Salmon (*Salmo salar*)			
Blue whale (*Balaenoptera musculus*)			
Mountain goat (*Oreamnos americanus*)			
Arabian camel (*Camelus dromedarius*)			
Pacific leatherback turtle (*Dermochelys coriacea schlegeli*)			
North American lobster (*Homarus amercianus*)			
Six-lined race-runner (*Cnemidophorus sexlineatus*)			
Gentoo penguin (*Pygoscelis papua*)			

(a) 45-degree angle of stoop. Cannot exceed 62·5 miles/h *100 km/h* in level flight.
(b) Vertical dive.
(c) Wind-assisted.
(d) Unconfirmed speeds up to 219·5 miles/h *353·25 km/h* claimed.
(e) Credited with burst speeds up to 65 miles/h *104 km/h*.
(f) Average over 440 yd *402 m*.
(g) Average over 410 yd *375 m*.
(h) Average over 200 yd *183 m*.
(i) Burst speeds up to 46 miles/h *74 km/h* claimed.
(j) Over 15 yd *13·7 m* (flying start).
(k) 14–17 miles/h *22·5–27·4 km/h* when ascending waterfalls.
(l) Gravity glide.
(m) On land.
(n) Jumping.
(o) Timed at speeds up to 1 mile/h *1·61 km/h* in water.
(p) Travelled 101·5 miles *163·3 km* in 29 years.

THE **GUINNESS** BOOK OF

Animal Facts and Feats

THIRD EDITION

"The wild life of to-day is not wholly ours to dispose of as we please. It has been given to us in trust. We must account for it to those who come after us and audit our records."

GERALD L WOOD FZS

GUINNESS SUPERLATIVES LIMITED
2 CECIL COURT, LONDON ROAD, ENFIELD, MIDDLESEX

PHOTO AND ILLUSTRATION CREDITS

Editor: Alex E Reid
Designer: David Roberts

© **Gerald L Wood and Guinness Superlatives Ltd 1982**

Published in Great Britain by
Guinness Superlatives Ltd, 2 Cecil Court,
London Road, Enfield, Middlesex EN2 6DJ

'Guinness' is a registered trade mark of
Guinness Superlatives Ltd

British Library Cataloguing in Publication Data
Wood, Gerald L
The Guinness book of animal facts and feats
– 3rd ed
1. Zoology
I. Title
591   QL 45.2

ISBN 0-85112-235-3

Typeset by Crawley Composition Ltd, in Bembo
Printed and bound in Yugoslavia by Mladinska Knjiga, Ljubljana

Contents

Acknowledgements

The superlatives of the Animal Kingdom are so diverse and prolific that no single person could possibly compile a book of this kind without leaning very heavily on the published researches and experiences of other people. I am, therefore, immensely indebted to the many men and women, some of them anonymous, who have contributed directly or indirectly to the text through their own zoological writings.

Similarly, this book could not have been written without the friendly cooperation of the Zoological Society of London, and I am extremely grateful to the Librarian, Mr Reginald Fish, and his assistant Mrs Susan Bevis, for once again very kindly placing at my disposal a veritable mountain of books, journals and scientific papers.

Special thanks are also due to the many experts at the British Museum (Natural History) who gave so generously of their time to answer my awkward enquiries, and in particular Dr Ailsa M Clark (Echinoderms), Mr John E Hill (Chiroptera), Mr Paul Hillyard (Arachnida), Mr S F Morris (Palaeontology), Dr Paul Whallcy (Insects) and Dr Alwyne Wheeler (Fishes); also Mrs Anne Datta (Zoology Librarian) and Mrs Joyce Pope (Information Officer) for their help with source material.

I would also like to express my special appreciation to the following people who supplied factual data or made suggestions for modifications or additions: Dr F Barker of the Department of Natural Resources (Wildlife), Konedobu, Papua New Guinea; Dr Kenneth J Campbell of the Natural History Museum, Los Angeles; Dr D K Lahiri Chaudhury of Calcutta; Dr Harold G Cogger of the Australian Museum, Sydney; Miss J Covacevich of the Queensland Museum, Brisbane; Prof Barry Cox of King's College, London; Mr A Fuller of the Imperial War Museum, London; Dr Peter C Harper of the University of Canterbury, Christchurch, New Zealand; James Jensen of Brigham Young University, Provo, Utah; Dr F Wayne King of New York Zoological Park (Bronx Zoo); Dr Lloyd Kiff of the Western Foundation of Vertebrate Zoology, Los Angeles; Dr Peter Merrett of the Institute of Terrestrial Ecology at Furzebrook, Dorset; Dr Eiichi Nakamoto of the Amami Kanko pit viper centre, Japan; Miss Elizabeth Pope of the Australian Museum, Sydney; Michael Pope of Port Moresby, Papua New Guinea; Dr John L Randall of Bernice P Bishop Museum, Honolulu; Dr W B Scott of the Huntsman Marine Laboratory, St Andrews, Nova Scotia; Dr Leighton Taylor of Waikiki Aquarium, University of Hawaii; Dr Gilbert Voss of Miami University, Florida; Mr Gwynne Watkins of the Fijian Cultural Centre, Orchid Island; Forrest G Wood of the US Naval Undersea Centre, San Diego and Professor Roger C Wood of Stockton State College, Pomona, New Jersey.

My thanks are also due to Marvin C Jones of San Diego, California for keeping me fully up to date on the longevity records set by captive mammals; David Moon of Crawley, Sussex and David C Williams of Tustin, California for details of superlative insects; E M Nielsen of Columbus, Nebraska for unpublished information on the largest African elephant killed in modern times; John Cheetham of Brighton, Sussex for material on captive giant snakes; Trevor Housby of Lymington, Hampshire; Jesse James Schroeder of New York and Jim McKay of Cairns, Queensland, Australia for data on the great white shark; Gordon Hull of London for statistics on captive gorillas; and F Boothman of Amersham, Bucks for his extremely valuable comments on the maximum sizes and weights reached by some dinosaurs.

Hundreds of other correspondents also very kindly supplied information and material for this new edition, but as the list of their names would be much too long to reproduce here, I hope I will be forgiven if I express my gratitude to them in one collective 'thank you'.

Finally, I wish to thank Mr Alex Reid and Mr David Roberts of Guinness Superlatives Ltd for their considerable assistance during the preparation of this book, and a very special note of appreciation is due to my wife/secretary/critic Susan for her enthusiasm throughout.

Introduction

In this book an attempt has been made to provide the answers to a vast number of interesting questions about animal extremes – answers which the average reader cannot find by consulting generally-available literature – and in the process expose many of the half-truths and exaggerated statements that are synonymous with this fascinating subject.

Since the last edition was published in 1976 an astonishing collection of new and sometimes bizarre superlative items has come to light, and much of this fresh information has been incorporated into the revised text.

Who would have believed, for instance, that the fabulous 'Fenykoevi Elephant', the largest recorded animal of modern times, would lose its title to another enormous bull shot in Angola; that a herd of whooper swans would be spotted by an airline pilot flying at a height of more than 27 000 ft *8230 m*; that a great white shark measuring an incredible 29 ft 6 in *9 m* in length and weighing over 10 000 b *4540 g* would be killed in Azorean waters; that the quahog, a thick-shelled clam, found in the North Atlantic, sometimes lives for 150 years; that a pit viper has been known to fast for more than 3 years; that the world's most valuable butterfly is a hybrid; and that the fossil remains of a vulture-like bird with an estimated wing-span of 24 ft *7·3 m* have recently been discovered in Argentina?

I have also devoted some space to endangered wildlife, because many of the creatures featured in this book are now on the verge of extinction.

The mass destruction of wildlife by man began with the age of discovery. Since 1600 at least 300 of our higher vertebrates have disappeared from the face of the earth, and if present trends continue it has been estimated that by the year 2000 one-fifth of all living species (5–10 million) will have gone forever as their habitats vanish. The world's tropical rain forests, for instance, which are home for about 40 per cent of the world's animal and plant life, are now being destroyed at the rate of 95 000 sq miles *246 000 sq km* a year, and in Britain alone 50 million trees have been lost in the past 25 years. Sea pollution from city sewage and farm pesticides being washed down rivers has also increased dramatically, and in addition an estimated 6 million tonnes of oil are spilled from ships each year.

The time has now come for civilised man – and I use this term in its broadest sense – to turn away from senseless destruction and concentrate instead on painstaking, long-range ecological planning on a world-wide basis. If he treated the living environment with the same reverence that he does the cultural treasures of the past, there would be no problems; unfortunately, however, man's future survival is not dependent on his ability to preserve valuable artifacts, but on his willingness to live with nature in peaceful coexistence, and at the moment there is very little evidence of this.

Finally, if this book can settle arguments on the extremes of the animal world, then its primary purpose will have been achieved. If there are factual errors or any important omissions, I would appreciate having them drawn to my attention.

Mammals

(class Mammalia)

A mammal is a warm-blooded, air-breathing vertebrate or backboned animal. It has a four-chambered heart and the body temperature is maintained by an insulating covering of hair or blubber. The brain is large and well developed. Young are usually born alive and are nourished on milk secreted from their mother's mammary glands.

The earliest known mammals were small, shrew-like creatures (*Morganucodon*, *Megazostrodon* and *Sinoconodon*) which lived about 210 million years ago. They had evolved from certain mammal-like reptiles (*Synapsida*), and their remains have been discovered in Britain, South Africa and China.

Living mammals are divided into (1) the primitive monotremes or egg-laying mammals (Ornithodelphia); (2) the marsupials or mammals with pouches in which the embryonic young are nurtured soon after birth (Metatheria); and (3) the placentals whose young remain in the womb until they have reached a comparatively advanced stage of development (Eutheria).

These infra-classes, in turn, are split up into 18 orders comprising 95 families and 4008 species. The largest order is Rodentia (1591 species) and the smallest Tubulidentata (1 species).

The largest and heaviest mammal in the world, and the largest marine animal ever recorded, is the blue whale or Sibbald's rorqual (*Balaenoptera musculus*).

Two races are recognised: the northern blue whale (*B.m. musculus*) of the North Atlantic and North Pacific Oceans and the larger southern blue whale (*B.m. intermedia*) of the Southern Hemisphere.

Since 1961 Japanese and Russian cetologists (Ichihara, 1961; Zemsky and Boronin, 1964) claim to have established the existence of a pygmy blue whale (*B.m. brevicauda*) in the subantarctic waters of the Indian Ocean near the Kerguelen Islands, but the validity of this subspecific ranking has been questioned by some Western experts. George L Small (1971), for instance, thinks these pygmy blue whales were probably a fairly independent stock of young individuals which podded in the area before migrating to the ice; he also contends that the subspecies designation was a 'fraud' perpetrated by the two countries so that they could carry on hunting blue whales in a lightly exploited segment of the Antarctic Ocean not yet covered by international whaling restrictions, and it is interesting to note that other blue whales described as pygmies (i.e. less than 65 ft *19·8 m* long at sexual maturity) have been discovered in other areas as far apart as South Africa and Australia.

The largest accurately measured blue whale on record (length taken in a straight line parallel to the body axis from the tip of the upper jaw to the notch in the tail flukes) was a female brought into the Cia Argentina de Pesca shore station, South Georgia, some time between 1904 and 1920 which measured 107 Norwegian fot (=110 ft 2½ in *33·59 m*) (Risting, 1922).

Another female caught near the South Shetlands, Falkland Island Dependencies in March 1926 was 109 ft 4¼ in *33·33 m* and an enormous male 107 ft 1 in *32·64 m* (Risting, 1928).

Seven other blue whales (all females) over 100 ft *30·48 m* in length were also taken in the Southern Ocean between 1922 and 1925. The largest specimen measured at South Georgia by the Tonsberg Whaling

Company was 104 ft 2 in *31·75 m* long and had a maximum girth of 45 ft *13·7 m*.

In another series of 711 blue whales measured by members of the Discovery Committee (London) in the Southern Ocean between 1923 and 1926 the lengths were not quite so impressive, the largest male and female measuring 26 m *85 ft 3½ in* and 28·5 m *93 ft 6 in* respectively (Mackintosh, 1942). This later prompted Scheffer (1974) to question the accuracy of the earlier figures, but although some of the measurements may have been obtained by untrained whaling personnel, it is doubtful whether the margin of error much exceeded 1–2 ft *0·3–0·6 m*.

The measurement from the point of the snout to the notch in the tail is known as the 'total' length. The 'over-all' length (projection of the lower jaw to the notch in the tail) is somewhat longer, but as the lower jaw was hardly ever in its natural position when this now protected whale was lying on the flensing platform, this reading was rarely taken (one blue whale measured 'over-all' at Leigh Harbour, South Georgia in *c* November 1913 was 95 ft *29·0 m,* but the 'total' length was 90 ft *27·4 m*).

To complicate matters further, when a baleen whale is on dry land the enormous weight tends to spread the body out in all directions, and in very large individuals this can add several feet to the true measurement.

According to the International Whaling Statistics 13 blue whales measuring between 100 ft and 102 ft *30·48–31·09 m* have been caught in the Southern Hemisphere since 1930.

Shortly after the First World War a female blue whale measuring 102 ft 4 in *31·19 m* was brought into the shore station at Donkergat, Saldanha Bay, Cape Province, South Africa, and another one processed there about the same time was longer than the 100 ft *30·48 m* flensing platform. Both whales were killed in Cape waters (Green, 1958).

On 23 January 1922 a 98 ft *29·9 m* female accidentally entered the Panama Canal from the Caribbean and was killed by machine-gun fire after threatening shipping. The carcase was later towed out to sea and bombed by US Army planes (Harmer, 1923).

Owing to the intensive exploitation of the Antarctic stock between 1925 and 1955 very large females – adult males are approximately six per cent shorter – are now extremely rare. During the 1957–58 season one measuring 96 ft *29·3 m* was taken, but this length was exceptional; by the time the blue whale was given complete protection in the Southern Hemisphere in 1965 the average length of adult females in the catch was only 73 ft *22·3 m*, thus indicating that the whalers had become increasingly dependent on immature animals.

The largest accurately measured northern blue whale on record was probably a 92 ft *28 m* female

brought into the Balaena shore station, Hermitage Bay, Newfoundland in May 1903 (Millais, 1904–06).

In the N Pacific the largest specimen in the 1919–20 American catches was a female measuring 90 ft 2 in *27·48 m*.

During the early days of whaling lengths in excess of 100 ft *30·5 m* were reported for blue whales taken in northern waters, but these measurements were probably exaggerated or taken along the curves of the body. Included in this category are a 120 ft *36·68 m* specimen cast ashore near Utrecht, Holland in *c* 1547; a 105 ft *32 m* long skeleton found near the mouth of the Columbia River, Oregon, USA on 8 January 1806 by Lewis and Clark during their expedition to the Pacific (the whale had been washed ashore a few days previously and the meat had been removed by the local Indians); another one the same length found dead in an inlet in the Davis Strait, Greenland in *c* 1815; a 117 ft *35·7 m* female driven ashore at Assateague Beach, near Snowhill, Maryland, USA in December 1833; another example measuring 105 ft *32 m* which stranded on the island of Lewis, Outer Hebrides in *c* 1870; a 102 ft 8 in *31·29 m* female brought into a shore station on the Murman coast (European Russia) in 1883; and a 102 ft *31·09 m male* killed near Derejford, Iceland in 1896.

Although the bodies of whales are supported by the buoyancy of water which distributes the compressive force over a broad area, even large rorquals cannot exceed certain dimensions. This is because the surface of the lungs, intestines, kidneys, etc. becomes relatively smaller with increases in body mass. Eventually, says Slijper (1962), a point is reached where these organs can no longer cope with essential metabolic processes, and in the case of the blue whale the crunch probably comes somewhere between 110 ft *33·5 m* and 120 ft *36·6 m*.

Four blue whales have been stranded on British coasts since 1912, at least two of them after being harpooned by whalers. The last occurrence (*c* 60 ft *18·3 m*) was at Wick, Highland, Scotland on 15 October 1923 (Harmer, 1927). According to Mr Sidney Brown formerly of the Whale Research Unit of the National Institute of Oceanography (cited by Fraser, 1974), small numbers of blue whales were captured by whalers operating from the Shetland Islands and the Outer Hebrides between 1903 and 1914 and 1920 and 1929. Most of the kills (57 in 1920) occurred west of St Kilda. Later, in 1950–51, a station was reopened at West Loch Tarbert in Harris, Outer Hebrides, and during this period six blue whales were captured.

The first piecemeal weighing of a blue whale took place at Balaena shore station, Hermitage Bay, Newfoundland in May 1903 under the supervision of Dr Frederick A Lucas, Director of the US National Museum, Washington, DC. The rather slender 77 ft

9 in *23·7 m* animal scaled 63 tonnes, including blood, which accounted for 8 per cent of the total weight. The meat weighed 40 tonnes, the blubber 8 tonnes, the blood, viscera and baleen 7 tonnes and the bones 8 tonnes (Andrews, 1916).

On 7 November 1926 a 27·2 m *89 ft 1½ in* long pregnant female was weighed piecemeal by Captain George Sørlle at Stromness shore station, South Georgia. It scaled 122 tonnes (Laurie, 1933).

Since then 40 other blue whales have been weighed piecemeal aboard factory ships in Antarctic waters, 35 of them by the Japanese during the 1947–48 season. Their heaviest specimen, a 27·1 m *89 ft* female, tipped the scales at 136·4 tonnes (blubber 31·9 tonnes, meat 61·43 tonnes, bones 18·5 tonnes including an estimated 8·7 tonnes for the blood and stomach contents). Six of the others (two males, four females) also exceeded 100 tonnes, their weights ranging from 107·8 tonnes to 127·8 tonnes (Nishiwaki, 1950).

Two very large females weighed piecemeal by the Russians during the first cruise of the 'Slava' whaling fleet in 1947 were even heavier. One of them (28·7 m *94 ft 2 in*) tipped the scales at 140 tonnes and yielded 32 tonnes of oil, while the other individual (27·6 m *90 ft 6 in*) weighed an incredible 190 tonnes, making it **the heaviest blue whale on record.** The meat and blubber of this giant weighed 66 tonnes and 30 tonnes respectively, the bones 26 tonnes and the tongue 4.3 tonnes (Voronin, cited by Tomilin, 1967).

According to Lockyer (1976) the estimate of blood loss for large baleen whales during flensing is likely to be at least 6 per cent, which means that the weighings of carcases by parts can only represent about 94 per cent of the true body weight.

The approximate weight (excluding blood) of a blue whale can also be calculated by totalling the number of known-capacity cookers filled by the animal's blubber, meat and bones. A very corpulent 29·5 m *96 ft 9 in* female brought into the shore station at Prince Olaf, South Georgia in 1931 and processed by the Southern Whaling and Sealing Company, was calculated to have weighed 163·7 tonnes using this method. The total weight was believed to have been 174 tonnes (Laurie, 1933).

Another female 91 ft *27·7 m* long killed in Walvis Bay, SW Africa on 13 July 1924 and described as 'very fat', yielded a record 305 barrels of oil weighing 51·85 tonnes (Risting, 1928). Unfortunately this enormous whale was not weighed piecemeal, but on the basis of its oil yield it must have scaled *at least* 200 tonnes!

Working on the principle that the weight is proportional to the cube of the linear dimensions, a blue whale 50 ft *15·24 m* long should weigh about 20 tonnes, and one measuring 100 ft *30·5 m* about 160 tonnes. Because of seasonal fluctuations in the thickness of the oil-rich blubber and muscles, however, there are wide variations in the weights of individual blue whales of approximately the same length. Also, during the seven-month lactation period a large female can lose up to 30 tonnes nursing her calf.

New-born calves measure 6·5–8·7 m *21 ft 3½ in–28 ft 6 in* in length and weigh up to 3 tonnes.

Since 1909 it has been calculated that at least 340 000 blue whales have been killed by man, 328 177 of them in the Antarctic. In 1930 there were still an estimated 100 000 blue whales roaming the world's oceans, and in the 1930–31 season alone 29 410 were caught in the Antarctic (Tomilin, 1967). By 1953, however, the southern stocks had been reduced to an estimated 15 000–20 000 through unrestricted slaughter, and in 1962 the blue whale was in a critical condition, with only an exploitable stock of 4000 left in the entire Antarctic (it had been protected in the N Atlantic since 1960). But despite the seriousness of the situation three more years were to pass before the blue whale was given full protection in the Antarctic, followed by the N Pacific in 1966, and during that time a further 3912 blues were killed. Finally, in 1967, all the members of the International Whaling Commission, including Russia and Japan, were banned from catching blues anywhere in the world. The Japanese promptly got round this by starting up whaling companies in Chile and Peru, both then non-member countries, and continued killing blue whales under flags of convenience. No blues have been killed in the N Atlantic and Arctic (excluding the Azores, Madeira and Spain) since 1969, but the species was listed in Spain's 1970–71 catch of 89 baleen whales. Nine others were also caught elsewhere during the same season, including five in the Indian Ocean. In the 1972–73 season seven blues were captured (International Whaling Statistics). In 1978 a 22 m *72 ft 2 in* long immature female was washed up dead near Lima, Peru. It had a gaping wound near the tail which had almost certainly been caused by a harpoon.

In 1980 the Peruvian representative at the annual meeting of the IWC announced that his country was planning to issue itself with a scientific permit to catch two or three blue whales in the summer of 1981 because the museums of Peru (and Ecuador) were crying out for skeletons. When Canada and the USA hastily offered substitutes, the official then explained that the permit was also needed to determine whether there was a link – as a result of competition for the same food – between the increasing number of baleen whales in Peruvian waters and the massive decline in the anchovy population!

Scientific assessment of existing stocks of blue whales indicate that the *exploitable* stock in the Antarctic is now about 8000, with another 1500–2500 in

The tremendously bulky right whale, which has been credited with piecemeal weights up to 106 tonnes.

the N Pacific and *c* 500 in the N Atlantic. As the *total* stocks of blue whales are about 50 per cent higher than exploited stocks, which do not include undersized specimens and females with calves, the world population (including a few thousand 'pygmy' blues) is now believed to be somewhere in the region of 21 000–23 000, but these figures are subject to error and are probably on the high side. The optimum population level for this species is reported to be about 60 000.

The only other whale credited with a piecemeal weight of more than 100 tonnes is the North Pacific right whale (*Eubalaena sieboldi*). In *c* 1960 10 specimens were caught in the Sea of Okhotsk under a special licence granted by the Russian Government and the largest, a 17·4 m *57 ft* female, scaled 106·5 tonnes inclusive of blood (Klumov, 1962). This species has been reliably measured up to 70 ft *21·4 m* (female) in the waters off Kamchatka, NE Russia, and Omura *et al* (1969) have calculated that one measuring 20·7 m *68 ft* would weigh 135 tonnes.

The Greenland right whale or bowhead (*Balaena mysticetus*) is even bulkier, but this animal has never been weighed piecemeal. Coffey (1977) says it grows to 20 m *65 ft 7½ in* in length and weighs over 122 tonnes, but this latter figure must have been based on mathematical formula. Of 322 bowheads killed by Scoresby (1820) the largest measured 58 ft 9 in *17·9 m*, but he did mention one caught near Spitzbergen which was a full 70 ft *21·3 m*. In 1963 a bowhead measuring 64 ft *19·5 m* was caught off Point Hope, N Alaska.

The largest marine mammal ever held in captivity was a female Pacific grey whale (*Eschrichtius gibbosus*) named 'Gigi' at Sea World, Mission Bay,

San Diego, California, USA. She was captured in Scammon's Lagoon, Baja California, Mexico, on 13 March 1971 by a collecting expedition from Sea World and arrived (by boat) in San Diego 4 days later. She was then approximately 6–10 weeks old and measured 18 ft 2 in *5·54 m* in length (weight 4300 lb *1950 kg*). By 30 March she had increased to 19 ft 10 in *6·05 m* and 5000 lb *2268 kg*, and 10 weeks later she was 22 ft *6·7 m* and 7500 lb *3402 kg*. On 13 March 1972, when she was one year old, and rapidly outgrowing her surroundings, Gigi was returned to the sea about 4 miles *6·4 km* north of Port Loma. She was then 27 ft *8·23 m* long and weighed an estimated 14 000 lb *6350 kg*. Her release was timed to coincide with the annual 6000 mile *9660 km* northwards migration of the grey whale herds from the calving grounds in the lagoons of Baja California to the Arctic. The whale was fitted with a compact radio and instrumentation package, and for five days her movements were tracked by a research vessel and aircraft as she joined up with the herd and moved northward. In the Autumn of 1979 Gigi was sighted in San Ignacio Lagoon, Baja, California with a newborn calf.

The largest marine mammal held in captivity today is a bull killer whale (*Orcinus orca*) named 'Orky' at Marineland, Palos Verdes Estates, California, USA. He was captured in Pender Harbour, British Columbia, Canada on 12 April 1968 and was moved to Marineland by air on 10 May. At that time he was 17 ft *5·2 m* long and weighed 4000–4500 lb *1814–2041 kg*. By January 1976 he had increased to 23 ft 8 in *7·21 m* and 11 000 lb *4989 kg*, and in October 1980 he measured 26 ft 6 in *8·08 m* and weighed an *estimated* 14 000 lb *6350 kg*. His mate 'Corky' is 20 ft 6 in *6·25 m* long and weighs 7000 lb *3175 kg*.

The largest animal ever killed underwater (as opposed to on the surface) was a 24 ft *7·3 m* long

Northern bottlenosed whale (*Hyperoodon ampullatus*) weighing 3½ tonnes. A diver sent down to investigate the damage done to a barge which suddenly sank off the coast near Flushing, Netherlands on 24 August 1958, found the animal trapped inside the hull and killed it with a knife (Bruyns, 1971).

The smallest totally marine mammal if body weight is used as the criterion of size is probably Commerson's dolphin (*Cephalorhynchus commersoni*), also known as Le Jacobite, which is found in the waters off the southern tip of South America and possibly Kerguelen Island in the Indian Ocean.

In one series of six specimens received at Duisburg Zoo, W Germany in 1978 after being captured off S Patagonia two mature females weighed 23 kg *50·7 lb* (length 1·39 m *4 ft 6¾ in*) and 28 kg *61·7 lb* (length 1·4 m *4 ft 7 in*) respectively, although they were not in good condition at the time (Wolfgang Gewalt, pers. comm.). Later the same year four more Commerson's dolphins were seized by government agents in New York City after they had been flown into the USA from Argentina without proper documentation. The only mature animal was a male which measured 1.36 m *4 ft 5½ in* in length and weighed 27 kg *59½ lb*, while the heaviest female (length 1.42 m *4 ft 8 in*) scaled 35 kg *77 lb*. Both dolphins were in fair condition (Spotte, Radcliffe and Dunn, 1979).

The widely distributed finless black porpoise (*Neophocaena phocaenoides*) is another strong contender. In one series of six specimens caught at the mouth of the Indus, W Pakistan the weights ranged from 25·4 kg *56 lb* (small male) to 38·1 kg *84 lb* (large female) and the lengths from 1.4 m *4 ft 7 in* to 1·55 m *5 ft 1 in* (Pilleri, 1972).

Heaviside's dolphin (*Cephalorhynchus heavisidei*), which lives off the Cape of Good Hope, South Africa, and the White-headed dolphin (*C. albifrons*) from New Zealand waters are also pygmies (maximum length 1·3 m *4 ft 3 in*), but both these species are bulkier and have been weighed up to 40 kg *88 lb*.

According to Nishiwaki (1972) the smallest known cetacean is the Tucuxi (*Sotalia fluviatilis*) of the Amazon and its tributaries which does not exceed 1·2 m *3 ft 11 in*, but this statement is in error. Two sexually mature animals measured 1·48 m *4 ft 10¼ in* (male) and 1·46 m *4 ft 9½ in* (female) respectively (Harrison and Brownell, 1971), and greater lengths have been reported for specimens taken off the Brazilian coast. It has recently been suggested that there may be two separate sub-populations of this species, one freshwater and one marine, the latter identified by its larger size and darker colour, but this has not yet been confirmed.

Until quite recently the greatest recorded depth to

The delightful Commerson's dolphin, probably the world's smallest cetacean if weight is the criterion of size.

which a whale had dived was 3720 ft *1134 m* by a 47 ft *14·32 m* bull sperm whale (*Physeter macrocephalus*) found entangled with a submarine telegraphic cable running between Santa Elana, Ecuador and Chorillo, Peru on 14 October 1955 (Heezen, 1957). It is now known, however, that large bulls can dive much deeper than this in pursuit of food. Berzin (1972), for instance, mentions a telegraph cable linking up Lisbon, Portugal and Malaga, Spain, which was found damaged at a depth of 2200 m *7218 ft*. 'In this case', he writes, 'there was no intact corpse in the cable, but from the character of the damage and the remains of the body it was assumed that . . . the culprit was a sperm whale.'

In 1970 American scientists, by triangulating the location clicks of sperm whales, calculated that the *maximum* depth reached by this species was 2500 m *8202 ft*. At that time, however, they were unaware that an even deeper dive had been recorded in South African waters the previous year.

On 25 August 1969 Dr Malcolm Clarke (pers. comm.) of the National Institute of Oceanography, Wormley, Surrey accompanied a pilot on spotter patrol for the Union Whaling Company at Durban.

During the flight he carried out some observations on two large sperm whales in an effort to determine the duration of their dives. One of them remained below for 53 minutes and the other for a record-breaking 1 hour 52 minutes. Soon afterwards both whales were caught by the whaling fleet, and inside the stomach of the whale which had remained submerged for nearly two hours were found two small sharks, which must have been swallowed about an hour earlier. These were later identified as *Scymnodon sp.*, a small family of selachians which are restricted to the sea-floor. At this point from land – 149 km *93 miles* – the depth of water is in excess of 3193 m *10476 ft*, which now suggests that the sperm whale sometimes reaches a depth of over 3048 m *10000 ft* when seeking food.

When a sperm whale goes into a deep dive the lungs collapse completely at the 100 m *328 ft* mark (=11 atmospheres) and the air is forced into the more rigid parts of the respiratory tract. When this happens the invasion rate of nitrogen into the blood is reduced to zero, and in this condition the animal can descend with perfect safety to any depth beyond because further increases of pressure will have no effect on its virtually incompressible body. By the same token, it is also able to make rapid ascents from deep dives without suffering any discomfort from 'caisson sickness' because it does not breathe air at pressure in deep water, and this comes in very handy when it spends too long below and nearly exhausts its oxygen supply.

The only other marine mammals definitely known to dive deeper than 3000 ft *914 m* are the northern bottlenosed whale (*Hyperoodon ampullatus*) of the N Atlantic, the Berardius (*Berardius bairdii*) of the N Pacific and – rather surprisingly – the killer whale. In 1965 a bull of the latter species was found entangled in a telegraph cable off Vancouver Island, British Columbia, Canada at a depth of 3378 ft *1029 m* (Scheffer, 1970).

Scoresby claimed that the Greenland right whale could descend to 4800 ft *1463 m* because that amount of harpoon line was frequently paid out, but when Ommanney (1971) was working in the Antarctic he said similar lengths were often taken by whales in quite shallow water. The northern bottlenosed whale and the berardius, on the other hand, always dive vertically when they are wounded, and there is one record of a harpooned berardius allegedly descending to 2400 m *7874 ft*.

The shark-like pygmy sperm whale (*Kogia breviceps*) probably also has a deep-diving ability.

Blue and fin whales rarely descend to depths greater than 100 m *328 ft* because the krill on which they feed is not found in abundance much below this level (Kooyman and Andersen, 1969), but when they are frightened they can dive much deeper. In one series of tests which involved fixing depth gauges to harpoons Scholander (1940) found that fin whales returned unaffected from dives down to 1164 ft *355 m*. On another occasion a harpooned fin whale dived to a depth of 500 m *1640 ft* and broke its 'neck' when it hit the bottom (Howell, 1930).

The fastest swimming marine mammals are the streamlined rorquals and dolphins, where the body is beautifully designed for low resistance.

The fastest swimming whale over short distances is the Sei whale (*Balaenoptera borealis*) which, when wounded, 'dashes off at a tremendous pace for perhaps a third of a mile or less' (Andrews, 1916). The same observer says this species can attain a velocity of 26 knots (30 miles/h *48 km/h*) during its initial rush on the surface.

The minke or piked whale is also extremely fast when danger threatens, and a family group of three has been timed at 25 knots (28·77 miles/h *46·3 km/h*) in South African waters (Gambell, 1968).

Both these rorquals have a normal cruising speed of 9–13 knots (10·4–15·0 miles/h *16·7–24·1 km/h*) which they can sustain for hours.

During the 1947–48 whaling season Gawn (1948) carried out some speed tests on the blue whale in Antarctic waters. He discovered that it could maintain a velocity of 20 knots (23 miles/h *37·0 km/h*) for 10 minutes when frightened, 14·5 knots (16·74 miles/h *26·9 km/h*) for 2 hours and could keep ahead of a whaling ship travelling at 10 knots (11·5 miles/h *18·5 km/h*) all day.

Fin whales can swim at a steady 18 knots (20·7 miles/h *33·3 km/h*) for 30 minutes before tiring, but they are generally slower than blues of the same size.

The fastest marine mammal over short distances is the killer whale which, despite its name, is classified as a dolphin. On 12 October 1958 a bull measuring an estimated 20–25 ft *6·10–7·62 m* in length was timed at 30 knots (34·5 miles/h *55·5 km/h*) as it approached the SS *Monterey* in the E Pacific. It then circled the ship, which was travelling at 20·6 knots (23·7 miles/h *38 km/h*) for 20 minutes before continuing on its original course. (Johannessen and Harder, 1960). Other observers (Maxwell, 1952; Blond, 1954) believe that this very powerful predator can reach 35 knots (40·28 miles/h *64·8 km/h*) in short bursts when chasing fast-moving prey like the minke whale.

There is also a record of a school of short-finned pilot whales (*Globicephala macrorhynchus*) circling a US Navy vessel moving at 22 knots (25·3 miles/h *40·7 km/h*) for several days in the tropical Pacific. 'They would pass the ship, go way out in front, and go back in the wake to look for food', said one of the ship's officers who watched their progress.

Of the smaller dolphins, the swiftest is probably

the common dolphin (*Delphinus delphis*), which has been timed at 24 knots (27·6 miles/h *44 km/h*) over 100 m *328 ft* (Tomilin, 1967). The Red Sea bottle-nosed dolphin (*Tursiops abusalam*) and the Pacific white-sided dolphin (*Lagenorhynchus obliquidens*) can elude boats making less than 22 knots (25·3 miles/h *40·7 km/h*) and the spotted dolphin (*Stenella attenuata*) and the euphrosyne dolphin (*Stenella coeruleoalba*) have been clocked at 21·4 knots (24·6 miles/h *39·6 km/h*) and 21 knots (24·17 miles/h *38·9 km/h*) respectively. The Pacific bottlenosed dolphin (*Tursiops truncatus gilli*), the Ceylon dolphin (*Stenella alope*) and the pygmy killer (*Feresa attenuata*) may also exceed 20 knots (23 miles/h *37·0 km/h*) (Nishiwaki, 1972; Bruyns, 1971).

As pelagic species have a very large blood-oxygen content, this might explain some of the more exceptional performances.

Speeds of up to 30–32 knots (34·5–36·8 miles/h *55·6–59·3 km/h*) have been reported for dolphins (probably *D. delphis*) riding the bow waves of destroyers, but this is not true swimming. In this form of locomotion the dolphin attains its propulsive power from the moving vessel and is 'squeezed' along by the water pressure; in other words, it is a form of surfing which requires little or no effort.

The longest migrations made by any mammal are those of the grey whale (*Eschrichtius gibbosus*). In the late autumn the California stock leaves its feeding grounds in the Bering Sea and travels 6000 miles *9650 km* southwards along the western American coastline to the calving and breeding lagoons off Baja, California and Mexico. The following spring it moves northwards again along the same route to the feeding grounds.

The largest single aggregation of cetaceans on record was probably a huge school of migrating common dolphins (*Delphinus delphis ponticus*) followed by observer aircraft in the Black Sea, European USSR. It contained an estimated 100 000 animals.

Although absolute age determination in whales has not yet been resolved, it is probable that the longest-lived mammals after man (116+ years) are the blue and fin whales. Studies of the alternating light and dark layers or laminae found in the wax-like plug deposited in the outer ear indicate a maximum life span of *c* 90 years under natural conditions (Roe, 1967; Nishiwaki, 1972), but results for baleen whales are not always consistent, and it is still not certain whether one or two growth layers represent a year of age.

A bull killer whale known as 'Old Tom', who had distinctive physical characteristics – a broad, green-white band encircling his body and an unusually shaped dorsal fin – was reportedly seen every winter from 1843 to 1930 in Twofold Bay, Eden, NSW, Australia. This claim (90+ years) has never been fully authenticated, but as the complete skeleton of this giant dolphin is preserved in the local museum it would be an easy matter to establish his age by counting the number of growth rings laid down in the dentine of the teeth. In the sperm whale these rings are laid down annually, and this probably applies to all toothed cetaceans.

The greatest age recorded for a captive cetacean is 29+ years for an Atlantic bottlenosed dolphin (*Tursiops truncatus*) which was still alive in 1982. It arrived at Marine Studios, Florida, USA in 1943 (M Jones, pers. comm.).

The largest living terrestrial animal is the African bush or savannah elephant (*Loxodonta africana*). The average adult bull stands 10 ft 6 in *3·2 m* at the shoulder and weighs 5.25 tonnes. The average adult cow is much smaller, standing 8 ft 6 in *2·59 m* at the shoulder and weighing about 2.5 tonnes.

At one time the bush elephant ranged over the entire African continent, but commercial exploitation, the expansion of cultivated land and the degeneration of grassy plains to desert have greatly reduced its range over the past one hundred years. Today its numbers (1 343 000) are largely concentrated in wildlife parks and game reserves in 35 African countries, but out of this total only five states have a stable or growing elephant population. The most important short-term threat to the survival of this species is ivory poaching (100 elephants=1 tonne of ivory), but despite stringent anti-poaching laws the trade is still flourishing, particularly in Zaire, where there are an estimated 377 000 animals.

The largest accurately measured African bush

E M Nielsen with the record-sized elephant he shot in southern Angola.

elephant on record, and the largest recorded land mammal of modern times, was an enormous bull shot by E M Nielsen, an American big-game hunter, 25 miles *40 km* NE of Mucusso, S Angola, on 7 November 1974. This giant measured 13 ft 8 in *4·17 m* in a projected line from the highest point of the shoulder to the base of the extended forefoot whilst lying on its side (Rowland Ward, 1975), thus indicating that its standing height must have been about 13 ft *4·0 m* (height measurements of wild elephants taken after death are about five per cent greater than the living height because the great weight tends to spread the body out laterally). Other measurements included: overall length 35 ft *10·7 m* (tip of extended trunk to end of extended tail); forefoot circumference 5 ft 11 in *1·80 m*; computed weight 26 998 lb *12·25 tonnes.*

According to Nielsen (pers. comm.) he and his colleague Alfredo Ferrari, a professional white hunter, first sighted the huge animal when they were tracking a small group of elephants through fairly dense bush late in the day. The grey colossus was in the company of ten other mature bulls, and fairly towered above the rest. For the two men, however, size was only of secondary importance. They were after a good tusker, and as it so happened this particular elephant fitted the bill nicely.

'As the bull passed close to our position', said Nielsen, 'I shot the first round . . . into the lower front chest of the elephant, and then proceeded to shoot three more into him as he started running off into the deepening gloom. I then quickly reloaded . . . and followed Alfredo as he chased after the herd in an attempt to catch up with the wounded bull. Upon reaching the elephants again we found they had moved into a densely-wooded area where they stood in a circle around their wounded companion . . . I then moved into a new position approximately 75 yards from the bull and tried a brain shot . . . but the bullet went a little too high . . . However, upon this frontal shot the bull turned slowly to the left and started to walk away. As the other elephants began to panic, I put three more solid bullets into various parts of his body. A few seconds later the bull crashed to the ground . . . I then moved in and finished him with shots through the heart and spine.'

The tusks (one broken) of this pachyderm measured 7 ft 5 in *2·26 m* and 5 ft 4 in *1·63 m* in length respectively (combined weight 165 lb *75 kg*), and it was only later when the two men measured this mountain of flesh that they realised just how huge this elephant was.

Nineteen years earlier, in November 1955, J J Fenykoevi, the Hungarian big-game hunter, had shot another colossal bull in the same area. This one measured 13 ft 2 in *4·01 m* on its side, which means it must have stood about 12 ft 6 in *3·81 m* at the shoulder. Other measurements included an over-all

length of 33 ft 2 in *10·11 m* and a girth of 19 ft 8 in *5·99 m* (measurement taken just behind the elbow and withers). The computed weight was 24 000 lb *10·9 tonnes.* The skin of this elephant reportedly weighed more than 4000 lb *1814 kg* alone and required a truckload of salt for preservation in the field. Fenykoevi says his crew of 23 native porters could not lift it between them.

On 6 March 1959 the mounted specimen was put on display in the rotunda of the US National Museum in Washington, DC.

In August 1960 P K van der Byl shot another huge elephant in the Cuando River region, southern Angola. This measured 12 ft 6½ in *3·82 m* on its side (standing height about 11 ft 11 in *3·63 m*), with over-all length 29 ft 11½ in *9·13 m* (Rowland Ward, 1962).

Before making his trip to the Dark Continent Nielsen said he researched various hunting areas, and most professionals agreed that the African elephant reached its maximum size in southern Angola, which is still largely unexplored, and in Damaraland in Namibia where a small population of the exceptionally tall desert elephant still survives. This latter animal has relatively longer legs and larger feet than other elephants, and one enormous bull shot recently measured 13 ft 6 in *4·11 m* between pegs (standing height *c*12 ft 10 in *3·41 m*). Tusk size in this extraordinary elephant, however, is very much smaller than that found in other parts of the continent.

Although Angola may now have a complete monopoly of abnormally large elephants, bulls of comparable size have been recorded in other parts of Africa in the past. At one time the Knysna Forest, Cape Province, South Africa was famous for its giant strain of elephants and this is confirmed by the height of the trees off which they browsed in the district. One enormous bull shot by the Duke of Edinburgh (Prince Alfred, second son of Queen Victoria) in this area in *c* 1875 was almost identical in size to the 'Fenykoevi Elephant', measuring 13 ft *4·0 m* at the shoulder and 32 ft *9·8 m* over-all. The girth of this individual was given as 28 ft *8·5 m*, but this extreme figure must have referred to post-mortem expansion of the belly (Bisset, 1875). Another Knysna bull shot by Major P J Pretorius (1947), the famous South African hunter, in *c* 1920 reportedly measured 12 ft 6 in *3·81 m* at the shoulder, but as the over-all length was only 22 ft 6 in *6·86 m* (*sic*) there was obviously something wrong somewhere (the standing height to over-all length ratio is 1–2·5). According to official museum records in Cape Town, where this specimen was stuffed and put on display, the shoulder height is only 9 ft 4 in *2·84 m* and indicates an immature animal.

Mention should also be made of the legendary 'Dhlulamithi' (Taller than the Trees), Rhodesia's greatest tusker, who was tragically shot at Nuanetsi in August 1967 after he had strayed temporarily from the Gona-Re-Zhou game reserve where he was a protected animal. Experienced game-rangers familiar with this lord of the bush said he stood at least 12 ft *3·7m* at the shoulder and was built on a massive scale, but because of the embarrassment caused by the killing of this celebrated beast, the whole episode was hushed up by the Rhodesian Government and no field measurements were taken. The tusks, however, were secured (naturally), and later presented by Col V R Verster, who fired the fatal shot, to the South African Embassy in Washington, DC. They measure 8 ft 6¼ in *2·60m* and 7 ft 7½ in *2·32m* respectively, the combined weight being 239 lb *108 kg* (Wright, 1970).

Much further north A Haig shot a bull on the Blue Nile (Sudan) which was estimated by him – on the basis of the circumference of the elephant's forefoot – to have measured over 13 ft *4·0m*. The ears of this animal were enormous, measuring 6 ft 5½ in *1·97m* in vertical diameter, and 4 ft 1½ in *1·26m* in transverse diameter, and probably constitute a *record* in themselves (Lydekker, 1907).

The shoulder height of an adult African bush elephant corresponds approximately to the width across the expanded ears or twice the circumference of the forefoot plus ten per cent.

In *c* November 1969 Dr Sylvia Sikes (1972), the leading authority on the African elephant, shot a huge bull ('the biggest elephant I have ever set eyes on') near Portofino, Lake Chad, Central Africa, which measured 11 ft 9¾ in *3·60m* at the shoulder. This individual, a member of an eight-bull herd which lived in the swamps along the Nigerian shores, had a forefoot circumference of 5 ft 11 in *1·82m* (equivalent to a shoulder height of 13 ft *4·0m*), thus indicating that swamp and lagoon-dwelling elephants have disproportionately large feet owing to the nature of their habitat. The weight of this giant was calculated to be 6·2 tonnes *13 669 lb* based on a 0·5 g *0·018 oz* heart-weight/100 g *3·54 oz* body-weight index.

Although the bull elephants of northern Kenya are renowned for their large tusks, their physical size is less than average, and ample proof of this was provided by the celebrated 'Ahmed' of Marsabit Mountain Reserve, who was described by the world's newspapers, television and certain commercial tour operators as 'the world's largest living elephant'. The only thing exceptional about this animal, however, apart from his magnificent tusks, was the fact that President Kenyatta of Kenya issued a protective decree in 1970 which virtually made this elephant a living national monument. Ahmed died on 17 January 1974 through a combination of old age and deterioration of feed and his body is now on display in the National Museum of Kenya, Nairobi.

The famous 'Jumbo', the largest elephant ever held in captivity. This picture was taken in 1882.

According to the Director, Dr A Mackay (pers. comm.) the mounted specimen stands a very modest 9 ft 10 in *3·00m* at the shoulder.

The largest African bush elephant ever held in captivity was probably the famous 'Jumbo', who was acquired by London Zoo on 26 June 1865 from the Menagerie du Jardin des Plantes, Paris in exchange for an Indian rhinoceros. (The elephant had been caught originally south of Lake Chad in the French Sudan.) In 1879 he measured 10 ft 9 in *3·28m* at the shoulder, and in January 1882, when he was purchased by Phineas T Barnum, the famous American showman, he allegedly stood 11 ft *3·4m* at the shoulder (weight 6·5 tonnes) and could reach – forefeet off the ground – an object 26 ft *7·9m* above him with his trunk (Bartlett, 1899).

The true standing height of Jumbo will never be known for certain because Barnum refused to allow anyone to measure his prize exhibit. He claims the elephant measured 11 ft 7 in *3·53m* in March 1883 and 12 ft *3·7m* shortly before his death on 15 September 1885 (hit by a train at St Thomas, Ontario, Canada), but both these figures were exaggerated for commercial reasons. According to 'Professor' Henry Ward of Ward's Natural Science Establishment in Rochester, NY, who was asked by Barnum to mount Jumbo for exhibition purposes, the elephant measured 11 ft 4 in *3·45m* on his side (maximum girth 16 ft 4 in *4·98m*), which suggests that this pachyderm must have stood about 10 ft 9 in *3·28m* in life as reported earlier. This measurement was also confirmed by Robert Gillfort, a pole-jumper with the Barnum and Bailey Circus who, in 1883, attempted to find out the true height of Jumbo by casually standing his pole alongside the elephant and carefully noting the mark on the wood that corresponded with the animal's highest point at the shoulder (Hornaday, 1911). The skeleton of Jumbo, which Barnum presented to the American Museum of Natural History, New York in 1889 has a mounted shoulder height of 10 ft 5¼ in *3·18 m*.

After touring North America for two years the model of Jumbo was dismantled and the 1538 lb *698 kg* hide reconstructed, stuffed and sent to the Barnum Museum at Tufts University, Massachusetts, where it was destroyed by fire in April 1975.

Another bull named 'Tembo' received at Copenhagen Zoo, Denmark in 1936 as a three-year-old and destroyed in August 1970 after turning violent, was also of comparable size although no measurements were taken after death. This animal had to lower his head when passing through his stall entrance (height 3·34 m *10 ft 11½ in*) (Arne S Dyhrberg, pers. comm.), and must have stood nearly 11 ft *3·4 m* in life.

Captive elephants, incidentally, should be measured like a horse, with a standard cross and bar, and not by means of a tape stretched over the rounded muscles of the shoulder.

The largest cow African bush elephant ever held in captivity was probably an individual named 'Sudana'. She was captured on the SE slopes of Mount Kilimanjaro, Tanzania on 6 May 1929 when aged two years, and arrived at New York Zoological Gardens on 9 November 1931. In 1947 she measured 8 ft 7 in *2·62 m* at the shoulder, and recorded the same height on 15 September 1958. She was destroyed on 11 August 1962 after being rendered immobile by arthritis (Crandall, 1964).

This size was matched by the famous 'Dicksie' of London Zoo (received October 1945 from Kenya) who measured 8 ft 7 in *2·62 m* in July 1965 when aged 25. She died tragically on 6 September 1967 from heart failure after falling (or was she pushed by a jealous comrade?) into the surrounding dry moat.

The African forest elephant (*Loxodonta africana cyclotis*), which is found in the rain forests of Guinea, French Equatorial Africa and the Congo, is a shorter animal than the bush elephant, although this subspecies is stockier and proportionately heavier.

The greatest standing height recorded for an African forest elephant is 3 m *9 ft 10 in* for a bull measured at Api by Commandant Pierre Offermann (1953) while Director of the Belgian Congo army-run elephant training centre. This centre was at Api from 1900 until 1926, and then at Gongala-na-Bodia.

A 2·85 m *9 ft 4¼ in* bull shot at the Api station in 1906 and immediately cut up and weighed was found to total an astonishing 6 tonnes – the weight of the blood and stomach contents was estimated at 340 kg *750 lb* – making it heavier than the average adult bush elephant (i.e. 5·25 tonnes).

The status of the African pygmy elephant (*Loxodonta africana pumilio*), which is found in the swampy forests of Gabon and the Congo, is still uncertain, but although this animal has been credited with subspecific rank (Noack, 1906; Hornaday, 1923), the modern consensus of opinion is that pygmy elephants (maximum shoulder height 6 ft 8 in *2·03 m*) are a race of undersized *forest elephants* living in an unfavourable environment.

The greatest weight recorded for an elephant is 6·64 tonnes for a huge bull shot by Captain Hewlett (with Dr G Crile) near Ngaruka, Tanganyika on 26 December 1935 (Benedict and Lee, 1938; Crile, 1941). The body was cut up into 176 parcels and weighed piecemeal on scales capable of registering 600 lb *272 kg*. The skin – except that of the four legs from the knees down and the tail – weighed 2005 lb *909 kg*, the stomach and intestines (with contents) 2034 lb *923 kg*, the muscles and fat 4365 lb *1980 kg*, the liver 235 lb *106·5 kg*, the heart 57·5 lb *27 kg* and the kidneys 40 lb *18 kg*. Because there was considerable loss of blood and body fluids due to evaporation and spillage into the gravel and sand of the dried river course where the animal fell, Dr Crile, an American endocrinologist, allowed 10 per cent of the total weight for seepage. It is reasonable to assume that this elephant must have weighed nearly 7 tonnes when alive.

The shoulder height was not recorded, but as the front foot measured 60 in *1·52 m* in circumference, it must have stood about 11 ft *3·4 m* in life.

In 1965 a relationship between dressed hind-leg weight and live body-weight was demonstrated for 26 bush elephants (13 of each sex) killed in the Murchison Falls National Park during cropping operations by Uganda National Parks rangers; and another 12 elephants (6 of each sex) were killed in Kenya's Tsavo National Park the following year to check the accuracy of the earlier findings. According to Laws *et al* (1967) the hind-leg weights of the 38 elephants accounted for between 5·3 and 6·3 per cent of the total body mass and could be used to predict live weight more accurately than by carefully weighing the animal in pieces with considerable blood and fluid losses. In the Murchison Falls experiment the greatest weight recorded for a dressed hind-leg was 308·4 kg *679 lb 14 oz* for a bull which weighed 5 tonnes, while in Tsavo National Park the maximum weight was 294 kg *648 lb* for another 5 tonne bull.

There is also a relationship between blood-free heart weight and total body mass (see page 15).

A few months before his death 'Tembo' (see this page) scaled 6·25 tonnes on a controlled weigh-bridge. **The greatest weight recorded for a cow bush elephant** is 4·39 tonnes in the case of 'Sudana' (see this page), who was euthanased on 11 August 1962. The heaviest wild specimen was one killed in Murchison Falls National Park on 16 January 1964 which weighed 3·23 tonnes (shoulder height 8 ft 6 in *2·59 m*).

Although the elephant is supposed to have an inborn fear of mice, and will panic if one of these creatures approaches its trunk, this is just a popular myth. It is, however, wary of small active animals like the mongoose or squirrel, showing alarm if a sudden darting movement is made in its immediate vicinity.

In an interesting experiment carried out at Frankfurt Zoo, W Germany a few years ago a group of tethered elephants showed no signs of fear whatsoever when a baby mouse was introduced to them; in fact, they sniffed the rodent with their trunks wide open and in such a position that if the mouse had decided to crawl into one of these nasal passages it could easily have done so. A rat and rabbit also drew the same reaction and behaviourists concluded that a small mammal foolish enough to crawl into the end of the trunks would be vigorously blown out and splattered over the walls of the stall. Sometimes, however, the freak accident does occur and in one case reported from Africa the elephant died as the result of such an encounter.

One evening Rennie Bere (1966) and a member of his staff found a dead cow elephant in Queen Elizabeth National Park, Uganda, lying on top of a very young bull calf which had obviously been crushed by her weight. There were no external injuries, but the mother was bleeding profusely from the mouth and the end of the trunk, and there was a trail of clotted blood leading back for 40 yards *36·6 m*. The animal had apparently been feeding normally when the tragedy occurred, but managed to stagger a short distance before toppling over. A makeshift post-mortem revealed that one of the lungs was badly congested, and the immediate cause of death appeared to be a burst blood vessel. The question was – how did it happen? Bere thinks a small tree-mouse may have been accidentally sucked up by the elephant while it was drawing in mud or sand with which to spray itself. The panic-stricken beast had then tried unsuccessfully to clear the blockage by violently beating its trunk against a tree, and died from apoplexy as a result. Unfortunately, no one thought of this possibility until a few days later, so the inside of the trunk was not examined.

At least eight races of the Asiatic elephant (*Elephas maximus*) have been described (Deraniyagala, 1955), but only four are generally recognised. They are: *E.m. indicus* of India, Burma, Thailand, Vietnam and Borneo (introduced a few hundred years ago); *E.m. maximus* and *E.m. ceylanicus* of Sri Lanka; and *E.m. sumatranus* of Sumatra (Chasen, 1940; Ellerman and Morrison-Scott, 1951).

The average adult bull Indian elephant stands 9 ft *2·7 m* at the shoulder and weighs 4·5 tonnes, and the average adult cow 8 ft *2·44 m* and 3·2 tonnes.

The two races of Sri Lanka elephant average rather larger and heavier than the typical race from the Indian mainland, while the race in Sumatra is generally slightly smaller.

Shoulder heights attained by the Asiatic elephant (wild population 28 000–43 000) have been greatly exaggerated in the past. This was mainly due to the fact that measurements were often obtained by throwing a tape over the shoulders, taking the ends down to the outside of each front foot and then dividing the result by two.

Benedict (1936) says an 8 ft *2·4 m* cow elephant measured by this method recorded a height of 8 ft 10 in *2·69 m* while a 10 ft *3·1 m* bull came out at 11 ft 4 in *3·45 m*! It is also known that some unscrupulous mahouts would measure their charges from the ground to the crown of the *raised* head and then claim the result as the elephant's shoulder height.

Twice the circumference of an Asiatic elephant's forefoot when resting on the ground and enlarged by pressure gives approximately its height at the shoulder (up to six per cent error), but this rule does not always apply in the case of young growing animals.

The largest Asiatic elephant on record was probably a single-tusked bull shot by the Maharajah of Susang in the Garo Hills, Assam, India in 1924 which, on the evidence of its forefoot circumference, measured an estimated 11 ft 3 in *3·43 m* at the shoulder. This fabulous animal had been lured into a stockade, and was killed as it attempted to break out (D K Lahiri Choudhury, pers. comm.). Another bull shot by Lalji, Kumar of Gouripur in the same area in 1945 measured 11 ft *3·4 m* (circumference of forefoot 5 ft 6 in *1·68 m*), and on 21 May 1965 Duncan Hay shot a very large tusker near the Reserve Forest, Lakhimpur, Assam which stood 10 ft 11 in *3·33 m* (circumference of forefoot 5 ft 5½ in *1·66 m*). In June 1950 H Mant shot an elephant in a Sri Lanka swamp, which had a forefoot circumference of 6 ft 1½ in *1·87 m*; normally this would be equal to a shoulder height of 12 ft 3 in *3·73 m*, but as mentioned earlier swamp-dwelling elephants often have disproportionately large feet because of the nature of their habitat. Another bull tusker shot by W M Smith at Bilkandi, Bengal on 19 January 1870 reportedly measured 12 ft *3·76 m* between pegs (standing height *c* 11 ft 5 in *3·48 m*), but this figure was exaggerated. According to Dr A P Kapur, Director of the Zoological Survey of India (pers. comm.) this elephant, now on display in the Indian Museum, Calcutta, has a mounted shoulder height of 10 ft 9·92 m in *3·30 m* and measures 11 ft 2¼ in *3·41 m* at the arch of the back. In 1882 another exceptionally large bull was shot by W H Varian at Chalampia Madua in the North Coast Province of Sri Lanka. The following measurements were taken immediately after death: height at shoulder 11 ft 1 in *3·38 m* (standing height *c* 10 ft 7 in

$3·23 m$); at arch of back 11 ft 9 in $3·58 m$; overall length 26 ft $7·92 m$; girth of body at thickest part 22 ft 4 in $6·81 m$; estimated weight about 8 tonnes.

In November 1967 a massively-built tusker measuring 10 ft 6 in $3·2 m$ at the shoulder (circumference of forefoot 5 ft 3 in $1·6 m$) was shot by D K Lahiri Choudhury near Filbari in the Garo Hills after it had killed a number of people.

One of the largest wild elephants surviving in India today is a single-tusked bull living in the Morghat Reserve Forest, N Bengal which, on the basis of a forefoot impression, measures about 10 ft 10 in $3·3 m$ at the shoulder.

The largest Asiatic elephant ever held in captivity was a 'makna' (tuskless bull) called 'Bholanath' owned by Kumar Jitendra Choudhury of Bengal, which measured 10 ft 11 in $3·33 m$ at the shoulder in $c1905$. The Maharajah of Nepal's famous tusker 'Hari Prasad' stood 10 ft 9 in $3·28 m$ in 1957 (Stracey, 1963), and another huge tusker belonging to the Rajah of Nahan-Sirmount in the Punjab was 10 ft 7½ in $3·24 m$ in $c1870$.

The Rajah of Gouripur's great tusker 'Jung Bahudar' stood 10 ft 5½ in $3·19 m$ a few months before his death in $c1964$, and during the Second World War another big tusker in the Maharajah of Gwalier's stable was measured by Stracey at 10 ft 5 in $3·18 m$.

The largest Asiatic elephant ever held in a zoo was probably the famous American circus elephant 'Tusko' (1894–1934), who spent the last part of his life in Woodland Park Zoological Gardens, Seattle, Washington. He stood 10 ft 2 in $3·10 m$ at the shoulder (Lewis, 1955).

In 1932 a shoulder height of 10 ft 4 in $3·15 m$ was reported for a huge tusker named 'Harry' (b 1880) at West Berlin Zoo, Germany, but this measurement cannot be confirmed because the zoo records were destroyed by Allied bombing during the Second World War (Heinz-George Klos, pers. comm.).

'Big Charlie', an Asiatic bull owned by Butlin's Ltd, the holiday camp people, reportedly stood 10 ft 6 in $3·2 m$ at the shoulder and weighed 7·5 tonnes in 1957 when he was 25 years old, but these figures owed much to commercial exaggeration. In reality he measured 9 ft 7 in $2·92 m$ and scaled 5·3 tonnes. This animal was so devoted to his trainer, Shaik Ibrahim, that when he died suddenly at Butlin's Holiday Camp, Filey, Yorkshire from pneumonia in 1959, the elephant refused to eat and became completely unmanageable. In the end the RSPCA were called in to put him out of his misery.

The greatest weight ever recorded for an Asiatic elephant is 6·49 tonnes in the case of 'Tusko', who has already been mentioned. Another 10 ft 2 in $3·10 m$ bull living in the elephant stables at Mysore, India in 1953 scaled 6·19 tonnes on a weigh-bridge

(Rensch and Harde, 1955).

On the basis of these statistics, a weight of 7·75–8·15 tonnes can be extrapolated for an 11 ft $3·35 m$ bull in good condition (cf 6·75 tonnes for an African bush elephant the same height).

The largest (and heaviest) Asiatic cow elephant ever held in captivity was a specimen named 'Zebi', presented to Bristol Zoo by the Maharajah of Mysore in 1868. At the time of her death in January 1910 she reportedly stood 10 ft $3·1 m$ at the shoulder and weighed 5 tonnes, and these figures are borne out by photographic evidence (Flower, 1931; G Greed, pers. comm.).

In August 1979 'Sally', a 44-year-old Asiatic elephant at Edinburgh Zoo, Scotland was measured at 9 ft 1½ in $2·78 m$, making her the largest cow living in captivity today. She was imported from Burma in 1939 when she was four years old.

At least 200 people are killed annually by elephants in Africa (as opposed to 50000–150000 elephants killed by man), and Carrington (1958) puts the yearly death-toll in India at $c50$.

In 1949 two rogue elephants killed five people near Kasungu, Malawi in the space of 24 hours (Debenham, 1955), and four years later another rogue bull crossed into the Sudan from Zaire and killed 11 people. There is also a record of a rogue elephant in N Zululand killing 12 natives in quick succession during a temporary bout of insanity.

In 1952 a single-tusked elephant killed 27 people in Bangladesh before it was shot, and one highly trained work elephant in India killed 18 men and still managed to avoid execution because it was considered too valuable an animal to be destroyed. In cases like this compensation is usually paid to the relatives of the unfortunate victims. Similarly, an elephant working in the teak forests of Burma killed a total of nine mahouts in 15 years before its tusks were sawn off as close to the lip as possible. In 1963 a rogue tusker overturned a crowded truck at Kooni Pahar, NE Frontier, India and pushed it down a 300 ft $91 m$ gorge. Nine people died as a result.

Circus and zoo bull elephants, 90 per cent of them Asiatic, probably account for another 10 deaths annually, and most of these fatalities occur when the animal is on 'musth' and frequently aggressive.

In September 1916 the Sparks Circus was playing in Kingsport, Tennessee, USA when their Asiatic cow elephant suddenly went on the rampage and killed a local man. The angry townsfolk immediately called for a trial and 'Murderous Mary', as she was dubbed by the local newspaper, was sentenced to death. The problem was: how do you execute a 3 tonne elephant? It wasn't easy. In the end they took the unfortunate animal 35 miles $56 km$ further south to Erwin where the Clinchfield Railroad yards were situated – and hanged her with a train crane! This is the only record of an elephant being killed in this barbarous manner.

Although elephants are supposed to be strictly vegetarian and will not eat meat in any shape or form, they will sometimes pick up and chew the dismembered limbs of victims, and this has led to claims that they are also carnivorous.

On 1 November 1944 an Asiatic bull called 'Chang' reportedly killed – and ate – a woman who had befriended him at Zurich Zoo, Switzerland. According to one writer (Clarke, 1969) the woman, a typist, had steadily built up a special relationship with the elephant over a period of time, and the zoo had even given her permission to sleep in a room directly adjacent to the animal's stall. One morning the keeper noticed blood on the floor of the stable. There was no sign of the woman, but a human hand and a toe lay half-buried in the straw. Some days later pieces of clothing were found in the elephant's droppings.

Klaus Huber (1954), on the other hand, who wrote the history of the first 25 years of this zoo, gives a totally different account of the tragedy. He says on the night in question a mentally-ill woman climbed into the elephant stall through an unfastened window and was promptly killed by the alarmed bull, who then proceeded to tear the body into small pieces. The following morning members of the Zurich City Police found the remains of the suicide scattered around the stable, but none of the flesh had been eaten.

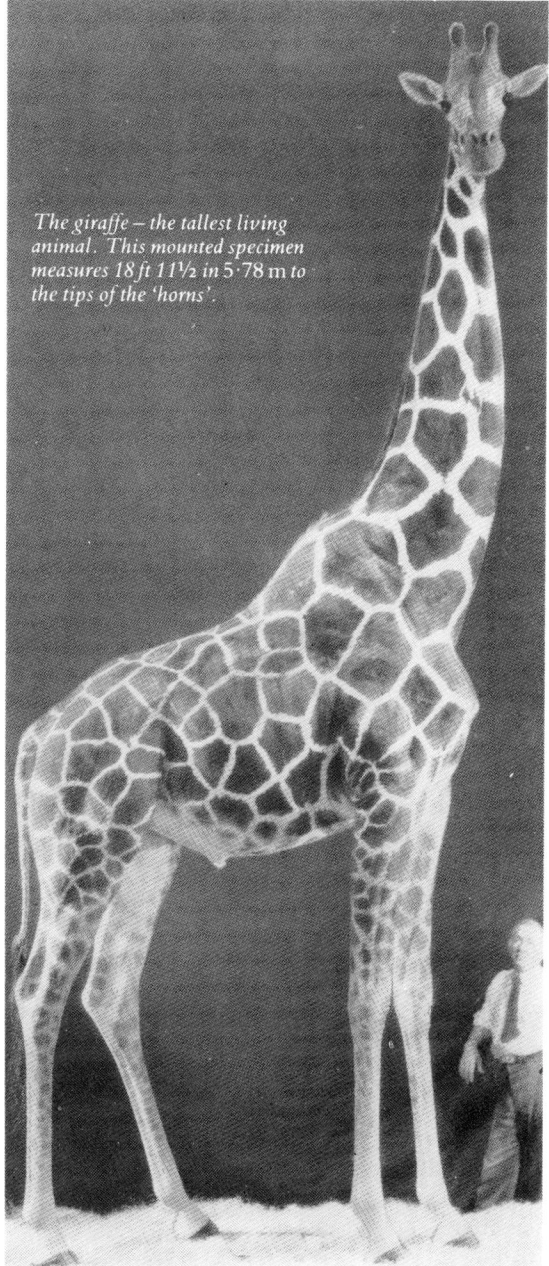

The giraffe – the tallest living animal. This mounted specimen measures 18 ft 11½ in 5·78 m to the tips of the 'horns'.

The tallest living animal is the giraffe (*Giraffa camelopardalis*), which is closely associated with the scattered acacia and thorny bush growth of the dry open plains of tropical Africa.

There are nine recognised races (up to 13 have been described), the distinctions being based on height, coat colour and pattern and the number of horns. The tallest are the Masai giraffe (*Giraffa c. tippelskirchi*) of Tanzania and S Kenya and the Cape or southern giraffe (*Giraffa c. capensis*) of SW Africa. In both sub-species adult bulls average 5·3 m *17 ft 4½ in* in a normal standing position (tip of forehoof to base of horn) and weigh about 1200 kg *2646 lb*. Adult cows are much smaller and lighter in build, averaging 4·4 m *14 ft 5½ in* in height and weighing about 567 kg *1250 lb*.

The greatest measurement recorded for a giraffe between pegs is 19 ft 3 in *5·87 m* (standing height of about 19 ft *5·8 m*) for a Masai bull shot by Caswell in Kenya (Shortridge, 1934), but this extreme figure may have included the horns as well (length 6–9 in *15–23 cm*). It was thus 4 ft *122 cm* taller than a London double-decker bus. This animal was not weighed piecemeal, but it probably scaled at least 1650 kg *3638 lb*. Another bull of the same race also shot in Kenya measured 19 ft *5·8 m*. The tallest Cape giraffe on record was a bull collected by Henry Bryden (1936) which measured 18 ft 11½ in *5·78 m*. This specimen was later mounted to the same height and put on display in the American Museum of Natural History, New York.

The greatest measurement recorded for a cow

giraffe between pegs is 16 ft 10 in *5·13 m* for a matriarch shot by Henry Bryden in the desert country near the Botletli River, Ngamiland in 1917.

The tallest giraffe ever held in captivity was a Masai bull called 'George', who arrived at Chester Zoo on 8 January 1959 from Kenya when he was an estimated 18 months old. At the age of 6 years he measured 18 ft *5·49 m*, and when he stopped growing a year later his horns almost brushed the roof of the 20 ft *6·1 m* high Giraffe House. He died on 22 July 1969 (G Mottershead, pers. comm.).

The tallest cow giraffe ever held in captivity was probably a specimen called 'Rosie', a member of the Baringo race (*Giraffa c. rothschildi*), who arrived at Whipsnade Zoo in June 1934 from Kenya. Her approximate height was 17 ft *5·2 m*, but measurements like these must be considered exceptional, because captive giraffes seldom reach their full height potential on artificial diets.

Although the most striking feature of the giraffe is its exceptional height, problems of restricted growth are not uncommon in this species. One of the most notable cases was a reticulated bull called 'Long John Silver', who was landed with this unfortunate name because he was born at London Zoo during the Queen's Silver Jubilee celebrations. He suddenly stopped growing at the age of one year when he was only 9 ft *2·7 m* tall, and was still the same height at 17 months. By then, his embarrassed father 'Robbie', at 16 ft 6 in *5·03 m* the tallest member of the zoo's herd, was starting to give him some funny looks, especially as his five-month-old baby half-sister 'Dawn' was now practically the same height. Finally, in October 1978, a specialist from a London children's hospital was called in to treat the animal for what was obviously a thyroid deficiency. Two years later 'John Silver', as he is now known, measured 13 ft 6 in

4·11 m, but there has been no increase in height since then (Susan Bevis, pers. comm.).

Because of its extraordinary anatomical shape the giraffe is one of the very few mammals that cannot swim – even in an emergency! Deep rivers are an impassable barrier to them, and they will avoid large expanses of water like the plague. On 26 September 1960 a giraffe escaped from its crate shortly after it had been unloaded from a ship at New York docks, panicked and fell into the water from a jetty. According to one eye-witness report the terrified animal sank like a stone without making any attempt to swim (Crandall, 1964).

The smallest living land mammals are the widely distributed pygmy and least shrews of the genera *Sorex*, *Microsorex* and *Suncus*. There is some controversy over which species is actually the tiniest, but most authorities give the title to Savi's pygmy shrew (*Suncus etruscus*) of the Mediterranean region, South Africa, Pakistan, India and Sri Lanka. According to Van den Brink (1967), mature specimens have a head and body length of 36–52 mm *1·42–2·05 in*, a tail length of 24–29 mm *0·95–1·14 in* and scale between 1·5 and 2 g *0·053–0·071 oz*, but weights up to 7 g *0·25 oz* have been reported for this species (pregnant female?) in Pakistan (Roberts, 1977). Another strong contender is the least shrew (*Sorex minutissimus*) of Scandinavia, Siberia, S China and Japan, which has a head and body length of 35–53 mm *1·38–2·09 in*, a tail length of 21–33 mm *0·83–1·30 in* and weighs 1·5–4 g *0·053–0·141 oz*, and mention should also be made of Hoy's pygmy shrew (*Microsorex hoyi*) of N America which has a normal weight range of 2·3–3·5 g *0·08–0·12 oz* (Walker *et al*, 1968).

These nimrods are so minute that they can scurry through the tunnels left by large earth-worms and are the lower limit of size postulated for warm-blooded animals.

The smallest land mammal found in Britain is the Eurasian pygmy shrew (*Sorex minutus*). Mature specimens have a head and body length of 43–64 mm *1·69–2·52 in*, a tail length of 31–46 mm *1·22–1·81 in* and weigh 2·4–6·1 g *0·085–0·215 oz* (Crowcroft, 1954). This species has been recorded from the top of Ben Nevis (4406 ft *1343 m*), Britain's highest mountain.

Apart from short, intermittent resting periods, shrews are active 24 hours a day and will consume their own body-weight in food during that time. A mammal any smaller than a shrew would be unable to eat fast enough to avoid starvation. In fact, without food, a shrew would starve to death within 2–3 hours.

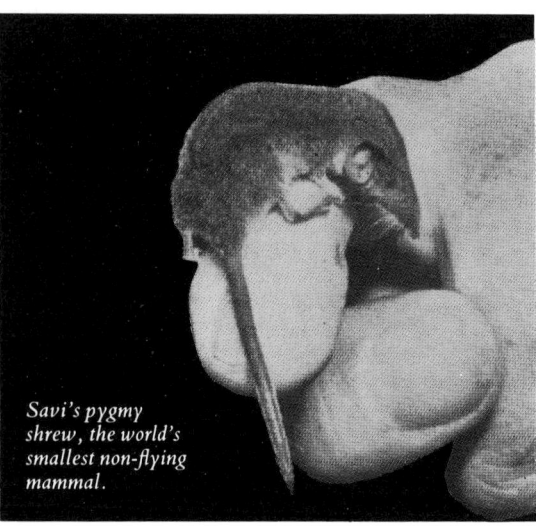

Savi's pygmy shrew, the world's smallest non-flying mammal.

The smallest totally marine mammal is Commerson's dolphin (see page 11).

The rare marine otter (*Lutra felina*), which ranges along the entire coast of Chile, south to Tierra del Fuego, and northwards to the coast of northern Peru, is considerably smaller (one adult male measured 91 cms *35·8 in* in length and weighed 4·08 kg *9 lb*), but it is not strictly marine because it ascends freshwater rivers in search of prawns on which it feeds.

The smallest marine mammal found in British waters is the common porpoise (*Phocoena phocoena*). Adult specimens measure 5–6 ft *1·52–1·83 m* in length and weigh 100–165 lb *45–75 kg*.

The smallest freshwater mammal is the southern water shrew (*Neomys anomalus*) of the Mediterranean area and Asia Minor. Adult individuals measure 106–152 mm *4·17–5·98 in* overall and weigh 7·5–16 g *0·27–0·56 oz*.

The best claimants to the title of the world's rarest land mammal are those species which are known only from a single (type) specimen. Most of them, however, are only in this group because their habits are imperfectly understood and/or they live in difficult terrain. One notable example is Fontoynont's hedgehog tenrec (*Dasogale fontoynonti*), which is represented in the Natural History Museum, Paris, by a single specimen collected in eastern Madagascar.

The rarest mammal (excluding bats) found in Britain is the common otter (*Lutra lutra*). Before the Second World War there were an estimated 14 000 otters living in Scotland, Wales, the Lake District, the West Country and East Anglia, one to every 3 mile *4·8 km* stretch of Britain's rivers, but since then their numbers have dropped dramatically. The main reasons for the alarming decline were hunting, increased leisure use of rivers and pollution (including pesticides) of waters, combined with the exceptionally bad winter of 1963 which decimated the population. On 1 January 1978 the species was accorded full legal protection outside of Scotland, but three years later the Joint Otter Group published two reports which showed that during the survey carried out by them in 1977–78 the presence of otters had been detected in only 6 per cent of the 1500 sites visited in England and 20 per cent of the 2030 survey sites in Wales. Even in Scotland (including Loch Ness), where it was thought to be reasonably abundant, it has now vanished completely from most of the central lowlands and parts of the eastern region, although signs of otters were found in 70 per cent of the 3205 sites visited in the Highlands and Islands.

The rarest marine mammal is Longman's beaked whale (*Indopacetus pacificus*), which is known from only two skulls. The type specimen was discovered on a beach near Mackay, Queensland, Australia in 1822 (Longman, 1926), and the second near Mogadiscio, Somalia, E Africa in 1955 (Azzaroli, 1968).

Britain's rarest marine mammal is the pygmy sperm whale (*Kogia breviceps*). The first recorded specimen was stranded on Creggstrand, County Clare, Ireland on 24 April 1966. It measured 8 ft 1½ in *2·48 m* in length. On 17 February 1949 a 12 ft 11 in *3·94 m* long female narwhal (*Monodon monoceros*) was found stranded in the Thames estuary at Rainham, Essex, and five months later another female 13 ft 1 in *3·99 m* long ran aground at Wouldham, Kent. The last stranding had been in the Shetlands in 1808. In 1950 a white whale (*Delphinapterus leucas*) was sighted at Rudha-Dunain, Soay, Highland, Scotland, and in 1965 another specimen was seen at Arrochar, Loch Long. Both these animals are usually limited to high Arctic latitudes (Fraser, 1974).

The fastest land animal in the world is the cheetah or 'hunting leopard' (*Acinonyx jubatus*), which can reach 54 miles/h *86·9 km/h* from trotting in 2·75 s, and the same speed from a standing start in 3 s over suitably level ground. Bourliere (1955) cites a record of a cheetah covering more than 700 yd *640 m* in 20 s (=71·6 miles/h *115·2 km/h*), but as this sprinter par excellence seldom runs at peak acceleration for more than 200–300 yd *183–274 m*, this claim must be discounted. Kruuk and Turner (1967) found that cheetah attacks in the Serengeti National Park, Kenya averaged 183·3 yd *167·6 m*, and that the cheetah-prey distance when the cat made its move was about 95 yd *86·9 m*.

Other writers have credited this racing machine with even more imaginative speeds (i.e. up to 92 miles/h *148 km/h*) but Hildebrand (1961), who carried out a locomotion study based on a film sequence of a running cheetah in the wild, found the maximum rate was 56 miles/h *90 km/h*. At this velocity it completed one stride (23 ft *7 m*) in 0·28 s. This figure is also confirmed by Guggisberg (1975), well known for his pioneer work on the habits of this creature, but Kruuk and Turner believe a somewhat higher speed (*c* 60 miles/h *97 km/h?*) may be attained during short bursts.

The cheetah lives on the open plains and semi-arid savannahs of Southern and East Africa, Iran, Baluchistan and Afghanistan (?). It was also found in India up until fairly recently, but the last reliable sighting of a wild specimen was near Chandragiri, southern India on the night of 28–29 March 1952 (Seshadri, 1969). The cheetahs used by Indian princes today for the hunt are imported from Kenya, which is now the centre of abundance for this species.

In September 1937 eight cheetahs imported into

The three-toed sloth, the slowest-moving land mammal.

England from Kenya by Gandar Dower, the well-known animal collector and writer, were matched singly against greyhounds in a series of races involving a mechanical hare on the oval dog-track at Harringay, London. Not surprisingly, cheetahs will never run flat out under domestic conditions, and this was subsequently proved in the trials. The fastest times were put up by a female cheetah called 'Helen' who, despite the fact she had difficulty negotiating the bends, recorded an average speed of 43·4 miles/h *69·8 km/h* over three 345 yd *315 m* runs, compared to 36·9 miles/h *59·km/h* for the fastest greyhound.

A few months later a cheetah was raced against a speedway rider at Belle Vue, Manchester. On this occasion, however, the animal stopped running when it caught the meat attached to the bike and waited for the man to come round again. When he drew level the cat sprang, knocking both rider and bike to the ground. Fortunately no damage was done.

Cheetah races were also staged at White City stadium, London, but they were not very successful. Apart from stopping to fight, they often took short cuts across the central barrier, which made betting on them virtually impossible!

That the cheetah is beautifully designed for speed is illustrated by the interesting hypothesis that an adult specimen *without legs* would still be able to propel its streamlined body along the ground at a speed of 5 miles/h *8 km/h* through sheer muscular contraction (Eaton, 1974).

The fastest land animal over a sustained distance is the pronghorn antelope (*Antilocapra americana*) of the Great Plains of the western USA.

On 10 October 1941 Mr Don Robins of the US Grazing Service paced four bucks for 4 miles *6·4 km* in Malheur County, Oregon. The antelopes had already run about 200 yd *183 m* before they came level with the car, and they travelled at 35 miles/h *56 km/h* for another 4 miles *6·4 km*. This was probably their *cruising* speed, because they showed no evidence of tiring (Einarsen, 1948).

Another small group of pronghorns which raced parallel with a car on a road near Rincon, New Mexico in 1918 averaged 30 miles/h *48 km/h* for 7 miles *11·3 km* (Carr, 1927), and other individuals have been timed at 42 miles/h *68 km/h* for 1 mile *1·6 km*.

When it is hard-pressed, however, this handsome ungulate really comes into its own. On 14 August 1939 three agricultural scientists from Oregon University were driving across the dried bed of Spanish Lake in Lake County when they were challenged by a small group of pronghorns led by a magnificent buck. As they closed in from the right the buck took a lead of about 50 ft *15 m* and the men had to increase speed to keep up with the beast.

'The buck was now about 20 ft *6 m* away and kept abreast of the car at 50 miles/h *80 km/h*', writes Einarsen. 'He gradually increased his gait, and with a tremendous burst of speed flattened out so that he appeared as lean and low as a greyhound. Then he turned towards us at about a 45 degree angle and disappeared in front of the car, to reappear on our left. He had gained enough to cross our course as the speedometer registered 61 miles/h *98 km/h*. After the buck passed us he quickly slackened his pace, and when he reached a rounded knoll about 600 ft *183 m* away he stood snorting, in graceful silhouette against the sky, as though enjoying the satisfaction of beating us in a fair race.'

If the car speedometer was *reliable* this particular pronghorn must have been travelling in excess of 70 miles/h *113 km/h* as it crossed in front of the vehicle, but as this would make it even faster than the cheetah this reading must be considered suspect. In any event, chasing an antelope over bumpy ground while watching a speedometer is not the best way to measure speed.

How does a creature lacking the more supple limbs and back of the cheetah manage to reach velocities nearly as high? Unlike the latter, the pronghorn has unusually well-developed bronchia and lungs, and when it runs it takes in a much greater volume of air than normal through its *open mouth*. (Most big game animals are tight-lipped in flight.) Another compensation is the heart, which is twice as big as that of other mammals of comparable size.

The blackbuck (*Antilope cervicapra*) of Pakistan and India and the Mongolian gazelle (*Procapra guttorosa*) are also very fast (45–50 miles/h *72–80 km/h*), but claims that they have been timed at 60 miles/h *97 km/h* over distances of 2 miles *3·2 km* or more must be put down to faulty readings.

A three-year-old male saiga (*Saiga tatarica*) chased by a motor-cyclist at a speed of 75–80 km/h *47–50 miles/h* in S Russia kept up the pace for 15–16 minutes before it collapsed totally exhausted (Gambaryan, 1974).

The fastest wild mammal found in Britain is the roe deer (*Capreolus capreolus*), which can cruise at 25–30 miles/h *40–48 km/h* for more than 20 miles *32 km*, with occasional short bursts of up to 40 miles/h *64 km/h*. The red deer (*Cervus elephus*) is normally slightly slower, but on 19 October 1970 a frightened runaway stag registered a speed of 42 miles/h *68 km/h* on a police radar trap as it ran through a street in Stalybridge, Cheshire.

The slowest-moving land mammal is the ai or three-toed sloth (*Bradypus tridactylus*) of the tropical rain forests of Central and South America, which crawls slowly along the ground like a mechanical toy in low gear. The usual speed is 6–8 ft/minute *1·83– 2·44 m/minute* (0·068–0·091 miles/h *0·110–0·146 km/h*), but one mother sloth speeded up by the calls of her infant was observed to cover 14 ft *4·3 m* in 1 minute (0·159 miles/h *0·256 km/h*). In the trees this speed may be increased to 1·36 miles/h *2·19 km/h* (Beebe, 1926). Peak acceleration is probably reached however during the courtship 'pursuit' when the males, prompted by the sexual urge, forsake their nocturnal and strictly arboreal habits to go in search of females. Sometimes they will even swim across small rivers, their long arms moving majestically overhead in what can only be described as the slowest crawl on record.

Thanks to the protective mimicry of its algae-covered body and the fact that it spends practically its entire life in the tree-tops, the wickedly-clawed three-toed sloth has virtually no natural enemies apart from the rare Harpy eagle (*Harpia harpyja*), which sweeps in when the dull-witted animal exposes the back of its neck and quickly severs the spinal cord with a series of sharp blows with its powerful beak. Even then, in death as in life, the sloth may still cling to the branch with a grip of iron, and the raptor sometimes has to content itself with eating parts of the carcase while the unfortunate creature hangs in the upside-down position.

The longest-lived land mammal after man (116+ years) is the Asiatic elephant (*Elephas maximus*).

The greatest age that has been verified with absolute certainty is 78 years in the case of an Asiatic cow named 'Modoc', who died at Santa Clara, California, USA on 17 July 1975. She was brought to the USA in 1898 at the age of two by the famous Carl Hagenbeck, who later sold her to a New York animal dealer. In 1904 she was purchased by the Barnum and Bailey Circus (later to become the Ringling Brother–Barnum and Bailey Circus). By 1930 she was the largest and heaviest elephant in the famous Ringling herd, measuring 7 ft 10 in *2·39 m* at the shoulder and weighing 9180 lb *4164 kg* (Benedict, 1936). During her long circus career she survived two deliberate mass poisonings that killed 11 of her companions and a fire that won her a heroine's reputation. At the height of the big top fire she hauled lion cages with crazed animals inside to safety. Later her own survival was jeopardised by her circus handler who accidentally blinded her in the left eye with a billhook. As a result of the injury Modoc was forced into early retirement and spent the next 20 years languishing at a roadside zoo in Tennessee. In 1959 she was rediscovered by Ralph Helfer of Creative Animal Techniques, Saugus, California, and later appeared in a number of television series including the popular *Daktari* (wearing false ears!) before being semi-retired in 1968.

In August 1974 Modoc made a special appearance at a fairground in Laguna Canyon, California and was visited by Fabian Redwood, who had previously worked with the animal. Redwood had been a strapping 24-year-old when he and Modoc last met in 1922. Now he was a lean, wizened 76. As soon as the elephant heard him speak she let out a trumpeting screech of recognition. Then, in a sudden burst of affection, she gently picked up her former trainer in her partially paralysed trunk and hoisted him level with her good eye so that she could gaze into his face.

A month before her death Modoc survived major surgery on the ingrowing toenail of her left front foot, but shortly afterwards complications set in (Ralph Helfer, pers. comm.).

Modoc's closest rival for age was probably a bull

timber elephant named 'Kyaw Thee' (Tusker 1342), who died in the Taunggyi Forest Division, Southern Shan States, Burma in 1965, aged 70. He was born and bred in captivity (Gale, 1974).

Of the 1700 elephants working in Burma for the famous Bombay Burmah Trading Company in 1938, 24 were classified as between 65 and 70 years and 144 between 55 and 65 years. These figures were based upon records that had been carefully kept for over 50 years.

Mention should also be made of the magnificent tusker 'Chandrasekharan', who died on 10 August 1940 aged 67 years. He was handed over by the Travancore Forest Department to the Royal Elephant Stables on 15 August 1883 when aged about 10 years.

The oldest zoo elephant on record was an Asiatic cow named 'Jessie', who was destroyed at Taronga Park Zoo, Sydney, Australia on 26 September 1939 after developing abscesses on the soles of her feet which eventually made walking impossible (Le Souef, cited by Flower, 1947–48). She arrived at Moore Park Zoo, Sydney in 1882 as a gift from the King of Siam (Thailand) and was transferred to Taronga Park Zoo just before the outbreak of the First World War. The exact age of Jessie on arrival in Australia was not recorded, but it was generally believed that she was about 12 years old. Patten (1940), on the other hand, thinks she was about 20, in which case she could have been c 77 years at the time of her death.

The greatest reliable age reported for an African bush elephant is c 70 years for the outsized bull 'Dhlulamithi' (see page 14), who was probably fully mature (i.e. 25 years old) when the Shangaan tribesmen of SE Rhodesia first came across him.

The magnificent tusker 'Ahmed' of Marsabit Mountain Reserve, Kenya who died in 1971 (see page 14) was believed to have been 55–62 years based on a count of seasonal and annual growth layers on the roots of the molars or grinding teeth (A MacKay, pers. comm.).

Unlike man, a wild elephant's life-span is determined by the persistence of its last molar teeth. Once these are gone the animal is literally toothless, with the result that it cannot masticate its food and dies of starvation. Laws (1966) found that the absolute age limit based on molar material for a series of elephants shot in Uganda was 60 years; Sikes (1971), on the other hand, says there is *evidence* that elephants living in certain unrestricted parts of Africa sometimes live for 80 or even 100 years, but these readings are only approximate and therefore subjective.

Captive elephants generally live longer than their wild counterparts because they are fed with softer foods; consequently, their teeth are not worn down naturally. In addition they suffer much less stress than their wild counterparts.

The greatest reliable age reported for a captive African bush elephant is 'over 41 years' for a cow named 'Jumbina', received at the National Zoological Park in Washington, DC, USA on 8 August 1913. She died there on 30 June 1952 after living in the zoo for 38 years 10 months 22 days. Her age on arrival was about 3 years (Mann, 1953).

The greatest reliable age reported for a forest elephant is 43+ years for a cow named 'Colonie' at the Gongala-na-Bodia training centre in the Congo, who was still alive in 1959.

The shortest-lived mammals are the extremely active shrews (*Soricidae*), which burn themselves out very quickly. Most species have a life-span of less than 18 months in the wild state, including the Eurasian common shrew (*Sorex araneus*), which usually dies before it is one year old (Crowcroft, 1956). The greatest age recorded for a captive specimen is 2 years 3 months 1 day in the case of a northern short-tailed shrew (*Blarina brevicauda*) which lived in the National Zoological Park, Washington, DC from 27 December 1957 to 28 March 1960 (Reed, 1961), as opposed to 3 months for a Eurasian shrew (M Jones, pers. comm.).

The highest living mammal is probably the yak (*Bos mutus*) of the Tibetan Plateau. In 1899 Edgar Phelps shot a bull 22 miles *35 km* south of Horpu Cho at an altitude of 18 500 ft *5639 m*, but this animal may pass the 20 000 ft *6096 m* line when foraging.

The bharal (*Pseudois nayaur*) and the pika or mouse hare (*Ochotona thibetana*) are also found above 18 000 ft *5486 m*, and the latter has been observed 'sunning' itself on a rock when the temperature was −17°C (=30 degrees of frost!). There is also a reliable record of a woolly hare (*Lepus oiostolus*) being seen at 19 800 ft *6035 m*.

The greatest elevation reported for a carnivore in the Himalayas is 19 000 ft *5791 m* for a woolly wolf (*Canis lupus chanco*), and the Tibetan fox (*Vulpes ferrilata*) and the red lynx (*Lynx lynx isabellinus*) have been sighted at 18 500 ft *5639 m* and 18 000 ft *5486 m* respectively (Napier, 1972). The snow leopard or ounce (*Panthera uncia*) has been observed at an altitude of 17 700 ft *5395 m* in the Ladakh Range, E Kashmir, and this predator will probably climb even higher when pursuing game like the bharal (blue sheep).

In May 1954 two members of the *Daily Mail* 'Abominable Snowman Expedition' to the Himalayas saw what appeared to be a red bear (*Ursus arctos isabellinus*) at a height of 18 000 ft *5486 m* on the Reipimu Glacier and later found a fresh set of footprints. Most of the sightings and discovery of tracks of the so-called 'yeti' can be attributed to this subspecies or other variants of the brown bear (*Ursus arctos*).

Sir Harry Johnstone (1886) reports seeing African elephants at an altitude of 13 000 ft *3962 m*, and tracks have been discovered on Mt Kilimanjaro, Kenya at 15 000 ft *4572 m*. In 1926 the frozen carcase of a leopard (*Panthera pardus*) was found near the rim of the Kobo crater (18 500 ft *5638 m*) on the same mountain.

On the other side of the world the vicugna (*Vicugna vicugna*) has been found above the snowline at 18 000 ft *5486 m* in the Peruvian Andes and the alpaca (*Lama pacos*) at 15 700 ft *4785 m*. On another occasion the tracks of a puma (*Felis concolor*) were discovered at an altitude of 18 375 ft *5600 m* in the same range. The mountain chinchilla (*Chinchilla laniger*) has also been found above the snowline in the Chilean and Bolivian Andes.

The largest herds ever recorded were those of the springbok (*Antidorcas marsupialis*) during migration across the high open plains of the western parts of southern Africa in the 19th century. These great *trekbokkes*, as the Boers called them, occurred at irregular intervals when overcrowding became acute and food and water supplies dwindled. The gazelles would join up to form a herd of almost inconceivable magnitude and then set off across the desert tracts and veld in search of fresh grazing. They moved in such densely packed masses that any unfortunate animals met on the way were either trampled to death or forced along with them, and the country was left completely devastated in their wake. Hardly any of the springbok survived the migration. Most of them died from starvation, drowning (attempting to cross the Orange River) or disease; others fell to predators (including man) or died from drinking salt water if they reached the sea.

Sometimes, it would take days for the living wave of animals to pass a given point. In 1849, for instance, Sir John Fraser saw a *trekbokke* that took *three days* to pass through the settlement of Beaufort West, Cape Province.

According to an eyewitness account of the last great migration in July 1896 the enormous herd covered 2070 miles² *5360 km²* (138 miles *222 km* long and 15 miles *24 km* wide) as it advanced towards Karree Kloof near the Orange River (Cronwright-Schreiner, 1925), and must have contained at least 10 million animals.

Fortunately these periodic movements are now a thing of the past. The migrations were so ruinous to crops and livestock that the farmers began destroying the springbok in great numbers, and this extermination, combined with outbreaks of rinderpest, reduced the enormous population drastically. Today springbok are found in reasonable abundance (*c* 3000 animals) only in the Kalahari Desert (especially around Etosha Pan) and some nature reserves in

SW Africa, and their numbers no longer threaten to disturb the delicate balance of nature.

With the possible exception of one or two other African game animals, the only other land mammals known to travel in herds numbering more than a million strong were the American bison (*Bison bison*) and the wapiti (*Cervus canadensis*) during migration. In 1873 a party of hunters reportedly took seven days to pass through a herd of bison moving between Medicine Hat, Alberta, Canada and the Red Deer Forest on the South Saskatchewan River, (during the five-year period 1870–74 more than 12·5 million animals were shot out of an original population of 50–60 million), and there were an estimated 10 million wapiti living in W America before the great slaughter started in the nineteenth century.

The longest of all mammalian gestation periods is that of the Asiatic elephant (*Elephas maximus*) with an average of 608 days or just over 20 months.

Burne (1943) gives a record of a cow named 'Mai Mai', captured in the Mongpan Forest, Burma who gave birth to a bull calf after a gestation period of 760 days – more than two and a half times that of a woman. The gestation period of the African bush elephant is reported to be 649–661 days (Lang, 1967).

The shortest of all mammalian gestation periods is probably that of the American opossum (*Didelphis marsupialis*), which is normally 12–13 days but may be as short as 8 days. This animal is born in a very immature state (litter size 8–18), and the young are immediately transferred to the ventral pouch, where they remain for 10 weeks until embryonic development is complete.

The shortest of all mammalian gestation periods in which the young are fully developed at birth is that of the golden hamster (*Mesocricetus auratus*) of Asia Minor with an average of 15–16 days. Gestations as low as 13 days have been reported for both the Eurasian common shrew and the cosmopolitan house mouse (*Mus musculus*), but the ranges of these two species are 13–19 days and 13–21 days respectively (Burton, 1965).

The greatest number of young born to a wild mammal in a single litter is 31 (30 of which survived) in the case of a tail-less tenrec (*Tenrec ecaudatus*) at Wassenaar Zoo, Holland in 1972. This species lives in Madagascar and the Comoro Islands. The normal litter size is 12–15, although females can suckle up to 24. In March 1961 a total of 32 (average litter size 6–13) was reported for a house mouse at the Roswell Park Memorial Institute in Buffalo, NY, but this specimen may have been treated with fertility drugs.

The opossums (*Didelphidae*) of the Americas also have large litters, and there is a record of a female (species not identified) being found with 27 mammae arranged in a circle on her abdomen.

The greatest number of litters produced by a mammal in a single year is 15 (average litter size 4–9) by the meadow vole (*Microtus pennsylvanicus*) of Canada and the N USA. Females start breeding at the age of 25 days, and the gestation period is 21 days. Mating recurs soon after the litter is born.

The smallest young produced by any mammal at birth are those of the mouse opossums (*Marmosa*) of Central and South America which, in some species, are no larger than a grain of rice (*cf* 3 tonnes for a new-born blue whale calf).

The fastest developing mammal in the world is the streaked tenrec (*Hemicentetes semispinosus*) of Madagascar. Two young born at Berlin Zoo, W Germany on 18 July 1961 could run almost immediately and on the sixth day they were eating worms, apparently fully weaned. Unlike the meadow vole (see above), however, this species has a gestation period of at least 50 days.

The heaviest brain in the animal world – and the most complex – is that of the sperm whale. During the 1949–50 Japanese Whaling Expedition to the N Pacific, Dr Tokuzo Kojima (1951) of the Brain Institute, University of Tokyo, weighed the brains of 16 adult bulls brought aboard the factory ship *Nissin Maru No 1*. The heaviest example, taken from a 49-footer *14·94 m*, weighed 9·2 kg *20·28 lb* and the lightest 6·4 kg *14·1 lb* (from a very old individual). The average weight was 7·8 kg *17·2 lb*. Pilleri and Gihr (1971) give the absolute brain size for this species as *c* 10 kg *22 lb* (*cf* 1424 g *3·14 lb* for an adult man).

By way of comparison, the brain of a 90 ft *27·43 m* long blue whale weighed 6·9 kg *15·21 lb* and that of a large fin whale 8·3 kg *18·30 lb*.

The heaviest brain recorded for a land animal is 7·5 kg *16·5 lb* for a semi-adult 7 ft 4 in *2·24 m* Asiatic cow elephant, but this exceptional figure probably included a certain amount of blood. The brain of an adult African bull elephant weighs 4·2–5·4 kg *9·26–11·9 lb* (cows 3·6–4·3 kg *7·9–9·5 lb*).

The heaviest mammalian brain in proportion to body weight is that of the common marmoset (*Callithrix jacchus*) of E Brazil, which accounts for 5·55 per cent of the total weight of the animal, but the Capuchin monkeys (*Cebidae*) of Central and S America are also strong contenders. In the blue whale the correlation is 0·007 per cent, the fin whale 0·016 per cent, the sperm whale 0·03 per cent, the elephant 0·12 per cent and man 1·93 per cent (Slijper, 1962).

The largest living terrestrial carnivore is the Kodiak bear (*Ursus arctos middendorffi*), which is found on Kodiak Island and adjacent Afognak and Shuyak

in the Gulf of Alaska, USA. The average adult male has a nose to tail length of 8 ft *2·44 m* measured along the back (not the belly), stands 52 in *1·32 m* at the shoulder and weighs between 1050 lb *476 kg* and 1175 lb *533 kg*. Females are about one-third smaller.

It should be noted here that the weight of an individual bear is not constant, and can fluctuate enormously during the course of a single year. At the end of the summer it may scale 60 per cent more than it did a few months previously, and when it emerges from hibernation the following spring after subsisting on its reserves of fat it is often in an emaciated condition.

The greatest weight recorded for a Kodiak bear in the wild is 1656 lb *751 kg* for a male shot at English Bay, Kodiak Island in 1894 by J C Tolman. The *stretched* skin (pegged to the side of a cabin on a frame and then weighted with rocks at the bottom edge for maximum effect) measured 13 ft 6 in *4·12 m* from the tip of the nose to the root of the tail, and the hindfoot was 18 in *46 cm* long (Phillips–Wolley, 1894).

The largest Kodiak bear ever held in captivity was a male at Cheyenne Mountain Zoological Park, Colorado, USA which scaled 1670 lb *757 kg* at the time of its death on 22 September 1955 (William Meeker, pers. comm.). Unfortunately nothing is known about the physical condition of this animal (or its nose to tail length), but it was probably 'cage-fat'. The bear was received at the zoo as a cub direct from Kodiak Island on 29 June 1940.

'Sam' and 'Erskine', twin Kodiak bears at Chicago Zoological Park, Illinois, USA were also very large. Sam, the *smaller* of the two – he could reach food suspended 10 ft 6 in *3·2 m* above the ground with his mouth – recorded a posthumous weight of 1412 lb *640 kg*, and Erskine weighed an estimated 1600 lb *726 kg* at the time of his death in *c* 1957 (Robert Bean, pers. comm.).

The largest Kodiak bear ever held captive in a British zoo was probably a male called 'Nick' (one of twins) received at London Zoo direct from N America on 29 January 1954. At the age of one year he scaled 595 lb *270 kg*, and when he died at Whipsnade Zoo in October 1963 he recorded a posthumous weight of 1148 lb *521 kg*. He could reach meat suspended 10 ft 3 in *3·12 m* from the ground.

The closely related Peninsula giant bear (*Ursus a. gyas*) of the Alaska Peninsula and other parts of the state has also been credited with the title of 'largest living land carnivore' and there is very little to choose between these two races of brown bear in terms of actual size.

On 28 May 1948 Robert C Reeve of Anchorage shot an enormous male near Cold Bay which measured 10 ft *3·05 m* nose to tail. Its weight was estimated at 1600–1700 lb *726–771 kg* (skin 193·5 lb

88 kg), and judging from photographic evidence this was not exaggerated. Reeve said the bear had recently come out of hibernation and carried little or no fat, and he believed that the animal would have scaled at least 1850 lb *839 kg* at the end of the summer. Another outsized male shot by Harold McCracken (1957) near Frosty Peak at the western end of the Alaska Peninsula in November 1916 weighed an estimated 1600 lb *726 kg*. The skin of this animal measured 11 ft 4 in *3·45 m* nose to tail and 10 ft 6 in *3·2 m* across the outstretched front paws. In June 1909 Dr J Wylie Anderson shot a male on Unimak Island which reportedly weighed 1320 lb *599 kg*, but Rowland Ward (1928) gives the weight of this specimen as 1460 lb *662 kg* and says its skin measured 11 ft *3·35 m* in length.

The largest Peninsula giant bear ever held in captivity was probably a male captured on 24 May 1901 near Douglas Settlement at the western entrance to Cook Inlet on the Alaska Peninsula and sent to the National Zoological Park, Washington, DC where it was received on 9 January 1902. On 20 January 1911 it recorded a weight of 1160 lb *526 kg*, but Seton (1925–27) says the bear was heaviest about 1 December 1910 when it scaled an *estimated* 1200 lb *544 kg*. According to the same authority the diet of this bear was very carefully regulated and at no time during its twelve-year stay at the zoo was it over-fat.

Bergman (1935) has described a giant race of Kamchatka bear (*Ursus a. piscator*) from the southern part of the peninsula which he says exceeds even the Kodiak and Peninsula giant bears in size, but this claim is only partially substantiated by Russian findings. Baturin, who shot a great number of bears in Kamchatka, says his largest example weighed 40 poods (653 kg *1440 lb*), while Novikov (1962) mentions a small number of others which scaled between 500 kg *1102 lb* and 685 kg *1510 lb*.

This sub-species is now probably extinct, because no individuals remotely approaching this size have been killed in Kamchatka in recent years. In one series of 40 bears collected by Averin (1948) the largest male weighed only 285 kg *628 lb*.

Weights in excess of 1000 lb *454 kg* have also been reliably reported for the grizzly bear (*Ursus a. horribilis*), although the average adult weight for males is 450–600 lb *204–272 kg* (females about one-quarter smaller). One huge male killed in the Okanogan Forest Reserve, Washington, USA in early August 1924 weighed over 1100 lb *499 kg*. It was a notorious cattle-killer, and over a period of three years had taken nearly 50 head of cattle and more than 150 sheep (Annual Report, Dept. of Agriculture, 1924). Another grizzly killed in Idaho in the 19th century was sold to a butcher in Spokane, who claimed that he paid for 1173 lb *532 kg* of meat. This figure was placed on the carcase as it hung in front of

The 1600 lb 726 kg giant brown bear shot by Harold McCracken on the Alaska Peninsula in 1916.

his shop (Wright, 1909).

Although the largest brown bears are now found in Alaska, it has been claimed by some authorities (Lydekker, 1901; Hittell, 1860) that the grizzlies which formerly inhabited the high peaks of the Sierra Nevada Range were, in fact, the heaviest of them all, weights of 1700 lb *771 kg* and 1800 lb *816 kg* being regularly attained. While these poundages must be considered somewhat excessive, it is interesting to see that Rowland Ward list a Nevada grizzly of 1536 lb *697 kg* in their 1907 edition. The bear, shot by W F Sheard in 1881, was stated to have measured 11 ft 6 in *3·5 m* in length (skin) and 10 ft 2 in *3·10 m* across the outstretched front paws.

The largest grizzly bear ever held in captivity was probably a male which lived for 18 years in the Lincoln Park Menagerie, Chicago, Illinois, USA. Shields (1890) says the bear 'was fed to suffocation by the thousands of visitors, and in his later years grew so fat that he could not walk, could only crawl around'. His weight was variously estimated at 1800 lb *816 kg* to 2200 lb *998 kg*, but he actually scaled 1153 lb *523 kg* at the time of his death. His nose to tail length was given as 7 ft 8½ in *2·35 m* and his shoulder height as 41¾ in *1·06 m*.

In 1977 a standing height of 10 ft *3·05 m* and a weight of 1390 lb *630 kg* were reported for a male grizzly bear called 'Teddy', star of an American 'terror' film called 'Grizzly', but photographic evidence suggests the animal in question was more probably a mighty 'silver-tip' from Alaska. Even so, it would still make him the largest Peninsula giant bear ever held in captivity.

Merriam (1918) lists seven full species and 15 sub-species of brown and grizzly bear in N America, but these identifications were largely based on variations in size and colours of pelt. The modern view is that they are all races of a single species, *Ursus arctos*.

The greatest reliable weight recorded for a European brown bear (*Ursus a. arctos*) is 480 kg *1058 lb* for a 2·43 m *8 ft* long male shot in the Oural district, N Russia. The average adult male weighs 144–204 kg *317–450 lb.*

The American black bear (*Ursus americanus*) rarely exceeds 400 lb *181 kg*, but weights in excess of 650 lb *295 kg* have been reliably recorded for exceptionally fat specimens. In December 1921 M E Musgrave, a hunter working for the Biological Survey, shot a confirmed cattle-killer on the Moqui Reservation, Arizona which scaled exactly 900 lb *408 kg*, but even this size was exceeded by another male shot by Joseph Allan at Millstream, New Brunswick, Canada in November 1976 after it had killed his German shepherd dog with one swipe of its paw. This bear tipped the scales at an astonishing 902 lb *409 kg* after it had been dressed (insides removed), which means it must have weighed nearly 1100 lb *499 kg* when alive! Its nose to tail length was 7 ft 11 in *2·41 m* (Aubrey Allan, pers. comm.).

The polar bear (*Thalarctos maritimus*) of the Arctic coastal regions has a proportionately longer neck and less massive skull than the giant brown bears already mentioned, and this streamlining tends to give an illusion of overall slimness. In reality, however, large males often bulk out heavier than their more terrestrial counterparts, and many informed Americans now hold the view that this species rather than the Kodiak is more probably the largest living member of the *Ursidae*. This may well be true where maximum poundages are concerned, but if average size is the criterion – the adult male measures 7 ft 9 in *2·36 m* nose to tail, stands 48 in *1·22 m* at the shoulder and weighs 850–900 lb *386–408 kg* – then the polar bear must yield to the brown bears of Alaska.

Capt George F Lyon (1825) describes how members of his crew killed a large polar bear at the entrance to Hudson Strait, NW Territories, Canada in July 1821 which measured 8 ft 7 in *2·62 m* nose to tail, 7 ft 11 in *2·41 m* in maximum girth and 4 ft 9 in *1·45 m* at the shoulder. 'On lifting him in, we were astonished to find that his weight exceeded 1600 pounds *726 kg*.'

According to Perry (1966) the French-Canadian explorer and hunter Andre Tremblay shot an enormous bear near Cape York, N Baffin Island, in the early part of this century which measured 11 ft *3·4 m* in length (skin), 4 ft 6 in *1·37 m* at the shoulder and weighed an estimated 1800 lb *816 kg*. The local Eskimos told him it was the largest bear they had ever seen. The same writer also mentions another polar bear killed on Franz Josef Island by members of the Russian research station there in the winter of 1931 which measured 12 ft 4 in *3·76 m* in length (skin) and scaled between 1300 lb *590 kg* and 1550 lb *703 kg*.

In October 1957 three Eskimo hunters returning to Point Barrow, N Alaska, reported they had seen a polar bear measuring over 30 ft *9·1 m* (sic) roaming the ice-shelf along the Arctic sea coast. A few months later Tom Bolock, an American sportsman, shot a huge bear which could have been the same animal as it was making a beeline for Siberia. The animal measured just over 10 ft *3·1 m* in length and its weight was conservatively *estimated* at 1800 lb *816 kg*. Another outsized male in the Carnegie Museum, Pittsburgh, Pennsylvania, USA tipped the scales at 1728 lb *784 kg*.

The greatest weight recorded for a polar bear in the wild is an incredible 2210 lb *1002 kg* for a white colossus shot by Arthur Dubs of Medford, Oregon, USA at the polar entrance to Kotzebue Sound, NW Alaska in 1960. In April 1962 the 11 ft 1½ in *3·39 m* tall mounted animal was put on display at the Seattle World Fair, but the present whereabouts of this exhibit is unknown.

It is interesting to note that the Boone and Crockett Club, which publishes details of North American big game records, take the position that bear records are 'meaningful' only if based on the size of the skull. That is why hunters who used to shoot the first large bear that came into their sights in the hope that it might be a record are now much more cautious, and this can only be a good thing. Unfortunately, in the case of Dubs' gargantuan polar bear, he couldn't submit the skull for measurement because a piece of it was accidentally chipped off in the dressing operation!

That it is possible for polar bears to exceed 2000 lb *907 kg* has also been confirmed by Ognev (1962), who says that some of the old males killed on the Taimyr Peninsula, NW Siberia have scaled as much as 60 pood (979 kg *2158 lb*) and yielded up to 12 pood (196 kg *432 lb*) of fat.

There are few records of captive polar bears exceeding 1000 lb *454 kg* in weight. A large male which died at the New York Zoological Park in 1960 scaled 1030 lb *467 kg* (Crandall, 1964). Another male named 'Carmichael', who died at Calgary Zoo, Alberta, Canada on 17 December 1970 recorded a posthumous weight of 1075 lb *488 kg*. He was received on 1 May 1948 as a five-month-old cub (David Banks, pers. comm.). On 21 February 1936 a posthumous weight of 1160 lb *526 kg* was reported for a male hybrid between a male polar and a female Kodiak bear at the National Zoological Park, Washington, DC, USA.

The polar bear is the only large land carnivore which does not instinctively fear man; in fact, it will deliberately stalk and kill humans for food at every given opportunity. On the other side of the coin, it also has an insatiable curiosity, and sometimes can be quite a clown – albeit a dangerous one!

Recently a woman working at an infants' school in

Anderma, a small settlement on the shore of the Kara Sea, N Russia, heard an urgent ring at the front door. When she hurried to admit the caller she found a large polar bear standing on its hind legs leaning against the bell! She quickly slammed the door shut, and shortly afterwards the unwelcome visitor shambled off in a huff.

In captivity bears are long-lived animals, and all seven species have been known to live more than 24 years.

The greatest age recorded for a bear is 47 years for a European brown bear at Skansen Zoo, Stockholm, Sweden (Kai Curry-Lindahl, cited by Crandall, 1964). Perry (1966) mentions a polar bear which lived for 41 years in Chester Zoo, and 40 years has been quoted for a sloth bear (*Melursus ursinus*) in an Indian zoo (Prater, 1965). A hybrid polar×Kodiak female born at the National Zoological Park, Washington, DC, USA on 21 February 1936 was euthanased on 19 April 1974 aged 38 years 1 month (M Jones, pers. comm.), and an Alaskan Peninsula giant bear (*Ursus a. middendorffi*) lived in New York Zoological Park from 23 August 1921 to 29 June 1958 (36 years 10 months 6 days). On 20 May 1977 the death was reported of a spectacled bear (*Tremarctos ornatus*) at Chicago's Brookfield Zoo aged 36 years 6 months, and this life span was also cited for a hybrid European brown×Asiatic black bear at Amsterdam Zoo, which died on 20 January 1955.

The rarest species of bear is the spectacled bear (*Tremarctos ornatus*) of NW South America, which was formerly distributed throughout the Andean forests of W Venezuela, Colombia, Ecuador, Peru and W Bolivia. Today it is found only in Ecuador and N Peru as a result of forest destruction, and the total Peruvian population is now less than 2000 animals.

Until recently the endangered giant panda (*Ailuropoda melanoleuca*) was believed to be a member of the raccoon family (*Procyonidae*). In 1973, however, Dr Vincent M Sarich, a biochemist at the University of California, Berkeley, declared that the animal was really a bear after studying blood and tissue samples taken from the famous 'Chi-Chi' after her death at London Zoo in July 1972. He also revealed that the giant panda was more closely related to the American black bear than it is to either the lesser panda (*Ailurus fulgens*) or the common raccoon (*Procyon lotor*). Since then, however, other scientists have pointed out that (1) the giant panda does not hibernate like the bear and (2) its genitals clearly resemble those of the raccoon, and the species has now been placed in a separate family of its own (*Ailuropodidae*) along with the lesser panda.

The giant panda is found in the intersecting mountain ranges of Sichuan (Szechwan), Hansu and Shanti provinces of central and NE China, and its habitat is so inhospitable that it is difficult to carry out a proper census. The total wild population, however, is estimated to be just under 1000 animals, including 200 in the Wolong reserve, NW Sichuan. In the winter of 1975–76 at least 140 giant pandas starved to death in Hansu province when their favourite type of bamboo came to the end of its natural 100-year life cycle, and four years later a number of other fatalities were reported in Sichuan province. In 1981 the World Wildlife Fund launched a major international campaign to help save the giant panda. The joint project includes construction of a research centre in the Wolong reserve, where a team appointed by the Fund is currently working with Chinese scientists.

The giant panda – like the bear! – is another long-lived species. A female called 'Li Li', who arrived at Peking Zoo in 1958 and later became the mother of the first zoo-born giant panda, was still alive in 1980 aged 28 years, and Canton Zoo had a male the same age (M Jones, pers. comm.).

The only performing giant panda in the world is a male owned by Shanghai Circus which, apart from doing some somersaults and foot-juggling, also rides a rocking horse and eats with a knife and fork! For a finale, he mounts a miniature carriage and blows on a horn as an Alsatian dog pulls him around the ring (Freiheit, 1979).

The largest land carnivore found in Britain is the badger (*Meles meles*). The average adult boar measures 3 ft *91 cm* in length (including a 4 in *10 cm* tail) and weighs 27 lb *12·2 kg* in the early spring and 32 lb *14·5 kg* at the end of the summer when it is in 'grease'. Adult sows are about 5 lb *2·27 kg* lighter.

In one series of 117 badgers collected in southern England the heaviest boar and sow weighed 37 lb *16·8 kg* and 30 lb 10 oz *13·9 kg* respectively.

Swayne (1908) mentions a 43 lb *19·5 kg* boar taken in Hereford, and a 42 lb *19 kg* boar and a 38 lb *17·2 kg* sow were killed on 5 May 1921 when they should have been at their lightest. Another boar shot near Llansannan, Denbighshire, N Wales also scaled 42 lb *19 kg* (Davies, 1936).

Dr Ernest Neale (1977), Britain's leading authority on the badger, quotes a weight of 52 lb *23·6 kg* for a badger trapped at Uckfield, Sussex in 1948, and says another one killed near Folkestone, Kent in February 1949 tipped the scales at 55 lb *25 kg*.

Weights of 61 lb *27·7 kg*, 62 lb *28 kg*, 63 lb *28·6 kg*, 66 lb *30 kg* and even 68 lb *30·9 kg* have been reported for badgers, the latter killed at Ampleforth, Yorkshire on 10 February 1942, but none of these extreme poundages have ever been authenticated.

Probably the heaviest badger on record was a

boar killed near Rotherham, Yorkshire in December 1952 which scaled exactly 60 lb *27·2 kg*. Neale says the animal was weighed by a group of Scouts under the supervision of the local vicar!

Although the common otter averages out smaller than the badger – in one series of 12 adult specimens the average weights for dogs and bitches worked out at 23 lb *10·4 kg* and 16 lb *7·3 kg* respectively – much larger individuals have been recorded. One dog otter killed by the Eastern Counties Otterhounds near Ipswich on 10 July 1907 scaled 34 lb *15·4 kg* (Clapham, 1922), and another one caught by the Darlington and Hurworth Otterhounds in 1840 weighed 35 lb *15·9 kg*. (This specimen is now on display at the Railway Tavern, Shincliffe, Co Durham.) The heaviest dog otter in the series already mentioned (Stephens, 1957) weighed 39 lb *17·7 kg*, and Daniel refers to another one caught in the River Lea, Essex in October 1794 which scaled 'upwards of 40 pounds' *18 kg*. Millais (1904–06) quotes a weight of 50 lb *22·7 kg* for an otter killed in Carmarthenshire which measured 5 ft 6 in *1·68 m* in total length (*cf* 4 ft *1·22 m* for average adult male), and in 1873 another specimen weighing '53 pounds and a few odd ounces' was caught in the River Avon near Ringwood, Hampshire (Corbin, 1873).

The largest marine carnivore (excluding the *Mysticeti*) is the sperm whale (*Physeter macrocephalus*), which has a world-wide distribution. The average adult bull measures 49 ft *14·93 m* in length at physical maturity and weighs 36 tonnes, and the average adult cow 36 ft *11 m* and 12 tonnes.

A bull sperm whale of 60 ft *18·29 m* is considered very large today, but individuals of much greater size were reported in the early days of whaling when they were not so molested. Bennett (1840), for instance, talks of one measuring 76 ft *23·16 m* in length and Beale (1839), in discussing the Australian sperm whale fishery, quotes a length of 84 ft *25·6 m* for 'the full-grown male of the largest size'. A length of 84 English feet *25·6 m* is also given by Van Mussechenbroek (1877) for the largest bull killed in the Moluccas or Spice Islands in the Malay Archipelago, and Scammon (1874) says the largest bulls measure 'from eighty to eighty-four feet'. There is also a record of a large sperm whale captured off the Galapagos Islands, E Pacific, by the British barque *Adam* in 1817 which produced 100 barrels of oil (the average yield is 50–55 barrels), and when Scammon was on a cruise in the barque *Rio Grande* in the same area in 1853 he took another cachalot which yielded 85 barrels of oil.

As no sperm whales approaching anything like this size have been caught this century, the general consensus is that these extreme measurements were either exaggerated or taken along the curves of the body, but this still does not explain the 5 m *16 ft 4¾ in* long lower jaw preserved in the British Museum which came from a bull caught between Cape Howe and New Zealand before 1851 and another outsized lower jaw measuring 15 ft 5 in *4·7 m* in length in the University Museum, Oxford, which came from a sperm whale allegedly measuring 88 ft *26·8 m*.

In this species the length of the lower jaw increases with age relative to the total body length. Thus, in a 14·7 m *48 ft 3 in* specimen the ratio was 1:6·2, as opposed to 1:5·4 for a 17·35 m *56 ft 10 in* bull (Tomilin, 1967). In a very old 16·28 m *53 ft 6 in* whale with completely worn teeth and very hard flesh, however, the ratio was only 1:5·1, and if we base the Tasman Sea jaw on this progression we get a total body length of 25·5 m *83 ft 8 in*, which is remarkably close to the maximum size quoted by the earlier writers.

The largest accurately measured sperm whale on record was a 20·7 m *67 ft 11 in* bull captured near the Kurile Islands in the NW Pacific by the Third Soviet Whaling Fleet in 1950. The whale was not weighed piecemeal, but it must have scaled – in good condition – at least 80 tonnes. Two other bulls taken (1) off the coast of Japan in 1946 and (2) off Kamchatka, NE Russia in 1964, both measured 19·8 m *65 ft* (International Whaling Statistics, 1945–66).

Since 1969 only eleven sperm whales reaching or exceeding 60 ft *18·29 m* in length have been caught in the N Pacific by Japanese and Russian whaling fleets. The largest specimen measured 61 ft *18·6 m*.

If we are to believe Millais (1904–6), the largest sperm whale ever taken in British waters was a 68 ft *20·7 m* long bull with a maximum girth of 40 ft *12·2 m* captured near Rona's Voe on 25 June 1903 and brought into the Norrona station in the Shetlands. However, as the oil yield (53 barrels) was exactly the same as that of a 54 ft *16·5 m* bull caught six days previously, this measurement must be considered suspect – unless, of course, it was taken over the curves.

In 1921 a length of 71 ft *21·6 m* was claimed for a sperm whale caught off the Aleutian coast and towed to the Akutan whaling station in Alaska (Henry Young, pers. comm.), but this was probably a curve measurement as well. Mr Sidney Brown (pers. comm.) of the Sea Mammal Research Unit in Cambridge has calculated from the photographic evidence and data he obtained personally on the lower jaw/total length ratios of four sperm whales caught in Icelandic waters in 1973 that the cachalot in question had a 'straight' length of *c* 61 ft *18·6 m*.

The sperm whales found in the Northern Hemisphere are generally larger than their southern counterparts.

The largest sperm whale ever recorded in the Southern Hemisphere was a 64 ft *19·5 m* bull caught near South Georgia during the 1948–49 whaling season.

On 15 May 1897 a length of 75 ft *22·9 m* was reported for a sperm whale killed in Algoa Bay on the SE coast of Cape Province, South Africa (Roberts, 1951), but this measurement was exaggerated. The skeleton of this animal, now in Port Elizabeth Museum, was originally assembled in a 63 ft *19·2 m* long hall and measured 58 ft *17·7 m* (G McLachlan, pers. comm.).

Fifteen sperm whales have been stranded on British coasts since 1913. The largest was probably a 61 ft 5 in *18·7 m* bull washed ashore at Birchington, Kent on 18 October 1914 (Harmer, 1927). Another one measuring *c* 60 ft *18·3 m* stranded at North Roe, Shetland on 30 May 1958. A huge bull which stranded at Derryloughan, Co Galway, Ireland on 2 January 1952 reportedly measured 65 ft *19·8 m*, but Fraser (1974) says the carcase had been badly damaged on the rocks and was so decomposed that there must have been some length extension.

There are very few authentic records of the cow sperm whale exceeding 40 ft *12·2 m* in length. In the summer season of 1969 two examples measuring 46 ft *14 m* were taken in the N Pacific (International Whaling Statistics). In 1947 a 55 ft *16·8 m* cow sperm whale was allegedly caught off Norway, but this was a wrongly identified bull.

The largest animal ever weighed in its entirety was an 18 m *59 ft* long bull sperm whale which stranded in the Westerschelde estuary, SW Netherlands on 24 February 1937. This cachalot, along with another bull measuring 16 m *52 ft 6 in*, were towed by tugs to Rotterdam and then raised out of the water by means of three floating cranes with a combined lifting capacity of 60 tonnes. The larger of the two animals weighed 53 tonnes (*cf* 53·37 tonnes for another 18 m *59 ft* bull weighed piecemeal in the Bering Sea on 28 June 1936) and the other 40 tonnes (Boschma, H. 1938).

The dental armament of the adult bull sperm whale is extremely formidable. The mandibular teeth can exceed 160 mm *6·30 in* in vertical height, and the author owns a specimen taken from a 56 ft *17 m* bull killed in South African waters which measures 203 mm *8 in* (245 mm *9·65 in* along the outside curve). The very large sperm whale captured off the Galapagos Islands in 1817 (see page 30) yielded a tooth measuring 241 mm *9·5 in* in vertical height (weight 3 lb *1·36 kg*), and one from the Azores measured 250 mm *9·84 in* (weight 4 lb 1¼ oz *1·84 kg*). Andrew Hermansen, the platform foreman at the now defunct Union Whaling Co Ltd in Durban, South Africa owns a specimen measuring exactly 254 mm *10 in*, and Yablokov (1958) says another tooth collected at a Russian shore station had a vertical height of 270 mm *10·63 in*. Trevor Housby (see page 134) has a tooth in his collection which has a vertical height of 235 mm *9·25 in*, but the specimen is broken and he estimates that it must have measured 317–330 mm *12·5–13·0 in* originally.

Probably the largest mandibular teeth on record are a pair in the collection of the Old Dartmouth

The largest animal ever weighed in its entirety – a 53-tonne bull sperm whale.

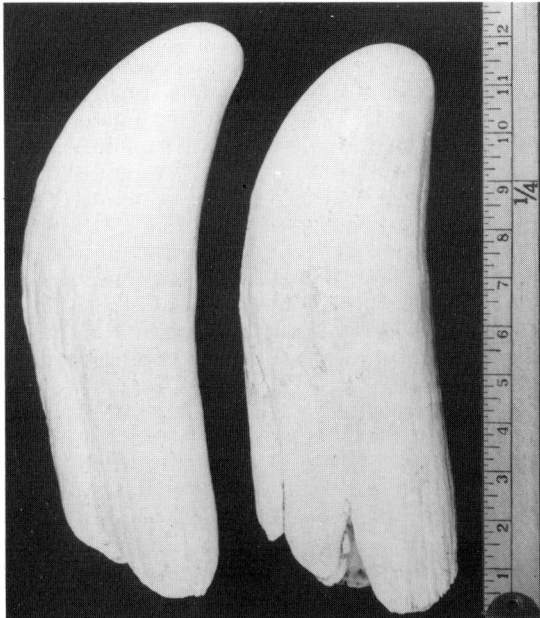

The largest pair of sperm whale teeth on record. They both measure 11 in 279 mm in vertical height and together weigh 8 lb 9 oz 3·88 kg.

Historical Society Whaling Museum, Massachusetts, USA which both measure 279 mm *11 in* in vertical height and weigh 4 lb 6 oz *1·98 kg* and 4 lb 3 oz *1·9 kg* respectively. They were cut out of a sperm whale allegedly measuring over 90 ft *27·4 m* taken by the American barque *Desdemona* off the River Plate (between Uruguay and Argentina) in the late 1870s (Ashley, 1926).

The smallest living carnivore (order Carnivora) is the least weasel (*Mustela rixosa*), also called the 'dwarf weasel', which is circumpolar in distribution. Four races are recognised (Hall, 1951), the smallest of which is *M.r. pygmaea* of Siberia. Mature specimens have a head and body length of 158–184 mm *6·22–7·24 in*, a tail length of 19–23 mm *0·75–0·90 in* and weigh between 35 and 70 g *1·23 and 2·5 oz*.

These bold and fearless cut-throats, which will readily attack animals nearly twice their own size without provocation, probably pack more nervous energy into their tiny bodies than any other living mammal, and their flashlike powers of movement are such that it is virtually impossible to follow them with the human eye. Yet despite their incredible quickness hawks, owls and even foxes sometimes succeed in catching them, though how they manage this feat of dexterity remains something of a mystery.

In Europe this family is represented by the larger *Mustela nivalis*, although a pygmy form has been found in Finland and eastern Europe which rivals

M.r. pygmaea for diminutiveness. This latter animal has a head and body length of 130–195 mm *5·12–7·68 in* and a tail length of 28–52 mm *1·1–2·05 in*.

The largest member of the cat family (*Felidae*) is the now very rare Manchurian or Amur tiger (*Panthera tigris altaica*). Adult males average 10 ft 2 in *3·10 m* in length (nose to tip of extended tail), stand 41–43 in *104–109 cm* at the shoulder and weigh 551–573 lb *250–260 kg*. Adult females are four-fifths this size.

The maximum size attained by this northern race of tiger has long been a matter of some conjecture. If we are to believe the claims of the old Russian hunters a number of the tigers killed before the advent of 'over-shooting' were very much larger than those that exist today. Yankovsky, for instance, says he killed one with the aid of dogs in the T'umen-Tzu region between NE Korea and SE Manchuria which measured 13 ft *4·0 m* over the curves of the body when the carcase was frozen (Taylor, 1956), and Barclay (1915) mentions another enormous tiger killed near Vladivostock which was adjudged to be 13 ft 5 in *4·09 m* long because the head and body measured 10 ft 5 in *3·18 m*! Both these measurements, however, are impossibly long for an animal of very symmetrical build, and the fact that Yankovsky himself estimated the weight of his tiger at no more than 500 lb *227 kg* would seem to confirm that these figures were actually taken from dressed skins.

Rowland Ward (1928) lists five Manchurian/Mongolian dressed skins ranging in size up to 13 ft 6 in *4·11 m*, and Cavendish (1894) speaks of a 14 ft 6 in *4·42 m* skin from Korea. Burton (1928), too, says he saw skins of immense size at the Nijni Novgorod Fair in 1893. Such measurements, however, are quite valueless and bear no relationship to the true length of the tiger (the skin of a 10 ft *3·0 m* tiger can be stretched to 13–14 ft *4·0–4·3 m*).

The *correct* way to measure a tiger is to lay the animal on its back and take a reading between pegs placed at the point of the nose and the tip of the extended tail, the result being some 5–6 per cent less than 'sportsman fashion', where the tape is stretched around the curves of the body (i.e. from the nose following a line between the ears and along the spine).

According to Baikov (1936) the man-eating tiger known as 'Great Van' which he shot in the Khailinkhe Forest, SE Manchuria, measured nearly 4 m *13 ft 1½ in* over the curves, but a published photograph showed a tiger of quite ordinary dimensions. Another tiger shot by the same hunter in Kirin Province, central Manchuria, reportedly measured 3·6 m *11 ft 9¾ in* over the curves, but as this specimen only weighed 560 lb *254 kg*, it could not have taped much more than 10 ft *3·1 m* between pegs.

Further evidence that the Manchurian tiger is not

much longer than its Indian counterpart is supplied by Morden (1930), who collected two male tigers in the Amur River region in 1929 while leading the American Museum of Natural History's North Asiatic Expedition. They only measured 10 ft *3·1 m* (weight 550 lb *249 kg*) and 9 ft 7 in *2·92 m* (weight 480 lb *218 kg*) respectively between pegs, although they were 'heavier and more powerfully built than any Indian tiger that I have seen'.

Another specimen measuring only 8 ft 6½ in *2·60 m* between pegs collected by two Russian zoologists was considered impressive enough to be sent to the Moscow Museum (Guggisberg, 1975), although this specimen may have been a female.

The tiger's length is also governed by its tail measurement. On an average this appendage is less than half the length of the head and body, but much longer measurements have been recorded. Baze (1957), for example, shot a heavily muscled tiger in Vietnam which, with the aid of a phenomenally long tail of 52 in *132 cm*, measured 11 ft 6 in *3·51 m* (between pegs?) and weighed more than 570 lb *258·5 kg*.

Very little information has been published on the weights attained by large Manchurian tigers. Filipek (1934) quotes a weight of 350 kg *772 lb* for a huge individual killed near the Amur River and Baikov shot a tiger in Manchuria which tipped the scales at 325 kg *717 lb*. There is also another record of a tiger killed in central Manchuria which weighed 320 kg *705 lb* (Novikov, 1962). All these weights, however, were eclipsed by a gigantic male shot in the Sikhote Alin Mts, Maritime Territory in 1950 which scaled 384 kg *846·6 lb* (Sysoev, 1960).

If all these poundages were proportional to length, then these four tigers would have measured 10 ft 10 in *3·30 m*, 10 ft 11 in *3·33 m*, 11 ft 2 in *3·40 m* and 11 ft 5½ in *3·49 m* respectively, but these figures are only hypothetical and in winter this northern race of tiger accumulates a thick layer of fat on the belly and flanks.

Not surprisingly, lengths in excess of 12 ft *3·7 m* have also been reported for the Indian tiger (*Panthera tigris tigris*). Buffon (1778) talks of one that measured 15 ft *4·6 m* and another tiger presented to the Nawab of Arcot in 1856 allegedly measured an incredible 18 ft *5·5 m* (sic).

Another tiger killed on Cozzimbazar Island, Bengal in 1807 reportedly measured '13 feet and a few inches from the tip of his nose to the end of his tail', and General W Rice (1857) states that the largest tigers shot by him and his friends in Rajputana and central India between 1850 and 1854 measured 12 ft 7½ in *3·85 m*, 12 ft 6¾ in *3·83 m* and 12 ft 2 in *3·71 m* respectively.

All these measurements, however, were (1) exaggerated; (2) taken from stretched skins; or (3) based on faulty tape readings, and in the old days there appears to have been a direct relationship between the recorded size of a tiger and the hunter's social standing or position. Perry (1964) says it was common practice for shikarees (native attendants) to carry with them specially made steel measures on which every inch *25 mm* was reduced by one-sixth. This meant that every 10 ft *3·05 m* tiger automatically measured out at 12 ft *3·7 m*, thus guaranteeing a handsome reward from a Viceroy or high-ranking military man.

Col F T Pollock (1903) says he shot a heavy, loose-skinned tiger in southern India which measured 10 ft 1 in *3·07 m* between pegs and yielded a 13 ft 4 in *4·06 m* long dried skin, and there is another record of an Indian tiger 1 in *25 cm* shorter yielding a 14 ft *4·3 m* skin when pegged out and dried.

Of the 200 tigers measured by Dunbar Brander (1923), a very reliable observer, only two exceeded 10 ft *3·05 m* in length between pegs and they were 10 ft 3 in *3·12 m* and 10 ft 1½ in *3·09 m*, respectively.

In reality, the average adult male Indian tiger measures 9 ft 3 in *2·82 m* in length, stands 36–38 in *91–97 cm* at the shoulder and weighs about 420 lb *190 kg*. Adult females are three-quarters this size.

If we exclude the freak male from Vietnam, **the longest accurately measured Indian tiger on record** was a 10 ft 7 in *3·23 m* individual (tail 3 ft 7 in *109 cm*) shot by Col Evans Gordon at Ramshai Hab, in the Duars, Bengal. It measured 40 in *102 cm* at the shoulder and weighed a surprisingly low 491 lb *223 kg* (Rowland Ward, 1907).

Until fairly recently the heaviest Indian tiger on record was a giant male shot in Nepal which weighed 705 lb *320 kg* (Smythies, 1942), while another tiger (length 9 ft 11½ in *3·04 m*) killed by Capt M D Goring-Jones in Central Provinces scaled exactly 700 lb *317 kg* (Rowland Ward, 1910).

Since then, however, Khan Seheb Jamshed Butt (1963) has claimed that tigers weighing up to 800 lb *363 kg* have been killed in India, and he was subsequently proved right in November 1967 when David J Hasinger of Philadelphia, Pennsylvania, USA shot an enormous individual in northern Uttar Pradesh some 50 miles *80 km* south of the Chinese border. This tiger measured a record 10 ft 7 in *3·23 m* between pegs (11 ft 1 in *3·38 m* over the curves) and tipped the scales at an astonishing 857 lb *389 kg* (D Hasinger, pers. comm.). In 1969 the mounted animal was put on display in the rotunda of the US Museum of Natural History, Smithsonian Institution, Washington, DC. It should be pointed out here that this tiger had killed a buffalo the previous evening and had probably eaten heavily. Schaller (1967) says the amount of food ingested by a very hungry tiger at one sitting can total as much as 20 per cent of its body-weight, which means a 700 lb *318 kg* male could – in theory – dispose of 140 lb *64 kg* of

The 857 lb 389 kg tiger shot by David Hasinger in Uttar Pradesh, northern India in 1967. The mounted specimen is now on display in the Smithsonian Institution, Washington DC.

meat. On the other hand, it also proves that this outsized individual must have weighed *at least* 715 lb *324 kg* – even with an empty stomach!

E H Morbey shot an exceptionally large male (length 10 ft 6 in *3·2 m*) in Kumaon, United Provinces, which scaled 645 lb *293 kg*, and a weight of 608 lb *276 kg* (length 10 ft 2 in *3·10 m*) was reported for another one killed by the Kumar of Bikaner in Gwalior (Rowland Ward, 1928).

Both these tigers were confirmed cattle-killers and consequently very bulky.

Although the African lion (*Panthera leo*) is smaller than the Manchurian tiger in terms of bulk, it rivals the Indian tiger for size. The average adult male measures 9 ft *2·7 m* in length, stands 37–38 in *94–97 cm* at the shoulder and weighs 380–400 lb *172–181 kg*. Adult females are one-fifth smaller. The now extinct Barbary lion (*Panthera leo leo*) and the Cape lion (*Panthera l. melanochaitus*) averaged out somewhat larger, the former weighing about 25 per cent more.

The longest accurately measured African lion on record was an 11 ft *3·4 m* long black-maned giant shot by G Gladney near Mucusso, S Angola in October 1973 (Rowland Ward, 1975). Another one shot by G Prud'homme in Uganda measured 10 ft 11 in *3·33 m*, and the same length was recorded for a male shot by J K Roberts in the Sudan (Rowland Ward, 1969).

Unlike the tiger, very few lions exceed a weight of 550 lb *249 kg* in the wild state. Roberts (1951) mentions a 9 ft 10 in *3·00 m* long male shot in the Sabi District, Transvaal, South Africa which scaled 553 lb *251 kg*, and a weight of 583 lb *264 kg* (length 9 ft 5 in *2·87 m*) was reported for another male taken in the Orange River Colony, South Africa in 1865. In *c* 1919 a lion weighing 610 lb *277 kg* was shot at Big Ben, Swaziland.

The heaviest wild African lion on record was a man-eater shot just outside Hectorspruit, E Transvaal, South Africa in 1936 by Lennox Anderson, which scaled 690 lb *313 kg*. This weight was so extreme – taken on the local railway scale – that it was checked by several people before being officially accepted (Campbell, 1937).

The protected Asiatic or Indian lion (*Panthera leo persica*), which is now confined to the Gir Forest preserve on the Kathiawar Peninsula, W India (total population *c* 200 in 1981), is about the same size as its African cousin, although a little stockier in build. An 8 ft 9½ in *2·68 m* long male shot by Capt Smeel weighed 490 lb *222 kg* excluding entrails (Sterndale, 1884).

The largest Asiatic lion on record appears to have been one shot by Lord Belper in the Gir Forest of Junagadh on 8 March 1935, which measured 9 ft 9½ in *2·98 m* between pegs.

The largest 'Big Cat' ever held in captivity was a 10 ft 6 in *3·20 m* long black-maned lion named 'Simba', who weighed a peak 826 lb *375 kg* in July 1970. Other statistics included a shoulder height of 44 in *112 cm* and a 52 in *132 cm* neck. Simba's owner, professional wild-animal trainer Adrian Nyoka, received the lion as a six-month-old cub from Dublin Zoo in November 1958 in exchange for an African serval. Up until the age of 3 years Simba grew along normal lines. Then suddenly, for some unknown reason, he started growing at an alarming rate. At 4½ years he tipped the scales at 500 lb *227 kg* and at 6 years he was 620 lb *281 kg*. Two years later he weighed in at 704 lb *319 kg* and by 1969 he had reached 756 lb *343 kg*. Simba died on 16 January 1973 and his stuffed body is now on display at Knaresborough Zoo, Yorkshire.

A Korean–Chinese tiger (*Panthera tigris coreensis*) at Peking Zoo recorded a weight of 812·5 lb *368·5 kg* on 20 February 1973 (Gary Smart, pers. comm.).

The Felidae is represented in Britain by the Scottish wild cat (*Felis silvestris grampia*), which is now confined to the Highlands. Male specimens rarely exceed 12 lb *5·4 kg* in weight and 3 ft *91 cm* in overall length, but one killed at Ardgay, Ross & Cromarty scaled 15 lb 10 oz *7·09 kg* (Pocock, 1951). The maximum weight recorded for a female is 12 lb 5 oz *5·6 kg*.

The smallest member of the cat family is the rusty-spotted cat (*Felis rubiginosa*). Two races are recognised: *Felis r. rubiginosa* of southern India and *Felis r. phillipsi* of Sri Lanka. The average adult male has a head and body length of 406–457 mm *16–18 in*, a tail length of 228–254 mm *9–10 in* and weighs about 1·35 kg *3 lb*, while adult females are slightly smaller.

According to Guggisberg the smallest wild cat in the world is the black-footed cat (*Felis nigripes*) of southern Africa, but although adult males are slightly shorter in overall length (i.e. 575–700 mm *22·6–27·6 in*), this species has been weighed up to 2·75 kg *6 lb*.

The rarest 'Big Cat' is the Bali tiger (*Panthera tigris balica*) which, up until the end of last century, was still fairly common. In the years that followed, however, indiscriminate killing by man virtually wiped out the population. The last individual killed in the wild was shot at Sumbar Kima, W Bali on 27 September 1937, and by 1963 there were believed to be only 3–4 left in a reserve in western Bali. Ten years later it was announced that this small race of tiger (the skull of an adult female was no larger than that of a male leopard) was almost certainly extinct, but in 1979 a team of scientists carrying out a survey in the northern mountains found claw marks estimated to be between 6 and 18 months old on a tree-trunk that they said were compatible with those of a Bali tiger, but the leopard is also found on this island (see below).

The Javan tiger (*Panthera t. sondaica*), which is similar in appearance to the Bali tiger but larger, is also on the brink of extinction through over-hunting. By 1955 there were only an estimated 20–25 tigers left in the whole of Java, of which 10–12 were in the Udjung Kulon Reserve at the western tip of this densely-populated island (Talbot, 1960). During the 1960s the tigers in Udjung Kulon and Baluran Reserves were killed, and by 1972 there were only three to seven in the Meru Betiri Reserve and another five in the Sukamati Reserve, SE Java. Those in the Sukamati Reserve were later exterminated and in 1978 the five tigers left in the Meru Betiri Reserve were accorded full protection by the Indonesian Government. By then, of course, it was too late.

In 1979 the fresh pugmark of a leopard was discovered by zoologists in a dried-up river bed in N Bali, and the animal was heard calling at night. Up until then the leopard had not been known to exist on the island, although two officers of the Indonesian Nature Protection and Wildlife Conservation Service had reported seeing what appeared to be a black specimen in the Prapat Agung area 4 years earlier.

The greatest reliable age recorded for a 'Big Cat' is *c* 29 years for a lion named 'Nero', who died in Cologne Zoo, W Germany in May 1907 or 1908 (Flower, 1931).

Another lion born at Dublin Zoo, Ireland on 26 June 1889 lived there for 25 years 18 days, dying on 14 July 1914, and one born at Carl Hagenbeck's Tierpark, Hamburg-Stellingen, W Germany in 1903 and later sent to Rotterdam Zoo, Netherlands died there on 13 November 1927 aged 24 years. The same figure was also quoted for a male named 'Brutus',

The 690 lb 313 kg man-eating lion shot just outside Hectorspruit, Eastern Transvaal, South Africa in 1936.

who died at the Orphanage in Nairobi National Park, Kenya in March 1972.

Lions rarely live longer than 20 years in the wild state, the normal expectation of life being 12–14 years.

According to Russian claims the Manchurian tiger lives up to 50 years in the wild, but this figure is not supported by zoo records. Guggisberg says one individual which died in Prague Zoo at the age of 26 years 'showed clear signs of advanced senility, and was found to have suffered from debility of the heart and lungs'.

Perry puts the maximum life potential in the wild at *c* 25 years, but he says few tigers live longer than 15 years.

The greatest reliable age recorded for a tiger is 26 years 3 months in the case of an Indian tigress which was born in Adelaide Zoo, S Australia in November 1931 and died there on 26 February 1958 (Marvin Jones, pers. comm.).

In July 1972 the death was reported of 'Shasta', a

liger at Hogle Zoo, Salt Lake City, Utah, USA aged 24 years. She was born there on 6 May 1948, the product of an African lion and an Indian tigress.

The greatest age recorded for a leopard is 23 years 7 months for a female born at Frankfurt Zoo, W Germany on 9 May 1950. It lived there until its death on 25 December 1973. There is also a record of a captive jaguar (*Panthera onca*) living for 22 years.

The greatest age recorded for any member of the Felidae excluding the domestic cat is 34+ years in the case of a bobcat (*Felis rufus*) captured locally by Fred Space of the Space Wild Animal Farm, Mear Sussex, New Jersey, USA in January 1942. It was put to sleep on 10 May 1974.

The only *established* man-eaters of the cat family are the tiger, lion and leopard.

The individual man-eating record is held by a notorious tigress known as the 'Champawat man-eater', which operated first in Nepal and then in Kumaon. She killed an incredible 438 people in eight years before being shot by Jim Corbett in 1911.

In 1869 a tigress reportedly killed 129 people in the Sunderbunds, a great swampy region in the Ganges Delta (Nott, 1886).

Man-eating lions prefer to do their killing in prides rather than individually, but there is one record from Malawi of a rogue lion which killed 14 people in the space of 1 month. Another man-eater shot in the Numgari District of Portuguese East Africa in September 1938 was responsible for the deaths of 22 natives in 8 weeks. There is also a reliable record of a lion killing 40 people in the Kasama District of N Rhodesia before it was shot in October 1943.

After a hunt lasting for several weeks in 1977, Tanzanian trackers shot a man-eating lion and found to their amazement that it only had three legs! Despite this handicap, the animal had attacked a dozen people in three months and killed eight of them.

During the period 1932–47 a pride of 17 man-eating lions and successive generations killed and ate between 1000 and 1500 people in a game area at the northern end of Lake Nyasa, Tanzania. The 'Njombe man-eaters', as they were called, were eventually shot out by George Rushby (1965) over a period of 15 months.

Recently hunters who paid to shoot lions on a game ranch at Ellisvas in South Africa discovered why they never had any luck, despite plenty of tracks. The owner was walking around with rubber lion paws on his feet!

The leopard also has a very unsavoury reputation. The infamous 'Man-eater of Panar', for instance, accounted for 400 victims before it was shot by Corbett in 1910, and as recently as October 1972 a leopard attacked and killed three boys aged 4, 7 and 12 respectively within the space of eight hours in villages near Junagadh, W India.

Strangely enough, a leopard which killed at least 18 people before it was captured in April 1978 turned extremely shy of humans when it was put in Lucknow Zoo, India for study. Not only did it spend most of the time hiding in its den, but it also rejected the keeper's offers of meat to tempt it into view.

Big cats turn man-eater for a number of reasons, but hunger is not always the deciding factor. According to animal experts in W Bengal many tigers take to drinking salty water and then develop a taste for salt. As human flesh has a salty taste, they then go after man.

The jaguar, which ranges from the SW USA through Central and South America to Patagonia is more a 'man-killer' than a 'man-eater', although Sasha Siemel (1954) makes several references to man-eating jaguars in Brazil.

The greatest number of live cubs produced by a big cat in a single litter is eight by an Indian tigress named 'Baghdad' (b 1972) at Marine World/Africa USA, Redwood City, California on 15 April 1979. It was her fifth litter in 2½ years (26 cubs in all) (Steve Castillo, pers. comm.).

The previous title-holder was a lioness named 'Maire' (b 1956) at Dublin Zoo who produced a live litter of seven in February 1964. She had earlier had at least three other litters of six live cubs by the same breeding male (Terence Murphy, pers. comm.).

In April 1972 a lioness named 'Pomone' at Bordeaux Zoo, France produced her third set of triplets in 13 months.

The largest member of the order Pinnipedia (*c* 34 species) is the southern elephant-seal (*Mirounga leonina*), which inhabits the circumpolar sub-antarctic islands and the coast of Patagonia. Adult bulls average 14–16 ft *4·3–4·9 m* in total length (snout to tip of hind flippers) and weigh 4000–5000 lb *1814–2268 kg*. Adult cows, who do not possess the characteristic proboscis of the bull, are much smaller, averaging 10 ft *3·1 m* in total length and weighing about 1500 lb *680 kg*.

The largest accurately measured southern elephant-seal on record was an enormous beach-master killed in Possession Bay, South Georgia on 28 February 1913 and subsequently examined by Murphy (1914). It measured 21 ft 4 in *6·50 m* after flensing (original length *c* 22 ft 6 in *6·9 m*) and must have weighed 4–5 tonnes. An animal this size could tower up to 10 ft *3·1 m* in height.

Another exceptionally large bull shot by Herbert Mansel 45 miles *72 km* west of the Falkland Islands in 1879 measured just over 21 ft *6·4 m* and 'must have weighed several tons'. The skeleton of this pinniped

The Indian tigress 'Baghdad' proudly showing off her record litter of cubs.

The same litter when they were half-grown.

is (or was) preserved in the Museum of the Royal College of Surgeons in London (Flower, 1884).

It should be pointed out here that seasonal variations in fatness can affect the total-length measurements of large bulls by as much as 15 in *381 mm*; also, the size of the proboscis is not constant.

According to Murphy the fattest bull seen by him at South Georgia measured 18 ft 4 in *5·59 m* in length. 'It was so round and distended that it had the appearance of being pneumatic and inflated under pressure. Seven men could barely turn its body over with the aid of ropes and hand holes in the blubber, even after half the blubber had been removed, and a trench had been scooped under one side of its carcase.'

Of 226 elephant-seals shot at South Georgia and examined by Laws (1953) the largest bull measured 18 ft 1 in *5·51 m* over the curve of the back (*c* 17 ft 2 in *5·23 m* straight-line measurement). Another bull measured photographically at Signy Island was 20 ft 6·1 m (*c* 19 ft 5·8 m), and an even larger individual was observed but not measured.

There are old records of beachmasters measuring 25 ft 7·6 m and even 27 ft 8·2 m, but although there is a tendency to over-estimate the size of this animal Laws says 'it is possible that formerly the bull elephant-seal reached a greater size than at present'. Today, however, bulls rarely exceed 18 ft *5·5 m*.

A 13 ft 4 in *4·06 m* bull weighed piecemeal by Messrs Christian Salvesen and Co at Leigh Harbour, South Georgia tipped the scales at 4357 lb *1976 kg*. The skin weighed 254 lb *115 kg*, the blubber 1469 lb *666 kg*, the heart 92 lb *42 kg*, the head 114 lb *52 kg* and the blood (estimated) 218 lb *99 kg*. 'It was a medium-sized bull,' writes Hamilton (1949), 'and in the absence of further data it is reasonable to believe that a large bull may weigh anything up to four or five tons.'

Elephant-seals occasionally stray to the coasts of South Africa and Angola. In 1924 a large bull hauled up on the beach at Simonstown, Cape Province, South Africa and caused a great deal of panic among the local population before it was shot. It measured 16 ft *4·9 m* in length and weighed 4500 lb *2041 kg*.

The largest accurately measured cow southern elephant-seal on record was an 11 ft 5 in *3·48 m* specimen obtained by Harris in the Falkland Islands in 1909. The weight of this animal was not recorded, but it probably scaled nearly 2000 lb *907 kg*. Another cow shot in South Georgia in *c* 1952 measured 11 ft 6 in *3·51 m*, but the length was taken along the curve of the back (Laws, 1953).

Most of the cows measured by Murphy at South Georgia were under 8 ft 6 in *2·59 m*.

The much less abundant northern elephant-seal (*Mirounga angustirostris*), now restricted to the islands off the Pacific coast of Mexico and southern Cali-

fornia, USA, is slightly smaller than its relative in the south and rarely exceeds 17 ft *5·2 m* and 5000 lb *2268 kg* (cows 11 ft *3·4 m* and 1700 lb *771 kg*).

In former times before they were over-exploited northern beachmasters reportedly reached a much greater size, but as the nasal tube is much more pendulous in this species and hangs down 12–15 in *305–381 mm* below the level of the chin, accurate comparisons are difficult. One fat bull taken in the Santa Barbara group, southern California by the brig *Mary Helen* in 1852 was 18 ft *5·5 m* long and yielded 210 gallons *795 litres* of oil; another seen by Scammon (1874) was credited with a length of 22 ft *6·7 m* 'tip to tip'.

The largest elephant-seal ever held in captivity was a bull of the southern race called 'Goliath' (one of several of that name) received at Carl Hagenbeck's Tierpark, Hamburg-Stellingen, W Germany in 1928 from South Georgia, who recorded a posthumous measurement of 20 ft 6 in *6·25 m* in 1930. Unfortunately this colossus was not weighed but – in good condition – it could hardly have scaled less than 8000 lb *3629 kg* at that length.

In 1970 a posthumous weight of 6287 lb *2852 kg* (excluding blood) was recorded for a 14 ft 8 in *4·47 m* long southern bull called 'Spot' at Edinburgh Zoo. As the blood usually accounts for about 5 per cent of the total body-weight in pinnipeds this rotund animal (maximum girth 14 ft 3 in *4·34 m*) must have weighed about 6590 lb *2989 kg* when alive (C Rushton, pers. comm.).

The largest northern elephant-seal ever held in captivity was a bull received at San Diego Zoo, California, USA in 1929 which measured 16 ft 6 in *5·03 m* in length and weighed 'nearly five thousand pounds' (Benchley, 1930).

The largest elephant-seal living in captivity today is a southern bull called 'Daikichi' at Enoshima Marineland, Fujisawa, Japan. He measures 18 ft 4 in *5·59 m* in length and weighs about 6500 lb *2948 kg*.

Although the walrus (*Odobenus rosmarus*) of the Arctic Ocean rarely exceeds 13 ft *4·0 m* and 3000 lb *1361 kg*, at least two bulls have been collected which were considerably larger. Capt Ole Hansen, who hunted walruses for more than 20 years, told Hagenbeck (1909) that on his last Arctic voyage he killed an enormous bull in Franz-Josef Land which yielded a 500 kg *1102 lb* hide. Unfortunately no length was quoted for this pinniped, but as the hide usually accounts for about 20 per cent of the total body-weight in adult bulls, this must have been an awful lot of walrus. Further proof that such outsized freaks do occur on very rare occasions was later supplied by Jack Woodson (1911), an American hunter, who shot what the local Eskimos described as 'the biggest walrus in existence' in the Chukchi Sea in August 1910. This bull measured an extraordinary 16 ft *4·9 m* from the nose to the first joint of the rear flippers, and a little over 18 ft *5·5 m* in total length. The hide alone tipped the scales at 1000 lb *454 kg*, and the total weight of this monster was put at 5000 lb *2268 kg*.

In May 1934 the body of a strange marine animal with a seal-like head was washed up on the shore at Tenes, Algeria. Unlike the Mediterranean monk seal (*Monachus monachus*), however, which does not exceed 10 ft *3·1 m*, this creature was over 40 ft *12·2 m* long and had a serpentine tail which gave it a peculiar humped appearance. It was never identified but, judging from photographic evidence, it wouldn't look out of place in Loch Ness!

The largest pinniped (two species) among British fauna is the grey seal (*Halichoeurus grypus*), also called the 'Atlantic seal'. It is found mainly on the western coasts of Britain, but the centre of abundance is the Farne Islands off the coast of Northumberland. Territorial bulls average 7½ ft *2·28 m* in total length and weigh 513 lb *213 kg* and mature cows 7¼ ft *2·2 m* and 340 lb *154 kg* (lactating females can be 100 lb *45 kg* heavier).

According to Hickling (1962) one of the largest grey seals killed by Blackett on the Farne Islands in *c* 1772 measured 9 ft *2·7 m* over the curve of the back, 7 ft 6 in *2·29 m* in maximum girth and weighed 658 lb *298 kg*. Edmondston (1838) says the largest bull collected by him on Shetland Island measured 8 ft *2·4 m* in length and weighed 672 lb *305 kg*, but as the maximum girth of this creature was only 6 ft *1·8 m* this poundage must be considered suspect. The largest of the 27 adult bulls measured by Millais (1904–06) was 9 ft 6 in *2·90 m*. He also mentions another bull shot by Sir Reginald Cathcart on South Uist, Outer Hebrides, which scaled 700 lb *318 kg*, and this is probably close to the upper weight limit for this species.

Adult cows have been recorded up to 7 ft 7 in *2·31 m* and 550 lb *249 kg*.

The smallest pinnipeds are the Baikal seal (*Pusa sibirica*) of Lake Baikal, a large freshwater basin in southern Siberia, USSR, and the ringed seal (*Pusa hispida*) of the circumpolar Arctic coasts. Both animals have their supporters, and in reality there is very little to choose between them in terms of size.

According to King (1964) adult specimens (both sexes) of *P. sibirica* grow to a length of *c* 4 ft 6 in *1·37 m* and a weight of about 140 lb *64 kg*, but Kozhov (1963) says the maximum size reached by this species is 5 ft 5 in *1·65 m* and 286 lb *130 kg*.

The ringed seal has been credited with a maximum length of 4 ft 10 in *1·47 m* and a weight of 200 lb *91 kg* (King, 1964), but measurements up to 5 ft 6 in *1·68 m* and a weight of 250 lb *113 kg* have also been reported.

Although these seals are classified as different

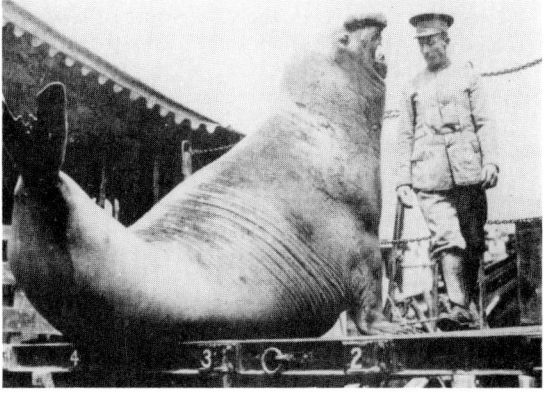

The famous southern elephant seal 'Goliath' of the Ringling & Barnum & Bailey Circus. This bull weighed over 6000 lb 2722 kg.

species, it has been suggested that *P. sibirica* may be a land-locked race of ringed seals because of the similarities in size and appearance.

The smallest pinniped found in British waters is the common seal (*Phoca vitulina*). Adult bulls measure 5½–6 ft *1·68–1·83 m* in total length and weigh up to 231 lb *105 kg*, and adult cows 4½–5¾ ft *1·37–1·75 m* and 193 lb *87·5 kg*. The main centre of abundance is the Wash area (*c* 6000), but other populations are found in the Shetlands, the Orkneys, East and West Scotland and N Ireland. In October 1980 a pregnant female set up a British record by giving birth to a pup over 60 miles *97 km* inland on the banks of the River Trent at Girton, Nottinghamshire. It was believed she was from a colony in the Wash and had lost her way during migration.

According to a Natural Environment Research Council report published in 1978 there were 70 000 grey seals and 19 500 common seals living in British waters.

Some species of seal are among the swiftest mammals in the sea.

The highest swimming speed recorded for a pinniped is 21·7 knots (25 miles/h *40 km/h*) for a Californian sea-lion (*Zalophus californianus*) (MacGinitie and MacGinitie, 1949). The graceful leopard seal (*Hydrurga leptonyx*) of the sub-antarctic islands is also capable of strong bursts when chasing prey like penguins, and when it wishes to sleep on an ice floe it sometimes shoots 6 ft *1·8 m* or more out of the water to land on the top with a thump.

The fastest-moving pinniped on ice or snow is the torpedo-shaped crabeater seal (*Lobodon carcinophagus*) of the Antarctic. One animal chased across tightly-packed snow on Signy Island, South Orkneys for dog food undulated along for 230 m *755 ft* at 19 km/h *11·8 miles/h* before it was finally killed. Most of the propulsive power comes from the hind-flippers which are held together as in swimming and are thumped down with tremendous vigour, while the front flippers are used to strike strong backward strokes.

'When disturbed suddenly the crabeater can escape rapidly', writes O'Gorman (1963). 'This remarkably quick escape reaction from sleeping to approximately 19 km an hour within seconds suggests that this more rapid locomotory pattern might be of considerable value to the crabeater seal when attacked by its hereditary enemy, the killer whale, which is probably quite capable of upsetting ice-floes in its pursuit of prey.'

The deepest-diving pinniped is the Weddell seal (*Leptonychotes weddelli*), the world's most southerly mammal, which is found along the Antarctic mainland and neighbouring islands. Adult bulls regularly descend to 900–1000 ft *274–305 m* in search of food, and dives can last for more than 20 minutes.

In March 1966 an elderly bull fitted with a depth-gauge recorded a natural dive of 600 m *1969 ft* in McMurdoe Sound, an inlet of the Ross Sea, and remained below for 15 minutes. At this depth the seal withstood a pressure of 875 lb/in² *6033 kPa* of body area (Kooyman, 1969).

The Weddell seal survives these tremendous dives because the lungs collapse at a depth of around 100 m *328 ft* from the external pressure. This means the nitrogen is driven into the bronchi and the trachea instead of being absorbed into the bloodstream, where the consequent embolisms or 'bubbles' would produce the fatal sickness known as the bends. Also, the surface blood-vessels are constricted to a minimum to ensure a steady supply of blood to the heart and brain, and large amounts of oxygen are tolerated in the blood.

Another seal under observation stayed underwater much longer (60 minutes) and must have travelled several miles under the ice looking for another breathing hole before being finally forced back to the station. How does the animal know when it has reached the point of no return? Unfortunately, science has not yet come up with an answer to this one, although Kooyman has speculated that the Weddell seal has some sort of control mechanism which sends out a warning when 50 per cent of the submersion capacity has been used up.

The elephant-seal also has a deep diving ability and can remain below for periods up to 40 minutes. One individual caught 40 miles *64 m* from the coast had a number of bottom-living small sharks, squids and rays in its stomach (Nishiwaki, 1967), and Martin (1977) says this pinniped sometimes descends to 2000 ft *610 m* when searching for food.

The greatest reliable age recorded for a pinniped

is 'at least 46 years' for a cow grey seal shot at Shunni Wick in Shetland on 23 April 1969. The age was determined by counting the cementum layers in the lower left canine tooth (Bonner, 1971).

The oldest ringed seal in a sample of more than 750 collected on the SW coast of Baffin Island in the eastern Canadian Arctic in 1954 by McLaren (1958) was a male aged 43 years.

The greatest reliable age reported for a captive pinniped is 43 years for a bull grey seal named 'Jacob'. He was captured off the Stockholm Archipelago in the Baltic Sea and arrived at Skansen Zoo, Stockholm, Sweden on 28 October 1901 when he was an estimated two years of age. He died there on 30 January 1942 (Kai Curry-Lindahl, pers. comm.).

Despite its great size, the life expectation of the elephant-seal is quite short by comparison. In one series of tooth counts of *M. leonina* by Laws (1953) the maximum ages recorded for bulls and cows were 20 years and 18 years respectively. In 1940 a cow of this species named 'Nixe' died at Carl Hagenbeck's Tierpark aged 15 years (Steinmetz, 1954).

The most abundant species of pinniped is the crabeater seal. In 1978 the total population was believed to be nearly 15 000 000.

The largest concentration of large mammals found anywhere in the world today is that of the northern fur seal (*Callorhinus ursinus*) in the Pribilof group, Bering Sea. The main colony is centred on St George and St Paul, and at the height of the breeding season there are an estimated 1 500 000 animals on these two islands alone. Another 500 000 pups are born each year.

If we exclude man, the northern fur seal is also something of a champion when it comes to keeping large harems. Forty to sixty wives is a good average, but an exceptionally strong individual may have as many as 150! These harem bulls, as they are known, have to defend their love nests against all challengers for periods lasting up to 2 months, and at the end of the season they are usually so thin and weak through lack of nourishment that some of them never make it back to the sea again.

The rarest of all pinnipeds is the Caribbean or West Indian monk seal (*Monachus tropicalis*). At one time this creature was the basis of a profitable seal fishery in both the Caribbean and the Gulf of Mexico, but it was so persistently slaughtered for its oil, meat and skin that by the end of the nineteenth century it was virtually extinct.

On 14 June 1909 an adult bull and two yearlings were received at New York Aquarium (Townsend, 1909). In March 1911 one of the young seals was still living, but Crandall says 'no further information concerning it is now available'.

In January 1911 some fishermen visited the Triangle Keys, a group of islets to the west of Yucatan and killed about 200 seals (Allen, 1942), and on 15 March 1922 one was killed near Key West, Florida (Townsend, 1923). In 1949 two seals were seen in the waters south of Kingston, Jamaica. They were probably from the last known colony on Serranilla Bank, which disappeared three years later. In 1962 a monk seal was seen on the beach at Isla Mujueres off the Yucatan Peninsula, and at least two individuals were spotted by fishermen between Cuba and the Bahamas in 1974. Two years later there was another sighting between Punta Gorda, Belize and Livingston, Guatemala (Knudson, 1977). In April 1980 a small team of scientists carried out a search of the SE Bahamas for a possible breeding colony, but no seals were found. Incredible as it may seem, this species has no protection whatsoever, the reason given being that it is now considered to be extinct!

The populations of the Mediterranean and Hawaiian monk seals (*M. monachus* and *M. schauinslandi*) are now estimated at 500 and 2000 animals respectively. In the case of the former the primary causes of mortality are pollution and accidental drowning in fish gear and its future survival is now in doubt. With the Hawaiian monk seal, however, the main problem is large predatory sharks, and these may have been responsible for the recent sharp decline.

The Juan Fernandez fur seal (*Arctocephalus philippi*) reportedly became extinct in 1917, but it was rediscovered on the Juan Fernandez Islands, E Pacific, in November 1965. It is now protected by the Chilean Government, and there are now believed to be about 700 of them living on Isla Robinson Crusoe and Isla Alejandro Selkirk.

Among the pinnipeds, the longest migrations are made by the northern fur seal which may travel 6250 miles *10 000 km* a year and spend 6–8 months at sea.

The only mammals capable of sustained flight are bats (*Chiroptera*), of which there are about 950 living species. They are found throughout the world with the exception of certain remote oceanic islands and the polar regions.

The largest bat in terms of wingspread is probably the Bismarck flying fox (*Pteropus neohibernicus*) of the Bismarck Archipelago and New Guinea. One specimen collected near Lae, NE New Guinea in July 1959 and now preserved in the American Museum of Natural History, New York has a head and body length of 455 mm *17·9 in* and measures 1650 mm *5 ft 5 in* across the outstretched wings. Peterson (1964) says he collected others of the same species measuring 'well over five feet six inches', and added that he was firmly convinced a 6 ft *1830 mm* specimen would be discovered one day.

The large flying fox (*P. vampyrus*) of S Burma, Thailand, Indonesia and the Philippines and the Indian flying fox (*P. giganteus*) have also been credited with measurements in excess of 5 ft *1520 mm* and weights up to 3 lb 0¾ oz *1·38 kg* and 3 lb 6¾ oz *1·54 kg* respectively, and the wingspread of *Acerodon jubatus* of the Philippines, which externally is indistinguishable from *Pteropus*, is given as 1510–1600 mm *4 ft 11½–5 ft 3 in* (Walker *et al*, 1968).

The largest bat found in Britain (14 species) is the very rare large mouse-eared bat (*Myotis myotis*) which has a wingspread of 365–450 mm *14·37–17·72 in* and weighs up to 45 g *1·6 oz* (females). This species was not added to the British list until 1956. Before then it was known only from a specimen collected in London (pre-1850) and a male taken alive at Girton, Cambridgeshire in 1888 and now preserved in the Museum of Zoology at Cambridge University. Today there are established colonies in Dorset and Sussex (Corbet and Southern, 1977).

The smallest known bat is the rare hog-nosed bat (*Craseonycteris thonglongyai*), also called the 'Bumblebee bat', of SW Thailand. This species, discovered in October 1973 by Kitti Thonglongya, a Thai mammalogist, and now the basis of a new family and genus (Hill, 1974), is restricted to two caves near the forestry station at Ban Sai Yoke on the Kawe Noi River, Kanchanaburi Province. Mature specimens (both sexes) have a wingspread of 160 mm *6·29 in*, a head and body length of 29–33 mm *1·14–1·29 in* and weigh 1·75–2·0 g *0·062–0·071 oz* (Lekagul and McNeely, 1977), which means it rivals the most diminutive pygmy shrews for the title of the world's smallest mammal. The tiny pipistrelle (*Pipistrellus nanulus*) of W Africa has a slightly smaller wingspread of 152 mm *6·0 in*, but this bat has a larger head and body (38 mm *1·5 in*), and scales about 2·5 g *0·088 oz* (Rosevear, 1965).

The smallest British bat is the common pipistrelle (*Pipistrellus pipistrellus*). Adult examples have a

The rare hog-nosed bat, which rivals Savi's pygmy shrew for the title of the world's smallest mammal.

wingspread of 190–250 mm 7·48–9·84 in, a head and body length of 35–45 mm 1·38–1·77 in and weigh 3–8 g 0·106–0·282 oz. The whiskered bat (*Myotis mystacinos*) is only fractionally larger.

At least three species of bat are known only from the type specimen: the small-toothed fruit bat (*Neopteryx frosti*) from Tamalanti, W Celebes (1938/9); *Paracoelops megalotis* from Vinh, Vietnam (1945); and *Latidens salimalii* from the High Wavy Mountains, S India (1948) (Walker *et al*, 1968). This does not mean, however, they are necessarily rare in occurrence but only that no more specimens have been collected since, and changes in collecting techniques will probably produce many more specimens eventually.

Of the species that were once reasonably abundant, probably the most seriously threatened one today is the flying fox (*P. tokudae*) of Guam and the Mariana Islands, W Pacific, which is still shot for food despite full protection. According to the Red Data Book (IUCN) it may now possibly be extinct, at least on Guam.

The Rodriguez flying fox (*P. rodricensis*), which is endemic to Rodriguez Island in the Mascarene group, W Indian Ocean, is also in a precarious state because it has no protection. In 1976 the total population was estimated at only 120–250 animals, but this was reduced to c70 in February 1979 after a severe cyclone. Fortunately Jersey Zoo has a small breeding colony, so all is not lost.

Ridley's leaf-nosed bat (*Hipposideros ridleyi*) of Malaysia was only known from a single specimen up until 1975, but that year a small colony (c50) was found in a forest only 25 miles 40 km north of Kuala Lumpur.

The rarest bat on the British list is Bechstein's bat (*Myotis bechsteini*), which is confined to southern England. Up until 1886 there was only one English record of this species (New Forest before 1837), but that year a small colony was discovered in a woodpecker's hole near Burley, Hampshire. Ten years later an adult male was shot near Battle, Sussex, and in 1901 one was found asleep in a chalk tunnel on the Berkshire side of the river at Henley-on-Thames. Two more specimens were shot at Newport, Isle of Wight in 1909, and since then there have been 21 further records, including 16 from Dorset (Corbet and Southern, 1977).

In January 1965 a small colony (c15) of grey long-eared bats (*Plecotus austriacus*) was discovered in the roof of the Nature Conservancy's research station at Furzebrook, Dorset (Stebbings, 1970). Up until then this species, which is found all over Europe, had only been recorded once in Britain (Hampshire 1875). In November 1976 another specimen was found in Sussex.

The greatest reliable age recorded for a bat is 31 years 5 months for an Indian flying fox (*Pteropus giganteus*) which died at London Zoo on 11 January 1979. A straw-coloured fruit bat (*Eidolon helvum*) at the same zoo lived for 21 years 10 months, dying in 1968 (Marvin Jones, pers. comm.), and 22 years 11 months has been cited for an Egyptian rousette bat (*Rousettus aegyptiacus*) at Giza Zoological Gardens, Cairo, (Flower, 1931).

The greatest reliable age reported for a bat under natural conditions is at least 24 years for a female little brown myotis (*Myotis lucifugus*) found on 30 April 1960 in a cave on Mt Aeolus, Vermont, USA. It had been banded at a summer colony in Mashpee, Massachusetts on 22 June 1937, at which time it was already fully adult. Another specimen found in a decomposed state in the same cave on 26 December 1964 was also believed to be 24 years old at the time of its death (Griffin and Hitchcock, 1965).

The greatest reliable age reported for a British bat under natural conditions is 22+ years for a greater horseshoe bat (*Rhinolophus ferrumequinum*) banded in Devon in March 1949 and recovered in 1970 (Stebbings, 1977). A Daubenton's bat (*Myotis daubentoni*) banded in 1949 was recaught in Suffolk in 1967 aged 18+ years (Yalden and Morris, 1975) and a whiskered bat (*Myotis mystacinus*) was recovered in Surrey 19½ years after it was banded.

Very little information has been published on the maximum speeds reached by bats because of their erratic flight patterns, but large species generally fly faster than small ones.

In one American experiment using an artificial tunnel the average velocity and individual variation of 17 different bats were determined, and only four of them exceeded 13 miles/h 20·9 km/h in level flight. The fastest was the big brown bat (*Eptesicus fuscus*), which recorded a maximum speed of 15·5 miles/h 24·9 km/h over a distance of 93 ft 28 m (Hayward and Davis, 1964).

Under totally natural conditions and in familiar territory flight rates are much higher, and on another occasion a small number of big brown bats were timed at speeds ranging from 17·8 to 23·6 miles/h 28·6–38·0 km/h as they left a maternity colony in Kentucky (Patterson and Hardin, 1969).

The noctule (*Nyctalus noctula*) and Schreiber's long-fingered bat (*Miniopterus schreibersi*) have both been timed at 31 miles/h 50·0 km/h in homing experiments (Kolb, 1955; Constant and Cannonge, 1957), but the swiftest flier of them all is the Brazilian free-tailed or guano bat (*Tadarida brasiliensis*), whose slim body and long, narrow wings are beautifully adapted to fast, vigorous flight. In one series of tests carried out at Davis Cave, Texas in June 1957 the top speed recorded over a 2-mile 3·2 km course was only

15 miles/h *24 km/h*, but the marked bats defeated the whole purpose of the exercise by making the characteristic high climb – they can reach an altitude of 10 000 ft *3048 m* in 8 minutes – and meandering before setting off for home. According to Davis *et al* (1962) this species can travel at speeds up to 60 miles/h *97 km/h* with the assistance of tail winds when chasing hordes of insects at great heights, but the maximum air speed attained by this bat in level flight is probably nearer 35–40 miles/h *56–64 km/h*.

During migration bats fly considerable distances. Buresch and Beron (cited by Krzanowski, 1964) mention three bats which flew 1697 km *1054 miles*, 1950 km *1212 miles* and 2347 km *1458 miles* respectively from the interior of the USSR to Bulgaria. The species concerned were the common pipistrelle (*Pipistrellus pipistrellus*) and the whiskered bat (*Myotis mystacinus*), both small, mediocre flyers, and the noctule, a strong powerful flyer.

The hoary bat (*Lasiurus cinereus*) of the Americas has been recorded in Iceland and the Orkneys, but Atlantic flights like those are impossible without the aid of prolonged westerly winds.

The largest concentration of wild mammals found living anywhere in the world today is the guano bat colony in Bracken Cave near San Antonio, Texas which has a summer peak population of up to 20 million individuals. Eight other caves in Texas also have a population of more than 1 million. They are: Goodrich 14–18 million; Rucker 12–14 million; Frio 10–14 million; Fern 8–12 million; Ney 10 million; Devil's Sink Hole 6–10 million; James 6 million; and Davis 4 million.

The most dangerous bat is the common vampire bat (*Desmodus rotundus*) of tropical and sub-tropical America, which not only drinks the blood of its victims, but also transmits disease, including the paralytic rabies virus (hydrophobia), which is almost 100 per cent fatal to livestock and man.

According to reliable estimates over 1 million head of cattle die every year in Latin America from rabies carried by vampire bats, and there are also a number of human fatalities. In 1933 over 40 people died of vampire bites in Trinidad, and there were five deaths in the Mexican State of Sinaloa in 1951.

Vampires usually alight on their sleeping or quiet victim and then crawl softly over the body until they find an attractive piece of bare skin. They then make a slight cut with their minute, razor-sharp incisor teeth and greedily lap up the blood oozing from the wound. Their saliva contains an anti-coagulant, which means the blood does not clot properly, thus allowing the nightmarish creatures to obtain full sustenance from the tiny puncture marks they have made. Sometimes the bats gorge themselves with blood to such an extent that they look like furry balls, and Eisentraut (1936) has described how one specimen which fed on the blood of a domestic goat for ten minutes became so bloated that it could not fly.

In recent years American Government scientists have discovered that an anticoagulant drug called 'diphenadione' provokes fatal haemorrhaging in vampires, and they have since come up with two satisfactory ways of controlling these bats. The most effective method is the application by brush of small amounts of the drug to the backs of the captive bats. The vampires are then released and make their way back to their colonies where they die shortly afterwards. As vampires have a habit of grooming each other like cats the drug has a multiplier effect, and in one series of nine individuals treated with the drug under laboratory conditions the vampires accounted for 310 of their companions. The other method is to inject the drug into the stomachs of cattle or simply spray them with the anticoagulant. The compound is harmless to cattle but renders the blood lethal to vampires for at least three days and nights.

Bats spend longer periods of time in *uninterrupted* hibernation than any other mammal.

Under natural conditions big brown bats have remained without movement for 64–66 days at ambient temperatures of 4–8°C *39·2–46·4°F*, and the little brown myotis has been known to spend up to 86 days in this death-like state (Menaker, 1964). In the laboratory, however, bats have been kept hibernating in controlled refrigerators for much longer periods. The most extreme case was that of a big brown bat which was imprisoned for an incredible 344 days before dying of starvation.

Similarly, in cooling experiments, temperatures as low as −1·3°C *29·7°F* have been recorded for the common pipistrelle without fatalities (Allen, 1939). At this extreme level, however, ice crystals start to form in the thin membranes of the wings, which means further cooling would clog the fluids in the lungs and heart and rapidly hasten death.

One of the hardiest species is the red bat (*Lasiurus borealis*) of the Americas. This tree-roosting bat sometimes hibernates in temperatures as low as −5°C *23°F* and can even tolerate parts of its body freezing solid.

Bats have the most highly developed sense of hearing of any terrestrial mammal. The ultrasonic frequencies used by these creatures normally range between 20 kHz (kiloherz or kilocycles per second) and 130 kHz, but vampire bats (*Desmodontidae*) and fruit bats (*Pteropodidae*) can hear frequencies as high as 160 kHz.

At the other end of the sound scale humans have a

range of only 20 Hz to 19 kHz, while the hearing of an elephant is even more restricted. In tests carried out on a young Asiatic elephant at the University of Kansas, USA the animal responded to a range of sound frequencies between only 17 Hz and 10·5 kHz, thus indicating that there is a simple relationship between the size of the head (i.e. the distance between the ears) and the ability to hear high frequencies (Heffner and Heffner, 1980).

The largest living primate is the mountain gorilla (*Gorilla gorilla beringei*) of the volcanic mountain ranges of W Rwanda, SW Uganda and E Zaire, which some primatologists think should be accorded full specific rank.

The average adult male 'stands' 5 ft 6 in *1·68 m* tall (because the gorilla cannot stand fully erect like man the measurement is taken between pegs placed at the crown and heel in the supine position), has a chest girth of 59 in *150 cm* and weighs about 430 lb *195 kg*. The average adult female is much smaller, standing about 4 ft 7 in *1·40 m* and weighing about 220 lb *100 kg*.

The other two races of gorilla, the eastern lowland gorilla (*Gorilla gorilla graueri*) of the lowland forests of E Zaire and SW Uganda, and the western lowland gorilla (*Gorilla g. gorilla*) of the lowland rain forests of SE Nigeria, the Cameroons, Gabon and the Congo, are both slightly smaller than *Gorilla g. beringei*, adult males averaging 5 ft 4 in *1·63 m* and 370 lb *168 kg* and 5 ft 3 in *1·6 m* and 345 lb *156 kg* respectively (Willoughby, 1978).

If we are to believe the claims of some of the early hunters a small number of really outsized gorillas have been killed in the past, but these assertions were either grossly exaggerated or the field measurements taken in such a way as to considerably enhance the true size of the primate.

For instance, one western lowland gorilla killed in the eastern Cameroons allegedly measured 7 ft 6½ in *2·30 m* in height, 3 ft 7 in *1·09 m* across the shoulders and weighed 770 lb *349 kg*, but Willoughby says a photograph published in the French journal *La Nature* on 29 July 1905 showed a gorilla of quite ordinary dimensions.

Another male of the same race shot by M Villars-Darasse in the Forest of Bambio, Haute-Lobaze, former French Equatorial Africa, in 1919 was stated to have measured 9 ft 4 in *2·84 m* (*sic*), but once again photographic evidence (*L'Illustration*, Paris, 14 February 1920) failed to substantiate this extreme stature. This particular specimen did, however, have unusually long legs for a gorilla and may have stood nearly 6 ft *1·8 m* tall (Cousins, 1972).

In the first gorilla the hunter probably obtained his measurement by running the tape over the contours of the body instead of in a straight line between sticks; while in the second, the 'height' must have been taken from the tips of the upraised hands to the end of the longest toe with the foot bent downwards while the animal was suspended in mid-air (lowland gorillas have relatively longer arms than those of the mountain race). Either – or both – of these methods were favoured by gorilla-hunters in the past who were anxious to make the total length as great as possible. The *correct* way to measure a gorilla in the field is to run the tape from the crown (excluding the crest) to the base of the heel, the feet being held at right angles to the lower legs.

In 1930 a height of 7 ft *2·1 m* was reported for an outsized mountain gorilla shot by a scientific expedition in the Albert National Park, Belgian Congo. Other statistics included a chest circumference of 73 in *185 cm* and an arm span of 10 ft *3·05 m* (Grzimek, 1963). Since none of these figures is proportional to the others, however, and no photographic evidence – or, for that matter, the embalmed body or skeleton – has ever been produced to substantiate this extreme claim, it must be assumed the dimensions of this primate were grossly exaggerated and/or the beast was merely a figment of the imagination.

As far as is known the only scientific expedition in the Belgian Congo that year was one led by Commander Attilio Gatti (1932) for the Royal Museum of Natural History, Florence, Italy. He shot a gorilla in the Tchibinda Forest near Lake Kivu which measured 8 ft 9 in *2·67 m* from the tips of the upraised hands to the soles of the feet in the hang position and weighed 482 lb *219 kg*. From this information (and photographic evidence) Willoughby was able to calculate that this gorilla must have stood about 5 ft 10 in *1·78 m* tall in life, although the animal was *stretched* to its fullest height when this value was determined.

Paul Belloni du Chaillu (1861), the French-American explorer-naturalist and father of gorilla-hunters, said adult male gorillas ranged in height from 5 ft 2 in *1·57 m* to 6 ft 2 in *1·88 m*. Of the nine specimens collected by him between 1856 and 1859 in Gabon, Equatorial Africa, the largest reportedly measured 5 ft 8 in *1·73 m*, but Gray (1861), who examined the limb-bones of this animal, believed that it was not possible for it to have stood more than 5 ft 3 in *1·60 m* in life.

The tallest gorilla ever shot in the field was probably a male of the mountain race collected by Commandant E Hubert and Dr Serge Freckhof at Alimbongo, N Kivu on 16 May 1938. This specimen measured 1·95 m *6 ft 4¾ in* from the crown of the head to the base of the heels, and had an arm span of 2·70 m *8 ft 10 in* (Heuvelmans, 1981). Another male of the mountain race collected by the Percy Sladen Expedition to the N Cameroons in 1932–33 measured 49 in *124 cm* from the crown of the head to the base of the spine, and 26·5 in *67 cm* from the point of the heel to the base of the spine. Allowing for some overlapping and the fact that it had a record span of 9 ft 2 in *2·79 m*, this gorilla must have stood about 6 ft 3 in *1·90 m* in life (Sanderson, 1940).

Fred G Merfield (1956), another reliable English observer, who collected 115 western lowland gorillas for European museums over a four-year period (1918–22) while he was a planter in the Mendjim Mey, French Cameroons, says he only shot one male standing over 6 ft *1·8 m*. This giant, taken in the Ambam district after a fierce battle in which the hunter received a deep thigh wound, was estimated to have weighed between 574 and 588 lb *260–267 kg*, although at the time he made this statement Merfield admitted that 'the abdomen was enormously extended, partly by a great quantity of vegetable matter in the intestines and partly by putrefaction'.

The skeleton of this gorilla was later presented to the Science Museum at the University of Texas, USA where primatologists estimated that the animal must have stood just over 6 ft *1·8 m* in life. Cousins (1972), who later saw a photograph of this gorilla in an advanced state of decomposition, said it was clearly 'a monstrous animal'.

In 1934 the George Vanderbilt African Expedition collected a very large male of the western lowland race which had been killed by natives in the neighbourhood of Aboghi in the Sanga River area, French Equatorial Africa. This gorilla measured exactly 6 ft *1·8 m* between sticks, had a 56 in *142 cm* chest and weighed about 500 lb *227 kg* (Coolidge, 1936). The mounted specimen is now on display at the Academy of Natural Sciences, Philadelphia, Pennsylvania, USA and has a standing height of 5 ft 10 in *1·78 m*.

Another gorilla killed on Mt Sabini by Edmund Heller's American expedition in 1925 and estimated to weigh over 500 lb *227 kg* measured 5 ft 11½ in *1·82 m* between sticks, and Burbridge (1928) shot a male on Mt Kiveno in the Kivu area which was 5 ft 11¾ in *1·82 m* and weighed over 400 lb *181 kg*.

The greatest reliable weight recorded for a gorilla in the field is the 482 lb *219 kg* already quoted for the large male shot by Commander Gatti in the Tchibinda Forest (see page 44). Another eastern gorilla shot by Henry C Raven (1931), leader of the Columbia University-American Museum of Natural History Expedition west of Lake Kivu in July 1929 stood 5 ft 8½ in *1·74 m* (chest 60 in *152 cm*) and weighed 467 lb *212 kg*. Another male killed at Tchibinda stood 5 ft 10 in *1·78 m* and had a chest circumference of 56 in *142 cm*.

On the basis of its height and girth measurements, Willoughby believes the large male in the Museum of the Philadelphia Academy of Sciences must have weighed about 530 lb *240 kg* when alive, and he says a shorter (5 ft 7¾ in *1·72 m*) but more heavily-built

specimen collected by the same expedition may have been even heavier.

The largest female mountain gorilla in a series of 60 skeletons examined by Schultz (1930) measured an estimated 4 ft 8½ in *1·43 m* in life.

The tallest gorilla ever held in captivity was a very slender male of the mountain race called 'Baltimore Jack', who measured a remarkable 6 ft 3 in *1·91 m* in the standing position. This exhibit, who had exceptionally long legs for a gorilla, was received at Baltimore Zoo, Maryland, USA in 1956 and was sold to Phoenix Zoo, Arizona in 1970 for breeding purposes. He died two years later and his body is now preserved in formaldehyde at Arizona State University (Cousins, 1979). It is interesting to note that this freak only weighed 300 lb *136 kg* and had a below-average reach of 7 ft 6 in *2·29 m*.

The famous western lowland gorilla 'Bushman' (1927–51) of Lincoln Park Zoo, Chicago, USA was credited with a standing height of 6 ft 2 in *1·88 m*, but Willoughby estimates that he was no more than 5 ft 8 in *1·73 m*. His mounted body may now be found on display in the Chicago Natural History Museum.

The heaviest gorilla ever held in captivity was probably a male of the mountain race named 'N'gagi', who died in San Diego Zoo, California, USA on 12 January 1944. He scaled 683 lb *310 kg* at his heaviest in 1943 (Willoughby, 1978), and weighed 636 lb *288 kg* at the time of his death. He was 5 ft 7¾ in *1·72 m* tall and boasted a record chest measurement of 78 in *198 cm*.

N'gagi and another mountain gorilla named 'M'bongo' arrived at San Diego Zoo on 5 October 1931. They had been captured the previous year by Martin and Osa Johnson in the Alumbongo Mts in the Kivu region of the Congo. At the time of their arrival they were both approximately five years of age, and their combined weight was 272 lb *123 kg*. N'gagi was about six months older than M'bongo and he weighed 147 lb *67 kg*. Throughout their life in captivity N'gagi was always the dominant animal, although when the gorillas did actually fight M'bongo always proved the fiercer and more crafty of the two. In February 1940 M'bongo overtook his big companion in weight for the first time, tipping the scales at 517 lb *235 kg*, compared to N'gagi's 501 lb *227 kg*. In May the same year they were weighed again and M'bongo scaled 602 lb *273 kg* to N'gagi's 525 lb *238 kg*, but this was only because the latter creature had been unwell for several months and had lost considerable weight. By then, however, M'bongo was 'round and paunchy with an enormously fat abdomen', while N'gagi was 'broad of shoulder and very trim and slender of waist and hips' (Benchley, 1940). In February 1941 N'gagi scaled 578 lb *262 kg*. During an attempt to weigh M'bongo shortly before his death on 15 March 1942 the platform scales 'fluctuated from 645 pounds to nearly 670' (Benchley, 1942), but his posthumous weight was given as 618 lb *280 kg*. This marked decrease in poundage was owing to the fact that the gorilla took very little food during his terminal illness, which lasted 45 days. His posthumous measurements were: height 5 ft 7½ in *1·71 m*; span 8 ft 1½ in *2·48 m*; chest 69 in *175 cm*; belly 72 in *183 cm*; wrist 14⅓ in *36 cm*; thigh 27¼ in *69 cm*; calf 15⅓ in *39 cm*; hand length 10½ in *27 cm* and foot length 12¾ in *32 cm*.

According to Groves (1967) both these primates were eastern lowland gorillas (*Gorilla g. graueri*). Willoughby, on the other hand, says an analysis of the measurements and proportions of the limb bones of both specimens showed a much closer link with *Gorilla g. beringei*, and he believes M'bongo and N'gagi may have been hybrids of both races.

The magnificent western lowland gorilla 'Phil' of St Louis Zoo, Missouri, USA was credited with a weight of 776 lb *352 kg* shortly after his death on 3 December 1958 aged 29 years, but this enormous poundage was not satisfactorily recorded. Apparently the body was placed in a truck and taken to a public scales in the city where the vehicle (with Phil inside) was weighed. Later on the empty truck was driven back to the scales again and the weight deducted from the original total. What is not known, however, is how much petrol was used on these round trips; also, was the truck utilised for other jobs before it was driven back to the scales for weighing? Willoughby, working on a posthumous chest circumference of 72¼ in *184 cm* and a standing height of 5 ft 5½ in *1·66 m* (taken from dry-bone dimensions) calculated that Phil must have scaled about 640 lb *290 kg* at the time of his death, but as the gorilla had eaten practically nothing during the previous six weeks this is probably an over-generous estimate. If the belly girth of 64 in *163 cm* had also been taken into consideration, then the weight (by formula) would have been about 550 lb *249 kg*, but Phil was probably nearly 100 lb *45 kg* heavier than this before his terminal illness.

That Phil was a massively-built animal goes without saying, but N'gagi and M'bongo were both taller, and also (with one exception) had larger vital statistics.

The much-publicised 'Gargantua' of Ringling Bros and Barnum and Bailey's Circus was billed as standing 6 ft 6 in *1·98 m* tall and weighing 750 lb *340 kg*, but this was showbiz propaganda. Gargantua – or 'Buddy' as he was originally called – was purchased by Mrs Gertrude Lintz of Brooklyn, New York in 1931 when he was one year old, and she kept the gorilla for five years before selling him to the circus for $10 000. According to Riess *et al* (1949) this top money-spinner weighed 550 lb *249 kg* at the time

of his death on 25 November 1949, but Dr S Dillon Ripley, Curator of Vertebrate Zoology at the Peabody Museum, Yale University, where the skeleton is now on display, told Plowden (1972) that the greatly dehydrated body only scaled 312 lb *141 kg*. In life Gargantua, who was not obese, weighed about 400 lb *181 kg*. His standing height was 5 ft 7½ in *1·71 m*.

Within days of Gargantua's passing the same circus acquired another 'world's heaviest captive gorilla' which, predictably, they called 'Gargantua II'. He was later credited with a height of 6 ft 3 in *1·91 m* and a weight of 700 lb *318 kg*, but although neither of these figures were ever confirmed he was probably much heavier than his predecessor at the time of his death. Gargantua II died in 1972 and his body was sent to the Yerkes Regional Primate Research Centre in Atlanta, Georgia for autopsy. The skin was later mounted and put on display at the Ringling Bros Circus World near Orlando, Florida and the measurements are given as follows: Height (heel to crown) 6 ft 3 in *1·91 m*; chest circumference 61·5 in *156 cm*; belly circumference 57·5 in *146 cm*; neck 34 in *86 cm*; upper arm 17 in *43 cm*; forearm 16 in *41 cm*; wrist 13 in *33 cm*; thigh 27.75 in *70 cm*; and ankle 14 in *36 cm* (Gordon Hull, pers. comm.). Judging from these statistics, this gorilla must have weighed about 475 lb *215 kg* when alive, which is not exactly King Kong material.

The largest gorilla ever held captive in a British zoo was the western lowland gorilla 'Congo'. He arrived at Bristol Zoo from the French Cameroons on 30 August 1954 and weighed 476 lb *216 kg* in February 1966. At the time of his death in December 1968 he scaled an estimated 560 lb *254 kg*. 'When I saw him a few months before his demise,' writes Cousins (1972), 'I was struck by the obesity of this animal. His abdomen was so vast that it almost touched the ground when he walked. His height was estimated at 5 ft 8 in, but I believe that he was smaller than this.'

The celebrated lowland gorilla 'Guy' of London Zoo, who died tragically on 8 June 1978 aged 32 years after failing to recover from an operation for the extraction of bad teeth, recorded a posthumous weight of 523 lb *237 kg*. For some unknown reason an anthropometric study of this much-loved animal was not carried out after death, but Cousins says brief details were taken at the British Museum where the body was later sent for mounting. These included a chest circumference of 72 in *183 cm* and a belly girth of 84 in *213 cm* (!) after the skin had been removed. A belly this size, however, is impossibly high for a 5 ft 7½ in *1·71 m* gorilla weighing only 523 lb *237 kg*, and as no reference was made to post-mortem inflation this figure must (assumedly) have been a misprint for 64 in *163 cm*.

The heaviest gorilla living in captivity today is a western lowland male called 'Zaak' who was received at Kobe Oji Zoo, Japan in December 1962. He weighed 555 lb *252 kg* in 1970, and tipped the scales at 628 lb *285 kg* in June 1976. He has not been weighed since, but Tadashi Yamagami (pers. comm.), the zoo's director, says the animal is now 'a little corpulent' and will be given reduced meals in future!

The huge lowland male 'Samson' (b November 1949) of Milwaukee Zoo, Wisconsin, USA scaled a very obese 652 lb *296 kg* in April 1971, but by May 1974 he had reduced to 582 lb *264 kg*. Shortly before his premature death on 1 December 1981 his weight fluctuated between 505 lb *229 kg* and 520 lb *236 kg*.

The heaviest captive female gorilla on record was a very obese specimen of the western lowland race called 'Susie' who was received at Cincinnati Zoo, Ohio, USA on 11 June 1931. In 1940 she weighed 305 lb *138 kg*, and shortly before her death on 29 October 1947 an astonishing 458 lb *208 kg*. Her standing height of 5 ft 2 in *1·57 m* was also a record for a female gorilla (Gordon, 1947).

Another female of the same race called 'M'Toto', who came to Ringling Bros and Barnum and Bailey's Circus via Mrs Maria Hoyt of Havana, Cuba in 1941 as a potential 'bride' for Gargantua, was credited with a peak weight of 438 lb *199 kg*, but this claim is suspect. If the poundage was authentic it would have made M'Toto heavier than Gargantua, despite the fact that he was a good 9 in *23 cm* taller, and this figure is not borne out in photographs. M'Toto died in Venice, Florida, on 17 July 1968.

The heaviest female gorilla ever held in a British zoo was 'Josephine', a member of the western lowland race, who arrived at Bristol Zoo on 28 September 1954 from the French Cameroons. At the time of her death on 3 March 1966 she weighed a very obese 355 lb *161 kg* (Cousins, 1972).

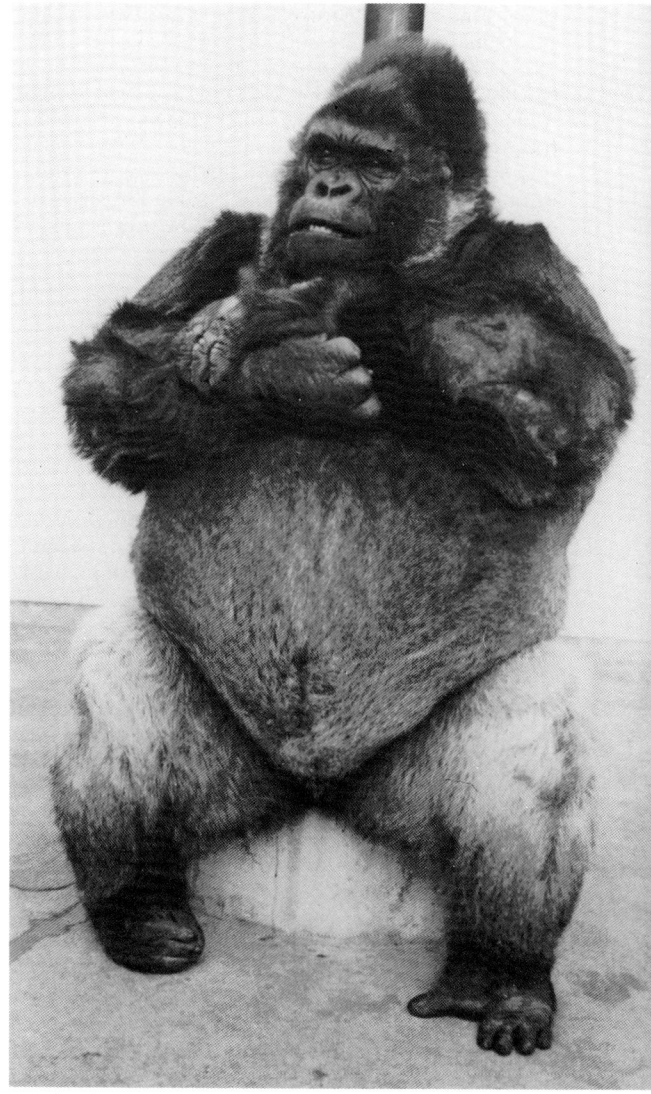

'Zaak', the world's heaviest captive gorilla.

Although the physical strength of the gorilla has often been exaggerated in print, it is still an immensely powerful animal.

On one occasion an explorer watched a group of gorillas upending large boulders in their search for grubs. They were casually flipping them over with one hand as though they were hollow, and some of the creatures were only half-grown. After the group moved off the man decided to test the weight of one of these rocks and found that it took him all his strength just to raise it a few inches off the ground with both hands!

Willoughby mentions a captive male gorilla which yanked up a steel cage door weighing over 600 lb *272 kg* with such tremendous force that it jammed, and M'Toto as a young gorilla once seized the rear axle of a station wagon with one hand and rammed the vehicle – the emergency brake was on – against a wall with a resounding crunch.

In a scientific experiment 'Congo', a 128 lb *58 kg* female mountain gorilla, registered a pull of 240 lbf *1068 N* on a spring-balance while working with both hands and feet braced, but Yerkes (1927) says she was only half trying. He concluded from this test that the arm strength of the young gorilla was two or three times greater than that of a human of comparative size.

Despite their fierce appearance, gorillas are generally timid and peaceful animals that shun human contact, but they can become extremely dangerous when wounded or alarmed. When this does happen, they usually attack the legs, thighs and buttocks of their tormentors with their powerful teeth and fingernails.

The only authentic record of a gorilla killing a human occurred in 1910. The victim, a native of the Boringo tribe, Uganda had apparently gone into the forest to cut some bamboo and had surprised a family of gorillas resting in an open space. The man was immediately attacked by a large male, and when his corpse was found later on it was minus the head and neck which were lying nearby. An arm had also been torn off in similar fashion (Akeley, 1923).

The strength of an ape that can calmly hold a man suspended while his head and neck are pulled off can only be imagined!

Apart from man, one would hardly expect such a formidable adversary as a full-grown gorilla to have any enemies in the natural state, so it came as something of a shock to zoologists in February 1961 when the bodies of a large silverback and a female were found within the space of three days on the slopes of Mt Muhavura in Kigezi game reserve, W Uganda. They had both been killed by a huge black leopard. The male had apparently been attacked in his night nest and had then rolled down a slope with his assailant. When found, he had severe neck injuries and a gash in the area of the groin which had laid bare the intestines. The female had also received groin injuries and her corpse had been partially eaten.

'At some months' interval more partly decomposed gorilla bodies were found and the pug marks around the spot left no doubt as to the identity of the killer', said Walter Baumgartel (1965), who owned a small hotel at the foot of the Virunga Volcanoes. 'We tried our best to punish him, but leopard hunting in dense undergrowth is a tricky task. These cats usually sleep by day in one of the numerous caves and hunt at night. Stalking them in the dark would be madness. The few times we were at his heels the black terror was clever enough to escape across the border where we could not follow him.'

At that time Kigezi game reserve was still the responsibility of the Belgian authorities, and they took the view that the leopard would sooner or later meet its match in the shape of a strong male gorilla and would be killed. Sadly, this was not to be. The leopard carried on its bloody vendetta, and Baumgartel said he had personal knowledge of seven gorillas of various ages and sex being killed by this ruthless predator; probably even more were slain and not discovered.

A gorilla taken by surprise (i.e. sleeping) would stand virtually no chance against a large leopard in a close-contact encounter, but natives familiar with this great ape say an adult male will kill one of these big cats with a mighty open-handed blow to the side of the head if it has time to take up a defensive posture.

The orang-utan (*Pongo pygmaeus*) of Sumatra and Borneo falls a long way behind the gorilla in terms of size, although the heavy coat of shaggy hair developed by old males tends to make them look much larger than they really are. In one series of ten Bornean adult males measured by Hornaday (1926) the heights ranged from 4 ft 0¾ in *1·24 m* to 4 ft 6 in *1·37 m*, while those of four females were 3 ft 6 in *1·07 m* to 4 ft *1·22 m*. The average adult weights of both sexes are 165 lb *75 kg* and 82 lb *37 kg* respectively (Schultz, 1941). The heaviest captive specimen on record was a very obese male called 'Andy' at New York Zoological Gardens who weighed 450 lb *204 kg* in 1959 when aged *c* 13 years. A 13-year-old female called 'Sandra' at the same zoo tipped the scales at 168 lb *76 kg* (Crandall, 1964).

In 1971 a budding young artist named D James Orang won first prize at an art contest held in Kansas, USA and later became an internationally known painter. What the judges didn't realise, however, was that Mr Orang (real name 'Djakarta Jim') was a six year old orang utan living at Topeka Zoo, Kansas. The ape's paintings were later sold and the money used to buy some female company for this hairy 'Rembrandt', but unfortunately this kind gesture quickly put paid to a promising artistic career. When a young thing named 'Daisy' entered his life the primate became completely infatuated with her and decided that there were better things to do than paint. He never put brush to canvas again.

The smallest known primate is the rare pen-tailed tree shrew (*Ptilocercus lowi*) of Malaysia, Sumatra and Borneo. Adult specimens have a head and body length of 100–140 mm *3·94–5·51 in*, a tail measurement of 130–190 mm *5·1–7·5 in* and weigh 35–50 g *1·23–1·76 oz*. The pygmy marmoset (*Cebuella pygmaea*) of the Upper Amazon Basin and the lesser mouse-lemur (*Microcebus murinus*) of SW Madagascar are also of comparable size but heavier, weighing 50–75 g *1·76–2·65 oz* and 45–80 g *1·59–2·82 oz* respectively.

The greatest irrefutable age reported for a primate is 57+ years for a male orang utan called 'Guas' at Philadelphia Zoo, Pennsylvania, USA who died of pneumonia on 9 February 1977. This ape arrived at Madame Abreu's colony in Havana, Cuba, in *c* 1928 and was received at Philadelphia Zoo on 1 May 1931. Photographic evidence, however, suggests that Guas must have been at least 13 years of age at the time of his arrival (Marvin Jones, pers. comm.), which would mean he was probably over 59 when he died. His mate 'Guarina' was euthanased in January 1976 at the estimated age of 56 years (Arleen Vandegrift, pers. comm.).

The oldest primate living in captivity today is

probably a male chimpanzee (*Pan troglodytes*) called 'Jimmy' at Seneca Zoo, Rochester, NY, USA who was still alive in December 1981) aged 51 years 6 months. He arrived at the zoo on 1 July 1931 when aged not less than one year.

Although the famous western lowland gorilla 'Massa' of Philadelphia Zoo officially celebrated his 50th birthday on 30 December 1980, Marvin Jones says this 300 lb *136 kg* primate is actually six months younger. He arrived in a shoebox at the home of Mrs Gertrude Lintz of Brooklyn, New York in September 1931 aged three months and was received at Philadelphia Zoo on 30 December 1935 when he was thought to be five years of age. One of his birthday presents was a T-shirt from film actor Clint Eastwood.

The rarest primate is the legally-protected hairy-eared dwarf lemur (*Allocebus trichotis*) of the rain forests of E Madagascar which, until fairly recently, was known only from the type specimen (Gunther, 1875) and three skins. In 1966 a live example was collected on the coast near Mananara (Fisher *et al*, 1969). This extreme rarity, however, may be owing to the fact that the species lives in a largely unexplored area.

The most seriously endangered primates are the golden lion tamarin (*Leontopithecus rosalia*) of SE Brazil and the liontail macaque (*Macaca silenus*) of SW India, both of which have a total population of 500 or less. Neither species has legal protection.

'Jimmy' the chimpanzee, the oldest primate living in captivity today, who is now in his 52nd year.

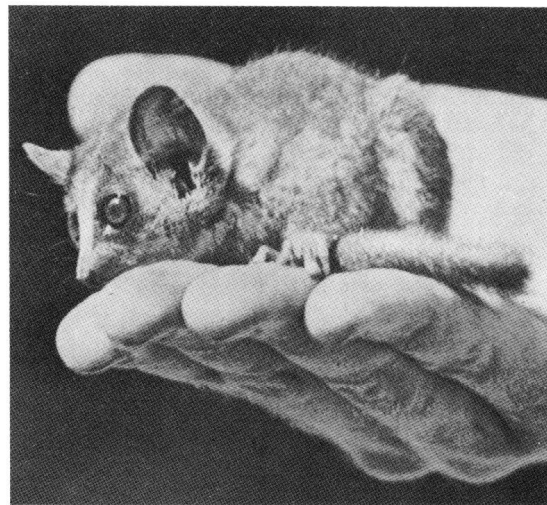

The lesser mouse-lemur, one of the smallest known primates.

The largest members of the monkey tribe are the mandrill (*Mandrillus sphinx*) of W Africa, the anubis baboon (*Papio anubis*) of Central Africa and the chacma baboon (*Papio ursinus*) of southern Africa. Adult males of all three species measure up to 40 in *102 cm* in length (excluding tail) and can weigh 90 lb *41 kg* or more. There is insufficient data for one species to be cited as consistently being the largest either in length or poundage, but the only species which has been reliably credited with weights in excess of 100 lb *45 kg* is the mandrill. One huge male tipped the scales at 119 lb *54 kg*, and an unconfirmed weight of 130 lb *59 kg* has been reported for another individual. Adult females are about half the size of males.

'Guas' and 'Guarina', the ancient pair of orang utans.

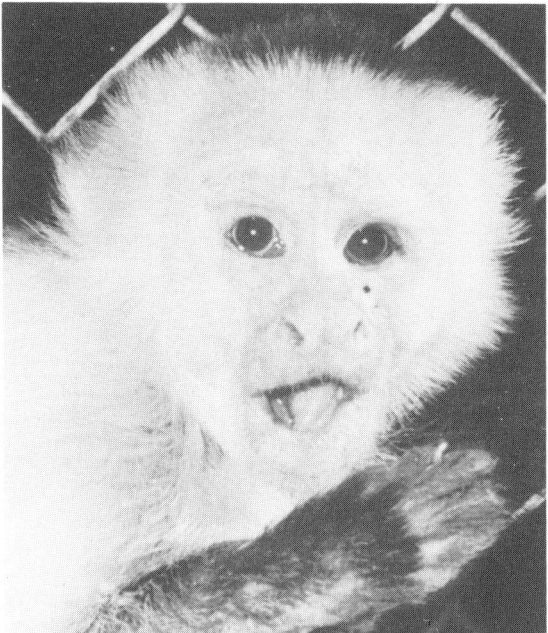

The oldest monkey on record – a 47-year-old white-throated capuchin.

The smallest known monkey is the pygmy marmoset (*Cebuella pygmaea*) of the Upper Amazon Basin.

The greatest reliable age recorded for a monkey is 46 years 11 months for a white-throated capuchin (*Cebus capucinus*) which died in Evansville Zoo, Indiana, USA on 12 April 1976. A black-capped capuchin (*Cebus apella*) lived for 45 years 1 month in Milwaukee Zoo, Wisconsin, USA, dying on 16 June 1979 (Marvin Jones, pers. comm.).

On 14 March 1916 a big male mandrill called 'George' died at London Zoo aged 'about 46 years'. The Hon Walter Rothschild who presented this animal to the zoo in November 1906, purchased it in Paris for £124, and later told Flower (1931) that he was 'practically certain' that it was the same mandrill as one that had been imported into Europe in 1869.

Flower also gives a record of a chacma baboon living for 45 years.

An emperor tamarin (*Saguinus imperator*) received at Jersey Zoo on 10 June 1961 died on 7 September 1981 aged at least 21 years 3 months, which is double the normal life-span (Phillip Coffey, pers. comm.).

The most intelligent of sub-human primates are the chimpanzees (*Pan*) of Central Africa, and especially the pygmy chimpanzee or bonono (*Pan paniscus*) of Zaire, which was not described until 1929.

One of the most notable characteristics of this extraordinarily placid creature, which is restricted to a relatively small area of rain forest on the south bank of the Zaire River, and is now on the endangered list, is that it spends much more time in the bipedal position than its larger cousin *Pan troglodytes*, which is more than double its size. In addition, it has several anatomical features that are more human-like. For instance, the forehead is higher and more domed, and the face flatter with less of a snout. The ears, too, are smaller and the teeth much more man-like. It also has a larger and more sophisticated vocabulary than *P. troglodytes*, and captive specimens have been known to laugh out loud. Another interesting point about this gentle and affectionate primate is that it shows no fear of man, even when freshly caught, and will allow itself to be touched without flinching.

Recently a small group of American anthropologists who have made a particular study of this animal have put forward the view that mankind is descended directly from a race of pygmy chimpanzee, and that the divergence between two species took place between four and six million years ago. They say the intelligence of pygmy chimpanzees and similarities in their blood group with humans make it probable that they were the common ancestors of humans, gorillas and modern chimpanzees, and that orang utans and gibbons diverged much earlier from this lineage.

Although monkeys are not as intelligent as the great apes, some species are not short on grey matter. One of them is the pigtail macaque (*Macaca nemestrina*) of Malaysia, which is trained from an early age to climb palm trees and throw down ripe coconuts, where senior monkeys grade them according to size.

For this work the monkeys receive a daily allowance of bananas in lieu of pay and are quite happy with the arrangement.

The situation at a coconut plantation near the town of Kuantan, Pahang State, was very much the same. One day, however, the work gangs left their posts for their customary mid-day meal only to find that their banana issue had been drastically reduced. In no time whatsoever the irate monkeys were protesting loudly outside the manager's office. There was even a bit of picketing, and the occasional blackleg who tried to climb up a tree to carry on with his job was quickly hauled down by his companions. This time, however, justice was on the side of the strikers. Apparently the manager of the estate had gone away and neglected to tell his deputy, who was new to the job, what the banana allocation should have been.

When he returned 36 hours later he quickly restored the status quo and the monkeys returned to work!

In America trained Capuchin monkeys (*Cebidae*) are now being used as help-mates to severely handicapped people, and their daily household chores include spoon-feeding, opening and closing doors, (including those of the fridge), turning lights on and off, cleaning and turning the pages of a book.

The fastest moving primates in the trees are the smaller gibbons of the genus *Hylobates* of SE Asia and Indonesia, which exceed all other mammals in agility. Because of the practical difficulties involved in recording speeds of this nature, practically nothing has been published in the way of statistics, but 'flights' in excess of 20 miles/h *32 km/h* are probably quite feasible.

The fastest primate on the ground is probably the langur (*Presbytis entellus*) of India and Sri Lanka, which has been timed at 23–26 miles/h *37–41·6 km/h*.

Some writers with fertile imaginations have credited charging gorillas with speeds up to 15 yd *13·7 m* a sec (=30·68 miles/h *49 km/h*) on all fours, but the legs of this animal were not designed for such sprints. Willoughby says a troop of gorillas will move off at a rate of about 5 miles/h *8 km/h* when pursued.

The largest rodent in the world is the capybara or water cavy (*Hydrochoerus hydrochaeris*), which reaches its maximum size in the tropical rain forests of South America. Mature specimens (females are larger) have a head and body length of 1·02–1·37 m *3 ft 4 in–4 ft 6 in* and usually scale 50–55 kg *110–121 lb*, but much heavier weights have been recorded for captive animals. According to Zara (1972) the largest male and female in a small breeding group at Evansville Zoo, Indiana, USA weighed 53 kg *117 lb* and 79 kg *174 lb* respectively. The smaller sub-species *Hydrochoerus h. isthmius* of Panama, Central America is about half this size.

The largest rodent found in Britain is *now* the coypu (*Myocastor coypus*), also known as the 'nutria' which was introduced into this country from Argentina by fur-breeders in 1929. Three years later the first escapes were recorded from a nutria farm at Horsham, Sussex, followed by break-outs at Tiverton, Devon in 1933, but it was not until 1937 when a number of coypus escaped from fur farms in the Yare valley, Norfolk that the major dynasty of wild specimens was founded (this rodent breeds three times a year and produces 6–10 in a litter). During the Second World War there were further escapes from the 51 nutria farms in East Anglia, and they quickly became established in Norfolk and parts of Suffolk where they began attacking crops and threatening drainage systems by burrowing in river banks. By 1960 the Ministry of Agriculture estimated there were at least 200 000 coypus living in the

Norfolk Broads area alone. Fortunately the very hard winter of 1963 killed about 80 per cent of the population, and by the end of 1965 the Ministry had exterminated more than 40 000 others. Between 1966 and 1970 their numbers further declined to around 1000, but then there were a succession of mild winters which allowed the coypu to re-establish itself, and by 1975 the population had gone up to 10 000. Two years later the Minister of Agriculture appointed a special study group to look into the coypu problem, and they set a target year of 1990 for the complete eradication of the species in Britain. In 1979 some 8000–12 000 coypus still survived in East Anglia, but in the first six months of 1980 two dozen professional hunters accounted for 4200 of them.

Adult male coypus measure 76–91 cm *30–36 in* in length (including a short tail) and average 11–12 lb *5·0–5·5 kg* in weight, but much larger individuals have been recorded. On 5 December 1951 a coypu measuring 106 cm *3 ft 6 in* in length and weighing 18 lb *8·2 kg* was killed in a dyke by three boys at Ditchingham, Suffolk. Another one shot at Orford, Suffolk in September 1959 scaled 22 lb *10 kg*, and a weight of 28 lb *13 kg* was reported for a coypu caught in Norfolk in 1962. In captivity weights up to 40 lb *18 kg* have been reported for cage-fat animals.

Like the capybara, these rodents are good swimmers and can remain submerged for long periods of time. One large male chased by dogs in Norfolk stayed underwater for 20 minutes. They have also been known to kill cats by luring them towards water and then drowning them.

The smallest known rodents are the northern pygmy mouse (*Baiomys taylori*) of the S USA and Mexico and the harvest mouse (*Micromys minutus*) of N Eurasia. There is very little to choose between them in terms of size and weight, but if one species has to be given the title then *B. taylori* is probably the more deserving of the two. Adult specimens have a head and body length of 50–80 mm *1·97–3·15 in*, a tail measuring 35–55 mm *1·38–2·17 in* and weigh 7–8 g *0·25–0·28 oz*.

The British form of *M. minutus* has a total length of 96–135 mm *3·78–5·32 in* and averages about 6 g *0·21 oz*, but weights up to 15 g *0·53 oz* have been recorded for pregnant females.

The most widely-distributed of all mammals is the house mouse (*Mus musculus*), which is found on every continent including Antarctica where it lives in the heated dwellings built by man.

Until quite recently the rarest rodent in the world was Swarth's rice rat (*Oryzomys swarthi*) of San Salvador in the Galapagos group, E Pacific. Four specimens were collected on the island by J S Hunter for the California Academy of Sciences in 1906 (Orr,

1938), and it was not heard of again until January 1966 when the skull of a recently dead animal was found (Fitter, 1968). Since then, however, no trace has been found of this rodent, and it is now believed to be extinct.

The Thornton Peak melomys (*Melomys sp.*) of NE Queensland, Australia, which was not discovered until 1975, is known from only a few specimens, but this mosaic-tailed rat lives in a very remote area and further field work may extend its range (Watts and Aslin, 1981).

The most seriously endangered rodent today is the Saltmarsh harvest mouse (*Reithrodontomys raviventris*) of San Francisco Bay and the bordering salt marshes in California, USA. Despite full protection the Red Data Book says the population is very low.

The longest-lived rodents are old-world porcupines (family *Hystricidae*).

The greatest reliable age recorded for a rodent is 27 years 3 months for a Sumatran crested porcupine (*Hystrix brachyura*) which died in National Zoological Park, Washington, DC, USA on 12 January 1965 (Marvin Jones, pers. comm.). On 18 April 1976 a common crested porcupine (*H. cristata*) died in Los Angeles Zoo, California aged 24 years 7 months, and on 6 May 1933 a female African brush-tailed porcupine (*Atherurus africanus*) died in Philadelphia Zoo, Pennsylvania after spending 22 years 10 months 1 day in captivity (Wilbur Amand, pers. comm.). In 1942 the death was reported of an Indian crested porcupine (*H. indica*) in Trivandrum Zoo, India aged 22 years (Simon, 1943), and on 9 January 1886 a female (*H. cristata*) died at London Zoo after spending 20 years 4 months 14 days in captivity (Flower, 1931).

On 2 January 1973 the death was reported of an American grey squirrel (*Sciurus carolinensis*) aged 23 years 6 months in Racine Zoo, Wisconsin, USA. The normal life-span for this species is 5–6 years.

The most dangerous rodents in the world are (indirectly) the black and common rats (*Rattus rattus* and *R. norvegicus*), both of which originated in Asia. They serve as reservoirs for a number of fatal diseases, including the devastating bubonic plague bacillus (*Pasteurella pestis*), which is transmitted to human beings by the rat flea (see page 177). According to one gloomy estimate rat-borne diseases have killed more people in the past 1000 years than all the wars and revolutions ever fought on this planet.

Mice have also been indirectly responsible for a large number of human fatalities, but for a much more bizarre reason! They love the sulphurous tips of matches, and if anyone is foolish enough to leave live ones lying around they will often gnaw off the ends and store them in their nests. Over a period of time the chemical undergoes changes and can sometimes burst into flame spontaneously.

The highest living rodent is the mountain chinchilla (see page 25).

The master engineer of the mammalian world is the American beaver (*Castor canadensis*) of N America and Finland (introduced). This very large rodent, which is exceeded in size only by the capybara, builds complex dams across slow-moving streams or rivers and then erects dome-shaped lodges of sticks and mud in the artificial ponds or lakes created by the impounded waters. Most dams average about 75 ft *23 m* in length, but Anthony (1937) saw one in Estes Park, Colorado, USA which was 1040 ft *317 m* long and had a series of shorter dams above and below it. Another one 1500 ft *457 m* long was 12 ft *3·7 m* high.

The largest beaver dam ever built is probably one on Jefferson River in Montana, USA which is 2296 ft *700 m* long and can bear the weight of a rider on horseback (Von Frisch, 1975). Other unconfirmed measurements up to 4000 ft *1219 m* have been claimed. Huge dams like this are maintained by succeeding generations of beaver families and are regularly adapted to meet changes in the water level. One industrious pair of adult beavers observed in a Canadian national park over a period of 15 months cut down 266 trees (mostly poplars and willows) between them and built three 50 ft *15·2 m* long dams across a stream plus a lodge with a capacity of 1000 ft³ *28·3 m³*.

Because beavers are such skilled hydro-engineers many people are convinced these rodents are exceptionally intelligent, but in reality most of their actions are instinctive and are governed by inherited behaviour patterns. Even when they are building dams beavers sometimes get it all wrong and flood adjacent land to no purpose, and there are numerous records of beavers being crushed by trees they had just gnawed through.

The brainiest rodent is the much maligned rat, which is in a class of its own in terms of ingenuity. On one occasion a psychologist placed a specimen in an 'activity wheel' while an automatic counter kept track of the number of revolutions. When the man returned to the cage to see how things were progressing he was somewhat taken aback to find the rat lying comfortably on its back outside the apparatus while it casually spun the wheel with one of its forefeet!

The world's champion burrowers are the Eurasian mole-rats (*Spalax*), which do most of their digging with their outsized incisors. One 152 mm *6 in* deep burrow found by Anisimov (cited by Hanney, 1975) in the southern USSR measured 363 m *1191 ft* in length, but he mentioned another example which was very much larger. This one had a total of 114 mounds, the last two being 169 m *554 ft* apart! These particular burrows were dug by *Spalax microphthalmus*, which can shift 50 times its own weight in soil in 20 minutes.

The mammals which spend the longest period of time in hibernation are the marmots (*Marmota*), which eat to excess in the early autumn and accumulate massive reserves of fat. They usually enter their winter quarters in September and do not emerge until the end of March, but in the very northern parts of their range like Alaska and Siberia they sometimes aestivate for up to eight months. Unlike bats, however, marmots wake up every 3–4 weeks for brief periods to stretch, scratch and urinate. There is also a British record of an edible dormouse (*Glis glis*) sleeping for 6 months and 23 days, but this species also wakes up at regular intervals. Habitual burrowers like the mole do not hibernate because they have to feed constantly on invertebrates. The colder it gets the deeper they dig.

The world's greatest mammalian lover is Shaw's jird (*Meriones shawi*) of N Africa, which is frequently used as an experimental laboratory animal. One 60 g *2·12 oz* male was observed to mate 224 times in two hours!

The largest insectivores in the world are the moonrat (*Echinosorex gymnurus*) of the forests of Malaysia, Sumatra and Borneo and the European hedgehog (*Erinaceus europaeus*), both of which have their supporters. In the case of the moonrat, adult specimens have a head and body length of 265–445 mm *10·43–17·52 in* and a tail measuring 200–210 mm *7·87–8·27 in*, while the stockier European hedgehog has a head and body length of 179–263 mm *7·05–10·35 in* and a much shorter tail (17–35 mm *0·7–1·38 in*). In one series of adult moonrats from N Borneo the weights ranged from 970 g *34·2 oz* to 1100 g *38·8 oz* (Findley, 1967), as against 800 g *28·2 oz* to 1200 g *42·3 oz* for *E. europaeus* (Herter, 1938). The maximum weight recorded for the moonrat is 1400 g *49·4 oz*, but well-fed European hedgehogs have been known to scale as much as 1900 g *67·0 oz*.

The African otter shrew (*Potamogale velox*) of W and Central Africa has also been credited with the title of 'largest living insectivore', but this species is a bit of a puzzle because no-one has yet got around to weighing a fully-adult animal. Mature specimens have a head and body length of 290–350 mm *11·4–13·8 in* and a tail measuring 245–290 mm *9·6–11·4 in*. Anteaters of the families *Tachyglossidae* and *Myrmecophagidae* are, of course, much larger, but although they feed on termites and other soft-bodied insects they are not classified as insectivores but belong to the orders *Monotremata* and *Edentata*. And to complicate matters still further, some insectivores are carnivorous like the African otter shrew which feeds on fishes, crabs and amphibians. It is not surprising, therefore, that the *Insectivora* has been described as the 'wastebasket taxon' to which groups of animals of uncertain affinities have been relegated. **The smallest known insectivore** is Savi's pygmy shrew (see page 20).

The greatest reliable age recorded for an insectivore is 15+ years for a lesser hedgehog-tenrec (*Echinops telfairi*), which was born in Amsterdam Zoo, Netherlands in 1966 and was later transferred to Jersey Zoo. It was still alive in September 1981.

The rarest insectivore is Fontoynont's hedgehog-tenrec (*Dasogale fontoynonti*), which is known only from the type specimen collected in eastern Madagascar and now in the Museum of Natural History, Paris, France.

In 1979 a tame European hedgehog set up a homing record for an insectivore when it travelled 77 km *48 miles* back to its first owner's home in the E Ukraine, USSR. The creature had originally been found lying injured in a country road by a woman doctor, who had cared for it until it was fully recovered. Later she gave the hedgehog to her granddaughter who lived in the town of Dimitrov. Two months afterwards the doctor found her former patient sitting on her doorstep when she returned home from work one evening, and now the pair are inseparable. This species rarely travels more than 1 km *0·62 mile* in any given direction during the space of one year.

The largest of all antelopes is the ox-like giant eland (*Tragelaphus derbianus*) of W and Central Africa, which is very 'bovine' in appearance and has a prominent dewlap. Adult bulls average 5 ft 9 in *1·75 m* at the withers and scale about 1575 lb *714 kg*, but weights up to 1980 lb *898 kg* have been reported for old individuals (Rowland Ward, 1971).

The common eland (*T. oryx*) of E and S Africa nearly matches the giant eland in height, but is not quite so massively built (average weight of adult bulls 1300–1500 lb *590–680 kg*). There are exceptions, however, and Meinertzhagen (1938) says he shot one in Nyasaland which tipped the scales at 2078 lb *943 kg*. Two other huge bulls collected by him in Kenya both weighed 1969 lb *893 kg*. Adult female elands are smaller, more lightly built, and rarely exceed 4 ft 9 in *1·45 m* at the withers and 800 lb *363 kg*.

The American animal collector Frank Buck with a diminutive lesser Malay chevrotain – the smallest member of the Ruminantia.

It is interesting to note that the giant eland 'browses', while the common eland 'grazes'.

The smallest antelope is the royal antelope (*Neotragus pygmaeus*), which lives in the dense forests of W Africa from Sierra Leone to Ghana. Mature specimens (both sexes) measure 10–12 in *254–305 mm* at the withers and weigh only 7–8 lb *3·17–3·63 kg*, which is the size of an adult brown hare (*Lepus capensis*).

A royal antelope received at London Zoo in 1938 reportedly had hooves so tiny that all four placed together barely covered a penny. Its legs were slimmer than pencils.

The more rangy Salt's dik-dik (*Madoqua saltina*) of NE Ethiopia and Somalia weighs only 5–6 lb *2·27–2·72 kg* when adult but this species is taller, standing 14 in *356 mm* at the withers. According to Lydekker (1911) dik-diks are so small that 'two or three may be killed at one shot'.

The rarest antelope in the world is the handsome Arabian oryx (*Oryx leucoryx*), which has not been recorded in the wild since 1972 when three were killed and four others captured by a motorised Arab

hunting party on the Jiddat-al-Harasis plateau, South Oman. Fortunately the Fauna Preservation Society had long foreseen this black day, and in 1962 had mounted a rescue operation in South Yemen which resulted in the capture of two males and one female. These 'unicorns' were sent to Phoenix Zoo, Arizona, USA where the climate is similar to that of their ancestral haunts, and later they were joined by six other specimens presented or loaned from other zoos. This captive breeding stock multiplied so successfully that by the end of 1977 there were 91 animals in the World Herd, including a number of surplus oryx which had been deposited at San Diego Zoo. There were also 38 others in Los Angeles Zoo and 80–90 in private collections (Fitter and Scott, 1978). Two years later the trustees of the World Herd agreed to send a small breeding herd of 12 oryx to Oman, and in April 1980 the first group of ten animals were placed in a special holding area within a reserve after being airlifted from San Diego. When the progeny of these zoo-bred antelopes are eventually released into the desert wilderness they will be guarded by a tough nomadic tribe who have sworn to protect them from international poachers.

The most seriously endangered wild antelope is Jentink's duiker (*Cephalophus jentinki*), which is thinly scattered in the deep forests of Liberia, Senegal and the Ivory Coast. The total population is 'unlikely to exceed a few hundred' (*Red Data Book*).

The greatest reliable age recorded for an antelope is 25 years 4 months for an addax (*Addax nasomaculatus*) which died in Brookfield Zoo, Chicago, Illinois, USA on 15 October 1960. An eastern white-brindled gnu (*Connochaetes taurinus albojubatus*) at the same zoo lived for 21 years 5 months (13 June 1934–20 November 1955) and a greater kudu (*Tragelaphus strepsiceros*) for 20 years 9 months (8 July 1936–16 April 1957). A nilgai (*Boselaphus tragocamelus*) at the National Zoo, Washington, DC lived for 21 years 8 months (15 February 1918–7 November 1939), and a blesbok (*Damaliscus dorcas*) at New York Zoological Park for 21 years 5 months (4 September 1920–18 February 1942) (Marvin Jones, pers. comm.). Flower (1931) mentions another eastern white-brindled gnu which died in Philadelphia Zoo, Pennsylvania, USA on 27 July 1928 aged 20 years 1 month 22 days, and a brindled gnu (*C. taurinus*) received at New York Zoological Park on 2 September 1920 was sold on 26 August 1940 after spending 19 years 11 months 22 days in captivity (Crandall, 1964).

In 1980 the death was reported of the last wild-born Arabian oryx at Phoenix Zoo aged *c* 20 years. During her time in captivity she produced and reared 13 young and eventually became the ancestress of the World Herd.

The largest deer in the world is the Alaskan moose (*Alces alces gigas*) of the forested areas of Alaska, USA and the W Yukon and NW British Columbia, Canada. Adult bulls average 6 ft *1·8 m* to the top of the humped shoulder and scale about 1100 lb *499 kg*. Cows are about 25 per cent smaller.

Shoulder heights up to 8 ft 6 in *2·59 m* and estimated weights up to 2600 lb *1179 kg* have been claimed for this sub-species, but as Seton (1925–27) points out the shoulder height of the Alaskan moose may be 8–10 in *203–254 mm* less than the same measurement taken between pegs. Similarly, no reliable weights have been published for large moose shot in Alaska, but a bull standing 6 ft 6 in *1·98 m* at the shoulder and in good condition would be expected to weigh about 1400 lb *635 kg*.

Two bulls shot at Funny River, Alaska measured 6 ft 6¼ in *1·99 m* and 6 ft 9¼ in *2·06 m* respectively between pegs, but although these statistics sound impressive both these animals were probably not much above average size. They are now on display in the American Museum of Natural History (Peterson, 1955).

Lockhart (1895), in a reference to the Alaskan moose, says: 'Those down at Peel River and the Yukon are much larger than up this way (Great Slave Lake). There I have known two cases of extraordinary moose having been killed, the meat alone of each of them weighing about 1000 pounds.'

This figure implies a live weight of 1700–1800 lb *771–816 kg*, but Seton says these poundages were guessed.

According to Whitehead (1972) the Alaskan moose reaches its maximum size on the Kenai Peninsula where exceptionally large bulls 'may' measure up to 7 ft 6 in *2·29 m* at the shoulder and weigh nearly 1800 lb *816 kg*, but as this is the height of an average adult cow Indian elephant this measurement needs to be authenticated. Rowland Ward (1910) are more cautious and say bulls of this race reach a maximum height of 6 ft 9 in *2·06 m* at the shoulder and a weight of 1600 lb *726 kg*.

Probably the largest Alaskan moose on record was a bull shot by Dall de Weese (1898) on the Yukon River in September 1897 which measured 7 ft 8 in *2·34 m* between pegs and weighed an estimated 1800 lb *816 kg*. Another massive bull killed in 1918 reportedly measured 8 ft 7 in *2·62 m* from heel to hump and had an antler spread of 63·5 in *1·61 m*.

In 1948 Clarence W McKeen shot a very large moose (*Alces a. andersoni*) near Jumbo Lake, Ontario, Canada which produced over 770 lb *349 kg* of dressed meat. On the basis of percentage weights, Peterson calculated that this animal must have scaled somewhere between 1300 lb *590 kg* and 1400 lb *635 kg* when alive. Another specimen shot on St Ignace Island, Ontario the following year recorded a weight

of 1177 lb *534 kg* (shoulder height between pegs 6 ft 3 in *1·91 m*).

The elk (=moose) of Northern Europe rarely exceeds 5 ft 9 in *1·75 m* and 900 lb *408 kg*, but the Eastern Siberian race (*Alces a. cameloides*) is taller. According to Flerov (1960) one outsized bull measured 2.35 m *7 ft 8½ in* between pegs, but this animal must have been a bit on the lean side because it only scaled 565 kg *1246 lb*.

The largest deer found in Britain is the red deer (*Cervus elaphus scoticus*) of Scotland, the Lake District and the West Country. A full-grown wild stag measures 3 ft 4 in–3 ft 8 in *1·02–1·12 m* at the shoulder and weighs 196–224 lb *89–102 kg*, while hinds are about two-thirds this size.

The heaviest wild red deer on record was a stag killed in Gordon Castle Park, Grampian, Scotland in 1831 which weighed 525 lb *238 kg* 'as he fell' (Millais, 1904–06). Another stag killed on the Isle of Islay, Strathclyde, Scotland in 1940 scaled 456 lb *207 kg* clean (without the liver), and another one taken in Glenmore Deer Forest, Highland, Scotland in 1877 weighed 462 lb *210 kg* (Whitehead, 1964).

The heaviest park red deer on record was a stag killed at Woburn, Bedfordshire in 1836 which tipped the scales at 476 lb *216 kg* (height at shoulder 4 ft 6 in *1·37 m*). Another stag weighing 472 lb *214 kg* was killed in Warnham Court Park, Sussex on 7 September 1926.

The red deer reaches its maximum size in Central Europe (*C. e. hippelaphus*), where weights up to 660 lb *299 kg* clean have been recorded for stags.

The smallest true deer (Cervidae) is the northern pudu (*Pudu mephistophiles*) of Ecuador and Colombia. Mature specimens measure 13–14 in *330–356 mm* at the shoulder and weigh 16–18 lb *7·26–8·16 kg*. The southern pudu (*P. pudu*) of Chile and Argentina is slightly taller (15–16 in *381–406 mm*) and weighs about 20 lb *9·07 kg*.

The lesser Malay chevrotain (*Tragulus javanicus*) of SE Asia, Sumatra and Borneo is much smaller, but this species is not a *true* deer because it has only three divisions to its stomach instead of the normal four. Adult specimens measure 8–10 in *203–254 mm* at the shoulder and scale 6–7 lb *2·72–3·18 kg*, which makes it the smallest member of the sub-order *Ruminantia*.

The smallest deer found in Britain is the Chinese muntjac (*Muntiacus reevesi*), which was introduced at Woburn, Bedfordshire in *c* 1900. It is now widely established in Southern and Eastern England as a result of escapes from deer parks. Adult bucks average 17–18 in *432–457 mm* at the shoulder and weigh about 30 lb *13·6 kg*, and adult does 15–16 in *381–406 mm* and 26 lb *11·8 kg*.

The rarest deer is Fea's muntjac (*M. feae*), which is

restricted to the mountainous forests on the borders of S Burma and W Thailand and up until very recently was known only from two specimens (Tate, 1947). No up-to-date information has been published on the status of this species, but the fact that it lives in very difficult terrain and is chiefly nocturnal must give it a strong measure of protection. In December 1977 a solitary female was received at Bangkok Zoo.

According to recent field observations muntjacs never sleep (i.e. lose consciousness) and even at times of total rest they never close their eyes for longer than 25 seconds. Most of their life is apparently taken up with the problems of searching for food, breeding, looking after their young and watching out for enemies like the leopard.

Pere David's deer (*Elaphurus davidianus*) of NE China had probably been extinct in the wild for nearly 3000 years when the Jesuit missionary and zoologist Pere Armand David obtained the skins and bones of a pair of deer from the herd in the Imperial Hunting Park near Peking in 1865 after bribing sentinels. This probably makes it the only living mammal (total population 801 at the end of 1978) that man has *never claimed* to have seen in its natural habitat.

The greatest reliable age recorded for a deer is 26 years 8 months for a red deer (*Cervus elaphus scoticus*) which died in Milwaukee Zoo, Wisconsin, USA on 28 June 1954. Another specimen at the National Zoo, Washington, DC, USA lived for 26 years 6 months 2 days (Jones, 1958). A female Malayan sambar (*Cervus unicolor equinus*) died in New York Zoological Park on 11 December 1955 aged 26 years 5 months 6 days (Crandall, 1964).

In November 1937 a hunter killed a large bull wapiti (*Cervus canadensis*) – the red deer of N America – near Winslow, Arizona, USA which carried a Biological Survey ear-tag showing that it had been transported to Arizona from Wyoming in 1913 when nearly a year old (Murie, 1951). The maximum potential for this species is *c* 30 years.

The largest living marsupial is the red kangaroo (*Macropus rufus*) of the inland plains of central, southern and eastern Australia.

In one series of 426 males collected by Frith and Calaby (1969) in western NSW the heaviest specimen weighed 169 lb *77 kg* and measured 8 ft 2 in *2·49 m* along the curves of the body. The longest individual (9 ft 5 in *2·87 m*) only scaled 154 lb *70 kg*, but the two researchers said it was a bigger framed animal than the heavier example and would have weighed more if it had been in better condition.

Lengths up to 11 ft *3·4 m* along the curve and weights up to 300 lb *136 kg* have been claimed for this species by hunters in the past, but the maximum size attained by this giant marsupial is probably in the region of 9 ft 6 in *2·90 m* (straight-line measurement *c* 8 ft 8 in *2·64 m*) and 200 lb *91 kg*. Such a boomer (old-man kangaroo), standing fully erect in a threatening posture, would be more than 7 ft *2·1 m* tall.

Adult females are about half the weight of adult males and rarely exceed 60 lb *27 kg*. The heaviest specimen in a series of 2942 females scaled an exceptional 80·3 lb *36·4 kg* and measured 6 ft 9 in *2·06 m* in total length.

The eastern grey kangaroo (*Macropus giganteus*) of the forest areas of eastern Australia averages out slightly smaller than *M. rufus*, but the males of the Tasmanian race (*Macropus g. tasmaniensis*) are much more heavily muscled, and some of them rival the largest reds for size. One 'forester' shot in northeastern Tasmania reportedly weighed 180 lb *82 kg* (total length 8 ft 8 in *2·64 m*), while Lydekker gives details of another outsized individual which measured 9 ft 7 in *2·92 m* along the curves and tipped the scales at a staggering 200 lb *91 kg*. (The preserved skin of this specimen has a 'flat' length of 8 ft 2 in *2·49 m*.)

Males of both species grow throughout their entire lives, but even under the best conditions they are never over-weight because the heavier they are the less efficient their means of progress.

Both the red and grey kangaroos can travel for miles at 25 miles/h *40 km/h*. One energetic grey chased by a man on horseback for 30 km *18·6 miles* in Tasmania eventually ran out of land and swam out to sea for another 3 km *1·7 miles* where it probably fell victim to sharks. It is only when hard-pressed (e.g. paced by a car), however, that these kangaroos reach maximum velocity, and in situations like this vigorous males have been timed at 35 miles/h *56 km/h* for short bursts and young mature females ('blue flyers') at 40 miles/h *64 km/h*. One large male red paced for nearly a mile *1·6 km* at 35 miles/h *56 km/h* dropped dead from its exertions and was obviously too heavy for sustained flight at that speed.

The long-jumping abilities of both animals are also impressive. During the course of a chase in New South Wales in January 1951 a female red made a series of bounds which included one of 42 ft *12·8 m*. On another occasion a female grey pursued by dogs cleared a pile of logs 6 ft *1·8 m* high and 40 ft *12·2 m* long. High fences, on the other hand, are not negotiated so easily and a 5 ft *1·5 m* barrier will deter most kangaroos. There are exceptions, however, and a captive male grey once cleared an 8 ft *2·4 m* fence when a car suddenly back-fired! There is also a record of a terrified red chased by hunting dogs clearing a stack of timber 10 ft *3·1 m* high and 27 ft *8·2 m* long (Troughton, 1965).

When females carrying young in their pouches are

chased by predators like the dingo or fox they will often eject their passengers, particularly large ones, in an effort to save their own lives. When this happens, usually at high speed, the unfortunate joey hits the ground with a bump and rolls some distance before picking itself up and shooting off in another direction. But even if it escapes, the young kangaroo is still doomed, because without its mother to supply nourishment it will soon starve to death. By then she could be miles away, and the chances of the two making contact again are very remote. It is certainly a fact that no independent young aged less than 235 days have ever been seen in the wild.

According to tests carried out by Dawson and Taylor (1973) kangaroos are far more efficient bounding along on two legs than other animals travelling on four because their oxygen consumption does not increase with acceleration. If anything, it drops slightly, which would seem to suggest that hopping is an inexpensive way of getting around in a hurry.

The newly-born 'fetus' of an average-sized female red kangaroo is so tiny that it would take 20 000 of them to match the 45 lb *20·4 kg* weight of the mother – a ratio record unequalled in the mammalian world.

The smallest known marsupial is the rare Ingram's planigale (*Planigale ingrami*) of NW Australia. Adult male examples of this flat-skulled mouse have a head and body length of 45 mm *1·77 in*, a 50 mm *1·97 in* long tail and weigh about 4 g *0·14 oz*. Females are smaller.

The rarest marsupial in the world is the thylacine (*Thylacinus cynocephalus*), also known as the 'Tasmanian wolf', the largest of the carnivorous marsupials which, if still extant, is now confined to the remote mountain regions of the north-western parts of the island.

A hundred years ago the thylacine was *reasonably* abundant in Tasmania. Its prey then was the kangaroo and the wallaby, but as man invaded the primitive forests and steadily exterminated much of the indigenous wildlife, the thylacine was forced to seek alternative prey. It developed a taste for sheep and poultry, and this soon brought it into sharp conflict with the farmers, who then began a relentless war of extermination. In 1888 the Government agreed to pay a bounty of £1 a head for each adult animal brought in and 10s for every pup, and official statistics show that between that time and 1909, the last year in which the bounty was paid, 2184 thylacine were killed, although the total figure was probably much higher. One man and his brother shot 24 in one day! On top of this, in 1910 the thylacine population was decimated by an outbreak of disease, possibly

The heavily-muscled body of a 'Big Red' kangaroo – the largest living marsupial.

distemper. Between 1914 and 1930 there were a number of confirmed killings, the last at Mawbanna in April 1930, but it was not until 1936 that the species was accorded full protection (Guiler, 1966).

The last thylacine held in captivity was a male called 'Benjamin' caught by a wallaby trapper in the heavily forested Florentine Valley some 60 miles *96 km* north-west of Hobart in 1933. It was later exhibited at Hobart Zoo but died there the following year.

In January 1957 an individual was reportedly photographed and kept in sight for two minutes on Birthday Bay Beach, 35 miles *56 km* SW of Queenstown by the pilot of a mining company helicopter, but experts who examined the picture said it was a large dog. A few months later three sheep were found dead in the Derwent Valley and it was claimed that their injuries corresponded with those that a thylacine might inflict. Brown (1973), however, says a dog was caught shortly afterwards in the trap-cage set up at the site.

The following year Walt Disney sent over a film team from Hollywood in an effort to catch this elusive animal on celluloid but the mission was unsuccessful.

In August 1961 two fishermen camping out at isolated Sandy Cape on the west coast heard a strange noise outside their tent one night and saw a shadowy figure trying to reach a basket of fish bait hanging up outside the entrance. One of the men attacked the creature with a piece of wood and eventually drove it off, and the following morning they found the body of a young Tasmanian wolf lying on the ground a short distance away. The fishermen later claimed the corpse was stolen from their tent by a person or persons unknown, but they did manage to collect some hair and blood samples. These were later positively identified as belonging to a thylacine by Dr Eric Guiler, senior lecturer in zoology at the University of Tasmania.

In December 1966 the traces of a thylacine lair in which a female and pups had been living were found in a disused mine boiler at Whyte River near Mawbanna, but although a trap-cage was set up in the vicinity it was not touched.

On 3 November 1969 the tracks of a thylacine were said to have been positively identified in the Cradle Mountain National Park, and other definite sightings were later reported in the Cardigan River area of the north-west coast and the Tooms Lake region, but all this information was purely circumstantial and it is interesting to note that the Tasmanian Griffiths-Malley Expedition mounted in the 1970s failed to find any trace of this animal. In the 12 months leading up to June 1978 ten sightings of the thylacine were reported to the Tasmanian National Parks and Wildlife Service, but Brown believes most of them referred to greyhounds of which there are several hundred in Tasmania. This dog is very similar in shape and size to the thylacine and, from a distance, could easily be mistaken for one of these marsupials. Today, nothing less than a body or clear photograph will convince the sceptics that the Tasmanian wolf still exists.

Other seriously endangered species include the long-tailed dunnart (*Sminthopsis longicaudata*) of W Australia (4 specimens); the northern rat-kangaroo (*Bettongia tropica*) of E Queensland (6 specimens) and the narrow-nosed planigale (*Planigale tenuirostris*) of E Australia (7 specimens).

The sandhill dunnart (*Sminthopsis psammophila*), also called the 'narrow-footed marsupial mouse', is known only from the type specimen collected by the Horn Expedition in 1894 near Lake Amadeus, Northern Territory, but this creature may eventually prove to be fairly common in this unworked area.

The crescent nail-tailed wallaby (*Onychogalea lunata*) of Central Australia has not been recorded since 1972, but the brindle nail-tailed wallaby (*O. fraenata*) which was thought to have become extinct in 1937, was rediscovered in the Emerald District, central Queensland in April 1974 during a fauna survey.

The pig-footed bandicoot (*Chaeropus ecaudatus*) was last sighted in the Musgrave Ranges between South Australia and Northern Territory in the mid-1920s, and there have been no records of the desert rat-kangaroo (*Caloprymnus campestris*) of central Australia since 1932.

Leadbeater's possum (*Gymnobelideus leadbeateri*), long believed extinct, was rediscovered in the Cumberland Valley, SE Victoria in 1961 and is now protected by law.

In August 1966 a male mountain pygmy possum (*Burramys parvus*) was captured in the kitchen of a ski-lodge on Mount Hotham in the Victoria Alps. Up until then this species was only known from a few fragments of fossilised bone found in a cave in New South Wales in 1896. Five months later a pair of dibblers (*Antechinus apicalis*), the first seen for 83 years, were collected near the Waychinicup River, east of Albany, SW Australia.

In September 1973 a marsupial mouse (family *Dasyuridae*) new to science was caught in a trap in the Billiatt Conservation Park 100 miles *160 km* east of Adelaide, South Australia. This type specimen, together with a mother and her recently-born young, were later taken to the Institute of Medical and Veterinary Science in Adelaide for study.

The greatest reliable age recorded for a marsupial is 26 years and 22 days for a common wombat (*Vombatus ursinus*) which died in London Zoo on 20 April 1906 (Flower, 1931). Another specimen lived for 26 years in Antwerp Zoo, Belgium (1928–30 November 1954).

Relating age to an index of molar progression for macropods, T H Kirkpatrick (pers. comm.) found that the oldest animal taken at the Jedburgh box, Queensland by professional kangaroo hunters was a male red kangaroo which had an estimated skull age of 30 years (possible error ±7 years).

He also mentioned a wallaroo (*Macropus robustus*) from Springsure which he had aged at 25½ years (possible error ±5 years).

According to Kirkpatrick (1965) the oldest kangaroo he had authentic record of was a *M. giganteus* which lived in captivity for 24 years. A female wallaroo (b 18 December 1960) and a female grey kangaroo (b 3 June 1961) in his possession were still alive in September 1980 aged 19 years 8½ months and 19 years 3 months respectively.

The greatest age recorded for a captive thylacine

is 8 years 4 months 18 days for a specimen at London Zoo (Flower, 1931).

The only marsupial found living wild in Britain today is the red-necked wallaby (*Macropus rufogriseus*) of eastern Australia and Tasmania. In 1939 a pair escaped from a private menagerie near Leek, Staffordshire and started a dynasty in what was to become part of the Peak District National Park. In the early 1960s there were an estimated 40–50 descendants of these two animals roaming the moorland and they appeared to be thriving, but the terrible winter of 1963 wiped out 75 per cent of the population. In 1977 the site colonised by the wallabies was sold for sheep-farming and stocked with 2000 ewes, and this extra competition for food, plus the hard winter of 1978, virtually exterminated the species. Fortunately the Nature Conservancy Council stepped in before it was too late, and as a result of their positive action and the earlier efforts of some private individuals, the Peak Park Planning Board purchased nearly 1000 acres *405 hectares* of the wallabies' habitat from the landowners. Now the future of these attractive creatures looks a lot more promising.

One of the most unusual members of the mammalian world is the little-known marsupial mole (*Notoryctes typhlops*) of the semi-deserts of central and south Australia, which has the peculiar habit of going into sudden, periodic torpors.

Wood Jones (1923–24), who kept one of these creatures under observation for a short time in captivity, said it started feeding ravenously on earthworms as soon as it was unpacked from its container. When it had finished eating it promptly fell asleep, breathing very rapidly as though it was trying to cram as much rest as possible into the short time available. It would then wake up, just as suddenly, and start searching feverishly for food again in what seemed to be a race against the clock.

'Apparently', writes Wood Jones, 'they need an extraordinary amount of food when active; but possibly when inactive they can sustain prolonged fasts. They seem to be animals which live either at fever pitch or remain almost wholly quiescent as season and circumstances demand.'

The swamp antechinus (*Antechinus minimus*) of SE Australia and Tasmania is another strange marsupial. During the mating season, which lasts only four days, the males become so excited that they collapse and die soon afterwards. Zoologists believe the act of copulation produces certain hormones which cause a breakdown of natural immunity to blood parasites.

The largest member of the Sirenia is the American manatee (*Trichechus manatus*) of the Caribbean, which ranges from the coast and coastal rivers of the SE USA to Guyana, northern South America.

Adult specimens (both sexes) average 9–10 ft *2·7–3·1 m* in total length and weigh 450–600 lb *204–272 kg*, although females tend to be heavier.

The largest American manatee on record was a captive male caught off the coast of Texas in *c* 1910 which measured 15 ft 3 in *4·65 m* in length and weighed a very light 1310 lb *594 kg* (Gunter, 1941). Under captive conditions a manatee this size would normally be expected to eat about 1 kg *2·2 lb* of vegetation a day for every 5 cm *2 in* of body length (Hartman, 1979), but in this particular case the amount of food consumed daily (i.e. 27–47 kg *60–99 lb*) was considerably less. In its natural environment this animal, in good condition, would probably have scaled at least 2000 lb *907 kg*.

The dugong (*Dugong dugon*) of the tropical Indo-Pacific region is also of comparable size, but in this species – the mermaid of legend – the weight-length relationship is much more variable. That is why an 8 ft 1¼ in *2·47 m* specimen scaled 565 lb *256 kg*, another of 9 ft *2·7 m* only 325 lb *147 kg* and a third of 11 ft 6 in *3·5 m* just under 840 lb *381 kg*. According to Mani (1960) the largest dugong on record was a 13 ft 4 in *4·06 m* female landed by fishermen at Bedi Bunder off the Sarashtra coast, W India on 23 July 1959 which weighed 'nearly a ton' (=2240 lb *1016 kg*), but an unconfirmed length of 19 ft *5·8 m* has been reported for a male caught in the Red Sea (Anderson and Jones, 1967). This latter measurement, however, must be considered suspect because the dugongs found in the Red Sea rarely if ever exceed 10 ft 4 in *3·15 m* in length.

In July 1905 the cargo steamer SS *Samshon* was passing Haramil Island in the Red Sea when the captain saw what looked like three people floating upright in the water with their heads and chests showing. Thinking they had been shipwrecked he stopped to pick them up, but when they submerged he suddenly realised they were a family of dugongs. Angry at being delayed, he waited until they reappeared and shot the biggest one in the neck. The wounded sirenian then headed for the shore, followed by the other two, where they were easily captured by the crew. Back on board the three dugongs were put in a big tank and fed on fish (*sic*) which the adults reluctantly accepted. Unhappily the female was still nursing her calf, and when her mate eventually succumbed from a combination of the injury and the unsuitable diet she pined and neglected her offspring. Within a week they were dead as well (Prater, 1929).

Both the American manatee and the dugong were dwarfed by the huge dugong-like Steller's sea cow (*Hydrodamalis gigas*), which formerly lived in the shallow waters around the Komandorskie (Commander) Islands in the Bering Sea, N Pacific.

When he was marooned on Bering Island with the Second Trans-Asiatic Expedition in 1741, George Wilhelm Steller dissected an adult cow after it had been killed and dragged ashore by forty of his companions to provide food and clothing. It measured 7·5 m *24 ft 8 in* in total length, had a maximum girth of 6·2 m *20 ft 4 in* and yielded 200 poods (=3265 kg *7200 lb*) of meat and blubber. After working out the approximate ratios of lung to total body volume from the detailed notes that were taken by the German physician and naturalist, Mackal (1976) calculated that the live weight of this giant sirenian must have been about 10 880 lb *4935 kg*, which is not unreasonable for a marine mammal of these known dimensions. As the maximum length attained by Steller's sea cow was said to be 9 m *29 ft 6 in* this would give a weight of 17 400 lb *7893 kg* by extrapolation (*cf* 18 293 lb *8298 kg* for a 29 ft *8·8 m* bull killer whale).

This slow, inoffensive creature (total population *c* 2000) reportedly became extinct only 27 years after its discovery in 1741 as a result of over-hunting for food, but there is some Russian evidence that it may have survived until 1834 in the same area.

In July 1962 the crew of the Russian whaler *Buran* saw half a dozen unusual-looking creatures in a shallow lagoon near Cape Navarin to the south of the Gulf of Anadyr, NE USSR. The animals, measuring 6–8 m *19 ft 8¼ in–26 ft 3 in* in length, were swimming around slowly and appeared to be browsing on seaweed, the staple diet of *H. gigas*. The description the men later gave to Russian biologists (Berzin *et al*, 1963) also fitted that of Steller's sea cow, but it has since been suggested that they were more probably a small group of male narwhals (*Monodon monceros*), which were surfacing from time to time with their bodies arched in such a way that their spiral tusks were not revealed on the surface. This species (maximum body length 6·1 m *20 ft*) is rarely seen outside Arctic waters.

The smallest sirenian is the little-known Amazonian manatee (*Trichechus inunguis*), which does not exceed 8 ft 3 in *2·51 m* and 308 lb *140 kg*. This species is also the most seriously endangered sea cow and is now confined to the Amazon basin, NE South America. It is protected by law, but there is no real enforcement, and it is still regularly harpooned or shot for its highly-prized meat.

Manatees have been credited with a potential lifespan of more than 50 years in the wild on account of their slow growth, but no definite information has been published.

The greatest authentic age recorded for a captive specimen is 30 years for an American manatee at Bradenton, Florida, USA which was still alive on 1 June 1979. It was born in captivity.

Very few dugongs have been kept in captivity for more than a few months, but Marvin Jones (pers. comm.) says one individual received at Manapan camp, Malaysia in 1960 was still alive in 1968.

The longest recorded elephant tusks (excluding prehistoric examples) are a pair from the eastern Congo. They were originally owned by King Menelek of Abyssinia (Ethiopia), who later presented them to a 'European political officer'. They were eventually put up for sale in London and were purchased by Rowland Ward Ltd, the famous Piccadilly taxidermists, who presented them in 1907 to the National Collection of Heads and Horns kept by the New York Zoological Society. The right tusk measures 11 ft 5 in *3·5 m* along the outside curve, the left 11 ft *3·35 m*; combined weight is 293 lb *133 kg*.

Another pair of tusks measuring 11 ft 1¼ in *3·38 m* and 10 ft 0½ in *3·06 m* respectively, with a combined weight of 244 lb 6 oz *111 kg* were collected by T Christensen in Kenya in February 1959 (Rowland Ward, 1969), and a bull with tusks measuring 10 ft 9 in *3·28 m* and 10 ft 8 in *3·25 m* respectively (combined weight 253 lb *115 kg*) was shot by Mrs P Fluckiger in Kenya in March 1970 (Rowland Ward, 1971).

The dugong – the mermaid of legend. This pair was captured by fishermen in the Red Sea.

In 1904 W R Foran shot an old elephant bull on the slopes of Mt Kenya which carried only one complete tusk measuring 11 ft 1 in *3·38 m* in length and weighing 169 lb *77 kg*. The other tusk, which was just a broken stump, scaled 30 lb *13·6 kg*.

The right tusk of a bull elephant is nearly always slightly longer and heavier than the left because the animal prefers to dig and root about with its left tusk. In the case of the Christensen elephant, however, the difference is rather pronounced.

The longest recorded Asiatic elephant tusks are a pair in the Royal Siamese National Museum, Bangkok which measure 9 ft 10 in *3·00 m* and 9 ft 2 in *2·74 m* respectively. They belonged to an elephant kept in the palace of King Rama V, and when this unfortunate creature had to walk in royal processions it had to raise its head so that the ivories would not scrape in the sandy road. Whenever the elephant stopped a special 12 in *30 cm* high platform was brought for it so that the tips of the tusks could rest on the ground.

The mighty tusker 'Ahmed' of Marsabit Mountain Reserve, Kenya.

The heaviest recorded tusks are a pair in the British Museum, London which were collected from an aged bull shot by an Arab with a muzzle-loading gun at the foot of Mt Kilimanjaro, Kenya in 1897. They were sold in Zanzibar in 1898 to an American company, Messrs Landesberg, Humble and Co, who in turn sent them to London for auction in 1901. The heaviest of the two tusks was bought by the Trustees of the British Museum for £350, and the other one was acquired by Joseph Rodgers and Sons Ltd, a cutlery firm in Sheffield. In 1932 this tusk was sold to W B Wolstenholme Ltd, also of Sheffield. The following year it was purchased by the Trustees of the British Museum. When they were fresh these tusks weighed 240 lb *109 kg* (length 10 ft 2½ in *3·11 m*) and 225 lb *102 kg* (length 10 ft 5½ in *3·19 m*) respectively, giving a combined weight of 465 lb *211 kg*, but when Hill (1957) examined them they totalled 440 lb 8 oz *200 kg*. This rather contradicts a recent statement by Rowland Ward (1975) that the loss of weight during the drying-out period is only 1–2 lb *454–907 g*.

Another huge pair collected by Major P H G Powell-Cotton from an average-sized bull shot near Lake Albert on the Uganda-Congo border in 1905 and now preserved in the Powell-Cotton Museum at Quez Park, Kent measure 9 ft *2·7 m* and 8 ft 11 in *2·72 m* respectively, and have a combined weight of 372 lb *169 kg* (198 lb *90 kg* and 174 lb *79 kg*).

According to Hallett (1967) the tusks of the famous 'Mohammed' of Marsabit Mountain Reserve, N Kenya were so long and heavy that the poor elephant could not raise his head properly and had to walk backwards to avoid getting them stuck in the ground. In 1950 game-wardens estimated that there was 10 ft *3·1 m* of tusk outside each gum and put their combined weight at 400 lb *181 kg*. When this elephant died of old age in 1960, however, the tusks were found to total just over 250 lb *113 kg*, the longest measuring 10 ft 9 in *3·28 m* in length and scaling 141 lb *64 kg* (Bere, 1966).

His even more celebrated successor 'Ahmed' was said to have had the longest and heaviest tusks of any living elephant, and in 1971 game circles estimated that they were both between 160 lb *73 kg* and 170 lb *77 kg*. But when this legendary pachyderm died on 17 January 1974 it was discovered that the tusks, measuring 9 ft 9 in *2·97 m* and 9 ft 4 in *2·85 m* respectively, totalled 296 lb *134 kg* (A MacKay, pers. comm.).

Ahmed's successor, 'Abdol', who was killed by poachers in Marsabit Mountain Reserve in February 1977, had even bigger tusks than his predecessor, but further details are lacking. In 1980 the tusks of 'Mapeni' (Big Boy) of Kenyatta National Park were so long that they reportedly dug into the ground.

Owing to selective shooting for sport and ivory very few large tusks are now left in Africa, and anything scaling over 100 lb *45 kg* must be considered exceptional.

The heaviest recorded Asiatic elephant tusks are a pair collected from a bull killed in the Terai jungle, N India and later presented to King George V. The tusks, now in the British Museum have a combined weight of 321 lb *146 kg* (lengths 8 ft 9 in *2·67 m* and 8 ft 6½ in *2·60 m*).

The heaviest single tusk on record was one weighing 258 lb *117 kg* collected in Benin, W Africa. It was put on display at the Paris Exposition of 1900, along with another tusk weighing 214 lb *97 kg* (a pair?). A H Neumann (1898) said another one weighing 250 lb *113 kg* was once on exhibition in the Zanzibar Customs Hall.

The longest (and heaviest) cow elephant tusks on record are a pair taken from an elephant shot by Peter Pearson, the well-known Uganda game-ranger on the NE shore of Lake Albert in 1923. The tusks, now in the British Museum, measure 6 ft 7 in *2·0 m* and 6 ft 3½ in *1·92 m* respectively, and have a combined weight of 98 lb *44 kg*.

Cow tusks rarely exceed 15–20 lb *7–9 kg* in weight (some cows never grow tusks at all), but they are more valuable than those of bulls because of their closer grain.

The longest horns grown by any living animal are those of the water buffalo (*Bubalus arnee*) of India. One huge bull shot in *c* 1955 had horns measuring 13 ft 11 in *4·24 m* from tip to tip along the outside curve across the forehead (Powell, 1958), and two other heads measured 13 ft 8 in *4·17 m* and 13 ft 4 in *4·06 m* respectively. It should be pointed out here that in this species two different types of horns are grown. In the cases already mentioned, the horns were spread outwards almost horizontally from the head and curved slightly upwards and inwards near the tips. In the second category, the horns curve upwards in a semi-circle and the tips are only separated by a small gap.

Texan longhorn steers (*Bos taurus*) have been credited with measurements up to 13 ft 6½ in *4·13 m* tip to tip along the outside curve, but very few authentic spreads (i.e. straight-line measurements) over 8 ft *2·42 m* have been recorded. Two sets of horns with 9 ft *2·7 m* spreads were reportedly shown at the Columbian Exposition, Chicago in 1893, but they may have been steamed and straightened. 'Horns contain the essence of glue', says Dobie (1943). 'They can be steam-heated or boiled and straightened out so that a certain amount of curve is transformed into horizontal length . . . Moreover, in mounting a pair of horns on wood – for few that are sold are on the original skull – unscrupulous dealers add several inches to the frontal piece, thus further increasing width.' The famous longhorn steer 'Champion' (b 1890), who was exhibited at the 'International Fair' in San Antonio in 1899, was said to have had a horn spread of over 9 ft *2·7 m*, but the actual measurement was believed to have been 8 ft 7½ in *2·63 m*. This magnificent longhorn was last seen in Davenport, Iowa in *c* 1902, but Dobie says the whereabouts of his horns are unknown. Ray Stone of Houston, Texas has four pairs of longhorn steer horns in his private collection which have a spread of more than 8 ft *2·4 m*. His largest head has an astonishing spread of 9 ft 9 in *2·97 m*, but this is explained by the fact that the horns, although showing various curves, grow out like handle-bars from the skull. Horizontal horns like these are extremely rare on live animals. Ivie (pers. comm.) says they belonged to a 16-year-old steer weighing an estimated 2200 lb *998 kg*.

Birds

(class Aves)

A bird is a warm-blooded, air-breathing bipedal vertebrate covered with feathers and having the forelimbs modified into wings which are sometimes rudimentary and useless for flight. The brain is well developed, and the jaws are covered with horny sheaths forming a beak. Young are produced from eggs. Other features include a four-chambered heart and an essentially high constant body temperature because flight requires a tremendous output of energy over a long period.

The earliest known bird was the reptilian-like glider *Archaeopteryx*, which lived about 165 million years ago. Unlike modern birds, it had well-developed teeth in its jaws and a long jointed bony tail, but the wings bore characteristic feathers. Its remains were first discovered at Solenhofen in Bavaria, Germany in 1861.

The class Aves is divided up into 28 orders of equal status comprising 161 families and about 8900 species. The largest order is Passeriformes (perching birds), which contains about 5100 species and the smallest Struthioniformes (one species).

The largest living bird is the ostrich (*Struthio camelus*) of Africa. There are now five geographical races – the last Syrian ostrich (*S. c. syriacus*) was killed and eaten by Arabs in Bahrein in 1941 – and they differ slightly in size, shape and colour. The largest sub-species is the northern ostrich (*S. c. camelus*), which is now found in reduced numbers south of the Atlas Mountains from Upper Senegal and Niger across to the Sudan and central Ethiopia. Adult cock examples of this flightless bird stand about 8 ft *2·4 m* tall (height at back 4 ft 6 in *1·37 m*) on the average and weigh 265–280 lb *120–127 kg* (Duerden, 1919), but

heights up to 9 ft *2·7 m* and weights up to 345 lb *156 kg* have been reliably reported. Adult hens are smaller, standing about 7 ft *2·1 m* tall and weighing 200–220 lb *90–100 kg*.

The southern ostrich (*S. c. australis*), which is now found only in the wilder parts of the NE Transvaal, South Africa, southern Zimbabwe and the adjoining part of Mozambique, as well as Botswana and SW Africa, is not as heavy as its northern cousin (220–250 lb *100–113 kg*) and has a shorter neck. Larger domesticated birds have been recorded, but these were usually crosses between *S. c. camelus* and *S. c. australis*. William A Hooper (pers. comm.), owner of the famous Highgate Ostrich Farm at Oudtshoorn, Cape Province, South Africa says abattoir birds measuring a few inches over 8 ft *2·4 m* and weighing up to 326 lb *148 kg* have been reported (a 320 lb *145 kg* ostrich yielded 21 ft² *2·0 m²* of skin). In 1979 St Augustine Alligator Farm, Florida, USA sold an exceptionally large cock bird (probably a hybrid) to a commercial animal dealer. It stood 8 ft 6 in *2·59 m* tall and was extremely fat, having been kept for 20 years in a relatively small paddock. According to Robert C Baudy (pers. comm.), who has bred many ostriches in his special animal compound and was familiar with this particular bird, it was 'a giant among giants'. Unfortunately the present whereabouts of this super-heavyweight is not known.

During the mating season the cock ostrich is one of the most dangerous animals on earth and its war-dance has to be seen to be believed. It stamps its feet, waves its neck in erratic circles and generally works itself up into a towering rage before charging at the object of its wrath, which it then proceeds to kick with its huge, powerfully-clawed legs.

One angry cock ostrich at Hanover Zoo bent a 13 mm *0·5 in* thick iron bar at right angles with a single kick, and another bird at Frankfurt Zoo ripped the clothes off an unsuspecting keeper's back with a well-placed blow and half threw him through a wire fence at the same time (Grzimek, 1970). There is also a record of an introduced ostrich kicking a young camel to death on a ranch near Nuevo Laredo, Mexico (Laycock, 1966).

Not surprisingly, there are a number of records of people being disembowelled or fatally kicked in the head by an irate ostrich. In 1965 a 21-year-old man died at Oudtshoorn after his skull was fractured, and Clarke (1969) says there are two or three serious accidents in that area each year.

Ostriches regularly swallow stones or quartz-pebbles as an aid to digestion, and if they can't find suitable ones in captivity, they will happily gulp down an amazing variety of articles as substitutes. In the stomach of one individual which died suddenly at London Zoo several years ago were found a 3 ft *91 cm* long piece of rope, a spool of film, an alarm clock key, a cycle valve, a pencil, a comb, three gloves, a handkerchief, glove-fasteners, pieces of a gold necklace, two collar studs, a Belgian franc, two farthings and four halfpennies.

When a post-mortem was carried out on a cock bird which choked to death at Highgate Ostrich Farm in February 1962 a total of 484 coins weighing 8 lb 4 oz *3·74 kg* were found in its stomach. Apparently South Africa had just converted from sterling to decimal currency, and the larger coin proved to be the bird's undoing.

Although the ostrich is not rated very highly in the intelligence stakes – the brain of a 270 lb *122 kg* cock bird weighed only 42·11 g *1·49 oz* or 0.03 per cent of the total bodyweight – it is not nearly so stupid as tradition would have us believe. The classic story that it will bury its head in the sand when frightened in the belief that it cannot be seen is based on the manner in which it sits on its nest. By laying its long neck flat on the ground the ostrich looks just like another hillock on the bare scrub-covered veld and – hopefully – is overlooked by predators. It is also interesting to note that the dull brown hen sits on the eggs during the daytime when her feathers are practically indistinguishable from the sandy earth, while the black cock bird sits during the hours of darkness.

Further evidence that ostriches are reasonably intelligent animals comes from SW Africa where they have been trained to herd sheep, and a farmer near Durban, Natal has taught an ostrich to chase off birds that attack his crops.

Unfortunately, they also have an inherent inquisitiveness, and if regimental mascot 'Osman' had not been quite so nosey, he would probably still be alive today.

This popular and entertaining character was attached to an artillery unit stationed in Kenya during the Mau Mau troubles, and when the Government declared a state of emergency in October 1952 he was given a free run of the lines when the battery was on operations. He was no bother, however, and spent most of the daylight hours foraging around the stables or the swill bins. At night-time one of his favourite tricks was to pad up silently behind a patrolling sentry and put his head over the man's shoulder just to see if he was missing anything. For those who knew him this was perfectly in order, but on the fatal night in question he tried it on a new sentry who had not been warned beforehand. The man, not unnaturally, literally jumped out of his skin when he suddenly saw the long, sinewy neck leaning over him and, in the ensuing panic, the poor ostrich got in the way of the frenzied man's rifle butt and suffered a broken leg. Osman was accorded full military honours after his untimely death, and his skeleton is now on display in the National Museum in Nairobi.

Ostriches seldom go near water, and it was not until April 1971 that floods in Cape Province solved a problem which had long puzzled ornithologists: can these huge birds swim? When the Victoria West nature reserve was swamped all the antelopes in the area drowned, but two ostriches swam serenely out of the valley. A South African Air Force helicopter pilot also spotted another one making its way down the swollen Sak River.

The largest marine bird is the Emperor penguin (*Aptenodytes forsteri*), which breeds on sea ice and islets off the coast of Antarctica. Adults stand up to 4 ft *1·2 m* tall and are massively built. In one series of 33 adult birds, weighed in November when they were fattest, by Dr Edward A Wilson, a member of the British National Antarctic Expedition of 1901-4, the average was 70·5 lb *32 kg*, but heavier specimens have been reported. One emperor penguin captured in the Ross Sea by another British Antarctic Expedition in November 1915 tipped the scales at 94 lb *42·6 kg* and boasted a chest measurement of 52 in *132 cm*, and this probably constitutes a weight record for this species.

Emperor penguins have tremendous strength and vitality and are extremely difficult to kill. One individual shot through the body with a solid bore carried on apparently unaffected for some time and led its pursuers, a party from James Ross's Antarctic Expedition of 1839–43, a merry dance across the packed snow. On another occasion five men from a Scottish whaling ship tried to pin an emperor penguin down on the ice without harming it, but they were quite unequal to the task and were bowled over like ninepins. They eventually managed to strap two leather belts around the lusty bird's body, but as they stood back to take a breath, so too did the penguin – and burst the belts! The 74 lb *33·6 kg* powerhouse was finally secured with a rope, but when it was hoisted on board it still managed to knock the ship's dog out cold with a blow from its muscular flipper.

According to Tucker (1977) the upper limit of size for a bird capable of *steady flapping flight* is reached when the mass approaches 12 kg *26 lb 7 oz*, but heavier weights have been recorded for various species that were still able to fly.

The world's heaviest modern flying bird is the Kori bustard or paauw (*Ardeotis kori*) of East and South Africa. Very little weight data has been published for this species, but a 30 lb *13·6 kg* cock bird would be considered a large example. Hens are smaller and much lighter in weight.

One of the heaviest birds on record was a paauw shot by H T Glynn, a well-known sportsman, in South Africa which weighed exactly 40 lb *18·2 kg*. The head and neck of this bird were presented to the British Museum (Bryden, 1936). Carl Schneritz told Harting (1906) that he shot two big bustards on the high veld between Scheenspruit and Rustenberg in the Transvaal in 1899. The larger of the two had a wingspread of 9 ft *2·7 m* and scaled 37 lb *16·8 kg*. In 1959 a scientific expedition from the Durban Museum shot a Kori bustard in SW Africa which weighed 35 lb *15·9 kg* and kept the camp in meat for nearly a week (P A Clancey, pers. comm.).

This long-legged bird runs swiftly when danger threatens, but when it does take to the air its relatively slow flight is powerful and sustained at low altitudes.

The great bustard (*Otis tarda*) of Europe, Africa and Asia has also been credited with the title of the world's heaviest flying bird, but this statement is based on an isolated record of a cock bird shot in the USSR which tipped the scales at 21 kg *46 lb* and probably could not fly. The normal weight range for adult cock birds is 24–35 lb *11–16 kg*. This species bred in England until 1832, and one bird shot illegally on the north Norfolk coast in *c.*1942 weighed 24 lb *10·9 kg* (span 6 ft 6 in *1·98 m*). In 1975 the Great Bustard Trust imported 11 birds (four cocks and seven hens) from Portugal and installed them in a wired-off enclosure on Porton Down, Salisbury Plain where it was hoped they would breed.

Weights in excess of 30 lb *13·6 kg* have also been reliably reported for the great Arabian bustard (*Ardeotis arabs*). Meinertzhagen (1954) says the average weight in a series of 19 adult cock birds collected by him in Iraq was 24 lb *10·9 kg*, the heaviest scaling 37 lb *16·8 kg*. The average weight of 18 adult hens was 17 lb *7·7 kg*.

Blandford (1895–8) claims that weights up to 40 lb *18·1 kg* have been recorded for the now extremely rare great Indian bustard (*A. nigriceps*), and he gives the normal weight range of adult cock birds as 25–30 lb *11·3–13·6 kg*. Stuart Baker (1922), on the other hand, says the heaviest weight he could trace for a cock bird was 26 lb 8 oz *12·0 kg*. Earlier a 'sportsman' writing in the *Oriental Sporting Magazine* of August 1830 revealed that between 1809 and 1830 he bagged 961 great Indian bustards near Ahmedmagar, Bombay Province. The cock birds weighed 18–32 lb *8·1–14·5 kg* and the hens 8–15 lb *3·6–6·8 kg*.

Gilliard (1958) says the Australian bustard (*A. australis*) 'is probably the heaviest of all flying birds', but Gould, who killed a great number of them on the plains of the Lower Namoi, NSW, and also in South Australia, gives the weight of the adult cock birds as between 13 lb *5·9 kg* and 16 lb *7·3 kg*. The maximum weight recorded for this species is 32 lb *14·5 kg* for a cock bird killed in Victoria (Serventy and Whittell, 1950).

The mute swan (*Cygnus olor*), which is resident in Britain, the trumpeter swan (*Cygnus c. buccinator*) of North America and the whooper swan (*Cygnus cygnus*) of North America, Europe and Asia also exceed 30 lb *13·6 kg* on occasion, the average weight of adult cobs being 26 lb 14 oz *12·2 kg*, 26 lb 4 oz *11·9 kg* and 23 lb 13 oz *10·8 kg* respectively (Boyd, 1972). Audubon (1840) mentions a trumpeter swan which scaled 37 lb 13 oz *17·2 kg*, and there is a record from Poland of a cob mute swan weighing an astonishing 49 lb 9½ oz *22·5 kg* at the height of the summer (Sanden, 1935).

There is also an isolated record of a Siberian white crane (*Grus leucogeranus*) weighing 33 lb *15·0 kg* (Fisher and Peterson, 1964).

The upper weight limit for a modern flapping bird is about 40 lb *18 kg*. If the body mass increased still further the flight muscles needed to provide the power output would take up a higher proportion of the weight than the bird could afford consistent with maintaining all its other functions.

A wandering albatross (*Diomedea exulans*) nestling weighed by Tickell (1968) on Bird Island, South Georgia, Falkland Island Dependencies shortly before its departure scaled 35 lb 7½ oz *16·1 kg*, but a third of this avoirdupois consisted of heavy fat deposition which would be shed in the first few weeks of flight. In one series of 108 adult *D. exulans* the average weight was found to be 18 lb *8·2 kg*. The heaviest bird scaled 25 lb *11·3 kg* and the lightest 13 lb *5·9 kg*. Gibson and Sefton (1960) point out, however, that 'being voracious feeders, the considerable stomach contents of well fed birds influence the weight accordingly'.

The heaviest raptor (bird of prey) is the Andean condor (*Vultur gryphus*), which ranges from western Venezuela southwards to Tierra del Fuego and Patagonia. Adult males and females scale 23–24 lb *10·4–10·9 kg* and 17–22 lb *7·7–10·0 kg* respectively.

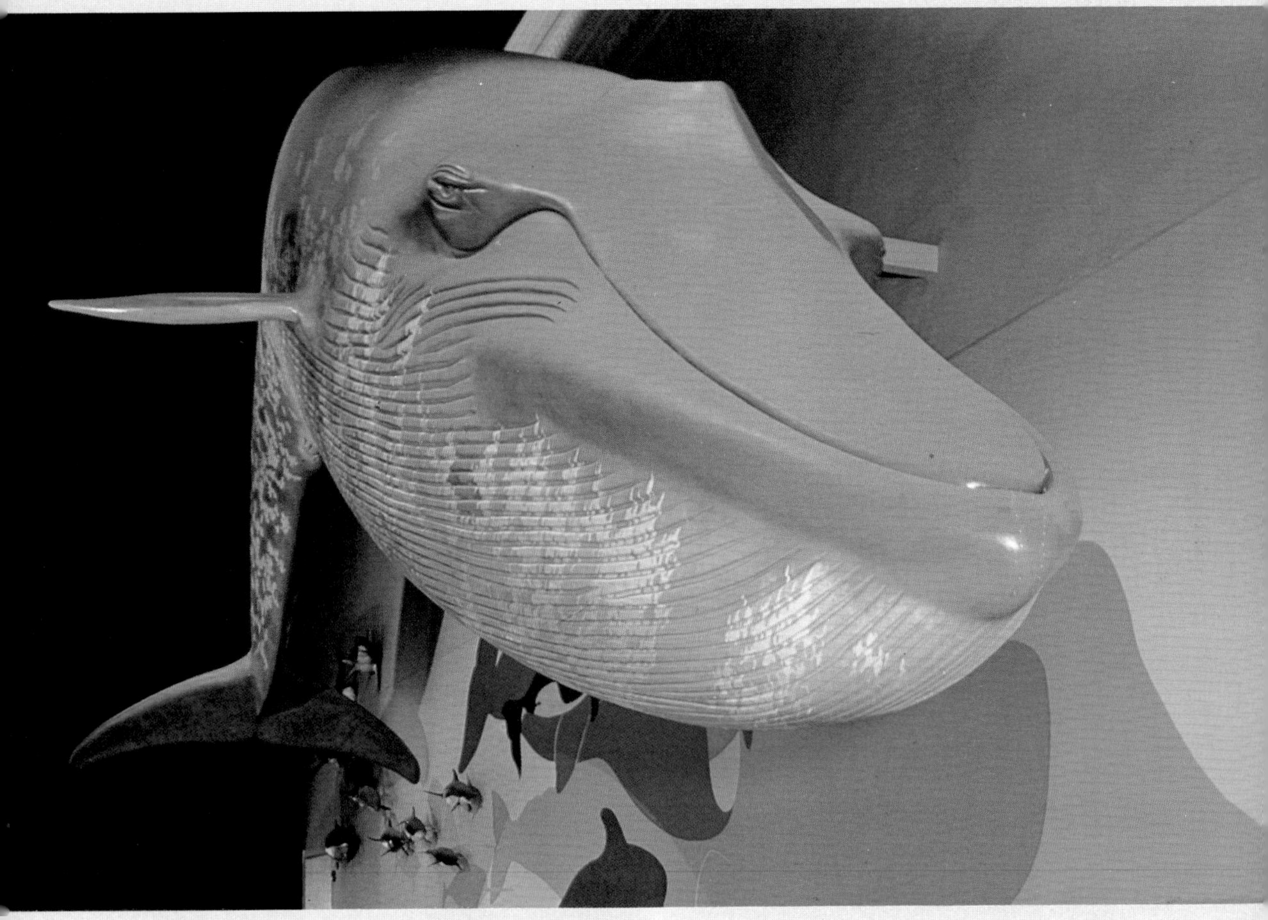

A 90 ft 27·4 m long model of a blue whale.

The bull killer whale 'Orky', the world's largest captive marine mammal.

The female Asiatic cow elephant 'Modoc', who lived for 78 years.

The Eurasian pygmy shrew, the smallest land mammal found in Britain.

The rusty-spotted cat, the smallest member of the Felidae.

Peking Zoo's record-sized 812½ lb 369 kg Korean-Chinese tiger.

One old male shot on San Gallen Island off the coast of Peru in *c*1919 weighed 26 lb 8 oz *12·0 kg* (Murphy, 1925). In October 1965 a weight of 11 kg *24 lb 4 oz* was reported for an Andean condor named 'Friedrich' at Frankfurt Zoo, W Germany but the bird (hatched 1959) was only 18 lb 6 oz *8·3 kg* at the time of his death on 24 February 1971 (Bernard Grzimek, pers. comm.).

The almost extinct Californian condor (*Vultur californianus*) – in 1980 the wild population was down to 13 known birds – is not quite as large as its South American cousin and rarely exceeds 20 lb *9·1 kg*. The heaviest bird collected by Stephens (1895) scaled 21 lb 8 oz *9·8 kg*, and Henshaw (1920) quotes a weight of 23 lb *10·4 kg* for another specimen. Three other examples (all males) formerly in the private collection of E B Towne, Jr, and now in the California Academy of Sciences, Los Angeles reportedly weighed 27 lb *12·3 kg*, 29 lb *13·2 kg* and 31 lb *14·1 kg* respectively, but Carl B Koford (1953) the leading authority on this species, believes Towne may have obtained these figures second-hand from the men who collected the birds for him. Certainly, it is difficult to believe that this species could ever outweigh the heaviest Andean condor.

The only other birds of prey which *regularly* exceed 20 lb *9·1 kg* are the European black vulture (*Aegypius monachus*) and the Himalayan griffon (*Gyps himalayensis*). In one series of 20 male specimens of *A. monachus* the weights ranged from 7 to 11·5 kg *15 lb 7 oz to 25 lb 6 oz* (average 9·22 kb *20 lb 5 oz*), and in another series of 21 females the range was 7·5 to 12·5 kg *16 lb 8 oz to 27 lb 8 oz* (average 10 kg *22 lb*). In *G. himalayensis* the weight ranged from 8 kg *17 lb 10 oz* to 12 kg *26 lb 7 oz*, giving an average of 10 kg *22 lb* for both sexes (Brown and Amadon, 1968).

The heaviest eagle in the world – and the most formidable – is the harpy eagle (*Harpia harpyja*), which ranges from southern Mexico to eastern Bolivia, southern Brazil and northern Argentina. Very little weight data has been published for this forest-dwelling species, but adult females (males are much smaller) average about 16–17 lb *7·3–7·7 kg*. Stanley Brock, former manager of the vast Dadanawa cattle ranch in Guyana, once owned an enormous female called 'Jezebel' who tipped the scales at 27 lb *12·3 kg*, and this probably represents the upper weight limit for a bird of prey that needs to glide and dodge through branches with great dexterity when hunting monkeys.

The Philippine eagle (*Pithecophaga jefferyi*) of Luzon, Samar and Leyte in the Philippines, is only fractionally smaller, although no weights are available for adult females. Adult males of both species average 10–11 lb *4·5–5·0 kg*.

Until quite recently this raptor (total population 150–250 pairs) was known as the monkey-eating eagle, but in 1978 the name was changed because the President of the Philippines felt it denigrated the qualities of a bird 'in whose rarity and confident bearing the Philippines can take pride'.

The huge Steller's sea eagle (*Haliaeetus pelagicus*) of NE Siberia is also of comparable size, adult females weighing 6·8–9 kg *15–19 lb 13 oz*, and there is an old record of a female white-tailed sea eagle (*H. albicilla*) killed at Stornaway, Lewis, Outer Hebrides in the nineteenth century which scaled 16 lb 8 oz *7·5 kg* – a weight record for a British eagle.

The Asian golden eagle or Berkut (*Aquila chrysaetos daphanea*) does not normally exceed 14 lb *6·4 kg* (adult females) but much heavier specimens have been recorded. Sam Barnes of Pwllheli, North Wales owns an outsized female called 'Atalanta', which he collected in the Tien Shan Mountains in the Kirghiz Republic, USSR some years ago. The Kirghiz tribesmen use these eagles to hunt deer and wolves – the bird is trained to grip the head of the animal it is pursuing and slow it down to a halt – and never trade them to Westerners, but because the eagle was sick and believed to be dying, Barnes was able to purchase her for two bottles of brandy and a few hundred cigarettes. On rabbit-hunting expeditions he flies this eagle at an extraordinary 26 lb 10 oz *12·1 kg*.

The greatest wingspread attained by any living bird is that of the Wandering albatross of the southern oceans, which has more wing feathers (88) than any other species. In one short series of birds examined by Tickell (1968) on Bird Island, South Georgia adult males averaged 10 ft 1¾ in *3·09 m* with wings tightly stretched, and adult females 10 ft 2¼ in *3·11 m*, but females are normally smaller than males.

In an earlier study during June–August 1959 at Malabar (Sydney) and Bellambi NSW, Australia, the average wingspread of the 119 birds netted while on the water was found to be 9 ft 10 in *3·00 m*, with a maximum of 10 ft 7¼ in *3·23 m* and a minimum of 8 ft 11 in *2·72 m*.

The largest accurately measured specimen on record was an 11 ft 11 in *3·63 m* male caught in the Tasman Sea on 18 September 1965 by the Antarctic research ship USNS *Eltanin*. The bird was measured by Dr Peter C Harper (pers. comm.), an ornithologist at the University of Canterbury, Christchurch, New Zealand after it became ensnared in some oceanographic gear trailing behind the vessel. 'I took it according to standard routine ornithological measurements – taken in the flesh without stretching the bird or its primaries', he said. 'The bird was . . . nearly pure white – a sign of great age.' Another one taken by banders in Western Australia in *c*1957 measured 11 ft 10 in *3·6 m* (H J Disney, pers. comm.), and a third male found stranded on the beach at Bunbury, 110 miles *177 km* south of Fremantle,

Western Australia on 17 July 1930 had a span of 11 ft 6 in *3·5 m* (Whitlock, 1931).

As these statistics cover only a few hundred birds out of a total world population of *c* 50 000, the law of averages says this dynamic soarer must reach and sometimes exceed 12 ft *3·7 m*, and this is confirmed by several nineteenth-century naturalists who had an opportunity to measure a number of large specimens. Scouler (1826), for instance, says he caught one bird which measured 12 ft *3·7 m* and weighed 18 lb *8·2 kg*, and the same measurement is given by Hutton (1865) for his largest albatross. According to Spry (1877) all the birds collected by him on Marion Island in the southern Indian Ocean were 11–12 ft *3·4–3·7 m*, and Lord Campbell (1877) claims he measured several birds of 12–13 ft *3·7–4·0 m* at islands in the Indian Ocean during the cruise of the *Challenger*.

Dr George Bennett (1860), who was a very competent observer, measured seven albatrosses ranging from 10 ft 4 in *3·15 m* to 11 ft 8 in *3·56 m*, but also mentioned another specimen in which the spread of wings reached 14 ft *4·3 m*.

Dr Robert Cushman Murphy (1936), one of the world's foremost authorities on the sea birds of the southern oceans, is more critical, however, and considers a measurement of 13 ft *4·0 m* to be excessive. The largest albatross examined by him in South Georgia taped 11 ft 4 in *3·45 m*, and he put the maximum wingspread of this species at 'about 11½ feet with the wings of the dead bird stretched out as tightly as possible'.

As already noted, this measurement has since been surpassed by 5 in *12·7 cm* for a *live* example, but more recently evidence has come to light which suggests the maximum expanse of wing attained by the wandering albatross may be more than 13 ft *4·0 m*.

In April 1929, while serving as an apprentice aboard the SS *Devon*, J Strand Jones (pers. comm.) says he helped capture an enormous individual which measured an astonishing 13 ft 10 in *4·22 m* across the tightly-stretched wings.

'We caught it by throwing a heavy nut attached to a cord across its back as it flew alongside the ship in the Indian Ocean, then hauling it aboard. The cord was thrown from the boat deck and the bird hauled in to the after well deck. What struck me about the bird apart from the incredible expanse of wing was the size of the beak, but that was too dangerous to measure. Afterwards we took out the stanchions as when loading cargo, and it flopped overboard.'

In the normal course of events the capture of such an outsized albatross would have been noted in the ship's log. As luck would have it, however, the superstitious Master had earlier blown his top when somebody had foolishly taken a few pot-shots at one of these birds with a ·22 rifle, and after this perfor-

The magnificent Andean condor 'Friedrich', who had a wing expanse of just over 10 ft 3·1 m.

mance it was decided that discretion was the better part of valour.

Figuier (1894) speaks of a wandering albatross in the Leverian Museum, London which measured 'thirteen feet from the tip of one wing to the tip of the other'. It was reportedly collected during one of Capt Cook's voyages, but further details are lacking, because the museum collection was auctioned in 1806 and went into a number of private hands. It is interesting to note, however, that Karl Mullenhoff (1885) mentions a *D. exulans* of almost identical size (4 m *13 ft 1½ in*) in a paper he had written about the dimensions of flying animals. This bird weighed 12·7 kg *28 lb*.

Another huge specimen shot off the Cape of Good Hope reportedly had a wingspread of 17 ft 6 in *5·33 m* (Parkinson, 1900), but the largest mounted example in the Australian Museum, Sydney, NSW where this avian giant is said to be preserved, measures exactly 10 ft *3·05 m*, although it is not fully adult (H J Disney, pers. comm.).

Nelson (1980) claims the largest and heaviest seabird in the world is the royal albatross (*Diomedea epomophora*) of the seas around New Zealand and Cape Horn, but Murphy says the wingspread is less than in *D. exulans* and probably does not exceed 3 m *9 ft 10 in*.

The wandering albatross's closest rival in terms of wing expanse is the Andean condor, which has the largest 'sail area' of any living bird. Very little accurate size data has been published for this gigantic soarer, but it is believed that the adult male has an average wingspread of 9 ft 3 in *2·82 m* and the female 9 ft *2·7 m*. Fisher (1946) quotes a measurement of 9 ft

The Weddell seal, which is probably the world's deepest-diving pinniped.
A vampire bat feeding off the leg of a chicken.

The famous emperor tamarin 'Whiskers' who exceeded the normal life-span recorded for this species of monkey by a factor of two.
Jersey Zoo's 15-year-old lesser hedgehog-tenrec, the oldest insectivore on record.

10 in *3·00 m* for a specimen preserved in alcohol, and the same span is given by Koford for another condor collected by J R Pemberton which is now in the Museum of Comparative Zoology at Harvard University. The old male shot on San Gallan Island (see page 68) measured a fraction of an inch over 10 ft *3·1 m* and Friedrich at Frankfurt Zoo (see page 68) had a wingspread of 10 ft 1¼ in *3·08 m*.

According to RP Emile Housse (1948), the leading Chilean ornithologist, the Andean condor has been reliably measured up to 3.2 m *10 ft 6 in* across the wings, and this is probably a reference to the huge bird examined by Edward Whymper (1892), the famous English mountaineer, at Antisana, north central Ecuador. Alexander von Humboldt, the German explorer and scientist, on the other hand, did not see a single condor in Ecuador over 9 ft *2·7 m*, although he was assured by the inhabitants of Quito that they had shot other birds measuring up to 11 ft *3·4 m*.

At one time the Berlin Tierpark, E Germany owned a magnificent pair of Andean condors which measured 3·15 m *10 ft 4 in* and 2·95 m *9 ft 8 in* across the wings and weighed 10·88 kg *24·0 lb* and 9·2 kg *20·3 lb*, respectively, but further details are lacking.

As stated earlier, the Californian condor is appreciably smaller than its South American relation, and there are few authentic records of adults (both sexes) spanning more than 9 ft *2·7 m*. Of five adults collected by Stephens, four measured 9 ft 4 in *2·84 m* or fractionally more. Wingspreads up to 11 ft *3·4 m* have been claimed for this species, but Koford gives the greatest substantiated measurement as 9 ft 7 in *2·92 m* for a male collected by E B Towne which is now in the Museum of Vertebrate Zoology at the University of California. Three other males preserved in the California Academy of Sciences measure 9 ft 6½ in *2·91 m*, 9 ft 6 in *2·90 m* (this is the bird which allegedly weighed 31 lb *14·1 kg*) and 9 ft 5 in *2·87 m* respectively, and a female in the Museum of Comparative Zoology, Harvard University has a span of 9 ft 6 in *2·90 m*.

The European black vulture and the Himalayan griffon are also of comparable size, and Brown and Amadon say large examples are as big as most California condors. In one series of *A. monachus* the spans ranged from 8 ft 3 in to 8 ft 10 in *2·51–2·69 m*, but a measurement of 9 ft 10 in *3·00 m* has been reported elsewhere for a female (Harting, 1906). There is also an authentic record of a female *G. himalayensis* which taped 10 ft 0½ in *3·06 m*.

Mention should also be made of the vulture-like marabou (*Leptoptilos crumeniferus*) of tropical Africa, which according to Fisher and Peterson (1964) has the largest wingspread (*c* 12 ft *3·7 m*) of any living bird!

Later Dr Roger Tory Peterson (pers. comm.),

doyen of American ornithologists, said: 'James Fisher and I based our report on personal correspondence with Col Meinertzhagen (now deceased) in which he indicated that he had taken a specimen with a wing span of 13 feet 4 inches. This was an unpublished record. When we pressed Meinertzhagen as to the accuracy of this size, he said, "Well, I may have stretched the wings just a bit." James Fisher attempted to confirm Marabou wing spans by measuring specimens from the British Museum. However, as there is considerable variance between a dried skin and that of a freshly taken specimen, we decided to stay on the conservative side of Meinertzhagen's large specimen and gave it as *c* 12 feet'.

Richard Meinertzhagen shot this marabou in Central Africa in the 1930s, and as he was a very reliable observer there is no reason to doubt his statement. In fact, even if he had stretched the wings of this bird to their maximum limit (which he didn't) this probably would not have added much more than 4–5 in *102–127 mm* to the true span. In other words, the actual wingspread was probably nearer 13 ft *4·0 m* than *c* 12 ft *3·6 m*.

Just how freakishly large this individual was can be judged by the fact that Stanley Flower shot what he considered to be a *large* marabou at Kaka, in the Sudan, in March 1900 and found it had a wingspread of 8 ft 4 in *2·54 m*. Two other marabous killed in East Africa measured 8 ft 8 in *2·64 m* and 8 ft 9½ in *2·68 m* respectively, and another specimen shot in Zambia in 1966 reportedly spanned 9 ft 1½ in *2·78 m*. In 1913 a wingspread of 10 ft 9 in *3·28 m* was reliably reported for a closely-related Greater adjutant stork (*L. dubius*) shot on the banks of the Godavari River, Bombay Province, India.

The only other species of birds which have been reliably measured over 10 ft *3·1 m* are the European white pelican (*Pelecanus onocrotalus*), the trumpeter swan (*Cygnus c. buccinator*) and the Dalmatian pelican (*Pelecanus crispus*), with maximum spans of 10 ft 4 in *3·15 m*, 10 ft 2 in *3·10 m* and 10 ft 1½ in *3·09 m* respectively.

The greatest wingspread recorded for an eagle is 9 ft 4 in *2·84 m* for a female wedge-tailed eagle (*Aquila audax fleayi*) killed in Tasmania (Fleay, 1952). In December 1931 another female spanning 9 ft 2 in *2·79 m* and weighing 12 lb 12 oz *5·78 kg* was found drowned in a dam near Molong, NSW after it had unsuccessfully attacked a large male red kangaroo which had taken refuge in the water (Wood, 1972). Less reliable is a claim that a female caught in a dingo trap on the Nullambar Plains, South Australia had a span of 10 ft 3 in *3·12 m*, and that another one shot by a boundary rider near the Werribee Gorge, Victoria in 1914 measured a full 11 ft *3·4 m* from tip to tip (Roche, 1914). In one series of 126 specimens measured by research workers near Adelaide, South

Australia in 1932 the average span was found to be 7 ft 5 in *2·26 m* and the average weight 8 lb *3·63 kg*, although Chisholm (1948) says some individual birds were much larger.

Mr Sam Barnes' enormous Asian golden eagle Atalanta (see page 68) has a wingspread of 9 ft 1 in *2·77 m*, and would probably make 9 ft 4 in *2·84 m* if her wings were stretched out tight after death. Adult females of this race normally have a span of *c* 7 ft 3 in *2·21 m*.

The greatest wingspread claimed for any race of golden eagle is 9 ft 4 in *2·84 m* for a female *Aquila c. chrysaetos* captured alive at Stockfield Park near Wetherby, Yorkshire on 29 November 1804 after being wounded by gunshot (Annual Register, 1805), but this measurement is not considered reliable. Earlier on 4 December 1796 another outsized golden eagle was captured in a fox trap near Wareham, in Dorset. This raptor had a more acceptable span of 8 ft 2 in *2·49 m* and was said to be the largest flying bird ever seen in England. Since then, however, this measurement has been exceeded by another golden eagle collected in Europe which spanned 8 ft 3½ in *2·53 m* and weighed 14 lb 7 oz *6·55 kg* (Brown, 1976).

In one series of seven adult males the spans ranged from 6 ft 2½ in to 6 ft 11½ in *1·89–2·12 m*, and in a series of five females the range was 7 ft 0¾ in–7 ft 5⅓ in *2·15–2·27 m*.

The harpy eagle is forced to hunt below the forest canopy because of its great weight and is compensated with wings that are relatively short and rounded but very broad. No one has yet recorded a series of measurements for this formidable bird, but Stanley Brock's enormous female had a wing expanse of 2 m *6 ft 6 in* (*cf* 2·2 m *7 ft 2½ in* for the Philippine eagle).

Although eagles are extremely powerful birds very few species can carry a load much in excess of their own bodyweight. Usually they kill animals half their own weight or less that can be lifted easily, but some raptors have been known to carry off much heavier prey.

One of the strongest eagles per pound of bodyweight is Pallas's sea eagle (*Haliaeetus leucogaster*). Alan Home (1879–80) writing of this bird says: 'A grey goose will weigh on the average seven pounds (much heavier are recorded), but I have repeatedly seen good-sized grey geese carried off in the claws of one of these eagles, the bird flying slowly and low over the surface of the water, but still quite steadily'.

Another time he watched a bird of the same species capture a fish on the River Jumna north central India, that was so large that it only just succeeded in reaching a low sandbank in the river with its prey. 'As it made for this bank it flew so low and with such difficulty that the writhing fish in its claws struck the water every few yards, and twice

seemed likely to pull its persecutor under water.' On reaching the sandbank some 250 yd *229 m* distant a shot from Hume's rifle caused the eagle to quit the fish, which was then recovered and found to be a carp, which scaled over 13 lb *5·9 kg*. As the weight of an adult *H. leucogaster* ranges from 5 lb 12 oz *2·6 kg* to 7 lb 3 oz *3·26 kg*, this particular individual must have been carrying about twice its own poundage!

Another formidable performer in the lifting stakes is Steller's sea eagle which, apart from large fish, also includes young seals and arctic foxes in its diet. According to Brown and Amadon the food of this bird is taken from the ground or water 'often with very little effort', which suggests that a very large female i.e. 19 lb *8·6 kg* is probably capable of carrying a 20 lb *9·1 kg* kill low over the ground (or sea) for a distance of several hundred yards.

Dan McCowan (cited by Lane, 1955) mentions two hunters in the Canadian Rockies who once saw an American bald eagle (*Haliaeetus leucocephalus*) descend from a considerable height with a 15 lb *6·8 kg* mule deer fawn in its talons, which it dropped when the men shouted at it. There is also a reliable account of another bald eagle carrying a lamb weighing at least 8 lb *3·6 kg* over a distance of 5 miles *8 km* to its eyrie with the aid of upcurrents of air or thermals. Females of this species have been weighed up to 14 lb *6·4 kg*.

Because of its short, broad wings the harpy eagle can lift large prey almost vertically, and there is one report of a female rising more than 60 ft *18·3 m* with a 13 lb *5·9 kg* sloth in her massive claws.

Although many lurid stories of eagles carrying off human babies or young children have appeared in print over the years, most ornithologists tend to look upon such accounts with suspicion because eagles normally kill their prey before bearing it away. At least one case, however, has been fully authenticated.

On 5 June 1932 4-year-old Svanhild Hansen was playing in the yard of her parents' farmhouse in the small village of Leka, a few miles north of Trond-

Mrs Svanhild Hantvigsen (née Hansen) showing the dress she was wearing when the sea eagle snatched her.

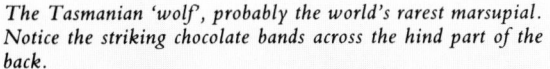

The Alaskan bull moose, the world's largest species of deer.

A demonstration of the amazing elasticity of an ostrich's throat.

The Tasmanian 'wolf', probably the world's rarest marsupial. Notice the striking chocolate bands across the hind part of the back.

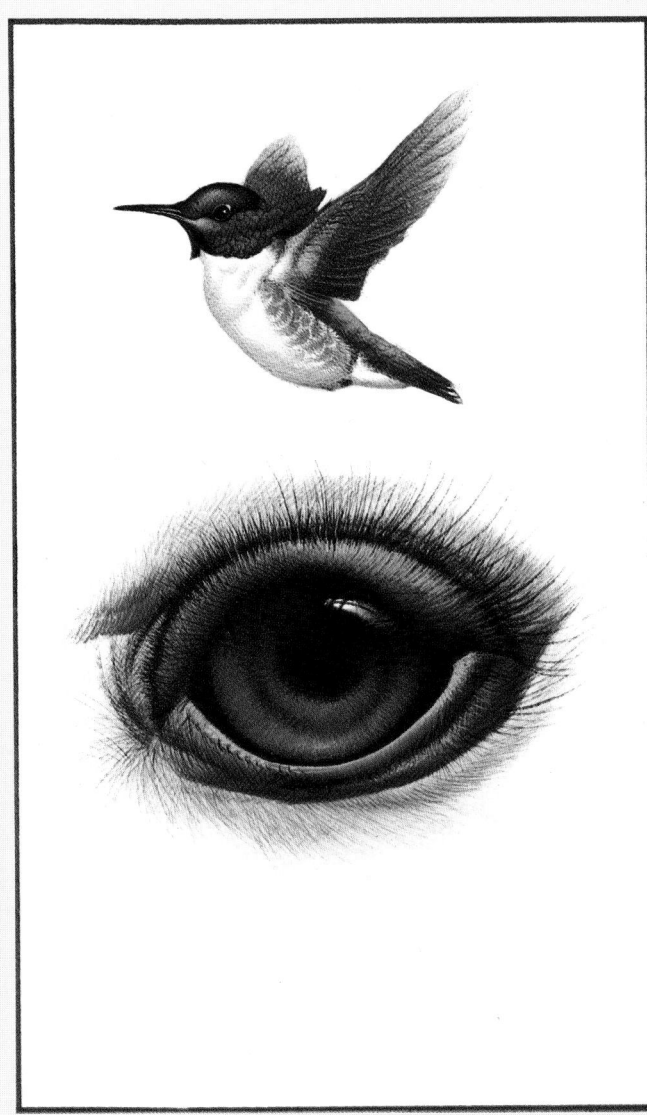

Left – Ray Stone with his record-sized pair of Texan longhorn steer horns. Right – A bee hummingbird drawn to actual scale compared with the eye of an ostrich. The ostrich is 97 000 times more massive.

heim, Norway when a huge white-tailed sea eagle suddenly swooped down and carried her off. The bird headed for its eyrie, which was located 800 ft *244 m* up the side of a mountain more than a mile *1·6 km* away, but in the end the load proved just a bit too much for it and the child was dropped on a narrow ledge about 50 ft *15 m* below the eagle's nest.

The frantic parents immediately organised a search-party from the village and, guided by the eagle which was still soaring over the high ledge, they eventually found little Svanhild asleep and unharmed, except for some scratches and bruises (Storer, 1963).

Apparently the girl was very small for her age and Caras (1964) says the eagle must have hit a powerful upcurrent of air at precisely the right moment to give it the height needed for the incredible flight. Svanhild still has the little dress she wore on that terrifying day, and the holes made by the eagle's talons are clearly visible.

In recent years there have been a number of reports from the USA of huge birds attempting to carry off children – and even fully grown men! Most of the published descriptions, however, fit an outsized vulture or buzzard, neither of which has claws designed for lifting feats.

The smallest living bird is the Bee Hummingbird (*Mellisuga helenae*) of Cuba and the adjacent Isle of Pines. Very little information has been published on this species, but adult males (females are slightly larger) measure 57 mm *2·24 in*, in total length, half of which is taken up by the bill and tail. The weight is 1·6 g *0·056 oz*, which means this bird is much lighter than a Privet hawk-moth (2·4 g *0·085 oz*) and only one-fifth the mass of a common wren.

The vervain hummingbird (*Mellisuga minima*) of Jamaica, Hispaniola, Gonave and Tortue is nearly as diminutive, adult males having a total length of 63 mm *2·5 in*. Three mature specimens netted by A W Diamond (cited by Lack, 1976), weighed 2·1 g *0·074 oz*, 2·1 g *0·074 oz* and 2·2 g *0·0778 oz* respectively.

A weight of 2·2 g *0·078 oz* has also been reported for the little woodstar (*Acestrura bombus*) of Ecuador and Peru, but this hummingbird is fractionally larger than *M. minima*.

Even smaller species have been claimed, but the measurements were based on skins that had shrunk.

The only other hummingbirds (315 species) known to weigh less than 3 g *0·10 oz* when fully grown are the frilled coquette (*Lophornis magnifica*) and the minute hermit (*Phaethornis idaliae*) of Brazil, the scintillant hummingbird (*Selasphorus scintilla*) of Costa Rica and Panama, the white-tailed emerald (*Elvira chionura*) of Costa Rica, the reddish hermit (*Phaethornis ruber*) of the Guianas and Amazon and

Orinoco basins, the amethyst woodstar (*Calliphlox amethystina*) of South America and the little hermit (*Phaethornis longuemareus*) of Central and South America.

These colourful masters of the air are extremely pugnacious creatures, and Greenewalt (1960) says they have even been known to engage hawks and eagles in aerial combat. Their weapon is their long, needle-like bill which they use to attack the eyes of their enemies, and this, coupled with their ability to fly straight up, down, sideways and backwards makes them a very dangerous adversary.

Not surprisingly, hummingbirds have the highest energy output per unit of weight of any living warm-blooded animal.

The smallest bird of prey is probably the sparrow-sized white-fronted falconet (*Microhierax latifrons*) of NW Borneo. Adult birds (both sexes) measure 140–152 mm *5·5–6·0 in* in length and weigh about 35 g *1·24 oz*. As befits its very modest size, this falconet feeds mainly on dragonflies.

The elf owl (*Micrathene whitneyi*) of the deserts of the SW USA and Mexico and the least pygmy-owl (*Glaucidium minutissimum*) of Central and South America are even shorter (*c* 130 mm *5·1 in*), but both birds probably bulk out heavier.

The smallest ratite and probably the smallest flightless bird that has ever existed is the Inaccessible Island rail (*Atlantisia rogersi*) of the Tristan da Cunha group, S Atlantic. This bird, which has degenerate, hair-like plumage, is only the size of a newly-hatched domestic chick (length 125 mm *5 in*). It lives in burrows among the tangled and matted undergrowth.

The smallest sea-bird is the least storm-petrel (*Halocyptena microsoma*), which breeds on many of the small islands in the Gulf of California, NW Mexico. Adult specimens measure about 140 mm *5·5 in* in length and weigh about 25 g *0·88 oz*. The White-vented storm-petrel (*Oceanites gracilis*), which breeds in the Galapagos Islands, E Pacific, is nearly as small, measuring 148 mm *5·8 in* in length.

The British storm-petrel (*Hydrobates pelagicus*) measures 152 mm *6 in* in length (wingspread 355 mm *14 in*) and weighs about 28 g *1 oz*.

The smallest regularly breeding British land bird is the Goldcrest (*Regulus regulus*). Adult specimens measure 90 mm *3·54 in* in length and weigh between 3·8 and 4·5 g *0·134–0·159 oz*. The firecrest (*Regulus ignicapillus*), a passage migrant which has bred in Hampshire in small numbers since 1961 and sometimes winters in SW England, also measures about 90 mm *3·54 in* in length but may be slightly heavier. The Common wren (*Troglodytes troglodytes*), Britain's second smallest regularly breeding land bird, measures only 95 mm *3·74 in* in length, but is twice as heavy as *Regulus*.

The total wild bird population of the world may be in the order of 100 000 million.

The most abundant species of bird living today – and the most destructive – is the Red-billed quelea (*Quelea quelea*) which is distributed throughout the drier parts of Africa south of the Sahara. Although it is impossible to calculate their numbers with any degree of accuracy, Dr Peter Ward (pers. comm.), who has made a long study of this bird, believes that the total population 'must be reckoned in thousands of millions – perhaps as many as 10 000 million'.

Today this 'feathered locust', as it is popularly known, poses a serious threat to the growers of cereal crops in many developing African countries, and its concentrations stretch from Senegal and Mauritania in the west across the continent to Ethiopia and Somalia, then south through Uganda, Kenya, Tanzania and Zambia to South Africa and up into Angola. Breeding colonies and night roosts – which may contain up to 10 million individuals – are attacked with flame-throwers, dynamite bombs and poisonous aerial sprays, but even though the birds are being slaughtered at an estimated rate of 1000 million a year it is not having any obvious permanent impact on the population size. The problem is that, contrary to the habits of most species of birds, this 20 g *0·70 oz* pest can breed three or four times a year – often in areas completely inaccessible to control units – and the eggs, usually three in number, hatch in 11–12 days.

The only other species of wild land bird credited with such prodigious numbers was the now-extinct passenger pigeon (*Ectopistes migratorius*) of North America, which may have been the most numerous species of bird that has ever existed on earth. It has been estimated that there were between 5000 million and 9000 million of these birds before 1840, forming 24–40 per cent of the total bird population of America. Thereafter the pigeons were killed in vast numbers by commercial hunters (pigeon pie was a popular table dish of the day), and the last recorded specimen, a female named 'Martha', died in Cincinnati Zoo, Ohio, USA at 1 pm Eastern Standard Time on 1 September 1914 aged *c* 12 years. She had been collected with several others in Wisconsin in 1902 (Deane, 1908). After death the carcase of this bird was frozen in a block of ice and shipped to Washington, DC, where Shufeldt (1951) made a detailed examination. The mounted specimen is now on exhibition in the US Museum of Natural History, Smithsonian Institution.

The commonest nesting birds found in Britain and Ireland are the blackbird (*Turdus merula*), the house sparrow (*Passer domesticus*), the starling (*Sturnus vulgaris*), the chaffinch (*Fringilla coelebs*), the robin (*Erithacus rubecula*), the blue tit (*Parus caeruleus*) and the dunnock or hedge sparrow (*Prunella modularis*), all of which have a peak breeding population in excess of 5 million pairs.

Between 1964 and 1974 the population of the wren increased tenfold after a series of mild winters, and at the end of this period there were an estimated 10 million pairs (Sharrock, 1976). This bird is severely affected by very cold weather, and during the exceptionally hard winter of 1963 it suffered heavy losses and again by the bad winter of 1978. The population today is probably around 4–5 million pairs.

Unlike land-birds, most species of sea-bird probably number more than 1 million individuals at the end of the breeding season.

The most abundant sea-bird in the world is probably the very small Wilson's storm petrel (*Oceanites oceanicus*) which breeds on the antarctic continent and adjacent sub-antarctic islands. Because it is widely distributed over the Atlantic, Indian and southern Pacific Oceans, this bird is rarely seen in large numbers, but the total population probably runs into hundreds of millions.

The short-tailed shearwater (*Puffinus tenuirostris*), which breeds on the islands in the Bass Strait separating Australia and Tasmania, is also extremely populous.

Matthew Flinders (1798), the English navigator, once saw a single flock of these 'mutton birds' in the Furneaux Group which took 90 minutes to fly past him at a speed almost equal to that of the pigeon.

'On the lowest computation, I think the number could not have been less than a hundred millions. Taking the stream to have been fifty yards deep by three hundred in width, and that it moved at the rate of thirty miles an hour, and allowing nine cubic yards of space to each bird, the number would amount to 151 000 000. The burrows required to lodge this quantity of birds would be 75 750 000 and, allowing a square yard to each burrow, they would cover something more than 18½ geographic square miles of ground.'

Even if this figure was greatly over-estimated, this species can easily sustain an annual loss of up to 500 000 fledgling birds through commercial exploitation for its meat and oil.

Britain's most abundant sea-bird is the common guillemot or murre (*Uria aalge*). According to a 1969–70 survey (Cramp *et al*, 1974) there were an estimated 577 000 pairs nesting along the coastlines, 80 per cent of them in Scotland, but Nelson (1980) believes the margin of error can be as high as 26 per cent in one-off counts like this.

Because of the practical difficulties involved in assessing bird populations in the wild, which vary according to species and habitat and whose numbers are constantly changing, it is virtually impossible to establish the identity of the world's rarest living bird.

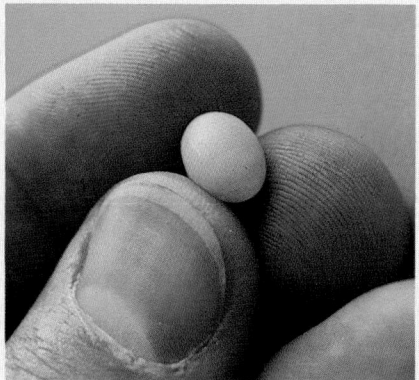

The egg of the bee hummingbird, the world's tiniest bird.

Fledglings being fed by the goldcrest – the smallest regularly breeding bird in Britain.

The Arctic tern – the greatest traveller in the avian world.

The pink pigeon, one of the world's most seriously endangered birds.

The strongest contender, however, must be the ooaa (*Moho braccatus*) of Kauai in the Hawaiian Islands, which was reportedly down to a single pair in 1979. It has been claimed by some writers that this swamp-dwelling honeyeater (rediscovered in 1960) was over-hunted for its magnificent plumes, which were much sought after by Polynesians for the manufacture of spectacular cloaks and as an adornment for helmets, but in view of the difficult terrain and the disagreeable climate found at the altitudes where these birds live, this could not have been the sole reason for their rapid decline. Examples of the ooaa can be found in the Royal Scottish Museum, Edinburgh and the University Museum at Cambridge.

In 1977 the total population of the Chatham Island robin-flycatcher (*Petroica traversi*) was down to seven, all of them confined to Little Mangare Island which covers only 1 acre 0·4 *hectare*. The Gorgeted wood-quail (*Odontophorus strophium*) of Colombia is known only from five specimens, and the Ivory-billed woodpecker (*Campephilus principalis*) of Cuba now numbers less than six pairs. The once abundant Colombian grebe (*Podiceps andinus*) of Lake Tota was down to 300 in 1968, and in 1977 only one (possibly three) were observed. In 1979 only eight Japanese crested ibis (*Nipponia nippon*) survived in a reserve on Sado, a small island off the north-west coast of Honshu, and the population of the echo parakeet (*Psittscula echo*) of Mauritius is now less than ten.

The Mauritius kestrel – the world's rarest bird of prey.

In 1978 the Mauritian government asked Gerald Durell, director of the Jersey Wildlife Preservation Trust, for help when the population of the pink pigeon (*Nesoenas mageri*) reached a critical 30. Eight birds were captured and two breeding colonies set up, one in Jersey Zoo and the other in Mauritius. So far they have produced about 40 young, and these have since been transferred to the wild.

During the 3-year period 1978-80, the population of the *protected* dusky seaside sparrow (*Ammospiza nigrescens*) dropped from 24 to 5, all of them males. (The last female was sighted in 1975.) This species came under threat when its habitat in Titusville Marshes, Florida, USA was flooded to stop mosquito attacks on personnel at the nearby Kennedy Space Centre. Now the last survivors are confined to two large cages in Federal Custody while various ornithological authorities decide whether the birds should be mated with females of similar species so that at least something of the dusky sparrow will continue to exist.

The kakapo (*Stringops habroptilus*) of New Zealand is in a similar position. In 1980 only 15 known examples still survived – all males.

The world's rarest bird of prey is probably the Mauritius kestrel (*Falco punctatus*), which is now confined to the Black River gorges in the south-west part of the island. Sixty years ago this raptor was quite common, but when monkeys were introduced to the Indian Ocean island they started destroying the forest habitat, and by 1975 the kestrel population was down to six. Fortunately that year the surviving birds built their nests on a cliff face where the monkeys couldn't reach them, and by December 1978 their numbers had increased to 23, including a breeding colony of eight which had been taken from the wild. Since then, however, all the captive birds have died from genetic deterioration as a result of interbreeding.

In October 1978 the German zoologists Drs B and C Meyburg announced that the Madagascar serpent eagle (*Eutriorchis astur*), which is known only from a few individuals and has not been collected since 1930, still survived in the Marojejy Strict nature reserve and probably in the primeval forests of the Masaola Peninsula. They also revealed that the population of the Madagascar fish eagle (*Haliaeetus vociferoides*) was down to *c* 10 pairs. Neither species is protected.

The rarest sea-bird in the world is the magenta petrel (*Pterodroma magentae*), also called the Chatham Island taiko, which, up until very recently, was known only from the type specimen collected in 1867 about 500 miles *800 km* east of the island (Giglioli and Salvadori, 1868). In 1978 however a New Zealand ornithological expedition exploring Chatham Island positively identified and photographed three of these birds.

The Bermuda petrel (*Pterodroma cahow*), rediscovered in 1951 when six nests were found in the islands of Castle Roads, is also seriously threatened as a result of DDT poisoning and depredation by rats. In 1977 there were less than 30 pairs left. This bird has never been identified at sea.

The status of the Reunion petrel (*Pterodroma aterrima*) of the western Indian Ocean remains uncertain. This species is known only from six specimens, the last two of which were collected in 1953 (Alexander, 1954), but since then very little effort has been made to find others.

Of the larger sea-birds, the most seriously endangered species is the short-tailed albatross (*Diomedea albatrus*), which breeds only on Torishima, Seven Islands of Isu, N Pacific. According to a recent survey the total population is only 57 pairs (Tuck and Heinzel, 1978).

Not surprisingly, 91 per cent of the bird species that have become extinct since 1680 lived on islands.

According to the British Ornithologists' Union more than 40 species of birds have been recorded only once in the British Isles – most of them since the end of the Second World War. That which has not recurred for the longest is the black-capped petrel (*Pterodroma hasitata*) of the West Indies. A specimen was caught alive on a heath at Southacre, near Swaffham, Norfolk in March or April 1850. This species is now confined to the highlands of Haiti, so it is extremely doubtful whether it will ever be seen again in Britain. A red-necked nightjar (*Caprimulgus ruficollis*) was shot at Killingworth, Northumberland on 5 October 1856. This bird breeds in Iberia and NW Africa. Other species recorded only once include the brown thrasher (*Toxostoma rufum*), the black-and-white warbler (*Mniotilta varia*), the yellow warbler (*Dendroica petechia*), the fox sparrow (*Zonotrichia iliaca*) and the rufous-sided towhee (*Pipilo erythrophthalmus*), all from North America (Sharrock, 1974).

In October 1975 a Siberian rubythroat (*Luscinia calliope*) was trapped on Fair Isle, Shetland, and in September 1976 a Pallas's reed bunting (*Emberiza pallasi*) was seen on the same island. The following year a Cape May warbler (*Dendroica tigrina*) was spotted at Paisley, Strathclyde and a Ruppell's warbler (*Sylvia rueppelli*) at Dunrossness, Shetland. In August 1978 an Eleonora's falcon (*Falco eleanorae*) from the south Mediterranean region was recorded at Formby, Merseyside, and four months later a greater sand plover (*Charadrius leschenaultii*) from southern Russia took up temporary abode in Pagham harbour, West Sussex (Rogers *et al*, 1978 and 1979).

On 17 October 1979 an adult American bald eagle was spotted at Llyn Coran, Anglesey, N Wales, but the origin of this bird remains a mystery. 'Genuine

The snowy owl, Britain's most tenuously established bird.

vagrancy is considered unlikely, but the escape likelihood is also slight' comment the Rarities Committee.

Even more incredible, on 28–29 May 1979 an Aleutian tern (*Sterna aleutica*) was sighted on the Farne Islands, Northumberland (Rogers *et al*, 1980). This bird breeds on the coasts of Alaska and eastern Siberia, and up until then had never been recorded outside the N Pacific but Chris Mead (pers. comm.) of the British Trust for Ornithology believes this species also embarks on quite long distance movements – possibly down to the southern Pacific. 'If this is the case, then the bird which turned up in Northumberland could quite easily have been blown round the Antarctic and simply missed the Pacific Ocean on the way back.'

Britain's rarest bird is a black-browed albatross (*Diomedea melanophris*) which joined a colony of gannets on Hermaness, Shetland in 1974 and has spent every summer with them since.

Albatrosses are normally confined to the southern hemisphere and rarely cross into the North Atlantic because they are essentially gliders and depend on air currents for sustained flight. In the doldrums, that region of calms and light winds near the equator, they would have problems remaining airborne, which is why this belt acts as a kind of invisible barrier. Sometimes, however, odd birds are carried over on freak winds and when this happens they become permanently 'lost' in the higher altitudes with no hope of ever getting back to their familiar haunts.

The most tenuously established British bird is now the snowy owl (*Nyctea scandiaca*), with one pair breeding regularly on Fetlar, Shetland from 1967 until 1975 and rearing a total of 21 young. Soon afterwards, however, the old male took off for an unknown destination, having driven off all the young males, and left the females without a mate.

On 19–22 April 1979 an adult male was seen on Fair Isle some 80 miles *129 km* further south, but it did not find its way to Fetlar where a small number of females were waiting hopefully. At one time this bird of the polar regions was a regular winter visitor to the Shetlands, Orkneys and the Hebrides, and it has also been recorded on the Scottish mainland and as a rare vagrant in England.

Britain's rarest regularly breeding bird is now Montagu's harrier (*Circus pygargus*) of Southern England, which is now down to 2–4 pairs.

The white-tailed eagle (*Haliaeetus albicilla*) became extinct as a breeding species in Scotland in 1916 when an *English vicar* took the eggs from the last nesting site on the Isle of Skye. In 1968 four Norwegian eaglets were released on Fair Isle, Shetland but the three that survived left the island over the next 14 months. In 1975 the Nature Conservancy Council made another attempt to re-introduce the bird on the island of Rhum in the Inner Hebrides, and during the next two years 13 eaglets were set free. Two of the females were later found dead, but some of the others still live in the area. In October 1978 eight more specimens obtained from Norway were also released (Love *et al*, 1978) and there are now around 40 sea eagles in this National Trust reserve.

The position of the Osprey (*Pandion haliaetus*), formerly Britain's rarest breeding bird, is now much improved. In 1980 about 20 pairs were nesting in Scotland at secret locations, and the previous year a total of 30 young were successfully reared.

According to the Rare Birds Breeding Panel, a Kentish plover (*Charadrius alexandrinus*) hatched out two chicks at a secret location in the Lincolnshire/Humberside area in 1980. It was the first time this rare spring passage migrant had successfully bred in Britain since the mid-1950s.

Britain's rarest breeding sea-bird is the roseate tern (*Sterna dougalli*), which winters off the coast of West Africa. In 1977 only 630 pairs were counted in six main colonies (Thomas, 1978).

There are at least 500 active egg collectors in Britain who will stop at nothing to get their hands on prized specimens.

Although birds are generally longer-lived than mammals of comparable size and activity, very few species reach or exceed 40 years in the captive or wild state and reports that they sometimes live for 100 years or more should be treated with extreme caution. A classic example was the Egyptian vulture (*Neophron percnopterus*) which died in the menagerie at Schonbrunn, Vienna, Austria in 1824 allegedly aged 118 years. Flower (1925) discovered the menagerie was not founded until 1752, 'so even if it were proved that it was one of the original inmates of that famous collection, there is still a previous 36

years to be accounted for'. Other dubious records in the same category include a sulphur-crested cockatoo (*Cacatua galerita*) of 140 years, a grey parrot (*Psittacus erithacus*) of 120 years, a griffon vulture (*Gyps fulvus*) of 117 years, a golden eagle (*Aquila chrysaetos*) of 104 years and a mute swan (*Cygnus olor*) of 102 years.

In July 1840 the death was reported of a mute swan named 'Old Jack' in St James's Park, London reputedly aged 70 years. He was said to have been hatched 'on the piece of water attached to Buckingham Palace' in 1770 (*Morning Post*, 16 July 1840).

A sulphur-crested cockatoo called 'Cocky Bennett', owned by Mrs Sarah Bennett, licensee of the Sea Breeze Hotel at Tom Ugly's Point, near Sydney, NSW, Australia was said to be over 120 years old when he died in 1916, but Kinghorn (1930) could not find any authentic information regarding the true age of this bird. The cockatoo was in the possession of Mrs Bennett for 26 years, and had previously been owned by Captain George Ellis, skipper of a South Seas sailing-ship, who claimed the bird was alive when he was only a nine-year-old apprentice. During the last 25 years of his life Cocky Bennett was practically featherless, and he was often heard to scream: 'One more ******** feather and I'll fly!'

The greatest authentic age recorded for a captive bird is 72+ years for a male Andean condor called 'Kuzya' who died in Moscow Zoo, USSR in 1964. This bird was already full-grown when he arrived at the zoo in 1892 and lived out of doors all the year round (Igor Sosnovski, pers. comm.).

In April 1973 the death was reported of another ancient Andean condor in the Menagerie du Jardin des Plantes, Paris, France aged 71+ years. It was received at the menagerie in 1902 (Dr Guy Chauvier, pers. comm.).

It is interesting to note that Comfort (1964) thinks the 68 years quoted by Flower (1925) for his longest-lived bird – a female Great eagle-owl (*Bubo bubo*) which was still alive in 1899 – is 'probably too low', and that the less fully authenticated records given by Gurney (1899) of birds living beyond 70 years are 'probably substantially correct'. These include a 73-year-old sulphur-crested cockatoo (1818–91) and a 72-year-old grey parrot (1797–1869).

On 5 January 1975 the death was reported of 'Jimmy', a red and green Amazon parrot (*Amazona* sp.) aged 104 years in Liverpool. The bird was allegedly hatched on 3 December 1870 and spent his entire life in his original brass cage.

The ostrich is another potentially long-lived bird under domestic conditions, but it is very accident prone and seldom dies of natural causes. According to one ostrich farmer with over 60 years' experience 90 per cent of ostriches die after breaking their legs.

Barring such accidents and bearing in mind that ostriches are rarely kept longer than 15 years for feather production because the quality and quantity of plumage decreases as the birds get older, there is nothing to prevent an ostrich from living 50 years or more. In 1972 a cock bird aged 62 years 7 months was killed in the unique ostrich abattoir at Oudtshoorn (Alex Hooper, pers. comm.). Another ostrich reportedly lived for 68 years (Clay, 1962).

An emu (*Dromaius novaehollandiae*) named 'Charlie', owned by Kay and Jim Whittle of Awakeri, North Island, New Zealand celebrated his 42nd birthday in July 1980. He was reared on their farm from a youngster.

On 22 March 1967 the death was reported of a Siberian white crane (*Grus leucogeranus*) called 'Pops' at the National Zoo, Washington, DC aged 62+ years. Three days earlier the bird had sustained a compound fracture of the left leg which was set and a cast applied, but the combination of shock and old age proved too much for the creature. Pops was received as a young adult on 26 June 1906 and spent a total of 61 years 8 months and 25 days in captivity (Hamlet, 1968).

In September 1980 a sulphur-crested cockatoo named 'Cocky', star of London Zoo's parrot house for 55 years, was presented with a medal by Piccadilly's Burlington Arcade Association for helping to make the capital a friendlier place. He is famous for his 'hello, hello, hello' greeting.

The domestic goose (*Anser anser domesticus*) normally lives about 25 years, but older examples have been reported. On 16 December 1976 a gander named 'George', owned by Mrs Florence Hull of Thornton, Lancashire died aged 49 years 8 months. He was hatched out in April 1927.

The greatest authentic age recorded for a sea-bird in captivity is 44 years for a herring gull (*Larus argentatus*) which lived in the Menagerie du Jardin des Plantes from 1830 to 1874 (Gurney, 1899).

Another specimen called 'Tommy', owned by Miss Olive Watson of Macduff, Banffshire, Scotland was still alive in November 1981 aged nearly 40 years. He was found in a street in 1943 with a damaged wing and has been a member of the family ever since.

Until fairly recently it was generally believed that sea-birds in aviaries lived longer on the average than those living under natural conditions because they had a regular food supply and were protected from enemies, but since the introduction of bird-banding it has been discovered that wild sea-birds live practically as long as captive ones, although fewer of them achieve real old age.

The greatest authentic age recorded for a wild sea-bird is 53 years for a Laysan albatross (*Diomedea immutabilis*) which was still alive in c 1978 (Nelson, 1980). A pair of royal albatrosses known as 'Blue White' (female) and 'Green White Green' (male)

Miss Olive Watson with her elderly pet herring gull 'Tommy'.

were 52 years and 39 years old respectively in 1980 when they nested at Taiaroa Head, Otago, New Zealand. A black-browed albatross which joined the gannet colony on Mykines in the Faroes in 1860 and was shot in 1894 was believed to have been about 40 years old at the time of its death. Westerkov (1936) believes the maximum age reached by albatrosses (*Diomedeidae*) may be as much as 80 years.

A northern fulmar (*Fulmarus glacialis*) aged 41+ years has also been reported, but further details are lacking.

Among the longevity records given by the late Prof W Rydzewski (The Ring 96-97 1978) are a brown pelican (*Pelecanus occidentalis*) of 31 years 1 month 26 days (20 September 1933 to 15 November 1964 Washington, USA), a herring gull (*Larus argentatus*) of 31 years 11 months 10 days (25 July 1929 to 5 June 1961 Gothenburg, Sweden), a sooty tern (*Sterna hirundo*) of 32 years 0 months ? days (June

1940 to 7 June 1972 Washington, USA), a black-headed gull (*Larus ridibundus*) of 32 years 1 month 0 days (14 May 1922 to 14 June 1954 Heligoland, Germany), a common guillemot (*Uria aalge*) of 32 years 1 month 3 days (2 July 1938 to 5 August 1970 Heligoland, Germany) and an Arctic tern (*Sterna paradisaea*) of 33 years 10 months 26 days (24 July 1936 to 19 June 1970 Washington, USA).

In 1979 a pair of oyster-catchers (*Haematopus ostralegus*) returned to the same house and family in Helgeland, Norway for the 21st year in succession. The male is so tame it can be fed on the kitchen floor. The birds are absent eight months of the year (Ola Veigaard, pers. comm.).

It has been calculated that some 60–75 per cent of all birds die between the ages of three and six months through disease, predation, starvation, bad weather and accidents. One of the shortest-lived species is the robin, which has a life expectancy of only 5–6 months in the wild, although one ringed bird managed to survive for 12 years 10 months 12 days.

A great deal of nonsense has been written about the maximum flying speeds attained by birds, the tendency being to exaggerate rather than under-estimate the velocity. It is extremely difficult to time a bird accurately over a measured distance, even using elaborate tracking and recording devices, because too many other factors are involved such as wind velocity, gravity, angle of flight, and other methods used to determine speed like a car running on a parallel course or an aircraft are not really reliable because the angles of ascent or descent are not measured. The question is also complicated by the fact that most published estimates of bird velocities are for ground speed – which is very different from air speed.

The air speed of a bird is defined as the velocity with which it flies in relation to the air, and ground speed as the velocity with which it flies in relation to the ground. Thus, a bird flying at 40 miles/h *64 km/h* with a tail wind of 30 miles/h *48 km/h* has an air speed of 40 miles/h *64 km/h*, but the ground speed is 70 miles/h *113 km/h*.

According to Meinertzhagen (1955) birds have two speeds – 'a normal rate which is used for every-day purposes and also in migration and an acceler-ation speed, which in some cases nearly doubles the rate of their normal speed'. This latter velocity, however, cannot be maintained for any length of time.

Probably 50 per cent of the world's flying birds cannot exceed an air speed of 40 miles/h *64 km/h* in level flight, and Fisher and Peterson (1964) believe only a very small number of the rest – most of them ducks or geese – can reach or exceed 60 miles/h *97 km/h*.

The two main features associated with very rapid flight are long, narrow wings swept back to mini-mise turbulence and a torpedo-shaped body, and the pinnacle of design is found in the white-throated spinetail swift (*Hirundapus caudacutus*) of Asia. This beautifully streamlined bird feeds on insects while travelling at 70 miles/h *113 km/h*, and in the USSR air speeds up to 170 km/h *105·6 miles/h* have been re-liably measured for this supreme flier in courtship display flights (Dement'ev and Gladkov, 1966). The Alpine swift (*Apus melba*) is also exceptionally fast, but although Swiss experts have credited this species with accelerations up to 150 miles/h *241 km/h* during wild dashes, this figure must refer to ground speed.

Heinrich Gaetke (1895) who spent 50 years in Heligoland, Germany studying bird migratory movements, was firmly convinced that much greater velocities were attained by birds flying at high alti-tudes than at low ones because of the more rarified air, but his statement that birds like the Eurasian golden plover (*Pluvialis aprocaria*), the Eurasian cur-lew (*Numenius arquata*) and the black-tailed godwit (*Limosa limosa*) reach speeds up to 240 miles/h *386 km/h* at heights of 40 000 ft *12 192 m* must be discounted because no birds can reach this altitude (see page 87).

The much-debated question of the maximum speed attained by the peregrine falcon (*Falco peregrinus*) in a controlled stoop has still not been satisfactorily resolved despite the development of modern elec-tronics. British falconer Philip Glasier once fitted miniature air speedometers to trained peregrines and found the maximum diving speed was only 82 miles/h *132 km/h*, but this aerial killer – the tiercel is the better flyer – can reach much greater velocities when stoop-ing from great heights during territorial displays. In experiments carried out in the USSR peregrines were timed at 270 km/h *168 miles/h* at a 25-degree angle of stoop and 360 km/h *224 miles/h* at steeper angles. During the period 1963–67 Hantge (1968) watched 191 peregrine hunts from beginning to end over a 1–2 km *0·62–1·24 mile* course in Germany. The highest speed recorded at a 30-degree angle of stoop was 270 km/h *168 miles/h*, and at 45 degrees the maximum velocity was 350 km/h *217 miles/h*, but he said the birds could not exceed 100 km/h *62·1 miles/h* in level flight. More recently Orton (1975), using precise mathematical formulae, has calculated that a peregrine weighing 2 lb 10 oz *1·19 kg* would reach a maximum velocity of 239 miles/h *385 km/h* in a 5000 ft *1524 m* free-fall, and a maximum dive-speed of 250 miles/h *402 km/h* if it went into the stoop with an initial velocity greater than that of the actual fall-speed from a standstill. How the peregrine – the fastest-moving living creature – manages to pull out of such incredible dives without tearing itself apart or at least blacking out has yet to be explained.

The fastest-flying sea-bird is the magnificent frigatebird (*Fregata magnificens*), also known as the 'Man-o-War' bird. One individual was timed at 95·7 miles/h *154 km/h* in still air, but ground speeds in excess of 200 miles/h *320 km/h* have been claimed for this species, which has the greatest wing area in proportion to weight (1·5 kg *3 lb 5 oz*) of any living bird. One observer reports seeing one of these superb flying machines (wingspread 8 ft *2·4 m*) pursue, overtake and seize a flying fish in the air while half a gale was blowing.

In the South Seas frigatebirds are trained by natives to carry messages to neighbouring islands like carrier pigeons, and these express postmen always return to the special posts erected for them on the beaches.

Despite their diminutive size hummingbirds (*Trochilidae*) have also been credited with amazing bursts of speed. In 1945 Wagner timed the courtship flight of a green violetear (*Colibri thalassinus*) between two trees and found the average velocity to be 55 miles/h *89 km/h*. He believed that two birds chasing each other in courtship flight reached speeds up to 90 miles/h *145 km/h*! Greenewalt (1960), on the other hand, using a wind tunnel equipped with a feeding-bottle, discovered that a ruby-throated hummingbird (*Archilochus colubris*) could only manage 29 miles/h *46·7 km/h*, although Scheithauer (1967) doubts whether this figure represented its maximum speed – 'there are far stronger driving factors than the stimulus of reaching a food site, for example, aggressive pursuit and the mad manoeuvres of the courtship flight'. The same authority timed the daily chases of two long-tailed sylphs (*Aglaiocercus kingi*) over a figure-of-eight course 67·3 m *73·6 yd* long during the courtship period and found that the average speed was 61 km/h *37·9 miles/h* and the maximum 75·5 km/h *46·9 miles/h*. He felt that on a straight course the birds might have attained a flight velocity of 88 km/h *55 miles/h*.

The winner of the 186 miles *299 km* Ulster race for pigeons in 1961 averaged 97·5 miles/h *157 km/h*, but this was wind-assisted and the average air speed was about 45 miles/h *72 km/h*. In level flight in windless conditions it is very doubtful whether any pigeon can exceed 60 miles/h *97 km/h*, although Schorger (1955) reckons the passenger pigeon had a potential top speed of 70 miles/h *113 km/h* when hard-pressed.

The fastest standard game bird is the Red-breasted merganser (*Mergus serrator*). On 29 May 1960 a flock of six birds was flushed from the river ahead of an aircraft on a low aerial reconnaissance flight for the USA Atomic Energy Commission along the Kukpuk River, Cape Thompson, northern Alaska. When the ducks took flight all the birds turned aside, except one male which flew slightly below and ahead of the plane. This loner, with a burst of speed, managed to keep his position in relation to the aircraft for about 1500 ft *457 m* before finally losing ground and turning aside. The air speed of the aircraft during the chase was 80 miles/h *129 km/h* (Thompson, 1961).

The spur-winged goose (*Plectropterus gambiensis*) has been timed at 60 miles/h *97 km/h* in level flight and 88 miles/h *142 km/h* in an escape dive.

Some birds can fly into a wind with a greater velocity than their own maximum speed and *still move forward*, although the reasons for this are not known. Meinertzhagen once saw a small group of common eider (*Somateria mollissima*) perform this remarkable feat in South Uist, Outer Hebrides during a 90–95 mile/h *145–153 km/h* gale. 'This particular wind was so strong', he writes, 'that shooting was out of the question, wild swans were grounded and unable to rise and we experienced the greatest difficulty in walking against it. Eider duck had come inland from the sea and were sitting about on the short grass. When disturbed they would rise into the wind and make headway against it at ground level, doing about 15–20 mph except for one bird who actually achieved a minus ground speed and slowly backed towards us.'

There is also a record of a flock of wood pigeons (*Columba palumbus*) moving forward at 40 miles/h *64 km/h* in the face of a 110 mile/h *177 km/h* gale when they should have been moving backwards! (McNabb, 1953).

The slowest powered flight without sinking to be actually measured is that of the American woodcock (*Scolopax minor*), with a speed of 5 miles/h *8 km/h*.

Only a small number of birds weighing less than 20 g *0·705 oz* are capable of true stationary hovering in still air. These include the hummingbirds (*Trochilidae*), the sunbirds (*Nectariniidae*) and the ringlets (*Regulus*). Some raptors like the common kestrel (*Falco tinnunculus*), the common buzzard (*Buteo buteo*) and the osprey (*Pandion haliaetus*) can remain airborne for short periods of time without forward movement, but unlike their much smaller relations such feats would be impossible without the aid of head winds and up-currents of air.

The undisputed master of hovering is undoubtedly the hummingbird, and its manoeuvring skill is quite extraordinary. A German ornithologist once picked up a caged hummingbird at the airport and placed it on the seat beside him for the one-and-a-half-hour drive back to his home. 'During the entire trip the bird hung, wings whirling, in the absolute centre of the cage even when he rounded corners or hit a bump' said George (1970). 'As it hung there, it turned its head from time to time to look at the man, never losing its dead centre position, and it never sat down to rest.'

Another hummingbird kept under observation at a zoo hovered continuously for four hours, during which time it must have beat its wings more than a million times.

The fastest-running bird is the ostrich, which can travel at 28–30 miles/h *45–48 km/h* for 15–20 minutes without showing undue signs of fatigue. The maximum velocity reached by a *frightened* ostrich has not yet been accurately determined, but Guggisberg (1964) claims he once timed a cock ostrich at 45 miles/h *72 km/h* over 800 yd *732 m*.

The emu of Australia, which ranks second in size to the ostrich among living birds (i.e. up to 5½ ft *1·68 m* and 120 lb *54 kg*) is nearly as fast, and has been credited with speeds up to 40 miles/h *64 km/h* over short distances.

The fastest-running flying bird is the roadrunner (*Geococcyx californianus*) of the SW USA, which has been clocked at 26 miles/h *42 km/h* over a short distance when hard-pressed by a car. On another occasion a horseman came upon one of these birds standing about 100 yd *91 m* ahead of him on a level road and decided to give chase. The roadrunner took up the challenge, and with straightened neck and slightly extended wings acting as stabilisers, tore furiously along the road for 440 yd *402 m* before seeking refuge in a thicket. Even then, the rider was still at least 50 yd *46 m* behind. This bird rarely flies, and when it does take to the air it is an awkward performer (Cottam *et al*, 1942).

The fastest-swimming bird is probably the gentoo penguin (*Pygoscelis papua*), which breeds on the subantarctic islands. In January 1913 Dr Robert Cushman Murphy was able to time a few of these birds under water in a transparent pool at the summit of a coastal hill south of the Bay of Isles, South Georgia. 'They dashed straight away under water the length of the pond and back again, with a velocity which I then had an opportunity to compute as about ten metres a second. They chased each other round and round, flashing into the air twice or thrice during their burst of speed, every action plainly revealed through the clear, quiet water.'

As ten metres a second (=36·0 km/h *22·3 miles/h*) is a respectable flying speed for some birds and a rate attained by very few dolphins, Kooyman (1975), not unreasonably, has questioned the accuracy of measurements like this, and it is certainly true that the general small size of penguins does tend to give an illusion of exceptional speed as they porpoise through the water. Stonehouse (1967) also believes the burst speeds of penguins have been over-estimated and he credits them with a maximum velocity of 13–17 miles/h *20·9–27·4 km/h* depending on the species. Two emperor penguins trained to swim between ice-holes 27 m *89 ft* apart recorded an average speed of only 7·5 km/h *4·7 miles/h* and a maximum of

9·6 km/h *6 miles/h* (Kooyman *et al*, 1971).

The fastest wing-beat rates are to be found among the hummingbirds, with the top prize going to the horned sungem (*Heliactin cornuta*) of tropical South America. One specimen measured with a stroboscope recorded a frequency of 90 beats a second, while the amethyst woodstar (*Calliphlox amethystina*) and the white-bellied woodstar (*Acestrura mulsant*) were not far behind with 80 and 79 beats respectively (Stolpe and Zimmer, 1939; Scheithauer, 1967). No measurements have been published for the bee hummingbird – the frequency *normally* increases in proportion to the decrease in wing length – but a 2 g *0·07 oz* reddish hermit (*Phaethornis ruber*) had a much less rapid rate of 50·5 beats a second (Stresemann and Zimmer, 1932).

In 1951 Edgerton *et al* reported up to 200 beats per second for the ruby-throated hummingbird (*Archilochus colubris*) and the rufous hummingbird (*Selasphorus rufus*) of eastern and western N America during courtship flights, but these frequencies were for the narrow tips of the primaries only and not the complete wing.

By way of comparison, large vultures sometimes exhibit a flapping rate as low as one beat per second and a condor can easily cruise 60 miles *97 km* in two hours without flapping at all!

The most aerial of all birds is the sooty tern (*Sterna fuscata*) of the warmer parts of the Atlantic, Indian and Pacific Oceans. After leaving the nesting-grounds the young birds do not come to land or alight on water until they return to their breeding-grounds on tropical and sub-tropical islands for the first time at the age of 3–4 years.

The common swift (*Apus apus*) also spends most of its life in the air and, after leaving the nest, remains aloft for 2–3 years until it is mature enough to breed. During this time it feeds, drinks, bathes and even sleeps on the wing, resting comfortably at night on the air currents found at high altitudes. Not surprisingly, swifts have very weak and tiny feet, which means they would have problems getting airborne again if they accidentally landed on flat ground.

Some 20 per cent of the world's birds migrate. **The greatest distance so far recorded for a ringed bird** is 14 000 miles *22 530 km* for an Arctic tern which was banded as a nestling on 5 July 1955 in the Kandalaksha Sanctuary on the White Sea coast about 125 miles *200 km* from Murmansk, European USSR, and was captured alive by a fisherman 8 miles *13 km* south of Fremantle, Western Australia on 16 May 1956. The bird had flown south via the Atlantic Ocean and then circled Africa before crossing the Indian Ocean. It did not survive to make the return trip. Another specimen banded at Valley, Anglesey, N Wales on 28 June 1966 was recovered near Bega, NSW, Australia on 31 December 1966 after a calculated flight of 11 285 miles *18 160 km* at 124°, and this may be a better record on a point-to-point basis (Chris Mead, pers. comm.).

This species also holds the record for the greatest distance covered in a year between breeding seasons – 25 000 miles *40 200 km*. It has been known to nest within 450 miles *720 km* of the North Pole and flies every year to the South Pole and back again.

Between breeding seasons the short-tailed shearwater (*Puffinus tenuirostris*) flies a figure-of-eight course from South Australia to the N Pacific and back again, a distance of 21 000 miles *33 800 km*, while the Sooty albatross (*Phoenetria fisca*) travels 19 000 miles *30 600 km* in some 80 days while flying round the world at 40° south latitude.

A Manx shearwater (*Puffinus puffinus*) ringed in Wales in June 1966 was recovered in NSW, Australia in December after flying 12 000 miles *19 300 km*.

The longest journeys made by a land-bird are probably those of the American golden plover (*Pluvialis d. dominica*) on their loop migration between northern Canada and Argentina. In just over 6 months they cover 15 000–17 000 miles *24 100–27 400 km*.

It has been calculated that the common swift which seldom perches from early morning to late at night and migrates to and from southern Africa annually, flies 15 000 miles *24 100 km* in a single year. This means the oldest specimen on record (21 years) must have travelled about 3 150 000 miles *5 070 000 km* before it called it a day!

Most hummingbirds do not migrate very far, but there are exceptions. One of the most remarkable avian flights is that made by the ruby-throated hummingbird, which every autumn travels up to 2000 miles *3200 km* across the eastern USA to its wintering grounds in Central America. For most of these birds this also includes a 500 mile *800 km* nonstop flight across the Gulf of Mexico, and it still remains something of a mystery as to how these 3 g *0·11 g* birds manage such an arduous journey on their limited food reserves.

Accurate records of migration speeds are difficult to obtain, but one of the fastest travellers must be the American golden plover (*Pluvialis d. fulva*), which flies nonstop from the Aleutians to Hawaii, a distance of 2050 miles *3300 km*, in only 35 hours. Stresemann (1934) has calculated that this journey requires 252 000 wing-beats! Ducks and geese are also very rapid flyers on migration. One flock of snow geese (*Anser caerulescens*) flew nonstop from James Bay, Canada to Louisiana, USA, a distance of nearly 1700 miles *2740 km*, in 60 hours (Cooch, 1955), and half a million ducks flying continuously from Saskatchewan,

Canada to the same American state did the 1500 mile *2400 km* trip in 36 hours (Bellrose and Sieh, 1960).

At the slower end of the table, the black-and-white warbler (*Mniotilta varia*) migrates across the northern USA at a steady 20 miles *32 km* a day.

The shortest bird migrations are made by species like the mountain quail (*Oreortyx pictus*), the black-capped chickadee (*Parus atricapillus*) and Clark's nutcracker (*Nucifraga columbiana*) of North America, which merely descend from exposed mountain ridges to the sheltered valleys below during the autumn months. The mountain quail, which nests at altitudes up to 9500 ft *2896 m* in the central California mountains, leaves the region of deep snow in September and, in groups of 10–30, *walk* in single file down below the 5000 ft *1524 m* mark. In the spring they make the return trek, again on foot, to the higher altitudes (Tyne and Berger, 1971).

At one time it was believed that most birds flew at heights of 20 000 ft *6096 m* or more during migration because of the physical advantages of low pressure at high altitudes (see Gaetke, 1895), but this is now known to be untrue. Most migrating birds, in fact, fly at relatively low altitudes (i.e. below 300 ft *91 m*); only a few dozen species fly higher than 3000 ft *914 m*.

Until fairly recently the greatest acceptable height recorded for a bird was 26 902 ft *8200 m* for a small number of Alpine choughs (*Pyrrhocorax graculus*) which followed the British Everest Expedition of May 1924 to Camp V (Hingston, 1936), but on 9 December 1967 a herd of about 30 whooper swans (*Cygnus cygnus*) flying in from Iceland to winter at Lough Foyle, Co Londonderry, Northern Ireland were spotted by the pilot of a civilian transport aircraft over the Outer Hebrides at a height of just over 27 000 ft *8230 m*. The altitude had earlier been confirmed by a radar controller at a Civic Air Traffic Control Radar Unit in Northern Ireland, who reported an echo moving southwards at a ground speed of about 75 knots (86 miles/h *139 km/h*) (Stewart, 1978). Unlike the alpine choughs, however, whose initial take-off point may have been only a few thousand feet lower, these particular swans must have taken off from a coastal lagoon at sea level and then climbed rapidly on a ridge of high pressure to 27 000 ft *8230 m* for a ride on the 'jet stream' in the lower stratosphere. According to Elkins (1979), who later investigated the meteorological conditions pertaining at the time, the temperature at that altitude was −48°C *−54·4°F*. He added: 'It seems incredible that sustained flight can occur under such physiologically rigorous environmental conditions. The atmospheric pressure at 8000 m is only one-third of that at the earth's surface, and both air density and oxygen concentration are only 40 per cent. The latter figure is an indication of the efficiency of the avian respiratory system compared with that of man, who normally requires an additional oxygen supply about 4000–5000 m (*13 000–16 500 feet*)'.

The celebrated record of a skein of 17 Egyptian geese (*Alopochen aegyptiaca*) photographed by an astronomer at Dehra Dun, N India on 17 September 1919 flying across the sun at an estimated height of 29 000 ft *8839 m* has long been discounted by experts because the picture is not clearly defined. But now that it has been established, however, that swans, which belong to the same family (Anatidae), can fly nearly as high, this may well have been accurate.

On 23 May 1960 the Indian Everest Expedition found three species of raptor lying dead on the South Col at a height of nearly 26 000 ft *7925 m*. One of the birds was brought down and later identified as the steppe eagle (*Aquila n. nipalensis*) (Gyan Singh, 1961). In 1921 a bearded vulture (*Gypaetus barbatus*) was seen at 25 000 ft *7620 m* on the same mountain (Wollaston, 1922), and this dynamic soarer *may* sail over the summit on occasion.

A wall creeper (*Tichodroma murina*), a jungle crow (*Corvus macrorhynchos*) and a rose-breasted finch (*Carpodacus puniceus*) have been sighted at 21 000 ft *6400 m* migrating across the Karakorum Range, N India (Ingram, 1919), a crane (*Grus grus*) at 20 000 ft *6090 m* in the Himalayas, an Andean condor (*Vultur gryphus*) at 19 800 ft *6035 m* in the Andes (Jacks, 1953), and black-tailed godwits (*Limosa limosa*), Eurasian curlews (*Numenius arquata*) and even jackdaws (*Corvus monedula*) at 19 700 ft *6005 m* on Mt Everest.

On 9 July 1962 a Western Airlines L-188 Electra was flying over Lander County, Nevada, USA at an altitude of 21 000 ft *6400 m* when the pilot heard a dull thud. When the plane landed one of the crew found a large blood-stained dent on the leading edge of one of the plane's horizontal stabilisers with a feather sticking to it, which was forwarded to the US Fish & Wildlife Service for identification. The unfortunate bird was a mallard (*Anas platyrhynchos*) (Terres, 1969).

In 1959 a radar station in Norfolk picked up flocks of small passerine night migrants flying in from Scandinavia at altitudes up to 21 000 ft *6400 m* on three separate occasions. According to Lack (1960) they were probably warblers (Sylvidae), chats (Turdidae) and flycatchers (Muscicapidae).

At the other end of the vertical scale, there is a very interesting record of three house sparrows which lived quite happily at a depth of 640 m *2100 ft* in Frickley Colliery, Yorkshire from the summer of 1975 to the spring of 1978. In 1977 a pair nested and actually reared three young, but they did not survive. Summers-Smith (1980) believes the sparrows entered the mine as 'naive juveniles'.

The deepest-diving bird in the world is the massive emperor penguin of Antarctica. In 1969 a team of American scientists carried out a series of experiments at Cape Crozier to determine the diving ability of this species. All the birds used for the experimental dives were collected from groups gathered at the edge of the ice and then taken to the diving station – an isolated hole in the ice to which the penguins were forced to return after each feeding dive. Depth measurements were obtained with small (4·5 g *0·16 oz*) capillary depth-recorders sutured to the backs of the birds' necks; these offered very little resistance to swimming and consequently did not have much of an inhibiting effect during the dives. About 2–3 hours after attaching the depth-tubes the birds were recaptured and the instruments removed. According to Kooyman *et al* (1971) a total of 238 dives were measured during the experimental studies and the greatest depth recorded in a vertical plunge was 869 ft *265 m* – by a small group of ten penguins. The duration of most of the dives was less than one minute, but one bird which did not return to the dive station was seen swimming near the observation chamber some 32 ft *9·8 m* from the hole after 18 minutes submersion. The birds were never seen to exhale under water, and diving was usually preceded by a few rapid breaths and then a deep inhalation.

How emperor penguins manage to avoid decompression sickness is not yet known, but the 'bounce' dives they normally make are probably too short for significant amounts of nitrogen to be absorbed into the blood.

The deepest-diving flying birds are the common loon (*Gavia immer*), also known as the 'great northern diver', and the oldsquaw duck (*Clangula hyemalis*), both of which can reach a depth in excess of 150 ft *46 m*. Jourdain (1913) quotes a record of a common loon caught in a trammel-net at 180 ft *55 m*, and Roberts (1932) was told by a fisherman living at the mouth of the Cascase River, Minnesota, USA that he had netted loons at a depth of 200 ft *61 m* in Lake Superior. There is also an unconfirmed report of a loon being caught at a depth of 240 ft *73 m*. Similarly, a fisherman at St Joseph, Michigan, USA told Barrows (1912) that he had taken oldsquaw ducks frequently at a depth of 180 ft *55 m*, and Butler (1898) says they were often caught at Michigan City, Indiana at the same depth. The greatest depth is recorded by Tarrant (1883), who was informed by Captain Nathan Saunders, that he had taken oldsquaw ducks on lines set in Green Bay, Wisconsin at a depth of 200 ft *61 m*.

It has been suggested that birds caught in nets at depths greater than 60 ft *18 m* became entangled in the net while it is being raised, but Schorger (1947) thinks it is 'wholly improbable that they were all caught during the raising of the nets'. He concludes: 'There are apparently no physical or physiological reasons why some exceptionally skilful individuals among diving birds cannot descend to a depth of 200 feet. There is ample evidence that this depth is actually reached'.

Another fine diver is the common guillemot. Tuck and Squires (1955) mention an individual found trapped in fishing gear set at 240 ft *73 m* off Newfoundland, and this could be a record depth.

Diving birds are anatomically adapted to resist pressure and physiologically adapted to stand shortage of oxygen.

For parental energy in supplying food to its young, the wren probably takes some beating. One mother was observed to feed her young 1217 times in a day of nearly 16 hours (Wing, 1956), and a pair of great tits (*Parus major*) fed their young 10 685 times during a 14–day period.

Birds have very large eyes for their size – they often weigh more than the brain – because they are more dependent on sight than other vertebrates, and the vision of diurnal raptors is the most acute in the animal world. Leslie Brown (1970) once watched a Verreaux's eagle (*Aquila verreauxii*) launch a stoop at a martial eagle (*Polemaetis bellicosus*) carrying a rock hyrax from a distance of 1·5 miles *2·4 km* and says this bird of prey has such keen eyesight that it could probably see a small green grasshopper 1 in *25 mm* long 300 yd *274 m* away. The same authority also goes on to say that a golden eagle (*Aquila chrysaetos*) can detect an 18 in *460 mm* long hare at a range of 2150 yd *1966 m* (possibly even 2 miles *3·2 km*) in good light and against a contrasting background, and insect–eating raptors like the red-footed falcon (*Falco vespertinus*) can spot a dragonfly at a distance of 880 yd *805 m*.

In laboratory experiments keen-eyed pigeons have been trained to work as quality inspectors on mock-up production lines for rewards of grain. They reject anything that is not perfect and are remarkably quick at spotting defects.

Owls (*Strigidae*) have a sensitivity to low light intensities that is 50–100 times greater than that of human night vision. Tests carried out at the University of Michigan, USA between 1938 and 1943 showed that under favourable conditions the barred owl (*Strix varia*) could swoop on a dead mouse from a distance of 6 ft *1·8 m* or more in an illumination of only 0·00 000 073 ft-candle (the light from a 6 watt inside-blue bulb, reduced by the rheostat, and passed through nine sheets of paper), equivalent to the light from a standard candle at a distance of 1170 ft *357 m*, and that the same bird could see dead prey (with difficulty) in an illumination of only 0·00 000 08 ft-candle, which is equivalent to the light from a standard candle at a distance of 3536 ft *1076 m* (Dice, 1945).

These nocturnal raptors also have the smallest range of eye movements ever recorded in animals. In one Canadian experiment using four awake, un-anaesthetised great horned owls (*Bubo virginianus*) the maximum rotation was found to be less than 1·5 degrees, compared to 40 degrees for the domestic cat and 100 degrees for man (Steinbach and Money, 1973).

The 'intellectual giants' of the bird world are generally considered to be the crows (*Corvidae*) and the parrots (*Psittacidae*), but the subject is so complex that it would need a separate study that cannot be undertaken here.

The question of the 'dimmest' bird, however, is much easier to resolve, and one needs to look no further than the domestic turkey (*Meleagris gallopavo*) for this title. On one occasion a farmer left an empty barrel in his yard. Six of his best turkeys promptly scrambled into it, piled up one on top of the other and died of suffocation because none had the sense to get out. Other breeders have known turkeys to stand out in the open during a heavy downpour and be drowned because they were not intelligent enough to walk a few yards to their hutches. Each year thousands of turkeys freeze to death on cold nights because they stubbornly refuse to seek refuge in their warm sleeping quarters, and some turkeys are so retarded that they even have to be persuaded to eat. Some farmers rear chickens alongside turkeys in the hope that the turkeys will copy the actions of their brighter companions, but this is generally wishful thinking. Turkeys are also great panickers, and on one occasion more than 13 000 being fattened for Christmas were trampled to death on a poultry ranch in Corning, California, USA when a low-flying jet suddenly flew over. There are even reports of turkeys being frightened to death by pieces of paper fluttering in front of their path.

The highest price ever paid for a stuffed bird is £9000 for an example of the extinct great auk (*Pinguinus impennis*) in summer plumage collected by the naturalist Count Raben in Iceland in *c* 1821. The bird was purchased at a London auction on 4 March 1971 by the Director of the Iceland Natural History Museum, who said later he would have bid up to £23 000 for this extreme rarity. Only about 80 stuffed specimens and four skeletons are preserved world-wide. The last great auk was killed on Eldey Island, Iceland in June 1844, although there was an unconfirmed sighting near the Grand Bank of Newfoundland in 1852. Another one captured alive in Waterford Harbour, SW Ireland in 1834 was later beaten to death by the local populace who thought it was a witch! (Halliday, 1978).

In December 1970 a passenger pigeon fetched a mere £75 at another London auction.

The highest price ever paid for a live bird is approximately £25 000 by a Japanese fancier for a Belgian-owned racing pigeon called 'De Wittslager' in October 1978. In 1971 an American zoo offered 35 000 dollars (then worth £14 463) for a live example of the now protected Philippine eagle, but the money was never claimed.

The longest feathers grown by any bird are those of the Phoenix fowl or onagadori, a strain of red junglefowl (*Gallus gallus*), which has been bred in SW Japan for over 300 years. Only the roosters have the very long tail coverts, which grow continuously for up to six years without moulting, and an extreme measurement of 34 ft 9 in *10·59 m* was reported in 1972 for a specimen owned by Masasha Kubota of Kochi (Ogasawara, 1972).

Among flying birds, the two central pairs of tail feathers grown by Reeves's pheasant (*Syrmaticus reevesii*) of the mountains of central and northern China sometimes exceed 8 ft *2·4 m* in length. These exaggerated feathers act as an escape brake, and when they are thrown up vertically in mid-air the bird drops to the cover of trees like a falling meteor.

The number of feathers on a bird varies with the species and the season, being most abundant immediately after a moult. In general, however, large birds have more feathers than small ones. In one series of 'feather counts' a whistling swan (*Cygnus columbianus*) was found to have 25 216 feathers, 20 177 of which were on the head and neck; a pied-billed grebe (*Podilymbus podiceps*) 15 016; a Mallard (*Anas platyrhynchos*) 11 903; and a domestic chicken (*Gallus gallus*) 9325. The house sparrow (*Passer domesticus*) has about 3500 in winter and 3000 in summer. A ruby-throated hummingbird (*Archilochus colubris*) had only 940, although hummingbirds have more feathers per gramme of body weight than swans (Wetmore, 1936; Wing, 1956).

Feathers can also account for a sizeable fraction of the total weight in some species of bird. One bald eagle weighing 4082 g *9 lb* had 677 g *1 lb 8 oz* of feathers, or 16.6 per cent of the total.

In 1938 2600 feathers weighing 10·3 g *0·363 oz* were counted in the nest of a long-tailed tit (*Aegithalos caudatus*) in north Yorkshire. As the farmyard where most of the feathers must have been collected was 500 yd *457 m* from the nest, it has been estimated that the parent birds flew over 738 miles *1188 km* during the building programme.

In general, relative egg weight diminishes as body weight increases.

The largest egg produced by any living bird – and the biggest single cell in the animal world today – is that of the North African ostrich. The average-sized example measures 156×136 mm *6·14×5·35 in* and weighs 1·65 kg *3 lb 10 oz*, compared to 152×127 mm *6×5 in* and 1·56 kg *3 lb 7 oz* for the southern ostrich (Duerden, 1919). The shell is 1·6 mm *0·063 in* thick and can support the weight of a 250 lb *113 kg* man.

One game warden reported seeing lions playing with a clutch of eggs for some time. When they had finished not a single one was broken.

The largest egg laid by any bird on the British list is that of the mute swan. In one series of 88 samples the measurements ranged from 100–122 mm ×70–88 mm *3·94–4·8 in×2·76–3·47 in*, the average being 112·5×73·5 mm *4·43×2·89 in* (Schonwetter, 1960–61). The weight is 336–364 g *12–13 oz*.

The largest egg produced by a sea-bird is that of the wandering albatross, which is highly variable in shape and size. In one series of 87 from Gough

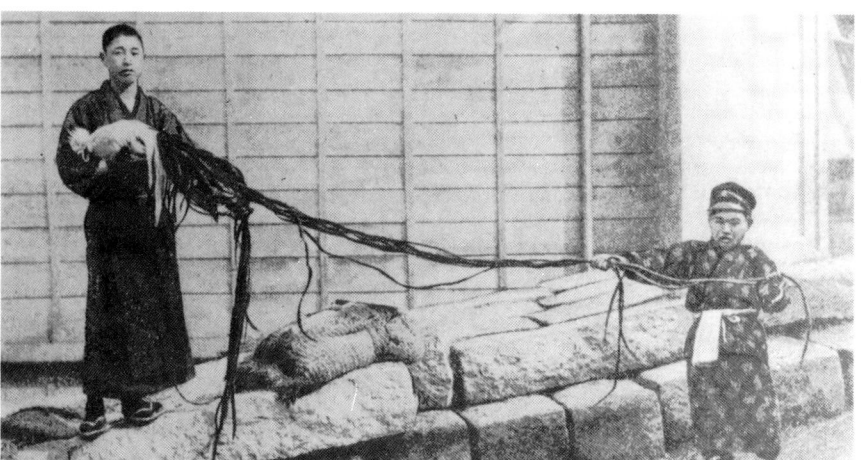

The exceptionally long tail coverts of the cock Phoenix fowl have been measured up to 34 ft 9 in 10·59 m in length.

Island, in the Tristan da Cunha group, S Atlantic, the average was 127×77 mm *5×3 in* (Verrill, 1895). The weights of six freshly laid South Georgia eggs ranged between 429 g and 487 g *15·1–17·2 oz* (Murphy, 1936), but weights up to 588 g *20·7 oz* have been reported for specimens collected on Auckland Island, 200 miles *320 km* south of New Zealand (Ross, 1847).

The eggs of the largest eagles, on the other hand, do not exceed 5–6 oz *142–170 g*.

On 3 May 1977 a white goose (*Anser anser domesticus*) named 'Speckle' owned by Donny Brandenberg of Goshen, Ohio, USA laid a 24 oz *680 g* egg. The average weight is 6–8 oz *170–227 g*.

The largest egg laid by any bird in proportion to its own size is that of the brown kiwi (*Apteryx australis*) of New Zealand. There is an old record of a 3 lb 12 oz *1·7 kg* hen laying an egg weighing 406 g *14·3 oz*, or nearly one-quarter her body mass, but weights up to 18 oz *510 g* have been reliably reported for other ova. The problems of producing such an enormous cell, however – the egg of the chicken-sized kiwi is more than ten times as large as that of the domestic hen's – can be disastrous, and not infrequently kiwis containing fully developed eggs have been found dead in their nesting burrows.

Most parasitic cuckoos lay relatively small eggs, but Tyne and Berger (1971) mention a single egg of a non-parasitic greater ani (*Crotophaga major*) which was one-third of the female's bodyweight.

The smallest mature egg laid by any bird is that of the Vervain hummingbird, which measures less than 10 mm *0·39 in* in length. Two examples collected in Jamaica weighed 0·365 g *0·0129 oz* and 0·375 g *0·0132 oz* respectively. (Diamond, cited by Lack, 1976). One egg of *Aepyornis maximus* (see page 219) could hold the contents of 33 000 eggs of this species. The eggs of the bee hummingbird (*Mellisuga helenae*), the world's tiniest bird, are only fractionally larger. On 8 May 1906 two specimens were collected at Boyate, Santiago de Cuba by O Tollin, who later presented them to the US National Museum of Natural History, Washington, DC, USA. One of these eggs has since been mislaid (which cannot be difficult!), but the other one measures 11·4×8 mm *0·45×0·32 in* and weighs 0·5 g *0·0176 oz* (J Watson, pers. comm.).

On 11 June 1905 Nelson Carpenter (1906) flushed a very small female Costa's hummingbird (*Calypte costae*) near Escondido, southern California, USA. Closer investigation revealed a nest placed on a small twig about 5 ft *1·5 m* from the ground, which contained two eggs. One of them was slightly incubated and measured 12·7×8·4 mm *0·5×0·33 in*, but the other one was only 7·36×5·33 m *0·29×0·21 in* and contained no yolk. This undersized egg, which was emitted from the oviduct *before reaching maturity*, is now preserved in the Western Foundation of Verte-

brate Zoology, Los Angeles (L Kiff, pers. comm.). Another 'sport' laid by a Zebra finch (*Taniopygis castanotis*) measured only 9·5×7 mm *0·37×0·28 in* (C Taylor, pers. comm.), and the smallest domestic chicken's egg recorded scaled 1·29 g *0·046 oz* or 98 per cent less than the average weight (Szuman, 1926).

The smallest egg laid by any bird on the British list is that of the Goldcrest (*Regulus regulus*) which measures 12·2–14·5 mm *0·48–0·57 in*×9·4–9·9 mm *0·37–0·39 in*. The weight is 0·6 g *0·021 oz*.

The smallest egg laid by any bird in relation to body weight is that of the emperor penguin, which constitutes only 1·4 per cent of the body mass.

As a general rule the eggs of large birds require longer incubation periods than those of smaller species. One notable exception, however, is the ostrich which takes only 42 days.

The longest incubation period of any bird is that of the wandering albatross with a normal range of 75–82 days, but Tickell (1968) says he observed two eggs on Bird Island, South Georgia which took 85 days to hatch. The royal albatross has a normal range of 75–81 days and the brown kiwi 75–80 days. The incubation period of the mallee fowl (*Leipoa ocellata*) of Australia is normally 62 days, but Petersen (1963) cites a record of an egg taking 90 days to hatch.

The longest incubation period of any bird on the British list is that of the northern fulmar with a range of 52–53 days.

The shortest incubation periods are to be found among the passerines or perching birds. A small number of species have been credited with a ten-day cycle – the time that has elapsed between the laying of an egg and the emergence of the young bird from the shell – but most of these birds are now known to require from 11 to 14 days. They include the Eurasian siskin (*Carduelis spinus*) 11–12 days, the house sparrow (*Passer domesticus*) 12–14 days, the wryneck (*Jynx torquilla*) 12 days and the common wren (*Troglodytes troglodytes*) 14 days.

The brown-headed cowbird (*Molothrus ater*) of North America has traditionally been given a ten-day cycle, but Nice (1953) found the duration in one series of 62 hatchings was 11–12 days. Sometimes, however, an egg may be retained for 12–24 hours in the oviduct, and the same writer mentions another observer (Hoffman, 1929) who caught a cowbird that appeared to be egg-bound and gave it a home for the night. The following morning he found two eggs in the cage. 'One of these eggs' says Nice 'would have had an extra day of development before it was laid, and if immediately incubated might conceivably have hatched in ten days'.

The only other species of birds with well-authenticated records of ten-day incubation periods are the great spotted woodpecker (*Picoides major*) of

Europe and the black-billed cuckoo (*Coccyzus erythropthalmus*) of the Americas. In the first case six eggs were laid between 26 April and 1 May. Four young hatched out on 10 May, and the last two were out by 10 am on 11 May (Bussmann, 1946). In the second, one egg was found on 2 July, additional eggs were laid on 3 and 6 July, and the last one hatched out on 16 July (Spencer, 1943). Nice, however, thinks the last egg in the cuckoo clutch may have been retained in the oviduct for an extra 24 hours and thus laid in a more advanced state than the others.

The shortest incubation periods reported for birds on the British list are those of the Eurasian siskin (*Carduelis spinus*) and the hawfinch (*Coccothraustes coccothraustes*), both averaging 11–12 days.

The number of eggs laid by a bird in a 'single clutch' varies considerably among species and is largely related to food supplies and the physical condition and age of the hens.

The bobwhite (*Colinus virginianus*) of North America is generally credited with laying the largest clutches, with a normal range of 12–24 eggs, followed by the blue tit (*Phasianus colchicus*) 6–22 eggs, the greater scaup (*Aythya marila*) 6–22 eggs, the red-crested pochard (*Netta rufina*) 6–21 eggs and the grey partridge (*Perdix perdix*) 12–20 eggs, but Campbell and Ferguson-Lees (1972) believe the larger numbers were probably the produce of two or even three hens laying in the same nest.

By continually removing eggs from a clutch, however, experimenters have succeeded in tricking a wryneck into laying 48 eggs, a house sparrow 51, a campo flicker (*Colaptes campestris*) 71 and a bobwhite 128 eggs before stopping (Wing, 1956). The mallard may lay 80–100 eggs, and there is an instance of one hen producing an incredible 146 eggs in an effort to achieve a nest complement (Mouquet, 1924).

In July 1977 a muscovy duck (*Cairina moschata*) owned by Mrs Emily Enderby of Boston, Lincs laid a clutch of 31 eggs and hatched out 25 ducklings.

At the other end of the range most true sea-birds – and at least 32 species of raptor – lay only one egg in a clutch, and the wandering albatross and the Philippine eagle, which breed only once in two years, have the lowest egg output of any living birds.

Although hen ostriches usually lay 12–15 eggs weighing 44–55 lb *20–25 kg*, these clutches represent only 20–25 per cent of the bird's body weight, as opposed to 50 per cent for the two-egg clutches of the bee hummingbird and 120–144 per cent for the 10–12 egg clutches of the goldcrest. But these performances are eclipsed by the ruddy duck (*Oxyura jamaicensis*) of the Americas, which lays a clutch of 14–15 eggs weighing three times as much as itself!

The largest egg collection in the world is housed in the Zoological Museum, Tring, Herts., which is part of the British Museum (Natural History). In 1980 it contained between 700 000 and 800 000 eggs (Michael Walters, pers. comm.). The collection in the Western Foundation of Vertebrate Zoology, Los Angeles, California, USA is also of comparable size. 'We presently have about 140 000 sets (clutches) of eggs here with accompanying data' says curator Lloyd F Kiff (pers. comm.), 'plus another 10 000 or so sets without adequate data . . . If we assume that each clutch contains an average of four eggs, probably a good estimate for a large generalised collection, then this yields a figure of approximately 600 000 eggs.'

The most palatable bird's egg is that of the domestic chicken – but only just!

During the period 1946 to 1951 a highly experienced tasting panel at the Low Temperature Research Station, Cambridge determined the relative palatability of the eggs of 212 species of birds belonging to 25 orders. The samples were tested in the form of a scramble prepared over a steam-bath and nothing was added. Marks were awarded for general palatability on a scale ranging from 10·0 (ideal), through 9·0 (very good), 8·0 (good egg flavour), 7·0 (barely perceptible 'off' or foreign flavour) to 5·0 (unpleasant) and finally 2·0 (repulsive and inedible). Not surprisingly, the domestic chicken came out top with 8·7 points, followed by the emu with 8·4, the coot and lesser black-backed gull 8·3, the kittiwake 8·2, Swainson's francolin 8·1 and the common rhea, Grant's guan and the golden plover, all with 8·0. The only bird to score 2·0 points was the black tit, but the wren was not much better at 2·7. It is interesting to note that the panel found the egg of the budgerigar was just as edible as the egg of the domestic duck, goose and pheasant, all of which scored 7·1 points, and that the North African ostrich did worse than was expected with only 7·3 (Cotts, 1954).

The largest nests (i.e. made of sticks or twigs) are built by eagles and storks. One example constructed by a pair of bald eagles in Vermilion, Ohio, USA and possibly their successors over a period of 35 years measured 8 ft 6 in *2·59 m* across and was 12 ft *3·66 m* deep. When it finally crashed to the ground during a storm – killing the eaglets inside – its weight was estimated at 4000 lb *1814 kg*. A much larger eyrie built by another pair of bald eagles near St Petersburg, Florida, was 9 ft 6 in *2·90 m* across and had a depth of 20 ft *6·10 m* (Petersen, 1963). In 1954 Seton Gordon (1955) saw a golden eagle nest in Scotland which was 15 ft *4·6 m* deep. It had been in use for 45 years.

In 1909 workmen removed the 6×5 ft *1·8×1·5 m* nest of a white stork (*Ciconia ciconia*) from the sum-

The Mallee fowl, builder of the world's largest nest sites.

The nesting mound of the Mallee fowl. The eggs are incubated by the heat generated from decaying vegetable matter.

A pigeon's nest made entirely of 6 in 152 mm nails built in a Sheffield foundry.

mit of the cathedral in Colmar, NE France when it started leaning over at a dangerous angle. Inside the walls of the 1456 lb *660 kg* nest, which was about 30 years old, were found 17 ladies' black stockings, five fur caps, the sleeve of a white silk blouse, three old shoes, a large piece of leather and four buttons that had belonged to a railway porter's uniform.

The incubation mounds of dry sandy earth with a core of vegetable matter scratched together by the mallee fowl of Australia are much larger. According to Frith (1962) most mounds measure about 15 ft *4·6 m* in diameter and 2–3 ft *60–91 cm* in height, but he saw one in southern Australia which measured 18 ft *5·5 m* in diameter. When dug out it was found to be 4 ft 6 in *1·4 m* deep, and when fully mounded in the summer was 4 ft *1·2 m* high. Other mounds have been discovered measuring up to 15 ft *4·6 m* in height and 35 ft *10·7 m* in diameter (Wetmore, 1931). It has been calculated that the nest site of a Mallee fowl may involve the mounding of 300 yd³ *229 m³* of matter weighing 300 tonnes.

The smallest nests are built by hummingbirds. The silk, cotton and lichen effort of the Vervain hummingbird is about the size of half a walnut shell, while the deeper one of the bee hummingbird is thimble-sized.

The most valuable nests are those constructed by the edible-nest swiftlet (*Collocalia inexpectata*) of SE Asia and Indonesia, which produce the raw material for bird's-nest soup. The most sought after nests – they take 33–41 days to build – are those made entirely of salivary mucus which do not require extensive cleaning.

There are also a number of birds which use very strange and sometimes uncomfortable materials to make their nests, and the crows are probably the leading exponents in this field. One avian masochist built a nest entirely of barbed wire, and a pair of crows in Bombay, India made theirs out of some gold spectacle frames they had stolen from an open shop window. A pigeon's nest in Sheffield was found to consist of 6 in *152 mm* nails plus a few feathers, and a wren made one entirely out of hair-pins. In August 1940 a chaffinch's nest built almost completely out of confetti was found in a garden at Reedham, Norfolk. It was later exhibited at Norwich Castle Museum. On an allotment in Bury St Edmunds, Suffolk a linnet built a nest in a cauli-flower and was found sitting on five eggs.

Reptiles
(class Reptilia)

A reptile is a cold-blooded, air-breathing vertebrate which is at least partly covered with protective scales or horny plates. Unlike mammals and birds it has no effective mechanism for the regulation of body heat, and its temperature rises and falls according to that of the surrounding air or water. The brain is relatively small and poorly developed. Paired limbs, when present, tend to lateral orientation in most forms. Young are usually produced from eggs, deposited on land, but in some species of lizard the eggs are retained within the oviduct and the young are born alive.

The earliest known reptile was the cotylosaur *Hylonomus*, which lived about 310 million years ago. Its remains have been found in the fossilised stumps of coal forest trees in Nova Scotia.

There are about 5175 living species of reptile and the class is divided into four orders. These are: the Crocodilia (crocodiles, alligators and gharials); the Chelonia (turtles, tortoises and terrapins); the Squamata (lizards and snakes); and the Rhynchocephalia (tuatara). The largest order is Squamata (sub-orders Sauria, Amphisbaenia and Serpentes) which contains about 4900 species, and the smallest is Rhynchocephalia (1 species).

The largest living reptile is the estuarine or saltwater crocodile (*Crocodylus porosus*), which ranges from India, Sri Lanka, S China and the Malay Archipelago to N Australia, Papua New Guinea and the Solomon Islands.

Mature males average 14–16 ft *4·3–4·9 m* in length and scale 900–1150 lb *408–522 kg*, but old individuals may be half as heavy again. Adult females do not exceed 14 ft *4·3 m*.

As with many other large animals the size attained by this crocodile has been much exaggerated. Sir Samuel Baker (1874), for instance, says those found in Sri Lanka – *Crocodylus p. porosus* – were usually larger than those found on the Indian coast and lengths of 22 ft *6·7 m* were quite common, but this measurement has never been substantiated. According to Deraniyagala (1939) the length record (between pegs) for the whole of this island is 19 ft 7 in *6 m* for a notorious man-eater shot in Eastern Province, and he also gives details of another one killed at Dikvalla, Southern Province, which measured 17 ft 8 in *5·38 m*. Two other crocodiles shot at Kantalia reservoir, Eastern Province, were 18 ft 8 in *5·69 m* and 18 ft 6 in *5·64 m* respectively. In 1924 a length of 21 ft *6·4 m* was reported for a saurian shot by game-wardens at Kumana, Northern Province who said it was so bulky that a man could leap over the body 'only with difficulty'. This measurement may have been reliable because the preserved skull has a 'dry' length of 724 mm *28·50 in*.

In *C. porosus* the ratio between skull length (tip of snout to the back of the cranium) and total length is a fairly constant 1:7·5 up to 16 ft *4·9 m*. In larger specimens the skull tends to become relatively broader with age, and in a 20 ft *6·1 m* individual the ratio is 1:8·6. Also the bone shrinks by approximately five per cent during the 'drying out' process.

In former times, before heavy persecution, this species reached a greater size than it does today because it was allowed full opportunity for un-interrupted growth, and measurements up to and even surpassing 30 ft *9·1 m* were reported. None of these claims, however, have been verified although, as we shall see later, such a length is not beyond the realms of possibility.

The most publicised crocodile in this 'outsize' category was a 33 ft *10·1 m* monster killed in the Bay of Bengal in 1840 which reportedly had a belly girth of 13 ft 8 in *4·17 m* and weighed an estimated 3 tonnes. Fortunately the skull of this reptile was saved and later presented to the British Museum by Mr Gilson Row, and the overall dimensions of this trophy were given as 36½ × 18¾ × 12⅓ in *927 × 476 × 313 mm* (Boulenger, 1889). These figures, however, were misleading inasmuch as the length was taken from the snout to the posterior edge of the lower jaw instead of to the back of the cranium. According to Greer (1974) the measurement from the snout to the occiput is a much more modest 655 mm *25·8 in*, which means the animal in question must have taped about 19 ft 4 in *5·89 m* in the flesh. It is interesting to note that another crocodilian skull in the same collec-tion which had long been mistaken for that of the Bay of Bengal 'giant' is somewhat larger. Nothing is known of its history, but its snout–occiput length of 715 mm *28·2 in* indicates it must have belonged to a saurian measuring nearly 21 ft *6·4 m* in length.

Earlier, in 1823, Paul de la Gironiere (1854) and a party of Indians killed another monstrous brute at Jala Jala, near Lake Taal on Luzon in the Philippines. The crocodile, a notorious man-eater, had recently attacked and eaten one of the settler's shepherds while he was crossing a river, and together with George R Russell, an American friend from Boston, he decided to avenge the man's death. After several weeks of patient waiting they managed to trap the killer in a small river. Even then, it took them more than six hours to subdue the animal, and it was still battling strongly when a lucky lance thrust severed its spinal column. The beast was so heavy it took the efforts of all forty hunters to beach it.

'When at last we had got him completely out of the water we stood stupefied with astonishment,' wrote the Frenchman, 'for it was a very different thing to see his body thus. Mr Russell, a very competent person, was charged with his measurements. From the extremity of his nostrils to the tip of his tail he was found to be twenty-seven feet long, and his circumference was eleven feet, measured under the arm pits. His belly was much more voluminous, but we thought it unnecessary to measure him there, judging that the horse upon which he had breakfasted must considerably have increased his bulk. In his stomach were found the horse, bitten into seven or eight pieces, plus about one hundred and fifty pounds weight of pebbles, varying from the size of a fist to that of a walnut.'

The head, which reportedly weighed 450 lb *204 kg* before the ligaments were detached, was later cleaned and presented to the Boston Museum of Natural History, Massachusetts, USA where it remained forgotten for nearly a hundred years. In 1924, how-ever, Dr Thomas Barbour, a leading American herpetologist, tracked down the unlabelled specimen and was able to identify it by marks on the palate which corresponded with a musket shot that La Gironiere had fired from close range into the reptile's open jaws. Once again, the skull failed to live up to its owner's reputation. Now in the Museum of Comparative Zoology at Harvard University, it has a snout–occiput length of 674 mm *25·5 in*, which means the Jala Jala man-eater must have taped about 20 ft *6·1 m* in the flesh. It would also indicate the original length of 27 ft *8·2 m* quoted for this crocodile was a curve measurement taken along the belly rather than a straight line between pegs.

If we exclude fossil remains, the largest crocodilian skull on record is probably one preserved in the Indian Museum, Calcutta which measures 750 mm *29·53 in* (Prashad, 1930). It reportedly belonged to a 25 ft *7·6 m* crocodile killed in the Hooghly River in the Alipore District of Calcutta and, judging from its size, this animal must have measured at least 22 ft *6·7 m* in the flesh.

In July 1957 Mrs Kris Pawlowski shot an estuarine crocodile on MacArthur Bank in the Norman River, SE Gulf of Carpentaria, north Australia which measured an astonishing 28 ft 4 in *8·64 m*.

In normal circumstances a claim like this would be rejected out of hand because nothing of this enormity was preserved, although a photographic record existed until 1968. On this occasion, however, Mrs Pawlowski's husband Ron, a leading authority on this species and a very reliable observer, was present when the crocodile was shot, so this record must be regarded as one with a high probability of accuracy.

Later he wrote: 'The type of ammunition used was a ·300 H & H Magnum, either Winchester or Norma, and the crocodile died instantly as was intended. As a tractor was not conveniently to hand there was no possible way we could drag the extremely bulky body onto dry land away from the tidal reach, and although the head was severed it was so heavy I could not lift it. That is why the skull was not pre-served . . . we had no means of moving such a weight.'

Mr Pawlowski also mentioned that of the 10 287 *C. porosus* he had examined personally, none had exceeded 18 ft *5·5 m* up until then.

Some very large estuarine crocodiles have also been killed in the Segama River, North Borneo.

According to James R Montgomery (pers. comm.), who ran a small rubber estate about half-way between Hilia and the mouth of the river during the period 1926–32, it was a veritable crocodile haven, both in number and size.

'My interest in this reptile,' he writes, 'arose firstly from the protection of my native labour force who bathed and laundered in the river, and my main difficulty at first was how to kill and not lose the body, which always managed to get back into the water even if dead. I eventually found that a soft-nosed ·375 bullet in the spinal column, just behind the head, was the answer.

'In most cases it was not possible to do a peg measurement as there was little means of moving the body. What we did was to straighten it out, drawing a line from the snout and tip of tail and measuring that. In the whole of this period, I shot and peg measured as best I could some 20 reptiles between 20 and 26 feet.'

Mr Montgomery also mentioned a fabulous brute which lived some 10 miles *16 km* down-river from his quarters. This reptile had been a legend for years and the River People (Seluke) estimated that he was more than 200 years old: 'On one memorable occasion I came across him asleep on a sand bank in the middle of the river. His snout was in the water at one end and the tip of his tail in the water at the other. We got him to move off and measured the sand bank very carefully with a 50-foot surveyor's tape. The sand bank was 32 feet 10 inches, making him in the region of 33 feet plus. We never shot at him as the Seluke looked on him as the Father of the Devil. Silver money was always thrown in the river whenever he was seen to ward off harm.'

On 26 June 1960 film-maker Keith Adams of Perth, Western Australia harpooned a 20 ft 2 in *6·15 m* long crocodile in the MacArthur near Barroloola, Northern Territory, and this is the 'official' length record for a *C. porosus* taken in Australia.

Two years later Fred Bennett, a Darwin professional crocodile-hunter, shot a huge semi-legendary saurian called 'Big Gator' in the River Adelaide, Northern Territory when it became too old and slow to hunt fish and started feeding on livestock instead. This ancient reptile measured exactly 20 ft *6·1 m* and weighed 2418 lb *1097 kg*.

The largest crocodile recorded in Australia in recent years was an 18 ft *5·5 m* character called 'Sweetheart' who had a penchant for outboard motors. In the space of two years he crunched his way through more than 20 of them in the Finniss River, Northern Territory, and also included a few petrol tanks to vary the diet. On one occasion two fishermen had to swim for their lives when the 1800 lb *816 kg* crocodile sank his teeth into their boat

and ripped the side off, and one of them described his escape as the 'best performance of walking on water in 2000 years!'

In the end, however, wildlife rangers were forced to take action when disgruntled fishermen threatened to shoot the playful brute. In July 1979 they managed to net him, and after being drugged he was towed to a quiet spot in the wilderness where it was hoped he would settle down and lead a more peaceful existence. But it was not to be. Shortly after being released in his new territory the still-drowsy crocodile was trapped under water by a floating log and drowned. Sweetheart was later stuffed and his body is now on display in Darwin Museum.

One of the last remaining strongholds for big estuarines is Papua New Guinea which is still largely unexplored. In May 1966 Herb Schweighofer shot a 'salty' at Liaga on the SE coast which measured 20 ft 9 in *6·32 m* in length and had a belly girth of 9 ft *2·74 m*. This size was closely matched by another crocodile which drowned after getting entangled in a fisherman's net at Obo on the Fly River in 1979. This specimen measured 20 ft 4 in *6·2 m* and yielded a 720 mm *28·35 in* skull which weighed 49·2 kg *108 lb* in the raw state and 26 kg *57 lb* when dried and cleaned out (Eric Balson, pers. comm.).

The largest estuarine crocodiles ever held in captivity are two males owned by George Craig of Daru Island, Gulf of Papua. One of them called 'Oscar' measures 18 ft *5·5 m* in length, and the other 'Gomik' is 17 ft 6 in *5·3 m*. Both these saurians were caught in the Fly River. Another large individual taken by Craig on a baited hook in the same river measured 19 ft 6 in *5·9 m* in length, but died shortly after being dragged on to a shelving mud bank (Pinney, 1976). The two largest examples at Moitaka crocodile farm measure 18 ft *5·5 m* and 16 ft *4·9 m* respectively, the latter being blind.

Lengths in excess of 20 ft *6·1 m* have also been reliably reported for the long-snouted gharial or gavial (*Gavialis gangeticus*) of the river systems of India and Pakistan, but in this species the head–total length ratio is only 1:5. A gharial measuring 21 ft 6 in *6·6 m* was killed in the Gogra River at Fyzabad, United Provinces in August 1920 (Pitman, 1925), and one of 21 ft *6·4 m* was shot in the Cheko River, Jalpaigur in 1934. Probably the largest gharial on record was one taken by Matthew George in the Kosi River, N Bihar in January 1924 which taped 23 ft *7 m* (Leo George, pers. comm.). Unconfirmed measurements up to 30 ft *9·1 m* have been claimed.

The Orinoco crocodile (*Crocodylus intermedius*) has also been credited with great size. Two specimens shot by Alexander von Humboldt and his companion Aimé Bonpland in 1800, while they were exploring the course of the Orinoco River, reportedly measured 22 ft *6·7 m* and 17 ft 2¾ in *5·25 m*, but these must

The body of the famous estuarine crocodile 'Sweetheart' who had a penchant for outboard motors and petrol tanks.

have been outsized freaks because the average adult length is only about 3 m *9 ft 10 in*. According to Neill (1971) the largest *C. intermedius* measured this century was just under 13 ft *4·0 m* in length.

The American crocodile (*Crocodylus acutus*) of the SE USA, Central America, the West Indies and northern South America is somewhat larger than *C. intermedius*, adult males averaging 11 ft 6 in *3·5 m*. The largest specimen to be accurately measured was probably a male shot by Jackson and Hornaday (1875) at Arch Creek, Biscayne, Florida which was 15 ft 2 in *4·62 m* long, with an estimated 6 in *152 mm* of tail missing. Another large male killed by an American alligator in 1952 after it had strayed into its rival's pen at the famous Ross Allen Reptile Institute in Silver Springs, Florida measured 14 ft 7 in *4·44 m* (Ross Allen, pers. comm.). There is also an old record of a *C. acutus* shot in Venezuela which measured 23 ft *7 m*, but Neill has queried the accuracy of this report. It is interesting to note, however, that the American Museum of Natural History, New York, possess a large skull of this species which measures 729 mm *28·7 in* (Bellairs, 1969).

In 1883 a huge saurian-like creature measuring 12 m *39 ft 4 in* in length was reportedly killed in the Beni River, Bolivia after receiving 36 balls. The preserved body was later sent to La Paz for scientific study, but further information is lacking.

The American alligator (*Alligator mississipiensis*) of the SE USA is slightly longer and bulkier than *C. acutus*, adult males averaging 12 ft *3·7 m*. During the last century three examples measuring over 18 ft *5·48 m* were collected in the vicinity of Avery Island, southern Louisiana. Two of them were credited with lengths of 18 ft 3 in *5·56 m* and 18 ft 5½ in *5·62 m* respectively. The largest, shot by E H McIlhenny (1935) on 2 January 1890, measured 19 ft 2 in *5·84 m*, which is a record for this species.

The maximum length attained by the Nile crocodile (*Crocodylus niloticus*) of Africa, Madagascar and adjacent islands is a matter of some controversy.

In ancient Egypt, where crocodiles – and rulers – were mummified, the word 'great' was applied to any saurian which measured over 7 Egyptian royal cubits (=12 ft 0⅓ in *3·67 m*). So far, however, no mummified crocodiles exceeding 15 ft *4·6 m* have been found by Egyptologists, so it is not surprising that Ditmars (1936), Schmidt (1944) and Pope (1956) all state that this species (average length 11–12 ft *3·4–3·7 m*) never exceeds 16 ft *4·9 m*. Dr Hugh B Cott (1961), on the other hand, begs to differ, and gives several reliable records from Central and Southern Africa of crocodiles measuring between 16 ft *4·9 m* and 19 ft *5·8 m*. They include a 16 ft 7 in

5·05 m specimen shot by L E Vaughan, a senior game-warden in N Rhodesia; one measuring just over 17 ft 5 in 5·31 m taken by W Hubbard in the Kafue River, also in N Rhodesia; an 18 ft 2 in 5·54 m individual killed by a game-ranger in the Semliki River, Uganda in 1950; a female (?) measuring 18 ft 4 in 5·59 m taken on the same river in June 1954; and one measuring 18 ft 10 in 5·74 m shot by C Yiannakis near Chipoko, Malawi.

Another huge saurian shot by a professional hunter named Erich Novotny near Nungwe in the Emin Pasha Gulf of Lake Victoria, Tanzania in 1948 measured exactly 21 ft 6·4 m, and he claims he saw another one in the same area which was even larger. The Juba River in Somalia also had a reputation for big crocodiles at one time, and Douglas Jones shot one which was just over 21 ft 6·4 m.

Of the 1406 crocodiles taken by the commercial hunters Glover and Van Bart on the Kafue River, N Rhodesia in 1950–51, the largest measured 17 ft 8 in 5·38 m when dry and 18 ft 5·49 m when landed, but the average length was only 9 ft 6 in 2·90 m (Foran, 1958).

Jack Bousfield, who claims he had a hand in killing 45 000(?) crocodiles in Lake Rukwa, Tanzania said the largest example measured 17 ft 4½ in 5·30 m, and the largest of 500 specimens collected by Graham and Beard (1973) on Lake Rudolf, Kenya in 1965 was 15 ft 9 in 4·80 m long and weighed 1500 lb 680 kg.

In November 1968 a legendary crocodile known as 'Kwena' was brought down by a professional hunter, Bobby Wilmot, in the Okavango Swamp, Botswana. This huge reptile measured 19 ft 3 in 5·87 m between pegs and had a belly girth of 7 ft 2·13 m. Its weight was estimated at between 1750 lb 794 kg and 1800 lb 816 kg, and the head alone weighed 365 lb 166 kg. Inside the stomach were found two goats, half a donkey and the still-clothed trunk of a native woman.

The largest accurately measured Nile crocodile on record was probably one shot by the Duke of Mecklenberg in 1905 near Mwanza, Tanzania which measured 21 ft 4 in 6·50 m in length (Hubbard, 1927). It was not weighed, but a Nile crocodile this length would be expected to scale somewhere between 2300 lb 1043 kg and 2400 lb 1089 kg in good condition. The 'official' record is 19 ft 6 in 5·94 m for a specimen taken on the Semliki River by a member of the Uganda Game and Fisheries Department in 1953. It had a belly girth of 7 ft 4 in 2·24 m.

At least six of the 21 members of the *Crocodylidae* will attack and eat man if given the opportunity, and several of the others are large enough to inflict serious injury or even death.

The most notorious man-eater of them all is undoubtedly the estuarine crocodile. Although no statistics are available, this saurian probably kills well over 2000 people annually, the majority of them unrecorded.

The most horrifying example of this reptile's taste for human flesh occurred in February 1944 when Allied troops invaded Ramree Island in the Bay of Bengal and trapped between 400 and 800 Japanese infantrymen in a coastal mangrove swamp. The Japanese attempted to run the naval blockade around the swamp and managed to get forty small craft inside the perimeter, but these were all sunk by gun-fire over a period of ten days. As soon as night fell the local crocodiles moved in *en masse*, attacking the dead, wounded and healthy alike, and the terrible screams of the dying men could be heard by the soldiers waiting just outside the swamp. The 'mopping-up' exercise lasted two weeks altogether, and only 20 prisoners were taken (A Fuller, pers. comm.).

In December 1975 more than 40 people were attacked and eaten when their holiday boat sank in the crocodile-infested Malili River in Central Celebes, Indonesia.

The Nile crocodile also has a very bad reputation, and probably accounts for nearly 1000 people (mostly women and children) annually, although at one time when this species was more numerous the figure may have been as high as 20 000. One 15 ft 3 in 4·65 m male shot in the Kihange River, Central Africa by a professional hunter allegedly killed 400 people over a period of years, but Guggisberg (1972) believes this figure was highly exaggerated and was only quoted 'to justify the mass slaughter of crocodiles'.

The strength of the crocodile is quite appalling. Deraniyagala (1939) mentions a crocodile in N Australia which seized and dragged into the river a magnificent 1 tonne Suffolk stallion which had recently been imported from England, despite the fact that this breed of horse can exert a pull of more than 2 tonnes, and there is at least one record of a full-grown black rhinoceros losing a tug-of-war with a big crocodile. Sometimes, however, even crocodiles over-estimate their own strength. One day in the 1860s a hunter named Lesley was a witness when a saurian seized the hind-leg of a large bull African elephant while it was bathing in a river in Natal. The crocodile was promptly dragged up the bank by the enraged tusker and then squashed flat by one of its companions who had hurried to the rescue. The victorious elephant then picked up the bloody carcase with its trunk and lodged it in the fork of a nearby tree (Stokes, 1953). Oswell (1894) says he twice found the skeletons of crocodiles 15 ft 4·6 m up in trees by the river's bank where they had been thrown by angry elephants. On another occasion a surprised crocodile suddenly found itself dangling

15 ft *4·6 m* in mid-air when it foolishly seized a drinking giraffe by the head.

Frank Lane (1955) says that tests carried out in France to determine the jaw strength of a 120 lb *54 kg* crocodile revealed that it could exert a crushing pressure of 1540 lbf *6·85 kN*. On this basis, a crocodile weighing 1 tonne could exert a force of nearly 13 tonnes-force (*cf* human jaws which can exert a 500 lbf *2·22 kN* crushing pressure).

Very little information has been published on the life-spans of crocodilians, but some species probably live longer than 50 years in the wild state. On the strength of its comparatively slow growth rate after sexual maturity, Cott is of the opinion that very large Nile crocodiles (i.e. 18 ft *5·5 m*) must be at least 100 years old, and that outsized examples may be as much as 200 years, but further study is needed before any definite statements can be made. According to Neill toothlessness and other signs of senility are always evident in alligators that have lived for about 50 years; he puts the maximum age as 'not much beyond this', and there is no reason to believe that crocodiles are longer-lived than alligators.

The greatest authentic age recorded for a croco-dilian is 66 years for an American alligator which arrived at Adelaide Zoo, S Australia on 5 June 1914 as a two-year-old and died there on 26 September 1978 after spending 64 years 3 months in captivity (Robert Baker, pers. comm.). Another female received at the Maritime Museum Aquarium, Gothenburg, Sweden on 17 May 1924 was still alive in December 1980 aged 58 years (Goran Sundstrom, pers. comm.).

Another example known as 'Jean-qui-rit' ('Laughing John') reputedly lived in the Menagerie du Jardin des Plantes, Paris for 85 years (1852–4 April 1937), but Flower has questioned the validity of this record. The same authority does cite, however, a reliable record of 50 years for a Chinese alligator (*Alligator sinensis*) which was still living in the Frankfurt Zoo, Germany on 8 September 1936 (probably killed during the Second World War), and says another one lived in Leipzig Zoo for 52 years.

London Zoo's famous American alligator 'George' was reputedly about 60 years old at the time of his death in 1952, but only 41 years were spent in captivity. When he was received in 1912 he was described as sexually mature, measuring 6 ft *1·8 m* in length, but this size is reached at the age of *c* six years. In other words, 'George' was probably nearer 47 years of age than 60.

The famous Nile crocodile 'Lutembe', who lived

The female American alligator which lived for 66 years.

for a number of years in a small bay in the Murchison Gulf, Lake Victoria and used to come ashore to be fed with fish when called, reputedly started her career in the nineteenth century as royal executioner to the Kings of Uganda, but this report was never substantiated. When she became world-famous in the 1920s, however, she was already a big animal (*c* 14 ft *4·3 m*) and must have been at least 25 years old. There is no record of her death, but Guggisberg says she 'disappeared' during the 1940s.

Today the commercial hunting of crocodilians for their skins, and man's hatred of them, has reduced the world's population to such an extent that 16 species have now been brought to the brink of extinction.

The rarest crocodilian in the world is the Chinese alligator of the lower Yangtze River of Anhwei and Kiangsi provinces which is now probably extinct in the wild state.

In 1980 there were less than 200 examples of the Siamese crocodile (*Crocodylus siamensis*) left in the wild, all of them confined to the Beung Borapet Reservoir in Nakorn Sawan Province, but this species is bred commercially in large numbers at Samut Prakan crocodile farm in Bangkok.

Crocodilians are excellent swimmers, and this ability was really put to the test in 1901 when Frank C Bostock, the English animal trainer, put a 7 ft *2·1 m* long Nile crocodile in the river above Niagara Falls to see what would happen. Up until then no creature of comparable size had ever survived a trip over the mighty cataract and Bostock was hoping his protege would be the first one to come through the terrifying ordeal with flying colours. Below the falls a dozen men were already in position on both banks of the river where they could see the crocodile if and when it swam into the calmer waters. Twelve minutes after being towed out into the fast current the unsuspecting saurian was swept over the top and plunged into the abyss. For 90 minutes there was no sign of life but, just as the observers were about to give up their weary vigil, the beast was spotted further up river making for the bank, apparently none the worse for its experience. After recapture it ate a hearty meal of fish!

The largest reptile – (excluding snakes) – found in Britain is the slow-worm (*Anguis fragilis*), which is widely distributed over England, Wales and Scotland. A female example collected in Midhurst, Sussex measured 460 mm *18·1 in* (head and body 215 mm *8·46 in*, tail 245 mm *9·65 in*), and a male from Dorset 427 mm *16·8 in*.

The smallest species of reptile is believed to be

Sphaerodactylus parthenopion, a tiny gecko found only on the island of Virgin Gorda, one of the British Virgin Islands, in the West Indies. It is known from only 15 specimens, including some gravid females, collected by Richard Thomas (1965) of Miami, Florida, USA and a colleague between 10 and 16 August 1964. The three largest mature females measured 18 mm *0·71 in* from snout to vent, with a tail of approximately the same length.

The smallest reptile found in Britain is the widely-distributed common lizard (*Lacerta vivipara*). Adult males measure 118–170 mm *4·56–6·69 in* in total length and adult females 121–178 mm *4·76–7·01 in* (Smith, 1951). The weight range is 8–15 g *0·28–0·53 oz*.

The highest speed ever recorded for a reptile on dry land is 18 miles/h *29 km/h* for a six-lined racerunner (*Cnemidophorus sexlineatus*) pursued by J Southgate Hoyt (1941) in a car near McCormick, South Carolina, USA. This lizard maintained its speed on all four legs for more than a minute before darting off the clay road into the undergrowth.

The largest living lizard is the Komodo monitor or Ora (*Varanus komodo*), a dragon-like reptile found on the Indonesian islands of Komodo, Rintja, Padar and Flores. Adult males average 8 ft 6 in *2·59 m* in total length and weigh 175–200 lb *79–91 kg*, and adult females 7 ft 6 in *2·29 m* and 150–160 lb *68–73 kg*.

As with crocodiles, the size attained by this giant lizard has been greatly over-estimated. Major P A Ouwens, the Curator of the Botanical Gardens at Buitenzorg, Java, who first described this animal in 1912, was informed by J K van Steyn van Hensbroek, Governor of Flores, that two Dutchmen working for a pearl-fishing company on Komodo had told him that they had killed several specimens measuring between 6 and 7 m *19 ft 8 in* and *23 ft*. Another ferocious monster seen by a Swedish zoologist on the shores of Komodo in 1937 was estimated to have 'measured seven metres', and the following year an American journalist reported that he had seen one measuring 14 ft 6 in *4·42 m*.

All of these statements, however, were based on visual estimates – the great girths of older specimens create an impression of enormous size – or referred to estuarine crocodiles which are also found in the area.

According to Ouwens the type specimen, now mounted in the Museum at Buitenzorg, measured 2·9 m *9 ft 6 in* between pegs. Another one collected by Nelly de Rooij (1915) on the west coast of Flores in 1915 was 2·66 m *8 ft 8¾ in* long, and the largest of the four monitors collected by the Duke of Mecklenburg in 1923 was just under 3 m *9 ft 10 in*. Of the 54 specimens collected by the Douglas Burden

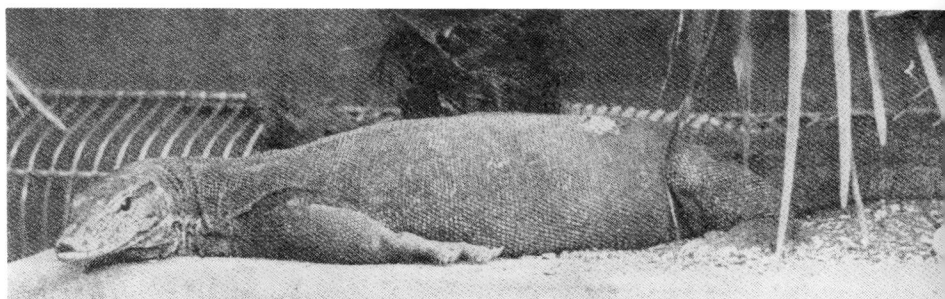

The world's smallest known reptile alongside a signet ring for comparison of size.

The Komodo monitor – the largest living lizard. This exceptionally bulky male specimen measured 10 ft 2 in 3·10 m in length and weighed 365 lb 165 kg.

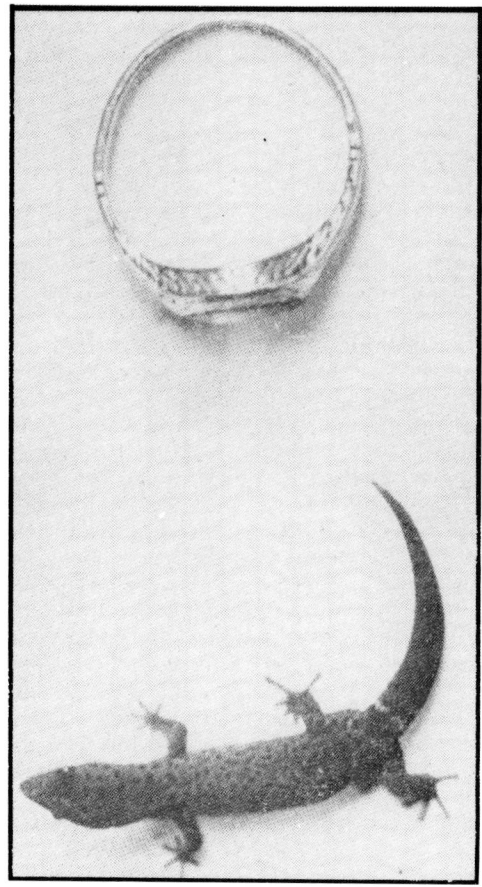

The Salvadori monitor, the longest known lizard. This semi-adult specimen was just over 9 ft 2·7 m in total length.

specimen, and the 10 ft 0¾ in 3·07 m male which the Sultan of Bima presented to an American zoologist in 1928, were probably one and the same animal.

Although the Komodo monitor is strictly protected by the Indonesian Government, it is now a threatened species mainly as a result of local hunting (the flesh is very palatable). The total population is estimated at c 6000 individuals, 900 of which are on Komodo itself and the rest in special reserves on Rintja, Padar, Gili Mota, Owadi Sami and Flores.

The longest lizard in the world is the Salvadori monitor (*Varanus salvadori*) of the E Highlands of Papua New Guinea, which was not described until 1878. Very little is known about this reptile, but adult males regularly exceed 10 ft 3·1 m in total length. Nearly 70 per cent of the measurement, however, is taken up by the exceptionally long tail. The largest specimen seen by Dr F Barker (pers. comm.) of the Dept of Natural Resources (Wildlife Branch) at Konedobu measured 10 ft 7 in 3·23 m, but on another occasion village collectors gave him a piece of rope measuring 15 ft 1 in 4·60 m which they claimed was the total length of a newly-killed individual, and he said there was no reason for him to doubt the accuracy of the report. Another male examined

Expedition to Komodo in 1926, the largest measured 9 ft 0½ in 2·76 m, and the biggest male taken by the Dutch zoologist De Jong (1932) on his second visit to the islands was exactly 9 ft 2·7 m.

The largest accurately measured Komodo monitor on record was probably a male which was exhibited in the St Louis Zoological Park, Missouri, USA for a short period c 1937. This specimen measured 10 ft 2 in 3·10 m in length and tipped the scales at a staggering 365 lb 165·6 kg. Nothing is known of this giant lizard's earlier history but this personally by Michael Pope (pers. comm.) of Port Moresby was 15 ft 7 in *4·75 m* long, and he was told this lizard sometimes reached a length of over 20 ft *6·1 m*. In 1980 an international team of scientists and young explorers from the around-the-world sailing expedition 'Operation Drake' reportedly caught an 18 ft *5·5 m* monitor in swampland near the Gulf of Papua, but this measurement was in error. The largest specimen brought into Masingara by a native hunter was an immature male measuring 2 m *6 ft 6¾ in*, but zoologist Ian Redmond later sighted another one which he estimated at 12 ft *3·7 m*. According to the local population this latter animal had killed and eaten a man two years previously, but although Salvadori's monitor is armed with fearsome claws and regularly feeds on carrion, it is basically a timid creature and takes rapidly to the trees when frightened. That is why the Papuans called it the 'pukpuk bilong tri' (tree-crocodile), although unlike its larger relative it is not known to swim or even like water.

In *c*1964 one of these very impressive looking reptiles measuring nearly 10 ft *3·0 m* in length was captured in the Fly River area and sent to Taronga Zoo, Sydney, NSW, Australia. The body was black, spotted with yellow, and the tail had irregular broad and narrow yellow bands.

This species is often confused with the similar-sounding Salvator monitor (*Varanus salvator*) of Malaysia which has been measured up to 9 ft *2·7 m*.

The greatest authentic age recorded for a lizard is 'more than 54 years' for a male slow-worm kept in the Zoological Museum at Copenhagen, Denmark from 1892 until 1946. At the age of 45+ years this specimen mated with a female known to be at least 20 years old (Kai Curry Lindahl, pers. comm.).

No other species of lizard lives anywhere near as long. The closest approach is made by the Komodo monitor which probably lives 20–30 years in the wild state, but the greatest authentic age recorded for a captive specimen is 9 years 3 months (Flower, 1937). The Gila monster (*Heloderma suspectum*) has lived for 20 years in captivity (Conant and Hudson, 1949).

The only known venomous lizards are the Gila monster and the bearded lizard (*Heloderma horridum*) of the SW USA and parts of Mexico. Both species carry sufficient neurotoxic venom to kill two adult humans, but this quantity is very seldom injected in natural bites. In one series of 34 cases of people bitten by these desert reptiles – they have very powerful jaws and hang on like grim death once they get a grip – there were eight fatalities. The majority of these attacks, however, took place in zoos or laboratories, and most of the dead victims were in bad health – or

drunk – at the time of the incident (Bogert and Del Camp, 1956). In their natural habitat these lizards are peaceful animals and rarely intrude into territory occupied by man.

In January 1979 a new species of iguana was discovered on Yaduatabu in the Fiji Islands, SW Pacific. Specimens of this new reptile (locally named the Fijian crested iguana) were later given to Mrs Ivy Watkins of the Fijian Cultural Centre, Orchid Island, and when one of the females laid three eggs she removed them to her home where they were successfully incubated. This was the first known occasion a new species of animal had been bred in captivity before it had been given a scientific name – *Brachophylus vitiensis* – (Gwyn Watkins, pers. comm.).

The largest living chelonian is the Pacific leatherback turtle (*Dermochelys coriacea schlegeli*), also known as the 'Leathery turtle' or 'Luth', which ranges through the Pacific and Indian Oceans from British Columbia to Chile and west to Japan and eastern Africa.

The average adult measures 6–7 ft *1·8–2·1 m* from the tip of the beak to the end of the tail (length of carapace 4–5 ft *1·2–1·5 m*), about 7 ft *2·1 m* across the front flippers and weighs anything up to 1000 lb *45 kg*.

The greatest authentic weight recorded for a Pacific leatherback turtle is 1908 lb *865 kg* for a male captured *alive* in Monterey Bay, California, USA on 29 August 1961. The turtle was purchased by Nelson (Bill) Hyler, owner of the Wharf Aquarium, Monterey 'for several hundred dollars' and placed in a large tank, but the unfortunate creature succumbed shortly afterwards from shock. This specimen measured 8 ft 4 in *2·54 m* in total length (L Bowhay, pers. comm.).

Another huge leatherback caught in a fisherman's net near San Diego, California on 20 June 1907 was credited with a weight of 1902 lb *863 kg*, but Pritchard (1971) has queried the accuracy of this poundage because he says the carapace length was only 5 ft 2 in *1·57 m* (*cf* 5 ft 5 in *1·65 m* for a 988 lb *448 kg* individual).

The Atlantic leatherback turtle (*Dermochelys coriacea coriacea*), which ranges through the Atlantic Ocean, the Gulf of Mexico and the Caribbean from Newfoundland to the British Isles and south to Argentina and Cape of Good Hope, is smaller than its Pacific cousin and rarely exceeds 800 lb *363 kg*.

The greatest weight recorded for an Atlantic leatherback is 800 kg *1764 lb* for a male found trapped in a fishing net at Longeville, Vendee Dept, W France on 10 July 1972 (Duron, 1978), although the roundness of the figure suggests this avoirdupois was only roughly correct. Another specimen harpooned off Courdouan, Charente-Maritime Dept, W France in 1826 scaled 650 kg *1433 lb* (total length 2·28 m *7 ft 5¾ in*) (Dugay, 1968), and one weighing 600 kg *1323 lb* (total length 2·45 m *8 ft 0½ in*) was caught 8 miles *12·9 km* east of Suroit de Chassiron in the same Dept on 22 October 1977 (now on display in Rochelle Museum). The leatherback also reaches an exceptional size in waters off Southern Africa and Pritchard mentions a specimen caught near Laaiplek, W South Africa which scaled 1420 lb *644 kg.*

Some large examples have also been taken in British waters. One of the heaviest actually to be weighed was a male which drowned after it became entangled with lobster lines off Crail, Fife, E Scotland on 27 November 1967. It measured 6 ft 4 in *1·93 m* in total length, 7 ft 4 in *2·24 m* across the front flippers and weighed 772 lb *350 kg.* A replica of this turtle is now on display in the Royal Scottish Museum, Edinburgh (A S Clarke, pers. comm.).

On 10 July 1962 what may have been the largest turtle ever recorded in British waters was caught in the fishing nets of the *Castle Moil* off South Minch, Barra, Outer Hebrides. Unfortunately the rope snapped when the crew tried to hoist the struggling giant aboard with a power-winch, and both net and turtle were lost. The men, however, estimated the total length of the animal at 12 ft *3·7 m* (Brongersma, 1972). This was obviously an exaggerated guess, but any chelonian heavy enough to break a nylon rope with a breaking strain of 1 tonne must be something of a superlative! According to the Rev Angus J McQueen of Barra (pers. comm.) this monster was later washed ashore on the west coast of North Uist still entangled in the net, 'but no measurements were taken.

The largest freshwater turtle in the world is the alligator snapping turtle (*Macrochelys temminckii*) of the SE USA. The normal upper weight limit for this species is about 200 lb *91 kg*, but there is an unconfirmed record of 403 lb *183 kg* for a monster caught in the Neosho River in Cherokee County, Kansas in 1937 (Hall and Smith, 1947).

The smallest marine turtle in the world is the Atlantic ridley (*Lepidochelys kempii*), which has a shell length measurement of 50–70 cm *19·7–27·6 in* and does not exceed 80 lb *36·3 kg.*

The smallest freshwater turtle is the striped mud turtle (*Kinosternon baurii baurii*) which ranges from southern Georgia south through the Florida Keys, USA. It has a maximum shell length of only 97 mm *3·82 in* (Oliver, 1955).

Several species of turtles are renowned for their aggressive behaviour towards man, but poor eyesight may have something to do with this! Probably the most vicious of them all is the Atlantic loggerhead (*Caretta caretta*) which occasionally enters the Mediterranean.

A 1323 lb 600 kg leatherback turtle caught near Lourenco Marques, Mozambique in May 1970.

During the Second World War an RAF plane was shot down off Malta and the crew took to a dinghy. Suddenly a huge loggerhead reared up before them and attempted to demolish the rubber craft with its strong, curved beak, and it was only after a desperate struggle that the airmen managed to drive off the chelonian.

The Pacific loggerhead turtle (*Lepidochelys olivacea*) also has a bad reputation, and in Sri Lanka it is known as the 'Nai amai' (dog turtle) because it bites savagely when caught (Deraniyagala, 1939).

In May 1972 a skin-diver was attacked by an amorous short-sighted Atlantic green turtle (*Chelonia mydas*) off the coast of Florida, USA during the breeding season and was lucky to escape with his life – let alone his honour! – because the males of this sub-species go in for 'love bites' which leaves deep, bleeding wounds.

The Pacific leatherback turtle is another dangerous chelonian on account of its great size, and there is a record of one biting off the big toe of a fisherman near Sydney, NSW, Australia.

The alligator snapping turtle also has an evil temper and is well named. Raymond L Ditmars (1936) complained that he could never take a photograph of this species without being confronted by a pair of enormously wide jaws, and on one occasion an angry male bit a leg off his camera tripod.

The greatest authentic age recorded for a turtle is 58 years 9 months 1 day for an alligator snapping turtle which was accidentally killed in Philadelphia Zoo, Pennsylvania, USA on 7 February 1949. This specimen was one of two alligator snapping turtles received at the zoo on 6 May 1890. The other example died on 10 December 1937 after living in captivity for 47 years 7 months and 4 days (Roger Conant, pers. comm.).

The stinkpot (*Strenotherus odoratus*) of the SE USA is another long-lived turtle, and there is a record of one living for more than 53 years 3 months in Philadelphia Zoo (Conant and Hudson, 1949).

The maximum life potential of marine turtles is not known, but a small group of Atlantic loggerheads lived in the Vasco de Gama Aquarium in Lisbon, Portugal from 1898 to 1931. Major Stanley Flower (1937) says they all died suddenly during an exceptional heatwave. It is virtually impossible to keep leatherback turtles in captivity for any length of time because their diet consists almost entirely of jellyfish which they eat in prodigious quantities; also, being soft-skinned, they are more prone to injure themselves in a confined space. In the natural state, however, they are probably very long-lived. According to a recent study of marked green turtles in Hawaiian waters this species may take as long as 50 years to reach maturity!

The rarest marine turtle is the protected Atlantic ridley which has been practically exterminated by over-fishing, nest robbing (unfortunately the eggs are supposed to be an aphrodisiac) and the slaughter of breeding females. In 1947 the total mature population exceeded 160 000. Today the only known breeding site is Rancho Nuevo, Tamaulipas, on the Gulf coast of Mexico, and in 1977 only 450 females hauled up on the beaches there (Cherfas, 1978). The following year, as part of America's aid programme to Mexico, the US Coastguard flew 2000 eggs to a remote island where it was hoped the hatched turtles would set up another breeding colony.

The fastest-swimming tetrapods are the powerful marine turtles, and in particular the beautifully streamlined leatherback. The normal cruising speed is 3–4 knots (3·5–4·6 miles/h *5·6–7·4 km/h*), but this can probably be increased fourfold in an emergency. Deraniyagala (1939) claims the green turtle can reach 10 m/s (19·4 knots 22·4 miles/h *36·0 km/h*) when travelling flat out, but although this chelonian is a remarkably good swimmer it is not a truly pelagic species like the leatherback which does not have the encumbrance of a heavy bony shell.

Some marine turtles also migrate over great distances. There is a record of a female *Chelonia mydas* tagged at Tortuguero, Costa Rica being recovered near Campeche, Mexico having swum 1219 miles *1960 km* in 275 days (Carr and Hirth, 1962), and in September 1972 another female tagged at Surinam, NE South America by members of the World Wildlife Fund organisation was found on a beach in Ghana, West Africa, having travelled 3700 miles *5950 km*. The Atlantic loggerhead is another confirmed wanderer, and one female tagged at Mon Repos, Australia was recovered 63 days later in the Trobriand Islands near New Guinea, having swum 2000 miles *3200 km* if the coastline was followed (Bustard and Limpus, 1970).

In 1980 American scientists strapped a satellite transmitter to the back of an Atlantic green turtle so that they could study its movements. For several months the animal dutifully swam around in the Gulf of Mexico, then – to the trackers' astonishment – suddenly moved 400 miles *640 km* inland! Later it was discovered that the chelonian had jettisoned the transmitter on a beach and a Kansas farmer was using it as a doorstop!

The largest living tortoise is *Geochelone gigantea* of the Indian Ocean islands of Aldabra, the Seychelles, the Amirante Islands and Mauritius (introduced).

The upper weight limit for males in the wild is about 450 lb *204 kg*, but much heavier captive specimens have been recorded. One male preserved in the Rothschild Museum at Tring, Hertfordshire has a carapace length between perpendiculars of 46·5 in *118 cm*, and the Hon Walter Rothschild (1915) says this giant tortoise weighed 593 lb *269 kg* when alive. Another male named 'Marmaduke' received at London Zoo in 1951 recorded a peak weight of 616 lb *279 kg* before his death on 27 January 1963 (David Ball, pers. comm.). Both these chelonians, however, were exceeded in size by an enormous *Geochelone g. daudinii* from Egmont Island in the Chagos Archipelago, which Rothschild deposited at London Zoo at the beginning of this century. Unfortunately the weight of this giant was not recorded, but as it had a carapace length of 55 in *140 cm*, it could hardly have scaled less than 700 lb *318 kg*.

Of the 11 surviving races of giant tortoise found in

An unusual upside-down view of a Galapagos giant tortoise. Notice its huge feet.

the Galapagos Islands, E Pacific only *Geochelone e. elephantopus*, *G. e. becki* and *G. e. guntheri* of Albemarle, *G. e. porteri* of Indefatigable and *G. e. darwini* of James regularly exceed 40 in *102 cm* in carapace length and a weight of 350 lb *159 kg*. The largest sub-species is *G. e. porteri*, and Pritchard (1967) says males have been known to measure 48 in *122 cm* in carapace length and weigh 600 lb *272 kg*. When Woodes Rogers, the English privateer, arrived in the Galapagos in 1708 he said he saw giant tortoises over 4 ft *1·2 m* high, and two of his crewmen came across one on Indefatigable which they estimated to weigh over 700 lb *318 kg*. Another specimen collected by Capt David Porter, the American naval officer, in *c* 1813, measured 66 in *168 cm* in length and 54 in *137 cm* across, but these figures must have been obtained over the curve.

Although tortoises are the longest-lived of all vertebrates, including man, reports that they sometimes survive for 250 or even 300 years can be discounted. Many exaggerated claims have been based on the mistaken belief that (1) tortoises have a very slow rate of growth and (2) scarred and rubbed shells are reliable evidence of great age. In reality, however, size is not a trustworthy indication of extreme longevity in reptiles, and in the wild chelonian shells are generally so badly worn after 20 years or so that it is difficult to trace the annual growth rings. Also, in hot weather, the tortoise might develop more than one ring that year.

On 19 May 1966 the death was reported of 'Tu'imalilia' (King of the Malilia), the famous but much-battered Madagascar radiated tortoise (*Testudo radiata*), reputedly presented to the King of Tonga by

Captain James Cook in 1773, but this record was probably a composite of two (or more) individuals whose periods of residence on the island overlapped.

The giant tortoises have also been credited with extreme life-spans on account of their great size, but since it has been discovered that males can attain a weight of 450 lb *204 kg* in only 15 years – one individual increased its weight from 29 lb *13 kg* to 350 lb *159 kg* in 7 years! – there is no reason to believe that they live longer than smaller species of tortoise.

In 1975 an unconfirmed age of 180 years was reported for a *G. gigantea* from Aldabra living in the Pamplemousses Royal Botanical Gardens, Mauritius, and in 1980 another individual reportedly celebrated his 140th birthday in the Menagerie du Jardin des Plantes, Paris, France (Marie-Claude Demontoy, pers. comm.).

The greatest authentic age recorded for a tortoise is 152+ years for a male Marion's tortoise (*Geochelone sumeirei*) brought from the Seychelles to Mauritius in 1766 by the Chevalier de Fresne, the French explorer, who presented it to the Port Louis army garrison. When the British captured Mauritius in 1810 the tortoise, the last surviving member of its species, was officially handed over to the British troops by the surrendering French forces. In 1908 the ancient mascot went blind, and 10 years later it was accidentally killed when it fell through a gun emplacement. This specimen is now preserved in the British Museum and as it was fully mature at the time of its capture Schmidt and Inger (1957) say its actual age 'may be estimated at not less than 180 years'.

A Mediterranean spur-thighed tortoise (*Testudo graeca*) lived in the grounds of Lambeth Palace, London from 1633 until 1753, and even then its death was attributed to the neglect of the gardener rather

The royal Tonga tortoise 'Tu'imalilia', which reputedly lived for nearly 200 years.

than to old age. In 1957 another specimen named 'Panchard' died in Paignton Zoo, Devon aged 116+ years. This tortoise was bought at a fair in 1851, at which time it was already fully adult (W E Francis, pers. comm.). There is also a reliable record of a European pond-tortoise (*Emys orbicularis*) living 120+ years (Rollinat, 1934).

Extreme longevity records based on dates carved in the shells of turtles (in the USA the word 'turtle' is used for a number of land species) are not generally considered reliable because they may have been put there by pranksters, but one or two claims may be genuine. A common box turtle (*Terrapene carolina*) found in Connecticut in June 1927 was marked with the date 1809, but Ditmars (1936) says the shell was so smooth that the figures could only be read with difficulty. Another turtle discovered in a backyard in Pensacola, Florida in 1979 had the date 1860 scratched on its shell, and Oliver (1955) mentions one which was 138 years old.

With the possible exception of chamaeleons (*Chamaeleonidae*) tortoises move slower than any other reptile. Tests carried out on a *Geochelone gigantea* in Mauritius revealed that even when hungry and enticed by a cabbage it could not cover more than 5 yd *4·6 m* in a minute (=0·17 mile/h *0·27 km/h*). Over longer distances its speed was greatly reduced.

In addition to being very slow in life, tortoises also take their time about dying. Francesco Redi, the 17th century Italian physician, once carried out a series of gruesome experiments to determine the vitality of these reptiles, and the results were staggering. One hapless tortoise which had its brain removed continued to grope its way about for another six months before it died, and when Redi examined the brain cavity afterwards he found it was as empty and clean as he had left it with the exception of one small clot of dry blood. Another individual which was decapitated did not expire until 23 days later, but although the headless trunk did not move about like the one which had been robbed of its brain it reacted to mechanical stimulus.

The rarest tortoise in the world is the protected Western Australian swamp tortoise (*Pseudomydora umbrina*) which is confined to Ellen Brook and Twin reserves about 12 miles *19 km* NE of Perth. In 1973 the total population was estimated at 150 animals, but by 1978 fewer than 50 still survived in the wild (each tortoise carries a homing device). In addition, Perth Zoo has held a total of 39 individuals since November 1963, 14 of which later died. Four others 'disappeared' including a very young one, which was later exhibited in Europe (Spencer *et al*, 1979).

Of the six recognised giant snakes (*Boidae*) the reticulated python (*Python reticulatus*) of the Indo-Malaysian region, Indonesia and the Philippines is the only species which *regularly* exceed 20 ft *6·1 m* in length.

One of the largest specimens on record was a female killed in Penang settlement, Malaysia in October 1859, and *The Times* carried the following report: 'A monster boa-constrictor was killed one morning this week by the overseer of convicts at Bayam Lepas, on the road to Telo' Kumbar. His attention was attracted by the squealing of a pig, and on going to the place he found it in the coils of the snake. A few blows from the changkolks of the convicts served to despatch the reptile, and on uncoiling him he was found to be twenty-eight feet in length and thirty-two inches in girth.'

A female shot near Taiping, Perak State, Malaya in the late 1800s measured 27 ft *8·2 m* in length and yielded a 33 ft *10·1 m* skin which is now preserved in the British Museum.

In June 1974 a length of 29 ft *8·8 m* was reported for another female killed by a group of Dyaks in Malaysia after it had just swallowed a pig.

The greatest authentic length recorded for a reticulated python is exactly 10 m *32 ft 9¾ in* for a monstrous individual shot near a mining camp on the north coast of Celebes Island in the Malay Archipelago in 1912. An account of this snake was given by Henry C Raven (1946), the American explorer and animal collector: 'I crossed the Strait of Macassar in my little schooner and sailed along the north coast of Celebes. Stopping near a mining camp at a place where there was a good harbour, I left the schooner and went inland a short distance to camp on the mountains, which were covered with virgin jungle.

'The white men at the mine told me of a huge python one of their natives had killed a few days before my arrival, and showed me a very poor photograph of it after it had been killed and dragged to camp. Though the print was dull, you could see a man standing on the huge body, which was about a foot thick. The civil engineer told me it was just ten metres . . . I asked him if he had paced off its length, but he said no, he had measured it with a surveying tape. No part of the animal was preserved. It had been rainy weather when it was killed, and on account of the dampness not even the skin was kept. I visited the place where the carcase had been cast aside. There was only the odour, and a few little pieces of bone left.'

This measurement is probably very near the upper size limit for any species of constrictor in terms of efficient locomotory power on land. This is because the surface of the internal organs becomes relatively smaller with increases in body mass. Eventually a point is reached where these organs can no longer cope with essential metabolic processes, which is why the biggest fossil snakes *Gigantophis* and *Madtsoia* did not exceed 10–11 m *33–36 ft*. Unfortunately many people often forget that all animals must live within the laws of physics and chemistry, and the height of absurdity was reached in February 1980 when an Indonesian newspaper carried the following item:

'A giant python was crushed by a bulldozer at a forest project in N Bengkulu, SW Sumatra. The snake contained four human corpses, two of which appeared to have been recently devoured as they were still in their shorts and trousers. The operator of the bulldozer battled for over an hour with the two mammoth snakes, each reported to be about 25 metres (82·5 ft) long, before one snake was killed and the other escaped. Larger snakes have been reported.'

The largely aquatic anaconda (*Eunectes murinus*) of the swamps, lakes and slow-moving rivers of tropical South America and Trinidad has also been credited with the title of 'longest snake in the world' but although it is the heaviest of the giant serpents – a 17 ft *5·2 m* anaconda will scale as much as a 24 ft *7·3 m* reticulated python – great bulk can often be misleading when it comes to estimating length.

To prove this point A Hyatt Verrill (1937) once asked the other members of an animal-collecting expedition he was leading in Guyana to estimate the length of an anaconda they had spotted curled up on a rock. The estimates varied from 20 ft *6·1 m* to 60 ft *18·3 m*, but when the snake was shot and straightened out it was found to measure exactly 19 ft 6 in *5·9 m*, although it was exceptionally bulky and scaled 360 lb *163 kg*.

Also complicating the issue is the fact that the anaconda has probably been the subject of more exaggerated claims regarding its size than any other living animal. The early Spanish settlers called it 'matatora' (bull-killer) and spoke of individuals measuring 60–80 ft *18–24 m*, but even larger snakes have been reported.

In January 1948, for instance, a 'sucuriju gigante' (giant boa) measuring 40 m *131 ft* in length and weighing an estimated 5 tonnes was allegedly captured *alive* after a band of Indians found it sleeping off a heavy meal on the banks of the Amazon. The snake was later towed to Manaos, W Brazil by river tug where it was the object of some curiosity until its life was snuffed out by a burst of machine-gun fire (Dinsdale, 1966). Later the same year another one measuring 35 m *115 ft* was reportedly killed at Fort Abunda in the Guapore District, SW Brazil after it had crawled into the old fortifications (Heuvelmans, 1958), and in 1954 a length of 36 m *118 ft* was quoted for another serpentine colossus shot by a Brazilian army patrol at Amapa on the French Guiana border (Gregor, 1962). Needless to say nothing was pre-

served of any of these outsized individuals, and two published photographs were valueless because no yardsticks were given.

Fortunately some of the early explorers and naturalists who visited South America were much more critical in their accounts of this giant snake. Capt J G Stedman (1796), for example, who travelled extensively in the Guianas between 1772 and 1777, said the largest anaconda killed by him measured 22 ft 4 in *6·8 m*. Sir Robert Schomburgk (1847–48), the German explorer, collected one in British Guiana which taped exactly 18 ft *5·49 m*, and Alfred Wallace (1853), who explored large parts of Amazonia, wrote that he never saw an anaconda over 20 ft *6·1 m*, although he was told by his native bearers that they were sometimes 60–80 ft *18–24 m*.

Nicholas Guppy (1963) collected an anaconda in the Yampari River, Guyana which measured 17 ft 3 in *5·26 m* and had a maximum girth of 28 in *71 cm* (it had just constricted an 8 ft *2·4 m* alligator), and on another occasion he shot a much larger example on the banks of the Kassikaityu River in the extreme south of that country. Unfortunately this one fell into very deep water and could not be recovered, but Guppy and the rest of his party all agreed that the snake must have been at least 27 ft *8·2 m* long.

Many extreme measurements have been based on the lengths of skins, but these records are unreliable. It is virtually impossible to remove the skin of a snake without stretching it by at least 10 per cent, and in the case of the anaconda and other heavy snakes the skin can be *deliberately stretched* without causing much distortion to the markings by 30 per cent or more.

The American Consul at Iquitos, Peru told Leonard Clark, the American explorer, that many of the anaconda skins brought to the city by traders each year measured 40 ft *12·2 m*, and Thomas Barbour claims he saw a 45 ft *13·7 m* skin (Perry, 1970).

In the 1920s Raymond L Ditmars, Curator of Reptiles at New York Zoological Park personally offered $1000 to anyone who could supply him with an anaconda skin measuring over 40 ft *12·2 m,* but the money was never claimed.

One of the longest anacondas ever captured was a tremendously bulky individual shot by W L Schurz (1962) in Brazil which measured 27 ft 9 in *8·46 m* in length and had a maximum girth of 44 in *1·12 m*. Its weight was not recorded, but a snake of these dimensions would probably scale about 450 lb *204 kg*. Clark collected another one near Iquitos which taped 26 ft 9 in *8·15 m*, and an anaconda measuring 26 ft 3 in *8·00 m* was killed in Pernambuco State, E Brazil in *c* 1948. A 26 ft *7·9 m* female shot in Nariva Swamp, Trinidad contained a 5 ft *1·5 m* alligator in her stomach (Oliver, 1963), while the 10 m *32 ft 10 in* skin in the Butantan Institute, Sao Paulo came from a specimen measuring over 25 ft *7·6 m* (Ditmars, 1933).

Another anaconda measuring more than 24 ft *7·3 m* and weighing 350 lb *159 kg* was over-powered by thirteen Indians near the mouth of the Kassikaitu River, Guyana after they found it asleep on the bank. It was later air-lifted to the USA but arrived in poor condition and died soon afterwards (Brock, 1967).

Some large anacondas have also been found on the tableland straddling the borders of Bolivia and Brazil which gave Sir Arthur Conan Doyle the idea for his book *The Lost World*. In 1980 British geologist Martin Litherland spent 3 months exploring this 100-mile *160-km* long tract of land, with a Bolivian geologist and four Indians, and he says they shot one anaconda measuring well over 20 ft *6·1 m* in length.

Dr Afranio do Amaral (1948), Brazil's leading herpetologist, accepted a record of an 11·28 m *37 ft* anaconda, and he said another snake killed in southern Brazil in 1913 by a group of Indians was over 11·6 m *38 ft*, but these measurements were based solely on written evidence supplied by witnesses. He concluded that the maximum length reached by the anaconda was somewhere between 12 m *39 ft 4 in* and 14 m *45 ft 11 in*.

If, for the sake of argument, we accept these extreme measurements, then we are talking about an animal weighing at least 1200 lb *544 kg*, and no constrictor could possibly drag that sort of poundage around on dry land without over-stretching its resources. Only the medium of water could support that kind of bulk, which would probably explain why so few large anacondas have been collected on terra firma. By the time a length of 28–30 ft *8·5–9·1 m* is reached the snake is so heavy that it is forced to live permanently in a river or lake.

In November 1956 an anaconda measuring 10·25 m *33 ft 7½ in* was reportedly killed on the lower Rio Guaviare, SE Colombia, but nothing of the snake was saved.

Another outsized individual shot near the Colombia–Venezuela border was credited with a length of 37 ft 6 in *11·43 m*, and this may well have been the largest accurately measured anaconda on record. Roberto Lamon, a petroleum geologist told Dr Emmett R Dunn (1944), a leading authority on Colombian reptiles, that he encountered the snake when he was exploring for oil in the steppes of the Upper Orinoco River. One day he and his men had sat down on the bank of a slow-moving river to have lunch when one of them suddenly noticed an enormous snake in the water. The party immediately opened fire with their ·45 automatics, and when all writhings had ceased they dragged the huge serpent out of its aquatic environment and measured it with a steel surveyor's rule. Afterwards they went back to work, but when they returned later to skin the

specimen they found it had disappeared! Apparently the bullets had only stunned the creature, and in so doing had deprived the scientific world of badly needed evidence that such monsters do exist.

Col P H Fawcett shot an anaconda on the Rio Abunda not far from the confluence of the Rio Negro, western Brazil in 1907 which he said measured 62 ft *18·9 m* (45 ft *13·7 m* out of the water and 17 ft *5·2 m* in it), but as this snake had a maximum diameter of only 12 in *305 mm* (=circumference of 37·7 in *958 mm*), this length must be considered excessive. (A 24 ft *7·3 m* anaconda shot by Paul Fountain [1914] in Brazil had a maximum girth of 42 in *1·07 m*.)

On 24 July 1979 fisherman Francisco Barretto was attempting to free a tangled net in one of the lakes near Rocinha, NW Brazil when he was attacked by a huge snake about 2 ft *610 mm* wide and pulled under. The following day what remained of his body was washed up, the flesh torn away and the chest crushed. Since then the 'monster' has been sighted on several occasions.

The smaller and more lightly built *Eunectes notaeus* of the Paraguay and Lower Piranha rivers does not exceed 7 m *23 ft* (Amaral, 1976).

The African rock python (*Python sebae*) of tropical Africa is another large constrictor whose size has been grossly exaggerated. According to the historians of ancient Rome the army of Attilus Regulus, while laying siege to Carthage (a suburb of modern Tunis) was attacked by an enormous serpent which was destroyed only after a fierce battle. The skin of this earth-shaker, measuring 120 ft *36·6 m* in length, was sent to Rome where it was preserved in one of the temples. Suetonius, the Roman biographer and antiquarian, says another giant python measuring 75 ft *22·9 m* was exhibited in front of the Comitium in Rome, and one captured alive in Ethiopia for Ptolemy II and put on view at the royal palace in Alexandria was credited with a length of 45 ft *13·7 m*.

As recently as 1932 a python allegedly measuring 130 ft *39·6 m* was killed in the Semliki Valley, Central Africa but the snake was conveniently converted into stew by the local Bwambwa tribe before any reliable measurements could be taken!

In reality the adult African rock python averages about 16 ft *4·9 m*, but much larger individuals have been recorded. Arthur Loveridge (1929) measured the freshly removed skin of a python speared by natives on the bank of the Nigeri River near Norogoro, Tanzania and found that it was exactly 30 ft *9·1 m* long. He estimated that the snake must have taped about 25 ft *7·6 m* in the flesh, and said he was quite prepared to believe that this species sometimes reached 30 ft *9·1 m*. Three years later he was proved right when a python measuring an incredible

9·81 m *32 ft 2¼ in* was shot by Mrs Charles Beart in the grounds of a school in Bingerville, Ivory Coast, W Africa after it had been found in a hedge of bougainvillea (Pope, 1961). This must have been an outsized freak, however, because no snakes approaching anything like this size have been collected since.

In 1958 K H Kroff killed a 23 ft *7 m P. sebae* in N Rhodesia while following elephants and found a 5 ft *1·5 m* long Nile crocodile in its stomach.

Much more recently a former Belgian army helicopter pilot has given details of an outsized python he once spotted in a forest clearing in the Congo; but although he took a series of pictures from a *claimed* altitude of 500 ft *152 m*, they give no clue as to the true size of the constrictor (estimated length 40–50 ft *12–15 m*) and the snake could just as easily have been a big python photographed from only 50 ft *15·2 m* up.

The amethystine python (*Liasis amethystinus*) of NE Australia, New Guinea and the Philippines rarely exceeds 15 ft *4·6 m*. One large specimen killed at Maxwellton, N Queensland in 1927 measured 19 ft 6 in *5·94 m* (Oliver, 1958), and Lewis Roberts (pers. comm.) shot another python at Shiptons Flat, near Cooktown, Queensland in *c* 1970 which was exactly 20 ft *6·10 m*. S Dean (1954) measured one at 23 ft 8 in *7·2 m*, and unconfirmed lengths up to 24 ft *7·3 m* have been claimed for pythons killed in New Guinea. In 1948 Louis Robichaux shot an outsized individual at Greenhills, near Cairns, Queensland which measured 25 ft *7·6 m* and yielded a 28 ft *8·5 m* skin.

In the late 1940s the New York Zoological Society offered a reward of $5000 for a *living* example of any snake 30 ft *9·1 m* or more in length, but although several people in Thailand have been feeding large captive reticulated pythons for years in an effort to claim the money, none of them have been successful.

'We did receive a report in 1971 of a reticulated python 11 m *36 ft* long captured in the Celebes', writes Dr F Wayne King, Curator of Reptiles, 'but by the time Indonesian officials got to the locality the snake had been killed and burned. As more and more time goes by, I doubt that our reward for the giant snake will ever be collected. Too many constrictors are killed as vermin every time they are found by local people. This argues rather persuasively that the really large specimens are becoming fewer and fewer in numbers. This is also supported by the size of skins that are reaching the leather industry from all parts of the world.'

Another problem with captive giant snakes is that until very recently there was no really practical method of obtaining a precise measurement. Fortunately snake-breeder and collector John Cheetham (pers. comm.) has recently discovered a simple method of measuring large constrictors accurately, unaided and regardless of the creature's temperament, and the pocket-sized device based on a carpenter's rule should prove a boon to zoos and dealers alike in future who buy and sell their snakes on a footage basis.

The longest (and heaviest) snake ever held in captivity was a female reticulated python named 'Colossus' who died in Highland Park Zoo, Pennsylvania, USA on 15 April 1963. She arrived at the zoo on 10 August 1949 after being shipped to the USA from Singapore and was probably of Malayan origin. Her length then was 22 ft *6·7 m*. In June 1951 she measured 23 ft 3 in *7·09 m*, and by February 1954 her length had increased to 27 ft 2 in *8·28 m* (weight 295 lb *134 kg*). On 15 November 1956 she measured 28 ft 6 in *8·69 m*, having grown 16 in *406 mm* in the intervening 33 months. Her maximum girth before a feed was measured at 36 in *914 mm* on 2 March 1955, and she scaled 320 lb *145 kg* on 12 June 1957 (Barton and Allen, 1961). Shortly before her death she was credited with a length of 30 ft *9·1 m*, but this was not borne out by posthumous examination.

'The snake was measured after its death but it was fairly hard to get a good measurement,' said William B Allen Jr, Curator of Reptiles (pers. comm.). 'It was stiffened up and vertebrae had pulled together shrinking the snake. We had a measurement of over 24 feet, but this being put on the same ratio as a smaller snake dying and shrinking, we could add the difference that would have given us our 28 feet alive!

An autopsy revealed that several segments of the vertebrae were eaten almost completely through, along with several rib sections, by reptilian tuberculosis, and it was this factor, along with a lung infection and possibly old age, that contributed to this snake's death.

London Zoo's famous 'Agamemnon' was also of comparable size. This specimen was 21 ft *6·4 m* long when it arrived on 20 December 1935, and grew to just over 28 ft *8·5 m* by the time of its death on 22 November 1942. Another reticulated python named 'Praggers', presented to London Zoo by the late Duke of Windsor on 22 May 1922, was credited with a measurement of 24–25 ft *7·3–7·6 m* in 1935 and a length of *c* 30 ft *9·1 m* at the time of its demise on 31 August 1942, but the latter figure was an estimate. Both pythons were collected in Malaysia and were probably females despite their names.

Another reticulated python caught by Charles Mayer, the French animal-collector, in the State of Negri Sembilan, Malaya and brought back by him to Europe was stated to have measured 32 ft *9·8 m*. This snake later came into the hands of Henry Trefflich, the well-known New York wild-animal dealer, who confirmed this length after running a string along the curves of the body. (It took eight men to hold and straighten it out on the floor.) Later, however, he told Dr James Oliver (1958), Director of the

A 25ft 7·6 m reticulated python being force-fed at New York Zoological Park.

American Museum of Natural History, that he sold it as a 34 ft *10·4 m* specimen to compensate for contraction of the body! If the size reported is genuine, and there is no reason to doubt Trefflich's statement, this is the only known record of a captive snake reaching and possibly exceeding 30 ft *9·1 m* in length, but it would be nice to have more information on this mysterious giant.

On 3 April 1980 the death was reported of Adrian Nyoka's famous 260 lb *118 kg* reticulated python 'Cassius' at Knaresborough Zoo, Yorkshire. Although credited with a length of 27 ft 6 in *8·38 m*, this female was somewhat shorter in reality and measured about 25 ft 6 in *7·77 m* in the flesh. She was collected in Malaysia in 1972 and yielded a 29 ft *8·8 m* skin.

Adrian Nyoka with his famous reticulated python 'Cassius'.

Very few large anacondas have been exhibited in zoos because their great weight and natural habitat make capture and transfer extremely difficult.

The largest anaconda ever held in captivity was probably a Brazilian specimen received at Highland Park Zoo, Pittsburgh, Pennsylvania, USA on 13 June 1950. At the time of its arrival it measured 16 ft 4 in *4·98 m* (108 lb *49 kg*), and on 26 February 1954 it was found to be 18 ft 7 in *5·66 m* (160 lb *73 kg*). By 21 March 1957 it had attained a length of 19 ft 6 in *5·94 m* and a weight of 200 lb *91 kg*. On 10 July 1960 it measured 20 ft 7 in *6·27 m*, but died shortly afterwards without being weighed (Barton and Allen, 1961).

The longest snake found in Britain (three species) is the grass snake (*Natrix natrix*), also known as the 'ringed snake', which is found throughout southern England, parts of Wales and in Dumfries and Galloway, Scotland. Adult males average 660 mm *26 in* in length and adult females 760 mm *29·9 in* (Appleby, 1971). The longest accurately measured specimen on record was probably a female killed in South Wales in 1887 which measured 1775 mm *5 ft 10 in*, while another female also collected in South Wales was 1750 mm *5 ft 9 in* (Leighton, 1901).

The longest venomous snake in the world is the king cobra (*Ophiophagus hannah*), also called the hamadryad, of eastern India, China, the Malay Archipelago and the Philippines. Adult examples average 12–13 ft *3·7–4·0 m* in length and weigh about 15 lb *6·8 kg*. In 1924 a native collector shot a huge specimen in the Nakhon Sritamart Mountains, S Thailand which measured 18 ft 4 in *5·59 m*. The head of this snake is preserved in the Museum of Comparative Zoology at Harvard University (Smith, 1943). Another hamadryad measuring 18 ft 2 in *5·54 m* was captured alive near Port Dickson in the State of Negri Sembilan, Malaya in April 1937 and kept in captivity for a time by Mr J Leonard of Ruthkin Estate (Gibson-Hill, 1948). Later it was sent to London Zoo where a length of 18 ft 4 in *5·59 m* was recorded for it shortly after arrival. At the time of its death a few days before the outbreak of the Second

World War – all of the venomous snakes in the collection were euthanased in case of escape – it measured a magnificent 18 ft 9 in *5·72 m* (David J Ball, pers. comm.).

The longest known sea snake (50 species) is the yellow sea snake (*Hydrophis spiralis*), which ranges from the Persian Gulf to the Strait of Macassar and the Philippines. The average adult length is about 6 ft *1·8 m*, but individuals measuring up to 9 ft *2·7 m* have been reliably reported.

The heaviest living snake is the anaconda, which has already been discussed. On the basis of the weight/length relationship of captive specimens measuring less than 20 ft *6·1 m* in length, Dowling (1961) has calculated that a 30-footer *9·1 m* in good condition would probably weigh over 600 lb *272 kg*, which means it would be nearly twice as heavy as a reticulated python of the same length.

The heaviest venomous snake is the eastern diamondback rattlesnake (*Crotalus adamanteus*) of the south-east USA. Adult examples average 5–6 ft *1·5–1·8 m* in length and scale 12–15 lb *5·4–6·8 kg*. One huge individual killed by Rutledge (1946) measured 7 ft 9 in *2·36 m* in length and tipped the scales at 34 lb *15·4 kg*. Two others killed in Florida reportedly measured 8 ft 9 in *2·67 m* and 8 ft 5 in *2·57 m* respectively, but these measurements may have been taken to the end of the rattle instead of to the base, thus adding an extra 4–5 in *102–127 mm* (Klauber, 1956).

The Gaboon viper (*Bitis gabonica*) of the tropical rain forests of Africa south of the Sahara is proportionately bulkier than *Crotalus*, but this species does not exceed 6 ft 9 in *2·06 m*. A 5 ft 8½ in *1·74 m* female killed in the Mabira Forest, Uganda scaled 18 lb *8·2 kg* with an empty stomach (girth 14½ in *37 cm*), and a weight of 25 lb *11·3 kg* has been reported for another individual which measured exactly 6 ft *1·8 m* (Pitman, 1974).

Mention should also be made of the king cobra, although this is a relatively slender species. In 1951 a weight of 26 lb 8 oz *12 kg* was recorded for a 15 ft 7 in *4·75 m* hamadryad captured alive on the golf-course at the Royal Island Club on Singapore Island and later taken to the Raffles Museum. On 26 February 1973 the death was reported of 'Junior', a 14 ft 5 in *4·39 m* king cobra at New York Zoological Park after establishing a longevity record for this species of 15 years 7 months. The posthumous weight of this snake was given as 28 lb *12·7 kg* despite the fact that it had suffered from a prolonged illness (Dresner, 1973).

The heaviest sea-snake is the very bulky Stoke's sea-snake (*Astrotia stokesii*) of the Pacific which reaches a maximum length of 6 ft *1·8 m*.

The shortest snake in the world is the very rare thread snake *Leptotyphlops bilineata*, which is known only from the islands of Martinique, Barbados and

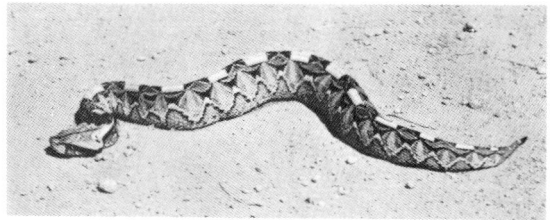

The Gaboon viper – the world's bulkiest snake in terms of overall body length.

St Lucia in the West Indies. Of eight specimens examined by Richard Thomas (1965) the two longest both measured 108 mm *4·25 in*. Thread snakes this size can glide through a cavity only 3 mm *0·12 in* wide, such as the hole left in a standard pencil after the lead has been removed.

Some of the worm-like blind snakes (*Typhlops*) of Africa are also very small. *T. fornasinii* of E Africa, *T. caecatus* and *T. hallowelli* of W Africa and *T. anchietae* of Angola all measuring 127–152 mm *5–6 in*, and Loveridge says that they are often kept and herded along by Driver ants (*Dorylinae*) like cattle on the hoof, although the reasons for this strange association have not yet been explained.

The shortest venomous snake in the world is the spotted dwarf adder (*Bitis paucisquamata*) of Little Namaqualand, SW Africa, with adults averaging 228 mm *9 in* in length. Perinquey's desert adder (*Bitis perinqueyi*) of SW Africa and the striped dwarf garter snake (*Elaps dorsalis*) of northern South Africa average 254 mm *10 in* and 267 mm *10·5 in* respectively.

When food is plentiful snakes often eat prodigious meals and can ingest up to 400 times their daily energy requirements in one session. They are able to do this because their jaws are highly elastic and can be stretched to a remarkable degree. Oliver (1955) says he once owned a 355 mm *14 in* long cottonmouth

A diminutive thread snake shown with a coin for comparison of size.

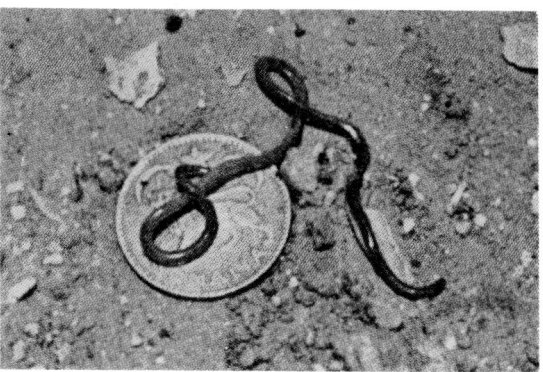

A python which had just swallowed a large bush pig.

moccasin (*Ancistrodon piscivorous*) which swallowed a very slender 736 mm *29 in* ribbon snake (*Thamnophis sauritus*) sharing the same cage, and the stomach of an exceptionally bulky 1511 mm *59·5 in* long file snake (*Mehelya capensis*) killed in the Kruger National Park, South Africa contained a 1086 mm *47·2 in* olive grass snake (*Psammophis sibilans*), an 851 mm *33·5 in* African rock python (*Python sebae*), a 540 mm *21·3 in* brown water snake (*Lycodonomorphus rufulus*) and a 489 mm *19·3 in* ring-necked spitting cobra (*Hemachatus haemachatus*).

Shortly after London Zoo's first king cobra arrived it was placed by a misguided keeper in a cage with six Asiatic cobras (*Naja naja*). The following morning only the hamadryad was in possession, the others having disappeared into its interior – a gastronomic extravagance which cost the Zoological Society £18 since they were only 'on deposit' from a dealer.

When it comes to eating *heavy* meals, however, the giant constrictors are the undisputed champions, although the actual size of the prey they swallow is sometimes exaggerated.

The largest animal on record to be swallowed by a snake was probably a 59 kg *130 lb* impala (*Aepyceros melampus*) which was removed from a 4·87 m *16 ft* African rock python (Rose, 1955). The weight of the snake was not recorded, but it was probably not much heavier than its victim. Lederer (1944) once induced a 24 ft *7·3 m* reticulated python to swallow a 120 lb *54·4 kg* pig, and a collared peccary (*Tayassu tajacu*) weighing an estimated 100 lb *45 kg* was removed from an anaconda measuring 25 ft 8 in *7·82 m*. Much less reliable is a claim for a 200 lb *91 kg* sloth bear (*Melursus ursinus*) swallowed by a dark phased Indian python of unknown length. Dr Walter Rose believes the maximum capacity of a very big constrictor is about 150 lb *68 kg* but a very large African rock python (i.e. 25–30 ft *7·6–9·1 m*) could probably surpass this poundage.

Although many lurid stories have appeared in print

of giant snakes attacking and swallowing human beings, there are only a small number of authentic cases on record, and most of the victims were either children or young babies.

Felix Kopstein (1927), an authority on the reptile fauna of Indonesia, mentions a 14–year-old boy who was killed and eaten by a 17 ft *5·2 m* python on Selebaboe Island in the Talaud group, and also cites the case of an Indonesian woman who was devoured by a serpent allegedly measuring more than 30 ft *9·2 m* in length.

In April 1960 a boy of eight was swallowed by a 20 ft *6·1 m* python while he was collecting rice from a paddy field near his home at Cox's Bazaar, E Pakistan, and 12 years later another boy the same age suffered a similar fate in Lower Burma, although this time the revengeful villagers ate the snake after they had removed the body!

As recently as November 1979 a 15 ft *4·6 m* African rock python attacked and killed a 13–year-old shepherd boy as he was driving home his flock in the N Transvaal, South Africa, but the victim was only partially swallowed.

It is extremely doubtful whether even a 30 ft *9·1 m* constrictor could swallow an average-sized man (i.e. 154 lb *70 kg*) using the head-first technique because the shoulders would get stuck in the gullet. And to succeed from the other end it would first have to manoeuvre both feet into its jaws at the same time, otherwise there would be an impasse at the crotch.

At the other end of the scale the giant snakes are also great fasters and there are a number of records of individuals going 12 months or longer without food. One female reticulated python at Frankfurt Zoo fasted for 570 days, took food for a time and then fasted for another 415 days before eating, and a much larger example at the same zoo went 679 days without food although it drank regularly (Lederer, 1944).

All of these achievements, however, pale by comparison with the fasts carried out by the highly venomous Okinawa habu (*Trimeresurus flavovirdes*) of the Ryukyu Islands, W Pacific. On 10 September 1977 the Amami Kanko Pit Viper Centre in Naze City, Kagoshima Prefecture, Japan started a fasting experiment with five of these snakes. Four of them died on the 207th, 696th, 1101st and 1184th days respectively, but the oldest individual aged *c* 12 years was still going strong – if approached it reared up in preparation for an attack – when the experiment was terminated on the 1189th day (12 December 1980), which is a record for a vertebrate animal. Although its weight decreased by 60·9 per cent during this period, its length actually *increased* much to the puzzlement of researchers. After its marathon fast the snake was given some milk and has since been restored to full physical health (Eiichi Nakamoto, pers. comm.). These creatures can adjust quickly to

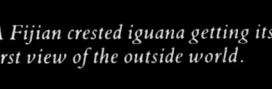

A Fijian crested iguana getting its
first view of the outside world.

The Okinawa habu, which has been
known to survive more than three
years without food.

The Round Island boa, which is now
the world's rarest species of snake.

The striking Gila monster, which
contains enough venom to kill two
adult humans.

changes in their environment, and by using very little energy they can exist for a long time on the layer of fat beneath the skin.

The most venomous snake in the world is the sea snake *Hydrophis melanocephalus* (=*H. belcheri*) of the Australo-Pacific region. In 1972–73 an eleven-man international team of herpetologists interested in sea snakes took part in a 6-week cruise of the Australian Timor Sea aboard the Schripps Institution of Oceanography research vessel R/V *Alpha Helix*, and collected 100 examples of this species around Ashmore Reef. Later one of the scientists, Dr Noburo Tamiya (1974) of Tohoku University, Japan carried out a number of MLD (minimum lethal dose) tests on live mice under laboratory conditions and discovered that this marine cobra has a neurotoxic venom 100 times more potent than that of any other sea or land snake. Fortunately *H. melanocephalus* is not an aggressive animal and has to be subjected to severe treatment before it can be induced to bite. Even then, it does not inject much of the venom because it has a very small head. If the skull wasn't much reduced in size the snake would not be able to enter the burrows of the small eels on which it feeds, and this probably accounts for the very high toxicity of the venom.

The most venomous land snake is the small-scaled or fierce snake (*Parademansia microlepidota*) of the arid interior of eastern central Australia. For many years this snake was considered a western form of the taipan (*Oxyuranus scutellatus*), but recent work by Covacevich and Wombey (1976) has shown that it is a distinct species. In tests carried out at the Commonwealth Serum Laboratories in Melbourne the venom of *P. microlepidota* was found to be four times as toxic as that of the taipan and nine times more toxic than the venom of the tiger snake (*Notechis scutatus*). This snake also has a fairly large venom yield. The average from 'milking' seven specimens was 44·2 mg *0·001 56 oz*, but one snake yielded 110 mg *0·003 88 oz* on a single occasion – enough to kill 125 000 mice (Sutherland *et al*, 1978). So far no human fatalities have been attributed to this species.

The kraits (*Bungarus*) of SE Asia and Indonesia are also highly venomous. The Indian krait (*B. candidus caeruleus*) is particularly nasty (MLD for man 2–3 mg *0·000 070–0·000 105 oz*) and about 50 per cent of bites are fatal even with antivenin treatment (Minton and Minton, 1971). The venom of the little-known Javan krait (*B. javanicus*) is reportedly even more toxic, and Kopstein (1932) cites the case of a father and son sleeping in a hut, being bitten in quick succession by the type specimen and dying soon afterwards.

The only snakes outside Asia which have a venom comparable in toxicity with that of the kraits are the North American coral snake (*Micrurus fulvius*) and the Boomslang (*Dispholidus typus*) of Africa, both of which have a MLD for man of 4–5 mg *0·000 140–0·000 175 oz*.

The most dangerous snake in the world is the saw-scaled viper (*Echis carinatus*) which ranges across Africa north of the Equator, through the Middle East to the Indian subcontinent and north Sri Lanka. It is an extremely prolific species and its venom is unusually toxic for man. Minton and Minton report that the lethal dose may be as small as 3–5 mg *0·000 105–0·000 175 oz* and this, coupled with the fact that the snake becomes extremely aggressive when frightened or disturbed, makes it a truly formidable adversary and one greatly feared by rural populations in Africa and India.

The king cobra, the Bushmaster (*Lachesis muta*) of tropical Central and South America, and the taipan of northern Australia and SE New Guinea have also been credited with the title of 'most dangerous snake' by various writers, but these species have a much more limited range than *E. carinatus* and are nothing like as abundant; in fact, these snakes are not naturally aggressive, despite claims to the contrary, and even when frightened they would probably try to escape.

In April 1980 a man was rushed to a hospital in Florida after being bitten on the finger by a venomous snake. After treatment he was discharged and told to keep the infected digit in an ice pack. Two weeks later the finger was amputated through frostbite!

Although all sea snakes are highly venomous they are not normally aggressive and there are comparatively few records of these creatures making unprovoked attacks on people in the water. Dr H A Reid (1956) gives details of two bathing tragedies at Penang, Malaysia in 1954, both off the same beach on the same day, but these cases were exceptional. The species responsible for most human fatalities, and thus the most dangerous sea snake, is the beaked sea snake (*Enhydrina schistosa*) of the Indo-Pacific region, which is on a par with the tiger snake for toxicity of venom (lethal dose for man 1·5 mg *0·000 052 oz*). During the period 1957–64 a total of 101 people, 80 of them fishermen, were admitted to Penang General Hospital suffering from sea snake bites, eight of whom died later. In seven of the fatalities the snake responsible for the lethal bite was *E. schistosa*, while the other one was not identified (Reid, 1975). The trouble with the sea snake is that the bite is painless and the neurotoxic venom very slow acting, so by the time symptoms develop like general debility, intense thirst and rapid, shallow breathing first-aid measures are too late. According to Reid the mortality rate due to sea snake bites is about 5 per cent of those bitten, and most victims die in 12 to 24 hours. The reason why the figure is so low is because the amount of venom injected is usually very small, despite the fact that sea snakes tend to hold on and chew.

The largest yield of venom ever recorded for a snake is 1530 mg *0·054 oz* dry weight for a jararacussu (*Bothrops jararacussu*) of Brazil (Schottler, 1952), but this was exceptional (average yield 150–200 mg *0·005–0·007 oz*). The Gaboon viper probably has the highest average yield. Three 'milked' at the serpentarium in Brazzaville Congo gave a combined weight of 2970 mg *0·1048 oz* (Grasset, 1946).

At the other end of the scale the highly venomous North American coral snake has a yield of only 2–6 mg *0·000070–0·000219 oz* (lethal dose for man 4–5 mg *0·000140–0·000175 oz*), and the even more toxic banded small-headed sea snake (*Hydrophis fasciatus*) less than 1 mg *0·000035 oz*.

Over a 10-year period ending December 1970 Bernard Keyter (*b* 1918), a supervisor at the South African Institute for Medical Research in Johannesburg milked 780 000 venomous snakes personally and obtained 870 gallons *3293 litres* of venom for serum purposes. He said he had never been bitten.

If we exclude China and the USSR, for which figures are not available, it is estimated that between 30 000 and 40 000 people die from snakebite each year – 10 000 to 15 000 of them in India where the rate is 5·4 deaths per 100 000 population (Swaroop and Grab, 1954). Latin America runs second to Asia in the snakebite table, and at the time of the 1954 World Health Organisation (WHO) survey there were about 2000 deaths annually in Brazil alone (*cf* 1000 for the whole of Africa).

The country with the highest fatality rate from snakebite is Burma, the average rate being 15·4 deaths per 100 000 population, but Swaroop and Grab claim the rate in some districts is as high as 30. During the period 1935–40 there were 12 733 *reported* deaths in Burma. With the advent of modern treatments, however, these statistics no longer stand up and Phelps (1980) believes the mortality rate today is probably less than half the quoted figures.

Recently a drug addict sleeping at his home in Faizabad, Central India, was bitten by an unidentified venomous snake but made a full recovery. The unfortunate snake died!

The highest incidence of snakebite in the world is found on the Amami Islands in the Rkukyu group, W Pacific, where one person in every 500 of the population is bitten by the aggressive Okinawa habu. Fortunately only three per cent of the victims die (Sawai *et al*, 1969).

The only venomous snake in Britain is the adder (*Vipera berus*), which is widely distributed throughout England, Wales and Scotland. Adult males average 500 mm *19·69 in* in length and adult females 550 mm *21·65 in* (Appleby, 1971). The largest accurately measured specimen on record was probably a 43·5 in *1·10 m* female killed at Pontrilas, Hereford and Worcester in August 1977.

Since 1890 ten people have died from snakebite in Britain, including six children, but there have only been two fatalities since 1950. One of them was a 14-year-old boy who was bitten on the right hand at Carey Camp, Dorset on 13 May 1957. He was rushed to Poole Hospital, but died three hours later from cardio-respiratory failure due to anaphylactic shock. On 1 July 1975 a five-year-old boy died in a Glasgow hospital 44 hours after being bitten on the ankle by an adder during a family outing to the hills near Callander, Perthshire. It was the first death from an adder-bite in Scotland since records began.

The longest-fanged snake in the world is the highly venomous Gaboon viper of tropical Africa. In a 4 ft 3 in *1·3 m* long individual they measured 29 mm *1·14 in*, and in one of 6 ft *1·8 m* the length was 50 mm *2·0 in* (Minton and Minton, 1971). The only other venomous snake with fangs comparable is the much longer bushmaster. Those of an 11 ft 4 in *3·45 m* individual measured 35 mm *1·38 in* (Cochran, 1943).

Like growth, the longevity of snakes has been greatly exaggerated and this largely stems from the ancient belief that periodic sloughing of the skin was a form of rejuvenation. That is why, in mythology, snakes are often 1000 years old.

The greatest irrefutable age recorded for a snake is 40 years 3 months and 14 days for a male common boa named 'Popeye' at Philadelphia Zoo, Pennsylvania, USA who was euthanased on 15 April 1977 because of medical problems associated with advanced age. He was purchased by Mrs Eugenie S Shorrock of Massachusetts from a London dealer in December 1936 and was later presented to the zoo (J Kevin Bowler, pers. comm.).

An Indian python purchased by Mrs Shorrock from the same dealer on 9 December 1936 died in Philadelphia Zoo on 20 February 1971 after being in captivity for 34 years 2 months and 11 days (Roger Conant, pers. comm.).

There is also an authentic record of a female anaconda living for more than 31 years. This specimen was received at Basle Zoo, Switzerland on 18 August 1930 and died on 8 May 1962 (H Wackernagel, pers. comm.).

The oldest venomous snake on record was probably a northern copperhead (*Agkistrodon contortrix mokeson*) collected in the Blue Hills near Boston, Massachusetts in May 1941. It died in Philadelphia Zoo on 7 April 1971 after having been in captivity for approximately 29 years 11 months. An African black-lipped cobra (*Naja melanoleuca*) hatched in San Diego Zoo, California, USA on 1 October 1928 died there on 12 November 1957 aged 29 years 32 days (Charles E Shaw, pers. comm.).

Although some of the slender species of snake give the impression of rapid movement as they glide smoothly over the ground this is in fact an illusion combined with ignorance of their metabolism. Except for short bursts of speed the vast majority of snakes cannot keep pace with a man walking at a normal pace i.e. 4 miles/h *6·4 km/h*, and their type of heart and circulation are such they tire rapidly.

In the early 1930s Dr Walter Mosauer (1935) carried out some speed tests on several species of desert snakes in California. The results were extremely disappointing. The maximum velocity recorded was 3·6 miles/h *5·8 km/h* for a Colorado desert whip snake (*Masticophis flagellus piceus*), while the allegedly swift sidewinder rattlesnake (*Crotalus cerastes*) could only notch up 2·04 miles/h *3·28 km/h*. The slowest of the six snakes tested was the rosy boa (*Lichanura roseofusca*) with a miserable 0·224 miles/h *0·36 km/h*.

On another occasion Dr James Oliver and his wife released a black racer (*Coluber constrictor*) on rough ground in Florida and invited a group of people to guess its speed. The estimates ranged from 10 to 15 miles/h *16–24 km/h*, but the best stopwatch reading was 3·7 miles/h *6·0 km/h*.

In similar trials carried out with Australian racers the maximum velocity recorded was 3·5 miles/h *5·6 km/h* (Kinghorn, 1964).

Even if we make due allowance for the fact that snakes rarely travel in a straight line between two points – a meandering course can add 25–35 per cent to the measured distance – probably only a very few species can exceed 5–6 miles/h *8–10 km/h* when travelling flat out.

On 23 April 1906 Col Richard Meinertzhagen (1955) timed an angry black mamba over a level distance of 47 yd *43 m* near Mbuyuni, Kenya after he and his men had baited it with clods of earth. The surface of the course was recently burned grass, and the 5 ft 7 in *1·7 m* long snake recorded a speed of 7 miles/h *11·3 km/h* before a bullet ended its career. As this species is said to be most active about the 8–9 ft *2·4–2·7 m* mark, a burst of speed of 10–11 miles/h *16–18 km/h* is probably within its capabilities.

The sand snakes (*Psammophis*) of Southern Africa are also exceptionally fast, and the karoo whip snake (*P. notosticutus*) has no difficulty catching the quick-moving lacertid lizards on which it preys.

The British grass snake has been timed at 4·2 miles/h *6·8 km/h*, which classifies it as one of the 'sprinters' of the serpentine world.

The fastest-swimming sea snake (*Hydrophiidae*) is the yellow-bellied sea snake (*Pelamis platurus*) of the Indo-Pacific region, whose body and tail are laterally compressed to aid movement through the water. This species, which is completely helpless on land, has been timed at 1 m/sec (=2·24 miles/h *3·60 km/h*) over short distances (Kropach, 1975), but it could probably improve on this in an emergency. In addition sea snakes can dive to 100 m *328 ft* and stay underwater for periods up to 5 hours.

The greatest concentration of snakes on record was one seen by Willoughby P Lowe (1932) while on board a steamer in the Malacca Strait between the Malay Peninsula and Sumatra.

'After luncheon on 4 May I came on deck and was talking to some passengers when, looking landward, I saw a long line running parallel with our course. None of us could imagine what it could be. It must have been four or five miles off. We smoked and chatted, had a siesta, and went down to tea. On returning to the deck we still saw the curious line along which we had been steaming for four hours, but now it lay across our course, and we were still very curious as to what it was. As we drew nearer we were amazed to find that it was composed of a solid mass of sea snakes, twisted thickly together. They were orange-red and black, a very poisonous and rare variety (*sic*) known as Astrotia stokesii . . . Along this line there must have been millions; when I say millions I consider it no exaggeration, for the line was quite ten feet wide and we followed its course for some sixty miles. I can only presume it was either a migration or the breeding season . . . it certainly was a wonderful sight.'

The rarest snake in the world is probably the Keel-scaled boa (*Casarea dussumieri*) of Round Island in the western Indian Ocean with a total wild population of less than 75 individuals. Another seven are currently housed in Jersey Zoo. The Round Island boa (*Bolyeria multocarinata*) has not been seen since 1974 when a single specimen was collected, and the *Red Data Book* says it may now be extinct.

The lizard-like tuatara (*Sphenodon punctatus*) of New Zealand is the sole survivor of an ancient group of reptiles which flourished 170 million years ago.

Adults measure 41–66 cm *16–26 in* in length and weigh up to 2 kg *4·4 lb*.

The most distinctive feature of this living fossil is its rudimentary third or pineal eye which is situated on the top of the head, but it also has the lowest body temperature (11°C *52°F*) of any living reptile and a rate of metabolism that is so reduced that it can go as long as 60 minutes without breathing (Milligan, 1924).

In addition, the incubation period of 13–15 months is the longest of any reptile.

Another peculiarity of this species is its remarkable indifference to pain, and one male injured in a fall showed no signs of distress even though it suffered two broken legs and crushed ribs.

This bizarre creature grows at a very leisurely pace and does not reach sexual maturity until it is at least

The tuatara – the world's most extraordinary reptile.

20 years old, although how it mates is a bit of a puzzle because the male does not possess a copulatory organ. One specimen received at Dublin Zoo, Ireland in 1911 lived there for 30 years, during which time it subsisted quite happily on a diet of two earthworms a week! Another individual kept by a European in New Zealand survived for 77 years, and the maximum expectancy of life in the wild may be 100 years or more.

The tuatara is now confined to about 20 islets off the NE coast of North Island and in Cook Strait, and is rigorously protected by the New Zealand Government. The total population has been estimated at between 10 000 and 15 000 animals.

Amphibians

(class Amphibia)

An amphibian is a cold-blooded, air-breathing vertebrate which lives both in the water and on land. It normally has four legs and is distinguished from reptiles by its naked and moist skin which is used in respiration. Throughout the class the brain is of a very low type. The majority of young are hatched from eggs deposited in water and breathe by means of external gills during the larval stage. At the completion of metamorphosis the gills close up and breathing is transferred to the skin and lungs so that the animal can live on land. In cold weather it burrows into the earth or mud at the bottom of a lake or pool where it passes into a state of hibernation.

The earliest known amphibian and the first quadruped was *Ichthyostega* which lived about 370 million years ago and evolved from the lobe-finned fishes (Crossopterygii). Its remains have been discovered in the freshwater beds of Greenland.

There are about 2400 living species of amphibian and the class is usually divided into three orders. These are the Salientia (frogs and toads); the Caudata (newts and salamanders); and the Gymnophiona (the wormlike caecilians). The largest order is Salientia, which contains about 1900 living species, while the smallest is Gymnophiona (160 species).

The largest amphibian in the world is the Chinese giant salamander (*Andrias davidianus*), which is found in the cold mountain streams and marshy areas of north-eastern, central and southern China. Adult specimens of both sexes average 1·14 m *3 ft 9 in* in total length and scale 25–30 kg *55–66 lb*.

The largest accurately measured giant salamander on record was a huge individual collected in Kweichow (Guizhou) Province, S China in *c* 1923 and described by Sowerby (1925) who says it measured 1·52 m *5 ft* snout to tail between pegs,

and 1·75 m *5 ft 9 in* along the curve of the body. Unfortunately this animal was not weighed, but it must have scaled nearly 100 lb *45 kg*.

The much rarer Japanese giant salamander (*Andrias japonicus*) of W Honshu and central Kyushu has also been credited with the title of 'largest living amphibian', but although it matches its Chinese counterpart in terms of length it 'bulks out' slightly smaller because the tail is proportionately longer. Apart from size, the two species can also be distinguished by the character of the tubercles on the head, those of *A. davidianus* being smaller and fewer (Ch'eng-Chao Liu, 1950).

According to Flower (1936) a very large Japanese giant salamander which died in Leipzig Zoo, E Germany on 31 May 1930 measured 1·44 m *4 ft 8¾ in* in a straight line and 1·64 m *5 ft 4½ in* along the curve of the body. This specimen weighed 40 kg *88 lb* when alive and 45 kg *99 lb* after death, the body having absorbed water from the aquarium.

The only other amphibians which approach *Andrias* in the length stakes are the eel-like three-toed amphiuma (*Amphiuma means tridactylum*) and the great siren (*Siren lacertina*), both of the SE USA, which have been measured up to 1003 mm *39·5 in* and 914 mm *36 in* respectively. Neither of these species, however, is as heavy as the hellbender (*Cryptobranchus alleganiensis*), also of the USA, built on the same lines as *Andrias* and reaching a weight of 4·5 kg *10 lb*.

The largest frog in the world is the rare Goliath frog (*Conraua goliath*) of Equatorial Guinea and Cameroon, W Africa. On 23 August 1960 the Spanish naturalist Dr Jorge Sabater Pi (1965) and his native helper caught a female in the cataracts of the River Mbia, Bata district, Rio Muni which had a snout-vent length of 340 mm *13·39 in* and measured 815 mm *32·1 in* overall. It weighed 3305 g *7 lb 4¾ oz*. A slightly longer female (356 mm *14 in*) collected in the same river by Dr Paul Zahl (1967) in December 1966 and now preserved in the museum of the

National Geographic Society in Washington, DC tipped the scales at 3100 g *6 lb 13¼ oz*. Another specimen killed in Cameroon in the early part of this century allegedly had a snout-vent length of 609 mm *24 in* and weighed 5890 g *13 lb*, but this record has never been verified and was probably exaggerated.

Most adult female frogs are considerably larger than the males because they produce enormous numbers of eggs within their bodies.

According to Oliver (1955) the heaviest American bullfrog (*Rana catesbeiana*) on record was a female which scaled 1 lb 4 oz *567 g*, but in 1949 Jim Pratt caught an outsized freak in Martha Lake, Alderwood Manor, Washington which reportedly scaled 7 lb 4 oz *3289 g* and measured 36 in *914 mm* in total length. Unfortunately further details are lacking, but the length-weight ratio is proportional.

Mention should also be made of the famous 'Coleman Frog', the most awesome exhibit in York-Sunbury Historical Society's museum in Fredericton, New Brunswick, Canada which allegedly weighed 42 lb *19 kg* (sic) when it was dynamited from Killarney Lake in the prime of its life in 1885.

The origins of this monster are obscure, but the story began in the early 1880s when Fred Coleman, who owned the Barker House Hotel overlooking the lake, struck up a friendship with the anuran. Every day the benevolent hotelier would walk to the lake's edge with the frog's favourite tidbits, fresh baked beans and buttermilk toddies, and guests would bring along other treats as well. As a result the frog prospered and grew fat. This happy state of affairs might have continued indefinitely if it had not been for a couple of local fishermen who were unhappy with their catch. One dark day they used dynamite to flush out the fish in the lake and killed the unfortunate frog as well. As a lasting memorial, Fred Coleman had his pet stuffed and put on prominent display in the hotel among the palm fronds, where it remained until the building was demolished.

A rumour then made the rounds of a musician from New York who had a stuffed, oversized frog which he used to advertise a patent medicine designed to relieve a croaking feeling in the throat. It was said the man had stayed at the Barker House Hotel the very same week the Coleman frog was dynamited from the lake, but the people of Fredericton would probably deny this!

The largest frog found in Britain is the marsh frog (*Rana ridibunda*), which was introduced into this country in February 1935 when 12 specimens from Debrecen, Hungary were released in a garden pond near Romney and Walland Marshes, Kent. Adult males and females have been measured up to 96 mm *3·78 in* and 133 mm *5·24 in* respectively and the weight can exceed 200 g *7·06 oz*.

The largest native British frog is the common

The largest Chinese giant salamander on record. It measured 5 ft 1·5 m between pegs and weighed nearly 100 lb 45 kg.

frog (*Rana temporaria*) which is found throughout Scotland, England and Wales. Females have been measured up to 95 mm *3·74 in* (Boulenger, 1893).

The largest toad in the world is the marine toad (*Bufo marinus*) of tropical South America which – thanks to man – is probably the most widely distributed amphibian living today.

An enormous female collected at Miraflores, Colombia on 24 November 1965 and later exhibited at New York Zoological Park had a snout-vent length of 238 mm *9·37 in* and weighed 1302 g *2 lb 14 oz* at the time of her death (Victor H Hutchinson, pers. comm.). This specimen is now preserved in the American Museum of Natural History, New York.

Some extraordinary feats have been attributed to this walking vacuum cleaner, especially in Queensland, Australia where it now poses a serious threat to wildlife after being introduced in 1935 to combat a

A unique photograph of a goliath frog with a dik-dik, one of the smallest members of the antelope family.

*The warty newt (*Triturus cristatus*), Britain's longest amphibian, which has been measured up to 162 mm 6·38 in in total length.*

The deadly two-toned arrow-poison frog, which secretes the most potent biotoxins known to man.

beetle which had been destroying sugar-cane crops. One straight-faced apiarist reported seeing sixteen of these ugly brutes standing on each other's shoulders in an effort to raid a hive (up to 300 bees have been found in the stomach of a single individual), and another Queenslander claims he once saw a big toad open a drain-cover 'to let his cobbers in for a drink' during a long, dry spell. In Proserpine, near the Great Barrier Reef, giant toad races are staged weekly in the local beer garden, and it was there in 1975 that champion 'Gerty', primed up as usual on the local beverage, staggered off the track in an alcoholic haze and ended up squashed under the metal chair of an excited onlooker. Her plaster replica is now on display in the Brisbane Museum.

The marine toad is closely matched in size by the Blomberg toad (*Bufo blombergi*) of Colombia, although this species is not quite so massively built. The type specimen, collected by Rolf Blomberg in the vicinity of Nachao, province of Narino on 11 September 1950 measured 207 mm *8·15 in* and weighed 1000 g *2 lb 3¼ oz* (Myers and Funkhouser, 1951). Probably the largest example on record was a female called 'Berta' housed at Ruhr Zoo, Gelsenkirchen, W Germany who measured 250 mm *9·84 in* and scaled 1125 g *2 lb 7½ oz* (Knobel, 1962).

The rococco toad (*Bufo paracnemis*) of Brazil and northern Argentina has also been credited with measurements up to 250 mm *9·84 in*, but this figure needs to be confirmed. One specimen collected in Brazil had a length of 205 mm *8·07 in*.

Giant toads appear to be widely distributed, and in most tropical or sub-tropical parts of the world there is at least one race which reaches an exceptional size.

The largest toad found in Britain is the common toad (*Bufo bufo*), which is found throughout England, Scotland and Wales. Adult males have been recorded up to 70 mm *2·76 in* and 40·4 g *1·43 oz* and females up to 102 mm *4 in* and 114 g *4·02 oz*.

The smallest frog in the world and the smallest known amphibian is the arrow-poison frog *Sminthillus limbatus* of Cuba. In one series of eleven adult specimens the lengths ranged from 8·5 mm *0·34 in* to 12·4 mm *0·49 in* (Schwartz and Ogren, 1956).

The smallest toad in the world is the sub-species *Bufo taitanus beiranus*, which was originally discovered in the Beira area of Mozambique, E Africa (Loveridge, 1932). The largest of the 13 specimens examined by Dr J C Poynton (1964) of the University of Natal had a length of 24 mm *0·95 in*.

The smallest amphibian found in Britain is the widely-distributed palmate newt (*Triturus helveticus*). Mature examples measure 75–88 mm *2·95–3·47 in* in total length and the weight ranges from 1·5 g *0·053 oz* to 2·39 g *0·084 oz* (Evans, 1894).

The greatest authentic age recorded for an amphibian is 51 years 7 months 3 weeks 2 days for a male Japanese giant salamander which was born in the Aquarium at Amsterdam Zoo, Netherlands on 10 November 1903 and died there on 6 July 1955.

On 28 March 1936 a Japanese giant salamander died in Blackpool Aquarium after having lived there for over 45 years. Its date of arrival was not recorded, but as Flower (1936) says it was fully grown in 1890, it must have been at least 50 years old. The potential life-span for this species is 60 years.

Toads, too, are also long-lived, but the popular belief that they can survive for decades – or even for a century or more – imprisoned in cavities in wood or solid rock without food, water or air is a myth.

This was neatly proved by Dr William Buckland, the famous English naturalist who, on 26 November 1825, enclosed two dozen common toads of different sizes in separate airtight compartments made of compact sandstone or porous limestone which he buried in his garden. When he examined them again on 10 November 1826 he found that all the toads in the sandstone compartments were dead and very much decayed, while most of the others in the larger cells of porous limestone were still alive, although emaciated. The survivors were buried again for a further year, but then were all found to be dead.

The toads in the sandstone compartments probably died within a few hours of being buried because they cannot live in dry air. The others in the porous limestone compartments only survived because they were getting a constant source of moisture and air, but in the end they died of starvation.

In July 1933 a live toad with eyes but no mouth was found in the solid chalk face of a greystone lime pit at Dorking, Surrey. It was exposed after blasting operations 50 ft *15·2 m* from the surface and 4 ft *1·2 m* into the face of the cliff. The amphibian was about 31 mm *1·22 in* long. When first captured it was pink in colour, but gradually got darker. It was later taken to the British Museum for examination.

According to Dr Doris M Cochran, Curator of Reptiles and Amphibians at the US National Museum, Washington, DC, who has made a special study of this subject, toad eggs often filter down through the soil and rock with surface water and get lodged in limestone, sandstone and coal cavities where the temperature is sufficient for them to hatch. The young animals feed on the insects which accumulate in these hollows until eventually they become too big to get out through the narrow apertures they have entered. Similarly, toads hatched above ground regularly hide in cool, moist holes and crevices during the summer in an effort to escape the heat and dryness, and the entrance to a mine or the bottom of a deep excavation must seem attractive.

The oldest toad on record was probably an *adult*

female *Bufo bufo* mentioned by Pennant (1776) which was kept under observation by an English family for 36 years and became so tame that it allowed itself to be put on a table and fed. Even then, it didn't die of old age – the family's tame raven suddenly took a dislike to it – and Malcolm Smith (1951) estimates that it must have been at least 40 years old at the time of its death.

The same authority also gives details of a natter-jack toad (*Bufo calamita*) which was bought from a dealer when fully grown and lived in a walled garden in Kensington, London for 15½ years before vanishing, and in 1975 a woman living in Brighton, Sussex claimed that another natterjack had been living in her little back garden for over 40 years!

Frogs are generally not as long-lived as toads, but there are exceptions.

In a letter published in the magazine *African Wild Life* (Vol 10, no 4, December 1956) D Cairncross described how he kept a live specimen of the very large African species *Pyxicephalus adspersus* for nearly 17 years, having acquired it in Pretoria West in November 1939 when it was already fully grown. He concluded by saying: 'In January 1940 a tadpole of this species metamorphosed in my aquarium and remained in my care for seven years when it unfortunately escaped. If this may be taken as a guide, it would appear that the animal requires about 28 years to reach its full size; and that the large specimen obtained in November 1939 hatched from an egg laid not later than November 1911. This would make it 45 years of age'.

Other amphibians reliably credited with a maximum life-span in excess of 20 years include the hellbender 29 years; the warty newt (*Triturus cristatus*) 28+ years; the three-toed amphiuma 27 years; the Japanese newt (*Triturus pyrrhogaster*) 26+ years; the great siren, the spotted salamander (*Ambystoma maculatum*) and the tiger salamander (*Ambystoma tigrinum*) 25 years; the fire salamander (*Salamandra salamandra*) 24 years and the California newt (*Taricha torosus*) 21 years (Flower, 1936; Koch, 1952; Oliver, 1955).

The finest jumpers among amphibians are frogs, the abilities of which are largely dependent on body-weight, hind-leg length and the surface from which they take off.

The jumper par excellence, not only for distance covered but also in terms of snout-vent length, is the 51 mm *2 in* long South African sharp-nosed frog (*Rana oxyrhyncha*). In 1950 Dr Walter Rose (1962) of Cape Town collected a small number of these frogs in Zululand and decided to test out the jumping ability of a 55 mm *2·17 in* long female. Her best leap was 9 ft 10 in *3·00 m* and in three consecutive jumps she covered a distance of 25 ft 5 in *7·75 m*. This in-

credible performance, however, was over very uneven ground and the jumps were not quite in a straight line. Some four years later, on 18 January 1954, a Frog Olympics was held on Green Point Racing Track, Cape Town in the presence of some 5000 spectators. Most of the contestants were examples of the long-toed frog (*Rana fuscigula*), which is about half as large again as *R. oxyrhyncha*, and only two of them managed a three-jump total in excess of 2·74 m *9 ft*. It was then the turn of a sharp-nosed frog named 'Leaping Lena' (later discovered to be a male) which had been hurriedly flown in from Durban to do his stuff.

'Seeing the tiny chap squatting there, the crowd began to laugh,' said Dr Rose, 'then, as he stayed blinking in the unaccustomed light, they commenced to jeer. Our hearts alternated between our mouth and our boots, for we were in effect his sponsor. Then, to our joy, the little fellow braced himself together, inflated his little chest, and leapt; once, twice, three times in a dead straight line. At the first leap the crowd gasped; at the second it cried out in amazement and at the third tumult broke out.'

The actual distance covered by this frog in three consecutive leaps was 24 ft 3½ in *7·4 m*, and shortly afterwards Dr Rose was a witness when 'Leaping Lena' achieved a three-jump total of 32 ft 3 in *9·83 m* under the same carefully observed conditions. After the competition this 'perfect little jumping machine' was released.

On 21 May 1977 another African sharp-nosed frog named 'Santjie' covered a distance of 33 ft 5½ in *10·20 m* in three consecutive leaps at a Frog Derby held at Larula Natal Spa, Paulpietersburg, (Piem Fourie, pers. comm.).

This species also holds the record for the greatest distance covered by a frog in a single leap. In 1975 a specimen named 'Ex Lax' jumped 17 ft 6¾ in *5·35 m* at the annual Calaveras County Jumping Frog Jubilee held at Angels Camp, California, USA.

The greatest number of consecutive jumps attributed to a frog is 120 for a freshly caught adult spring peeper (*Hyla crucifer*) on a grassy lawn. Not unnaturally the distance between each hop gradually decreased (Rand, 1952). This species is found in the eastern USA.

The leaping ability of toads is not nearly so impressive, although they probably have more stamina than frogs. Rand tested a small number of Fowler's toads (*Bufo woodhousei fowleri*) on the same lawn and found that they jumped from 304 mm *12 in* to 571 mm *22·5 in* per hop, or up to 7·8 times the snout-vent length; on sand, however, the distance covered was only 152–368 mm *6–14·5 in*.

One of the strongest contenders for the title of 'poorest jumper' among anurans is the diminutive greenhouse frog (*Eleutherodactylus ricordi planirostris*) of the south-eastern USA, whose scientific name is longer than the animal itself! One specimen tested by Oliver with a snout-vent length of 31 mm *1·22 in* could only manage a personal best of 120 mm *4·72 in* in five trials, or just under four times its own length. The Goliath frog is only slightly better. This species can cover 10 ft *3·05 m* in a single leap, but after 3 or 4 in quick succession it is completely exhausted.

The greatest altitude at which an amphibian has been found is 26 246 ft *8000 m* for a common toad collected in the Himalayas. This species has also been found at a depth of 1115 ft *340 m* in a coal-mine.

The rarest amphibian in the world is probably the Israel painted frog (*Discoglossus nigriventer*), which has only been recorded from the eastern shore of Lake Huleh. Since its discovery in 1940 only five specimens have been collected and it may now be extinct.

In March 1980 four examples of the Puerto Rican crested toad (*Bufo lemur*), thought to have been extinct since 1974, were collected in the NW part of the island.

Britain's rarest amphibian is the protected natterjack toad which is now extinct at all but one breeding site in its inland range.

Although many amphibians carry at least a trace of poison in their body or secrete this substance from glands in the skin, Caras (1964) says most of the members of this class 'are more colourful and musical than dangerous'. There are exceptions, however, and some of the arrow-poison frogs (*Dendrobatidae*) of Central and South America produce the most potent biotoxins known to man.

The most active poison is the batrachotoxin derived from the two-toned arrow-poison frog or kokoi (*Phyllobates bicolour*), which is found in the dense forests near the headwaters of the Rio San Juan and its tributaries, NW Colombia. Only 0·01 mg *0·000 000 35 oz* is sufficient to kill an average-sized man, which means that 1 oz *28·3 g* of this poison would be enough to wipe out 2 830 000 people!

According to Marki and Witkop (1963) the Cholo Indians of the region use a little trick to capture these frogs. 'They imitate the frog's peeping, which sounds like fiu-fiu-fiu, with great skill, by whistling and at the same time beating their cheeks with the fingers. Their imitation is so perfect that a frog present not too far away usually answers the call and thus can be located. Trying to find these small frogs, which live well hidden among the plants near the ground, by any other means, would seem hopeless.

'The Indians are quite reluctant to touch the frogs without protecting their hands with leaves. We have found that the poisonous secretion of the frog has no

effect whatsoever on the intact skin. However, in contact with even the smallest scratch it causes a long-lasting, pungent pain not unlike a bee's sting.'

When the frogs have been collected and taken back to the village they are pierced through the mouth and body with a specially cut stick and then held over an open fire. The heat and pain contract the skin and force out a milky secretion, especially on the back of the unfortunate creature. The tips of the arrows are dipped in the secretion and then left to dry in the shade. One tiny frog (length 20–30 mm *0·79–1·18 in*; weight 1 g *0·035 oz*) produces enough poison to tip up to 50 arrows.

Today the Cholo Indians use the arrows for hunting game such as the jaguar, deer, monkeys and birds, but in earlier times Wassen (1957) says the blowguns were used with deadly effect against neighbouring hostile tribes.

'An animal struck by a poison arrow becomes paralyzed almost immediately and dies within a short time,' adds Marki and Witlop. 'The Indians then cut out the arrow from the flesh together with a small piece of meat immediately surrounding it. This is only done as a precaution, since the kokoi venom – like curare – is usually completely harmless when taken orally. A small scratch in the mouth, however, or an ulcer in the digestive tract of a person eating such meat may, quite obviously, cause a dangerous situation.'

The poison of the kokoi is ten times more powerful than the deadly tetradotoxin produced in the body of the death puffer fish (*Arothron hispidus*) (see page 147), which causes rapid respiratory paralysis in humans and has no known antidote (Halstead, 1959).

The nerve poison tarichatoxin produced by the abundant and well-developed glands of the California newt (*Taricha torosus*) is also particularly virulent and experiments have shown that 9 mg *0·000 31 oz* is sufficient to kill 7000 mice. The eggs of this newt are also extremely toxic.

The most fecund amphibian in the world is the marine toad. Females may lay 35 000 eggs a year, while the arrow-poison frog *Sminthillus limbatus* lays one single egg.

The longest gestation of any terrestrial animal is that of the alpine salamander (*Salamandra atra*). According to Hafeli (1971) females living above an altitude of 1400 m *4593 ft* in the Swiss Alps produce two young in the fourth summer after fertilisation, which means the gestation period must be an incredible 37–38 months (*cf* maximum 25 months for the Asiatic elephant). At lower heights – this species is not found under 600 m *1969 ft* – the young are usually born in the third summer, i.e. 25–26 months (C B Goodhart, pers. comm.).

Fishes

(superclasses Agnatha, Gnathostomata)

A fish is a cold-blooded vertebrate which lives in water and takes in oxygen by means of gills. Usually it has a muscular, streamlined body covered with scales and limbs modified into paired fins for swimming, but in some species the skin is unprotected or concealed by bony plates, and others have no recognisable fins at all. A few primitive fish also move on land and breathe with lungs. The brain is basically a simple structure, but bony fish are capable of association and show a capacity for learning. The majority of young are hatched from eggs deposited in the water.

The earliest known fish and the first vertebrate was the fixed-jaw *Anatolepis*, which lived about 510 million years ago. Its remains (scales) have been found in the western USA.

There are about 30 000 living species of fish, 2300 of them freshwater, and each year about a hundred new ones are discovered. They are divided into two superclasses: the Agnatha (lampreys and hagfishes) and the Gnathostomata (sharks, rays, chimaeras, lungfishes, coelacanth, bichirs, sturgeons and bony fishes).

The largest and bulkiest fish in the world is the comparatively rare plankton-eating whale shark (*Rhiniodon typus*), which is found in the warmer areas of the Atlantic, Pacific and Indian Oceans. This species was first discovered in April 1828 when a 15 ft *4·6 m* long specimen, one of the smallest on record, was harpooned in Table Bay, South Africa after fishermen had noticed its unusual coloration (greenish grey with white spots). The body was examined by Dr Andrew Smith, a military surgeon attached to the British troops stationed at Cape Town, who published a brief description the following year, and a more detailed one in 1849. The dried skin, which he purchased for £6 sterling, is now in the Museum d'Histoire Naturelle, Paris.

More than 40 years elapsed before *Rhiniodon* was heard of again. In 1868 a young Irish naturalist named E Perceval Wright spent six months in the Seychelles, a group of islands in the western Indian Ocean. During his stay there he heard of a monstrous fish called the 'Chagrin' and offered a reward of $12 for the first example to be killed and delivered to him on shore. Eventually two individuals measuring 20 ft *6·1 m* and 18 ft *5·5 m* respectively were secured, both of which he photographed and dissected. Two years later, in Dublin, he wrote: 'I have seen specimens that I believe to have exceeded fifty feet in length, and many trustworthy men, accustomed to calculate the length of the sperm whale (one of the most important stations for this cetacean is off Ile Denis, one of the Seychelles group) have told me of specimens measuring upwards of seventy feet in length'.

He also revealed that Mr Swinburne Ward, Civil Administrator of the Islands, had informed him that he had personally measured one whale shark at slightly over 45 ft *13·7 m* in length.

Since then more than 100 of these marine giants of varying sizes have been stranded or rammed by ships. Only a few have been scientifically examined.

In the early part of 1919 an exceptionally large whale shark swam into the entrance of a bamboo fish-trap set in 50 ft *15·2 m* of water off Kaoh Chik on the east side of the Gulf of Thailand where it became firmly wedged. 'The fish remained stuck for seven days, during which time all fishing had to be suspended', said Dr Hugh M Smith (1925), Fisheries Advisor to the Thai Government. 'It was finally killed with rifle bullets and hauled out of the trap, but the combined efforts of the local fishermen were insufficient to drag it ashore.'

The enormous toad-like mouth of the whale shark, the largest fish in the world.

The Devil's Hole pupfish, the world's most restricted fish.

On the evidence of Dr Smith's statement this immense fish must have measured at least 17 m *55 ft 9 in* in length, which would also give it an estimated weight of 37 tonnes by formula.

In September 1934 the liner *Maurganui* collided with a whale shark 60 miles *97 km* NNE of Tikehau Atoll in the South Pacific and cut so deeply into the body of the fish that it was literally impaled on the bow. Gudger (1940) says about 15 ft *4·6 m* of the shark hung on one side of the bow, and another 40 ft *12·2 m* on the other, making a total length of 55 ft *16·8 m*. More than two dozen such collisions have been recorded around the world, and they are attributed to the sluggish nature of this surface-feeder and its apparent indifference to danger.

Lengths of 60 ft *18·3 m* or even more have been claimed for this species on the strength of visual assessments, but this sort of guesswork is notoriously unreliable because it is very easy to over-estimate the size of a large shark in the water. Gudger, for instance, mentions a huge individual known as 'Sapodilla Tom', who frequented the waters off Honduras for fifty years and was estimated to measure 60–70 ft *18·3–21·3 m* in length, and fisheries inspector Frederick Wallace (1923) was told by the red-snapper fishermen working in the Gulf of Campeche on the western Yucatan Peninsula that a local whale shark nicknamed 'Big Ben' was more than 75 ft *22·9 m* long!

The largest scientifically measured whale shark

on record – length taken from the tip of the snout to the notch in the tail in a straight line – was a 41 ft 6 in *12·65 m* long specimen captured off Baba Island near Karachi, Pakistan on 11 November 1949. This 'Mohr', as it is known locally, measured 23 ft *7·0 m* round the thickest part of the body (i.e. the fifth gill-slit) and weighed an estimated 21·5 tonnes.

In May 1912 another large individual measuring 38 ft *11·6 m* in length was killed by Captain Charles Thompson and some local fishermen just below Knight's Key, southern Florida, USA. It took them 9 hours to beach this monster, and it only succumbed after a piece had been cut out of its head and the small brain pierced by a knife attached to a long pole. The huge carcase was then towed to Miami, where it was hauled out of the water and placed on a railway flat-car, which promptly collapsed under the weight! The shark was later purchased by an enterprising promoter who, after having it skinned and *over-stuffed*, took it on a very successful tour of the eastern USA.

Gudger worked out the weight of this shark as 26 594 lb *12·06 tonnes*, basing his calculations on a length of 38 ft *11·6 m* and a girth of 18 ft *5·5 m*, but this poundage is probably too low. Another whale shark killed near Marathon in the Florida Keys on 9 June 1923 after a fight lasting 54 hours measured 31 ft 6 in *9·6 m* in length and had a circumference of 23 ft *7·0 m* directly in front of the pectoral fins and 17 ft 6 in *5·33 m* over the first gill-slit.

Other reliable records over 30 ft *9·1 m* (most of them taken from Gudger) include: a 10 m *32 ft 9¾ in* example caught in a drift-net off Cape Inubo on the SE coast of Japan in June 1901 (the stuffed fish measures 8 m *26 ft 3 in* in length and 4·3 m *14 ft 1¼ in* in circumference); one measuring 31 ft *9·4 m* taken near Cape Sable, Florida on 11 June 1919; a 10 m *32 ft 9¾ in* specimen caught at Salinas, Luzon in the Philippines on 19 January 1925 and another one 36 ft *11·0 m* long which stranded at Silay, Negros in the Philippines about the same time; a 32-footer *9·8 m* washed ashore at Jaimanitas, a village situated about 5 miles *8 km* west of Havana, Cuba on 20 November 1927 (this fish was weighed piecemeal and totalled about 18 000 lb *8165 kg* excluding oil and blood losses), and one measuring 34 ft *10·4 m* captured off Cojimar, Cuba, on 10 March 1930; a specimen measuring 'about 40 feet' which ran aground in Southport Harbour, North Carolina, USA on 6 June 1934 (the most northerly record); a 35 ft *10·7 m* individual which blundered into a fish trap off Fire Island Light, on the south shore of Long Island, NY, USA on 9 August 1935; one measuring 37 ft *11·3 m* and weighing an estimated 15 tonnes caught off Bimini in the Bahamas in 1958 and towed to Miami; a 32-footer *9·8 m* caught by a party of fishermen in the Arabian Sea in 1959 and towed to Mangalore on

the Malabar Coast, India; and a 30 ft 3 in *9·22 m* individual weighing an estimated 7 tonnes washed ashore in Anno Bay, NSW, Australia in April 1964.

A 34 ft *10·4 m* whale shark taken off the coast of Sri Lanka in *c* 1889 is now on display in the Fish Gallery at the British Museum.

An interesting account of the capture of a large whale shark appeared in the March 1951 issue of *Nature*. Although the capture occurred on 23 November 1940 near Pangkor Island off the west coast of the Malay Peninsula, it became known only in 1950 when the director of the Fisheries Dept at Penang examined some records of the Japanese occupation. The fish, which measured 35 ft *10·7 m* in length and 23 ft *7·0 m* across the outstretched pectorals, was caught in a beach seine operated by the Madras fishermen who migrated to Malaya. They tried to weigh it piecemeal, but after recording just over 13 000 lb *5·89 tonnes* of flesh they grew tired and dumped the rest of the carcase in the sea.

It would appear from the extensive literature regarding the whale shark that the average adult specimen measures about 32 ft *9·8 m* in length (weight 9 tonnes), and that the upper size limit for this species is somewhere in the region of 45–50 ft *13·7–15·2 m* if the length is taken in a straight line.

Apart from being the largest fish in the world, *Rhiniodon* also has the thickest skin of any living animal. In a 30 ft *9·1 m* individual it is 4 in *102 mm* thick, and this external covering has been likened to the solid rubber tyre of a heavy truck. Also interesting is the fact that when it is harpooned this shark can strengthen its 'armour plating' by tightening its dermal muscles, with the result that other irons simply bounce off its body.

On one occasion Dr William Beebe (1938) was aboard his yacht *Zaca* in the Gulf of California when a whale shark (estimated length 42 ft *12·8 m*) was sighted. He ordered the vessel to draw alongside, and it kept pace with the great fish for several hours. Eventually two of his brawny Samoan crew leapt on to the inoffensive creature's back from the deck and rammed home a large harpoon, which was attached by a long line to an empty petrol drum. The shark immediately went into a crash dive, and when it reappeared 15 minutes later the large drum was crushed in the middle, the result of the tremendous pressure encountered at great depths (the minute eyes and very thick skin are indicative of a deep-diving animal). Two more attempts were made to harpoon this fish, but each time the irons came back buckled 'as if they had struck steel'.

One would hardly expect a creature this size to have any natural enemies, but apparently there is at least one. In the early 1970s the tail of a large individual was washed up on a beach near the small village of Dhabab on the Gulf of Aqaba, the NE extension of the Red Sea. The caudal appendage had been severed as though by a knife, but there was clear evidence of teeth marks (Kendall McDonald, pers. comm.). The only marine predator capable of such a neat piece of surgery, which must have resulted in the death of the shark through loss of blood (a main artery is located at the base of the tail) is the killer whale (*Orcinus orca*), although what it was doing in that part of the world remains something of a mystery.

The only other fish comparable in size with the whale shark is the basking shark (*Cetorhinus maximus*), another filter-feeder which is found in all the temperate waters of the world, although it is most common in the North Atlantic. The average adult specimen measures 26 ft *7·9 m* in length and weighs 4·65 tonnes. Two basking sharks measuring approximately 28 ft *8·5 m* and 30 ft *9·1 m* landed at Monterey, California, USA in 1931 reportedly scaled only 6580 lb *2·98 tonnes* and 8600 lb *3·9 tonnes* respectively, but as a weight of 6600 lb *2·99 tonnes* has been cited for a 23 ft *7·0 m* individual both these measurements must have been taken round the curves of the body.

The maximum length reached by this shark is a matter of some controversy, and the literature abounds with exaggerated statements. Legendre (1923), for example, credits it with measurements up to 12–14 m *39·4–46·0 ft*, while Bigelow and Schroeder (1948) speak of basking sharks reaching lengths up to 50 ft *15·2 m*, with 35–40 ft *10·7–12·2 m* not being exceptional. There is no definite evidence to support these extreme measurements, however, and the total catch of the modern fishery, which now runs into tens of thousands, has produced only a few specimens that have exceeded 30 ft *9·1 m*.

Matthews and Parker (1950), who measured nine basking sharks in great detail at a Hebridean fishery in 1947, found their lengths ranged from 20 ft 6 in *6·25 m* to 24 ft 6 in *7·47 m*, the average being 23 ft 4 in *7·11 m*. They commented: 'The exaggerated lengths recorded by many writers appear to owe their origin, either to guesswork or to measurement round the curves of the body. An example may be quoted to show the ease with which the length of these enormous fishes may be over-estimated. In May 1947, when one of us (LHM) was in the hunting ship, a large shark was secured and its length was guessed at well over 30 ft. When it was lashed alongside for towing home, the length was estimated at 34 ft by pacing out the deck beside it. When it was measured after it had been removed from the water the length from the tip of the snout to the notch of the tail was found to be 7·36 m or *24 ft 1 in*. Even if an additional metre is allowed for the distance from the caudal notch to the perpendicular from the tip of the tail fin

an extreme length of 27 ft 4½ in only is given . . . If the body is measured round the curves and along the anterior edge of the caudal fin, lengths of over 30 ft may well be manufactured, but the only measurements of any value are those in a straight line'.

The three longest basking sharks for which Bigelow and Schroeder could find definite measurements for the western Atlantic taped 32 ft 2 in *9·80 m*, 32 ft *9·75 m* and 30 ft 3 in *9·22 m* respectively. Two others caught in the English Channel measured 31 ft 10 in *9·70 m* (De Blainville, 1812) and 31 ft 8 in *9·65 m* (Day 1880–84), and the largest basking shark taken by Gavin Maxwell (1952), who ran a shark fishery on Soay in the Inner Hebrides, Scotland between 1945 and 1949, was 30 ft 5 in *9·27 m*. Other reliable records over 30 ft *9·1 m* include a 32 ft 10 in *10·00 m* specimen (maximum circumference 18 ft *5·5 m*) captured near Brown's Point, Raritan Bay, New Jersey, USA in 1821; one measuring 30 ft 6 in *9·30 m* which stranded at Portland, Victoria, Australia in November 1883; a 34 ft *10·4 m* shark with a 5 ft *1·5 m* high dorsal fin caught near Auckland, New Zealand in 1885; another one the same length which ran aground near San Francisco, California, USA in *c* 1896 (this fish was embalmed and put on exhibition); a 32 ft *9·8 m* individual caught in a cod-trap at Petty Harbour, near St John's, Newfoundland, Canada in 1934; one measuring 34 ft *10·4 m* killed in Fortune Harbour, Newfoundland, on 13 August 1937 (tail 9 ft *2·74 m* wide); a 33-footer *10·1 m* harpooned in Monterey

The 4-tonne carcase of a basking shark being hoisted ashore from a French fishing vessel.

Bay, California, USA in 1948 (weight of liver 2100 lb *953 kg*); and a 32 ft *9·8 m* individual found entangled in a net at Grand Bruit, Newfoundland in July 1962.

The ten largest basking sharks taken on the Norwegian coast during the period 1884 to 1901 were credited with the lengths of 45 ft *13·7 m*, 40 ft *12·2 m* (3), 36 ft *11·0 m*, 32 ft 2 in *9·80 m*, 32 ft *9·8 m*, 31 ft *9·5 m*, 30 ft 6 in *9·30 m* and 30 ft 3 in *9·22 m* respectively (Collett, 1905), but it is extremely doubtful whether any of these measurements were taken in a straight line (*cf* 29 ft 2 in *8·89 m* for the largest basking shark taken in Icelandic waters).

The largest accurately measured basking shark on record was probably a 40 ft 3 in *12·27 m* giant which became entangled in a herring-gill net in Musquash Harbour, Bay of Fundy, New Brunswick, Canada on 6 August 1851 (Perley, 1852). This specimen weighed an estimated 16 tonnes, and its liver yielded 320 gallons *1211 litres* of oil (*cf* 102 gallons *386 litres* for a 28 ft 10 in *8·79 m* shark caught off the Irish coast). Another exceptionally large fish captured near Concarneau, Brittany, northern France in 1917 recorded a length of 38 ft *11·6 m* (Heuvelmans, 1968), and Gudger (1915) gives details of a 36 ft *11·0 m* basking shark taken in Monterey Bay, California, which he examined in a travelling museum.

According to Maxwell he narrowly missed catching a basking shark between Uisenish and Lochboisdale, South Uist, Outer Hebrides which he estimated was 'a full forty feet', but the 3 in *76 mm* manilla rope snapped when the harpooned beast went into a crash dive.

In 1806 a length of 36 ft 6 in *11·13 m* and a weight of 8 tonnes were reported for a basking shark washed ashore at Brighton, Sussex, but this tonnage is more proportional to a length of 31 ft 6 in *9·60 m*.

In October 1808 the rotting carcase of an unknown marine animal was washed up on the island of Stronsay in the Orkneys. It was serpentine in appearance, measuring 55 ft *16·8 m* in total length, 12 ft *3·7 m* in circumference and having a 15 ft *4·6 m* long neck.

Details of this monster and part of the skull were forwarded to the Royal Museum in Edinburgh University, and at a meeting of the Wernerian Society in Edinburgh on 19 November 1808 Mr Patrick Neill, a well-known naturalist and secretary of the Society, read 'an account of a great sea-snake lately cast ashore in Rothiesholm Bay, in the Island of Stronsay'. At a later meeting he described the unique specimen as a new genus, *Halysdryus pontoppidiani*, in honour of Bishop Erik Pontoppidan, who 50 years earlier had described a similar beast in his *Natural History of Norway*. Eventually news of the strange creature reached the ears of Sir Everard Home, the celebrated surgeon and anatomist of the Royal College of Surgeons in London, who was also a competent ichthyologist, and he asked Malcolm Laing, MP, a Justice of the Peace in Orkney, if he could borrow some of the remains. A few weeks later he received several vertebrae and part of the pectoral fin and, after a close study, he announced that they came from a large basking shark. He also queried the length of 55 ft *16·8 m* quoted for this animal, saying that the vertebrae corresponded in size with those of a 30 ft 6 in *9·30 m* specimen he had recently examined at Hastings (Home, 1809). The vertebrae of this fish are now preserved in the Royal Scottish Museum in Edinburgh. In 1933 they were examined by Commander Rupert T Gould of Loch Ness monster fame, who said that their huge size – they measure 6 in *152 mm* in diameter – led him to believe that the length of 55 ft *16·8 m* originally reported for this shark was reliable. He was mistaken, however, in thinking that these particular vertebrae were exceptionally large. In fact, they are slightly smaller in diameter than the largest vertebrae of a 25 ft *7·6 m* basking shark washed up on a beach near Provincetown, Massachusetts, USA in 1939 (Schroeder, 1940).

The decomposing body of a basking shark provides the basis for more than 90 per cent of the 'monster on the beach' stories that appear in the world's Press. This is not altogether surprising, because when the body of one of these great selachians is found in an advanced state of decomposition it does *look* more like a sea serpent than a basking shark. This is because the gill apparatus and the massive lower jaw have long dropped off and been washed away by the sea leaving behind a tiny box-like cranium and fleshy backbone which could pass as a small head on a long slender neck.

In November 1970 a 30 ft *9·1 m* long 'sea serpent' was washed up on a beach near Scituate, Massachusetts, USA. The strange-looking creature, which reportedly weighed between 15 and 20 tonnes (*sic*) and looked like a giant camel without legs, attracted a great deal of publicity and thousands of people visited the spot. The body, however, was later identified as being that of a basking shark.

A similar case occurred in April 1977 when the crew of the Japanese fishing vessel *Zuiyo Maru* trawled up the decomposing carcase of a huge marine animal 'like a snake with a turtle's body and front and rear flippers' off the Pacific coast of South Island, New Zealand. Most of the meat was gone, the internal organs were missing *and the lower jaw had fallen out*, but what was left measured 32 ft *9·8 m* in length and weighed 2 tonnes. After a member of the crew had photographed and sketched this weird denizen of the deep the trawler's skipper ordered the stinking carcase to be thrown back into the sea because he feared it would contaminate the rest of the

Above, the decomposing remains of a 25 ft 7·6 m long basking shark washed ashore at Cherbourg, NW France in May 1934.

Right, the huge filter-feeding shark Megamouth, which was not discovered until 1976.

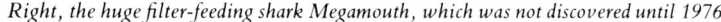

catch. After studying the photographs a palaeontologist at Yokohama University reported that it could not be a type of fish or even a mammoth seal – one leading marine biologist claimed it was an outsized Hooker's sea-lion! – because it was simply much too big and had too long a neck. He thought it was probably a plesiosaurus, a long-necked marine reptile which was known to have existed off eastern Australia about 100 million years ago. Fortunately samples of fibrous material from one of the fins were saved for scientific analyses, and later Dr Shigeru Kimura, a biochemist at Tokyo University, announced that the tissue contained a type of protein (elastoidin) found only in sharks and rays. The seaman's sketch of the Pacific monster also supported the 'rotting basking shark' theory.

On 15 November 1976 another huge filter-feeder new to science with mammoth jaws and a luminescent mouth interior was accidentally discovered by a US Navy research vessel 26 miles *42 km* NE of Kahuku Point, Oahu, Hawaii. The monstrous fish measured 14 ft 6 in *4·42 m* in length and weighed 1650 lb *748 kg*. Dr Leighton Taylor (1977), Director of the Waikiki Aquarium at the University of Hawaii, where 'Megamouth', as it was nicknamed, is now preserved in an 800 gallon *3028 litres* tank of formaldehyde, later described the animal's startling appearance: 'From the gills on the back it looks like a normal shark, but the head is notable because of the mouth which opens up and protrudes like a scoop.

The lower jaw swings out and expands, unlike other sharks'. He also said the gargantuan jaws contained more than 1000 tiny teeth arranged in four parallel rows on top and bottom.

The bizarre creature was caught at a depth of 500 ft *152 m* after it had half-swallowed a parachute anchor deployed to hold the 50 ft *15·2 m* research vessel steady in water over 14 000 ft *4267 m* deep. It was dead when it was hauled up with the stabilising equipment.

'Since we have only one specimen we don't know whether the Megamouth we have is a large or small one, nor do we know how many Megamouths exist', writes Dr C Scott Johnson (1978) of the Bioscience Department of the Naval Oceans Systems Center in San Diego, California. 'We do know that it appears to be a mature male, and was not caught before, most probably because it is a filter-feeder and would not bite a baited hook. Why it became entangled in the parachute is unknown. Since it had part of the chute in its mouth, we can only assume either it blundered into the chute while feeding with its mouth wide open or it was trying to eat it.'

The largest carnivorous fish (excluding filter-feeders) is the comparatively rare great white shark (*Carcharodon carcharias*), also called the blue pointer, white death shark, white pointer or man-eater which ranges from tropical waters to cool, temperate zones. Adult specimens (females are larger than males) average 14–15 ft *4·3–4·6 m* in length and generally scale between 1150 lb *522 kg* and 1700 lb *771 kg*, but much heavier weights have been recorded for carcharodons in approximately the same length category. One tremendously bulky 15-footer *4·6 m* caught near San Miguel Island off the coast of California on 18 March 1958, for example, weighed 3031 lb *1375 kg* (girth 9 ft 8½ in *2·96 m*), and a 13 ft 3 in *4·04 m* blue pointer captured at Hermanus, Cape Province, South Africa in 1928 tipped the scales at 2176 lb *987 kg*. These marked variations in poundages reflect the physical condition of the shark.

Although the general literature abounds with stories of enormous carcharodons, there are very few authentic records of their reaching or exceeding 20 ft *6·1 m* in length and/or 3000 lb *1361 kg* in weight.

In 1758 a great white shark measuring 20 ft *6·1 m* in length, 9 ft *2·7 m* across the pectoral fins and weighing 3924 lb *1780 kg* was harpooned from a French frigate in the Mediterranean after it had swallowed a sailor who had fallen overboard. Another man-eater caught by fishermen near Aix, southern France in 1829 was 22 ft *6·7 m* long and weighed over 4000 lb *1814 kg*. Among the undigested remains in its stomach was the headless body of a man in complete armour (Smith, 1833).

In October 1906 whaleman Archer Davidson killed a 20 ft *6·1 m* white pointer at the entrance to the Kiah River in Twofold Bay, NSW, Australia which measured an incredible 18 ft 6 in *5·64 m* in girth. The shark had been feeding heavily off a dead fin whale and was despatched with a razor-sharp boat spade from a 10 ft *3·0 m* dinghy. The combined measurement across the pectoral fins and the tail of this fish was 18 ft *5·5 m*, and the largest teeth in the jaws had an enamel height of 2·5 in *64 mm* (Caldwell, 1937). This monster was not weighed but, in view of its extraordinary bulk, it must have scaled at least 7000 lb *3175 kg*. On another occasion Davidson's brother George harpooned a white pointer near the try-works which measured 17 ft 8 in *5·38 m* in length and 12 ft *3·7 m* in circumference (Mead, 1962).

In November 1932 a 26 ft *7·9 m* great white shark was found trapped in a herring weir at Harbour de Loutre, Campobello Island, New Brunswick, Canada (Piers, 1934) and one measuring 25 ft 7·6 m stranded in the Gulf of St Lawrence between Newfoundland and the Canadian mainland in 1935 (Melancon, 1958). On 5 January 1941 a 20 ft *6·1 m* blue pointer weighing an estimated 3100 lb *1360 kg* was harpooned in Table Bay, Cape Town, South Africa and another blue pointer taken by a whale catcher about 100 miles *160 km* off the coast of Durban, Natal in July 1952 was 5 m *16 ft 5 in* long and weighed an estimated 1500 kg *3307 lb* (the jaws of this shark are preserved in Durban Aquarium). An 18 ft 2 in *5·54 m* gravid female caught off Fort Pierce,

Florida in the 1940s yielded a 790 lb *358 kg* liver and weighed an estimated 3160–3950 lb *1433–1792 kg* and a measurement of 18 ft 4 in *5·59 m* has been reliably reported for another gravid female taken in the same waters (Bigelow and Schroeder, 1948). On 5 June 1964 professional shark fisherman Capt Frank Mundus – the man on whom Peter Benchley based the character of 'Quint' in his best-selling novel *Jaws* – harpooned an enormous carcharodon off Montauk Point, at the tip of Long Island, New York, NY USA. This one measured 17 ft 6 in *5·33 m* in length, 13 ft *3·96 m* in circumference and weighed an estimated 4500 lb *2041 kg*. It was boated after a five-hour battle. In July 1965 an 18 ft 6 in *5·64 m* female with a girth of 10 ft 9 in *3·28 m* and weighing an estimated 3500 lb *1588 kg* was killed by rifle fire at Fremantle, Western Australia after it had eaten two sharks hooked on lines and was in the process of swallowing a third (Mark Andrews, pers. comm.). A white pointer measuring 20 ft *6·1 m* in length and weighing 3234 lb *1467 kg* was captured in King George Sound, Western Australia on 20 April 1975, and another one 16 ft *4·9 m* long (girth 10 ft 2 in *3·10 m*) and scaling 3388 lb *1537 kg* was taken in the same waters on 26 April 1976. In September 1977 an 18 ft *5·5 m* individual weighing an estimated 4000 lb *1814 kg* was caught at Point Albany, Western Australia, and the same weight was reported for one of 17 ft 6 in *5·33 m* captured in Moreton Bay, Queensland on 16 July 1979. On 16 April 1980 a white shark measuring 16 ft 6 in *5·03 m* in length and weighing an estimated 3500–4000 lb *1588–1814 kg* was caught off the Santa Catalina Islands, California and an 18 ft 2 in *5·54 m* specimen with a half-jaw circumference of 1·14 m *44·9 in* was taken in Israelite Bay, Western Australia in July 1980. In May 1981 a *5·06 m* 16 ft 7 in long carcharodon weighing 1750 kg *3860 lb* was trapped in a longline set off Iejima Island, Okinawa, Japan (Jesse James Schroeder, pers. comm.).

William Travis (1961) says a great white shark caught by him while drift-fishing off the Seychelles and raised to within 20 ft *6·1 m* of the surface was only 3 ft *91 cm* shorter than his 32 ft *9·8 m* shark cutter, but the rope holding this monstrous fish snapped like a piece of cotton when it suddenly made a determined dash ahead and it was not seen again.

Jordan and Evermann (1896) mention a 30 ft *9·1 m* man-eater taken off Soquel, California in 1880 which had a 100 lb *45 kg* sea lion in its stomach, but Dr Stewart Springer (pers. comm.), formerly of the US Fish and Wildlife Service, does not consider this record to be reliable. 'I can find no confirmation of the measurement of this shark and rather doubt that Jordan saw it. Perhaps he accepted the report on hearsay, feeling that if it could swallow a hundred pound sea-lion entire it was really very large. But of course, a 14–16 ft White shark can swallow a hundred pound sea-lion, or two for that matter.'

Another carcharodon caught in Santa Monica Bay, California after 1950 was credited with a length of 32 ft *9·8 m*, but this measurement was put out by local practical jokers. John E Fitch (pers. comm.), Research Director of the Department of Fish and Game at Long Beach, said the shark in question measured 14 ft *4·27 m*.

In 1975 Sea World of Mission Bay, San Diego, California offered a lucrative reward for any great white shark exceeding 20 ft *6·1 m* in a straight line, but although several commercial swordfishermen have since sunk harpoons in sharks which they estimated measured from 22 ft *6·7 m* to 26 ft *7·9 m*, they have not been successful. In each case the fish pulled loose or snapped off the gear, sometimes after 8–10 hours of struggling. The two largest sharks delivered so far measured 18 ft 2 in *5·54 m* (weight 4150 lb *1882 kg*) and 16 ft 8 in *5·08 m* (weight 4750 lb *2155 kg*), the latter being **the heaviest carcharodon ever recorded in American waters.** Another large individual measuring 16 ft *4·9 m* and scaling 3100 lb *1406 kg* harpooned by Larry Mansur near Los Angeles in July 1976 had two whole sea lions in its stomach weighing 175 lb *79 kg* and 125 lb *57 kg* respectively.

In 1977 a great white shark measuring an estimated 31 ft *9·5 m* in length was seen on several occasions by swordfishermen and by the pilot of their spotter plane in Californian waters. Several of the men put their boats alongside the outsized fish for comparison of size but did not attempt to harpoon it. 'Sufficient reports came to Department of Fish and Game personnel from these fishermen – all agreeing within a foot of this length, plus or minus, that I feel it is quite reliable', said John E Fitch (pers. comm.). 'These professional commercial fishermen have proven their judgment both reliable and extremely accurate on many occasions. However, it still must be placed in the realm of being an estimate.'

On 5 July 1975 Captain Paul O Sundberg (pers. comm.) was 21 miles *34 km* SSE of Montauk Point, Long Island, New York with a party of fishermen aboard his charterboat when a carcharodon estimated to measure more than 27 ft *8·2 m* in length passed under the vessel. As it approached again both Sundberg and his mate managed to get two swordfish-type harpoons into the animal but they were unable to subdue it and eventually, after a two-hour struggle, it broke free from the lines. Later it was discovered that the shark had left a lower-jaw bite mark approximately 30 in *76 cm* wide at the bottom of the stern, and closer examination revealed a portion of tooth embedded in the wood. There was no upper jaw mark, because when it made the bite a blue shark was hanging over the side from the gin pale. Thus, its bite encompassed the bottom of the boat and the blue shark's head.

According to Dr John E Randall (1973), senior ichthyologist at the Bernice B Bishop Museum, Honolulu, Hawaii, the size of bite inflicted by the great white shark is a good guide to approximation of length, a 16 ft *4·9 m* individual producing a wound area measuring 11×13 in *279×330 mm*. C Ostle of the Department of Fisheries and Fauna at Albany, Western Australia, told him that a whale killed in South Australian waters on 26 May 1972 had five enormous bites on its body measuring 19×24 in *483×610 mm* when it was found the next day, from which it was deduced that the carcharodon must have measured about 25–26 ft *7·6–7·9 m* in length. (Man-eaters this size can probably exert a crushing pressure of more than 50 tonnes per square inch *154 Pa* at the tips of the teeth.) Even larger bites were seen on a whale in 1968, but Ostle said they were not measured. On the basis of this information Captain Sundberg's monster must have measured over 30 ft *9·1 m* in length. The circular outline of another shark bite of comparable size (i.e. 30 in *76 cm* wide) was found on the mutilated body of a 770 lb *349 kg* bluefin tuna (*Thunnus thynnus*) netted on Long Beach, Simonstown, S Africa on 18 December 1962.

In June 1978 charter skipper John Sweetman harpooned another huge carcharodon estimated to measure 25 ft *7·6 m* off Montauk Point. This time, however, the shark towed the boat stern-first 30 miles *48 km* out into the Atlantic before it broke loose. Two days later another skipper harpooned what he thought was the same monster off Long Island, but this one quickly snapped the line when it went into a crash dive. It has since been suggested that the 'Montauk Monster' was nothing more than a harmless basking shark, which is also found in the same waters, but Capt Sundberg, who was in the area at the time, positively identified Sweetman's fish when it passed directly under the bow of his own boat. (The much higher and triangular-shaped dorsal fin of the basking shark is easily identifiable).

The popularly held view is that the largest great white shark on record of which there is evidence was a 36 ft 6 in *11·13 m* example caught off Port Fairy, Victoria, Australia in 1852, the jaws of which are preserved in the British Museum (Gunther, 1870), but this measurement was grossly exaggerated. Judging by the size of its teeth – the largest tooth in the upper jaw has an enamel height of 57 mm *2·24 in* – this particular selachian probably taped less than half this length, and Randall, who personally examined the jaws, calculated that it must have measured about 5·4 m *17 ft 8½ in* in the flesh. (One American ichthyologist has suggested that the 36 ft 6 in may have been a printer's error, and that the original length should have read 16 ft 6 in.)

According to Vladykov and McKenzie (1935), the largest great white shark ever recorded in Canadian

waters was a 37 ft *11·3m* brute found trapped in a herring weir at White Head Island near Grand Manan, New Brunswick in June 1930. Both these men are still alive and a few years back Mr R A McKenzie (pers. comm.), long since retired and living in St Andrews, New Brunswick, revealed that

this particular record was supplied by Dr Vadim Vladykov. He also said his co-author did not arrive on the Atlantic coast of Canada until the summer of 1931, which means that he did not examine the carcharodon personally but obtained his information second-hand. The important question is: would the

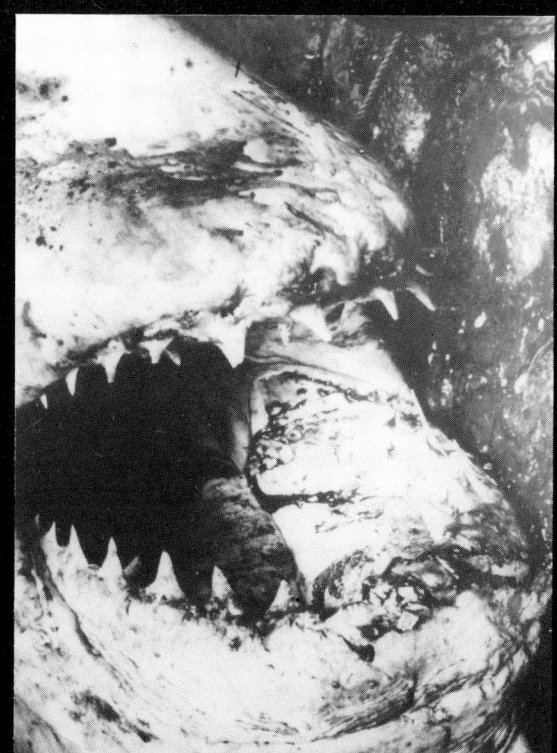

Left, the enormous bulk of the 29 ft 6 in 8·99 m great white shark harpooned by Azorean fishermen in May 1978.

Above, the jaws of the largest great white shark ever recorded.

Canadian ichthyologist, a man of high reputation, have included hearsay data unless he was positive it was accurate? In other words, did he have proof in the way of teeth, the jaws or even a photograph to substantiate this extreme measurement? Unfortunately only Dr Vladykov can supply an answer to this one, but so far all attempts to contact him have proved fruitless. The huge fish may, of course, have been a wrongly identified basking shark, which is the only really large selachian found in the area, but it is difficult to believe that a fisherman – presumably the source of Dr Vladykov's information – could have made such a mistake, because even if the carcase was in a bad state of decomposition the broad, triangular serrated teeth would have been an immediate means of identification.

As chance would have it – and unbeknown to the author – Dr W B Scott, Director of the Huntsman Marine Laboratory at St Andrews, had also been trying to either validate or discount Vladykov's outsized man-eater since 1976 with varying degrees of success, but it was not until November 1980 that he was able to confirm that the selachian was indeed a *white shark* as originally stated. 'There can be no doubt that the fish reported by Vladykov and McKenzie was a white shark for I have a tooth from it that is assuredly a white shark tooth,' he said in a letter. 'The specimen I have is the last one owned by an old gentleman who was present at the capture. Unfortunately he cannot remember the exact size, and has since given away all the other teeth that he saved. He told me that this was the smallest tooth he had.'

Dr Scott is now trying to uncover newspaper accounts or possibly even a photograph that would corroborate the 37 ft *11·3 m*, but judging from his statement an unbelievably huge carcharodon died in Canadian waters in June 1930.

In another letter Mr McKenzie said: 'There have been many more White Sharks taken on the Canadian Atlantic coast since our account of the Nova Scotian fishes was prepared. The most recent was not too far from here and was around 16–17 ft long. However, a few years ago a fantastic story concerning a White Shark was relayed to us by a fisheries officer, and if the fish was only half as long as indicated it was still a big shark. Since none of our men saw it or measured it, however, nothing has been published about it'.

Capt J S Elkington of Queensland, Australia told Stead (1963) that one day in 1894 an enormous white pointer drew alongside his launch just outside Townsville breakwater and lay there virtually motionless for half an hour. He said the shark was at least 4 ft *1·2 m* longer than his 35 ft *10·7 m* launch.

Lawrence Green (1958), the popular South African writer, improved even on this size by mentioning a 43 ft *13·1 m* blue pointer which ran aground in False Bay, Cape Province many years ago after it had followed a ship with plague on board. Later Green (pers. comm.) said: 'I gathered a great deal of information on whaling and shark fishing in those waters from a Tristan islander named George Cotton who settled at Simonstown towards the end of the last century. He died only a few years ago, almost a centenarian. Cotton was very vivid and accurate in his descriptions, but vague about dates. Thus it would be almost impossible to give the date of the 43-footer. In any case the newspapers of those days

gave little or no space to such events'.

The carcharodon also reaches an exceptional size in the waters off the Azores, which is the only area in the world apart from Flores, Indonesia, where open boat whaling is still carried on. In May 1978 an enormous individual swam into the harbour of San Miguel and made a general nuisance of itself for over an hour before a well-aimed lance thrust through the gills ended its life. This particular shark had been patrolling up and down outside the harbour entrance waiting for the dolphin fishermen to bring in their catch, and when a canoa (open whale boat) finally came into view the smell from the bloody carcases proved too much for the hungry beast and it threw caution to the wind. Unfortunately for science the Azorean fishermen treat these big sharks very casually, which is not altogether surprising when one remembers that sperm whales measuring up to 61 ft *18·6 m* have been captured off these islands, and when the jaws have been removed they invariably dump the bodies back in the open sea. On this occasion, however, Trevor Housby (pers. comm.), the well-known European big-game fishing consultant and writer on the subject, happened to be present when this monstrous fish was winched up on to the basalt setts, and he was able to take some measurements and two photographs before dashing off to catch an inter-island ferry. The man-eater measured an astonishing 29 ft 6 in *9·00 m* in straight-line length, 13 ft 8 in *4·17 m* across the outstretched pectoral fins and had a maximum girth of practically 20 ft *6·1 m*. Housby estimated the weight at 10 000 lb *4536 kg*, although he did admit later on that the carcharodon was even bulkier than a basking shark he had seen in the same length category (*cf* 13 440 lb *6096 kg* for a 27 ft 6 in *8·38 m Cetorhinus maximus* which had a maximum girth of 16 ft *4·9 m*). The jaws and teeth, the largest of which had an enamel height of just over 3 in *76 mm*, were later acquired by a dealer in curios living on Terceira.

Since then three more carcharodons over 6 m *19 ft 8 in* in length have been caught in Azorean waters. The most recent example, measuring 6·4 m *21 ft*, was harpooned off Lages de Pico in August 1980. Some big whites (i.e. 5–5·5 m *16 ft 5 in–18 ft*) have also been taken off Madeira, another island group southeast of the Azores.

The largest great white shark actually to be weighed was a 21 ft *6·4 m* long female caught by fishermen at a depth of 1800 ft *549 m* off Castillo de Cojimar, Cuba in May 1945 and beached with the aid of trucks. The monstrous animal, which measured 14 ft 9 in *4·5 m* in circumference just behind the pectoral fins, tipped the scales at an astonishing 7302 lb *3312 kg* and yielded a 1005 lb *456 kg* liver. The gutted shark was later mounted and put on display in the Museo de la Academia Naval del Mariel, Havana, but was eventually discarded when it started to decompose. The only evidence left today is a single tooth with an enamel height of 57 mm *2·24 in* and a vertebra measuring 80 mm *3·15 in* in diameter and 37 mm *1·46 in* in depth (L Howell Rivero, pers. comm.; Guitart and Milera, 1975).

The largest fish ever caught on a rod was a great white shark weighing 2664 lb *1208 kg* and measuring 16 ft 10 in *5·13 m* in length taken on a 130 lb *59 kg* test line by Alf Dean at Denial Bay, South Australia on 21 April 1959. Five other white pointers caught by Dean also weighed over 1 tonne. They scaled 2536 lb *1150 kg* (16 ft 9 in *5·11 m*), 2372 lb *1076 kg* (15 ft 11 in *4·85 m*), 2344 lb *1063 kg* (15 ft *4·57 m*), 2333 lb *1058 kg* (16 ft 3 in *4·95 m*) and 2312 lb *1049 kg* (16 ft 1 in *4·90 m*) respectively. On 26 April 1976 Clive Green caught another white pointer weighing 3388 lb *1537 kg* off Albany, Western Australia on a 130 lb *59 kg* test line (see page 130) but this record was not ratified because whale meat was used as bait.

Although several attempts have been made to keep the great white shark in captivity, none have been successful. On 19 August 1980 a 7 ft *2·1 m* 300 lb *136 kg* female nicknamed 'Sandy' was deposited in Steinhart Aquarium, San Francisco, but after three days in her new surroundings she started to fade away. In the end aquarium officials decided to return their star exhibit to her natural habitat. She was released near the Farallon Islands about 30 miles *48 km* off the Californian coast and quickly sped off.

Apart from being the man-eater par excellence, the voracious nature and indiscriminate feeding habits of the carcharodon have also resulted in many unusual objects being found in its stomach. One individual caught in the Adriatic had three over-coats, a nylon raincoat and a motor car licence inside it, and a 14 ft *4·3 m* 1250 lb *567 kg* shark yielded an old boot, a plastic pail, the remains of a seaman's oil-skins, a full bottle of chianti and a large iron cashbox containing 1670 Yugoslav dinars in notes and coins! A white pointer taken near Port Jackson, NSW, Australia contained half a ham, several legs of mutton, the hindquarters of a pig, the head and forelegs of a bulldog with a rope tied round its neck, a quantity of horseflesh, a piece of sacking and a ship's iron scraper. A 16 ft *4·9 m* brute captured in Hobson's Bay, Victoria, Australia in 1877 after look-ing through the fence surrounding the ladies' bath-ing section in 'a disagreeable manner', contained a large Newfoundland dog which had disappeared the previous day (McCoy, 1878–90). Bricks, bottles, tin cans and even a porcupine have been found in the stomachs of other carcharodons.

On 18 April 1968 Henri Bource, a 28-year-old Australian, was shooting an underwater film about sharks in the sea off Melbourne, Victoria when he was attacked by a white pointer which bit off his artificial left leg and swallowed it! His original left leg had been lost to another shark of the same species.

Jim McKay, an Australian marine biologist from Cairns, Queensland is planning to be the first person to **hand-feed a great white shark without the aid of cages, back-up divers or any weapons**. He has already made three attempts off Dangerous Reef, South Australia, but on each occasion the project had to be abandoned because of adverse weather con-ditions and other problems. In a letter he explained: 'Many years ago, about ten to be exact, I had a speared fish torn from my grasp by a whaler. I didn't see the shark approach for the attack, nevertheless it happened. I received not a single scratch from the encounter, so I tried it again at a later date. I enticed sharks to me and hand-fed them. I fed whalers, tigers, makos and many other species of sharks. As the years have gone, I have carried out these feedings with 100 per cent success. After the first few years of these feedings, I began to realise that it was a little more complex than I would have myself believed. I realised that my own behaviour had a direct effect on the animal in question. If I simulated panic, the shark became quite excited and aggressive towards me. If I behaved normal and in total control of myself, then I could confront the creature not only to feed it, but also to tag the animal.'

During his most recent attempt in early 1981 McKay spent 60 minutes on the sea-bed with two white pointers measuring 14 ft *4·3 m* and 12 ft *3·7 m* respectively. At first, he said, the sharks were very cautious, but they soon became very interested in the proceedings and eventually one of them made a few passes at the tuna bait. Unfortunately soon after-wards the No. 1 camera sprang a leak and filming had to be abandoned.

McKay has promised to supply details if and when he successfully hand-feeds a great white shark. 'Hopefully', he says, 'I'll be able to write the letter myself.'

Although Britain's coasts should fall comfortably within the range of the great white shark, the presence of *C. carcharias* in home waters has never been confirmed. Specimens were reportedly caught or washed ashore in 1769, 1813 and 1868, but these particular fish were all blue sharks (*Prionace glauca*), which was previously accorded the scientific name *Carcharias glaucus*. Hence the mix-up. An 11 ft 6 in *3·5 m* shark weighing 1120 lb *508 kg* caught off the Scilly Isles on 27 June 1937 was alleged to have been a man-eater, but this may have been a tiger shark which has been positively sighted in the English Channel and ranges as far north as Iceland. The great white is definitely known to occur off the Portuguese coast, however, and there have reportedly been sightings in the Bay of Biscay.

The tiger shark which allegedly measured 20 ft 9 in 6·32 m in length.

The only other species of sharks known to exceed 20 ft *6·1 m* or 3000 lb *1361 kg* are the cosmopolitan tiger shark (*Galeocerdo cuvieri*) of warm coastal waters, and the Greenland or sleeper shark (*Somniosus microcephalus*) of the arctic and northern seas.

Lengths up to 30 ft *9·1 m* have been claimed for the tiger shark, but the longest accurately measured specimen on record was an 18-footer *5·5 m* caught in a shark net at Newcastle, NSW, Australia in 1954 which scaled 3360 lb *1524 kg* (Grant, 1972; P R Wilson, pers. comm.). A Cuban specimen of about 18 ft *5·5 m* has also been reported (Bigelow and Schroeder, 1948). F A Mitchel Hedges (1923) quotes a length of 20 ft 9 in *6·32 m* and a weight of 1760 lb *798 kg* for a tiger shark he caught off the island of Taboga in the Gulf of Panama in 1922, but photographic evidence and the weight quoted – the rod and line record is held by a 13 ft 10½ in *4·23 m* specimen which scaled 1780 lb *807 kg* – suggests this measurement was taken over the curves of the body. Another one caught near the entrance to Port Jackson, NSW, Australia was credited with a length of 18 ft 6 in *5·64 m* and an estimated weight of 1800 lb *816 kg*, but this measurement has not been confirmed. On 16 May 1980 a length of 21 ft *6·4 m* was reported for a tiger shark netted at Mackay, Queensland, Australia, but when officers responsible for the Government shark-fishing programme made enquiries they found the fish in question was actually 18 ft *5·5 m*, which is still a record size (J Leech, pers. comm.). Dr John E Randall (pers. comm.) was once diving in 150 ft *45·7 m* of water at Enewatak in the Marshall Islands, W Pacific with a partner when a tiger shark slightly longer than their 20 ft *6·1 m* boat swam overhead.

The Greenland shark usually averages 10–12 ft *3·0–3·7 m* in length, but it sometimes reaches a much greater size. One monstrous individual caught off May Island in the Firth of Forth, Scotland in January 1895 was 21 ft *6·4 m* long and weighed 2250 lb *1021 kg*. Among the contents of its stomach was a

seaman's boot containing part of a human leg! (Jenkins, 1925). In the spring of 1929 another Greenland shark measuring 15 ft *4·6 m* in length and weighing 2352 lb *1067 kg* was found entangled in cod-nets in the Moray Firth. After a struggle lasting more than an hour it was hoisted over the side of the steam drifter *Bon Ami*, where it promptly disgorged four young seals, one of them 4 ft *1·2 m* long. This fish has been credited with lengths up to 8 m *26 ft 3 in*, and one example caught off the Greenland coast weighed 3080 lb *1397 kg*.

In 1966 oceanographer Dr Eugene LaFond and pilot Joseph Thompson were probing and photographing the 4000 ft *1219 m* deep bottom of the San Diego Trough in the 18 ft *5·5 m* research submarine 'Deepstar 4000' when suddenly they found an enormous shark looking into the lens of their camera. 'The eyes were as big as dinner plates', said Thompson afterwards, 'then came the huge pectoral fins and finally the tail.' By comparing its size with the known distance between scientific instruments placed on the seabed the two men calculated that the giant was about 30 ft *9·1 m* long. The fish was later identified as an outsized Pacific sleeper shark (*Somniosus pacificus*) by Dr Carl Hubbs, a marine biologist at the Scripps Institution of Oceanography, after studying photographic evidence.

On 19 February 1846 a six-gilled shark (*Hexanchus griseus*) with a reported length of 26 ft 5 in *8·05 m* was caught by fishermen at Polperro, Cornwall (Day, 1880–84), but this measurement was in error and should have read 26·5 in *67·3 cm*! This deep-water species has been recorded up to 15 ft 6 in *4·72 m* and 1682 lb *763 kg* off Cuba.

Although no reliable statistics are available, it is estimated that at least 100 people are killed annually by sharks, most of them unprovoked attacks off the coasts of Africa, South America and Asia where fatalities often go unrecorded. Of the 40–50 shark attacks actually reported worldwide each year, mostly in warmer waters, about 60 per cent survive the ordeal, although possibly with fewer appendages than they had originally. The waters around Australia are particularly dangerous, and at least 420 people have died since 1898, although a recent report contends that Australians have as much chance of being eaten by a shark as they have of being struck by a piece falling off an aircraft.

Research has shown that most shark attacks on humans were quick lunges inflicting a slashing wound, followed by departure. Man, however, is not the natural prey of carnivorous sharks, so why do they attack swimmers? Apparently they have such highly developed senses that they can pick up signals like splashing and the minute traces of ammonia found in urine at great distances, and anything upright in the water means only one thing to this magnificent predator – a dying fish! In December 1979 a shark (probably a carcharodon) killed a swimmer off the north coast of Madeira in the E Atlantic – the first recorded case of such an attack off the holiday island.

Even when dead these engines of destruction can still be dangerous, as fisherman Mark Green can bear painful testimony. In October 1977 he was driving along a road in Perth, Western Australia when his car was involved in a crash. He was hurled on to the razor-sharp teeth of a dead shark's jaws resting on the seat behind him and received gashes needing 22 stitches!

Recently scientists have discovered what they believe to be the perfect defence against man-eating sharks – a striped bathing costume! After months of experiments off the Australian coast, William Dunson, Professor of Biology at Pennsylvania State University, reported: 'Sharks usually eat anything. But they have never been known to attack the banded sea snake, a brightly striped ocean reptile which is one of the most poisonous creatures in the world.' He thought a brightly striped bathing costume would be enough to keep a swimmer safe, but warned: 'We are not yet ready to experiment with a human being. We have more research to do.'

Probably the greatest mass attack on man by any large animal occurred on 28 November 1942 when a German U-boat fired a salvo of torpedoes into the hull of the Liverpool steamer *Nova Scotia* (6796 tonnes) some 30 miles *48 km* off the coast of Zululand, South Africa. On board were 900 men, including 765 Italian prisoners of war bound for colonial work camps. The ship went down in seven minutes, and as the hundreds of men in the water thrashed around or clung desperately to pieces of wreckage (only one lifeboat was launched) packs of hungry sharks moved in for the kill. When a Portuguese rescue ship eventually arrived on the scene, there were only 192 survivors, the rest having been eaten by sharks in a bloody orgy of horror (Davis, 1964).

In January 1981 sharks attacked and killed 25 sailors when their Israeli freighter sank in the notorious Bermuda Triangle. Rescuers reported having to drag mutilated bodies from the jaws of the frenzied animals.

The largest fish ever killed underwater by a spear fishermen was a 16 ft *4·9 m* long basking shark weighing 2100 lb *953 kg* taken by Robert Lorenz off Santa Monica, California, USA in November 1955. In 1963 a 14 ft *4·3 m* white pointer weighing 1600 lb *726 kg* was killed in Australian waters by a skin diver using an explosive head fitted to a hand spear.

The 4928 lb 2235 kg *ocean sunfish captured off Bird Island in September 1908.*

The largest fish ever held in captivity was a whale shark weighing several thousand pounds which was exhibited at the Mito Aquarium, Japan for several months many years ago. The fish was kept in a small bay separated from the open sea by a net septum (Gilbert, 1963).

The largest of the bony fishes is the ocean sunfish (*Mola mola*), which is found in all tropical, subtropical and temperate waters. Adult specimens average 6 ft *1·8 m* from the tip of the snout to the end of the tail fin, 8 ft *2·4 m* between the dorsal and anal fins (vertical length) and weigh up to 1 tonne.

The largest ocean sunfish ever recorded was one accidentally struck by the SS *Fiona* shortly after 1 pm on 18 September 1908 off Bird Island, some 40 miles *64 km* from Sydney, NSW, Australia. A full account of this incident appeared in the *Wide World* magazine for 10 December 1910: '. . . all hands were alarmed by a sudden shock, as though the steamer had struck a solid substance or wreckage. The result was strange and remarkable, for the port engine was brought up all standing. The starboard engine was quickly stopped and a boat lowered and sent to investigate. On getting under the steamer's counter the boat's crew were astonished to find that a huge sun-fish had become securely fixed in the bracket of the port propeller. One blade was completely embedded in the creature's flesh, jamming the monster firmly against the stern-post of the vessel. It was impossible to extricate the fish at sea, so the boat was hoisted on board again and the steamer proceeded on her passage to Sydney with the starboard engine only working.

'On reaching Port Jackson, the *Fiona* was anchored in Mosman Bay, where all hands were set to work to remove the fish. After much difficulty and with the aid of the steamer's winch, the sun-fish was hoisted clear and swung on board.'

The fish was later taken to a nearby wharf and put on a weighbridge where it registered 2235 kg *4927 lb*. It measured 10 ft *3·1 m* in length and 14 ft *4·3 m* between the dorsal and anal fins.

Like the whale shark, the ocean sunfish is very tough skinned. Gilbert Whitley (1940) reports that one large individual caught in Botany Bay, NSW, Australia was impervious to bullets fired from Winchester rifles. Another one encountered off Montevideo, Uruguay resisted all attempts to harpoon it and was only secured after an iron had been inserted into its gill-cleft.

The largest ocean sunfish ever recorded in British waters was one weighing 800 lb *363 kg* which ran aground at a salmon fishing station at Montrose, Scotland on 14 December 1960. It was sent to the Marine Research Institute in Aberdeen. Another specimen exhibited in London in 1883 measured 8 ft *2·4 m* in length and 11 ft *3·4 m* between the dorsal and anal fins. It was caught in Swedish waters (Smitt, 1892).

In former times, when it was more abundant, the Russian sturgeon (*Huso huso*) or 'beluga' also grew to an enormous size, and one female caught at Saratov on the west bank of the Volga in 1869 scaled 2760 lb *1252 kg*. According to Dr Leo S Berg (1962), the Russian ichthyologist, the largest beluga on record was a gravid female taken in the estuary of the Volga in 1827 which measured 24 ft *7·3 m* in length and weighed 3249 lb *1474 kg*. Another gravid female caught in the Caspian Sea in 1836 scaled 3218 lb *1460 kg*, and a third weighing 3200 lb *1452 kg* was taken in the Volga in 1813. On 11 May 1922 a female weighing 2645 lb *1200 kg* was caught in the estuary of the Volga. The head weighed 635 lb *288 kg*, the body 1470 lb *667 kg* and the eggs or caviare 323 lb *147 kg*. Another female weighing 2706 lb *1227 kg* caught in the Tikhaya Sosna River in 1924 had 7 700 000 eggs weighing 541 lb *245 kg* in her ovaries.

The kaluga or Daurian sturgeon (*Huso dauricus*) of the Amur River and adjacent lakes of eastern Siberia is also worthy of mention. The largest specimen listed by Soldatov (1915) measured 13 ft 8½ in *4·18 m* and weighed 1193 lb *541 kg*, but Berg (1932) quotes weights of 1807 lb *820 kg* and 2513 lb *1140 kg* for two others.

A white sturgeon (*Acipenser transmontanus*) caught in the Columbia River at Astoria, Oregon, USA in 1892 and exhibited at the World's Fair in Chicago the following year, was stated to have weighed more than 2000 lb *907 kg*, but Gudger (1934) says he was unable to confirm this poundage. There are also two claims for a 1500 lb *680 kg* white sturgeon on record:

one taken from the Weiser River, Washington in 1898 after it had blundered into a salmon gill-net, and the other from Snake River, Oregon in 1911 (Brown, 1962). The official record is held by a 12 ft 6 in *3·81 m* fish taken in the Columbia River near Vancouver, Washington in May/June 1912 which weighed 1285 lb *583 kg*.

The largest sturgeon found in British waters is the now rare common sturgeon (*Acipenser sturio*). The heaviest recorded specimen was a female measuring 10 ft 5 in *3·18 m* and weighing 700 lb *318 kg* netted by the trawler *Ben Urie* off the Orkneys and landed at Aberdeen on 18 October 1956. Another female measuring 12 ft *3·7 m* and weighing 672 lb *305 kg* was caught by the trawler *King Athelstan* in the North Sea and landed at Lowestoft, Suffolk on 4 April 1937. **The largest river specimen** was a 9 ft 2·7 m male weighing 507½ lb *230 kg* accidentally netted in the River Severn at Lydney, Glos on 1 June 1937. Its captor, James Legg, a Blakeney lave net salmon fisherman, said the fish had a severe wound on its back, which was thought to have been inflicted by the propeller of a boat (S E V Jones, pers. comm.).

Frank Buckland, the eccentric Victorian naturalist, once arranged for a 9 ft *2·7 m* 212 lb *96 kg* sturgeon to be delivered to his London home so that he could take a plaster cast for his Museum of Economic Fish Culture. Unfortunately the rope attached to the tail went adrift as the weighty beast was being eased down the stone stairs leading to the area below and the next moment the armour-clad monster was off like an avalanche. It burst through the facing door like a battering ram, slid right into the kitchen and glided smoothly along the oil-cloth until it came to rest under the table. According to Buckland the cook screamed when she saw 'the master's horrid great fish', the housemaid nearly fainted, the cat jumped on the dresser, upsetting the best crockery and the parrot was so badly shaken it never spoke another word.

During a voyage from Firth of Clyde to Loch Eriboll in January 1955 a fault in the engine room of the aircraft carrier HMS *Glory* led to the discovery of a sturgeon trapped in a condenser pipe!

The longest bony fish in the world is the laterally compressed oarfish (*Regalecus glesne*), also called the 'King of the Herrings', which has a worldwide distribution. In *c* 1885 a 25 ft *7·6 m* long example weighing 600 lb *272 kg* was caught by fishermen off Pemaquid Point, Maine, USA, and a second one measuring 21 ft *6·4 m* was washed ashore near Santa Ana, California in June 1901. In December 1947 the steamship *Santa Clara* decapitated another oarfish estimated to measure 45 ft *13·7 m* in length and 3 ft *0·91 m* in diameter off the North Carolina coast while on a voyage from Baranquilla to New York. On 18 July 1963 a 50 ft *15·2 m* oarfish was seen

swimming off Asbury Park, New Jersey by a team of scientists from the Sandy Hook Marine Laboratory. At the time they were aboard the 85 ft *26 m* research vessel *Challenger*, which gave them a yardstick for measuring the fish's length.

The longest oarfish recorded in British waters was a 15 ft *4·6 m* specimen caught near Hartlepool, Durham in 1866 and now preserved in the Dorman Museum, Middlesbrough (C Thornton, pers. comm.). In February 1981 another one of these rare creatures measuring 12 ft 6 in *3·81 m* in length was washed up at Sandsend near Whitby, Yorkshire. It was later presented to the British Museum. Many reports of sea serpents can be attributed to sightings of oarfish on the surface.

The largest fish which spends its whole life in fresh or brackish water is the rare pa beuk or pla buk (*Pangasianodon gigas*), a giant catfish found in the deep waters of the Mekong River of Laos, Thailand, Cambodia, Vietnam and parts of China. According to Seidenfaden (1923) this fish attains a length of up to 3 m *9 ft 10 in* and a weight of 240 kg *529 lb*, and he says he saw one personally which measured 2·5 m *8 ft 2½ in* in length, 1·7 m *5 ft 7 in* in circumference and weighed 180 kg *397 lb*.

In June 1974 A E Davidson, the British Ambassador in Vietiane, Laos and a keen amateur ichthyologist, served up fillet of pa beuk ('Pa beuk de ban Sai') at a banquet given in honour of the Laotian Prime Minister, Prince Souvanna Phouma, but there were few takers. The 108 lb *49 kg* head of this 375 lb *170 kg* fish was later presented to the British Museum. Mr Davidson (pers. comm.) said the season for the pa beuk fishery at Ban Houei Sai was usually in April and May, and that between 20 and 30 fish were caught in a normal year. In 1974, however, only 14 examples were caught in a very short season lasting just four weeks. Of this total only two were females,

Above, an old drawing of an oar fish – the longest bony fish in the world.

Below, the formidable mouth of the wels, which has been dubbed a man-eater.

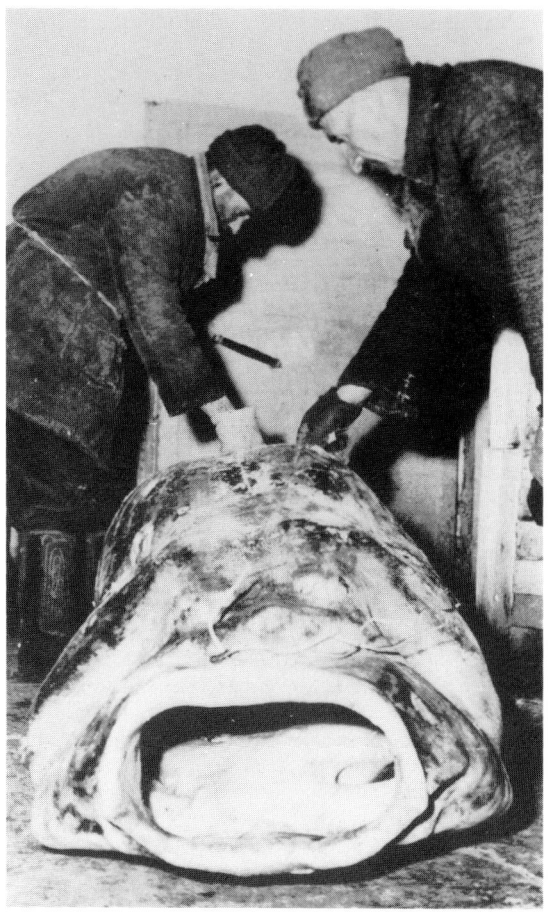

The rare pa beuk, the largest fish which spends its whole life in fresh or brackish water.

and they weighed 364 lb *165 kg* and 353 lb *160 kg* respectively. The twelve males ranged from 297 lb *135 kg* to 441 lb *200 kg*. In this series of fish the lengths were not recorded, but the measurements probably ranged between 7 ft 6 in *2·29 m* and 8 ft 6 in *2·59 m*.

In earlier times, before it was over-fished, the European catfish or wels (*Silurus glanis*) was considered the largest freshwater fish in the world, but today this species is no longer in contention. Kessler (1856) claims the catfish found in the Dnieper River, European Russia reached a length of 8–14 ft *2·4–4·3 m* and weighed up to 600 lb *272 kg*, and he says the largest one on record measured 15 ft *4·6 m* and tipped the scales at 720 lb *327 kg*. Seeley (1886) writes: 'It is often from six to nine or ten feet long, and occasionally reaches a length of thirteen feet. In the Danube it often attains a weight of 400 or 500 pound, and in South Russia may exceed 600 pound. With age it increases chiefly in circumference, and sometimes is as much as two men can span (*sic*)'.

The largest accurately measured wels of which there is reliable evidence was a 3 m *9 ft 10 in* female caught in the Danube in Rumania which is now preserved in the Museum d'Histoire Naturelle, Paris (Pellegrin, 1931). Another exceptionally large example from Rumania measured 2·85 m *9 ft 4¼ in* in length and weighed 170 kg *375 lb*. The heaviest Russian fish listed by Berg (1949) was taken in the Desna River in the Ukraine in September 1918. It weighed 565 lb *256 kg*. Another one caught in the Dnieper River near Kremenchug allegedly weighed 300 kg *661 lb*, but further details are lacking. Berg says catfish weighing 200 kg *441 lb* are not a rarity in the Syr-Darya and Chu Rivers, but this statement would not stand up today.

This species, incidentally, has been dubbed a maneater by some of the earlier writers. Grossinger (cited by Gudger, 1945) for instance, has been quoted as saying that two young girls in Hungary who had gone to fetch water from a river were devoured by great catfish, and the same naturalist also mentions another wels caught by a fisherman near the Turkish frontier with Europe which contained the body of a young woman. Gudger (1945), on the other hand, although admitting that a large wels has a mouth and gullet big enough to swallow a small child, believes that most human parts recovered from giant catfish have been taken from rotting corpses, particularly of children 'which in some way – by drowning or some other accident – have gotten into rivers.'

There are also several huge catfishes in South America. The longest – although not the heaviest – is the lau-lau (*Brachyplatystoma filamentosum*), found in the rivers of Guyana as well as the Amazon, which has been credited with a maximum length of 12 ft *3·7 m*, but 8 ft *2·4 m* is probably a more realistic figure. Dr William Beebe and John Tee-Van told Gudger (1943) that the two largest specimens taken by them at Kartabo at the junction of the Cuyuni and Mazaruni Rivers in Guyana in 1927 were 6 ft 2 in *1·88 m* and 6 ft 3½ in *1·92 m* respectively, but these measurements did not include the tail fin, which would account for about another 12 in *305 mm*. Eleven years earlier Beebe had measured another lau-lau caught at Kartabo which taped 6 ft 11 in *2·11 m* (about 8 ft *2·4 m* with the tail fin).

The pirahyba (*Piratinga piraiba*) of the Amazon River, which is closely related to the lau-lau, has been called the goliath of catfishes, but very little information has been published concerning size and weight. Ex-President Theodore Roosevelt (1914) was told by the doctor attached to his Brazilian expedition that while he was working at Itacoatira, a small town at the mouth of the Madeira River, he had seen a pirahyba measuring 3 m *9 ft 10 in*. It had been killed by two men with machetes after it had attacked their canoe. Another specimen collected by Dr J D Haseman (cited by Gudger, 1943) in the Guapore tributary of the Mamore River in 1909–10 for the Carnegie Museum in Pittsburgh, Pennsylvania, was so heavy that it required the efforts of four sturdy men to pull it up on to a sandbar. This fish measured 6 ft 1 in *1·85 m* in length and weighed an estimated 350 lb *159 kg*. Dr Haseman put the maximum length and weight of this species at 7 ft *2·1 m* and 400 lb *181 kg*.

Some writers claim that the largest freshwater fish in the world is the pike-like arapaima (*Arapaima gigas*), also called the 'pirarucu', which is found chiefly in the Amazon drainage of Brazil and Peru, but the size attained by this fish has been much exaggerated. When Schomburgk (1841) visited Brazil in 1836 the natives of the Rio Negro told him that they had caught pirarucu measuring 15 ft *4·6 m* in length and weighing 400 lb *181 kg*, but the naturalist-explorer did not see any fish remotely approaching that size. The two longest specimens collected by him measured 8 ft 1½ in *2·48 m* and 7 ft *2·13 m* respectively.

Paul Fountain (1914) claims he killed an arapaima on the Rio Negro which scaled 628 lb *285 kg* piecemeal, and weights up to 1000 lb *454 kg* have been reported elsewhere (Norwood, 1964), but these poundages are much too extreme to be acceptable.

Dr Haseman told Gudger that he measured an 8 ft *2·4 m* arapaima at Meura on the Rio Negro which scaled 264 lb *120 kg*, and heard from the local fishermen that they had caught a 10-footer *3·0 m* weighing 440 lb *200 kg* in the same spot a few days earlier. 'Haseman did not see the fish', says Gudger, 'but he saw the head. This was so much larger than the head of the one he measured that he thought the report of length and weight reasonably accurate.'

Three individuals caught by Edward McTurk, a rancher at Karanambu, Guyana on 13 May 1947 were 6 ft 11½ in *2·12 m* and 203 lb *92 kg*, 6 ft 8 in *2·03 m* and 148 lb *67 kg* and 5 ft 11 in *1·80 m* and 110 lb *50 kg* respectively. McTurk, who had probably seen more arapaima than any other white man, told McCormick (1949) that he once killed a fish measuring 9 ft *2·7 m*, but it was not weighed.

The largest freshwater fish found in North America is the alligator gar (*Lepisosteus spatula*) of the Mississippi River and its tributaries. The largest specimen listed by Gudger (1942) was a female taken in Belle Island Lake, Louisiana in *c* 1925 which measured 9 ft 8½ in *2·96 m* in length and weighed 302 lb *137 kg*. Another one caught by Dr Henry Thibault in the Arkansas River near Little Rock was 9 ft 2 in *2·79 m* and 232 lb *105 kg*, and there is also a record of an alligator gar taken in Moon Lake, Mississippi which measured 10 ft *3·0 m* and scaled 230 lb *104 kg*. The rod and reel record is 279 lb *127 kg* for an exceptionally bulky 7 ft 9 in *2·36 m* long individual caught by Bill Valverde in the Rio Grande River, Texas on 2 December 1951.

Africa's only giant freshwater fish is the widely-distributed Nile perch (*Lates niloticus*). Mature specimens usually measure 4–4½ ft *1·2–1·4 m* in length, but much larger individuals have been recorded. One huge female taken a few miles up the Sobat River, a southern tributary of the Nile, was 6 ft 1 in *1·85 m* long and weighed 266¾ lb *121 kg* (Boulenger, 1907), and another one caught in Lake No at the junction of the Bahr al Ghazal with the Bahr el Jebel or Nile proper tipped the scales at 280 lb *127 kg* (Gudger, 1944). There is also a record of a 246-pounder *112 kg* from Lake Rudolf, northern Kenya, and a Nile perch said to weigh 360 lb *163 kg* was caught in a seine net on Lake Albert (Gordon, 1969). The largest female caught in Lake Nasser, Egypt measured 2 m *6 ft 6¾ in* in length and weighed 175 kg *386 lb*, and another one from Nozha Hydrodrome near Alexandria scaled 168 kg *370 lb* (length 1·73 m *5 ft 8 in*). Sudan's record female was 1·75 m *5 ft 9 in* and 160 kg *353 lb* (Bishri, 1981). In September

The dwarf pygmy goby shown in actual size.

1978 a Kenyan fisherman netted a Nile perch measuring more than 6 ft *1·8 m* in length and weighing 416 lb *189 kg* in Lake Victoria where it has been introduced. The fish, which was the largest on record, was purchased by a research institute for the sum of £40.

The largest freshwater fish found in Britain and Ireland is the pike (*Esox lucius*), and Buller (1979) gives details of 202 individuals scaling 35 lb *15·9 kg* or more. The grand-daddy of them all was reportedly a 92 lb *41·7 kg* pike lifted out of the River Shannon, Ireland in *c* 1815, but the largest specimen for which there is visual evidence (preserved head) was a 72 lb *32·7 kg* monster caught in Loch Ken, Scotland by John Murray in 1774.

The smallest known fish in terms of length is the dwarf pygmy goby (*Pandaka pygmaea*), a colourless and nearly transparent creature found in the streams and lakes of Luzon in the Philippines. Adult males measure 7·5–9·9 mm *0·30–0·39 in* in length and weigh 4–5 mg *0·000 14–0·000 18 oz*, and adult females 9–11 mm *0·35–0·43 in* and 5–6 mg *0·000 18–0·000 21 oz*. This fish, which was discovered in 1927 off the shores of Malabon-Navotas near Metro Manila, is so tiny that it has to be studied with a microscope rather than a strong magnifying glass.

The world's smallest commercial fish is the now endangered sinarapan (*Mistichthys luzonensis*), another goby found only in Lake Buhi, Luzon. Adult males measure 10–13 mm *0·39–0·51 in* in length and adult females 12–14 mm *0·47–0·55 in* (Smith, 1902). Despite its diminutiveness this fish is much in demand as *food* and has considerable commercial importance. The natives of the region catch

The huge arapaima of the Amazon drainage of Brazil and Peru.

them with large close-web nets, pack them tightly into woven baskets until all the water drains out leaving a compact mass, and then sell them in dried cake form. A 1 lb *454 g* cake contains about 70 000 fish!

The smallest known marine fishes are the Marshall Islands goby *Eviota zonura* and the goby *Schindleria praematurus*, of the tropical Pacific which measure 12–16 mm *0·47–0·63 in* and 12–19 mm *0·47–0·75 in* respectively. Mature examples of the latter fish, which was not described until 1940, have been known to weigh only 2 mg *0·000 07 oz*, equivalent to 14 175 to the ounce – the lightest of all vertebrates and the smallest catch possible for any fisherman.

The smallest fish found in British waters is Guillet's goby (*Lebetus guilleti*), which does not exceed 24 mm *0·94 in*. It has been recorded from the English Channel, the west coast of Ireland and the Irish Sea (Wheeler, 1978).

The smallest species of shark is the very rare dwarf shark *Squaliolus laticaudus* of the W Pacific. The type specimen (male) taken in Batanga Bay on the island of Luzon on 8 June 1908 measured 150 mm *5·9 in* in length (Smith and Radcliffe, 1912), but this was exceptional. Of the few examples collected since none have exceeded 127 mm *5 in*. In Japan this fish is known as the Tsuranagakobitozama ('dwarf shark with a long face').

The most abundant fish in the world are the bristlemouths of the genus *Cyclothone* which have a world-wide distribution, except for the Arctic. They measure 1–3 in *25–76 mm* in length, and weigh about 500 to the 1 lb *450 g*.

The world's most abundant large animal (i.e. over 100 lb *45 kg*) is probably the whitetip shark (*Carcharhinus longimanus*) of the tropical, subtropical and warm temperate areas of the Atlantic, Pacific and Indian Oceans, which reportedly grows to 13 ft *4·0 m*.

The most restricted fish in the world is the diminutive devil's hole pupfish (*Cyprinodon diabolis*) which is confined to a small area of water directly above a rock shelf in a spring-fed pool in Ash Meadows, Nevada, USA. Because the pool is located 50 ft *15 m* below ground, the population is completely dependent on the amount of sunshine received. 'During the summer, when the sun shines on the ledge for several hours a day, the population rises to 700 or more', writes Nappe (1974). 'But during the winter when no sunlight can enter the spring the algae and the small invertebrates upon which the pupfish depend, dwindle; the pupfish numbers then drop to about 200.'

Longevity in fishes is associated with slow growth in the early stages of development, which means cold-water species have a greater life potential than those from warmer areas. The longest-lived species of fish is difficult to determine because (1) aquaria are of too recent origin, and (2) interpretations of age are not uniform, but early indications are that it is the lake sturgeon (*Acipenser fulvescens*) of eastern North America. Between 1951 and 1954 the ages were assessed of 966 specimens caught in the Lake Winnebago region, Wisconsin, USA by examination of the growth rings (annuli) in the marginal ray of the pectoral fin. The oldest sturgeon was found to be a male measuring 6 ft 7 in *2·01 m* which gave a reading of 82 years and was still actively growing. The next oldest was a 6 ft *1·83 m* example aged 49 (Probst and Cooper, 1954). Another lake sturgeon measuring 6 ft 9 in *2·06 m* and weighing 215 lb *98 kg* caught in the Lake of the Woods, Ontario, Canada on 15 July 1953 was believed to be 152 years old based on a growth ring count (Anonymous, 1954), but this record has not been confirmed and is probably too high. According to Magnan (1966) females live longer than males, and he gives 55 years as the usual maximum age for males and 80 years for females in Quebec province, the maximum age being reached in the more northern, slower-growing populations.

A 7 ft 7 in *2·31 m* white sturgeon caught in the lower part of the Fraser River, British Columbia, Canada in the summer of 1962 was believed to be 71 years old based on an annuli count (Semakula and Larkin, 1968), and another specimen 11 ft 6 in *3·51 m* long taken from the same river was estimated to be 82 years old.

Petrov (1927) says a 13 ft 11 in *4·24 m* Russian sturgeon caught on 3 May 1926 in the estuary of the Ural River and weighing over 1000 kg *2205 lb* was about 75 years old, and Solatov (1935) quotes a figure of 55 years for a 656 kg *1446 lb* kaluga.

A sterlet (*Acipenser ruthenus*) lived in the Royal Zoological Society Aquarium in Amsterdam for 69 years 8 months (Nigrelli, 1959). It was received in 1883 when 15 in *380 mm* long.

Dr Alex Comfort (1964) puts the upper age limit for the exceptionally large sturgeon at about 120 years.

There is a popular belief that certain species of fish live to a great age, and stories of carp living up to 300 years and pike for more than 200 years occur in some of the works on natural history published during the 18th and 19th centuries. Probably the most celebrated case of them all was the 'Emperor's Pike', which was said to have been caught in the Kaiserwag Lake in Wurttemburg, Germany in 1497. This enormous fish reportedly had a copper ring encircling its gill region which carried an inscription to the effect that the pike had been put in the lake by Emperor Frederick II in 1230, no less than 267 years before its final capture. Its length was given as 19 ft *5·8 m* and its weight as 350 lb *159 kg* (*sic*). The skeleton of this 'record breaker' was later preserved in Mannheim Cathedral. In the 19th century the bones were examined by a famous German anatomist, who found that the vertebrae were too numerous to belong to a single fish and must have come from several different individuals!

Exaggerated claims apart, though, the pike is still one of the longer-lived fishes. Francis Bacon (1645) says it sometimes lives to the 40th year, and this view is also shared by Dr Tate Regan (1911), who remarks that 'it is probable that fish of 60 or 70 lb are at least as many years old.' Comfort (1964), on the other hand, is much more cautious and refers to a record of a 34 lb *15 kg* pike caught in 1961 which had a scale reading of only 13–14 years, while Frost and Kipling (1949) give the maximum scale reading for 5000 pike taken in gill-nets from Lake Windermere during the period 1944–47 as 'slightly in excess of 15 years'. In June 1980, however, the death was reported of a huge pike at the Tierpark Berlin, aged 55 years. It was the zoo's oldest inhabitant.

Recently some incredible ages have been claimed for the Koi fish of Japan, a form of fancy carp. One specimen allegedly lived for 250 years, and in 1974 a 16 lb *7·3 kg* female named 'Hanako' reportedly celebrated her 223rd birthday in a pond at Shirakawa village in Gifu Prefecture after her age had been *determined* by a scale reading. Later, however, the fish's owner, Dr Kimiyaki Koshihara, whose ancestors served as the village headmen for three centuries, revealed that his family records *only* verified Hanako's age back to 1853!

According to Regan the carp lives up to 50 years under artificial conditions. 'Clarissa', London Zoo's famous 44 lb *20 kg* common carp (*Cyprinus carpio*), who died in May 1971 after spending 19 years in the aquarium there, was believed to have been about 30 years old when she was received in 1952, which means she must have been *c* 49 years at the time of her death.

After the sturgeons, the European eel (*Anguilla anguilla*), the European catfish (*Silurus glanis*) and the halibut (*Hippoglossus hippoglossus*) are probably the longest-lived fishes.

In 1948 the death was reported of an 88-year-old female European eel name 'Putte' in the aquarium at Halsingborg Museum, SW Sweden. She was reportedly born in the Sargasso Sea, North Atlantic in 1860 and was caught in a river as a three-year-old elver (Moriarty, 1978). Flower (1935) says two European catfish placed in a lake at Woburn Abbey, Bedfordshire in 1874 were still alive on 16 January 1935 aged 60+ years, and a specimen weighing 60 lb *27·2 kg* was removed when the lakes were netted in 1947 (Lever, 1977). In 1957 a female halibut measur-

ing 10 ft *3·0 m* in length and weighing 504 lb *229 kg* was caught in the North Sea and landed at Grimsby. It was aged at 60+ years by scale examination and was apparently both fertile and growing (Comfort, 1964). Another one caught off Iceland in October 1963 weighed 588 lb *267 kg*.

The life-span of most sharks is less than 25 years, but there are exceptions. One of them is the relatively small Australian school shark (*Galeorhinus australis*) which, from the evidence of tag returns, lives at least 32 years (Davies, 1964). A white pointer marked in South Australian waters and caught off Tasmania 25 years later had only grown 15 cm *5·9 in* in that time, and a tagged Greenland shark captured 16 years later was found to have increased its length by only 8 cm *3·15 in*. (Muus and Dahlstrom, 1974). The virtually indestructible whale shark must also reach a great age, and a figure of 70 years has been quoted for this fish.

Although the life-span of small fishes is much more limited, one notable exception is the goldfish (*Carassius auratus*). Bateman (1890) cites a record of 29 years 10 months 21 days for a specimen kept in an aquarium at Woolwich, London from 20 May 1853 until 11 April 1883, and Mennel (1926) gives details of several others which lived up to 25 years. On 1 August 1980 the death was reported of an ancient female called 'Freda' aged 41 years at Worthing, Sussex. Her owner, Mr A R Wilson, later had her stuffed.

The shortest-lived fishes are probably certain tooth carp of the sub-order *Cyprinodontidae* which live about eight months in the wild state. These include *Nothobranchus guentheri*, *N. rachovii* and *N. melanospiius* of Africa, and *Cynolebias bellottii*, *Pterolebias longipinnis* and *Austrofundulus dolichopterus* of South America. These small fishes are found in temporary ponds, drainage ditches and even in the water-filled footprints of large animals, and the fertilised eggs are buried in the mud at the bottom of the water. When this dries up, the fish die and the eggs, protected from drying out completely by morning dew and the moisture-retaining properties of the sub-stratum, aestivate until the next wet season when they hatch, grow at great speed and spawn, dying in the next drought.

Because of the practical difficulties of measurement very little accurate information has been published on the speeds attained by fishes, particularly the larger forms (over 1 m *39·4 in*). A good insight into rate of performance, however, is provided by the shape of the tail and body. Those with deeply forked or crescent shaped tails and a spindle-shaped body are capable of high speeds, while slow swimmers usually have square or round tails and short, laterally compressed bodies. Streamlined fish have three levels of speed: sustained, prolonged and burst – the latter reached at maximum effort but lasting only about 30 seconds. In laboratory aquaria swimming bursts up to 26 body lengths per second have been recorded for 10 cm *3·94 in* fish, including the sprat (*Sprattus sprattus*) (Wardle, 1975). Larger species were unable to exceed six body lengths, although hooked fish often react quite differently.

Most ichthyologists share the view that the fastest fish in the world over short distances is the sailfish (*Istiophorus platypterus*), which is beautifully adapted for swift movement through the water. The maximum burst speed reached by this species, which is found in all tropical waters, is not yet known, but Hamilton M Wright (cited by Hunt, 1935), says that in a series of speed trials carried out with a stopwatch at the Long Key Fishing Camp, Florida, USA between 1910 and 1925 one sailfish took out 100 yd *91 m* of line in 3 seconds, which is equivalent to a velocity of 109 km/h *67·7 miles/h* (*cf* 96 km/h *60 miles/h* for the cheetah).

'The speed of the sailfish is sometimes such that I have known a man on his first fishing trip to think that there were two fish when only one was on the line', reports Wright, 'because the fish reappeared on the surface so quickly in another quarter.'

When it is travelling at high speed the long dorsal fin of the sailfish folds back into a slot in the back, and the pectoral and ventral fins are pressed flush against the body to cut down drag to a bare minimum.

Marine biologists have long credited the swordfish (*Xiphias gladius*) of the tropical and temperate seas of the world with superior bursts of speed, but the evidence is based mainly on bills that have been found deeply embedded in ship timbers. A velocity of 50 knots (93 km/h *57·6 miles/h*) has been calculated from a penetration of 22 in *56 cm*, but this figure has been questioned by some authorities. According to Gray (1968) a 600 lb *272 kg* swordfish travelling at 10 miles/h *16 km/h* would hit a wooden vessel travelling at the same speed in the opposite direction with a force of about 0·5 tonne, all of it compressed into the 1 in² *645 mm²* area of the bill tip. This, he says, would be equivalent to a 1 lb *450 g* projectile hitting the ship at a speed of 30 miles/h *48 km/h*. Most experts put the maximum burst speed of this fish at somewhere between 30 and 35 knots (34·5–40·35 miles/h *55·5–64·8 km/h*). Anything higher, they say, would be impossible because the drag from the non–depressible dorsal fin and the distributed roughness of the much longer bill would be too great.

Some American fishermen believe that the bluefin tuna (*Thunnus thynnus*) is the fastest fish in the sea, and burst speeds up to 56 knots (64 miles/h *104 km/h*) have been claimed for this species. Certainly it is endowed with a perfect fusiliform shape, and when it is travelling flat out its first dorsal, pectoral and pelvic fins are withdrawn into grooves in its body to facilitate swimming. (The second dorsal and anal fins remain fixed because they have to act as stabilisers). The bluefin tuna also has one of the smallest abdomens among oceanic fishes, the whole mass comprising only 3–4 per cent of the total weight.

The question of how fast a bluefin tuna can swim was answered by H Earl Thompson off Liverpool, Nova Scotia, Canada in 1938. Using a device he and a friend has invented called a 'Fish-o-Meter', which consisted of a motor-cycle speedometer, a flexible cable and V-pulley mounted on a rod and reel, Thompson hooked a young bluefin weighing 59·5 lb *27 kg* which registered a speed of 43·4 miles/h *69·9 km/h* in a 20-second dash. He said individuals weighing 500–600 lb *227–272 kg* were the fastest swimmers (Patterson, 1939).

The yellowfin tuna (*Thunnus albacares*) and the wahoo (*Acanthocybium solandri*) are also extremely fast. Walter and Fierstine (1964) timed both species running out a light line in open water off the Pacific coast of Costa Rica at 74·59 km/h *46·35 miles/h* (=21·11 body lengths/s) and 77·05 km/h *47·88 miles/ h* (=18·93 body lengths/s) respectively, and Zane Grey once hooked a bonefish (*Albula vulpes*) off Long Key, Florida which dashed off at a calculated speed of 40 miles/h *64 km/h* for 400 ft *122 m*.

The torpedo-shaped mackerel sharks (*Isuridae*) must also be mentioned, and the fact they are warm-blooded – a feature shared only with the spearfishes, tunnies and bonitos – and thus have greater muscle efficiency would seem to indicate that these death-dealing animals are among the swiftest of all fishes. The fastest member of this family is the mako shark (*Isurus oxyrinchus*). One 12 ft *3·7 m* example chased by Thomas Helm (1961) and a colleague in the Florida Keys kept ahead of their speed-boat travelling at 27 knots (31 miles/h *50·0 km/h*) for 880 yd *805 m* before it disappeared, and other writers have credited this prodigious jumper – one hooked 600 lb *272 kg* mako cleared the surface by nearly 30 ft *9·1 m* – with burst speeds up to 40 knots (46 miles/h *74 km/h*).

The cosmopolitan great blue shark (*Prionace glauca*) is also capable of high bursts of speed. In one experiment carried out by Magnan and Saint-Legue (1928) in which the fish was tethered by an extremely fine thread to a tachometer, a great blue shark measuring 6 ft 6 in *1·98 m* in length and weighing 70·5 lb *32 kg* recorded a speed of 21·3 knots (39·5 km/h *24·5 miles/ h*). Elsewhere, in another test using water current, a very young specimen measuring 2 ft *61 cm* in length and weighing only 1·3 lb *580 g* held its own against a current of 26 ft/s (=17·7 miles/h *28·5 km/h*), and in short bursts of speed reportedly reached an astonishing 43 miles/h *69·2 km/h* (Budker, 1971), but as this is equivalent to 32 body lengths/s this measurement must have been wrongly converted.

The two-winged flying fish (*Exocoetus volitans*) of tropical and sub-tropical waters breaks the surface at speeds up to 20 miles/h *32 km/h* when fleeing from fast underwater predators like tunnies. It then 'taxis' along the top briefly with the lower part of its tail beating in the water up to 50 times a second, and then accelerates to something like 30–35 miles/h *48– 56 km/h* before rising into the air like a tiny sea-plane with its fins held taut. Schultz (1948) timed hundreds of these aerial ventures with a stopwatch and found that the majority of them lasted from two to ten seconds. He clocked one wind-assisted flight of 10 seconds and said the longest on record was one of 42 seconds, but this latter time has since been beaten. On 29 November 1972, while serving aboard the USS *Davis*, Lt Stephen J Kuppe (pers. comm.) watched a flying fish about 10 in *254 mm* long with a 14 in *356 mm* wing-span remain airborne 'for no less than 90 seconds while maintaining the same relative position alongside my ship at a distance of about 30 feet'. At that particular time the vessel was moving through the Mozambique Channel off East Africa at a speed of 24 knots (27·62 miles/h *44·45 km/h*), which means the flying-fish must have travelled a total airborne distance of 1214 yd *1110 m*.

A few years ago an ocelot (*Felis pardalis*) which earned its keep as a ship's cat was lost overboard in the Atlantic while attempting to catch one of these elusive creatures!

The fastest fish over sustained distances are the marlins (*Istophoridae*) of the warmer areas of the world. They have an estimated maximum burst speed of 40–50 miles/h *64–80 km/h* (Norman and Fraser, 1948), but can also swim at a very rapid rate for many hours.

The fastest moving *totally* freshwater fish is probably the pike, which has been timed at speeds up to 20·5 miles/h *33·0 km/h* over very short distances when lunging at prey. There is an isolated record of a common carp being timed at 30 miles/h *48 km/h* after it had been hooked (Soskin and Clark, 1976), but the highest speed reported for this species in the literature is 7·5 miles/h *12 km/h*. The anadromous Atlantic salmon (*Salmo salar*) has been credited with speeds up to 23 miles/h *37 km/h* in short bursts and 14–17 miles/h *22·5–27·4 km/h* when ascending waterfalls.

The greatest distance covered by a migrating fish is 5800 miles *9335 km* for a bluefin tuna dart-tagged off Baja California, USA in 1958 and caught 300 miles *483 km* south of Tokio, Japan in April 1963. During its marathon swim its weight increased from 35 lb *16 kg* to 267 lb *121 kg*. Two other individuals dart-tagged in the Gulf of Mexico and caught off Bergen, Norway travelled 4200 miles *6760 km* in 118 and 119 days respectively (Mather, 1962); while a fourth bluefin tagged off the Bahamas did the 4000 miles *6440 km* journey in only 50 days. There is also a record of an albacore (*Thunnus alalunga*) swimming at least 4900 miles *7885 km* from Los Angeles harbour, California, USA to the waters off southern Japan in 11 months (Soule, 1974). A blue shark tagged off Penzance, Cornwall was recaptured by a Russian ship 900 miles *1450 km* off French Guiana, northern South America after travelling 3200 miles *5150 km*, while two others were recaptured by sport fishermen off Long Island, New York, USA, a distance of 3500 miles *5630 km* (R Westerling, pers. comm.).

The slowest-moving marine fishes are the sea-horses (*Syngnathidae*). The major source of their propulsive power is the oscillating dorsal fin, and some species like the 1 in *25 mm* dwarf sea-horse *Hippocampus zosterae* of the Gulf Stream probably never get above 0·01 mile/h *0·016 km/h*.

The greatest depth from which a fish has been recovered is 8299 m *27 230 ft* for a 6·5 in *165 mm* brotulid, *Bassogigas profundissimus* (only the fifth ever recorded) sledge-trawled by the American research vessel *John Elliott Pillsbury* in the Puerto Rico Trench in April 1970 during a National Geographic Society/University of Miami Deep-Sea Programme. The previous record had been held by another specimen sledge-trawled by the Royal Danish research vessel *Galathea* in the Sunda Trench, south of Java, at a depth of 23 392 ft *7130 m* in September 1951 (Bruun, 1956). In 1910 the Norwegian Michael Sars Expedition trawled several rat-tailed fish (family *Macrouridae*) from a depth of 4700 m *15 420 ft* in the North Atlantic (Marshall, 1954). There is also a record of a deep-sea eel (family *Synaphobranchus*) in a state of metamorphosis being taken at a depth of 4040 m *13 255 ft* in the Indian Ocean, and the sea snail *Careproctus amblystomopsis*, a benthic fish, has been

The striped marlin travelling at speed.

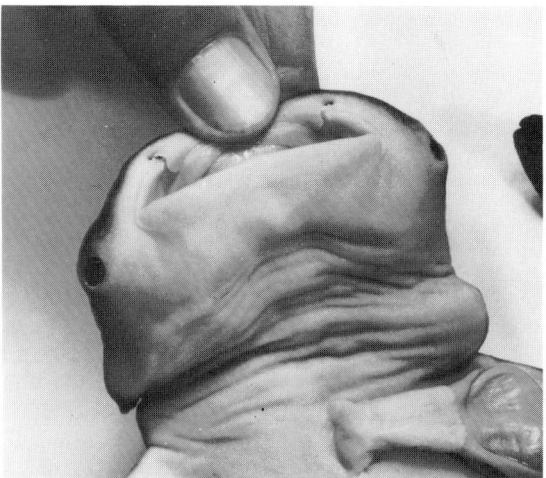

The whale shark lays the largest egg of any living animal. This infant was removed from a case measuring 11 in × 5 in 28 cm × 13 cm.

taken in the Kurile-Kamchatka Trench at a depth of 7230 m *23 720 ft* (Marshall, 1979).

On 24 January 1960 Dr Jacques Piccard and Lt Don Walsh, US Navy, sighted a sole-like fish about 12 in *305 mm* long (tentatively identified as *Chascanopsetta lugubris*) from the bathyscaphe *Trieste* at a record depth of 10 911 m *35 797 ft* in the Challenger Deep, Mariana Trench in the W Pacific. 'Slowly, very slowly this fish . . . moved away from us, swimming half in the bottom ooze, and disappeared into the black night, the eternal night which is its domain', relates Piccard (1960). This sighting has been questioned by some ichthyologists who still regard the brotulids of the genus *Bassogigas* as the deepest-living vertebrates. The two men had earlier sighted and photographed a *Bathypterois*, which is related to lantern-fishes, and a *Haloporphyrus* at 8010 m *26 280 ft*.

The world's highest living fish is the Tibetan loach (family *Cobitidae*), which is found at an altitude of 5200 m *17 060 ft* in the Himalayas.

Some fishes lay an enormous number of eggs, fecundity increasing with weight. A carp had 2 000 000 in its ovaries, a halibut 2 750 000, a cod 6 652 000, a turbot 9 000 000, a conger eel 15 000 000, and a common ling 28 361 000. The most fertile fish of them all, however, is the ocean sunfish. According to Johannes Schmidt, the famous Danish marine biologist, the ovaries of one female contained 300 000 000 eggs, each of them measuring about 0·05 in *1·27 mm* in diameter. It has also been established that there is a greater size difference between a newly-born ocean sunfish (length 0·1 in *2·54 mm*) and an adult than between any other living animal. Gudger (1936) says 'the larval sunfish is to its mother

as a 150 lb rowboat is to 60 Queen Marys!'

The bony fish which produces the least number of eggs is probably the tooth-carp *Jordanella floridae* of Florida, USA. Mature females deposit about 20 eggs over a period of several days (Innes, 1945). The average yield of the guppy *Poecilia reticulatus* is 40–50, but one female measuring 30 mm *1·2 in* in length had only four in her ovaries, while another measuring 2 in *51 mm* had 100.

The largest egg produced by any living fish is that of the whale shark. On 29 June 1953 Captain Odell Freeze of the shrimp trawler *Doris* was fishing in 31 fathoms (186 ft *57 m*) of water about 130 miles *209 km* south of Port Isabel, Texas, USA when he noticed a very large egg case in one haul of the net. 'I saw this thing in the net and, on picking it up, felt something kicking around in it. When I opened it with a knife, out flopped this little shark, very much alive. 'The egg case measured 12×5·5×3·5 in *305×140×89 mm*, and the embryo was 350 mm *13·78 in* long (Baughman, 1955).

The most venomous fish in the world are the beautifully camouflaged stonefishes (*Synanceidae*) of the tropical waters of the Indo-Pacific region. These hideous-looking creatures (up to 15 in *38 cm* and 2·5 lb *1·13 kg*) administer their extremely virulent neurotoxic poison through 13 erectile dorsal spines and direct contact – the tough spines can penetrate rubber soles – causes excruciating and persistent pain followed by delirium and in some cases death due to cardiac or respiratory arrest. They are equally as dangerous when found on a beach, because their secondary respiratory system allows them to live out of water for periods up to ten hours. In January 1950 a stonefish victim at Bundaberg, Queensland, Australia was saved by inhaling trilene (trichlorethylene) which served to numb the body and counteract the shock. The most dangerous member of the family is *Synanceja horrida*, which has the largest venom glands of any known fish, and in fatalities involving this species the victim usually dies within six hours in intense agony. An antivenin is available.

Despite their bristling armament, stonefishes have enemies. They are sometimes eaten by bottom-feeding sharks and rays without apparent ill-effects, and young ones often fall victim to large conches like *Strombus goliath* and *S. gigas*.

The most venomous fish found in British waters is the lesser weever (*Trachinus vipera*), which is found in shallow bays and coastal waters including the Thames estuary. This aggressive creature likes to half-bury itself in the sand with its dorsal spines erect and is easily trodden on by unwary bathers. People with heart conditions have been known to die within minutes of being stung, and the resultant wound is so agonisingly painful that fishermen stung on the hands or forearms sometimes become mentally un-balanced and throw themselves overboard. In one case a man cut off his own finger to obtain relief and other victims have been known to thrust an affected hand into fire as a counter-irritant – the attempted cure being more disastrous in its effects than the original injury!

In 1961 Dr David Carlisle, head of the Plymouth Marine Biological Association, blamed the lesser weaver for many of the 200 mysterious drownings that had occurred in the shallow waters off the south and west coasts of England in the previous three years. 'It has a powerful poison that causes acute pain and immediate panic. I believe that many of the drowned people have been poisoned and have then fallen headlong in the sea.' He added: 'Woe betide the swimmer who accidentally touches one. It will chase and poison, usually under the armpit.'

In an interesting case reported by Halstead (1957) a lesser weaver attacked a skin diver, driving its dorsal fins into the victim's right jaw.

The antidote to the weever sting is as much hot water as the person can bear, because the poison is easily broken down by heat.

The greater weever (*T. draco*) is equally as danger-ous, but this fish tends to occur in deeper waters and presents less of a threat to bathers.

The venom potency of *Trachinus* is nearly matched by that of the sting ray (*Dasyatis pastinaca*), which is widely distributed in shallow, coastal waters. In addition, the sting or dagger of this fish can cause severe lacerations, and the result can be fatal if the barbed tail is driven into the chest or stomach.

The most poisonous – as opposed to venomous – fish in the world is the death puffer (*Arothron hispidus*) of the Red Sea and the Indo-Pacific region. The ovaries, liver, intestines, skin, bones and even blood of this species contain a nerve biotoxin (tetrodotoxin) which is 200 000 times more potent than curare, the deadly plant poison used by the natives of South America for their arrow tips, and in fatal cases the victim usually dies within two hours of ingesting this hazardous meal. The dominant symp-toms are a creeping numbness, followed by pain and vomiting or diarrhoea, and the cause of death is usually muscular paralysis. Scientists have dis-covered that the toxicity of the fugu, as it is also known, is related to sexual activity and reaches its peak shortly before the breeding season starts.

During his second voyage of exploration and discovery in 1774 Captain James Cook suffered a severe attack of poisoning after eating part of a puffer fish. He wrote: 'This afternoon a fish being struck by one of the natives near the watering-place my clerk purchased it, and sent it to me after my return on board. It was of a new species, something like a sunfish, with a large, long, ugly head. Having no

suspicion of its being of a poisonous nature, we ordered it to be dressed for supper; but, very luckily, the operation of drawing and describing took so much time that it was too late, so that only the liver and roe were dressed, of which the two Mr Forsters and myself did but taste. About three o'clock in the morning we found ourselves seized with an extra-ordinary weakness and numbness over our limbs. I had almost lost the sense of feeling; nor could I distinguish between light and heavy bodies, of such as I had strength to move; a quarter pot, full of water, and a feather being the same in my hand. We each of us took an emetic, and after that a sweat, which gave us much relief. In the morning, one of the pigs, which had eaten the entrails, was found dead.'

Extraordinary as it may seem, the flesh of this fish and other puffers of the same family (*Tetrodontidae*) is considered a great delicacy in Japan – connoisseurs claim it produces a tremendously exhilarating feel-ing – and in the specially-licensed restaurants where this gourmet equivalent of Russian roulette is served, highly-qualified fugu chefs with a three-year ap-prenticeship behind them (good eyesight is a must!) remove the poisonous parts without contaminating the rest of the fish. Despite these elaborate pre-cautions, however, fugu still accounts for about 20 victims annually. In 1963 Japanese statistics revealed that of 168 persons taken ill after eating this fish, 82 died. Most of them, however, were uneducated villagers who served up the puffer for dinner and wiped out half the family, and Caras (1964) says there is a proverb in Japan: 'Great is the temptation to eat fugu, but greater is the dread of losing life.'

There is no known antidote (induced vomiting at a very early stage might help), but the Japanese claim that burying a victim up to the neck in earth acts as a cure!

The only species of puffer fish found in British

The death puffer, the most poisonous fish known to science.

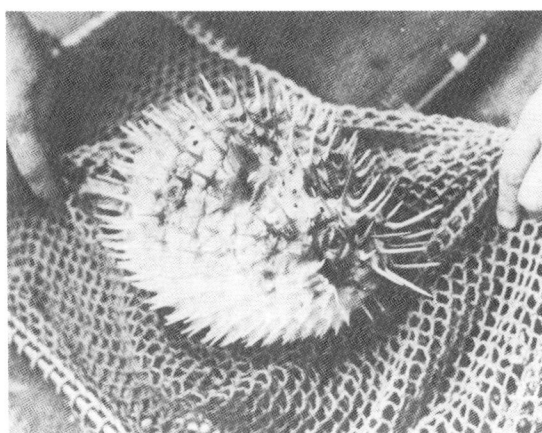

waters is *Lagocephalus lagocephalus*, which has been recorded in the English Channel as a rare vagrant (Wheeler, 1978).

The most powerful electric fish in the world is the electric eel (*Electrophorus electricus*), of the rivers of Brazil, Colombia, Venezuela and Peru. An average-sized specimen can discharge 400 V at 1 A, but a measurement of 650 V has been registered for a 90 lb *41 kg* individual in the New York Aquarium (Coates, 1937). This latter discharge would be sufficient to kill a man on contact or stun a horse at a distance of 20 ft *6 m*.

The electric catfish (*Malapterurus electricus*) of the rivers and lakes of tropical African can also produce a powerful discharge, and measurements up to 350 V at 1 A have been recorded.

The most powerful electric marine fishes are the torpedo rays (*Torpedinidae*) which are found in all warm and temperate waters. The black torpedo ray (*T. nobiliana*) of the Mediterranean and adjacent parts of the eastern Atlantic, including the English Channel and the western coasts of Britain, normally produces 50–60 V at 1 A, but discharges up to 220 V have been measured. These fish do not need very high voltages to stun or kill their prey because salt water is a better conductor of electricity than fresh water.

Some years ago an enterprising longshore fisherman at Brighton, Sussex made a tidy sum of money out of a large black torpedo ray he found caught in his net. He exhibited the fish on the seaside promenade as 'the heaviest fish on earth' and invited the public to guess its weight for a small fee. Needless to say no one held the fish long enough to gain any idea of its poundage – or win the prize offered in the competition to anyone who could lift the ray above his head. An excellent day's business was done until the fish, showing signs of battery exhaustion, was wisely withdrawn from public exhibition for a period of rest and feeding.

The most ferocious marine fish is the bluefish (*Pomatomus saltatrix*) of the temperate and subtropical waters of the Atlantic and parts of the Indo-Pacific oceans. This fast-moving predator, which travels in large schools, is best described as an animated chopping machine whose sole aim in life is to destroy as many other fishes as possible in the shortest space of time. It will attack mackerel, weakfish and herring with unbelievable fury, leaving behind a trail of oil, blood and pieces of its victims, and often destroys ten times as many fish as it can eat. In fact its gluttony is so great that when its stomach is full to bursting point (up to 40 fish have been removed from captured specimens) it often disgorges the contents and starts the slaughter all over again just for the sheer joy of it.

It has been estimated that an average-sized bluefish weighing 5 lb *2·32 kg* will eat over 1·5 tonnes of food a year. In April 1976 a large school of bluefish pursuing mullet went on a feeding frenzy along a section of the Florida Gold Coast, USA injuring at least a dozen people. One 17-year-old surfer bitten on the foot at Haulover Beach, North Miami had to have 60 stitches inserted, and a young boy emerged from the water with a bluefish hanging bulldog-fashion from his middle finger. The wounds were described as oval or circular gouges (De Sylva, 1976). This raises an interesting question: would a school of hungry bluefish skeletonise a human unfortunate enough to fall overboard in their midst? The answer is probably yes, if the person was not taken out of the water very quickly.

The most ferocious freshwater fish in the world are the ever-hungry piranhas of the genera *Serrasalmus*, *Pygocentrus* and *Pygopristis*, which live in the sluggish waters of the large rivers of South America. These utterly fearless cannibals have razor-sharp teeth, and their jaw muscles are so powerful that they can bite off a man's finger or toe like a carrot. They quickly congregate whenever anything out of the ordinary takes place, and will attack with lightning speed any creature, regardless of size, if it is injured or making a commotion in the water. There is a record of a 100 lb *45 kg* cabybara being reduced to a skeleton in less than a minute, and a wounded alligator has been stripped of all flesh in under five minutes.

Luckily only four out of the 16 species of piranha are considered dangerous to man (*Serrasalmus natterei* has the worst reputation), but although many fatalities have been attributed to these 'river sharks', most of the experiences have been largely based on hearsay. When Guppy (1963) visited Guyana he did not hear of a single death, but when he went to Apoera on the Courantye River he found most of the adult population had lost fingers, toes or penny-sized chunks out of their arms or legs after bathing or washing clothes. One boy at nearby Orealla had most of his foot bitten off and spent months in hospital. Harold Schultz (1963) of the Museu Paulista, Sao Paulo, Brazil, who spent 20 years travelling in the interior, said of all the many thousands of people he met during that time only *seven* had been injured by piranhas, and these were only slight bites. He admitted, however, that he himself had once nearly lost a toe to one of these freshwater devils.

In September 1981 more than 300 people were reportedly killed and eaten by piranha fish when an overloaded passenger-cargo boat capsized and sank as it was docking at the Brazilian port of Obidos on the Amazon. According to one official only 178 of the estimated 500 people aboard the boat survived

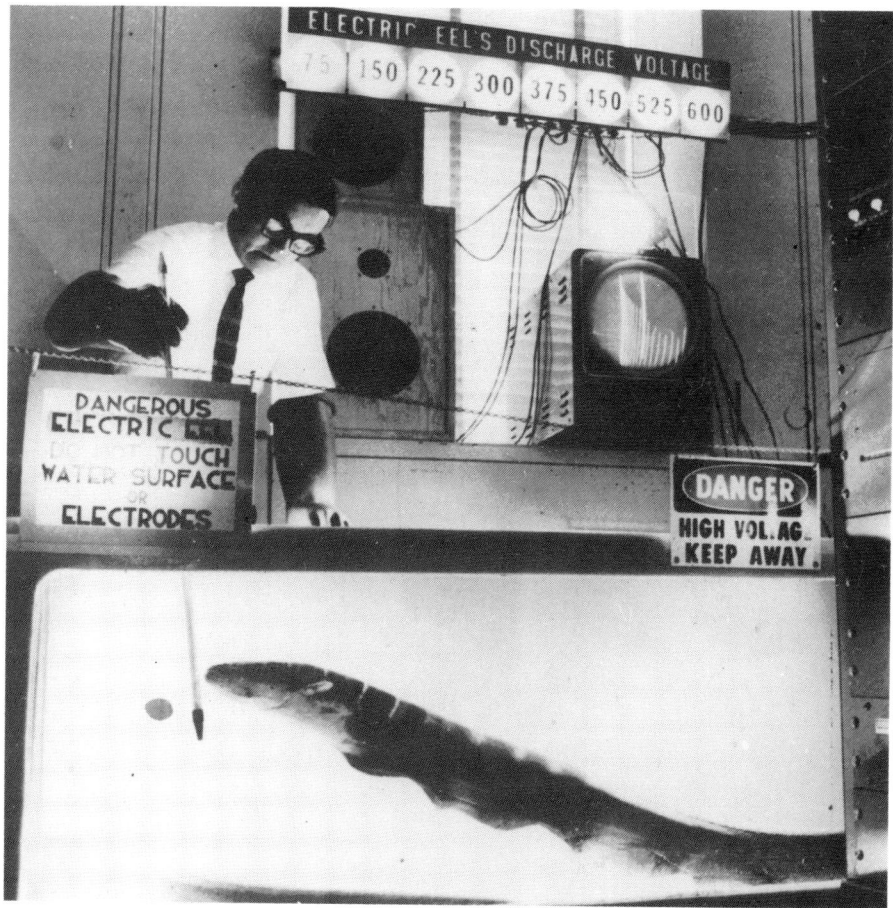

and only four bodies were recovered from the 250 ft *76 m* deep water, but the majority of the deaths were probably due to drowning rather than from attacks by these voracious fish.

The Amazonian dolphin or boutu (*Inia geoffrensis*) and the giant Brazilian otter (*Pteronura brasiliensis*) both feed on this fish with impunity.

On 10 April 1980 an outsized piranha named 'Percy', said to be the largest example of its kind held in captivity (length 13·25 in *337 mm*; weight 3 lb 6 oz *1·53 kg*), was electrocuted when he hungrily bit through the heating cable in his tank at Marineland in Morecambe, Lancs.

If we exclude the female beluga, which has been known to contain up to 323 lb *147 kg* of best quality caviar, the most valuable fish in the world is the Koi of Japan (see page 143). Prices rise according to size and perfection of colour and markings, but some prized females fetch well over £1000. The current world champion has been valued at more than £15 000.

The costliest fish on record was the obscure Tennessee snail darter (*Etheostoma sp.*), a 3 in *76 mm* long variety of perch, whose preservation by US environmentalists stopped a major Tennessee Valley Authority engineering project. The saga of the snail darter started in 1973 when it was first discovered in the Little Tennessee River during preliminary surveys for the Tellico Dam project. The fish was quickly declared an endangered species because the snails on which it feeds can only survive in fast-flowing water, and after a lot of litigation the Supreme Court finally ruled in June 1978 that the $116 million dam (then £66 million) would have to be abandoned. But the fight still went on, and the following year Congress approved a special amendment exempting the controversial dam project from the provisions of the Endangered Species Act despite the fact it had already been ruled uneconomic to complete. It was probably just as well, because since then another flourishing colony of these 'unique and irreplaceable little swimmers' has been found in another river 80 miles *129 km* away!

Echinoderms

(phylum Echinodermata)

An echinoderm is a spiny-skinned, exclusively marine invertebrate animal with a hard calcareous internal skeleton sometimes reduced. It occurs in all depths of the sea, and the shape and size of the body is exceedingly varied. The main characteristic is radial symmetry, which means the different parts of the body are arranged round a central axis or disc. Another feature is the water-vascular system which operates hydraulically a large number of hollow tube feet which serve for locomotion, attachment and respiration. Most species lay eggs and these hatch into free-swimming planktonic larvae.

Echinoderms are a very ancient order of animal, and their fossil remains have been found in rocks dating back nearly 600 million years.

There are about 6200 living species and the phylum is divided into five classes. These are the Asteroidea (starfishes); the Ophiuroidea (brittle-stars and basketstars); the Echinoidea (sea-urchins); the Holothuroidea (sea-cucumbers) and the Crinoidea (feather-stars and sea-lilies). The largest class is Ophiuroidea, which contains about 2100 species.

The largest known species of starfish in terms of span is the very fragile brisingid *Midgardia xandaros*. A female of this new genus collected in a dredge by the Texas A & M University research vessel *Alaminos* in the southern part of the Gulf of Mexico at a depth of 1500 ft *457 m* on 18 August 1969 measured 1380 mm *54·3 in* from arm tip to arm tip (R=major radius 680 mm *26·8 in*), but the diameter of the disc was only 26 mm *1·02 in*. Shortly after capture this starfish threw off all its eleven or twelve arms, and further damage occurred during subsequent handling. The dry weight of the fragmented parts was given as 70 g *2·47 oz* (Downey, 1972). Other brisingids probably grow even larger.

Midgardia's nearest challenger is the five-armed *Evasterias echinosoma* of the N Pacific. In June 1970 a Russian expedition from the Institute of Marine Biology in Vladivostock collected a huge example in the flooded crater of a volcano in Broughton Bay, Semushir, one of the Kurile Islands. It measured 960 mm *37·8 in* from arm tip to arm tip (R=505 mm *19·9 in*) – *more than twice the width of an average dustbin lid* – and weighed just over 5 kg *11 lb* when alive (P Lukin, pers. comm.).

The bulkiest starfish is the five-armed *Thromidia catalai* of the W Pacific. One specimen collected off Ilot Amedee, New Caledonia on 14 September 1969 and later deposited in the Noumea Aquarium weighed an estimated 6 kg *13·2 lb* (total arm span 630 mm *24·8 in*). It is now preserved in Bernice P Bishop Museum, Hawaii (Pope and Rowe, 1977).

The sunflower or twenty-rayed star (*Pycnopodia helianthoides*) of the N Pacific is also massively built. This species reaches its greatest size in Puget Sound, Washington, USA and spans up to 4 ft *1219 mm* have been claimed (Williams, 1952). Fisher (1928), however, says the largest recorded *Pycnopodia* had a major radius of 400 mm *15·75 in*, which is equivalent to a span of *c* 800 mm *31·5 in*.

Some members of the genus *Luidia* also reach an impressive size. One *L. superba* collected in Tagus Cove, Isabela in the Galapagos Islands, E Pacific spanned *c* 790 mm *31·1 in* (Downey and Wellington, 1978), while a *L. magnifica* from Hawaii measured *c* 770 mm *30·3 in* (Downey, 1972).

The largest five-armed *Pisaster brevispinus* captured in the 1968 'World Championship Starfish Grapple' held in Hood Canal, Puget Sound, Washington weighed 10 lb *4·54 kg*, although it only spanned 18 in *457 mm* (Furlong and Pill, 1970), but unconfirmed measurements up to 650 mm *25·6 in* have been reported for this species. *Oreaster reticulatus* (span up to 20 in *508 mm*) of the West Indies is also massively built and is practically all disc.

The largest starfish found in British waters is the spiny starfish (*Marthasterias glacialis*). In January 1979 Jonathon MacNeil of the Isle of Barra, Western Isles, Scotland found a specimen on the beach which spanned 30 in *762 mm*.

Among the smallest known starfishes is the Mediterranean deep-sea species *Marginaster capreensis* which does not exceed *c* 20 mm *0·79 in* total diameter.

The smallest starfish found in British waters is the cushion starfish (*Asterina gibbosa*), which has a maximum span of 60 mm *2·36 in* but is usually 25 mm *1 in*.

Although very little information has been published on the longevity of starfishes (each species having its own average life-span), they most probably live less than 4 years. Notable exceptions include *Marthasterias glacialis* and *Asterias rubens*, which do not reach sexual maturity in captivity until they are 7 years old and 5 to 6 years old respectively (Comfort, 1964; Bull, 1934), and there is also a record of an *Astropecten irregularis* living for 6 years 6 months (Feder and Christensen, 1966).

The only really venomous starfish is the crown-of-thorns (*Acanthaster planci*) of the Indo-Pacific region. Apart from a painful wound, spine pene-

Above, a huge five-armed starfish collected by a Russian expedition in the Kurile Islands, N Pacific in 1970.

Right, the five-armed Thromidia catalai – *the bulkiest known starfish.*

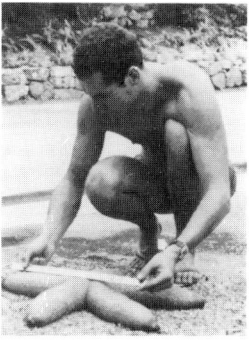

tration can also produce numbness and vomiting in humans.

The greatest depth from which a starfish has been recovered is 9990 m *32 776 ft* for *Hymenaster* sp. collected by the Russian research vessel *Vityaz* in the Philippine Trench, W Pacific in *c* 1960 (Belyaev and Mironov, 1977).

All starfishes can renew arms, and in some species even half a body from the remaining part, but only one family (Ophidiasteridae) can grow an entirely new starfish from a piece of one arm without retention of the disc or any part of it. In one of their experiments using the species *Linckia columbiae* (span 101 mm *4 in*) MacGinitie and MacGinitie (1949) found that a section of arm measuring only 10 mm *0·39 in* in length could grow into a full-sized animal, although they admitted that this regeneration often went haywire, the starfish sometimes ending up with eight arms instead of the usual six.

The starfishes with the greatest number of arms are found in the genus *Heliaster* of the E Pacific. Up to 50 have been reported.

Most of the brittlestars are small creatures averaging less than 12 mm *0·5 in* across the disc with a span of 101–127 mm *4–5 in*. There are some exceptions, however, and the largest brittlestar is probably the tropical variety *Ophiarachna incrassata* which has a disc diameter of over 51 mm *2 in* (Clark, 1962) and a span of *c* 508–609 mm *20–24 in*.

The basketstars (*Euryalae*) are much larger (up to 101 mm *4 in* across the disc) and most species with arms *fully extended* probably reach 609 mm *24 in*, but the long branching arms are normally coiled in such a tangle (except when feeding) that it is difficult to obtain accurate measurements.

The largest known ophiuroid (2100 species) is the Antarctic euryalid *Astrotoma agassizii*, which has unbranched, elongated arms. One giant specimen with its arms broken off spanned 57 mm *2·24 in* across the disc, and Fell (1966) says it must have measured about 1000 mm *39·37 in* in diameter when complete. Other individuals collected by Mortensen (1936) at South Georgia had discs measuring up to 60 mm *2·36 in* across, but these also had their arms broken off and the over-all size was not recorded.

The largest ophiuroid found in British waters is the gorgon's head basketstar (*Gorgonocephalus caputmedusae*). The diameter of the disc sometimes reaches 90 mm *3·54 in* and the total diameter 350 mm *13·78 in* in the Faroe Channel (Mortensen, 1927).

The smallest known ophiuroid is the brittlestar *Ophiomisidium mirabile* of the Southern Ocean having a total span of only 9 mm *0·35 in* (Smirnov, 1978).

As with starfishes, published information on the life-span of ophiuroids is sparse. Very small species like the one just mentioned may live only 2–3 years, but Fell (1966) believes 'most ophiuroids continue to grow for a period of 8 years at least, and probably for 10 or 15 years'. Buchanan (1964) found that it takes *c* 15 years for the brittlestar *Amphiura chiajei* to attain a disc diameter of 8·8 mm *0·35 in*, which suggests that large euryalids like *Astrotoma* and *Gorgonocephalus* must take 20 or even 30 years to reach their maximum size; but, as Fell points out, these giant forms usually live in plankton-rich waters and consequently may have a more rapid growth rate than other ophiuroids.

At least four genera of brittlestars (*Ophiura*, *Amphiophiura*, *Ophiacantha* and *Ophiosphalma*) live at depths in excess of 4 miles (*6430 m* 21 120 ft).

The greatest depth from which an ophiuroid has been recorded is *c* 8100 m *26 575 ft* for *Perlophiura profundissima* collected by the *Vityaz* in the N Pacific

(Belyaev and Litvinova, 1972).

The sea-urchins are generally small to moderate-sized echinoderms.

The largest of the 800 known species is *Sperosoma giganteum* of the deep waters off Japan, which is known only from a few specimens. It has a horizontal test (shell) diameter of 320 mm *12·6 in*. The tropical hatpin urchin *Diadema setosum* has been credited with measurements up to 457 mm *18 in*, but this figure was obtained *vertically* and included the uppermost spines which may reach 304 mm *12 in* in length in calm waters. (The lateral and lower spines are much shorter.)

The largest British species is *Aroeosoma fenestratum*. One specimen had a test diameter of 280 mm *11·02 in* (Mortensen, 1927), but the average measurement is 140–180 mm *5·5–7·1 in*.

The smallest known sea-urchin is *Echinocyamus scaber*, which is found in the waters off NSW, Australia. It has a test diameter of only 5·5 mm *0·21 in* (Clark, 1925). Of British species, the cake urchin *Echinocyamus pusillus* has a test length of only 6·3 mm *0·25 in*.

As with other classes of echinoderms, very little is known about the maximum life potentials of sea-urchins. It has been claimed that they live indefinitely (*sic*), but this is not borne out by scientific investigation. According to Moore (1935) the oldest *Echinus esculentus* dated by annual rings in the plates was 7 years old, but the potential maximum age was *c* 10 years. *Psammechinus miliaris* has been known to live 8 years under laboratory conditions (Bull, 1938), and 6 years has been reported for specimens of *Strongylocentrotus drobachiensis* collected off the coast of Norway (Grieg, 1928). In a study of the growth curves of two settlements of *Echinocardium cordatum* it was ascertained that the maximum age reached was *c* 15 years (Buchanan, 1967). Most other sea-urchins live less than 4 years, but some deep-sea species may remain active three to four times as long, depending on the availability of food.

The greatest depth from which a sea-urchin has been recovered is 7250 m *23 786 ft* for an unidentified specimen collected by the Galathea Deep Sea Expedition in the Banda Trench near Indonesia in 1951 (Bruun, 1956).

All members of the flattish Echinothuriidae, including *Sperosoma giganteum*, have toxic spines, but the only species found in shallow water is *Asthenosoma varium* of the Indo-Pacific. Although no human fatalities have been attributed to this animal, it is said to be greatly feared by pearl divers. The long-spined *Diadema setosum* of the same region is less toxic, but the barbs are difficult to remove and take a long time to dissolve. Probably the sea-urchin with the nastiest reputation is *Toxopneustes pileolus*, also of tropical waters. Unlike the other species already mentioned, this creature has stinging jaws (pedicellariae) which can produce intense radiating pain, followed by muscular paralysis, respiratory distress and – exceptionally – death (Halstead, 1971).

The sea-cucumbers are mostly moderate-sized echinoderms, but the class has wide limitations.

The bulkiest sea-cucumber (1100 species) is *Stichopus variegatus* of the Philippines, which has been measured up to 1000 mm *39·37 in* in length when fully extended and 210 mm *8·27 in* in diameter (Semper, 1868). Some of the worm-like sea-cucumbers of the genus *Synapta* can stretch themselves out to lengths of 1000 mm *39·37 in* or even 2000 mm *78·74 in*, but they have very thin body-walls and only measure about 12 mm *0·5 in* in diameter.

The largest sea-cucumbers found in British waters are *Cucumaria frondosa* and *Stichopus tremulus*, both of which have been measured up to 500 mm *19·69 in* (Mortensen, 1927).

The smallest known sea-cucumber is *Psammothuria ganapatii* from the waters off southern India, which does not exceed 4 mm *0·16 in* in length (Chandrasekhara Rao, 1968). The smallest British species, *Echinocucumis hispida*, has a maximum length of 30 mm *1·18 in*.

Most sea-cucumbers probably live at least 3 years. The Pacific species *Paracaudina chilensis* takes 3 to 4 years to reach maximum size (Tao, 1930), and the Japanese sea-cucumber *Stichopus japonicus* lives at least five years (Mitsukuri, 1903). One of the longest-lived species may be *Cucumaria elongata*, found in British waters, which reportedly lives 10–12 years.

The greatest depth from which an echinoderm has been recovered is 10 630–10 710 m *34 875–35 138 ft* for a number of *Myriotrochus bruuni* collected by the *Vityaz* in the Mariana Trench, W Pacific in 1958 (Belyaev, 1970).

Although some species of sea-cucumber are toxic, the poison does not seem to affect man and they are regularly eaten by Pacific Islanders.

During the 1975 *Alpha Helix* South East Asia Bioluminescence Expedition, 36 parasitic carapid fish were collected from the Banda Islands in the South Moluccan Sea. Fifteen of them (*Carapus mourlani*) were found in the intestine of a single host sea-cucumber, later identified as *Bohadschia argus*, which they may have entered for spawning. 'If indeed the 15 fish entered the holuthurian for sexual reasons', writes Meyer-Rochow (1977), 'one cannot help but think of the orgy that must have taken place inside the sea-cucumber.'

The largest crinoid (650 species) in terms of span is the unstalked feather-star *Heliometra glacialis maxima* of the NW Pacific. Measurements up to 914 mm *36 in* have been claimed for this race, but the largest recorded specimen had an arm length of 350 mm *13·8 in* and a span of c 700 mm *27·6 in*.

Although feather-stars tend to *decrease* in size in warmer waters, some of the tropical multibrachiate *Comasterids* are also very large, reaching nearly 609 mm *24 in* in total diameter. They are also much heavier than *Heliometra* because they can have as many as 200 arms (cf 10 arms for *Heliometra*).

The largest stalked crinoids are probably some sea-lilies of the genus *Metacrinus*, widely distributed throughout the Japan-Malay-Australian region. They have a maximum stalk (stem) height of about 609 mm *24 in*, plus another 152 mm *6 in* for the arms.

The strongest contenders for the 'smallest crinoid' title are probably the feather-stars *Antedon parviflora* and *Comissia minuta*, both found in Japanese waters. They have spans of c 40 mm *1·58 in*.

The smallest extant sea-lily is *Bathycrinus gracilis*, which has a total height of 70–80 mm *2·76–3·15 in*.

Most of the small feather-stars probably have a life-span of only 2–3 years. Some of the longest-lived species are the tropical comasterids, and Catala (1964) says he has kept a number of them alive in the aquarium at Noumea, New Caledonia, for 'several years'. The Antarctic feather-star *Promachocrinus kerguelensis* has an even greater age potential because it does not reach maturity until the tenth year, and Fell – on the basis of the known life-spans in other classes of echinoderms – estimates the maximum age attained by a crinoid at '20 or more years'. Nothing is known about the rate of growth in sea-lilies and the age potential, but the ascending axis probably develops fairly rapidly. 'Consequently', says Fell (1966), 'the great length of the stem in some extinct sea-lilies does not necessarily imply a correspondingly lengthy life span.'

The majority of feather-stars – their centre of abundance is the Indo-Pacific region – are found in relatively shallow waters, i.e. c 200 m *656 ft*, but some species of sea-lily are found at much greater depths.

The greatest depth from which a crinoid has been recovered is 9735 m *31 939 ft* for a sea-lily (*Bathycrinus australis?*) dredged up from the Bonin Trench, W Pacific by the *Vityaz* in c 1961 (Belyaev, 1969).

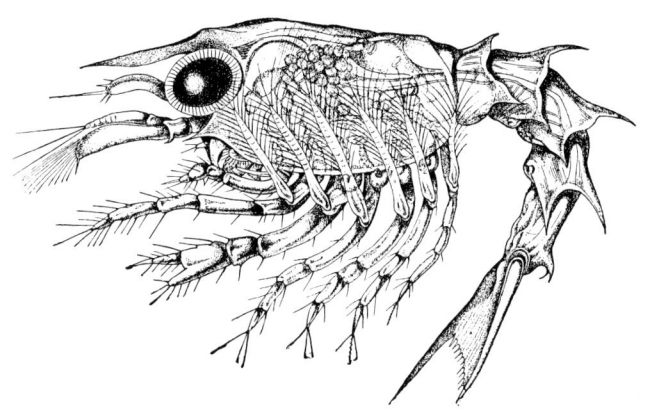

Crustaceans

(phylum Crustacea)

A crustacean is an aquatic invertebrate which breathes through gills. It has a segmented body, paired jointed limbs and a tough outer integument or shell which is pliable at the joints. This external skeleton, which is incapable of growth, is periodically cast off and replaced by a lime-impregnated coat. Another characteristic is the two pairs of antennae in front of the mouth which are used as feelers. The young are produced from eggs shed freely into the water or carried by the female.

The earliest known crustacean was the twelve-legged sea spider *Karagassiema* which lived about 650 million years ago. Its remains have been found in the Sayan Mountains in the USSR.

There are about 26 500 living species of crustacean and the phylum is divided into eight classes. These are: the Cephalocarida (primitive blind shrimps); the Branchiopoda (branchiopods); the Ostracoda (mussel or seed shrimps); the Mystacocarida (mystacocarids); the Copepoda (copepods); the Branchiura (fish lice); the Cirripedia (barnacles); and the Malacostraca (shrimps, prawns, lobsters, crabs). The largest class is the Malacostraca with 19 000 species, while the Cephalocarida and the Mystacocarida contain three and four species respectively.

The largest known crustacean is the Japanese spider crab (*Macrocheira kaempferi*), which is confined to the deep waters off the SE coast from NE Honshu to the Island of Kyushu.

Very little information has been published on this bizarre-looking creature, but adult males (females are smaller) usually have a biting-claw span of 183–213 cm *6–7 ft* and a shell measurement of 254×305 mm *10×12 in*.

According to R W Ingle (pers. comm.), a carcinologist at the British Museum, the largest giant spider crab on record is a male which spans 330 cm *10 ft 10 in*, but this size is exceeded by another specimen in Calcutta Museum, Bangladesh which measures 345 cm *11 ft 4 in*. An even larger male with a claw-span of 370 cm *12 ft 1½ in* weighed 18·6 kg *41 lb*, but the present whereabouts of this marine daddy-long-legs is unknown.

The maximum size attained by *M. kaempferi* has not yet been established with any degree of certainty. One monstrous crab caught in a fisherman's net off Honshu in November 1921 reportedly had a claw-span of 5·8 m *19 ft*, but further details are lacking. The American naturalist Charles Holder (1886) says the first European to set eyes on one of these crustaceans saw two biting claws leaning against a fisherman's hut which both measured 10 ft *3·0 m* in length and must have belonged to an animal with a span of 22 ft *6·7 m*! – 'at first the traveller thought they were some curious toy or grotesque plaything made in exaggerated imitation of the common rock crab'. The deep sea may hide still larger forms.

The Australian giant spider crab (*Leptomithrax spinulosus*) has also been credited with great size, but this species rarely has a claw span of more than 3 ft *91·4 cm*, although unconfirmed measurements up to 213 cm *7 ft* have been claimed.

The largest spider crab found in British waters is the thornback (*Maia squinado*) of the English Channel. This species has been measured up to 7 in *178 mm* across the spiny shell and the leg span may reach 2 ft *610 mm*. It weighs up to 4 lb *1·81 kg*.

Although the much more compact offshore xanthid *Pseudocarcinus gigas* of the Bass Strait separating Australia from Tasmania cannot compete with *M. kaempferi* in overall dimensions, the body size is about the same (up to 430 mm *16·9 in* across the shell), and one huge specimen caught off King Island with a fearsome 17 in *432 mm* long pincer tipped the scales at 27 lb *12·25 kg*.

The heaviest crab found in British waters is the Edible or Great crab (*Cancer pagurus*), mature individuals measuring 110–120 mm *4·33–4·72 in* across the shell and weighing 1–2 lb *450–900 g*. In 1895 an enormous specimen measuring 11 in *279 mm* across the shell and weighing 14 lb *6·35 kg* was caught off the coast of Cornwall. Another large one captured off Dartmouth, Devon in October 1952 scaled 8 lb 12 oz *3·97 kg*, and a third weighing 9 lb *4·08 kg* was taken off the Norfolk coast by Cromer fishermen on 7 September 1958. In June 1972 David Rollinson of Barnsley, Yorkshire collected the largest edible crab recorded in British waters this century while skin-diving off Brixham, Devon. It had a nipper span of 36·5 in *927 mm* and weighed 11 lb *5·0 kg*. Another one caught in the North Sea by fishermen out of Vadso, N Norway in January 1977 scaled 12 lb *5·4 kg*.

The heaviest land crab and the largest land crustacean is the robber crab (*Birgus latro*), which lives on tropical Indo-Pacific islands and atolls. Mature examples of this shell-less hermit scale 5–6 lb *2·3–2·7 kg* and have a leg span of 3 ft *914 mm*, but weights up to 9 lb *4·1 kg* have been reliably reported.

As its name implies, this crustacean is a bit of a freebooter, and when Gibson-Hill (1947) was studying a group of them on Christmas Island in the Indian Ocean they regularly made off with cooking utensils, knives, forks and even sandals that had been left lying around. On another occasion a wrist-watch went missing.

The smallest crabs in the world are the parasitic pea crabs (*Pinnotheridae*), which live in the mantle cavities of bivalve molluscs such as oysters, mussels and scallops. Some species have a shell diameter of only 0·25 in *6·35 mm*, including *Pinnotheres pisum* which is widely distributed in British waters.

Some crabs travel great distances during migration. In one series of tagged specimens released in the North Sea in 1962 a female *C. pagurus* of commercial size (shell width 115 mm *4·53 in*) walked 230 miles *370 km* from Whitby, Yorkshire to Fraserburgh, Scotland in under two years. Another one turned up in a seine-net in Aberdeen Bay about 175 miles *282 km* away 18 months later, and a third female travelled 124 miles *200 km* from Norfolk to Yorkshire in 21 months. The fastest female covered 13 miles *21 km* in 23 days (=0·0236 mile/h *0·0379 km/h*). It should be pointed out here that these measurements represented the shortest possible distances between the points of release and the location of recapture, and there is no guarantee that the crabs kept strictly to these routes; in other words, their actual journeys were probably longer.

Male edible crabs are much less venturesome and rarely go further than 5 miles *8 km* in any given direction. There is one record, however, of a male released off the Yorkshire coast in 1962 and found 40 miles *64 km* further north 61 weeks later, and an even more ambitious individual tagged off Norfolk in 1965 travelled 57 miles *92 km* in 5 months (Edwards, 1979).

One of the strongest contenders for the 'slowest crab' title on the other hand must be *Neptunus pelagines*. One specimen tagged in the Red Sea took 29 years to travel the 101·5 miles *163 km* to the Mediterranean via the Suez Canal at an average speed of 3·5 miles *5·6 km* a year.

The largest species of lobster is the American or North Atlantic lobster (*Homarus americanus*), and there are several authentic records of specimens weighing over 20 lb *9·1 kg*.

Dr Francis Herrick (1911), in a lengthy paper on the subject, mentions a very large male captured near Salem, Massachusetts in 1850 and now preserved in the Peabody Academy of Science which weighed 25 lb *11·3 kg* when alive, and says another one scaling 24·5 lb *11·1 kg* was taken at Lubec, Maine in September 1892. He concluded from his diligent researches that although very large lobsters weighing 20 lb *9·1 kg* or more had been caught on occasion, there was no reliable evidence to support claims in excess of 25 lb *11·3 kg*. 'Where lobsters are said to have attained a greater weight', he said, 'measurements of the parts of the skeleton which have been preserved invariably prove that the figures have been exaggerated. I do not maintain that the American lobster does not reach a greater weight than twenty-five pounds, but that I have been unable, up to the present time, to discover any well-authenticated evidence that this is the case.'

Two years later an enormous lobster was caught off the Atlantic Highlands, New Jersey. It measured 23·75 in *603 mm* from the rostrum to the end of the tail-fan (total length 40 in *1016 mm*) and weighed 34 lb *15·4 kg* (Firth, 1939).

This record stood until the autumn of 1934 when Capt Wheeler of the smack *Hustler* caught another lobster weighing 42 lb 7 oz *19·25 kg* off the Virginia Capes, Virginia. A few months later he took another outsized specimen weighing 38 lb 12 oz *17·58 kg* in the same area. Both these heavyweights, known as 'Mike' and 'Ike', are currently on display in the

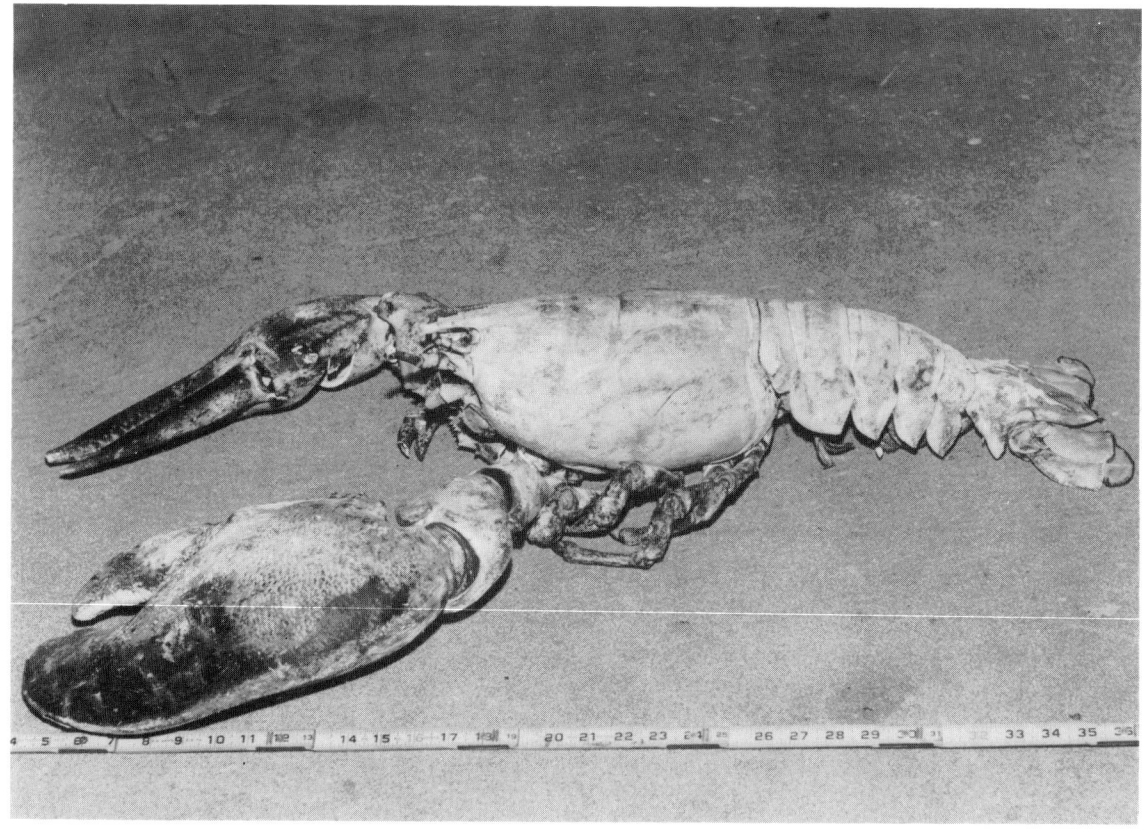

The 44 lb 6 oz 20·13 kg lobster caught off Nova Scotia, Canada in February 1977.

Museum of Science, Boston, Massachusetts (Gurney, 1950).

During the summer of 1939 an unconfirmed weight of 47 lb *21·3 kg* was reported for a lobster netted off the coast of New Jersey, and another huge individual allegedly scaling 48 lb *21·8 kg* was captured off Chatham, Massachusetts.

On 11 February 1977 a lobster measuring 42 in *1067 mm* from the tip of the crushing claw to the end of the tail-fan and weighing 44 lb 6 oz *20·13 kg* was caught off Nova Scotia, Canada and later sold to the owner of a New York restaurant where it is currently on display (Alan G Eisen, pers. comm.). **This is the heaviest crustacean ever recorded of which there is definite evidence**.

Probably all exceptionally large lobsters are males because they grow faster than females. This is because the latter moults only every second year after reaching maturity, while the male sheds its shell and increases in size annually.

The largest crustacean found in British waters is the common or European lobster (*Homarus gammarus*).

The maximum size attained by this species has been greatly exaggerated in the older literature. Olaus Magnus (1555), the Archbishop of Uppsala,

Sweden, for instance, says some of the lobsters found between the Orkneys and the Hebrides were so gigantic that they could seize a strong human swimmer and crush him to death in their claws, and Erik Pontoppidan (1753), the Bishop of Bergen, claims that one lobster seen by fishermen near Utaver in the Bay of Erien, Norway was so huge – it reputedly had a claw-span of 6 ft *1·8 m* – that no one dared to attack it.

Fortunately the common lobster of today is built along much more *modest* lines (average weight 2–3 lb *0·9–1·4 kg*), but in earlier times before it was overfished it reached a much greater average size, and probably rivalled *H. americanus* for length – although not weight.

In 1875 a lobster measuring 23·25 in *591 mm* in length and weighing 14 lb *6·4 kg* was caught in a trammel-net off the coast of southern Cornwall. The same year another outsized example scaling 12 lb *5·4 kg* was taken in Saints Bay, Guernsey in the Channel Islands, and Frank Buckland (1877) mentions one of 13 lb *5·9 kg* caught off Durgan, southern Cornwall.

Other reliable records over 12 lb *5·4 kg* include a 12 lb 4 oz *5·56 kg* male caught by a fisherman in Skelmorlie Bay, SW Scotland on 13 August 1935; a 12 lb 8 oz *5·67 kg* individual netted in Colwell Bay, Isle of Wight in January 1960; and one weighing 13 lb 8 oz *6·12 kg* caught by hand off Bournemouth, Hampshire in November 1974.

On 17 August 1967 a skin-diver caught a lobster weighing 14 lb 8 oz *6·58 kg* off St Ann's Head, Pembrokeshire, W Wales. It is now mounted in the bar of the Amroth Arms, Amroth, Pembrokeshire.

Until fairly recently the largest common lobster on record was believed to be a huge example in the Museum of the Academy of Natural Sciences of Philadelphia, Pennsylvania, USA which measures 32·5 in *826 mm* in total length and weighed an estimated 21–22 lb *9·5–10·0 kg* when alive. In 1966, however, this monster was re-examined and found to be an American lobster (C W Hart, pers. comm.).

In June 1931 a male lobster weighing 20·5 lb *9·3 kg* was caught in a caisson during the construction of No 3 jetty at Fowey, southern Cornwall. The crushing claw of this specimen, now preserved in the Museum of Toronto University, Ontario, Canada weighed 2 lb 10 oz *1·19 kg* after the meat was removed.

On 20 June 1964 an enormous crushing-claw was collected in a trawl near Skagen, the northernmost tip of Jutland, Denmark at a depth of 40 m *131 ft*. The still reasonably fresh appendage measured 351 mm *13·8 in* in length and 400 mm *15·7 in* in maximum girth. Dr Torben Wolff (pers. comm.), Curator of the University Zoological Museum in Copenhagen, said later: 'When comparing with the list of giant American lobsters compiled by Dr Herrick . . . the living weight of the whole animal must have been about 13 kg or 30 pounds, or perhaps somewhat more as the claws of the American lobster are somewhat larger compared to the body than those of the European lobster.' Although Dr Wolff's weight estimate is probably a bit too high, the owner of this crushing-claw probably scaled at least 10 kg *22 lb*, making it **the largest common lobster on record**.

The New South Wales crayfish (*Jasus verreauxi*), also known as the 'green cray', of the waters off the coast of eastern Australia, averages between 10 lb *4·5 kg* and 15 lb *6·8 kg* at maturity, but individuals weighing up to 25 lb *11·3 kg* have been reliably reported.

The largest crawfish or spiny lobster (*Palinurus vulgaris*) ever recorded in British waters was a female weighing 12 lb *5·4 kg* caught off Plymouth, Devon in August 1971 and later shipped to France.

The smallest known lobster is the Cape lobster (*Homarus capensis*) of South Africa which usually measures 100–120 mm *3·9–4·7 in* in total length.

Frank Buckland (1875) says the 'chicken lobsters' caught off Bognor Regis, Sussex averaged 14–20 to the pound, but this diminutiveness (the lobsters were in fact undersized *H. gammarus*) was due to over-fishing in the area.

The largest freshwater crustacean in the world is the crayfish *Astacopsis gouldi* which is found in small streams in Tasmania. Not much is known about this animal, but it is reported to reach a total length of 24 in *610 mm* and a weight of 8–9 lb *3·6–4·1 kg* despite the restricting nature of its habitat (Schmitt, 1973). The Murray River 'lobster' (*Euastacus armatus*) of South Australia also reaches an impressive size, having been credited with weights up to 6 lb *2·7 kg* (Francois, 1960).

Britain's largest freshwater invertebrate is the crayfish or whiteclaw *Astacus fluviatilis* which lives in fast-moving streams. It measures 4–6 in *102–152 mm* in length and weighs up to 4 oz *113 g*.

The smallest known crustaceans are the microscopic water fleas of the genus *Alonella*, some of which measure less than 0·25 mm *0·0098 in*. They are found in British waters.

The longest-lived of all crustaceans is the American lobster. One male weighing 35 lb *15·9 kg* was estimated to be about 50 years old (Schmitt, 1973), and this probably represents the upper age limit for this species. Very large examples of the common lobster may also exceed 30 years, and the crayfish *Astacus fluviatilis* has been credited with a maximum life-span of 15–25 years (Friedel, 1880). Some crabs also reach great ages, as shown by the *Neptunus pelagines* mentioned earlier which took 29 years to walk the length of the Suez Canal, and the edible crab lives 15–20 years (Bennet, 1974).

The fastest-moving crustaceans over short distances are the lobsters *Homarus* and *Palinurus*. When danger threatens they leap backwards with astonishing rapidity, and Lockhead (1977) says they may reach a speed of 8 m/s (=28·8 km/h *18 miles/h*) when making their escape bids.

The fastest-swimming crustaceans are the lightly-built portunid crabs (*Portunidae*). In most species the propulsive power comes from the last pair of legs which are flattened into paddles and are used like sculls, but in the saucer-shaped *Polybius* all four pairs of walking-legs are adapted for swimming. Henslow's swimming crab (*Polybius henslowi*) of the E Atlantic has been timed at 1·33 m/s (=4·79 km/h *3 miles/h*), but the maximum potential for these very pugnacious creatures must be much higher because they regularly overtake and catch fish in the open sea.

The fastest-moving crustaceans on land are the long-legged ghost crabs (*Ocypode*) of the tropics which are equally at home running forwards, backwards or sideways. These constantly-alert predators have been timed at speeds up to 2 m/s (=7·2 km/h *4·5 miles/h*) over short distances (Warner, 1977).

The greatest depth at which a crustacean has been seen is 35 802 ft *10 912 m* for an unidentified red shrimp sighted by Jacques Piccard and Lt Don Walsh of the US Navy through the window of the bathyscaphe *Trieste* shortly after it settled at the bottom of the Challenger Deep near Guam in the W Pacific on 23 January 1960 (Piccard, 1960).

The greatest depth from which crustaceans have been recovered is 10 500 m *34 449 ft* for a number of shrimp-like amphipods as yet unnamed taken *alive* by the American research vessel *Thomas Washington* in the Challenger Deep in November 1980. The technology required to trap and maintain life under great pressure was developed by research scientists at the Scripps Institution of Oceanography in La Jolla, California. The ingenious device (called a barotram) consists of a baited, high-pressure titanium trap that free falls to the ocean floor, where it remains for 10–30 hours before jettisoning its ballast and returning to the surface. The container is connected to a water circulation system and the marine life can be observed through tiny view ports. 'We were able to recover the animals and keep them alive up to one week on board ship, where they were observed', said Dr A Aristides Yananos, chief scientist of the expedition. The previous record had been held by a small number of isopods (*Macrostylis galatheae*) sledge-trawled from a depth of 9790 m *32 119 ft* in the Philippine Trench by the Danish Galathea Deep Sea Expedition of 1950–52 (Bruun, 1956). The blind lobster *Willemoesia* has been trawled off the Pacific coast of Central America in 3700 m *12 139 ft* of water (Idyll, 1964), and the deep-sea crab *Ethusina abyssicola* has been taken from a depth of 4815 m *15 797 ft*. The deep-sea hermit crabs *Parapagurus* and *Tylaspis* may also range beyond 3000 m *9843 ft* (Menzies *et al*, 1973), and some of the squat-lobsters of the genus *Munidopsis* may reach deeper levels (*c* 5000 m *16 400 ft*).

At the other end of the vertical scale Alexander Agassiz, the Swiss-born marine zoologist, collected nine different species of crustacea at an altitude of 12 500 ft *3810 m* when dredging Lake Titicaca on the Peru–Bolivian border in 1875, and amphipods and isopods have been found in the Ecuadorean Andes at a height of 13 300 ft *4054 m*.

The only living organism that has a greater biomass than the human population of the world (an estimated 180 million tonnes in mid-1980s) is probably *Euphausia superba*, the small shrimp-like krill of the Southern Ocean, which is a prime source of food for baleen whales and a central link in the economy of life. In March 1981 an enormous swarm of krill estimated to weigh 10 million tonnes was tracked by American scientists off Antarctica. According to the National Science Foundation in Washington it was so dense it equalled about one-seventh of the world's yearly catch of fish and shellfish. It has been calculated that over 300 million tonnes of krill (average length 50–60 mm *1·97–2·36 in*) could be harvested annually without affecting the food-chain, but recent research in Norway and West Germany on the edibility of this crustacean (it contains about 15 per cent protein) has revealed that the fluoride levels are so high that it is extremely doubtful whether krill could ever be rendered safe for human consumption. Commenting on the biomass of krill Dr Fincham of the British Museum, who works on *Euphausia*, says: 'As far as I know there are no figures available or even "guesstimates" of total weight of krill. However, some figures which may be of interest are estimates of annual production (which is not the same as standing crop) ranging from 330+ (derived from predation models) to 500+ (derived from food availability models) million tonnes.'

Although the crushing claw of a large lobster is powerful enough to pulp a man's arm at the wrist, and one skin-diver had the brass tubing of his snorkel nipped in two by an outsized individual which he valiantly tried to pull from the wreck of a wartime minesweeper in Bridlington Bay, Yorkshire, no serious injuries have been attributed to these crustaceans. In July 1938, however, a lobster fisherman, Robert Anthony of Portland, Dorset was nearly drowned by one of his catch. After emptying his pots, one of the more curious lobsters yanked out the boat plug, and the sea poured in through the hole! The robber crabs also have tremendously powerful pincers which can easily sever a human finger, but these giant land crustaceans are basically vegetarian and feed mainly on fruits including coconuts which they drill open in the region of the eyes. In 1951 hordes of robber crabs allegedly attacked a sleeping party of Moslem pilgrims marooned on an island in the Red Sea and killed 26 of their number by puncturing their skulls, but this story probably owed a lot to journalistic licence.

The only really dangerous crustaceans are the freshwater crabs and crayfishes of the Orient which serve as intermediate hosts to the common lung fluke. Humans infected by these very unpleasant parasites as a result of eating the uncooked meat often show TB-like symptoms, and if the fluke invades the brain as well it can cause cerebral haemorrhage, encephalitis and even infantile paralysis. In Africa fresh-water crabs eaten raw often cause blindness, and Warner (1977) says the condition is caused by a roundworm transmitted by the blackfly.

Arachnids

(class Arachnida)

An arachnid is a terrestrial invertebrate which breathes through gill-like structures called 'book-lungs' or by means of a network of air-filled tubes. The body is divided into two main parts: the cephalothorax (head and thorax fused together) bearing four pairs of legs and two pairs of pincer-like appendages, and the abdomen which is limbless. It has a rigid exoskeleton which it casts off periodically but no antennae. The function of these organs is served instead by the sensory bristles which cover the body and appendages. The young are usually hatched from eggs after leaving the female, but some are born alive.

The earliest known arachnid was the aquatic scorpion *Paleophonus nuncius* which lived about 400 million years ago. Its remains have been found on the Isle of Gotland, Sweden.

There are about 65 000 known species of arachnid and another 800 are discovered each year. The class is divided into eleven orders. These are: the Araneae (spiders); Opiliones (harvestmen); Chelonethi (false scorpions); Acareae (mites and ticks); Scorpiones (scorpions); Solifugae (sun-spiders); Amblypygi (tailless whip scorpions); Holopeltida (whip scorpions); Palpigradi (micro-whip scorpions); Ricinulei (ricinuleids); and the Schizopeltida (schizomids). The largest order is Araneae with 30 000 species and the smallest Ricinulei (25 species).

The largest known arachnids are the exceptionally bulky theraphosid spiders of the genera *Lasiodora* and *Grammostola* of Brazil. In 1973 an enormous female *Lasiodora* sp. with a leg-span of *c*270 mm *10·63 in* when fully extended and a body length of 92 mm *3·62 in* (front edge of the chelicerae or pincers to the end of the abdomen) was caught at Puraque, W Brazil (Ted Sasscer, pers. comm.). Another female of the same genus collected by Tom Gilliard at Manaos, W Brazil in 1945 had a leg-span of 241 mm *9·49 in* and scaled almost 3 oz *85 g* (Gertsch, 1979). *Grammostola mollicoma* is also of comparable size, and Bucherl (1971) mentions an outsized female kept in the laboratories at the Butantan Institute, São Paulo which, at the time of writing, had a body length of 90 mm *3·54 in* and a leg-span of at least 260 mm *10·24 in*.

As befits their awesome size, these spiders are extremely voracious, and Brazil and Vellard (1925) give details of a captive *Grammastola* which killed and devoured two frogs, a small rattlesnake and a highly venomous Jararaca snake within the space of four days. At the end of this eating orgy it went into retirement and fasted for two weeks!

The little-known *Xenesthis immanis* and *X. monstrosa* of Colombia also have massive bodies, and both species have been credited with leg-spans in excess of 230 mm *9·06 in*.

The Guyanan 'bird-eating' spider (*Theraphosa blondi*) of NE South America has long been credited with the 'largest spider' title, but this species bulks out lighter than the arachnids already mentioned. A male specimen with a leg-span of 254 mm *10 in* and a body length of 89 mm *3·5 in* collected by Mrs Joseph H Sinclair at Montagne la Gabrielle, French Guiana in April 1925 weighed just under 2 oz *57 g* (Willis J Gertsch, pers. comm.).

The 'tarantulas' of the genera *Dugesiella* have a much wider range of size, but one extremely large *D. crinita* collected by Baerg (1958) in Tlahualilo, Mexico in 1935 had a body length of 85 mm *3·35 in* and weighed 54·7 g *1·93 oz*.

Some of the running spiders (*Ctenidae*) of Central America also have a very impressive leg-span and the exceptionally long-legged *Cupiennius sallei* has been measured up to 254 mm *10 in* across. All of the members of this family, however, are light-bodied creatures and the species just mentioned cannot compete with a large theraphosid in terms of bulk or weight.

Ivan Sanderson (1937) tells of collecting a 'giant hairy spider' in the Assumbo Mountains, British Cameroons, W Africa in 1932 for the British Museum which covered an enamel dish measuring 12 in *305 mm* by 8 in *203 mm* when its legs were fully extended in all directions, but these dimensions were exaggerated. The largest spider sent by the zoologist to the Museum actually measured 178 mm *7·01 in* across the legs and belonged to the genus *Hysterocrates*. The largest African spider is probably *H. hercules*, which has a body length of 76 mm *3 in* and a leg spread of 203 mm *8 in* (D J Clark, pers. comm.).

Of the 617 known British species of spider, the cardinal spider (*Tegenaria parietina*) has the greatest leg-span. In August 1979 a male specimen with an extended leg-span of 140 mm *5·5 in* (body length 18 mm *0·7 in*) was collected in Slough, Berkshire (Paul Hillyard, pers. comm.). This house spider is found only in southern England and is so called because Cardinal Thomas Wolsey (1475-1530) is said to have lived in abject fear of them at Hampton Court.

The well known 'Daddy-Long-Legs' spider (*Pholcus phalangioides*) rarely exceeds 76 mm *3 in* across the legs, but Savory (1928) mentions an exceptionally large male collected in the south of England which measured 152 mm *6 in* across (length of body 7·6 mm *0·31 in*).

The heaviest spider found in Britain is probably the very bulky orb weaver *Araneus quadratus*. On 30 August 1981 a specimen weighing 1·698 g *0·06 oz* was captured at Canterbury Field Study Centre, Canterbury, Kent by Mr T W Harman and Mrs K Ironside (T W Harman, pers. comm.). This weight may be matched by the six-eyed spider *Segestria florentina* of southern England, which has been measured up to 23 mm *0·91 in* in body length and has been referred to as 'the largest British spider' (Locket and Millidge, 1951–53), and more especially by the very thick-set swamp spiders *Dolomedes fimbriatus* of southern England and *D. plantarius* of Redgrave and Lophan Fen nature reserve, Suffolk, which are almost identical in size (up to 22 mm *0·87 in* body length). The largest British spider seen by Bristowe (1971) was an outsized Water spider (*Argyroneta aquatica*) collected in Kent which had a body length of 28 mm *1·10 in* (normal range 9–13 mm *0·35–0·51 in*), but this female was not weighed. Another spider worthy of mention is the widely-distributed *Drassodes lapidosus*, which usually has a body length of 10–15 mm *0·39–0·59 in*. Recently, however, a giant variant measuring up to 22 mm *0·87 in* has been discovered on Skellig St Michael off the coast of County Kerry, Ireland (Bristowe, 1971).

The smallest members of the order Araneida are the midget spiders (*Symphytognathidae*), the tiniest of which is the pale yellow *Patu marplesi* of Western Samoa, SW Pacific. The type specimen (male) found in moss at an altitude of 2000 ft *610 m* near Malolelei, Upolu in January 1956 by T E Woodward of the Queensland Museum, Brisbane, Australia, measured 0·43 mm *0·017 in*, which means it is half the size of a full-stop on this page! (Forster, 1958).

The smallest recorded British species is the money spider *Glyphesis cottonae*, which is known only from a swamp near Beaulieu Road railway station in the New Forest, Hants and Thursley Common, Surrey (Locket and Millidge, 1951–53). Another money spider, *Saloca diceros*, found among mosses in Dorset and Staffordshire, and the widely-distributed comb-footed spider *Theonoe minutissima* are almost equally as diminutive, their body lengths being 1–1·2 mm *0·039–0·047 in* and 1–1·25 mm *0·039–0·049 in* respectively (Bristowe, 1958).

The largest spider webs are the aerial ones spun by the tropical orb weavers of the genus *Nephila*. Several examples found by Sherwill (1850) in the Karrakpur Hills near Monghyr, central Bihar, India measured 5 ft *1·5 m* in diameter (=15 ft 9 in *4·79 m* in circumference) and had long supporting guy-lines up to 20 ft *6·1 m* in length, and Haekel (1883) saw 'immense cobwebs one to two metres across' while on an excursion from Bombay. In the lower steppes of central Australia Spencer and Gillen (1912) found the webs made by *N. eremiana* so large and strong that they proved quite a hindrance to them as they rode through the scrub. 'The web stretches across from tree to tree for a distance of often twelve to fifteen feet and reaches a height in the middle of fully six feet.'

Some other web-building spiders show a tendency towards social habits, and the Australian species *Ixeuticus socialis* (formerly *Amaurobius*) constructs communal webs measuring up to 12 ft *3·7 m* in length and 4 ft *1·2 m* in width.

The silk produced by *Nephila* spiders is incredibly strong and possesses great elasticity. The tensile strength is much greater than that of steel, and some threads will stretch to twice their own length or more before breaking. According to Gertsch (1979) the natives of the New Hebrides have a very bizarre use for this silk. They make a conical cap out of the material which is then pulled down tightly over the head of an adulteress, causing death by suffocation.

Keith McKeown (1952) reports that it is not unusual for a man to have his hat knocked off his head by one of these snares, and F Ratcliffe (cited by Lane, 1955) describes how he blundered into a huge web 'and almost literally bounced off'.

The smallest webs in the world are the aerial ones spun by midget spiders. That of the orb weaver *Chasmocephalon armatum* of New Zealand only measures about 9–10 mm *0·35–0·39 in* in diameter, which means it is half the size of a small postage stamp. These spiders feed mainly on springtails and other minute insects.

The longest-lived of all spiders are the primitive *Mygalomorphae* ('tarantulas' and allied species). One female theraphosid collected by Baerg at Mazatland, Mexico in 1935 and estimated to be 10–12 years old at the time, was kept in his laboratory for 16 years, making a total of 26–28 years in all, and he believed that this was the normal life-span for females. Another female (*Eurypelma* sp.) from South America lived in the British Museum for 14 years and was thought to have been about 20 at the time of her death (Vesey-Fitzgerald, 1967), and Petrunkevitch (1955) mentions a female theraphosid which lived in the Museum d'Histoire Naturelle, Paris for 25 years.

Most male 'tarantulas' reach maturity in 8 to 9 years and die a few months later, but Baerg reared specimens of the Arkansas species *Dugesiella hertzi* under laboratory conditions which lived for 10, 11 and even 13 years.

Some of the funnel-web spiders (family Dipluridae) are also long-lived and Barrett (cited by McKeown, 1952), observed one (*Atrax* sp.) which occupied a cavity in a staghorn fern in his garden at Elsternwick, Victoria, Australia for 17 years.

The longest-lived British spider is probably the purse-web spider (*Atypus affinis*), which is found in southern England, parts of Wales and the Channel Islands. Females of this mysterious species spend practically most of their life in a *sealed* silken tube buried in the soil and normally live 5½–7 years in this tiny underground prison, which also serves as a dining room for any insect unfortunate enough to alight on the 2 in *51 mm* part of the tube sticking above the ground. When the 'dinner gong' vibrates the lady of the house dashes upstairs, punctures the tube with her massive fangs and then drags the struggling victim through the rapidly tearing slit she has made. One fully mature female collected by Bristowe (1971) and kept in a cool greenhouse survived for five years, which means she must have been at least nine years old at the time of her death.

The house spider *Tegenaria domestica* is also long-lived, and two individuals kept by Dr Oliver of Bradford lived for five and seven years respectively (Savory, 1928). Some of the large wolf spiders may also live as long as seven years.

The majority of spiders, however, complete their life-cycle in 10–12 months. One of the shortest-lived species is the deadly 'black widow' (*Latrodectus mactans*) of the Americas, Hawaii and the West Indies. A number of males reared under laboratory conditions lived on an average about 100 days, while females averaged 271 days (Deevey and Deevey, cited by Gertsch, 1979).

The most elusive of all spiders are the rare trap-door spiders of the genus *Liphistius*, which are found only in SE Asia. Like the purse-web spider, these creatures also live in silken tubes buried in the ground, but they are much more difficult to detect because the hinged circular door which secures the entrance to the lair is coated on the outside with plant matter and is beautifully camouflaged.

The most elusive spiders in Britain are the four species which are known only from the type specimen. These are the jumping spiders *Salticus mutabilis* (one male Bloxworth, Dorset 1860) and *Heliophanus melinus* (one female Bloxworth, 1870); the crab spider *Philodromus buxi* (one female Bloxworth, pre-1879), and the cobweb spider *Robertus insignis* (one male Norwich, 1906). The first three were all collected by O Pickard-Cambridge (Locket, Millidge and Merrett, 1974). The species most sought after by collectors, however, is the handsome lace-web or carmine spider (*Eresus niger*). Up until very recently this species was known only from seven specimens (six males and one female) collected in Hampshire and Dorset between 1816 and 1906. The females are dull black in colour, but the smaller males have a brilliant crimson body with six black spots and a series of iridescent white rings round the black legs. In the early summer of 1932 another male was seen at Kynance Cove, southern Cornwall, but was not captured (Bristowe, 1971), and in the early 1950s there was a second sighting at Sandown, Isle of Wight (Savory, 1966). In June 1979 two males were caught in a spider trap on heathland near Corfe Castle, Dorset. The following year Dr Peter Merrett of the Institute of Terrestrial Ecology at Furzebrook near Poole discovered 30–40 individuals on the same site and brought a pair back to the laboratory where they successfully bred. The female hatched 90 eggs. 'Only a handful of us know exactly where these spiders were found', says Dr Merrett (pers. comm.), 'and we shall release them when we have studied them. Hopefully all ninety will survive and breed a substantial colony there within a few years.'

The highest speed recorded for a spider on a level surface is 1·73 ft/s *53 cm/s* (=1·18 miles/h *1·90 km/h*) in the case of a female house spider *Tegenaria atrica*. This may not seem very fast, but Bristowe (1971) has calculated that this particular individual must have covered a distance equivalent to 330 times her own body length in ten seconds (*cf* 100 times own body length for fast-swimming fish). The same authority also found that although a mature female *Tegenaria* would run at top speed as soon as she was prodded with a pencil, she could not maintain this 'furious pace' for much longer than 15 seconds before collapsing in a heap. In other words, as the size increases the stamina decreases.

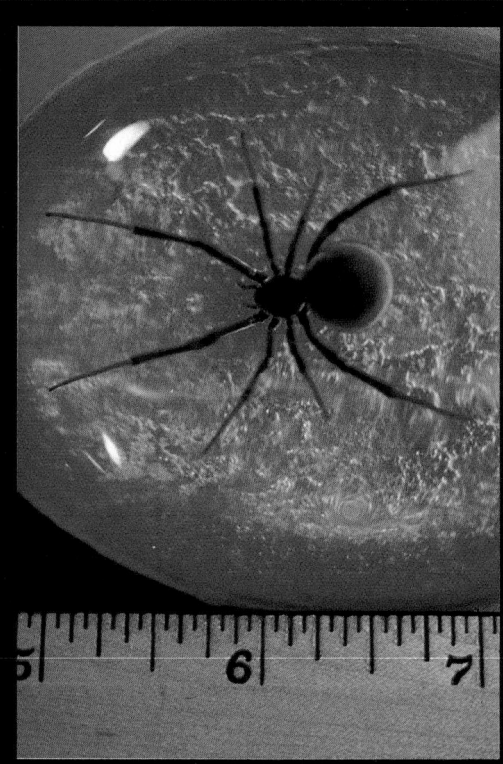

The formidable robber crab, the world's largest land crustacean.

Above – The deadly female 'Black Widow', the most feared of all spiders. This outsized specimen was collected in California.

The whiteclaw, Britain's largest freshwater invertebrate.

Below – The small blue of southern England, Britain's smallest butterfly, shown approximately actual size.

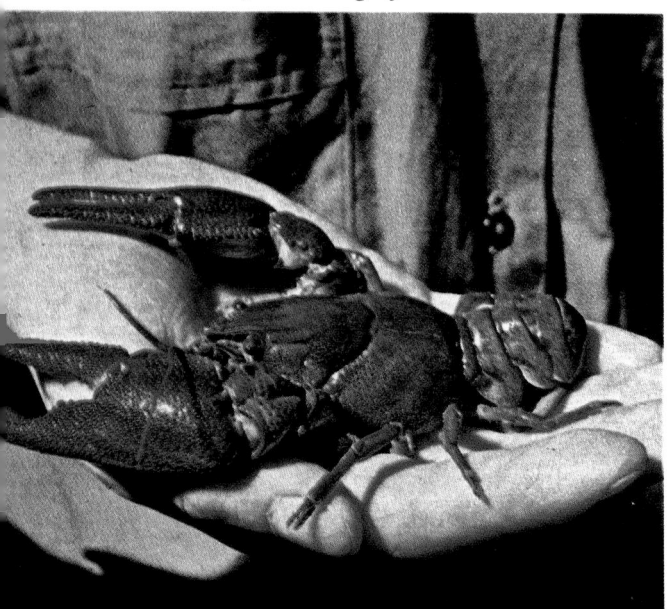

The magnificent birdwing Ornithoptera allottei, *the most highly prized of all butterflies.*

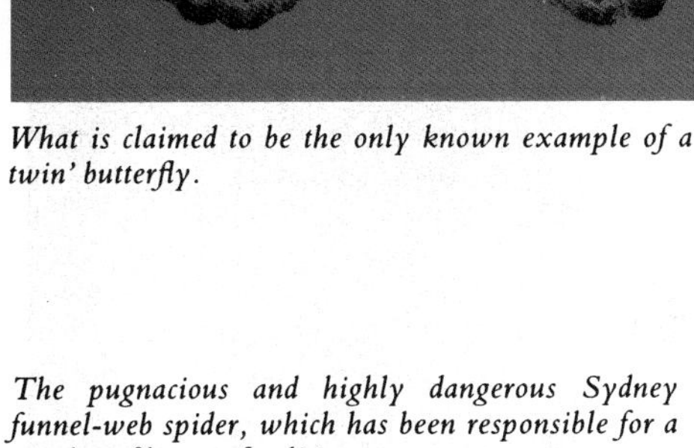

The goliath beetle, the world's heaviest insect, drawn to actual scale.

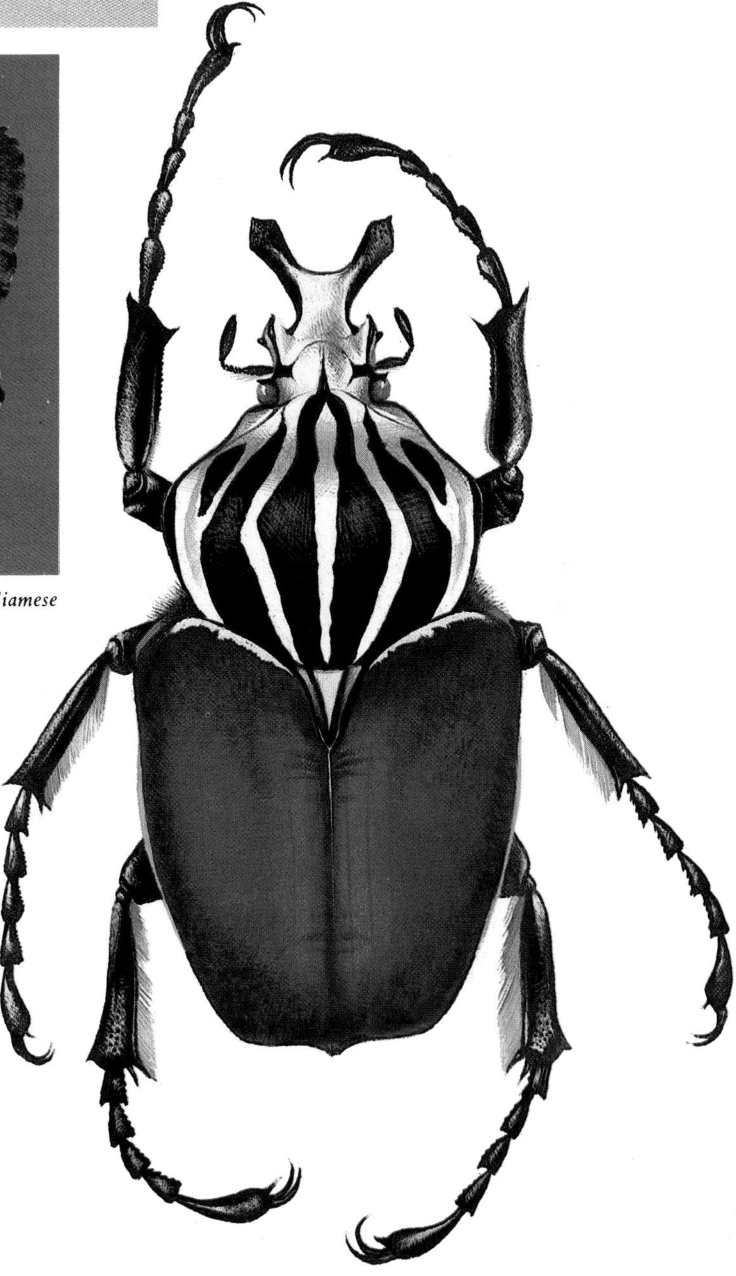

What is claimed to be the only known example of a 'Siamese twin' butterfly.

The pugnacious and highly dangerous Sydney funnel-web spider, which has been responsible for a number of human fatalities.

The swiftest terrestrial invertebrates are the long-legged sun-spiders of the genus *Solpuga*, which live in the arid semi-desert regions of Africa and the Middle East. They have well-developed tracheae as opposed to book-lungs and are incredibly fast over short distances including almost vertical surfaces.

In discussing the lightning-quick reactions of these creatures, Dr R F Lawrence (1965), former Director of the Natal Museum, says: 'One Cape coloured worker, on a farm in the Eastern Cape Province, told me how once when driving his team of mules home in the heat of the day he looked up and saw to his utter terror a large and hairy *Solpuga* rushing towards him down the stock of the long bamboo whip he was holding. He only just had time to throw the whip into the bushes before the *Solpuga* reached his hand. This story is not at all improbable, as the lash of the whip had probably been trailing on the ground near a wandering *Solpuga* which could easily have run up the long leather lash of the whip in a few seconds.'

Because they tend to run erratically, no accurate measurements have been recorded for these highly-carnivorous arachnids, but some species probably have a burst sprint capability of at least 10 miles/h *16 km/h.*

The greatest altitude at which a spider has been found is 22 000 ft *6706 m* for a jumping spider *Europhrys* sp. collected by R Hingston, the British naturalist-mountaineer, on Mt Everest in 1924, but immature specimens probably balloon even higher in their own gossamer. Spiders have also been found deep down in coal-mines and caves.

Although most of the 30 000 known species of spider have venom glands, only a few are dangerous to man.

The most venomous spiders in the world – and the most dangerous – are the Brazilian wandering spiders of the genus *Phoneutria*, and in particular *P. fera* which has the most active venom of any living spider. These large and highly aggressive arachnids frequently enter human dwellings and hide in clothing or shoes. When disturbed they bite furiously several times, and hundreds of accidents involving these species are reported annually. Fortunately an effective antivenin is available, and when fatalities do occur they are usually children under the age of seven who die during the first five hours of illness.

Bucherl says two little children sleeping in the same bed in a rural house near São Sebastiao in São Paulo State, Brazil were killed on the same night by one spider, a *Phoneutria*, which was brought to him for identification.

The venom is neurotoxic in action, which means it attacks the junction between the nerves and the muscles they control. The symptoms are excruciating pain, profuse sweating and salivation followed by hallucinations, spasms and finally respiratory paralysis. *Phoneutria* also has the largest venom glands of any spider (up to 10·4×2·7 mm *0·4×0·1 in*). Specimens 'milked' by electric shock at the Butantan Institute, São Paulo yielded an average dry venom weight of 1·25 mg *0·000 044 oz* and a maximum of 8 mg *0·000 28 oz*, the latter amount being enough to kill over 500 mice if injected intravenously. The MLD for an average sized man is not known, but as 0·10 mg *0·000 003 5 oz* is said to seriously endanger human life, the amount must be extremely small.

Second only to *Phoneutria* in terms of neurotoxic potency is the large funnel-web 'tarantula' *Trechona venosa*, also of South America. Fortunately this creature is sedentary by nature and no fatalities have been reported, but Vellard (1936) says rats bitten by this arachnid died *within seconds.*

The large and pugnacious Sydney funnel-web spider (*Atrax robustus*) of NSW, Australia also has a very nasty reputation, and it was not until 1980 that an antivenin was developed for this species. *A. robustus* first made the news in 1927 when a two-year-old boy was bitten by one and died within 90 minutes. Since then 11 more fatalities, half of them children under the age of ten, have been recorded. All but one of them died from respiratory failure followed by cardiac arrest within 12 hours of being bitten. In this species the male's venom is five times more toxic than that of the female which has not been known to cause serious illness. On 28 December 1970 a 17-year-old pregnant woman was bitten by a funnel-web spider while walking through bushland near Nowra, 95 miles *152 km* south of Sydney. She was on a camping holiday with her husband and suddenly felt something crawling inside her blouse, then a bite on the breast. Shortly afterwards she collapsed and was rushed to hospital, where doctors worked through the night in a vain attempt to save her and the unborn baby. In December 1971 doctors saved the life of a three-year-old girl in Sydney who had been bitten twice by a funnel-web spider by treating her with the drug athrophine. The child was found with the spider still clinging to her arm. The smaller *Atrax formidabilis* of Eastern Queensland is also potentially dangerous, but Sutherland (1974) says no fatal cases are on record. In January 1979, however, a 32-year-old woman died in Sydney after being bitten. Other species of *Atrax* are found in Victoria and Tasmania, but considered relatively harmless.

Thanks to the popular press, the most feared of all spiders is the notorious 'black widow' (*Latrodectus mactans*) but although females have a neurotoxic venom capable of killing a human being – the much smaller male cannot inject a lethal dose – fatalities are comparatively rare. This is because it is timid by nature and only bites when frightened. According to Thorp and Woodson (1945) there were 1291 *reported* cases of black widow bites in the USA during the period 1726–1943 (578 in California), but only 55 proved fatal, and most of these were young boys or elderly men with heart problems living in rural areas. This spider likes to make its home under the seats in outdoor privies and external genitals are a prime target! More recently Parrish (1963) has recorded 65 spider-bite fatalities in the USA for the period 1950–59, 63 of which were attributed to *Latrodectus* species. The symptoms are intense pain, temporary paralysis, nausea and dizziness, followed by nervousness and anxiety which can become so acute that several hospital patients have told doctors they thought they were going mad (Vellard, 1936).

In 1936 D'Amour, Becker and Van Riper carried out a series of experiments to determine the toxicity of the venom and found that on a dry weight basis it was 15 times more potent than the venom of the Prairie rattlesnake. This is interesting, because at one time the Gosiute Indians of Utah smeared their arrowheads with a lethal mixture of macerated black widow and rattlesnake venom when hunting big game (Chamberlain and Ivie, 1935).

More recently American scientists have discovered that there is a very marked 'seasonal variation' in the toxicity of *Latrodectus* venom. According to the findings of Keegan *et al* (1960) specimens collected near San Antonio, Texas in the autumn and 'milked' in the laboratory had a venom which was ten times as toxic as that taken from others in May. Although the reason for this is not known, the tests did reveal that if you are a Texan you stand a much better chance of survival if you are bitten by one of these creatures in the early summer!

In October 1977 Brian Wilson (pers. comm.) collected an exceptionally large female 30 miles *48 km* south of Barstow, California which measured 63 mm *2·5 in* overall (tip of front legs to tip of back legs) and had a body length of 17 mm *0·7 in*. As the normal overall length for females of this species is 25 mm *1·0 in*, this formidable individual must have packed quite a wallop!

In September 1978 four dead black widow spiders were found in a packing case at the British Government's secret aircraft and armaments experimental establishment at Boscombe Down, Wiltshire. The case was among the equipment which had been used in a military exercise in the Mojave Desert, California.

The closely-related red-back spider (*Latrodectus m. hasselti*), which ranges from Arabia right across southern Asia and the Pacific Islands to Australia and New Zealand, where it is known as the Katipo ('night-stinger'), has also been responsible for a number of fatalities. Keith McKeown (1952) says

this little demon has killed at least ten people in Australia this century, and there have been five deaths in New Zealand in the past 65 years. Two of the victims were a girl aged 7 and her 3-year-old brother who were bitten while asleep after hundreds of these spiders invaded the country town of Raetihi, South Island in June 1969 after a minor earthquake. No fatalities have been reported, however, since an antivenin was developed at the Commonwealth Serum Laboratories.

Latrodectus is also found in all Mediterranean countries and the typical sub-species *L. m. tredecimguttatus* was responsible for the virulent epidemics which occurred in Spain in 1833 and 1841, and in Sardinia in 1833 and 1839. In untreated victims the duration of the illness was up to 8 days, followed by a long convalescence, but a small number of fatalities were reported. There was also another epidemic in Italy and Yugoslavia during the period 1938–58, but in the 946 cases studied only two people died (Bettini, 1964).

The button-spider (*L. m. indistinctus*) of South Africa is also greatly feared, and Bucherl (1971) says a number of deaths have been recorded, although Clark (1969) could find only one fatality since 1945 – an 8-year-old girl.

It should be pointed out here that there is still a certain amount of disagreement among arachnologists regarding the taxonomy of some of the better-known widow spiders. 'Fortunately for clinicians' writes Minton (1974) '*Latrodectus* bites in man produce much the same symptoms and respond to the same treatment.'

Unlike *Latrodectus*, the recluse spiders (*Loxosceles*) of the Americas have a powerful necrotic venom. This means the bite produces an ulcerating wound which often turns gangrenous, and infections are common. In some cases victims suffer internal damage as well from blood poisoning. The most dangerous member of this genus is the 'arana de los rincones' (corner spider) of Chile and Uruguay which has been responsible for at least 50 deaths. The venom of the much-publicised Brown recluse spider (*L. reclusa*) of central and southern USA is not so potent.

Although the large theraphosids can inflict a very nasty wound with their huge fangs, the venom they secrete is only highly toxic to cold-blooded animals, and has only a local effect in man. There have been a small number of cases, however, of people collapsing and dying from shock after being bitten by one of these formidable-looking spiders.

The largest living scorpion (750 species) is *Heterometrus swammerdami* of southern India, males averaging 180 mm *7·1 in* from the tips of the pincers to the end of the sting. A specimen collected in Madras

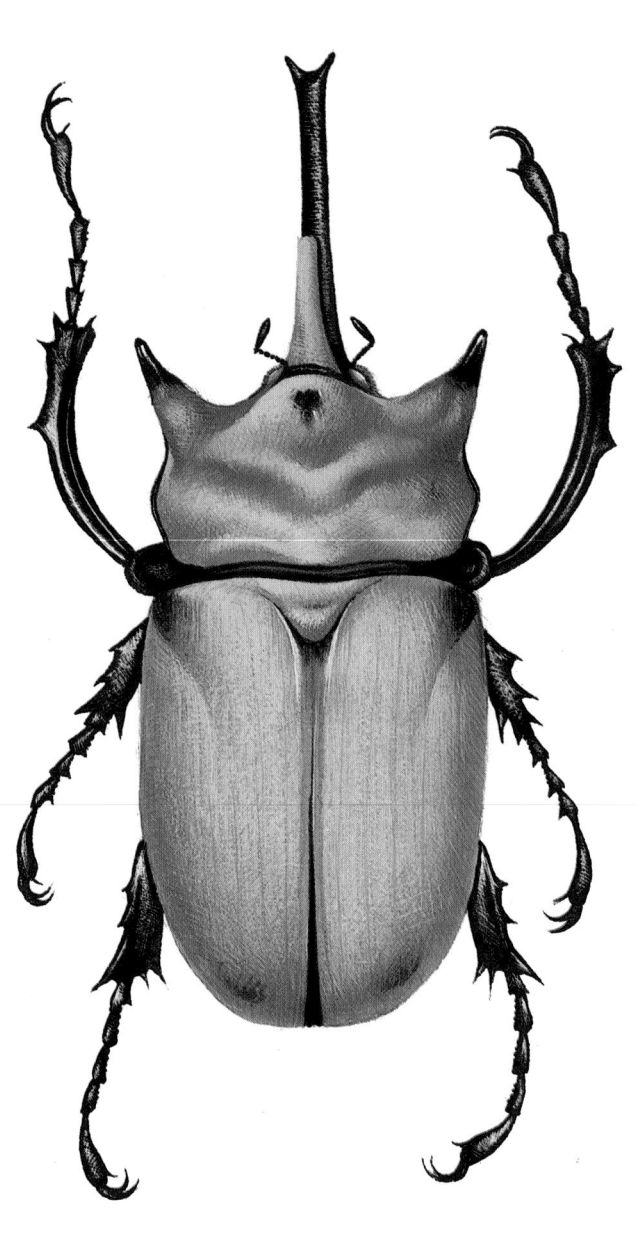

The huge elephant beetle, one of the world's heaviest insects, drawn to actual scale.

Forewing of the Queen Alexandra birdwing butterfly, drawn to actual size, as are the other butterflies on this page.

Dwarf blue butterfly.

Small blue butterfly.

Swallowtail butterfly.

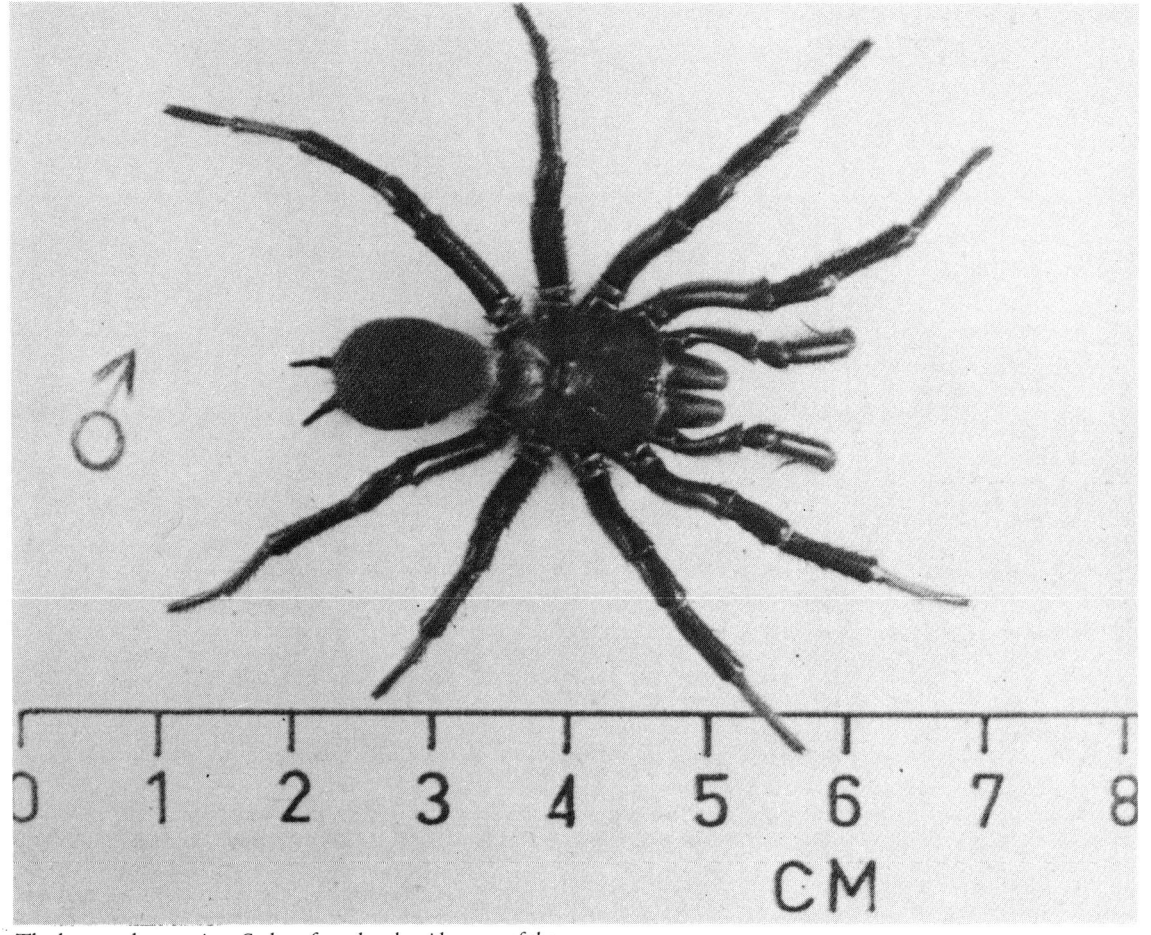

The large and pugnacious Sydney funnel-web spider, one of the world's most venomous arachnids.

Province on 14 September 1869, and now in the possession of the Bombay Natural History Society, measures 247 mm *9·7 in* (tip of head to point of sting 187 mm *7·4 in*, length of body 82 mm *3·2 in*). Another one found under a rock in the village of Krishnarajapuram, W Bengal during the Second World War and taken to the local military hospital for examination was even larger, measuring 292 mm *11·5 in* (Burgess, 1941).

The forest-dwelling imperial scorpion (*Pandinus imperator*) of W Africa is also of comparable size. One example preserved in the British Museum measures 215 mm *8·5 in*. In October 1931 an exceptionally large male was received at London Zoo from Ghana. It measured 228 mm *9·0 in* and was described as the biggest and most perfect example in living memory. In 1977 London entomologist Bernard Betts (pers. comm.) caught another huge male in Sierra Leone while mapping the westward distribution of this species. It measured just over 9 in *229 mm*

('it's a bit difficult to measure a live *imperator!*') and weighed 50 g *1·76 oz*, making it one of the heavyweights of the *Arachnida*. *Hadogenes troglodytes* and *H. trichiurus* of South Africa are also large species, males having been measured up to 180 mm *7·1 in* (Bucherl, 1971).

The smallest scorpion in the world is *Microbothus pusillus* from the Red Sea coast, which measures about 13 mm *0·5 in* in total length (Savory, 1964).

Although the scorpion has a very evil reputation, it is largely undeserved because the venom of most species produces only a mild to severe local reaction in man (i.e. a sharp burning sensation which may last anything from a few minutes to several hours). The most dangerous scorpions are the Buthids. All the members of this family carry very powerful venoms, but they vary greatly in the degree of virulence.

The world's most dangerous scorpion is the large fat-tailed scorpion (*Androctonus australis*) of the Atlas

Mountains and the northern Sahara. This animal can deliver a massive dose of neurotoxic venom which has been known to kill a man in 4 hours and a dog in about 7 minutes (Millot and Vachon, 1949).

Between 1936 and 1950 *A. australis* was responsible for nearly 80 per cent of the 1300 reported cases of scorpion stings in Algeria, 377 of which proved fatal, but the death-roll would have been much higher if the victims had not been treated with an antivenin produced by the Pasteur Institute in Algiers.

In September 1938 a total of 72 cases of dangerous scorpion sting (mostly *A. australis*) were reported in a *single day* from districts near Cairo, Egypt.

Three scorpions of the genus *Centruroides* (*C. noxius, C. suffusus* and *C. limpidus*) found in Mexico are also extremely dangerous. Data compiled by the State Statistical Dept 1940–49 show that annual deaths from scorpion stings in the Mexican Republic varied between a minimum of 1588 deaths in 1943 up to a maximum of 1933 deaths in 1946. In another survey covering the period 1957–58 the Institute of Health and Tropical Diseases found that there was a decrease in the number of deaths, the figures being 1494 and 1107 respectively. The total number of fatalities was 20 352 (mostly juveniles), while during the same periods 2 068 people died from snakebite, 274 from spiderbite and 1933 from the bites or stings of unidentified venomous animals (Mazzotti and Bravo-Becherelle, 1963).

Two other species, *C. sculpturatus* and *C. gertschi*, which are restricted to the southern parts of Arizona and New Mexico, USA were responsible for 64 deaths in Arizona between 1929 and 1948 – twice as many fatalities as all other venomous animals combined in that State (Stahnke, 1950).

A number of deaths have also been attributed to the Brazilian scorpions *Tityus serrulatus* and *T. bahiensis*. During one seven-year period 1331 stings with eight fatalities were reported in the city of Ribeirao Preto, most of them involving *T. serrulatus* which frequently enters houses and outbuildings.

During the Second World War a number of soldiers fighting on both sides in the Western Desert, North Africa died after being stung by scorpions of the genus *Buthus* (probably the widespread *B. occitanus*).

In South Africa scorpions of the genus *Parabuthus* have been responsible for a small number of fatalities among children. In February 1936 a plague of scorpions descended on Malmesbury, Cape Province and stung three African children to death, and in November 1959 a 2-year-old girl died in the village of Kenhardtt, Cape Province 10 minutes after being stung by one of these creatures. If the sting enters a vein death comes very quickly, and in one case reported in December 1966 a 12-year-old girl in Palapye, Botswana succumbed within 5 minutes.

Although the huge *Pandinus* and *Heterometrus* scor-

The huge imperial scorpion of the rain forests of West Africa.

pions have the largest stings and can inject a massive dose of venom, the potency is low and human fatalities are rare.

The most venomous scorpion in the world is the Palestine yellow scorpion (*Leiurus quinquestriatus*), which ranges from the eastern part of North Africa through the Middle East to the shores of the Red Sea. Happily the amount of venom it delivers is very small (0·255 mg *0·000 009 oz*) and adult lives are seldom endangered, but it has been responsible for a number of fatalities among young children under the age of 5.

Persons stung by scorpions carrying a powerful neurotoxic venom quickly develop a tightness in the throat and speech becomes slurred. They then become restless and start perspiring profusely, followed by vomiting and involuntary twitching of the muscles. Eventually breathing becomes laboured, and shortly before death the arms and legs sometimes turn completely blue.

At one time it was strongly believed that a scorpion would sting itself to death if surrounded by a ring of fire, but as it is immune to its own venom and also lacks the power to reason, this must be put down to faulty observation. When it is threatened a scorpion – not unnaturally – will lash out with its tail, and these actions can easily be wrongly interpreted as self-induced stinging.

Unknown to most people a colony of yellow-tailed scorpions (*Euscorpius flavicaudis*) has been living in the perimeter wall of the old dockyard at Sheerness Port, Isle of Sheppey, Kent for over a hundred years now. Before there is a mass exodus of the human population, however, it should be stated that this 40 mm *1·57 in* species which originates in southern Europe is quite harmless and its sting nothing more than a mere pinprick (Wanless, 1974).

Insects

(class Insecta)

An insect is primarily a terrestrial invertebrate which breathes through a system of air tubes. The body is divided into three main parts, the head, thorax and abdomen, and is covered by a horny material or exoskeleton which is shed periodically. The head bears a pair of antennae and three pairs of feeding appendages, and there are usually one or two pairs of wings rising from the thorax and three pairs of legs. The capacity for flight is one of the most striking features of adult insects, but not all species have wings. The young usually hatch from eggs after leaving the female, and some are born alive as fully developed larvae.

The earliest known insect was the springtail *Rhyniella praecursor*, which lived about 370 million years ago. Its remains have been found in the Rhynie Chert, Aberdeenshire, Scotland.

There are about 1 million living species of insect, and about 8000 new ones are discovered each year. The class is divided into 29 orders, the largest of which is Coleoptera (beetles) which contains about 330000 species. The smallest orders are Grylloblattodea and Zoraptera, both with 16 species.

The largest living insects in terms of bulk and weight are probably the heavily-armoured goliath beetles *Goliathus regius* and *G. goliathus* (=*giganteus*) of Equatorial Africa. Adult males of these species (females are smaller) have been reliably measured up to 110 mm *4·33 in* and 108 mm *4·25 in* respectively from the tips of the small frontal horns to the end of the abdomen, and the weight ranges from 70 g *2·47 oz* to 100 g *3·53 oz*. All the members of this genus have a massive build-up of heavy chitin forming their thorax and anterior sternum which gives them a distinct weight advantage over other giant scarabs of comparable size. Goliath beetles are also the heaviest flying insects – a 103 mm *4·06 in* speci-

men measured 245 mm *9·65 in* across the wings when mounted for display purposes – and native children sometimes amuse themselves by tying a piece of string to one of these creatures and flying it in circles like a model aeroplane.

According to Arrow (1951) the elephant beetles (*Megasoma*) of Central America and the West Indies are 'the largest of all known beetles, and indeed the most bulky of all insects', but although he may be right on the second count it is difficult to see how they could exceed *Goliathus* in weight because more than a quarter of the length is taken up by the cephalic horn. The longest species are *Megasoma elephas* and *M. acteon*, which have been measured up to 131 mm *5·16 in* and 126 mm *4·96 in* respectively, but *M. chiron* (110 mm *4·33 in*) has a shorter horn and is larger-bodied than the other two. It has been claimed that *Megasoma* must be lighter than *Goliathus* because there is more air space below the elytra (wing cover) where the greatest width is, but American collector David C Williams (pers. comm.) says he weighed two 104 mm *4·09 in* goliath beetles and a 108 mm *4·25 in M. acteon* in the dry state and found the latter specimen was the heaviest beetle of the trio.

The very rare longicorn beetle *Titanus giganteus* of the Amazon Basin – natives consider the 250 mm *9·84 in* larvae a great delicacy – has also been credited with the title of largest insect, and visually it certainly looks the part, but although this Cerambycid is 95 per cent solid beetle it lacks the body depth of the giant scarabs and the chitinous armour of *Goliathus*. Up until 1957 less than 20 examples of *T. giganteus* were known to science, but that year Dr Paul Zahl (1959), a naturalist working for the *National Geographic Magazine* in Washington, DC obtained 15 more specimens in northern Brazil, four of which measured more than 152 mm *5·98 in* in length (tip of jaws to end of abdomen).

Lengths up to 180 mm *7·09 in* and even 200 mm

7·87 in have been claimed for females of this species, with post-mortem abdomen elongation, but measurements like these tend to be artificially high.

Outside of the giant scarabs, the only other insects known to exceed 50 g *1·76 oz* are the very rare giant wetas *Deinacrida heteracantha* and *D. rugosa* of New Zealand, and the spiny stick-insect *Heteropteryx dilatata* of Malaysia. In one series of eleven adult female *D. heteracantha* (maximum length 100 mm *3·94 in* including the ovipositor) the average weight was found to be 49·7 g *1·75 oz*, but one formidable specimen reached 71·3 g *2·52 oz* after several matings and then proceeded to lay 25 g *0·88 oz* of eggs in 9 days! (Richards, 1973). In October 1977 a weight of 51·2 g *1·81 oz* was recorded for an extremely bulky female *H. dilatata* at London Zoo (R. Humphreys, pers. comm.). This particular individual had a nose to tail length of 140 mm *5·51 in* and measured 35 mm *1·38 in* across the thickest part of the abdomen, but collector Paul Brock of Slough, Bucks, has a much larger specimen (160 mm *6·30 in*) which probably scaled at least 65 g *2·29 oz* in its egg-laying prime. *Euryacantha horrida* of New Guinea is another exceptionally large spiny stick-insect (up to 145 mm *5·71 in*) and widths up to 40 mm *1·57 in* have been reported for this species.

The largest aquatic insect is the giant water bug *Lethocerus maximus* of Venezuela and Brazil which has been measured up to 115 mm *4·53 in*, but this underwater assassin has a relatively long and narrow body and is nothing like as heavy as the biggest members of the Scarabaeidae and the Phasmida.

The heaviest insect found in Britain is the stag beetle (*Lucanus cervus*) which is found in an area stretching from Cornwall to Kent and north just into Suffolk. An adult example of each sex collected by J T Clark (pers. comm.) weighed 4510 mg *0·159 oz* and 4075 mg *0·144 oz* respectively, and one of his larvae tipped the scales at 10 575 mg *0·373 oz*. In one series of 324 males collected in the Colchester area between 1963 and 1966 by the same authority the body lengths (including mandibles) ranged from 31 mm *1·22 in* to 68 mm *2·68 in*, with a mean value of 49·8 mm *1·96 in*. **The largest recorded specimen** is a male in the British Museum which measures 77·4 mm *3·05 in* in length and probably weighed at least 8000 mg *0·282 oz* when alive. It was collected in Sheerness, Kent in 1871. Another male measuring 76 mm *2·99 in* was captured at Priest Hill, Caversham, Berkshire in June 1969 and later presented to Reading Museum.

In October 1939 London Zoo received a large male stag beetle which came with the following note: 'The defendant was found lying on the pavement in Regent Street, outside the Café Royal, at 11.35 pm on the evening of the 4th inst. As he was unable to

A goliath beetle and an elephant beetle shown together for comparison of size.

stand, was causing an obstruction, and inclined to resist, I took him in charge. He did not appear to have any visible means of support and would give no account of himself. A strong tendency to alcoholism was shown by the fact that he refused a meal of drops of ten per cent cane sugar solution, but voraciously attacked the same solution when fortified with two or three drops of sherry. He had probably been overcome at a stag party.'

The rare great silver water-beetle (*Hydrophilus piceus*) of southern England is also of comparable size. Males of this species have been measured up to 48 mm *1·89 in* in length, and one adult pair weighed 5212 mg *0·184 oz* and 4950 mg *0·175 oz* respectively.

The longest insect in the world is the giant stick insect *Pharnacia serratipes* of Indonesia, females of which have been measured up to 330 mm *13 in* from the tip of the head to the end of the body. A female example of *Phobaeticus frustorferi* from Burma preserved in the US National Museum, Washington, DC measures 300 mm *11·81 in*, and a 270 mm *10·63 in Pharnacia maxima* in the British Museum has a total length of 510 mm *20·08 in*, with the legs fully extended (Judith Meadows, pers. comm.).

The longest members of the Coleoptera are the hercules beetles *Dynastes hercules* and *D. neptunus* of Central America and northern South America, males of which have been reliably measured up to 190 mm *7·48 in* and 180 mm *7·09 in* respectively. More than half the length, however, is taken up by the prothoracic horn. The two largest *D. neptunus* collected by Dr William Beebe (1947) in Avagua National Park, Venezuela measured 74 mm *2·91 in* and 76 mm *2·99 in* excluding the horn and weighed 15 g *0·53 oz* and 16·3 g *0·57 oz* respectively. The longhorn beetle *Batocera wallacei* of New Guinea has been measured up to 266 mm *10·47 in* in total length, but 190 mm *7·48 in* of this was antennae.

The smallest recorded insects are the parasitic wasps of the family *Mymaridae*. One species ironically named *Alaptus magnanimus* measures only 0·21 mm *0·0083 in*. The 'hairy-winged' dwarf beetles of the family *Ptilidae* (= *Trichopterygidae*) are also very tiny, and some species like *Nasonella fungi* of tropical America can easily crawl through the eye of a needle. Despite their minuteness these creatures retain all the external characteristics of insects, and the internal organ systems are contained in a space smaller than some of the Protozoa.

The most numerous of all insects are the springtails (Order Collembola) which are distributed throughout the world including the polar regions. It has been calculated that the top 9 in *229 mm* of soil in one acre of grassland contains 230 000 000 springtails or more than 5000 per square foot *50 000 per m²*.

The majority of insects live less than a year, but there are a number of exceptions. One of them is the periodic cicada (*Magicicada septemdecim*) of North America. Northern broods of this species live underground in a larval state for 17 years before digging to the surface and living as adults for a few weeks. The southern broods have a shorter life cycle of 13 years.

Some beetles are also long-lived. In 1846 Sir John Richardson showed some members of the British Association a specimen of the burying or sexton beetle (*Necrophorus germanicus*) which had been found embedded in concrete and must have been at least 16 years old. The insect was still alive when it was brought to Sir John and lived for another 6 weeks (Timbs, 1868). A cellar beetle (*Blaps gigas*) kept by Labitte (1916) lived for 14 years 233 days.

The longest-lived insects are the metallic wood borers (*Buprestidae*), and there are a number of well-authenticated records of adult beetles emerging from poorly-seasoned wood many years after it had been used in building or furniture. In 1889 a *Buprestis splendens* crawled out of the step of a staircase in the library of the University of Copenhagen, Denmark. The stairs, made from foreign pine, were laid in 1860, which meant the insect was at least 29 years old. Another specimen lived in the wood of a pencil-box for 30 years. *B. aurulenta* also has a very long larval life. In 1964 one of these beetles emerged from a doorpost of a house in Ipswich, Suffolk which had been built in 1934–35, and two years later another individual was found on the step of a staircase in a house at Thorpe Bay, Essex after living in the Canadian pine for more than 30 years. Even longer periods of 37 and 42 years have been reliably reported for these living jewels, and Packard (cited by Burr, 1939), mentions a wood borer which apparently lived for 45 years.

Certain species of ant (*Formicidae*) also have relatively long life-spans. Sir John Lubbock (1892) says he kept a female small black ant (*Formica fusa*) from December 1874 until August 1888 when it was at least 15 years old and a queen Westwood's ant (*Stenamma westwoodi*) held captive by Donisthorpe (1936) for 15 years was believed to have been about 18 years old at the time of her death on 2 October 1935. A longevity of 18 years has also been reported for a queen ant of the species *Myrmecina graminicola* kept in a laboratory, but she was already adult when collected, so her total lifespan must have been in excess of this figure (Joyce Pope, pers. comm.).

Although queen termites (*Isoptera*) have been credited with laying eggs for 50 years and life-spans twice as long (Klots and Klots, 1961), recent studies indicate that these insects do not usually survive more than 15 years.

Most butterflies live between two and eight months, depending on the time of year they were hatched, but some large migratory species like the monarch butterfly may live for 12 months or slightly longer.

In 1926 Father Cambouet, a missionary in Madagascar and a noted entomologist, reported to the Academy of Sciences in Paris that decapitated butterflies live longer than those which are left intact. He said he had found that when certain caterpillars were decapitated in such a way as to cause the minimum loss of blood, they could continue the natural course of their development and, after passing through the chrysalis stage, emerge as perfectly healthy but headless butterflies. Scientists who have studied this phenomenon since have come to the conclusion that headless butterflies are longer lived because they lead a much less active life. A perfect butterfly quickly spends its strength in activity, whereas its headless companions, leading much more placid lives, wear out their vital forces at a slower rate and thus attain a comparatively ripe old age.

The shortest lived of all insects is probably the common house-fly (*Musca domestica*). In one study of over 8500 specimens males had an average life-span of 17 days and females 29 days (Rockstein, 1959). Some may-flies (*Ephemeroidea*) survive only a few hours in the adult stage, but they spend 2 to 3 years as larvae.

The loudest of all insects are the cicadas (*Cicadidae*) which have a world-wide distribution. The strident songs of the males – most females are mute – can be detected more than a quarter of a mile away, and the sound made by the vibrating tymbal organs at the base of the abdomen has been likened to a knife-grinder, a locomotive letting off steam and even fat spitting in a hot frying-pan depending on the species.

According to scientists at Princeton University, New Jersey, USA the noise produced by thousands of cicadas under a single tree registered between 80 and 100 db at a distance of 60 ft *18·3 m* (*cf* 70–90 db for a pneumatic drill). The only thing in nature that will stop this deafening racket is the Cicada-killer (*Sphecius speciosus*). When one of these hunting wasps approaches an infested tree the sound stops immediately and there is an uncanny silence.

The only British species is the very rare mountain cicada (*Cicadetta montana*), which is confined to the New Forest area in Hampshire.

The highest gravity force encountered in nature is the 400g endured by the click beetle *Athous haemorrhoidalis* when jack-knifing into the air to escape predators. Unlike the flea (see page 178), however, this British species takes off from a prone position and *without using its legs*. Dr Glyn Evans (1972), who has done some research on this 12 mm *0·47 in* long insect at Manchester University, found it can catapult itself into the air to a height of at least 300 mm *11·81 in* when threatened by utilising a trigger mechanism similar to the back-breaker type of mousetrap. He also discovered that (1) the parts of the beetle farthest from the central pivot travel at an even greater acceleration, the brain being subjected to a peak deceleration at the end of the movement of 2000g; and (2) that while leaping into the air it both somersaults and rotates on its axis. He concluded: 'Yet the beetle is prepared to click again and again, so one assumes that it doesn't even get a bad headache. Presumably the secret lies in the very small mass and inertia involved, and the fact that it probably isn't a very intelligent animal to start with.'

The most dangerous insects in the world are the malarial mosquitoes of the genus *Plasmodium* which, if we exclude wars and accidents, have probably been responsible directly or indirectly for 50 per cent of all human deaths since the Stone Age. Even today these tiny horrors still kill at least 1 million people a year in Africa and SE Asia, and an estimated 600 million are constantly exposed to the disease. Four species of malarial mosquito are found in Britain, but they can only carry malaria if they come into contact with someone suffering from the disease. The North Kent marshes have long been breeding grounds for this creature, and when soldiers carrying the disease returned to the area from abroad after the First World War it was quickly spread by the mosquitoes.

At one stage half the population of the Isle of Grain was affected, and as recently as the 1940s malaria cases were still being noted. In 1974 workers building the new Grain power station at the edge of the marshes complained of being bitten by mosquitoes and a specialist firm was called in to deal with the menace. There are also a small number of cases of people dying in this country from mosquito dermatitis after being bitten on the face or neck. In each instance the person was highly allergic to the salivary secretion of the insect.

The most potentially dangerous insect in the world is the common house-fly. It can transmit thirty diseases and parasitic worms to man, including cholera, typhoid, dysentery, bubonic plague, leprosy, cerebro-spinal meningitis, diphtheria, scarlet fever, smallpox and infantile paralysis via 'vomit drop' – ingested food which has been allowed to flow back to the outer end of the proboscis.

If we exclude disease carriers, then the most dangerous insects are bees (Apidae) and wasps (Vespidae) in that order. Between them they kill more people each year than the estimated 40 000 who die from snakebite. There are at least four or five fatalities in this country each year, and an estimated 60 000 Britons are allergic to stings to the point where they suffer from acute breathlessness, a rapid drop in blood pressure and possible death. A very effective vaccine for this dangerous and potentially fatal condition is now available on the National Health Service.

In September 1964 a young Rhodesian set up an unenviable world record when he was stung 2243 times by a swarm of wild bees (*Apis adonsonii*). The attack took place on a river bank, and the youth was forced to take refuge in the water where he remained for four hours with only his head showing. When he was eventually rescued his scalp, face, neck, trunk and arms were black with stings. More than 2000 were removed from his eyelids, lips, tongue and mouth alone. To the astonishment of everyone he made a full recovery. As it so happens, the sting of this African bee is no more potent than that of the ordinary honey-bee, but unlike their relative these winged killers attack in great numbers and with ferocious intensity. In one experiment a scientist juggled a leather ball outside a hive and saw it stung 92 times in 5 seconds, before he himself was chased for half a mile by the angry insects.

In 1956 Prof Warwick Kerr of the Ribeirao Preto School of Medicine near São Paulo, Brazil imported 170 queen bees from Tanzania in an experiment to improve honey production, but the following year 26 of the queens and their swarms escaped. They mated with local honey-bees and soon afterwards the new vicious hybrids (*Apis mellifera adonsonii*) began moving northwards at a rate of 200 miles *320 km* a year. Since then these 'assassinos voadores' (flying killers) have stung to death at least 150 people – Prof Kerr has had his life threatened several times by bereaved families – and the most recent attack was in Barquisimeto, Venezuela where one person was killed and 13 injured in March 1981. At their present

The desert locust, the world's most destructive insect.

rate of progress they should cross the southern borders of the USA in 1985, but by then it is hoped that their aggressive behaviour will have been considerably diluted by further hybridisation with millions of docile bees set down in their migratory path.

The most destructive insect in the world is the desert locust (*Schistocera gregaria*), the locust of the Bible, whose habitat is the dry and semi-arid regions of Africa, the Middle East, through to Pakistan and northern India. This short-horn grasshopper can eat its own weight in food a day, and during long migratory flights a large swarm will consume 20 000 tonnes of grain and vegetation a day and bring famine to whole communities. In Ethiopia one huge concentration destroyed sufficient cereals in six weeks to feed a million people for a year, and only American famine relief staved off total disaster.

The greatest swarm of desert locusts ever recorded was probably one covering an estimated 2000 miles² *5180 km²* seen by Fletcher in South Africa in 1784. He says this multitude was blown out to sea by a strong wind, and when the tide washed back their bodies they formed a bank 4 ft *1·2 m* high along the beach for 50 miles *80 km*. In 1889 another swarm containing an estimated 250 000 000 000 locusts weighing about 500 000 tonnes was observed crossing the Red Sea.

Because of the practical difficulties of measurement very little reliable information has been published on the flight speeds of insects, but their general small size gives them the false impression of being very much faster than they really are. One of the first men to carry out experiments in this field was Demoll (1918), the German entomologist. He released a number of different species in a room lit by a single window and timed them by stopwatch as they flew directly from the dark side of the room to the light.

It was found that the swiftest flier was a hawk-moth (*Sphingidae*) which travelled at a rate of 53·6 km/h *33·3 miles/h*. A horse-fly (*Tabanus bovinus*) and a dragonfly (*Agrion* sp.) were not far behind with a speed of 50 km/h *31·1 miles/h*. The other insects tested were much slower. A common house-fly (*Musca domestica*) achieved a velocity of 8·19 km/h *5·09 miles/h*, a honey-bee (*Apis mellifera*) 11·6 km/h *7·21 miles/h* and a bumble-bee (*Bombus lapidarius*) 17·85 km/h *11·09 miles/h*.

The most accurate lists of insect flying speeds published so far, however, are still those of Magnan (1934), the French entomologist, who obtained his measurements by two methods. In one series of experiments he tethered the insect to a thread wound round a small drum mounted on ball-bearings, the revolutions of which were recorded on a kymograph as the creature was in flight. In the other series he timed the insect with a chronometer (aided with cinephotography) as it flew between two markers set against a grid at a measured distance. Of the 32 species of insect tested the fastest was the dragonfly *Anax parthenope* which travelled at a rate of 28·57 km/h *17·75 miles/h*. A hornet (*Vespa crabro*) recorded a velocity of 21·42 km/h *13·31 miles/h*, and the fastest of the five species of fly tested was the horse-fly, which travelled at 14·28 km/h *8·87 miles/h*.

As can be seen from the above, these speeds are much lower than those given by Demoll, but Magnan did emphasise that his measurements were not *maximum* flight capabilities. In the final analysis he felt that certain insects could reach speeds of 10 m/s (= 36·00 km/h *22·37 miles/h*).

From these observations it would appear that hawk-moths, horse-flies and certain species of dragonfly are the fastest-moving insects, all of which can exceed an air speed of 20 miles/h *32 km/h* over short distances, but Malcolm Barcant (pers. comm.), a leading authority on the butterflies of the West Indies, believes there are a number of small-bodied tropical species which are probably even faster. He writes: 'The vast family of the Hesperiidae contains several species with flight speeds which, if recorded, would be found to be well in the 30–40 mph range. One or two of them could possibly threaten a humming-bird. In the family Nymphalidae the genus *Prepona* which spans South and Central America (tropics) in all its species could all sustain flights of well over 30 miles/h *48 km/h*, particularly if disturbed. There are many others.'

Dr R J Tillyard (1917), the Australian entomologist, says he once timed a large dragonfly of the species *Austrophlebia costalis* at 98 km/h *60·9 miles/h* along a stretch of stream 80–90 yd *73–82 m*, but this was ground speed. According to the calculations of

Hocking (1953) a dragonfly this size could not possibly fly faster than 36 miles/h *57·9 km/h* – even in short bursts – over a level course, and the absolute maximum air speed over a sustained distance would be about 24 miles/h *38·6 km/h*. He added, however: 'This does not necessarily mean that Tillyard's observation is not reliable: a following wind, downhill flight and the short distance (850 × body length) taken together could account for the difference in the figures. It is well known that muscle may develop power much greater than normal for very brief periods. It is worth noting that even the great fossil species *Meganeura monyi*, with its 29-inch wing-span, would, on a similar basis, only have been capable of 43 mph; indeed, it probably had to fly at close to this speed in order to remain airborne.'

In April 1926 Dr Charles Townsend, an American zoologist, startled the scientific world by announcing that the deer bot-fly *Cephenemyia pratti* was the fastest-moving living creature. Writing in the *Journal of the New York Entomological Society*, he said: 'On 12 000 foot summits in New Mexico I have seen pass me at an incredible velocity what were certainly the males of *Cephenemyia*. I could barely distinguish that some had passed – only a brownish blur in the air of about the right size for these flies and without a sense of form. As close as I can estimate, their speed must have approximated 400 yards per second.'

Astonishing as it may seem, a great number of people took this claim seriously (=818 miles/h *1317 km/h*!) despite the fact that no instruments were used to measure the speed and there was no supersonic bang as they went through the sound barrier, and the figure was widely quoted for a number of years. It was eventually demolished by Dr Irving Langmuir (1938), the Nobel Prize winner for chemistry in 1932, who carried out some calculations and experiments on a model of a deer bot-fly in his laboratory. He said the fly would have to develop the equivalent of 1·5 hp *1·1 kW* and consume one and a half times its own weight in food per second to acquire the energy that would be needed to reach a velocity of 800 miles/h *1288 km/h*, and even if this was possible the fly would still be crushed by the air pressure and incinerated by the friction. He also revealed that a whirling piece of solder the same size as the fly was 'barely-visible' at 26 miles/h *41·8 km/h*, 'a very faint line' at 43 miles/h *69 km/h* and 'wholly invisible' at 64 miles/h *103 km/h*. He deduced from these tests that 'a speed of 25 miles per hour is a reasonable one for the deer fly, while 800 miles is utterly impossible'.

Despite these very careful calculations, however, Langmuir's figure of 25 miles/h *40 km/h* is probably a bit on the low side. This is because he carried out his tests in *normal* air conditions and used a model of a 10 mm *0·39 in* deer bot-fly (*Chrysops*) instead of a 15 mm *0·59 in* *Cephenemyia* – there was some confusion over identity. But even if we make due allowances for these small differences, it is still doubtful whether this high-altitude fly ever exceeds 30–35 miles/h *48–56 km/h* in level flight, even in the rarified air of its normal habitat.

The frequency of wing-beat among insects varies enormously and is closely linked to body size.
The highest wing-beat frequency so far recorded for any insect under natural conditions is 1046 Hz (=62 760 a minute) by a tiny midge of the genus *Forcipomyia*. This measurement was based on an aural estimate by Dr Olavi Sotavalta (1947), the remarkable Finnish entomologist, whose sense of absolute pitch was accurate to within 2·5 per cent of a cycle. Later he told Lane (1955) that another specimen which had been truncated and exposed to a temperature of 37°C *98·6°F* produced a flight tone equivalent to a frequency of 2218 Hz (=133 080 a minute). The muscular contraction-expansion cycle in 0·000 45 or 1/2218th of a second further represents the fastest muscle movement ever recorded. Measurements calculated from pitch-of-sound experiments, however, have been questioned by some scientists who contend that such values are 50 per cent too high. The highest reading obtained by Magnan using high-speed cinematography and a tuning fork was 250 Hz (=15 000 a minute) for the honey-bee.
The lowest frequency of wing-beat reported for any insect is 5 Hz (=300 a minute) for a swallowtail butterfly (*Papilio machaon*). Most butterflies beat their wings at a rate of 460–636 a minute.

Insects are the toughest creatures in existence. Some flies live in hot springs, and certain larvae of the family Enhydridae have been found in waters with temperatures up to 60°C *140°F*. At the other end of the scale, many springtails are active at temperatures well below freezing point, and the lower limit for the snow flea *Isotoma saltans* is – 15°C *5°F*. The midge larva *Polypedilum* is even more incredible. It can survive for years in a desiccated state; when dried it can be kept in liquid nitrogen at –196°C *–321°F* for 3 days or survive 102°C *215·6°F* for one minute (Wigglesworth, 1964). Insects can also withstand high concentrations of carbon monoxide, while others can live in an environment completely devoid of oxygen. The burnet moth (*Zygaenidae*) can even survive for long periods in cyanide-charged killing bottles, while the extraordinary fly *Helaeomyis petrolei* spends most of its life in pools of crude petroleum! Probably the most hard-bitten insect of them all, however, is the little beetle *Niptus hololeucus*, which appears to be virtually indestructible. According to Burr no less than 1547 specimens were found living in a bottle of casein that had been stoppered for 12 years, and he says others have been known to survive in a tin of leaves of the powerful poison *Datura stramontium* for 15 years. They also flourish on cayenne pepper and sal ammoniac.

The largest ant in the world is the ponerine ant *Dinoponera gigantea* of Brazil, workers of which have been measured up to 33 mm *1·30 in* from the top of the mandibles to the end of the abdomen. Two other Brazilian species, *D. longipes* and *D. mutica*, reach 30 mm *1·18 in* (Kempf, 1971). Workers of the rare bulldog ant *Myrmecia brevinoda* (=*gigas*) of Queensland and northern NSW, Australia, have been measured up to 37 mm *1·46 in*, but this species has much longer mandibles than *Dinoponera* and loses out in terms of bulk. The queen ants of the genera *Dorylus* and *Anomma* of Africa are even larger after hypertrophy, and Step (1924) says the huge wingless queens of the species *Dorylus helvolus* of South Africa are sometimes nearly 2 in *51 mm* in length.

The largest ant found in Britain (27 species) is the wood ant (*Formica rufa*), males reaching 9 mm *0·35 in* and queens 11 mm *0·43 in*. The blood-red robber ant (*F. sanguinea*) and the meadow ant (*F. pratensis*) are approximately the same size, and a measurement of 11·5 mm *0·45 in* has been reported for a queen of the latter species (Donisthorpe, 1927).

The smallest ant in the world is the worker minor of *Oligomyrmex bruni* of Sri Lanka, which measures 0·8–0·9 mm *0·031–0·035 in* (I H Yarrow, pers. comm.).

The smallest ant found in Britain is *Solenopsis fugax*, workers measuring 1·5–3·0 mm *0·059–0·118 in*.

The most dangerous ant in the world is the bulldog ant *Myrmecia pyriformis* (=*forficata*) of the coastal regions of Australia and Tasmania which uses its sting and jaws simultaneously when attacking. In November 1936 a 50-year-old man died at Mount Macedona, Victoria after being stung by one of these aggressive ants. Another fatality occurred in September 1963 when a woman was stung on the foot by a bulldog ant in her surburban garden at Launceston, Tasmania and died 15 minutes later.

The fire-ants (*Solenopsis*) of South America and now the southern USA are also highly dangerous because they often act in unison when danger threatens. Once they are in position on the intruder's body they all sting simultaneously and if hundreds of them are involved the pain can be excruciating. The venom can also induce hypersensitivity and trigger shock. In 1974 an elderly man died in Silsbee, Texas several months after he had been repeatedly stung in the leg, and the very same year a woman in Gulfport, Mississippi died from gangrene after she was attacked by fire-ants in her backyard.

The harvester ants (*Pogonomyrmex*) of the southern USA have also been responsible for a small number of fatalities, and Wheeler (cited by Step, 1924) makes the following comments about the Texan harvester: 'The sting of these ants is remarkably severe, and the fiery numbing pain which it produces may last for hours. On several occasions when my hands and legs had been stung by several of these insects while I was excavating their nests, I grew faint and almost unable to stand. The pain appears to extend along the limbs for some distance and to settle in the lymphatics of the groin and axillae. If it be true, as has been reported, that the ancient Mexicans tortured or even killed their enemies by binding them to ant-nests, *Pogonomyrmex barbatus* was certainly the species employed in this atrocious practice.'

The army ants (*Eciton*) of South America and the driver ants (*Dorylinae*) of Africa also deserve a mention – but for an entirely different reason. When searching for food they move off in highly organised columns numbering anything up to 500 000 individuals and will devour any animal that is too slow to get out of the way (even anteaters reluctantly step aside when they see a horde of army ants on the march). As far as humans and other mammals are concerned, however, the fearsome reputation of these ants is not really justified because their marching speed is only 0·0135 mile/h *0·0220 km/h*, but a tethered horse, an injured man or a baby in a cot would be doomed. In December 1973 a column of army ants 1 mile *1·6 km* long and half a mile *800 m* wide reportedly marched on the town of Goianira, central Brazil, and devoured several people including the chief of police before being driven back into the jungle by 60 militiamen armed with flame-throwers, but this story is as reliable as the earlier one about the 120 ft *36·6 m* long anaconda machine-gunned to death in the same country.

The desert ant *Cataglyphis bicolor* has the most sophisticated colour system of any insect, and its ability to discriminate between colours surpasses that of the human in certain parts of the spectrum.

The master builders of the insect world are termites which, although often referred to as 'white ants', are not related to true ants. Some of the mounds of these industrious workers found in northern Australia measure up to 20 ft *6·1 m* in height and nearly 100 ft *31 m* in diameter at the base, and Howse (1970) has calculated that if termites were man-sized their largest citadels would be four times as high as the Empire State Building and measure 5 miles *8 km* in diameter. The African termite *Macrotermes bellicosus* builds even taller mounds (heights up to 42 ft *12·8 m* have been reported in the Congo), but the bases are usually less than 10 ft *3·0 m* in diameter. Eugene N Marais (1971) once asked an engineer friend of his to calculate the weight of earth making up one enormous termitary and found it consisted of 11 750 tonnes of sand which had been piled up grain by grain over a period of centuries. Some desert termites also drive bore holes down to water, and one shaft was traced to a depth of 40 m *131 ft*.

Apart from their architectural ability, termites are best known as destroyers of wood which they digest with the aid of intestinal protozoa, but that's not all! Their tiny bodies can also distil an acid which eats through lead, manufacture a liquid capable of dissolving glass, and spread a substance on metal which rusts it and enables the insects to bore through. In 1949 termites quickly and quietly penetrated the walls of the Vatican in Rome and made their way to the library where they damaged valuable books and manuscripts. Five years later another hungry lot ate through the concrete floor of the almost completed Legislative Council Chamber at Darwin, Northern Territory, Australia and then attacked the doors and other woodwork. There is also a record of a man coming home one night and finding four of his framed pictures missing. All that was left were the glass coverings which the termites had cemented to the walls.

The largest termite in the world is *Macrotermes bellicosus* of Africa, queens of which have been measured up to 140 mm *5·51 in* in length and 35 mm *1·38 in* across the abdomen after hypertrophy. Specimens this size can produce up to 30 000 eggs a day!

The smallest known termite is *Afrosubulitermes* sp., which measures about 3·5 mm *0·14 in*.

The largest dragonfly in the world is *Megaloprepus caeruleata* of Central and South America. The largest specimen in the British Museum has a body length of 120 mm *4·72 in* and measures 191 mm *7·52 in* across the wings (Paul Whalley, pers. comm.). *Tetracanthagyna plagiata* of NE Borneo is also of comparable size, but this species is much bulkier than the fragile *M. caeruleata*. One individual in the same collection has a wing expanse of 176 mm *6·93 in* (body length 118 mm *4·65 in*) (Stephen Brooks, pers. comm.).

Dragonflies this size have the largest eyes and the most efficient vision of any insects. Each optic contains up to 28 000 facets, compared to only 6–9 facets for the virtually blind underground worker ants of the genus *Solenopsis*.

The largest dragonfly found in Britain is the emperor dragonfly (*Anax imperator*) of SE England which has been measured up to 106 mm *4·17 in* across the wings. In July 1974 Stephen Coates (pers. comm.) found a golden-ringed dragonfly (*Cordulegaster boltoni*) floating in the sea at Amroth, South Wales which measured 86 mm *3·39 in* in body length and spanned 105 mm *4·13 in*, but this specimen was softened by water immersion and probably gave an artificially high reading.

A queen termite after hypertrophy.

The smallest dragonfly in the world is *Agriocnemis naia* of Burma. A specimen in the British Museum has a wing expanse of 17·6 mm *0·69 in* and a body length of 18 mm *0·71 in* (P Ward, pers. comm.).

The smallest dragonfly found in Britain is *Lestes dryas* which has a body length of 20–25 mm *0·79–0·98 in*.

The largest known fly is *Mydas heros*, which is found in tropical South America. It has a body length of up to 60 mm *2·36 in* and measures about 100 mm *3·94 in* across the wings. This aerial ogre is so formidable it will attack even well-armed bees and wasps, diving on their backs and paralysing them with a well-placed bite in the soft region of the neck. Some of the craneflies (*Tipulidae*) of the tropics have a wing expanse of nearly 100 mm *3·94 in* and a length with legs extended of about 200 mm *7·87 in*, but these insects have very little bulk. A specimen of *Holorusia brobdignagius* in the British Museum measures 228 mm *8·98 in* from the tips of the front legs to the tips of the hind legs (B H Cogan, pers. comm.).

One zoologist has calculated that if all the eggs laid by a common house-fly hatched and the young ones survived and carried on through six generations the progeny of a single pair, if pressed together in a solid mass, would occupy 250 000 cubic feet *23 225 m³* of space, allowing 200 000 flies to each cubic foot *7·06 million per m³*.

The largest known flea is *Hystrichopsylla schefferi*, which was described from a single specimen taken from the nest of a Mountain beaver (*Aplodontia rufa*) at Puyallup, Washington, USA (Scheffer, 1969).

The largest British flea is the mole flea (*Hystrichopsylla talpae*) which measures 5–6 mm *0·20–0·24 in* (Rothschild and Clay, 1952). This flea is also found on other animals, and there is a record of a 6 mm *0·24 in* specimen being collected from a pigmy shrew (*Sorex minutus*)! In human terms, this would be equivalent to a man carrying an adult rat around with him (Lehane, 1969).

The most dangerous flea in the world is the widely-distributed oriental rat flea (*Xenopsylla cheop-*

sis), carrier of the dreaded bubonic plague bacterium *Pasteurella pestis*. In the fourteenth century this blood-sucking parasite caused the deaths of 25 million people in Europe or approximately one-quarter of the total population, and in the great Indian plague of 1896–1917 over 10 million people died. Since then the incidence of human plague cases has markedly decreased through the use of antibiotics.

Apart from their danger as carriers of disease, fleas are best known for their jumping abilities. In 1910 M B Mitzmain of the US Public Health Service carried out some tests on these insects and found that the jumper par excellence was the common flea (*Pulex irritans*). One energetic performer allowed to leap at will executed a high jump of at least 196 mm *7·72 in* and a long jump of 330 mm *12·99 in*, but these measurements were exceptional. According to Rothschild *et al*, (1973), unfed fleas can jump nonstop for long periods. The oriental rat flea has been known to jump 600 times an hour for up to 72 hours without a break, and on another occasion ten fleas stimulated by each other's presence executed 10000 jumps an hour, or one jump every 3·5 seconds. In jumping 130 times its own height a flea subjects itself to a force of 200g, the energy coming from the elasticity of resilin protein situated above the jumping legs.

The largest bee in the world is the leaf-cutter bee *Megachile pluto*, which is found only on Batjan, the largest island in the Moluccas, Malay Archipelago. It measures up to 38 mm *1·50 in* in length (Curran, 1945). Some of the carpenter bees (*Xylocopidae*) also exceed 25 mm *0·98 in*, and when the large and powerful males of this family are in an amorous mood they will try to seduce anything that flies – including jet airliners! According to Dr Edward Barrows of Georgetown University, Washington, DC, who spent two years studying the sexual habits of these bees, the males will intercept birds and even dandelion puff-balls in the mistaken belief that they are female bees, and some of these winged Casanovas have even been seen chasing jet airliners coming in to land at Washington International Airport!

The largest bee found in Britain is the large garden humble-bee (*Bombus ruderatus*), workers of which measure about 23·5 mm *0·93 in* in length.

The smallest bee is *Trigona duckei*, a dwarf stingless variety found in Brazil, which measures 2–5 mm *0·08–0·20 in*.

The smallest bee found in Britain is the least mining bee (*Halictus minutissimus*), which does not exceed 5 mm *0·20 in*.

The largest wasps in the world are the 'tarantula hawks' of the genus *Pepsis* of tropical South America, and Lucas (1894) gives the following measurements:

P. frivaldzskyi – body length 40–45 mm *1·57–1·77 in*; wing-span 74–82 mm *2·91–3·23 in*. *P. heros* – body length 40–54 mm *1·57–2·13 in*; wing-span 80–102 mm *3·15–4·02 in*. *P. hyperion* – body length 54–60 mm *2·13–2·36 in*; wing-span 86–102 mm *3·39–4·02 in*. *P. pulszkyi* – body length 56–67 mm *2·20–2·64 in*; wing-span 102–106 mm *4·02–4·17 in*. Some of these figures, however, are a bit on the low side, particularly those for *P. frivaldzskyi*, because the British Museum has a specimen which has a wing expanse of 114 mm *4·49 in* (I Yarrow, pers. comm.). *P. atrata* is another large species, and a body length of 63 mm *2·48 in* (excluding the 13 mm *0·51 in* stinger) and a wing span of 101 mm *3·98 in* have been recorded for a female (Zahl, 1959). Obviously a lot of work is needed in *Pepsis* systematics before the identity of the largest wasp can be definitely established.

These wasps (females) hunt the largest spiders, and each prefers a different species. One *Pepsis* even attacks and kills the enormous *Theraphosa blondi*, and one of these metallic-blue predators and its female victim are preserved in the British Museum.

The largest social wasp is *Vespa mandarina* of Japan which has a body length of 35 mm *1·38 in*.

The largest wasp found in Britain is the wood-boring greater horntail (*Urocerus gigas*), females of which have been measured up to 40 mm *1·57 in*. If, however, *U. gigas* is considered to be a saw-fly, then the largest British wasp is the hornet, queens of which measure 30 mm *1·19 in*.

The smallest known wasps are the Mymaridae (see page 172).

The largest wasps' nest on record was one found on a farm at Waimaukau, New Zealand in April 1963 which had grown so heavy that it had broken off and split into two pieces. It originally measured 12 ft *3·7 m* in length and 5 ft 9 in *1·75 m* in diameter. In 1971 a wasps' nest with a circumference of 6 ft *1·8 m* was discovered between two roof beams in a hospital at Bovey Tracey, South Devon.

The largest known butterfly is the rare Queen Alexandra birdwing (*Ornithoptera alexandrae*), which is restricted to the lowland forests of Papua New Guinea. Females (the more colourful males are smaller) average 210 mm *8·27 in* across the wings, but D'Abrera (1975) says specimens have been collected which exceeded 280 mm *11·02 in*. For the purpose of this book, the distance from the wing-apex to the centre of the thorax represents *half* the total span in butterflies and moths. In some older references the wing expanse is obtained by measuring along a straight line from apex to apex in a set specimen (i.e. the lower angle of each forewing at right angles to the body), but the result is less impressive. One *O. alexandrae* measured by the first method recorded a span of 264 mm *10·39 in*, but only

226 mm *8·90 in* by the second (Haugum and Lowe, 1978–9). This protected birdwing is also the heaviest known butterfly, females weighing up to 12 g *0·42 oz*. The Queen Victoria birdwing (*O. victoriae*) of the Solomon Islands, SW Pacific is somewhat smaller, females averaging 200 mm *7·87 in*, but measurements up to 254 mm *10 in* have been reliably reported. Birdwings are difficult to catch because they frequent the canopy of foliage at the tops of high trees, and in the past collectors had to resort to 'shooting' them with sporting guns loaded with dust or water. When they do fly lower, however, they are an easy target because their flight is slow and direct, and native children often tie lengths of fibre to captured specimens and fly them like small kites.

The largest butterfly found in Britain is the monarch or milkweed butterfly (*Danaus plexippus*), a rare vagrant which breeds in the southern USA and Mexico. Adult females average 38 mm *1·50 in* in length and have a wing expanse of 89 mm *3·50 in*. On 2 October 1937 a specimen with a wing-span of 109 mm *4·29 in* was caught in a garden at Lydney, Gloucestershire and later presented to Gloucester Museum (A Darknell, pers. comm.). The first monarch butterfly ever recorded in Britain was caught at Neath, South Wales on 6 September 1876 by Sir John Llewelyn. Since then more than 200 examples have been observed or captured.

Britain's largest native butterfly is the swallowtail (*Papilio machaon britannicus*), which is now confined to the Norfolk Broads and Wicken Fen, Cambridgeshire where it has been reintroduced. Females have been measured up to 100 mm *3·94 in* across the wings and weigh 500–600 mg *0·018–0·021 oz*.

The world's smallest known butterfly is the Dwarf blue *Brephidium barberae* of South Africa. It has a wing-span of 14 mm *0·55 in* and weighs less than 10 mg *0·000 35 oz*. The pygmy blue *Brephidium exilis* of the southern USA to Guatemala has a wing-span of 14–20 mm *0·55–0·79 in*.

The smallest butterfly found in Britain is the small blue (*Cupido minimus*) of southern England, which has a wing-span of 19–25 mm *0·75–0·98 in*.

Some butterflies have extraordinary powers of flight and migrate great distances. The champion is the painted lady (*Cynthia cardui*). In the early spring hundreds of thousands of these seemingly fragile insects leave their homes in North Africa and Asia Minor to fly across the Mediterranean and Europe to southern England where they arrive in late May or early June after a journey of 2000–3000 miles *3200–4800 km*. Some take a further trip to Scotland, and individual stragglers have even been seen in the extreme north of Iceland within a few degrees of the Arctic Circle, which means they must have flown nearly 4000 miles *6400 km*!

Monarch butterflies also cover enormous distances during migration. The northern population (*Danaus p. plexippus*) leaves the Canadian border in September and travels up to 1850 miles *3000 km* to reach its wintering grounds on the Californian and Florida coasts and along the Gulf of Mexico. The following March their progeny, who have inherited the ancestral memory, return along the same route. This species is also found in the Hawaiian Islands 2000 miles *3200 km* from the North American continent, where it was unknown until milkweed (*Asclepiadaceae*), its staple food, was first grown in 1845 and has since established itself in New Zealand and Australia. The occasional flights made by vagrants across the Atlantic are not nearly so arduous because they are assisted by strong westerly winds, and in calm conditions they can settle on the sea and take off again without difficulty. Many of the monarchs recorded in Britain, however, may have flown the shorter distance from the Canary Islands where they are also found.

Like migrating locusts, butterflies often travel in huge swarms. One mass migratory flight of painted ladies observed moving on a 40-mile *64 km* wide front in California and estimated to contain at least 3000 million individuals, reportedly took 3 days to pass a given point, and Williams (1958) says he witnessed a single flight of the pale form butterfly (*Catopsilia florella*) in East Africa in 1928–29 which continued steadily for more than *3 months*!

The majority of butterflies fly 5–8 ft *1·52–2·43 m* above the ground during migration, but some species travel at great heights. According to Williams dead large cabbage whites (*Pieris brassicae*) have been found in the Alps above the 12 000 ft *3658 m* mark, and butterflies of the genera *Cosmosalyrus*, *Lymanopoda* and *Pedialiodes* have been seen crossing the Andes at heights up to 4700 m *15 419 ft* (Klots and Klots, 1961).

The greatest height reliably reported for migrating butterflies is 19 000 ft *5791 m* for 'a few small tortoiseshells' seen flying over the Zemu Glacier (Sikkim) in the eastern Himalayas. This altitude is probably also reached by the Queen of Spain fritillary (*Argynnis lathonia*) which has been sighted at nearly 6000 m *19 685 ft* in the Himalayas.

Although the monarch butterfly and other members of the Danaidae are distasteful and poisonous to birds and other insectivorous animals if ingested, their effect on man is unknown because entomologists – not unnaturally – are reluctant to sample such lepidopteral delights. A meal of a large *Danaus plexippus*, however, would probably be fatal for somebody with a serious heart condition. These insects obtain their poisons from the toxic plants they eat, which are then stored or synthesised in the body after extraction. Some caterpillars of the *Nymphalidae* are also nasty inasmuch as they have urticating hairs which can cause severe irritation or dermatitis.

The most aggressive butterfly is the very powerful flier *Charaxes candiope* of Uganda which dive-bombs people intruding on its territory.

What is reported to be the only known example of a 'Siamese twin' butterfly with the abdomens fused together is currently on display in the Jumalon Museum in Cebu City, Cebu in the Philippines, but the authenticity of this claim has been questioned.

'The thought of a double caterpillar hatching from the egg, crawling and eating together, successfully skin-changing and pupating to survive to the adult stage is beyond credibility', comments Robert C Goodden (pers. comm.), a lepidopterist of international renown, 'and I would dearly like to be able to examine the butterfly to see whether the thoracic exoskeleton is in fact all one piece or whether there appears to be a join.'

The butterfly, a specimen of *Parthenos salentia*, was collected at Consolacion in 1954.

The most valuable of all butterflies and the most sought after by collectors is the very rare birdwing *Ornithoptera (=Troides) allottei* of Bougainville, the largest island in the Solomon group, W Pacific which is known from less than a dozen specimens. A male from the collection of G Rousseau Decelle, the French lepidopterist, was sold for £750 at an auction in Paris on 24 October 1966 (Howarth, 1967). It should be noted here that the specific ranking of this magnificent butterfly has been questioned by some experts who claim it is a natural hybrid of the blue birdwing (*O. urvillianus*) and the Queen Victoria birdwing (*O. victoriae*), but although these two species sometimes pair in nature fertilisation rarely occurs, and Haugum and Lowe say 'final proof of hybrid origin cannot be fully accepted until *allottei* is actually bred in captivity.' In recent years lepidopterists on the island have discovered a way to produce these prized birdwings by artificial hybridisation, and knowledge of this new technique has no doubt proved to be highly remunerative!

In November 1955 a collector paid DM 1500 (then about £125) at the annual Insect Trading Day in Frankfurt, Germany for the only known example in Europe of the Kaiser-I-Hind butterfly (*Teinopalpus imperialis*), a species found in the mountains of N India and SE China. Abnormally coloured butterflies also fetch high prices. In 1921 Lord Rothschild paid £75 for a black swallowtail (*Papilio machaon britannicus*) caught by a fisherman on the Norfolk Broads. At a London auction in April 1941 the sum of £49 was paid for an entirely white marbled white (*Melanargia galathea*), and an all-black specimen was sold for £41. In 1958 a black large cabbage white (*Pieris brassicae*) was sold in London for £44, and in 1962 the British Museum paid £50 for a chalk hill blue (*Lysandra coridon*) which was pure white. Some high prices have also been paid for butterflies in private deals between collectors, but no details are available.

Britain's rarest butterfly – about a quarter of the 59 species are under threat – is the chequered skipper (*Carterocephalus palaemon*), which is now confined to one site near Fort William, Inverness-shire, Scotland. Other species on the danger list include the large tortoiseshell (*Nymphalis polychloris*) of Essex and the Kent/Sussex border (20 sites); the black hairstreak (*Strymon pruni*) of Huntingdonshire and adjacent counties; the heath fritillary (*Melitaea athalia*) of Kent and the West Country (9 sites) and the silver-spotted skipper (*Hesperia comma*) of southern England (40 sites). The last large copper (*Lycaena dispar*) was captured at Bottisham, Cambridgeshire in July 1851, but in 1927 the very similar Dutch race *Lycaena d. batavus* was introduced to Woodwalton Fen, Huntingdonshire where it is artificially maintained.

The superb large blue (*Maculinea arion*) of the West Country was officially declared extinct in 1979 despite valiant efforts to save it. Thirty years ago this butterfly was found on at least 30 sites in the Cotswolds, Somerset, Devon and Cornwall but during the next decade the majority of them disappeared because of the intensification of agriculture and the loss of rabbits which kept the turf down, and by 1965 only four sites remained. In 1979 just 22 adults emerged from the last known colony, but they failed to mate and only a few sterile eggs were laid by virgin females. One of the main problems with this species is its strange eating habits. For the first 3 weeks or so of its life it feeds entirely on wild thyme which it needs through its first two skin changes. At the end of this time it falls to the ground where hungry red ants (*Myrmica sabuleti*) milk it of the honeydew which it secretes from two glands near the tail. Once it is covered in ants' scent the caterpillar blows itself up so that it smells and even feels like an ant grub and is then carried back to the underground nest, where the ants allow the imposter to feed on their ant larvae in exchange for a regular supply of the sugary fluid. It spends the winter hibernating in their subterranean chamber. In the spring it re-awakens, starts feeding again and then turns into a chrysalis before crawling to the surface as a butterfly about four months later.

If the Nature Conservancy Council and the Large Blue Committee had realised earlier that the red ant will only flourish on well-grazed sites this butterfly would probably still be with us today, but unfortunately the species died out before the right con-

The largest death's-head hawkmoth ever recorded in Britain. This specimen had a wingspan of 5¾ in 146 mm.

servation measures could be taken.

Since its demise this butterfly has reportedly been seen in various parts of Britain, but most of these sightings were male examples of the widely-distributed common blue (*Polyommatus icarus*).

'There is still a faint hope that some colony exists', writes Dr Jeremy Thomas (1980), 'but this is un-likely in the light of the many surveys that have been made and the rarity of suitable habitat occurring, by chance, as a result of modern farming practices . . . If no British colony is discovered in the next few years an introduction using continental stock may be considered.'

The largest moth in the world is the bulky hercules moth (*Coscinoscera hercules*) of tropical Australia and

New Guinea. In 1977 Carl Nilson of Napier, New Zealand caught a female at Lae, Papua New Guinea which had a wingspread of 280 mm *11·02 in* and a wing area of more than 100 in² *645 cm²*. It took him two hours to kill this specimen with a household fly spray! Another outsized female found near the post office at the coastal town of Innisfail, Queensland, Australia reportedly measured 355 mm *13·98 in* across the wings (Lord, 1948), but the Australian Museum in Sydney have no knowledge of this giant. The largest examples in their collection measure 228–254 mm *9–10 in* (C N Smithers, pers. comm.).

Another candidate for the title is the great owlet moth (*Thysania agrippina*), which ranges from the southern USA to southern Brazil. This moth is the largest member of the *Lepidoptera* in terms of wing expanse, but it lacks the bulk of *C. hercules* and the wings are much narrower. The largest specimen in the British Museum – collected in Chiriqui province, Panama – has a wing-span of 304 mm *11·97 in* (A Nye, pers. comm.), and another female preserved in the Dorman Museum, Middlesbrough measures 281 mm *11·06 in* (Cliff Thornton, pers. comm.). Chevalier Charles Oberthur, the French millionaire collector, once purchased a *T. agrippina* which measured an astonishing 360 mm *14·17 in* across the wings, but the present whereabouts of this monster is not known. The Oberthur Collection of 1 140 000 butterflies and moths was sold in 1927 and 70 per cent of the specimens were acquired by the British Museum, but the superlative moth was not among them.

Some of the giant atlas moths (*Attacus*) are also of comparable size. The largest member of this genus is probably *Attacus crameri caesar* (=*Attacus atlas caesar*) of the Philippines, females of which have been reliably measured up to 280 mm *11·02 in*, but *Attacus a. aurantiaca* from the Kai Islands in the Moluccas, Malay Archipelago would also be in strong contention (David Moon, pers. comm.). *Attacus atlas* of SE Asia has been credited with unconfirmed measurements up to 300 mm *11·81 in*, but an exceptionally large female in the Dorman Museum has a wing expanse of 264 mm *10·39 in*. Edward's atlas moth (*A. edwardsi*) of northern India is somewhat smaller (up to 240 mm *9·45 in*), but the females of this species have very fat abdomens and may bulk out heavier than their larger relatives.

The world's heaviest lepidopteran is the giant carpenter moth *Xyleutes boisduvali* of Australia which has an abdomen as large as a small banana. No weights have been published for this giant wood-boring moth, but adult females of the maximum size must scale at least 20 g *0·705 oz*. The largest specimen in the British Museum measures 250 mm *9·84 in* across the wings (Allan Watson, pers. comm.).

The largest moth found in Britain is the very rare death's head hawk-moth (*Acherontia atropos*), which breeds in Africa and occasionally reaches these shores during migratory flights in the late summer. One specimen with a wing-span of 118 mm *4·65 in* weighed 2500 mg *0·088 oz*. In June 1930 an outsized female with a wing expanse of 146 mm *5·75 in* was found dead in a garden in South Devon (Stuart Wilton, pers. comm.). Since 1978 Bill and Margaret Beer, the first people to successfully breed this moth in Britain, have produced female specimens measuring up to 150 mm *5·91 in*, at their home in Marlow Bottom, Buckinghamshire.

The largest native moth is the Privet hawk-moth (*Sphinx ligustri*). Adult females of this species have been measured up to 110 mm *4·33 in* and reach a weight of 2400 mg *0·085 oz*.

The smallest micro-moths are found in the family *Nepticulidae*, none of which exceed 6 mm *0·24 in*. The tiniest member is *Stigmella ridiculosa* of the Canary Islands which measures 2 mm *0·08 in*. The British species *Johanssonia acetosae* and *Nepticula microtheriella* measure 3 mm *0·12 in* and 3–4 mm *0·12–0·16 in* respectively (A M Emmett, pers. comm.).

The most phenomenal eating machine in nature is the larva of the Polyphemus moth (*Antheraea polyphemus*) of North America. In the first 48 hours of its life this ultimate in gluttons consumes an amount equal to 86 000 times its own birthweight!

The most acute sense of smell on record is that of the male Indian moon moth (*Actias selene*) which can trace, through its olfactory receptors, the love scent released by the female to its source from an almost unbelievable distance of 11 km *6·8 miles* (Chapman, 1971). This sex attractant or pheromone has been identified as one of the higher alcohols ($C_{16}H_{29}OH$).

Britain's rarest moth is the protected Essex emerald (*Euchloris smaragdaria*) which was thought to be to be extinct until 20 larvae were discovered in 1978.

Although moths are not generally considered dangerous to man, the caterpillars of several genera have sting hairs or spines associated with venom-secreting glands which produce varying degrees of irritation and swelling on contact with skin. Some of the most severe envenomations have been attributed to larvae of the flannel moth (*Megalopyge*) of the southern USA and Latin America, and especially the puss caterpillar (*M. opercularis*). Children 'stung' by larvae of this moth often develop a high fever and nervous symptoms (Riley and Johannsen, 1932), and the venom secreted by a closely related species, *M. lanata*, is said to be *potentially lethal*, although no human fatalities have been reported. Cases of caterpillar dermatitis have also been described from other parts of the world. The stinging larva of the moth caterpillar *Lonomia achelous* of tropical S America can cause internal bleeding in man, and at least one fatality has been reported.

There are also a small number of blood-sucking moths which have evolved from fruit-piercing *Noctuids*. The most unsavoury species is *Calpe* (=*Calyptra*) *eustrigata* of Malaysia which has been studied by Hans Banziger (1968), a Swiss entomologist. This large moth uses its strong barbed proboscis to extract blood from water-buffalo, deer and tapir, and he says its nasty habit of regurgitating some of the blood it has drunk makes it a potential disease carrier. In the laboratory this 'vampire' has been induced to feed on man – 'it felt like being stabbed with a hot needle' – but so far this performance has not been witnessed under natural conditions.

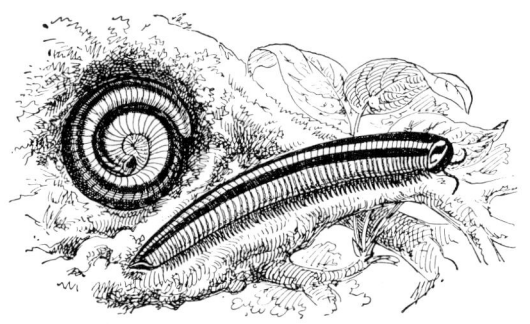

Centipedes & Millipedes

(classes Chilopoda and Diplopoda)

A true centipede is basically a carnivorous land-dwelling invertebrate (a few are marine) which breathes by means of tracheae or air tubes distributed throughout the body. It has a distinct head bearing a single pair of antennae and a mandible, and the appendages of the first body segment are modified into poison fangs called maxillipeds. The elongated trunk is composed of a number of similar segments, each one except the last two bearing a single pair of jointed legs. During growth it frequently sheds its exoskeleton. Young are hatched from eggs after leaving the female. The earliest known centipede, *Kampecaris*, lived about 250 million years ago, and today there are about 2800 living species which are divided into four orders. These are: the Scolopendrida; the Geophilida; the Lithobiida (including Craterostigmus) and the Scutigerida.

The millipede is a herbivorous, land-dwelling invertebrate which also breathes by means of tracheae. It has a distinct head bearing a single pair of antennae like the centipede, but there are two pairs of legs to each segment of the trunk except the first four, which bear one pair. It also differs from the centipede in having two rows of stink glands down each side of the body which secrete an evil-smelling substance capable of repelling insect enemies. The young, however, are oviparous. The earliest known millipede, *Archidesmus*, lived about 395 million years ago, and today there are about 8000 living species which are divided into thirteen orders. These are: Polyxenida; Glomeridesmida; Glomerida; Spirobolida; Stemmiulida; Polyzoniida; Siphonophorida; Julida; Spirostreptida; Callipodida; Platydesmida; Chordeumida and Polydesmida.

The longest known species of centipede is the 46-legged giant scolopendrid *Scolopendra gigantea* of the rain forests of Central and South America, adults measuring 250–265 mm *9·84–10·43 in* when fully extended and 25 mm *1 in* in diameter (Bucherl, 1971). Measurements of 12 in *305 mm* and even 15 in *381 mm* have been reported for individuals collected in Guyana, and Alexander von Humboldt says some of the centipedes he encountered in Venezuela were 18 in *457 mm* long, but these figures need confirmation. Much less reliable is the statement made by the Spaniard Ulloa, Christopher Columbus's gold assayer, that he saw centipedes on the north coast of South America which were 36 in *914 mm* long and 6 in *152 mm* in diameter (*sic*).

The widely-distributed *Scolopendra morsitans* usually measures 80–120 mm *3·15–4·72 in* when fully extended, but some giant forms are found in India and Malaysia. On one occasion H S Wood, the English naturalist, saw a 10 in *254 mm* electric blue centipede with bright coral-red fangs in the Kubbo-Kale Valley, India and described it as 'the most terrible thing I have ever seen in my tramps through the forest.' Another exceptionally large variant is found on the Andaman Islands in the Bay of Bengal, specimens having been measured up to 330 mm *12·99 in* when fully extended and 38 mm *1·50 in* in diameter, and an unconfirmed length of 12·5 in *318 mm* has been reported for another outsized individual collected in West Africa. *Scolopendra subspinipes* also reaches an impressive size (average length 215 mm *8·46 in*), and a measurement of 10 in *254 mm* has been reported for one Brazilian specimen.

These giant centipedes have a wide range of diet, and Cloudsley-Thompson (1958) says one large *S. gigantea* at London Zoo was quite happy with a regular supply of small mice 'which it devoured with alacrity.' Another voracious specimen was seen devouring the side of a living toad, and other scolopendrids have been known to kill and eat small birds and snakes.

Outside of the *Scolopendra* the only other centipede worthy of mention in terms of length is the worm-like *Orya barbarica* (Geophilida) of N Africa which has been measured up to 7 in *178 mm*.

The longest centipedes found in Britain are *Haplophilus subterraneus* and the sub-species *Nesoporogaster souletina brevior*, which have been measured up to 87 mm *3·43 in* and 70 mm *2·76 in* respectively. The latter animal, which may have been introduced from abroad, is confined to a single wood in Cornwall. Britain's longest scolopendrid is *Cryptops anomalans* of southern England which measures a modest 40 mm *1·57 in*.

The shortest known centipedes measure only 5 mm *0·20 in*.

The shortest centipede found in Britain is the widely distributed *Lithobius duboscqui*, which reaches a length of 5·5–9·5 mm *0·22–0·37 in* (Eason, 1964).

Although the word 'centipede' means 'hundred-legs', only some of the Geophilida justify this name. The centipede with the greatest number of legs is *Himantarum gabrielis* of southern Europe. It has 171–177 pairs when adult, all of which move separately. Half of the known species of centipede only have 15 pairs of legs when adult, but they all start life with six pairs, including *H. gabrielis*.

The fastest-moving centipede is probably *Scutiger coleoptrata* of southern Europe which can travel at a rate of 50 cm/s (=1·80 km/h *1·12 miles/h*) over short distances (Manton, 1952). The giant scolopendrids are less rapid, but Cloudsley-Thompson (1955) says he once had a large female *S. cingulata* which could snatch bees and wasps on the wing with her poison claws.

Centipedes are reasonably long-lived creatures. The maximum ages are reached by the giant scolopendrids, which do not reach maturity until they are 4 years old and probably live at least 10 years. The longest-lived British species is *Lithobius forficatus* which has a maximum life-span of 5–6 years. The geophilid centipede *Pachymerium ferrugineum* also lives at least 4 years (Palmen and Rantala, 1954).

Although all centipedes are provided with poison glands for paralysing or killing prey, the bite is not inflicted by the jaws but by the curved horny claws of the front pair of legs which serve as fangs. Most centipedes are relatively harmless to man, bites occurring very rarely and without serious consequences, but some species can administer a damaging bite and

necrosis sometimes develops on the site of the fang puncture. The most dangerous species are the large tropical and subtropical scolopendrids which can secrete a considerable amount of venom. When he was bivouacked with a group of soldiers in Northern Territory, Australia during the Second World War, Southcott (1973) says there were a few cases of centipede bite. 'I can remember one soldier in extreme pain following a bite on the leg; the pain was unrelieved by morphine. Another soldier was bitten on the right side of the mouth, and suffered pain and vomiting.' One of the most feared centipedes is a variant of *S. subspinipes* found in the Solomon Islands, W Pacific which reportedly has a bite that defies description. According to one writer the pain is so intense that victims have been known to plunge their bitten hand into boiling water as a counter-irritant – the attempted cure being more disastrous in its effect than the original injury! An unidentified Malayan centipede (probably a variant of *S. morsitans*) is said to be particularly dangerous, the symptoms being more severe than those from the bite of indigenous vipers, and victims are sometimes laid up for as long as three months (Keegan *et al*, 1964).

Some people, particularly small children, are especially sensitive to the toxins of centipedes capable of puncturing human skin, and a number of deaths have been claimed (Wood, 1886; Chalmers, 1919; Faust, 1928), but Bucherl (1971) has questioned the validity of these reports. Charles L Remington (1960) could find only one authentic case of a person dying after being bitten by a centipede, and that was a 7-year-old Filipino boy on the island of Leyte who succumbed 29 hours after a *S. subspinipes* had bitten him on the top of the head. Another case has since been reported from Arizona, USA, but Stahnke (1956) says this death was due to secondary infection. The chemistry of centipede venom is unknown and no antivenins have yet been developed.

Pseudoparasitism is another hazard, and there are a number of records of centipedes having been found living inside the nasal sinus or the alimentary canal of man after being accidentally introduced. Tartaglia (1961), for instance, describes a case of an intestinal pseudoparasitism lasting 9 hours after a Yugoslav woman had accidentally swallowed one of these unwelcome visitors (later identified as *S. cingulata*). Symptoms included vomiting, cold perspiration and irregular heartbeat.

The longest millipedes in the world are *Graphidostreptus gigas* of Africa and *Scaphistostreptus seychellarum* of the Seychelles in the Indian Ocean, both of which have been measured up to 280 mm *11·02 in* in length and 20 mm *0·79 in* in diameter (Kaestner, 1968). A 230 mm *9·06 in* long *Spirobolus* sp. collected in Nigeria weighed 61·13 g *2·16 oz* (David Moon, pers. comm.).

The longest millipede found in Britain is *Cylindroiulus londinensis* which reaches 50 mm *1·97 in*. The common black millipede *Tachypodoiulus niger* is also of comparable size, males and females having been measured up to 45 mm *1·77 in* and 49 mm *1·93 in* respectively.

The shortest millipede in the world is the British species *Polyxenus lagurus*, which measures 2–3 mm *0·08–0·12 in*. Another British species, *Macrosternodesmus palicola*, is 3·5 mm *0·14 in* long.

Despite the fact that the word 'millipede' means 'thousand-legged', very few species have more than 200. The record appears to be held by an unidentified South African species mentioned by Schubart (1966) which has 355 pairs (710 legs). *Siphonophora panamensis* discovered by H Loomis (1964) in Panama, has 175 segments, but not every segment has two pairs of legs. Interestingly enough, a millipede with 60 pairs uses only eight of them to woo its mate into submission; also, these creatures start off life with even fewer legs than centipedes, the usual number being three pairs.

Unlike the centipede, which has a wriggling movement, the gait of the millipede can only be described as an effortless, dignified glide. On 21 March 1977 David J Moon (pers. comm.) timed a giant *Spirobolus* sp. of supposed Kenyan extraction as it passed through its own length (150 mm *5·9 in*) at different temperatures.

'The trials were carried out during the evening under artificial light. To this end I prepared a special aluminium tray, about a foot square, into which damp garden soil, collected the same evening, was compressed to give a firm, fairly flat surface. With this arrangement the fastest time recorded was 20·3 s at 67°F *19·4°C*. However, on the surface of a smooth nylon carpet at almost the same temperature (66·5°F *19·2°C*) the time improved to 7·2 s – which gives a reasonable indication of the odorous distractions provided by the soil! 5·6 s was recorded at 73°F *22·8°C*, and at 87·5°F *30°C*, the merest shade under 4·0 s was notched up, to give a top speed at this temperature of 0·135 km/h *0·084 mile/h*.'

The fastest-moving Diplopods are the extraordinary jumping millipedes of the order *Stemmiulida*. In one scientific experiment Evans and Blower (1973) found that a 20–30 mm *0·79–1·18 in* long example of the West African species *Diopsiulus regressus* recorded a take-off speed of 48 cm/s (=1·73 km/h *1·074 miles/h*) when making a typical jump.

The rarest millipede found in Britain is *Osobates littoralis*, which lives on the sea-shore between high and low tides. It is known only from three specimens collected from the Isle of Man, Lancashire and Llandudno, NW Wales. *Cylindroiulus parisiorum* is known only from four specimens, all of them collected in churchyards (Gordon Blower, pers. comm.).

Most millipedes have a life-span of 1 to 2 years, but some species like *C. londinensis* may live up to 7 years.

Millipedes are not venomous because they do not possess fangs, but some of the large tropical species can squirt a very strong hydrocyanic acid secretion through the pores on the body surface which is unpalatable to other animals.

One of the nastiest members of the *Diplopoda* is *Rhinocricus lethifer* of the West Indies which can discharge this repugnatorial fluid quite a distance from the body. J F Loomis (cited by Sheals and Rice, 1973) found this to his cost when he picked up a specimen and was hit in the face and left eye from a distance of about 18 in *457 mm*. 'The pain was instantaneous, intense and of a burning and smarting nature. It persisted for several hours despite immediate bathing with ice-water. Swelling of the eyelid and cheek progressed rapidly and soon the eye was closed. The following morning the pain was gone but the eyelid again was swollen shut. On the day following the attack the skin over the affected area had turned dark brown and was raised into blisters where the concentration of the secretion had been greatest. The blisters persisted for nearly a week after which the discoloured skin peeled off without leaving any scars.'

Rhinocridium lethifer also has an unsavoury reputation, and the natives of New Guinea claim droplets striking the eye can cause blindness (Haneveld, 1958).

A large *Spirostreptus* found in the Sunda Isles, Malay Archipelago is also much feared by the natives, and a species of *Julus* on Amboina Island in the Central Moluccas is reported to have a venomous secretion, although this seems doubtful.

Segmented Worms
(phylum Annelida)

A segmented worm is a soft-bodied invertebrate which lives on land or in water and breathes through the skin or by means of gills. Its body is divided into equal parts and the muscular part of each segment is covered by a thin transparent skin from which bundles of horny bristles protrude. The main function of these bristles is to aid locomotion, but they are also used to anchor the worm firmly in its burrow. Young are hatched from eggs deposited on land or shed in water.

The earliest known Annelids lived about 620 million years ago and were marine.

There are about 8000 living species of segmented worms and the phylum is divided into three classes. These are: the Oligochaeta (earthworms); the Polychaeta (marine worms); and the Hirudinea (leeches). The largest class is Polychaeta, which contains about 5450 species, while the smallest is Hirudinea (300 species).

The longest known species of giant earthworm is *Microchaetus rappi* of South Africa. An average-sized specimen measures 1360 mm *4 ft 5½ in* in length (650 mm *25·6 in* when contracted), but much larger examples have been reliably reported. In 1936 a giant earthworm measuring an incredible 22 ft *6·7 m* when naturally extended and 20 mm *0·79 in* in diameter was collected by Van Heerden (1937), and when P O Ljungstrom and A J Reinecke of the Institute of Zoological Research at Potchefstroom University visited the Eastern Cape in November 1967 they were told by a resident of Debe Nek that earthworms had recently been seen reaching over the national road (width 6 m *19 ft 8¼ in*).

According to Ljungstrom and Reinecke (1969) the only enemies of this outsized annelid are the hammerhead stork (*Scopus umbretta*) and the common night adder (*Causus rhombeatus*), the latter being the only known viperid that eats earthworms.

The only other giant earthworm that approaches anything like the size of *Microchaetus rappi* is the better known *Megascolides australis* first discovered in Brandy Creek, southern Gippsland, Victoria, Australia in 1868. An average-sized example measures 1·22 m *4 ft* in length (0·61 m *2 ft* when contracted) and nearly 2·13 m *7 ft* when *naturally* extended. The longest accurately measured *Megascolides* on record was a specimen collected before 1930 in southern Gippsland which measured 2·18 m *7 ft 2 in* in length and over 3·96 m *13 ft* when naturally extended. Measurements up to 4·57 m *15 ft* have been claimed for earthworms collected near Loch, but Barrett (1931) believes these figures were probably obtained by 'stretching' the worm to its utmost limit – 'megascolides is liable to break under such barbarous treatment, despite a generous allowance of rings and its surprising elasticity.'

When it is travelling underground *Megascolides* is the only earthworm that can actually be *heard* going about its business. In fact, the usual way of locating these giants is for the searcher to stamp hard on the ground at likely spots. Any worms in the vicinity take fright at the disturbance and rapidly retreat downwards through their well-lubricated tunnels, making a distinctive and easily heard 'glugging' sound reminiscent of a bath being emptied.

In 1962 excavations at West Burleigh, Queensland uncovered another giant earthworm belonging to the species *Digaster longimani* which measured 0·91 m *3 ft* in length, 22 mm *0·87 in* in diameter and weighed 254 g *9 oz*. Five years later a scientific expedition from the Australian Museum, Sydney collected another 44 examples in Toonumbar State Forest, southern NSW. The largest worm measured 1·65 m *5 ft 5 in* in length and over 25 mm *1 in* in thickness when suspended alive by the tail, but it contracted to 1·06 m *3 ft 6 in* on being preserved in alcohol (Pope, 1958).

Giant earthworms are also found in other parts of the world. They include *Rhinodrilus fafner* and *Glossoscolex giganteus*, both of Brazil, which have been measured up to 2·1 m *6 ft 10¾ in* and 1·26 m *4 ft 1½ in* respectively when naturally extended, *Drawida grandis* of India which reaches 1·08 m *3 ft 6½ in* and *Spencerielle gigantea* of New Zealand which has been measured up to 1·3 m *4 ft 3 in* (Stephenson, 1930).

In May 1961 Mrs Marte Latham, an American explorer and animal-collector, discovered a new genus of giant earthworm near Popayan in the Colombian Andes at a height of 14 000 ft *4267 m*. The following month she presented a *live* specimen measuring 5 ft 6 in *1·68 m* when naturally extended to London Zoo. Unfortunately 'Gertrude' (also known as 'Willie') died ten days later and its body is now preserved in the British Museum.

The heaviest giant earthworm must be *Microchaetus rappi*. No weight details have been published for this species, but the 22 ft *6·7 m* example already mentioned could hardly have scaled less than 3 lb *1361 g*.

The longest earthworm found in Britain is the widely-distributed *Lumbricus terrestris*. The normal range is 101–254 mm *4–10 in*, but this species has been reliably measured up to 350 mm *13·78 in* when naturally extended. Lengths up to 508 mm *20 in* have been claimed, but in each case the body was probably macerated first.

The longest segmented worm found in Britain is the King ragworm (*Nereis virens*) which lives on the foreshore. This bristleworm regularly exceeds 300 mm *11·81 in*, and on 19 October 1975 an outsized specimen measuring 969 mm *38·15 in* was dug up at Hawkley Bay, Northumberland (James Sawyer, pers. comm.).

The smallest known annelid is the earthworm *Chaetogaster annandalei* which measures less than 0·5 mm *0·020 in*. Two other earthworms, *Aeolosoma kashyapi* and *Chaetogaster langi*, are both 1 mm *0·039 in* long.

Some segmented worms are relatively long-lived. *Lumbricus terrestris* and *Allolobophora longa* have been credited with 5–6 years and 5–10 years respectively in protected culture conditions (Rabes, 1901; Korschelt, 1914), and Wilson (1949) says the peacock bristleworm (*Sabella pavonina*) is not sexually mature until it is 10 years old. Nothing is known about the longevity of giant earthworms like *Megascolides*, but they probably live at least 8 years. **The longest-lived annelids** are leeches. Most species go on growing for 5 years, and 27 years has been reliably reported for a medicinal leech (*Hirudo medicinalis*).

The ability to replace lost parts is well-developed in many annelids, and in one experiment using an earthworm (*Lumbriculus* sp.) the head was regenerated 21 times from the available material. Growing an entirely new body from a single segment is much more difficult, but both *Myxicola* and *Chaetopterus* have this capability, and Dales (1963) says the remark-

The giant earthworm of Gippsland, Victoria, Australia, which has been measured up to 13 ft 3·9 m when naturally extended.

able *Dodecaceria caulleryi* eclipses even this performance by producing a series of individuals from each segment when its body fragments spontaneously.

Several of the marine worms of the Indo-Pacific region (e.g. *Eurythoe* and *Hermodice*) have venomous spines which can cause painful rashes, and at least one case of gangrene, possibly from secondary infection, has been reported (Minton, 1974).

Molluscs

(phylum Mollusca)

A mollusc is a soft-bodied unsegmented invertebrate which lives on land or in water, and breathes by means of a mantle cavity folded to form a lung or by gills. The body, which does not have a standard shape, is divided into four sections: a well-developed head with tentacles (missing in bivalves); a muscular foot or 'arms' which serve for locomotion or are modified to perform other functions; a rounded visceral mass in which the internal organs are housed; and a protective shell or mantle which grows with the body and is not shed periodically. It also has a highly complex nervous and circulatory system, and young are usually hatched from eggs.

The earliest known mollusc was the limpet-like *Neopilina galathea*, which lived about 510 million years ago and was thought to have been extinct since the Devonian Period. In 1952, however, ten living specimens were brought up from a deep-sea dredge off Costa Rica and three other species in the same genus have been discovered since in the eastern Pacific.

There are about 47000 known species of mollusc, and the phylum is divided into six classes. These are: the Monoplacophora (monoplacophs); the Amphineura (chitons); the Gastropoda (snails and slugs); the Scaphopoda (tusk shells); the Bivalvia (clams and oysters); and the Cephalopoda (squid, cuttlefish and octopuses). The largest class is Gastropoda, which contains about 35000 species, and the smallest is Monoplacophora (4 species).

The largest living invertebrate is the giant squid (*Architeuthis* sp.), the many-armed Kraken of Scandinavian legend, which allegedly dragged small fishing vessels down to their doom.

Although some of the great museums of Europe had physical evidence of this fabulous sea monster in the shape of preserved fragments of arms or bodily remains from as early as the sixteenth century, the scientific world remained dubious of the existence of the giant squid right up to the middle of the nineteenth century.

Then, in December 1853, a gigantic cephalopod was washed up on Aalbaek Beach, in Jutland, Denmark. Unfortunately the body of this specimen, which 'represented a full cartload', was cut up for fish bait before it could be secured for scientific examination, but the black horny parrot-like jaws measuring 114×82 mm *4½ × 3¼ in* and the attached muscles came into the hands of Prof Japetus Steenstrup, the eminent Danish zoologist, who described the specimen under the name *Architeuthis monachus* in 1857.

In 1856 the mutilated remains of another giant squid found floating in the sea near the Bahama Islands by Capt Hygom the previous autumn were brought back to Copenhagen and described by Steenstrup under the name *Architeuthis dux*. This animal had a 189 cm *6ft 2¼ in* long head and mantle and arms the same length (the two long tentacles or tentacular arms were missing).

Four years later a giant squid (*A. monachus*) was stranded between Hillswick and Scalloway on the west coast of Shetland. This one had a head and mantle length of 2·13 m *7ft* and measured 7 m *23ft* from the tip of the caudal fin to the end of the longest tentacles.

The scientific doubters were knocked back even further on their heels in 1861 when the crew of the French steam despatch-boat *Alecton* tried unsuccessfully to capture a giant squid weighing an estimated 2000 kg *4409 lb* some 192 km *120 miles* NW of Tenerife in the Canary Islands. After a 2-hour chase, during which the animal was seriously wounded by musket-fire, the sailors managed to pass a slip noose along the body until it was held fast over the junction of the caudal fin. But when they attempted to hoist the squirming creature aboard, the rope cut through the base of the fin like a knife through butter and the rest of the brick-red monster crashed back into the sea and disappeared.

The head and mantle of this cephalopod was estimated to have measured 15–18 ft *4·6–5·5 m* in length and its eight arms 5–6 ft *1·5–1·8 m* (the two tentacles were missing). The section of the caudal fin sliced off by the rope weighed about 40 lb *18 kg*, and when the *Alecton* arrived at Tenerife ten days later Lt Frederick-Marie Bouyer, the commander of the vessel, showed it to M Sain Berthelot, the French Consul there, who sent a full report to the French Academy of Sciences in Paris, together with a drawing of the squid sketched by one of the ship's officers. The animal was subsequently named *Architeuthis bouyeri* (Cross and Fischer, 1862).

If any doubts still lingered in the minds of men after this dramatic incident that there was such a creature as the giant squid, they were finally put to rest in 1873 when two herring fishermen and a 12-year-old boy were attacked by a huge individual off the coast of Newfoundland. The men, Theophilus Piccot and Daniel Squires, and Piccot's son Tom, were fishing in a dory off Portugal Cove, Conception Bay, about 9 miles *14 km* from St John's on 26 October when they saw a dark floating mass.

Thinking it was the debris of a wreck they decided to investigate, and one of the men prodded the matter with a boat hook. Suddenly the 'mass' opened out like a gigantic umbrella to reveal two huge green eyes and a parrot-like beak 'as big as a six-gallon keg' (*sic*), and the fishermen saw to their horror that they had accidentally disturbed a kraken.

The monstrous creature immediately launched an attack and hit the gunwale with its horny beak. Then it wrapped one arm and a tentacle round the flimsy craft and threatened to drag it, occupants and all, below the surface. The two men were terrified and sat there virtually paralysed as water began pouring into the boat, but fortunately young Tom was made of sterner stuff. With great presence of mind for a person of such tender years he snatched up a small axe and cut through the two appendages; whereupon the injured cephalopod ejected a tremendous amount of ink into the surrounding water and slowly sank from view.

When the badly shaken trio returned to shore the severed arm was thrown to the ground and eaten by dogs. But the long, thin tentacle was kept by Tom Piccot, who later sold it to the Rev Moses Harvey, a local amateur naturalist interested in kraken lore, after whom the giant squid (*Architeuthis harveyi*) was subsequently named.

According to Harvey (1874), who had the pale pink specimen preserved in strong brine, the tentacle measured 19 ft *5·8 m* in length and 3·5 in *89 mm* in maximum circumference, but the fishermen told him that 6 ft *1·8 m* had already been destroyed and there had been a further 6–10 ft *1·8–3·0 m* still attached to the creature.

From these data – and the diameter of the largest sucker – it was possible to estimate the size of this giant squid: head and mantle length 12 ft *3·7 m*, tentacles 32 ft *9·8 m*, total length 44 ft *13·4 m*.

There was also a stranding in Coomb's Cove, Fortune Bay. This one had a total length of 52 ft *15·9 m* (head and mantle 10 ft *3·0 m*, tentacles 42 ft *12·8 m*). Another very large example washed up at West St Modent in the Strait of Belle Isle, Labrador also measured 52 ft *15·9 m* (tentacles 37 ft *11·3 m*) and must have been much heavier (Verrill, 1879–81).

The giant squid was now *legitimate*, and in the next decade there were numerous sightings and strandings in Newfoundland waters. In October 1875 alone more than 30 dead specimens were found on the Grand Banks by the vessels of the Gloucester fishing fleet and cut up for bait. Most of them measured over 30 ft *9·1 m* in length.

In the 1900s and 1930s there were further sightings and strandings in the same waters, and during the period 1963–67 ten giant squids were brought to the Marine Science Research Laboratory at the Memorial University of Newfoundland, St John's for scientific examination. The largest example (*Architeuthis dux*), stranded at Conche on White Bay on 24 October 1964, measured 31 ft 6 in *9·6 m* in total length (head and mantle 10 ft 6 in *3·20 m*, tentacles 21 ft *6·4 m*) and weighed 331 lb *150 kg*, and none was under 18 ft *5·49 m* (Aldrich, 1967).

The largest giant squid so far recorded ran aground in Thimble Tickle Bay, Newfoundland in 1878. The capture of this monster (*Architeuthis princeps*) was described by the Rev Harvey in a letter to the *Boston Traveller* (30 January 1879):

'On the second day of November last, Stephen Sherring, a fisherman, residing in Thimble Tickle . . . was out in a boat with two other men; not far from the shore they observed some bulky object, and supposing it might be part of a wreck, they rowed towards it, and, to their horror, found themselves close to a huge fish, having large glassy eyes, which was making desperate efforts to escape, and churning the water into foam by the motion of its immense arms and tail. It was aground and the tide was ebbing. From the funnel at the back of its head it was ejecting large volumes of water, this being its method of moving backwards, the force of the stream, by the reaction of the surrounding medium, driving it in the required direction. At times the water from the siphon was black as ink.

'Finding the monster partially disabled, the fishermen plucked up courage and ventured near enough to throw the grapnel of their boat, the sharp flukes of which, having barbed points, sunk into the soft body. To the grapnel they had attached a stout rope which they had carried ashore and tied to a tree, so as to prevent the fish from going out with the tide. It was a happy thought, for the devil-fish found himself effectually moored to the shore. His struggles were terrific as he flung his ten arms about in dying agony. The fishermen took care to keep a respectful distance from the long tentacles, which ever and anon darted out like great tongues from the central mass. At length it became exhausted, and as the water receded it expired.

'The fishermen, alas! knowing no better, proceeded to convert it into dog's meat. It was a splendid specimen – the largest yet taken – the body measuring 20 feet from the beak to the extremity of the tail . . . The circumference of the body is not stated, but one of the arms measured 35 feet. This must have been a tentacle.'

Very little is known about the weight attained by exceptionally large giant squids and some incredible estimates have been made. Dr Bernard Heuvelmans (1968), for instance – comparing the shape of a giant squid with its arms (excluding tentacles) held together to that of a cigar – has calculated that the Thimble Tickle giant may have weighed as much as 27 tonnes (sic) provided it was 'very thickset' (i.e. maximum bodily circumference 12–15 ft *3·7–4·6 m*). He is saying an *invertebrate* with a head and mantle length of 20 ft *6·1 m* and a maximum bodily girth of 15 ft *4·6 m* is *twice as heavy* as a whale shark with a body length of 38 ft *11·6 m* and a maximum girth of 20 ft *6·1 m*, and *five times as heavy* as an adult African bull elephant!

In actual fact, if we apply the Belgian zoologist's weight formula to the 31 ft 6 in *9·60 m* Conche giant squid already mentioned it comes out at 603 lb *274 kg* – an error by almost a factor of 2!

Earlier MacGinitie and MacGinitie (1949), basing their calculations on a maximum bodily girth of 12 ft *3·7 m*, had arrived at a weight of 29 tonnes, or 30 tonnes including the arms and tentacles (sic) for this individual, but in 1968 they admitted that this figure was exaggerated and corrected it to a more reasonable 7·63 tonnes. Even this revised weight, however, is still excessive.

According to Dr Igor Akimushkin (1965), the Russian teuthologist, a 12 m *39 ft 4 in* long giant squid will weigh 1 tonne if the head, mantle and arms combined make up half the total length. Since there is a cubic relationship between the linear dimensions of *Architeuthis* and its volume or weight, this means the Thimble Tickle monster must have scaled about 2·8 tonnes (i.e. the weight of a large bull hippopotamus), although 2 tonnes is probably a more realistic figure.

Giant squids are also found in other parts of the world, but the lengths they attain outside the N Atlantic are generally less spectacular. This has prompted one or two teuthologists to query the accuracy of some of the measurements given by Verrill, but although a small number of them may have been taken roughly, i.e. paced out, there is no real reason to suppose that any of the lengths were deliberately exaggerated.

On 16 April 1930 an *Architeuthis* was washed ashore on the Miura Peninsula, Japan. Its head and mantle measured 3·59 m *11 ft 9¼ in* in length and its tentacles 3·57 m *11 ft 9 in*, making a total length of 7·16 m *23 ft 6 in* (Tomilin, 1967).

On 2 November 1874 a French expedition to the uninhabited island of St Paul in the southern Indian Ocean found 'a great calamary' (*Architeuthis sanctipauli*) cast up on the northern shore which had a head and mantle length of 2·13 m *7 ft* and tentacles measuring 4·87 m *16 ft*, making a total length of 7 m *23 ft* (Velain, 1877).

On 1 November 1922 the badly mutilated carcase of what was described as an outsized giant squid was washed up on the beach at Baven-on-Sea near Margate, Natal, South Africa after it had been involved in a three-hour fight with two whales about 1300 yd *1189 m* from the shore. All of its arms and tentacles had been bitten off leaving just stumps, but the former were estimated to have measured 30 ft *9·1 m* in length when intact. If the 47 ft *14·3 m* long marine giant was an *Architeuthis* – a span of 32 oxen failed to move it – this would presuppose a total length of more than 100 ft *30 m*. As it turned out, however, the 9 ft *2·7 m* thick mound of flesh was nothing more than the decomposing body of a whale with its half-detached blubber lying around in shapeless masses. Ten days later it was carried away by a spring tide.

There are also several records from New Zealand. One of the largest specimens (*Architeuthis kirki*) was discovered *alive* among the rocks at Cape Campbell on 30 June 1886. It had a head and mantle length of 10 ft *3·0 m* and measured 28 ft 10 in *8·79 m* overall (Robson, 1887).

In October 1887 a giant squid with exceptionally long tentacles was washed up in Lyall Bay, Cook Strait. This bizarre creature was described by T W Kirk of the Dominion Museum, Wellington, who wrote: 'Early last month, October 1887, Mr Smith, a local fisherman, brought to the Museum the beak and buccal mass of a cuttle which had that morning been found lying on the "Big Beach", and he assured us that the creature measured 62 feet in total length. I that afternoon proceeded to the spot and made a careful examination, took notes, measurements and also obtained a sketch. Measurements showed that, although Mr Smith was over the mark in giving the total length as 62 feet (probably not having a measure with him, he only stepped the distance), those figures were not so very far out; for, although the body was in all ways smaller than any of the hitherto-described New Zealand species, the enormous development of the very slight tentacular arms brought the total length up to 55 feet 2 inches, or more than half as long again as the largest species yet recorded from these seas.'

It should be pointed out here that the tentacles of *Architeuthis* are highly elastic and can be extended or retracted at will by the animal: so it is quite feasible that the length of 62 ft *18·9m* paced out by the fisherman may have been correct at the time he found the squid. This probably also explains the discrepancy in Kirk's figures, because in the table of measurements for this individual he gives the total length as 57 ft *17·4m* (head and mantle 7 ft 9 in *2·36m*, tentacles 49 ft 3 in *15·01m*).

Architeuthis longimanus, as it was named, is the *longest* giant squid so far recorded, although nothing like the heaviest (this specimen probably weighed less than 300 lb *136 kg*). Unfortunately nothing has survived of this specimen apart from a possible tentacle club and a beak preserved in the Dominion Museum, but Dell (1970) says the labels have deteriorated so badly that no detail can be read. This means that *A. longimanus* is only known from Kirk's description – and there are certain anomalies in that.

Some of the squids found in the rich feeding-grounds of the Antarctic Ocean also reach an impressive size. The largest cephalopod discovered so far in these waters is the gelatinous cranchid *Mesonychoteuthis hamiltoni*, which has been measured up to 3·1 m *11 ft 6 in* in length excluding the tentacles, but Clarke (1966) says this size was exceeded by other individuals collected by the British research vessel *Southern Harvester* in the Bellingshausen Sea in 1955–56. One outsized example preserved in a tank of formalin at the British Museum has a mantle length of *c* 3 m *9 ft 10 in*, but Dr Anna M Bidder (pers. comm.) of the Department of Zoology at Cambridge University, possesses a transverse slice of the pen of another *Mesonychoteuthis* which, judging by its width, must have come from a cranchid measuring at least 5 m *16 ft 5 in* in mantle length. The only source for these active swimmers, incidentally, is the digestive tracts of captured sperm whales!

When they were in the vicinity of the Ross Barrier in the Antarctic in December 1964 scientists aboard the Russian survey ship *Gnevny* lowered special instruments several thousand feet to determine the depth and salinity of the ocean. Suddenly a sharp tug was felt, and when the *steel* cable was pulled up they found it had been severed by an unknown marine animal of unbelievable strength.

Four years later almost to the day the two-man helicopter crew of a Soviet whaling flotilla operating in the Indian sector of the Antarctic Ocean spotted what appeared to be the body of a giant squid moving convulsively just below the surface. When they flew lower to investigate, the observer saw through binoculars that the half-submerged monster

was bright brown in colour and had tentacles (arms?) about 1 m *39·4 in* thick. Unfortunately no photographs were taken.

Although Norway is closely associated with kraken lore, very few giant squids have been stranded on her coasts or captured at sea in the past 100 years. The largest known *Architeuthis* was one killed by fishermen near Tromso on 10 October 1939 which measured over 13 m *42 ft 8 in* in total length and had 8·7 m *28 ft 6 in* long tentacles. It was not weighed, but as it had a maximum girth of 3 m *9 ft 10 in* and its longest arm measured 3·1 m *10 ft 2 in*, it must have scaled more than 1000 kg *2204 lb* (Karl Basilier, pers. comm.). Another giant squid found on a beach at Kyrksaeterora (formerly Heven) in 1896 measured about 37 ft *11·3 m* in total length (Heuvelmans, 1968), and a third which stranded at Ranheim on Trondheim Fjord in October 1964 was just under 30 ft *9·1 m* (estimated weight 200–300 kg *441–661 lb*). All three belonged to the species *Architeuthis dux*, which Aldrich (1968) contends is the only giant squid found in the N Atlantic. He says *A. princeps* and *A. harveyi* are the same species at different stages of decomposition, which would seem to suggest the systematics of the N Atlantic forms need revising.

The largest giant squid recorded this century was a 47 ft *14·3 m* long specimen captured by a US Coast Guard vessel near the Tongue of the Ocean on the Great Bahamas Bank in 1966 after being involved in a fight with a sperm whale. The carcase, or what was left of it, was later handed over to the Institute of Marine Sciences at the University of Miami, Florida but Dr Gilbert L Voss (pers. comm.) says much of this material was spoiled when a graduate student attempted to preserve a couple of sharks' heads in the same formalin tank. Fortunately the head was saved, and one arm is now on deposit in the Natural History Museum at Vienna, Austria.

In July 1968 two doctors fishing off the resort of Luanco on the NW coast of Spain found a dead giant squid and towed it to shore where it was weighed and measured before being cut up for fish bait. It scaled 256 kg *564 lb* and was 9·5 m *31 ft 2 in* long. On 4 July 1972 the Portuguese fishing trawler *Elisabeth* caught another *Architeuthis* near the Flemish Cap Bank which had a mantle length of 1·6 m *5 ft 3 in* and a total measurement of 8·2 m *26 ft 11 in*. It weighed 207 kg *456 lb*. This specimen is now on display in the Aquario Vasco da Gama, Lisbon (Marcelo de Vasconselos, pers. comm.).

Very few giant squids have been stranded on British shores. The largest recorded example was probably one found at the head of Whalefirth Voe, Shetland on 2 October 1949 which had a 4 ft *1·2 m* long head and mantle and a total length of 24 ft *7·3 m*. It was identified as *A. monachus* (Stephen, 1950). On 1 February 1957 the Aberdeen trawler *Viking Prestige* caught another *A. monachus* off Rattray Head which measured 23 ft 11 in *7·29 m* in total length (Stephen *et al*, 1957). Both these cephalopods were dwarfed, however, by another *Architeuthis* killed off the west coast of Ireland just over a century ago. An account of its capture was given in the *Zoologist* (June 1875) by Sgt Thomas O'Connor, Royal Irish Constabulary.

'On the 26th of April, 1875, a very large calamary was met with on the north-west of Boffin Island, Connemara. The crew of a curragh . . . observed to seaward a large floating mass, surrounded by gulls. They pulled out to it, believing it to be a wreck, but to their astonishment found it was an enormous cuttle-fish, lying perfectly still, as if basking on the surface of the water. Paddling up with caution, they lopped off one of its arms. The animal immediately set out to sea, rushing through the water at a tremendous pace. The men gave chase, and, after a hard pull in their frail canvas craft, came up with it, five miles out in the open Atlantic, and severed another of its arms and the head. These portions are now in the Dublin Museum. The shorter arms measure, each, eight feet in length, and fifteen inches round the base; the tentacular arms are said to have been thirty feet long. The body sank.'

The head of this monster, devoid of all appendages, weighed about 84 lb *38 kg* and, judging by the size of its arms and tentacles it must have approached the overall dimensions of the wounded *Architeuthis* taken off the Great Bahamas Bank in 1966.

At the moment nobody really knows what the absolute size limit is for a giant squid, but it would be foolish to suppose that the one which ran aground in Thimble Tickle Bay represents the ultimate in terms of length and bulk. Capt A Kean claims he found a huge individual stranded in Flowers Cove, Newfoundland which measured 72 ft *22·0 m* in total length (Frost, 1934). Another one washed up on the same coast in *c* 1882 was credited with a length of 88 ft *26·8 m* (head and mantle 30 ft *9·1 m*, tentacles 58 ft *17·7 m*), and Murray (1874) says two giant squids stranded on the coast of Labrador before 1870 measured 80 ft *24·4 m* and 90 ft *27·4 m* respectively.

Measurements of 90 ft *27·4 m*, 130 ft *39·6 m* and even 200 ft *61·0 m* have been conjectured for giant squids from the size of sucker marks found on the skins of captured sperm whales, but it is dangerous to place too much reliance on this evidence. Verrill says the largest suckers on the tentacles of a 32 ft *9·8 m* long specimen measured 1¼ in *32 mm* in diameter, and those on a 52-footer *15·9 m* about 2 in *51 mm*. Daniel (1925), however, examined sucker marks on the head of one cachalot which measured 3½ in *89 mm* across, and others measuring up to 5 in *127 mm* in diameter have been found on the skins of sperm whales captured in the North Atlantic. Ivan Sanderson (1956) goes even further and claims that sucker marks over 18 in *457 mm* have been found on the heads of cachalots, but he does not explain how the poor whales managed to escape from the clutches of such colossi!

The general consensus of opinion is that exceptionally large sucker marks, i.e. over 2 in *51 mm* in diameter, are old scars that have increased in size as the sperm whale grew. Thus, if a cachalot grows by a factor of 4 after being marked by a squid, and the original tooth ring was 25 mm *1 in* across, it will end up with a 4 in *102 mm* wide scar.

The 405 lb 184 kg giant squid taken from the stomach of a 47 ft 14·3 m sperm whale caught in the Azores.

In an unpublished letter to Frank W Lane, author of the definitive *Kingdom of the Octopus*, Prof E Bullock of the Memorial University of Newfoundland, St John's gave details of some calculations he had made regarding the weight of a hypothetical squid with a tooth ring measuring 12 in *305 mm* across. The answer came out at 255 tonne provided the creature had the same proportions as the 31 ft 6 in *9·60 m* Conche specimen already mentioned, or an even more nightmarish 1038 tonnes if the squid was 'thick set'! In other words, 'there ain't no such animal'.

Another possibility is that other giant squids exist which have much larger suckers in proportion to arm length than *Architeuthis*: for instance, an exaggerated form of *Stenoteuthis caroli* (the largest suckers on a 2·15 m *7 ft ½ in* female stranded on the beach at Withernsea, Yorkshire after a gale in February 1925 measured 25 mm *1 in* in diameter).

It is more likely, however, that the animal responsible for most of the abnormally large sucker marks is not a squid at all but the blood-sucking sea lamprey (*Petromyzon marinus*). This species, which can grow to a length of more than 3 ft *91 cm*, is closely associated with the sperm whale and feeds by pressing the circular edge of its mouth hard against the skin until it is punctured.

Huge fragments of squid arms (not tentacles) said to have been recovered or vomited up from the stomachs of sperm whales have also been cited as *evidence* for the existence of really monstrous specimens. Heuvelmans (1968), for instance, speaks of arms measuring 27 ft *8·2 m*, 35 ft *10·7 m* and even 45 ft *13·7 m* in length and up to 2 ft 6 in *76 cm* thick, but as none of these appendages have ever found their way into a museum or research institute, such measurements must be considered spurious.

The only known enemy of the giant squid in its natural habitat is the adult bull sperm whale which sometimes swallows its victims whole (female cachalots feed on smaller squids), although killer whales and large sharks will attack dying or disabled specimens on the surface. A cachalot harpooned off São Lourenco, Madeira on 12 June 1952 vomited a giant squid which still showed signs of life. This one measured 34 ft *10·4 m* in total length and weighed 330 lb *150 kg* (Rees and Maul, 1956). On 4 July 1955 an intact *Architeuthis* was found in the stomach of a 47 ft *14·3 m* long bull brought into the whaling station at Fayal Island in the Azores. It measured 34 ft 5 in *10·49 m* in total length and weighed 405 lb *184 kg* (Clark, 1955). In 1956 the remains of another squid estimated to have measured 12 m *39 ft 4½ in* in total length when alive were discovered in the stomach of a 15·8 m *51 ft 10 in* sperm whale captured by the Russian whaling flotilla *Slava* in the Atlantic off the southern Orkneys. Another one taken *alive* from the stomach of a large bull caught by a Russian whaling flotilla in the N Pacific on 31 December 1964 weighed 450 lb *204 kg* (total length 12 m *39 ft 4½ in*).

Young basking sharks measuring up to 3 m *9 ft 10 in* in length have also been recovered from this cetacean's stomach, which suggests that a weight of 450–500 lb *204–227 kg* is probably about the most an adult bull can get down its gullet in one go.

The giant squid has the largest eye of any living or extinct animal. In a 12 m *39 ft 4½ in* specimen the ocular diameter was 180 mm *7·09 in*, and that of the Thimble Tickle monster *c*400 mm *15·75 in* (*cf* 304 mm *12 in* for a long-playing record!). In the latter case the eyeball must have weighed several pounds, but most of this bulk would have been fluid. By way of comparison, the eyes of the largest blue whales have an ocular diameter of 100–120 mm *3·94–4·72 in*, the southern elephant seal *c*70 mm *2·75 in* and Man 24 mm *0·94 in*.

The smallest squid so far recorded is *Parateuthis tunicata*, which is known only from two specimens collected at depths of 3000 m *9843 ft* and 3425 m *11 237 ft* respectively in the Antarctic Ocean by the German South Polar Expedition of 1901–03. The larger of the pair had a head and mantle length of only 7·87 mm *0·31 in*, and a total length of 12·7 mm *0·50 in* (Thiele, 1921).

The smallest squid found in British waters is *Alloteuthis media*, which has a maximum total length of 177 mm *7·00 in*.

The most dangerous squid is *Ommastrephes gigas* of the Humboldt Current off Peru, which may reach a total length of 12 ft *3·7 m* and a weight of 350 lb *159 kg*. This extremely aggressive predator is greatly feared by native fishermen, and Lane believes that anyone unfortunate enough to fall overboard in the vicinity of these demons would be torn to pieces in less than half a minute (the chitinous jaws of this species are so powerful that they can bite through the extra-tough wire leaders used by fishermen to catch tunny). So far, however, no human fatalities have been reported, although American big-game fishermen now regularly angle for this cephalopod.

On 25 March 1941 the British troopship *Britannia* was attacked and sunk by a German raider in the Atlantic about 1400 miles *2253 km* west of Freetown, Sierra Leone, W Africa. Eleven survivors managed to cling to a tiny raft and took it in turns to sit on the floating platform. One moonlit night a large squid (probably an Atlantic version of *O. gigas*) seized one of the men and dragged him screaming below the surface as his horrified companions looked on helplessly. **This is the only known record of a man**

being attacked and killed in the water by a large squid.

On 12 January 1952 PC John Morrison (pers. comm.) was walking along the beach at Broadford Bay, Isle of Skye, Scotland after a heavy storm when he saw a strange, fleshy-looking object lying half-buried in the sand. He gave it a hefty kick, thus making him the aggressor, and the next moment a long tentacle whipped out and seized him by the foot. After a few seconds of violent struggle the Constable managed to get free – but left his wellington boot in the determined animal's clutches. He later managed to kill the squid with a pair of garden shears borrowed from a nearby home. The cephalopod, which had a total length of nearly 9 ft *2·7m*, was later identified as a specimen of *Stenoteuthis caroli* by Dr A C Stephen of the Royal Scottish Museum, Edinburgh.

Nature gave the squid a jet propulsion unit long before man ever thought of using similar methods for his own transport, and Bartsch (1917) claims that decapods 'inch for inch will compete in swimming power with any other creature that lives in the sea.' Certainly some of the smaller surface-dwelling varieties like *Stenoteuthis bartrami* and *Onychoteuthis banksii* are among the swiftest marine denizens, and it has been calculated from their flight trajectory – there is a record of an *O. banksii* landing on a ship's deck 7 m *23 ft* above sea level – that squids of these genera leave the water at speeds up to 55 km/h *34·2 miles/h* when they are being pursued by swift enemies like tunny (Akimushkin, 1965).

Fast-swimming squids are very popular with neurological researchers because they have the largest nerve fibres (axons) of any living animal. In the case of *Ommastrephes gigas*, they have been measured up to 18 mm *0·7 in* in diameter, which means they are about 100 times thicker than human nerves.

Very little is known about longevity in squids, but most species probably have a natural life-span of less than four years once they have reached the adult stage. Akimushkin believes it must take 'several decades' for giant squids like the one caught in Thimble Tickle Bay to reach such dimensions, but in marine animals there is no real relationship between size and age.

The largest known octopus (more than 100 living species) is *Octopus apollyon* (=*O. dofleini*) of the coastal waters of the N Pacific, which regularly exceeds 12 ft *3·7m* in radial spread and 55 lb *25 kg* in weight. One huge individual trapped in a fisherman's net in Monterey Bay, California, USA had a radial spread of over 20 ft *6·1m* and scaled 110 lb *50 kg* (MacGinitie and MacGinitie, 1949) but this size was exceeded by another giant octopus which scuba diver Donald E Hagen 'wrestled' to the surface single-handed in Lower Hoods Canal, Puget Sound, Washington, USA on 18 February 1973. This monster measured 12 ft 8½ in *3·87m* overall – several lengths were actually obtained ranging from 11 ft 8 in *3·56 m* to 13 ft 3 in *4·04 m* – and had a relaxed radial spread of 23 ft *7·0m* (the arms in this species account for about 78 per cent of the total length).

Another huge individual caught off Dungeness, Washington, reportedly weighed 125 lb *57 kg*, but further details are lacking.

Jerry Brown of Seattle, Washington told Jacques-Yves Cousteau (1973) that the largest octopus he had ever seen had a radial spread of over 30 ft *9·1 m* and probably weighed over 200 lb *91 kg*, while Heuvelmans credits this species with measurements up to 32 ft *9·85 m* across ('some say 38 feet') and a weight of 275 lb *125 kg*, but nothing in the way of evidence has been offered to substantiate these extreme claims.

Some of the octopods found on the coral reefs off Port de Papeari, Tahiti, S Pacific also reach a large size. Wilmon Menard (1947) was present on the Rimaroa atoll when one spanning 18 ft *5·5m* was killed by the local male population with clubs and spears and this was not considered a record specimen.

In 1874 Dr William H Dall, the Curator of Molluscs at the US National Museum in Washington, DC speared an octopus of the N Pacific variety *Octopus hongkongensis* in Illiuliuk Harbour, Unalaska Island, Alaska which had a radial spread of 32 ft *9·8m*, but the body of this cephalopod was diminutive by comparison – 12×6 in *305×152 mm* – and the creature probably weighed no more than 20 lb *9·1 kg*.

At the end of November 1896 the remains of a large marine animal were found by two boys on a beach 12 miles *19 km* south of St Augustine, Florida, USA. At first the fleshy mass was thought to be part of a large whale, but after a careful examination Dr DeWitt Webb, president of the local scientific society, pronounced it to be a gigantic octopus of a type unknown to science. On 3 January 1897 the *New York Herald* devoted considerable space to the story, the following being an extract:

'It had evidently been dead some days and was much mutilated. Its head was nearly destroyed and only the stumps of two arms were visible. Its gigantic proportions, however, were astounding. The body, as it lies somewhat embedded in the sand, is 18 feet long and about 7 feet wide, while it rises 3½ feet above the sand. This indicates that when living its diameter must have been at least 5½ feet. The weight of the body and head would have been at least four or five tons. If the eight arms held the proportions usually seen in smaller species of the octopus, they would have been at least 75–100 feet in length and about 18 inches in diameter at the base.

'The form of the body and its proportions show that it is an eight-armed cuttlefish, or octopus, and not a giant ten-armed squid like the devil fishes of other regions. No such gigantic octopus has been heretofore discovered.'

Full details of the monster, together with photographs taken by Dr Webb, were sent to Prof A E Verrill of Yale University, the leading authority on giant squids and other cephalopods, who later wrote in the *American Journal of Science* (1897): 'These photographs show that it is an eight-armed cephalopod, and probably a true octopus of colossal size. Its body is pear-shaped . . . The head is scarcely recognisable, owing to mutilation and decay. Dr Webb writes that a few days after the photographs were taken . . . excavations were made in the sand and the stump of an arm was found, still attached, 36 feet long and 10 inches in diameter, where it was broken off . . . This probably represents less than half of their original length . . . The length, given as 18 feet, includes the mutilated head. The parts cast ashore probably weighed at least 6 or 7 tons, and this is doubtless less than half of its total mass when living . . . this species is evidently distinct from all known forms, and I therefore propose to name it *Octopus giganteus*.'

Soon afterwards, however, Verrill had second thoughts about the true identity of this animal and made a retraction in a later issue of the same journal.

'Additional facts have been ascertained and specimens received, that render it quite certain that this remarkable structure is not the body of a Cephalopod. It was described by me . . . as the body of an Octopus, from the examination of a number of photographs, and the statement made to me that, when it was first cast ashore, stumps of arms were found adherent to one end, one of which was said to have been 36 feet long. Subsequently, when it was excavated and moved, this statement proved to be erroneous. Apparently nothing that can be called stumps or arms, or any other appendages, were present.'

He also said the tissue samples Dr Webb had sent him were not from a cephalopod, and suggested that the great mass might be part of the head of a creature like a sperm whale, although he admitted that it was decidedly unlike the head of an ordinary cachalot.

Dr F A Lucas, Curator of Comparative Anatomy at the US National Museum, also had an opportunity to examine some of the preserved tissues, and he supported Verrill's view that they showed whale affinities. 'The substance looks like blubber, and smells like blubber and it is blubber nothing more or less', he said.

Interest in the mysterious carcase rapidly waned after that, and within a few years the St Augustine monster had been forgotten. The story, however,

Donald Hagen with his record-sized octopus.

did not quite end there . . .

In 1970 Joseph Gennaro, Jr, Associate Professor of Biology at New York University, carried out some microscopic tests on one of the tissue samples of '*Octopus giganteus*' preserved in the Department of Molluscs at the US National Museum along with control specimens of the squid and octopus, and his findings, along with a detailed article on the strange creature by F G Wood, former Curator of the Marineland Research Laboratory at St Augustine, were published in *Natural History* (March 1971), the journal of the American Museum of Natural History.

The mysterious creature washed up on a beach near St Augustine, Florida, and which is thought to have been the remains of a giant octopus.

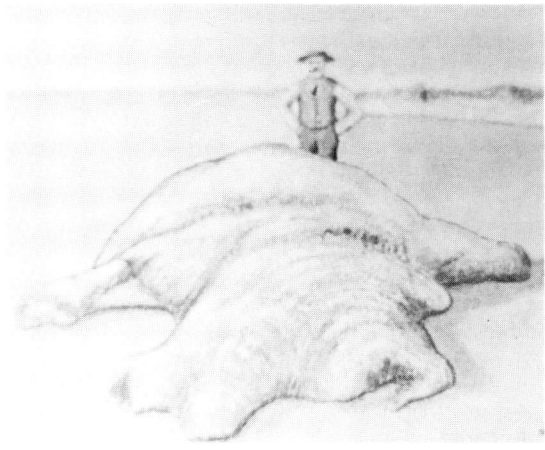

The decomposing remains of the strange animal cast ashore at Machrihanish, Scotland.

Professor Gennaro concluded: 'Viewing section after section of the St Augustine sample, we decided at once, and beyond any doubt, that the sample was not whale blubber . . . the connective tissue pattern was . . . similar, if not identical, with that in my octopus sample. The evidence appears unmistakable that the St Augustine sea monster was in fact an octopus.' Since then the same authority has carried out further biochemical tests on the sample and these 'indicate rather conclusively that the creature was not a decapod'.

Although these histological analyses would appear to confirm Dr Webb's original pronouncement that the animal found on the Florida beach was a giant octopus, not everyone agrees with this assessment, however, and Dr Gilbert L Voss, a leading American expert on the cephalopods, thinks the remains may have been part of a large mammal – or even a whale shark – the skeleton having fallen out as the floating body rotted. Certainly it is difficult to believe that a *positive identification* could be made of connective tissue after such a length of time, and the fact that neither suckers nor a beak, the two characteristics

that could have placed this enigma firmly among the cephalopods, were seen or mentioned is another minus. Cephalopod beaks are extremely resistant, and even if the mandibles had fallen out some trace of suckers would have remained at the bases of the arms around the mouth. Another point worth noting is that the soft, gelatinous flesh of these invertebrates is extremely prone to decomposition – Verrill remarked upon the 'extreme firmness and toughness' of the tissue samples sent to him – and Dr Webb could not seem to decide whether the thick skin was muscular or tendonous. Finally, although the so-called giant scuttle of the Bahamas is traditionally an immense octopod, Dr Voss says all of the sightings of large cephalopods in the Gulf Stream off Florida have been of the giant squid *Architeuthis* which are quite common in the area, but are quickly eaten by the rather large shark population when they are disabled and brought to the surface. He also mentioned that the head and brachial crown of one individual collected off Bimini by a charter-boat skipper in the 1960s weighed approximately 500 lb *227 kg* and must have come from a very big specimen.

According to Lloyd's shipping paper of 27 April 1903 the SS *Colorado*, on her arrival in New York, reported that on 7 April, in latitude 45·26, longitude 36·45, she had sighted the body of an elephant floating on the surface. The animal, an African bush elephant named 'Jingo', had apparently been dumped overboard when he died from sea-sickness while en route to the USA from England. Other elephants had suffered the same fate on earlier voyages across the Atlantic.

In July 1960 the remains of another 'sea monster' measuring 20×18 ft *6·1×5·5 m* and weighing an estimated 8 tonnes were found on a desolated beach 14 miles *23 km* south of Sandy Cape on the west coast of Tasmania, but it was not until March 1962 that the carcase was scientifically examined. By that time it had shrunk to 8×3 ft *2·4×0·9 m* due to decomposition. Like *O. giganteus* this animal lacked any recognisable feature, and there was no trace of vertebral structure in the *tough, fibrous material*. After taking away samples for laboratory analysis the Commonwealth Scientific and Industrial Research Organisation (CSIRO) announced in Sydney that the creature was nothing more than 'a large lump of decomposing blubber, probably torn off a whale'.

Britain's answer to the giant octopus was a tremendously bulky monster with enormous eyes washed ashore at Machrihanish, Mull of Kintyre, Scotland on 30 September 1944. The decomposing carcase measured 30 ft *9·1 m* in length and had huge gaping wounds in its side. Unfortunately no one was available to carry out a scientific examination, and the unidentified creature was later carried out to sea.

The largest octopus found in British waters is the common octopus (*Octopus vulgaris*), which is confined mainly to the English Channel. A specimen with a radial spread of just over 6 ft *1·8 m* and weighing 7 lb *3·2 kg* was spear-gunned by a member of Brighton Swimming Club near the Palace Pier, Brighton, Sussex in September 1960, but spans up to 8 ft *2·4 m* and a weight of 10 lb *4·5 kg* have been claimed for other individuals.

This species reaches a much greater size in the warmer waters of the Mediterranean. The largest males examined by Packard (1961) at the famous Zoological Station at Naples, Italy weighed between 8 kg *17 lb 10 oz* and 10 kg *22 lb*, and the largest female was 6·3 kg *13 lb 14 oz*. Verany (1851) speaks of one caught at Nice, France which had a radial spread of 3 m *9 ft 10 in* and scaled 15 kg *33 lb*, and weights up to 25 kg *55 lb* have been reported for other examples (Nixon, 1969).

The smallest known octopus is *Octopus arborescens* of Sri Lanka which has a radial spread of less than 2 in *51 mm*. The smallest species found in British waters is the lesser octopus (*Eledone cirrosa*) which has a wide distribution. It has a maximum radial spread of less than 2 ft *61 cm*.

Although a lot of blood-curdling stories have been written about octopuses, they are normally shy, inoffensive creatures and rarely attack humans deliberately. They are curious, however, and will sometimes investigate the arm or leg of a diver simply because it is moving, but if the person is experienced and remains motionless, the octopus soon loses interest. The diver is only in danger if he struggles and the cephalopod is firmly anchored to a rock, because it then gets excited and holds on tightly to the limb it has seized.

The total adhesive power of an octopod's suckers is tremendous. According to Lane, (1957) a 14-stone (196 lb *89 kg*) man can be held under water by a pull of only 10 lb *4·5 kg* if he does not struggle, and Parker (1921) says the 2000 suckers of an average-sized octopus (i.e. 5 ft *1·5 m* radial spread) can theoretically exert a pulling force of over 700 lb *318 kg*!

In April 1935 a large *O. apollyon* seized a fisherman while he was wading waist-high in the surf at a point south of Golden Gate – the entrance from San Francisco Bay, California to the Pacific Ocean. The arms were wrapped round the man's body, legs and left arm. Fortunately a friend who was scraping shellfish off the rocks nearby heard his companion's cries and rushed to his assistance as he was being slowly dragged out of his depth. As fast as he severed one arm, another seemed to replace it, but after a desperate struggle he managed to mortally wound the creature with a knife thrust between the eyes. Shortly after he had helped his friend ashore in an exhausted condition the octopus was washed up dead. It had a radial spread of 15 ft *4·6 m* and weighed 43 lb *19·5 kg*.

In May 1960 another fisherman was attacked by an octopus while he was collecting oysters from the rocks at Spitskop, Cape Agulhas, South Africa. After a struggle he managed to free his arms from its suckers, only to find that the cheeky cephalopod had made away with his gold wrist-watch!

Unlike squids, the majority of octopods die within two years of hatching, but large species like *O. apollyon* may live much longer.

The most venomous cephalopods in the world are the two closely related species of blue-ringed octopus, *Hapalochlaena maculosa* and *H. lunulata*, which have a combined range around the coasts of Australia and are common in tidal pools. The fast-acting neurotoxic venom carried by these small molluscs (radial spread 4–6 in *101–152 mm*; weight up to 90 g *3·17 oz*) is so potent that scientists at the Commonwealth Serum Laboratories in Melbourne, Victoria say the amount ejected through the horny beak in one bite is sufficient to kill seven people.

Curiously enough persons bitten by these demons do not feel any initial pain. The first symptoms are usually a dryness of the mouth and difficulty in swallowing, followed by vomiting, loss of co-ordination, failing eyesight and a paralysis which spreads to all parts of the body.

On 18 September 1954 a 21-year-old skin diver was bitten on the shoulder by a blue-ringed octopus as he was coming ashore at East Point near Darwin, Northern Territory and collapsed shortly after-wards. He was immediately rushed to hospital where he was given emergency treatment, and then placed in an iron lung, but he died from respiratory failure less than 2 hours after being bitten. The octopus was almost certainly *H. lunulata* (Flecker and Cotton, 1955). In 1967 there were two more fatalities in Australian waters, including a 23-year-old soldier who was bitten on the hand while paddling in a rock pool near Sydney, NSW and died from respiratory failure 90 minutes later. In both cases the octopus was believed to have been *H. maculosa*.

On the credit side, however, at least four poeple are known to have survived a bite from *H. maculosa* despite the potency of its venom. Two of them developed only mild paralysis and were discharged from hospital after 24 hours' treatment, and the others made a gradual recovery over a period of several days.

Finally, it should be noted that all of the victims were bitten *after they had picked the octopus up*. There are no authentic records of this animal deliberately attacking swimmers in the sea.

In October 1947 a fisherman was bitten on the hand by an *O. apollyon* near San Francisco, but apart from profuse bleeding, tingling and a pulsating sen-sation confined to the area of the punctures there were no after-effects other than a swelling which gradually subsided over a period of four weeks (Halstead, 1949).

The greatest depth at which an octopus has been recovered is 8100 m *26 575 ft* for a single specimen collected in a trawl by the Russian research vessel *Vityaz* at Station 162 in the Kuril–Kamchatka Trench in *c* 1950. Unfortunately the animal was lost before it could be positively identified (Zenkevitch *et al*, 1955).

The largest of all existing bivalve molluscs is the giant clam *Tridacna gigas*, which is found on the Indo–Pacific coral reefs. Weights up to 1000 lb *454 kg* have been claimed for this species, but there are very few authentic records of this invertebrate reaching even half that poundage. The largest *T. gigas* ever recorded is one now on display in the American Museum of Natural History, New York which measures 45×29 in *114×74 cm* and weighs 579·5 lb

263 kg. It was collected on the Great Barrier Reef off the north-eastern coast of Queensland, Australia in 1917 and probably scaled about 600 lb *272 kg* when alive. (The soft parts weigh up to 20 lb *9·1 kg*). Another example in the same museum measures 52 in *132 cm* in length and weighs 507 lb *230 kg*. It was collected at Tapanoeli on the north-western coast of Sumatra in 1963. *T. derasa* of the same region is also of comparable size, and two specimens in the Aus-tralian Museum, Sydney, and the Milan Museum, Italy weigh 500 lb *227 kg* and 472 lb *214 kg* respectively.

Although the giant clam is popularly believed to be a man-killer, and there have been a number of stories of pearl divers and others drowning after getting their foot or leg caught in the steel-trap jaws of one of these creatures (the serrated edges fit so tightly that they can grip a piece of wire) not one single case has ever been authenticated. Roger Caras (1976) says the huge purple-green mantle of this bivalve is so conspicuous that only a fool or a very unobservant person would tread on it, and even if somebody did accidentally put a foot between the giant teeth he would still have plenty of time to withdraw it because the jaws close very slowly (small specimens close much more rapidly than large ones).

According to Dr R T Abbott of the Philadelphia Academy of Natural Science (cited by Breland, 1963), the first attempt by one of the Dayak divers to recover the famous 'Pearl of Laotze' (see page 200) ended in tragedy when the giant clam closed on the man's arm and he drowned, but this report has never been proven and is probably a glamorous extension of the story. Caras solicited the opinions of 13 specialists (six of them Australian) regarding the danger or otherwise of the giant clam to man, and the general consensus of opinion was that evidence incriminating this species was 'circumstantial and largely hearsay'. Certainly none of them knew of a human fatality or injury due to this mollusc. This does not mean though that *Tridacna* is not dangerous. On the contrary, if a large specimen did trap a limb and the man was unarmed and unable to sever the great adductor muscle controlling the huge valves, then he would surely drown.

In 1963 Dr Joseph Rosewater, Curator of Molluscs at the US Museum of Natural History, Washington, DC, received a personal communication from a Malaysian named Johnny Johnson, who attributed the loss of one of his legs to a giant clam, but further details are lacking.

Leon Vaillant, the French naturalist, once put the strength of the giant clam to the test in 1883 by fastening an exceptionally large specimen (560 lb *254 kg*) to a post and then hooking buckets of water to the lip of one of the valves until the weight forced it open. By using this method he discovered that the

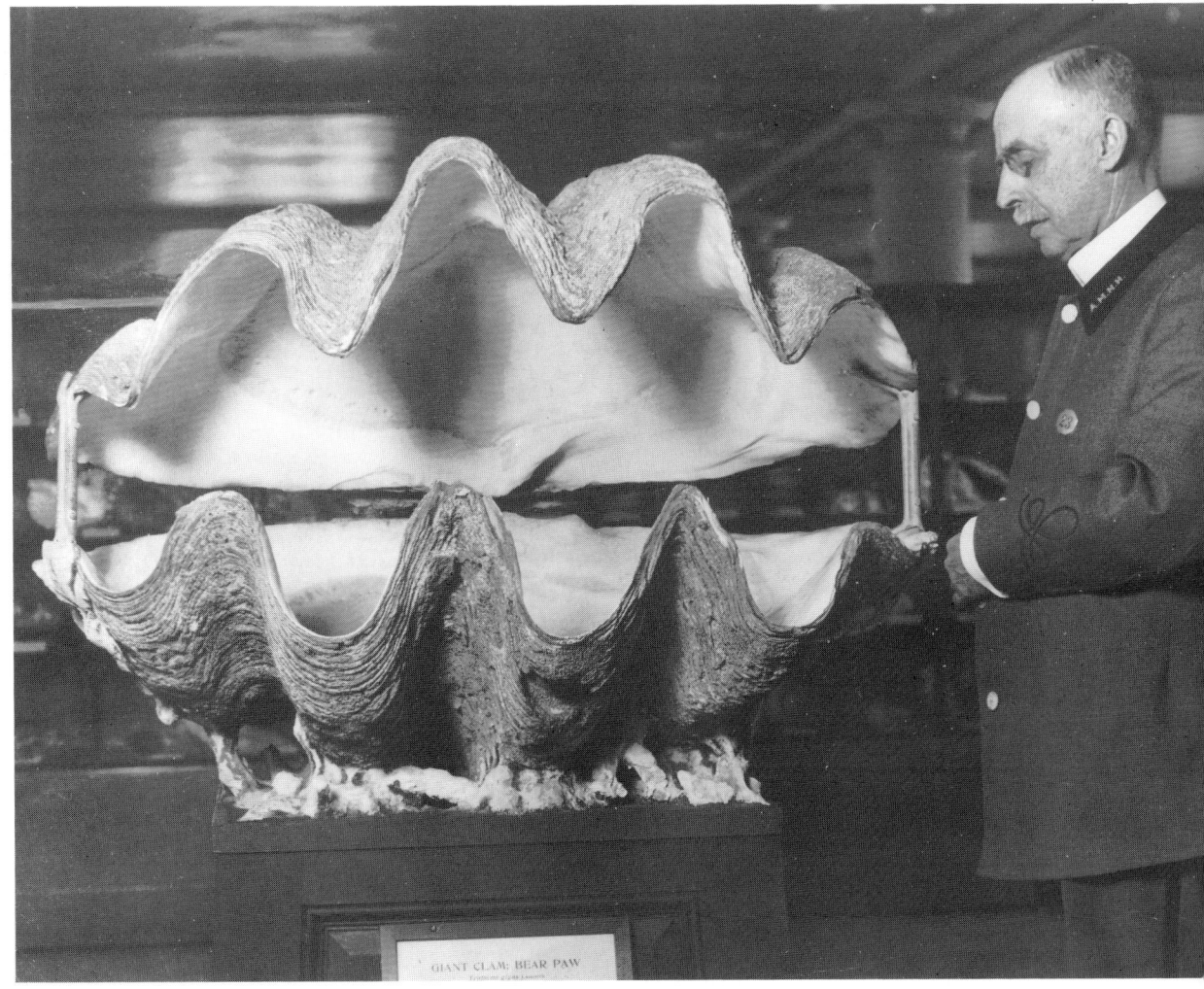

The 579½ lb 263 kg giant clam preserved in the American Museum of Natural History, New York.

clam yielded to a pressure of 1960 lb *889 kg*, or three and a half times its own weight, which means it would be impossible for a trapped man to wrench open the two valves of a *Tridacna* this size with his bare hands.

The largest bivalve mollusc found in British waters is the fan mussel (*Pinna fragilis*), which is most abundant off the southern coast of England. One example found at Torbay, Devon measured 370 mm *14·6 in* in length and 200 mm *7·9 in* in breadth at the hind end. The smallest British species is the coin-shell *Neolepton sykesi*, which measures 1·2 mm *0·047 in* in length. This species is only known from a few specimens collected off Guernsey, Channel Islands and Mounts Bay Cornwall.

The smallest British shell is the scarce but widely distributed univalve *Ammonicera rota*, which measures 0·5 mm *0·02 in* in diameter, while *Tornus unisulcatus* measures 0·4×0·8 mm *0·0157×0·0315 in* (McMillan, 1968).

The value of a sea-shell does not necessarily depend on its rarity or its prevalence. Some rare shells are inexpensive because there is no demand for them, while certain common shells fetch high prices because they are not readily accessible. In addition, 'live' shells with the extant creature inside fetch higher prices than 'dead' examples, and exceptionally large specimens in good condition are more valuable than ones of average size. In theory the most valuable shells in the world should be some of the unique examples collected in deep-sea trawls, but these shells are always dull and unattractive and hold very little interest for the collector.

The most highly prized of all shells in the hands of conchologists is the white-tooth cowrie (*Cypraea leucodon*), which is found in the Philippines. Up until 1960 this species was known only from the type specimen preserved in the British Museum which was included in the Broderip Shell Collection purchased by the Trustees of the British Museum in 1837 for £1575 – but that year a second specimen was 'rediscovered' in the Shell Collection of the Boston Society of Natural History and is now preserved in the Museum of Comparative Zoology at Harvard University. In 1965 a third example was found in the stomach of a fish caught in the Sulu Sea, a large inter-island body of water in the Philippines.

The rarest highly prized shell is the cone *Conus dusaveli*, which is known only from the type specimen recovered from the stomach of a fish caught off Mauritius in the Indian Ocean before 1872. It originally changed hands for £80, but was later acquired by J C Melvill for £20. It now forms part of the Melvill-Tomlin collection in the National Museum of Wales, Cardiff (Dance, 1969). In August 1977 a second example of the lost species *Tibia serrata* was found near Bandar Abbas in the Strait of Hormuz, S Iran. The type specimen was collected in 1811.

The highest price ever paid for a sea-shell is $7000 (then equivalent to £3300) by a Japanese collector in November 1975 for a 'gem' specimen i.e. live-taken, fully adult and without any growth marks, of the very rare cowrie *Cypraea valentina* found off Mactan Island in the Philippines. It was the seventh known specimen. In 1978 a sum of $10000 (then £5000) was refused by Phillip Clover of Glen Ellen, California, USA for a *Conus cervus* from the Indonesian Archipelago. The last specimen sold at auction in 1873 fetched £16 5s 0d.

The curvaceous precious wentletrap (*Epitonium scalare*) of the Indo-Pacific region was once so scarce that Kaiser Franz I Stephan, husband of Maria Theresa, paid 4000 guilders for a perfect specimen in *c* 1750. Today, however, they are collected in quantity and now sell for only a few pounds.

Pearl is a dense, lustrous concretion that is formed in various molluscs by deposition of thin concentric layers of nacre about a foreign particle (e.g. a minute parasitic worm) within or outside the mantle. Biologically speaking all shelled molluscs are capable of producing a pearl of sorts but the specimens fit for use in jewellery come chiefly from the large tropical pearl oysters (*Pinctada*) and the freshwater mussels (*Quadrula*).

The largest known natural pearl is a milky-white nacreous mass known as the 'Pearl of Laotze', formerly owned by the late Wilburn Dowell Cobb of San Francisco, California, USA, which measures 9·5 in *241 mm* in length by 4·0–5·5 in *102–140 mm* in diameter and weighs 127 374 grains or 6·37 kg *14 lb 1 oz* (one pearl grain=50 mg). According to Cobb's romantic account of how he came to own this huge gem, which is shaped like a human brain and has the same convolutions and furrows, Dayak divers recovered the pearl from a giant clam (*T. derasa*) off Palawan in the Philippines on 7 May 1934. They presented it to Panglima Pisi, lieutenant to a Moro chief who, in return, gave them a sack of rice which was considered generous payment. Later the same year Cobb, a collector of early Chinese pottery, saw the misshapen freak and tried to buy it, but Panglima refused to sell because he looked upon the pearl as a talisman. Two years afterwards the American revisited southern Palawan and went to see Panglima again. On his arrival he found the man's only son critically ill with malaria and, by applying his small fund of medical knowledge, he was able to effect a cure. The grateful father then offered him the pearl as a gift if he would return for it in a year – for Panglima had vowed to pray by it for 12 months in thanksgiving for the recovery of his son. Cobb accepted the offer and took possession of the pearl in July 1937. Shortly afterwards the specimen was examined by Dr Hilario A Roxas of the Bureau of Science of the Philippine Commonwealth Government in Manila who found that part of one of the valves of the *Tridacna* fitted the pearl 'almost like a glove'. He suggested that a detached piece of brain coral may have accidentally lodged between the valves of the mollusc. The clam, unable to eject the coral, then tried to minimise the irritation by covering the

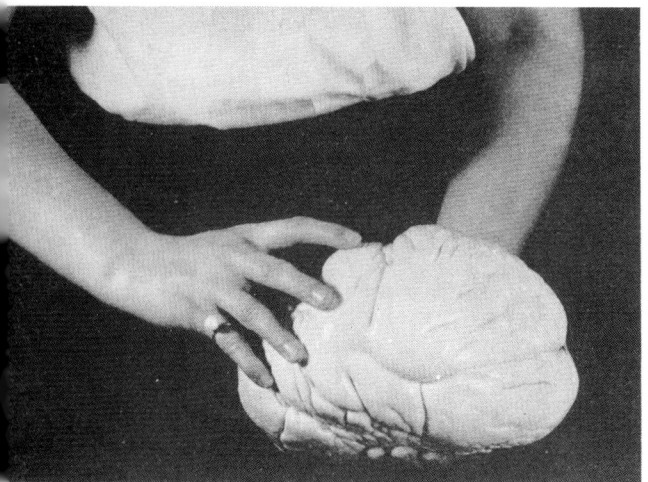

The 'pearl of Laotze', the largest known natural pearl.

unwelcome guest with mother-of-pearl.

In April 1969 the 'Pearl of Laotze' was put up for sale in London with a price tag of £1 458 333, but there were no takers and one appraiser put its value at less than one-twentieth of this amount. This estimate was not far out. After Cobb's death in 1980 the pearl was auctioned in San Francisco and went for a more modest $200 000 (then £85 000).

If we exclude this giant, then the largest pearl in the world is probably the poorly-formed 'Hope Pearl' of 1800 grains (=90 g *3·18 oz*). It is fractionally over 3 in *76 mm* in length and has a circumference at its globular end of 4·5 in *114 mm*.

The largest known pearl of regular shape is the celebrated 111½-grain (=5·57 g *0·197 oz*) 'La Peregrina' (The Wanderer), which was discovered by a Negro slave in the Gulf of Panama in the early sixteenth century. It was taken to Europe, and Philip II of Spain gave it to Princess Mary Tudor (later Mary I) of England when he married her in 1554. Later it came into the possession of the Bonaparte family. Napoleon's brother Joseph, King of Spain, is said to have taken the pearl when he abdicated in 1813, and the Duke of Abercorn's family acquired it from Napoleon III (1808–73), who spent his last years in exile at Chislehurst, Kent. In January 1969 the gem was sold in New York to Richard Burton, the Welsh actor, for £15 420. He wanted it as a present for his wife, Elizabeth Taylor.

The largest known freshwater pearl is the famous 'Little Willie', which measures 0·5 in *12 mm* in length and weighs 41·45 grains (2·07 g *0·073 oz*). The gem was found in a freshwater mussel (*Margaritifera margaritifera*) collected by William Abernethy, a professional pearl wader, in the River Tay, Perthshire, Scotland in August 1967 (pearl waders scan the river bed through glass-bottomed drums). He sold the pearl to A & G Cairncross, jewellers, of Perth for an undisclosed sum, but it has since been valued at £14 000. Freshwater pearls lack lustre, but can still be attractive.

The greatest number of pearls found in a single oyster is 1716 for a specimen collected by two Chinese fishermen off the south coast of Kwantung province in September 1958.

Pearls vary in colour from a full white, pink, apricot, gold and rose through to green, purple and black. The most sought after pearls are rose or greenish-black in colour, but blue-black ones are nearly as costly and true gold pearls also fetch extremely high prices. In 1947 an oyster was found with one pink and one black pearl inside it.

The longest-lived of all molluscs is the Quahog (*Venus mercenaria*), a thick-shelled clam found along the eastern seaboard of North America and, more recently, the Solent, Southampton Water and Portsmouth Harbour where there are now permanent colonies (introduced via the kitchens of Atlantic liners). Research in the USA involving the study of the microscopic rings laid down annually on the tooth holding the shells together indicates that this species sometimes lives for 150 years.

The deep-sea clam *Tindaria callistiformis* is also worthy of mention, because it has **the slowest rate of growth in the Animal Kingdom**. It takes an estimated 100 years to reach a length of 8 mm *0·31 in*. This figure was obtained by a team of scientists from Yale University, Connecticut, USA after they had dredged up a number of these clams from a depth of 3800 m *12 467 ft* in the North Atlantic and measured the amount of radioactive element radium 228 in their shells at different stages of growth. The greatest age recorded using this method was 98 years for a clam in the largest size category, and this tied in nicely with the number of rings, i.e. *c* 100 found in its shell (Turekian, 1975). The freshwater mussel has also been credited with a potential maximum lifespan of 100 years (Israel, 1913), but the giant clams probably do not exceed 30 years.

The largest known gastropod is the trumpet or baler conch (*Syrinx aruanus*) of Australia. One outsized specimen collected at Bunbury, Western Australia in 1974 and now owned by Morton Hahn of Randolph, New Jersey, USA weighed 35 lb *16 kg* when alive. Its shell measures 28·1 in *71 mm* in length and has a maximum girth of 38 in *965 mm*.

The largest gastropod found in British waters is the sea-hare *Aplysia limacina*, which has been measured up to 380 mm *15 in* in length. It has been recorded from Salcombe, South Devon (McMillan, 1968).

The largest known land snail is the giant African snail (*Achatina* sp.). The average adult specimen measures 8 in *203 mm* in length when fully extended (shell 5 in *127 mm*) and weighs about 8 oz *227 g*, but much larger individuals have been recorded. One outsized *Achatina* collected by Christopher Hudson (pers. comm.) in Aberdeen, Sierra Leone, West Africa in June 1976 was 13·5 in *343 mm* long and scaled 1 lb 7 oz *652 g*, but it later increased its size to 15·5 in *394 mm* (shell 10·75 in *273 mm*) and 2 lb *907 g*. On the same expedition Hudson was shown an empty shell which measured 14 in *356 mm* in length. This species was originally found only in East Africa and Madagascar, but at the beginning of the nineteenth century it turned up in Mauritius, the Seychelles and Reunion in the Indian Ocean. Since then it has spread to India, the Far East and the USA. The Japanese also took it to all the Pacific Islands they occupied during the Second World War for use as food, and several thousand were accidentally brought back to California with American army surplus

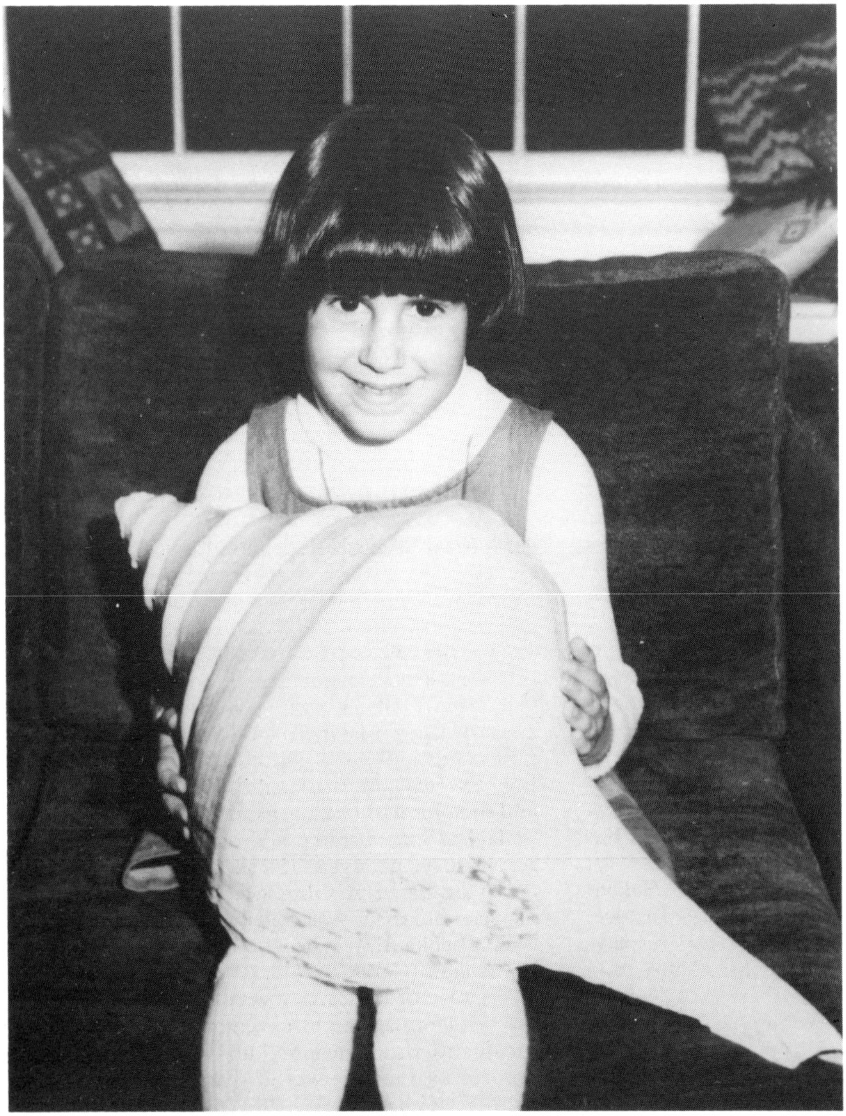

Left, the trumpeter conch, the largest known gastropod. This specimen weighed 35 lb 16 kg when alive.

Below, the giant snail Achatina with a smaller relative.

material after the war. Today this nightmarish destroyer of almost any growing thing is a major pest, and although countless millions of them are wiped out annually by fire and poison, they reproduce at such a staggering rate – it has been calculated that one snail can theoretically produce 11 million descendants in 5 years – that their numbers remain virtually unaffected.

The largest land snail found in Britain is the Roman or edible snail (*Helix pomatia*) of SE England which measures up to 4 in *102 mm* when fully extended (shell 50×50 mm *1·97×1·97 in*). The weight is 3 oz *85 g*.

The smallest land snail found in Britain is the widespread *Punctum pygmaeum*, which has a shell breadth of only 1·2–1·5 mm *0·047–0·059 in*.

The greatest age recorded for a captive land snail is 15 years for a *Helix spiriplana* (Vignal, 1923). *Rumina decollata* has been known to live 12 years (Vignal, 1919), *Helix aspersa* 8–10 years, *Cepaea hortensis* 9 years (Lang, 1904), *C. nemoralis* 7 years (Brockmeier, 1896), *Helix pomatia* 6–7 years (Kunkel, 1916), *Geomalacus maculosus* 6½ years (Oldham, 1942), and *Eulota fruticum* 5–6½ years (Kunkel, 1928). A desert snail (*Helix desertorum*) from Egypt presented to the British Museum as a dead specimen in 1846 and gummed to a card in an open case, awoke from its protracted sleep in 1850 and took a long walk in another gallery. It lived for another two years. The giant African snail has a maximum life-span in captivity of *c* 10 years, but probably lives less than 6 years in the wild state. Of the marine gastropoda, the red abalone (*Haliotis rufescens*) and the Japanese limpet (*Acmaea dorsuosa*) are known to live to 13 years and 17 years respectively, and observations made by MacGinitie and MacGinitie (1949) on the growth rate of another limpet, *Lottia gigantea*, indicate a life-span of at least 15 years.

The most fertile gastropod is probably the sea hare *Tethys californicus*. MacGinitie and MacGinitie give a record of a 5 lb 12 oz *2·6 kg* female which laid 478 million eggs in 4 months 1 week (41 000 eggs per minute), but they say larger females lay considerably more. At the other end of the scale, some gastropods lay less than 1000 eggs a year, and a black slug (*Arion ater*) deposited only 477 eggs in 480 days.

The most dangerous snails in the world are the tiny aquatic creatures of Africa, the Far East and South America which carry the flukes responsible for the terrible wasting disease schistosomiasis (formerly called bilharzia).

Three species of the genus *Schistosoma* – *S. haematobium*, *S. mansoni* and *S. japonicum* – habitually live in man, and in some countries schistosomiasis causes more sickness and death than any other single disease. In many parts of Africa and tropical America it is ranked second only to malaria, and an estimated 250 million people have died after being infected. At the present time there are over 200 million people round the world with the disease, traces of which have been found in ancient Egyptian mummies, and it is the only major tropical disease actually on the increase. This is mainly due to the spread of irrigation and hydro-electric schemes which create new breeding-grounds for the water snails.

The most venomous gastropods are the very attractive cone shells (*Conidae*) of tropical and sub-tropical waters. These molluscs all possess a highly-developed neurotoxic venom apparatus consisting of a single poison gland plus duct and a retractable proboscis which contains a number of harpoon-like rasping teeth.

The most dangerous species is the very rare *Conus geographus* of the Indo-Pacific region, which has been responsible for at least five fatal stings – all of them amateur shell-collectors. Three of the victims were natives of New Caledonia Territory, SW Pacific, one of them a 9-year-old girl. In the case of Charles Garbutt, 27, who was stung at Hayman Island off the coast of Queensland, Australia on 27 June 1935, the first symptom was a numbness which spread to the lips. Twenty minutes later his eyesight started to fail and then his legs became paralysed. After 60 minutes he lapsed into a coma, and died 4 hours later from respiratory paralysis (Flecker, 1936). The other death occurred at Okinawa, Japan. The victim, a 32-year-old man, was collecting shells on a beach in Nakagusuka Bay when he was stung. He died 4 hours later (Caras, 1976).

Because of its scarcity very little is known about the virulent nature of the venom of *C. geographus* or the quantity a single individual can produce, but it is reportedly more powerful than that of the Asiatic cobra (*Naja naja*).

Conus omaria also has a bad reputation. In November 1963 a 9-year-old native girl died on Tanga Island, New Guinea after being stung by a cone shell (probably *C. omaria*), and on 27 August 1964 another native girl aged 8 nearly succumbed on Manus Island, New Guinea after being stung by another *Conus* which was later positively identified as belonging to this species. In the latter case the symptoms were slurred speech, palsy and laboured breathing and her life was only saved by artificial respiration.

C. tulipa, *C. catus*, *C. striatus*, *C. obscurus*, *C. textilis*, *C. imperialis*, *C. aulicus*, *C. marmoreus*, *C. pulicarius*, *C. quercinus*, *C. litteratus*, *C. lividus* and *C. sponsalis* have also been implicated in injuries to man (Kohn, 1963).

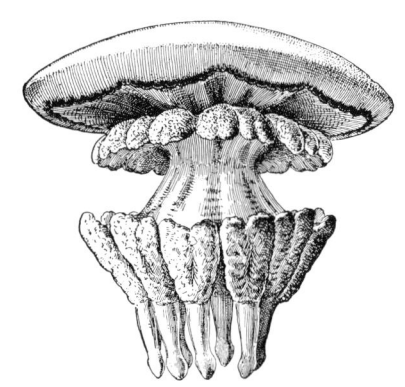

Cnidarians

(phylum Cnidaria, formerly Coelenterata)

A cnidarian is a soft-bodied marine invertebrate (a few hydroids live in freshwater) with a radially symmetrical body which is little more than a stomach. It occurs in two forms: the cylindrical polyp which attaches itself to rocks, and the gelatinous, umbrella-shaped medusa which is free-swimming. Both groups, however, have a mouth fringed by stinging tentacles which are used to capture prey. Young are either reproduced from eggs discharged in the water where they are fertilised (medusae), or from larva buds which detach from the parent and grow directly into adults (polyps).

The earliest known cnidarians, the Late Pre-Cambrian jellyfishes *Kimberella quadrata* and *Eoporpita medusa*, lived about 600 million years ago.

There are about 8500 known species of cnidaria, and the phylum is divided into three classes. These are: the Scyphozoa (jellyfishes); the Anthozoa (sea anemones and corals); and the Hydrozoa (sea firs, hydras and siphonophores). The largest class is Anthozoa which contains about 6500 species, and the smallest Scyphozoa (c 200 species).

The largest living cnidarian is the Arctic giant jellyfish (*Cyanea capillata arctica*), which is found in the relatively shallow coastal waters of the NW Atlantic from Greenland to North Carolina, USA. One huge specimen examined by Alexander Agassiz (1865) in Massachusetts Bay, Massachusetts had a bell measuring 7 ft 6 in *2·29 m* across and tentacles stretching 120 ft *36·6 m*, thus giving a theoretical tentacular spread of c 245 ft *75 m*. A medusa this size would weigh about 200 lb *91 kg*.

The largest cnidarian found in British waters is the 'Lion's mane' jellyfish (*Cyanea capillata*), which is probably a smaller version of *Cyanea c. arctica*. One specimen washed ashore near St Andrews, Fife, Scotland in c 1885 had a bell diameter of 910 mm *35·8 in* and tentacles more than 45 ft *13·7 m* long (M'Intosh, 1875), and Russell (1970) saw the impression of another jellyfish in the sand at Newton-by-the-sea, Northumberland in September 1967 which may have been slightly larger.

At the other end of the size range some jellyfishes have a bell diameter of less than 20 mm *0·79 in*, including the deep-sea species *Crossota brunnea* which measures 8·5 mm *0·33 in*.

The longest-lived cnidarians are sea anemones (*Actiniaria*). A small number of *Actinia mesembryanthemum* have been kept in captivity for 70 years without showing signs of deterioration (Dalyell, 1848), and a group of *Cereus pedunculatus* collected 'some years prior to 1862' and deposited in the aquarium of Edinburgh University's Dept of Zoology were observed continuously for 80–90 years before they all died suddenly in 1940 or 1942 (Warwick, cited by Comfort, 1964). There is also a record of a beadlet anemone (*Actinia equina*) living for 66 years. Most of the small jellyfishes probably live less than a year, but there are exceptions. In July 1928 some freshwater medusae suddenly reappeared in the great water-lily tank at the Royal Botanic Gardens at Kew after an absence of 45 years. They were first seen in the tank in 1880 after being brought over with aquatic plants from Brazil, but 'disappeared' 3 years later. Some hydroids are seasonal inasmuch as they die down in winter and regenerate new polyps in the spring.

Although all cnidarians are potentially harmful to man, only a few have stinging cells or nematocysts capable of penetrating the skin.

The most dangerous species is the transparent Australian box-jelly (*Chironex fleckeri*), also known as the 'sea wasp', which has been responsible for at least 60 fatalities in the tropical waters off the coast of Queensland since 1880 compared to 13 deaths due to sharks (Barnes, 1967). The cardiotoxic venom carried by this invisible killer works so rapidly it can paralyse the heart in 30 seconds, and one Australian scientist has commented that 'only a bullet kills faster than a sea wasp'. The pain from the massed batteries of nematocysts – a single box-jelly may have nearly 40 million stinging cells – is said to be the most excruciating known to man, and victims frequently scream out in terrible agony and become irrational.

The clinical symptoms in severe stinging are intense muscular pain and violent spasms, followed by rapid weak pulse, prostration, respiratory failure and death. Sutherland (1974) says death usually occurs within two or three minutes, and in many cases the victim expires before he or she can struggle the few yards to the shore. One man died *within 30 seconds* of being stung, and small mammals injected in a laboratory with *Chironex* venom diluted 10000 times have succumbed before the hypodermic needle could be removed.

In May 1953 a man died after being stung by a box-jelly while in shallow water with his 11-year-old son at Townsville. Elizabeth Pope (1953) writes: 'The boy . . . and his father waded out with a box to reset their fish trap. They were about 10 yards out from the shore in water that was knee-deep. They took a rest and were about to lift the box up again and proceed when . . . father stooped down, placing his hands between his legs. As he stood up the boy

The 'Lion's mane' jellyfish, the largest cnidarian found in British waters.

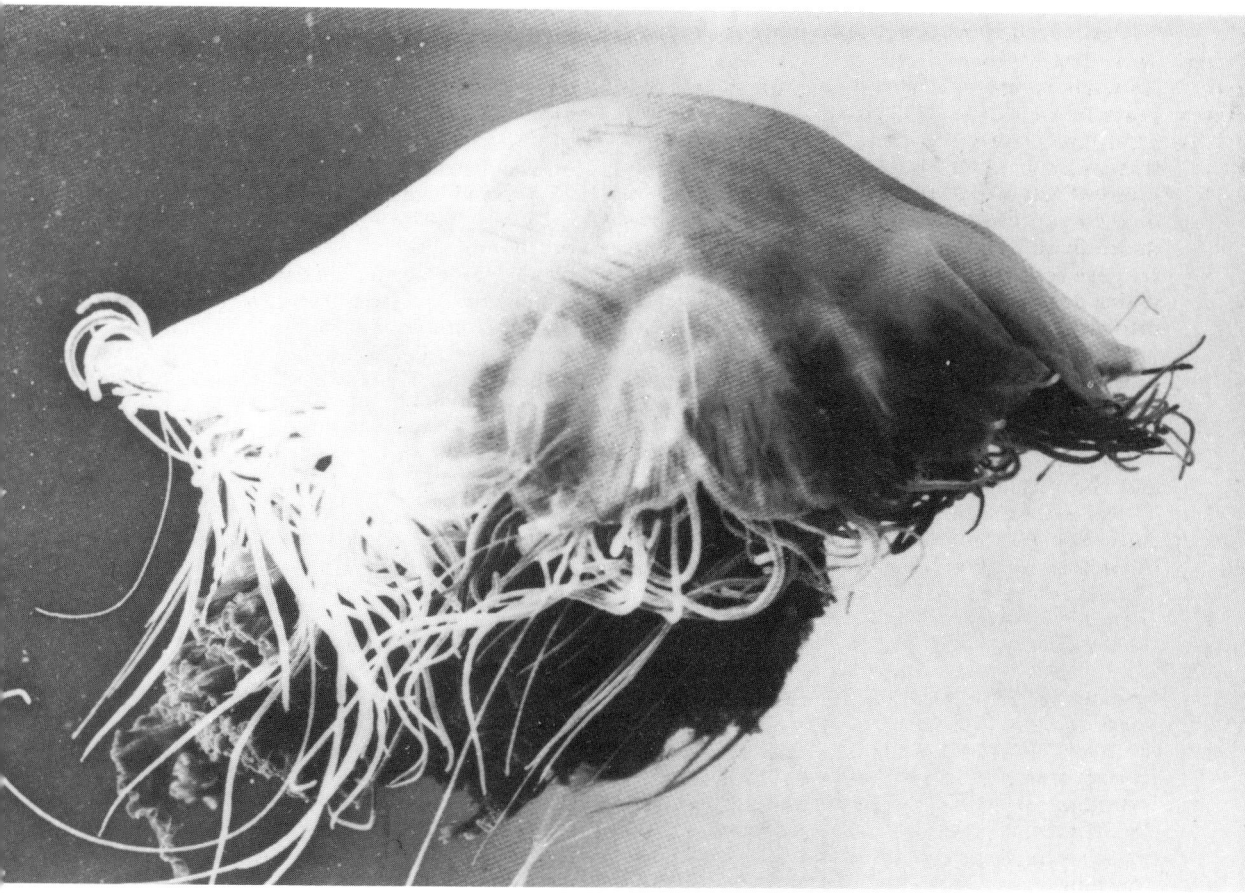

noticed thick cobweb-like looking stings on his father's arms and legs. His father went pale immediately and said "Get out of the water quick, Ken." The boy climbed upon the top of the trap and so got out of the water. His father staggered ashore and said "I copped the lot". He died within a matter of from three to four minutes.'

According to the autopsy findings of this fatal case and that of an 11-year-old girl, the lungs and air passages of both victims were blocked by enormous quantities of frothy mucus. The child had been standing in 2 ft 6 in *76 cm* of water off North Mission Bay, Tully.

It has been calculated by Southcott that 'a large *Chironex fleckeri* swimming along may present 200 ft (about *60 m*) of trailing tentacle in a volume of sea water, say a cylinder less than a foot across and 3–6 ft long. Observations on victims of fatal stings indicate that only a small fraction of this (about 20 ft or *6–7 m*) in vigorous contact with the skin is sufficient to cause death.'

Although a toxoid for active immunisation of humans is now available, virtually any type of protective clothing will ward off *Chironex* stings because the nematocysts have very limited penetrating power. One very effective defence is women's panty hose, outsize versions of which are worn by Queensland life-savers at surf carnivals.

Chiropsalmus quadrigatus of the SW Pacific also has a nasty reputation, and it has been responsible for a small number of fatalities in the Philippines, but *Chironex* is the more massively built, with thicker and longer tentacles, and appears to be the more dangerous form.

The most dangerous cnidarian found in British waters is the Portuguese man-o'-war (*Physalia physalis*) which is not a true jellyfish but a colony of polyps (*Siphonophora*). This highly-coloured float has been measured up to 12 in *305 mm* in length and 6 in *152 mm* across, and the tentacles have an amazing capacity for contraction, reducing from 100 ft *30 m* to less than 6 in *152 mm* in a few seconds when food is trapped.

Most people stung by the fishing tackle of this spectacular organism experience a burning pain followed by a large reddish weal which may last for up to a week before fading. Others, however, who are particularly sensitive to the venom, which in its crude form is about 75 per cent as toxic as that of the Asiatic cobra, can become seriously ill and may have to spend weeks in hospital. It is particularly dangerous to small children or adults with weak hearts, and a severe shock could lead to drowning.

In August 1955 a 6-year-old boy drowned at Camber Sands, Sussex after coming into contact with one of these creatures, and in March 1964 a 73-year-old man died from heart failure after stagger-ing ashore at Miami Beach, Florida with tentacles clinging to his chest, arms and legs.

The dried tentacles of *Physalia* have even been used in a murder attempt, but it is doubtful whether the soup made from this rather unusual recipe would have the desired effect!

This siphonophore is sometimes encountered in prodigious numbers, and the captain of one vessel reported sailing through a shoal for 96 miles *155 km* in the W Pacific (Fish and Cobb, 1954).

Apart from a few small fishes that associate with *Physalia* as commensals and are not affected by its neurotoxic venom, some turtles are also apparently immune, and a loggerhead was once seen happily chomping its way through a shoal of these creatures with no worse effect than swollen eyes!

Young octopods of the Pacific species *Tremoctopus violaceus* also have good reason to be grateful to this siphonophore. They use the stinging cells as a defensive weapon and for capturing food by attaching pieces of the tentacles to specially adapted suckers on their four dorsal arms.

'It is interesting to speculate on the method *Tremoctopus* might use in obtaining the tentacle fragments', writes marine biologist Everett C Jones (1963), who himself was once severely stung when he lifted a small female from a dip net one dark night. 'Unless the octopod is immune to *Physalia* toxin, the approach to the coelenterate must be made quite cautiously, and one can only imagine the pickpocket type of dexterity which would be required to obtain enough tentacle fragments to cover the eight rows of suckers.'

Certain sea slugs (e.g. *Glaucus* and *Glaucilla*) also use the stinging cells for defence purposes, but unlike *Tremoctopus* they feed on *Physalia* first and then transfer the undischarged nematocysts to specialised sacs on their backs by way of the stomach!

In 1968 hundreds of bathers at Port Stephens, NSW, Australia were treated for sea slug stings, but the injuries were far less serious than those normally inflicted by the rightful owners (Thompson and Bennett, 1969).

Despite the fact that the 'murderer' in one of Sherlock Holmes' classic cases was a 'lion's mane' jellyfish, no deaths have ever been attributed to this animal. In August 1959 twelve bathers were treated for serious stings at Aldeburgh, Suffolk, but there were no complications and they all made complete recoveries. There are no records of people being stung by the Arctic giant jellyfish because bathing is not exactly a popular recreation in the very cold waters it inhabits. If, for the sake of argument, a man did get entrapped in the tentacles and was rapidly swept upwards towards the bell in a stunned condition a very large *C. c. arctica* might – instinctively – try to engulf him; whether it would succeed, however, is another matter.

The largest sea-anemone is probably *Discoma* sp. of the Great Barrier Reef, Queensland, Australia which has an expanded oral disc measuring up to 2 ft *610 mm* in diameter. *Stoichactis* of the Indo-Pacific area reportedly attains a diameter of 1·5 m *4 ft 11 in*, but this measurement refers to the distance between the tips of the outspread tentacles. Some tube-anemones (*Ceriantharia*) reach a *length* of 2 m *6 ft 6¾ in*.

The largest sea-anemone found in British waters is *Bolcera tuediae* of the North and Irish Seas, which may exceed 12 in *305 mm* in diameter and have inner tentacles measuring 100 mm *3·94 in* or more in length.

The smallest British species is probably the tube-anemone *Gonactina prolifera* of the North Sea which has 'a total length in extension' of up to 4 mm *0·16 in* (Stephenson, 1935).

The most toxic sea-anemone is *Rhodactis howesii* of the tropical reefs of the Indo-Pacific region which, when cooked, forms part of the native diet. This species has been responsible for a number of fatalities in Polynesia after accidental or deliberate ingestion of the raw material, death being due to respiratory failure. The beadlet anemone of the E Atlantic and Mediterranean and the rosy anemone (*Sagartia elegans*) of the same waters have stings powerful enough to cause severe local pain, vomiting and prostration, and Mediterranean sponge divers have reportedly died after coming into contact with the European stinging anemone (*Anemonia sulcata*), but Zervos (1934) says these mortalities may have been due to infection rather than envenomation.

Although the hermit crabs (*Paguridae*) are closely associated with sea-anemones and both animals benefit from the partnership, *Triactis producta* of the Pacific is much less fortunate. The crabs of the genus *Lybia* like to carry these reluctant passengers around in their claws for protection, and when one of them is molested by a fish or another denizen of the deep it thrusts these 'fire-brands' into the face of the enemy!

In July 1965 a Pacific sea-anemone caused some consternation when it engulfed a 30 in *76 cm* long leopard shark (*Triakis semifasciata*) at Niagara Falls Aquarium, NY, USA. The aquarium director said the fish was 'not overly bright' and had probably irritated the cnidarian.

Sea-anemones have been dredged up from depths of over 33 000 ft *10 058 m* in the Philippine Trench, W Pacific.

The largest structure ever built by living creatures is the 1260 mile *2028 m* long Great Barrier Reef off Queensland, NE Australia, which covers an area of 80 000 square miles *208 000 sq km* and contains more life per square inch than anywhere else on earth. It consists of countless millions of dead and living stony corals (*Scleractinia*) and took 600 million years to build. Modern man will probably destroy it in less than 300 years if eventual plans to drill the reef for oil are carried out indiscriminately.

Prehistoric Animals

A prehistoric animal is an organism which no longer exists on the face of the earth in a living state, although at one time it flourished. It is known only from skeletal remains, impressions or the traces of burrows preserved in sedimentary rocks laid down during the passing of geological time, and for a living creature to become a fossil it must be buried soon after death so that it cannot be eaten by scavengers or destroyed by oxygen-breathing bacteria. The exact age at which an animal qualifies for this category is uncertain, but it is probably at least 25 000 years.

The oldest fossils discovered so far are the bore holes of marine worms (Metazoa) which thrived about one thousand million years ago.

It has been calculated that the biomass of all the organisms that have lived and died since the Cambrian era (600 million years) would equal the weight of the earth itself – 5796×10^{18} tonnes.

The first dinosaur to be scientifically described was *Megalosaurus bucklandi* ('great fossil lizard') in 1824. A lower jaw and other bones of this reptile had been found by workmen before 1818 in a slate quarry at Stonesfield near Woodstock, Oxfordshire and later placed in the University Museum, Oxford, where they were examined by William Buckland the first Professor of Geology. This 30 ft *9·1 m* long bipedal theropod, which stood over 12 ft *3·7 m* tall in the erect position and weighed about 2 tonnes, stalked across what is now southern England about 115 million years ago. In March 1822 Dr Gideon Mantell (or rather his wife Mary Ann) discovered some large fossilised teeth of another bipedal dinosaur of the same period (early Cretaceous) near

Cuckfield, Sussex which he described in 1825 under the name *Iguanodon mantelli* ('iguana-tooth'). Unlike the flesh-eating *Megalosaurus*, however, this 30 ft *9·1 m* long reptile (standing height 16 ft 6 in *5·0 m*; weight 4·5 tonnes) was herbivorous. Seven years later Dr Mantell found fragmentary remains of a 30 ft *9·1 m* long armoured dinosaur in Tilside Forest, Sussex, which he called *Hylaesaurus armatus* ('toad lizard'), and in 1834 he obtained a large number of *Iguanodon* bones from a quarry in Maidstone, Kent. It was not until 1841, however, that the name *Dinosauria* ('terrible lizards') was given to these newly discovered giants by Dr (later Sir) Richard Owen, the great English anatomist and vertebrate palaeontologist.

The longest dinosaur so far recorded is *Diplodocus*, an attenuated titanosaurid with a remarkably long whiplash tail, which ranged over the late Jurassic of western North America. The original specimen, discovered in Albany County, Wyoming by a collecting party from Carnegie Museum, Pittsburgh, Pennsylvania in 1899, measured 68 ft *20·7 m* along the curve of the body, but this skeleton lacked the skull and the last 24 tail vertebrae (Richard Lund, pers. comm.). When Andrew Carnegie, the museum's patron, later arranged for a life-size plaster reconstruction of *Diplodocus carnegiei*, as it was named, to be made at his expense, bones from other collections were incorporated into the skeleton to fill the missing gaps. This composite reconstruction measures 87 ft 6 in *26·6 m* in total length – head and neck 22 ft *6·7 m*; body 15 ft *4·6 m*; tail 50 ft 6 in *15·4 m* – and has a mounted height of 11 ft 9 in *3·58 m* at the pelvis, the highest point on the body. As can be seen from this breakdown, the trunk is relatively short compared to the overall length, which is why *Diplodocus* only weighed an estimated 10·56 tonnes in the flesh (Colbert, 1962).

In May 1905 the steel tycoon presented an exact replica of this magnificent exhibit to the British Museum, and later donated nine more plaster casts to other museums.

According to De Camp and De Camp (1968) these giant sauropods may have been able to regenerate lost parts, and they mention another skeleton collected in Wyoming which appeared to have lost about 25 per cent of its tail to a carnosaur and then regrown it – along with 21 new vertebrae!

Britain's longest dinosaur was probably *Cetiosauriscus oxoniensis* ('whale lizard') from the upper beds of the Great Oolite at Enslow Bridge, near Oxford. This creature, which measured 68 ft 6 in *20·88 m* in total length and weighed over 30 tonnes, was already known to Prof Owen when he made his famous address to the British Association for the Advancement of Science in 1841, but at that time he was firmly convinced the huge vertebra he had seen in a private collection belonged to an archaic crocodile. In 1868, however, a 5 ft 4 in *163 cm* long thigh bone was found and the following year more gigantic remains were uncovered in the same quarry. In May 1898 Alfred N Leeds dug out a partial skeleton (*C. o. leedsi*) in the No 1 Brickyard of the New Peterborough Brick Co, Northamptonshire, and in 1968 quite a good specimen ('the best so far') was found near Stamford, Lincolnshire (Charig, 1979).

In 1975 an amateur fossil-hunter working on the cliff-face near Brighstone, Isle of Wight, discovered an unusual 9 in *229 mm* long bone; later identified as the haemal arch (a bone running beneath the vertebrae of the tail) of a diplodocus-type sauropod.

The heaviest land vertebrates of all time were the massive brachiosaurids ('arm lizards') of the late Jurassic of the SW USA, East Africa, the Sahara (Niger) and Portugal. Unlike the rest of the giant sauropods, these giraffe-like dinosaurs had high shoulders and sloping backs, and their necks were relatively much thicker. During the period 1909–11 a German expedition under the direction of Dr W Janensch excavated the first complete skeleton of a brachiosaurid at the famous Tendaguru site in Tanzania and later shipped the bones back to the Humboldt Museum fur Naturkunde, East Berlin for preparation and assembly. It proved a monumental task in more ways than one, and another 26 years were to elapse – the work continued throughout the First World War – before *Brachiosaurus brancai*, as it was named, was finally put on display in the great hall of the museum in 1937. Two years later, however, when hostilities broke out again, the skeleton was hurriedly taken apart and the bones buried in the cellar to protect them from the devastating Allied air raids. After the war they were brought out again and

reassembled. As it stands today, the world's largest mounted dinosaur measures 74 ft 6 in *22·7 m* in total length (height at shoulder 21 ft *6·4 m*) and has a raised head height of 39 ft *11·9 m* (42 ft *12·8 m* from the level of the ground).

Until fairly recently this giant among giants was estimated by palaeontologists to have weighed 40–50 tonnes when alive, which is a staggering weight for a terrestrial vertebrate. Then, in 1962, Dr Edwin Colbert, Curator of the Department of Vertebrate Palaeontology at the American Museum of Natural History, New York carried out a series of experiments to determine *more accurately* the tonnage of this immense sauropod and other dinosaurs. His calculations were based on miniature models carefully scaled at 0·041–0·037 natural size. First of all, he worked out the volume of each restoration in cubic centimetres. Then he multiplied the result by the cube of the linear scale of the model to give the volume of the dinosaur when it was alive. It was now possible to calculate the weight fairly easily by multiplying the metric volume by the *assumed specific gravity* of a young alligator, a living reptile closely related taxonomically to the dinosaurs.

Most of the calculated dinosaur weights ran very close to earlier estimates, but the biggest surprise of all was the tonnage worked out for *Brachiosaurus*. This was 78·26 tonnes or double the weight of an average-sized adult bull sperm whale! Even Dr Colbert was startled by this finding.

'It has been generally supposed that 40 to 50 avoirdupois tons constitute about the upper limit for the weight of a land-living vertebrate', he said, 'the assumption being that greater weights would exceed the limitations of the supporting strength of bone, ligament and muscle. Yet here is a dinosaur that, on the basis of the calculations, weighed as much as a large whale. Extra volumetric measurements of the model were made, and linear measurements of the model . . . checked several times. After all possible checks of method and measurements had been made, the figure still held. Therefore, unless one is prepared to reject the . . . model of *Brachiosaurus* as being completely inaccurate, a proposition that I for one cannot accept, it appears that *Brachiosaurus* was indeed a gigantic sauropod, in weight almost two and a half times the size of *Brontosaurus* . . . Certainly no other land-living vertebrate ever approached it in massiveness and weight.'

Dr Colbert's model for his *Brachiosaurus* was the East Berlin colossus, but since then museum officials have revealed they also possess isolated bones from other individuals which are up to one-third as big again as their equivalents in the mounted specimen! (F Boothman, pers. comm.).

In the summer of 1972 field palaeontologist Dr James Jensen, Director of the Earth Science Museum

The 8 ft 2·44 m long shoulder-blade of 'Supersaurus' alongside its 6 ft 3 in 1·91 m discoverer James Jensen.

at Brigham Young University, Provo, Utah, USA unearthed the remains of another huge brachiosaurid while he was working with a small team in the Upper Jurassic deposits of the Dry Mesa Quarry, western Colorado. This outsized sauropod, which has been christened 'Supersaurus', is still being dug out, but up to mid-1979 the finds included 8 ft *2·4 m* long matching scapulae or shoulder blades, two 10 ft *3·0 m* long ribs and most of the cervicals, the largest of which measured over 4 ft 6 in *137 cm* in length. Because the latter series of vertebrae are about three-quarters complete in number, James Jensen (pers. comm.) was able to calculate the total length of the neck based upon the B. cervical formulae very early in the proceedings, and found it added up to ±39 ft ±*11·9 m*. 'This is due to the fact that the shortest neck vertebrae collected – one near the anterior end – is 3 ft in length and the longest one is nearly 5 ft long. When you calculate these dimensions in a series having 13 vertebrae it adds up to a long neck.'

From the evidence of the bones already excavated this new discovery is generally some 22 per cent larger than the mounted specimen in the Humboldt Museum. If the anatomical design is similar, this would give it an overall length of *c* 90 ft *27·4 m*, a

shoulder height of 26 ft *7·9 m* and a raised head measurement of nearly 50 ft *15·2 m* in the natural position; even more startling, however, would be its weight (the cube of the linear dimensions) which would be an earth-shaking 140 tonnes, making it comparable in mass to a large blue whale.

In 1979 'Dinosaur Jim', as he is popularly known, found another shoulder blade in the same quarry which measured an even more amazing 8 ft 10 in *2·69 m* in length. If the rest of 'Ultrasaurus', as it has been nicknamed, is built on the same gigantic scale this presupposes a total length of 100 ft *30·5 m* and a weight of 187 tonnes by extrapolation, which would put it in the same size category as the largest members of the East African group of brachiosaurids, but further discoveries need to be made – the shoulder blades of these two monsters differ in shape – before any definite calculations can be worked out.

How these mind-boggling quadrupeds managed to support the crushing weight of their tremendous bulk *in locomotion* without questioning the laws of physics and chemistry remains something of a mystery, particularly as one would have thought that the amount of weight required for the massive development of the skeleton would have left insufficient over to build the enormous muscles needed to supply the force to move these immense bones. Some palaeophysiologists – who study the physical make-up of extinct animals – believe the secret may lie in the increased area of support provided by the relatively short but extremely massive tail, but they would also like to know more about the complex hydraulic control system needed for the heart to pump a column of blood 50–60 ft *15·2–18·3 m* high!

Until fairly recently it was firmly believed that the brachiosaurids and the other long-necked saurischian dinosaurs spent most of their time in the waters of swamps or lakes because their legs could not support their vast bulk on land, and the fact that the nostrils and eyes of these reptiles were placed high up on the head like those of the hippopotamus and they also had snorkel-like necks certainly seemed to suggest an aquatic existence. This theory, however, has now been discarded because (1) the pressure at the depth indicated would prevent them from inhaling and crush the blood vessels in the neck; and (2) their fleshy, compact feet would soon become hopelessly mired in the mud at the bottom and they would quickly starve to death (Kermack, 1951; Bakker, 1971). It has recently been suggested that these peaceful herbivores were fully terrestrial, and their long necks were used to browse the tops of high trees as they roamed the plains and forests, but this method of feeding would probably require too much effort to meet the daily needs of these group animals.

The largest flesh-eating dinosaurs ever to stalk

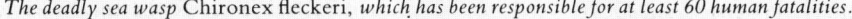

The giant millipede Scaphistostreptus seychellarum *of the Seychelles, which has been measured up to 280 mm 11·02 in in length.*

The deadly sea wasp Chironex fleckeri, *which has been responsible for at least 60 human fatalities.*

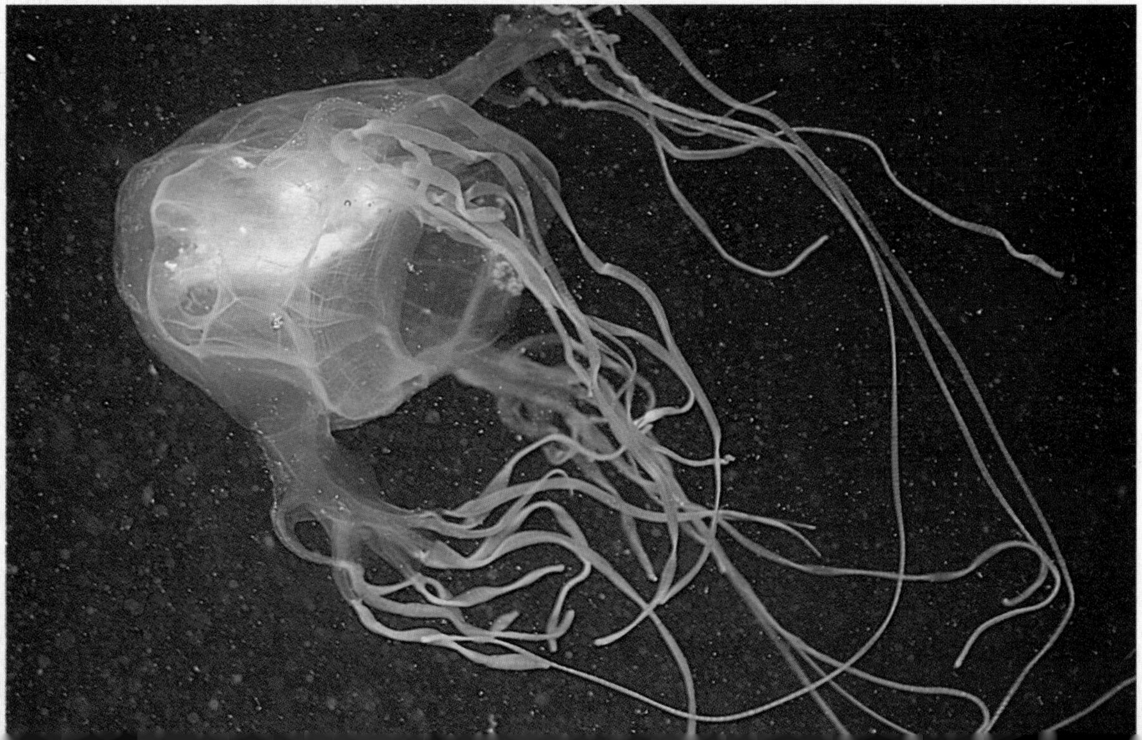

across the earth were the tyrannosaurids ('tyrant lizards') of the late Cretaceous, which culminated in the seven-tonne *Tyrannosaurus rex* of the NW USA. A composite skeleton of this terrifying creature mounted in the American Museum of Natural History has a standing height of 18 ft *5·5 m* and measures 47 ft *14·3 m* in total length but Newman (1970), in a revised estimate, has chopped 12 ft *3·7 m* off the tail of this specimen (only 20 of the caudal vertebrae are authentic) to give it a more bird-like posture. If this radical departure from orthodox restorations of *Tyrannosaurus* is generally accepted then *Tarbosaurus efremovi*, its Mongolian counterpart, may be more deserving of the title because it is known from 15 well preserved skeletons. This scavenger had a bipedal height of 16 ft *4·9 m* and measured about 40 ft *12·2 m* in total length, but although it had a slightly longer skull (4 ft 2 in *1·27 m*) than its North American relation, its head was less massive, and it may have lost out in terms of overall bulk.

During the period 1924–29 a British expedition working at the famous Tendaguru site discovered another huge carnosaur (*Megalosaurus ingens*) which, on the sole evidence of its 14·5 cm *5·7 in* long teeth, must have been nearly as large as *Tyrannosaurus*.

In 1934 labourers working on Highway 64 near Kenton in Cimarron County, Oklahoma, USA accidentally unearthed a huge rib 7 ft *2·1 m* long and 12 in *30 cm* in circumference. Dr J W Stovall, a palaeontologist at Norman University, was hurriedly called to the site of the discovery, and over the next few months he and a picked team excavated the bones of an exceptionally large carnosaur new to science. This mysterious giant, which measured 42 ft *12·8 m* in total length and had a bipedal height of 16 ft *4·9 m*, was even more heavily built than the tyrannosaurids and had arms more than twice as long (Ray, 1941). Dr Stovall named this fearsome beast *Saurophagus maximus* ('lizard-eater'), but after his death the bones were re-examined and found to be those of a very large *Antrodemus* (=*Allosaurus*), which up until then had been credited with a maximum length of 33 ft *10·1 m*.

Torvosaurus ('savage lizard') of the Morrison Formation of Utah, which was not described until 1979, was another extremely bulky carnosaur. Its discoverer, Jim Jensen, thinks it may have weighed as much as 6 tonnes although it was only 30 ft *9·1 m* long.

During the summer of 1965 a Polish-Mongolian expedition led by Prof Zofia Kielan-Jaworowska discovered parts of a new theropod in the Nemegt Basin which would have exceeded the tyrannosaurids in height (but not in weight) if the rest of the skeleton was built on the same enormous scale. Only the shoulder-blades and forelimbs of this bizarre

The 18 ft 5·5 m high skeleton of Tyrannosaurus rex, *the largest of the flesh-eating dinosaurs.*

creature were uncovered, but the appendages measured an astonishing 8 ft *2·4 m* in length and ended in huge three-finger hands armed with 14 in *36 cm* sickle-shaped claws. According to Ostrom (1978), however, the bones of *Deinocheirus mirificus* ('amazing terrible hand'), as it has been named, are very similar to those of the 7 ft *2·1 m* tall ostrich dinosaur, *Struthiomimus altus* of Canada's Late Cretaceous, which measured 13 ft *4·0 m* in total length (tip of horny beak to end of tail) and weighed in the region of 200 lb *91 kg*. If it is an exaggerated version of the 'bird-mimic', as seems likely, this particular specimen must have been at least 40 ft *12·2 m* long in order to carry such huge arms, although it probably scaled less than 3 tonnes. The relatively low weight – less than half that of the tyrannosaurids – is explained by the fact that the ostrich dinosaurs were slender and graceful bipeds with small heads and long necks.

Although the ornithomimids were technically carnivorous, and Ostrom thinks the huge hands of *Deinocheirus* were designed 'for grasping and tearing apart what must have been very large victims', these fast-moving dinosaurs had weak and toothless jaws, and probably lived for the most part on tubers and small animals (e.g. termites) which they dug out of the ground with their heavy fore-claws.

Therizinosaurus ('scythe lizard'), also from the Nemegt Basin, had even larger sickle claws (up to 70 cm *27·6 in*) but Rozhdestrensky (1971) says this dinosaur had a feeble skull partially or entirely lacking teeth.

In 1937 the American Museum-Sinclair Expedition to the Mesaverde coal measures returned home with the tracks of a gigantic bipedal dinosaur which had been cut out of the roof of the Red Mountain mine near Cedaredge, Colorado. The footprints, which measured 34 in *86 cm* from the heel to the end of the middle toe and occurred at 15 ft *4·6 m* intervals, were identical in shape to smaller tracks made by the herbivorous iguanodonts of England and Belgium, although Colbert (1962) thought they were made by a huge carnosaur – 'perhaps a dinosaur very much like *Tyrannosaurus*'. Dr Barnum Brown (1938), the leader of the expedition, estimated that this mysterious ornithopod (its remains were never discovered) must have stood 35 ft *10·7 m* tall, but as this monster had a calculated hip height of 3·44 m *11 ft 3½ in*, the actual measurement was probably nearer 25 ft *7·6 m*. Even so, this animal still scaled an estimated 11 tonnes, which is the combined weight of two African bull elephants (Russell and Beland, 1976). Earlier, in 1931, another iguanodont footprint measuring an even more nightmarish 44 in *112 cm* in length and 32 in *81 cm* across the side toes was taken from the Chesterfield coalmine at Sego, Utah.

Some of the crested duck-billed dinosaurs (*Hadrosauridae*) also reached tremendous size. One of the giants of the group, *Lambeosaurus*, of the Upper Cretaceous of North America, may have reached a total length of 16 m *52 ft 6 in* (standing height *c*8·5 m *28 ft*), and Russell and Beland give the estimated weight of a Mexican lambeosaur (based on humeral length) as 13·8 tonnes, which means it was twice as heavy as *Tyrannosaurus*! No dinosaur, however, could possibly support that sort of weight on two legs for long periods, and the very large ornithopods were probably quadrupedal for much of the time when not feeding.

The largest known dinosaur eggs are those of *Hypselosaurus*, a 30 ft *9·1 m* long sauropod of the Late Cretaceous of Europe. Some examples found in the Valley of the Durance near Aix-en-Provence, southern France in October 1961 would have had – uncrushed – a long axis of 304 mm *12 in* and a shorter axis of 254 mm *10 in* giving a capacity of 3·3 litres *5·77 pints*. These eggs probably represent the maximum size to which a reptilian egg can grow. This is because the shell is much more fragile than that of a bird's egg. In a larger cell the pressure of the internal fluid would have been too great and the egg would have burst; also, if the shell had been thicker the embryo would not have been able to break out of its limey prison. As the largest hatchlings were probably no bigger than a domestic cat, the huge *Brachiosaurus* and its allies probably gave birth to live young weighing at least 1 tonne which could move with the herd almost immediately without fear of being trampled underfoot.

Despite the fact that most of the dinosaurs had exceptionally small brains for their large bodies – that of *Brachiosaurus* weighed less than 1 lb *454 g* and *Stegosaurus* only 70 g *2·47 oz* – the general shape of their skull cavities show they possessed a good sense of smell and hearing and knew what was going on around them. Their routine movements, however, were not determined by the brain but by greatly enlarged ganglia above the shoulders and hips, and these nerve centres unconsciously controlled the functions of the huge legs and tail.

If we are to believe the latest catastrophist theory, the sudden disappearance of the dinosaurs and many other forms of life at the end of the Late Cretaceous was caused by a runaway asteroid hitting the earth. According to a team of scientists at the Lawrance Berkeley Laboratory, California, USA concentrations of the rare metal iridium recently found in the fossil record indicate that the impact, a million times more violent than the biggest H-bomb explosion, threw up an enormous cloud of dust which blotted

The 1¾ tonne *Stegasaurus, which had a walnut-sized brain weighing only 2½ ounces* 71 g. *Man appeared 140 million years after it became extinct.*

An artist's impression of what 'ultrasaurus', *the largest land vertebrate so far discovered, might have looked like in life.*

Baluchitherium, *the largest land mammal ever recorded, towering over a Steppe mammoth and a record-sized African bull elephant.*

out the sun for 3–5 years and suppressed photosynthesis. When the plant life died so did the rest of the animals in the food-chain, and they claim the seeds only regerminated when the dust containing the element fell to the ground and the sunlight returned. How other large reptiles such as crocodiles managed to survive the calamity, however, is not explained!

The largest flying creature ever to inhabit the earth was probably the pterosaur *Quetzalcoatlus northropi*, which soared over the SE USA about 65 million years ago. This ultimate in flying machines, which is known only from a small number of wing bones excavated in Big Bend National Park, SW Texas during the 3-year period 1972–74 (Lawson, 1975), measured an estimated 11–12 m *36–39 ft* across the wings (weight 86 kg *190 lb*), which means it was half as big again as *Pterodon ingens* (up to 8 m *26 ft 3 in*) the previous record-holder. Earlier, this pterosaur had been credited with a wing-span of 15·5 m *51 ft*, based

on an extrapolation of the length of the humerus, the wing bone corresponding to the upper arm, but Langston (1981) says this calculation had to be adjusted downwards when it was realised that the corresponding weight of 136 kg *300 lb* would have ruled out any possibility of flapping flight.

'If creatures with such large spans really existed steady flapping flight would be impractical for them', writes Tucker (1977). 'They could carry enough muscle mass for flapping flight only if they were extremely delicately built, with a total mass of about 5 kg, of which only 16 g would comprise the body, exclusive of wings, for a span of 15 m. This body mass would be half that of a house sparrow, and such a creature could flap steadily only if the boundary layer over the wings and body could be kept laminar. Any attempt to carry a bulkier body with more powerful muscles would result in the animal being too heavy to fly by flapping.'

It is interesting to note that the bones of this

carrion eater, which probably used its long neck to probe the insides of rotting dinosaur carcases, were dug out of rocks which are essentially non-marine: so how did an animal this size, living some 400 km *250 miles* from the nearest coastline, with no cliffs or mountains in the area from which to launch itself, ever manage to get airborne? Apparently this dweller of the open plains just waited, vulture-fashion, with its wings extended and elevators raised until a strong thermal upcurrent lifted it off the ground. Once it was in the air and had gained altitude it could then wheel around the sky for long periods like its modern avian counterpart, its keen eyes constantly searching for food on the ground below, and it probably only flapped its wings on take-off and when it needed to restore its equilibrium in flight. Landing was much less of a problem because it had a very low stalling speed, and touchdowns must have been a very gentle affair.

In the 1940s a single neck vertebra of another pterosaur which must have been almost as big as *Q. northropi*, and may in fact have been identical, was uncarthed in Jordan. Until further discoveries are made, however, *Titanopteryx* as it was named must be considered a distinct species.

Britain's largest pterosaur was *Ornithodesmus latidens* from the Wealden shales of Atherfield, Isle of Wight. It had a wing expanse of 5 m *16 ft 5 in* (Hooley, 1913).

The largest marine reptile so far known to science is the short-necked pliosaur *Stretosaurus macromerus* from the Kimmeridge Clay of Oxfordshire. A mandible found in Cumnor, Oxfordshire and now in the University Museum, Oxford has a restored length of over 3 m *9 ft 10 in* and must have come from an individual measuring at least 50 ft *15·2 in* in total length. *Kronosaurus queenslandicus*, which swam in the seas around what is now Australia about 80 million years ago, was also of comparable size, and a complete skeleton in the Museum of Comparative Zoology at Harvard University, Cambridge, Massachusetts, USA measures 42 ft *12·8 m* in total length. It was collected at Army Downs, northern Queensland in 1931, and the 9 ft *2·7 m* long triangular-shaped skull contains 80 spiked teeth, each measuring up to 9 in *23 cm* in length (Fletcher, 1959). In the early 1960s the partial remains of another giant pliosaur were discovered in a clay pit being worked by the London Brick Company at Stewartby, Bedfordshire. This animal measured 21 ft *6·4 m* across the paddles and had a calculated overall length of 36 ft *11·0 m* when it was alive. A reconstruction at the British Museum has since revealed that pliosaurs had a fin on the upper part of the tail and were much more streamlined than had hitherto been realised (Newman and Tarlo, 1967).

The long-necked plesiosaurus *Elasmosaurus platyurus*, which swam in the shallow sea over what is now the state of Kansas, USA in the Late Cretaceous, measured up to 47 ft *14·3 m* in total length, of which the extremely flexible neck accounted for 25 ft *7·6 m*. Most of the ichthyosaurs were less than 30 ft *9·1 m*, but *Leptopterygius acutirostris* of the Late Jurassic of Europe had a 7 ft *2·1 m* long skull and measured about 40 ft *12·2 m* in total length.

The largest known crocodile was *Deinosuchus hatcheri* from the Upper Cretaceous of North America, which measured up to 53 ft *16·2 m* in overall length and probably weighed about 15 tonnes. It is thought to have preyed on the great dinosaurs. The huge gharial *Rhamphosuchus* from the Upper Pleistocene rocks of the Siwalik series, northern India, was even longer, reaching 60 ft *18·3 m*, but it lacked the massive skull of *Deinosuchus* and was less heavily built.

The largest known prehistoric turtle was *Stupendemys geographicus*, an enormous aberrant pelomedusid chelonian of the Pliocene. Fossil remains discovered by a Harvard University palaeontological expedition working on an outcrop of the Urumaco Formation, northern Venezuela during the summer of 1972 indicate that this turtle, which may have been a freshwater form, had a carapace (shell) measuring 2·18–2·30 m *7 ft 2 in – 7 ft 6½ in* in mid-line length and a total absolute length of at least 3·65 m *12 ft* despite a relatively short neck (Wood, 1976). This animal weighed a computed 4500 lb *2041 kg* in life.

The marine turtle *Archelon ischyros* of the Late Cretaceous of North America was also of comparable size. An almost complete skeleton discovered near the south fork of the Cheyenne River, in Custer County, South Dakota in August 1895 and later exhibited in the Peabody Museum of Natural History at Yale University, Connecticut has an overall length of 3·4 m *11 ft 2 in* (straight-line carapace length 1·93 m *6 ft 4 in*), but the 64 cm *25·2 in* long head belongs to a different individual (Wieland, 1909) and the actual skull may have been a bit bigger. This turtle weighed an estimated 6000 lb *2722 kg* in life, but 4000 lb *1814 kg* is probably a more realistic figure because, unlike *Stupendemys*, this animal had a weakly ossified carapace.

The largest prehistoric tortoise was probably *Geochelone (Colossochelys) atlas* of the Pleistocene of India, Burma, Java, Celebes and Timor. When this giant land vertebrate was first discovered in the Upper Siwalik series near Chandigarh, northern India in 1837 and composite reconstructions of the fragmentary material made, the carapace length (over the curve) was given as 12 ft *3·7 m* (Falconer and

Cautley, 1844), but this measurement was in error. In 1923 Dr Barnum Brown, Curator of Fossil Reptiles at the American Museum of Natural History, found the first complete (although fragmented) carapace in the same locality and shipped back the pieces to the museum. When reconstructed, this tortoise proved to be an old male whose shell measured 223 cm *7 ft 4 in* over the curve (straight-line length 180 cm *5 ft 11 in*), 152 cm *5 ft* in width and 89 cm *2 ft 11 in* in height. The weight of this specimen was computed to be 2100 lb *955 kg*. Much more recently *Geochelone*

shells of similar size have been collected from the Pleistocene of Florida and Texas, USA (W Auffenberg, cited by Wood, 1976).

The longest prehistoric snake was the python-like *Gigantophis garstini* of the Egyptian Eocene. Parts of a spinal column and a small piece of jaw discovered at Fayum in the Western Desert, indicate a total length of about 37 ft *11·3 m*. Another fossil giant snake, *Madtsoia bai*, from the Eocene of Patagonia, South America measured about 10 m *32 ft 10 in* in length (Simpson, 1933).

The largest known prehistoric amphibian was

The enormous carapace of Stupendemys geographicus, *the largest known turtle.*

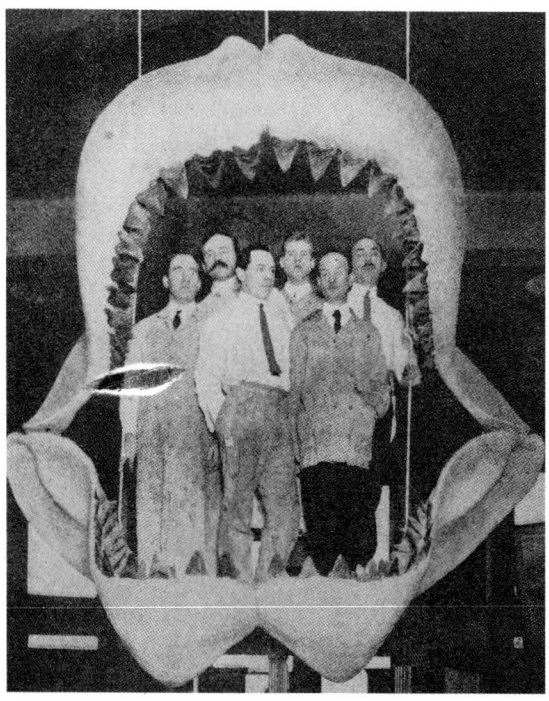

A reconstruction of the jaws of the extinct great shark, which was made at least one-third too large.

the gharial-like *Prionosuchus plummeri* of the Triassic of South America. In 1972 the fragmented remains of a specimen measuring an estimated 9 m *29 ft 6 in* in overall length were discovered in northern Brazil by a team from the University of London (Barry Cox, pers. comm.).

The largest prehistoric fish was the great shark (*Carcharodon megalodon*), an ancestor of the present-day great white shark (*C. carcharias*), which abounded in Miocene seas. In 1909 the American Museum of Natural History undertook a restoration of the jaws of this enormous marine predator, basing the size on 4 in *102 mm* long fossil teeth, and found that the jaws measured 9 ft *2·7 m* across and had a gape of 6 ft *1·8 m*. The shark was estimated to have measured 80 ft *24·4 m* in length when alive, but Randall (1973) says the reconstruction was made at least one-third too large in the mistaken belief that *all* the teeth were nearly the same size as the large ones medially in the jaws. 'Actually', he points out, 'the lateral teeth are very small compared to those at the symphysis.'

According to Randall's own calculations, based on a projection of a curve of tooth size of *C. carcharias* and the enamel height of the largest fossil tooth (115 mm *4·53 in*) in the American Museum of Natural History and the largest (117·5 mm *4·63 in*) in

the US National Museum, Washington, DC, the *maximum* length attained by *C. megalodon* was more probably in the region of 43 ft *13·1 m*. This figure, however, may be a bit on the low side because larger fossil teeth are known. In fact the same writer states that the South Australian Museum has a number of *Carcharodon* teeth collected from Lake Bonney, South Australia which have an enamel height of 127 mm *5 in*, and some of the fossil teeth collected at Shark-tooth Hill, near Bakersfield, California, USA reportedly measure nearly 6 in *152 mm* in height and weigh 12 oz *340 g*. The owner of the latter dentition must have measured about 55 ft *16·8 m* in length and weighed at least 25 tonnes.

The largest prehistoric insect was the dragonfly *Meganeura monyi*, which inhabited the Carboniferous swamps and marshes of western and central Europe about 280 million years ago. Fossil remains (i.e. impressions of wings) found at Commentry, central France indicate that it had a wing expanse of up to 70 cm *27·6 in* and may have weighed as much as 1 lb *454 g*.

Britain's largest dragonfly was *Typus* sp. (family Meganeuridae), which is known only from a wing impression found on a lump of coal in Bolsover colliery, Derbyshire, in July 1978. It had an estimated wing span of 50–60 cm *19·69–23·62 in* and lived about 300 million years ago, making it the oldest flying creature so far recorded (Paul Whalley, pers. comm.).

None of the prehistoric spiders could compare in size with the modern bird-eating varieties. The largest fossil so far recorded is probably *Eophrynus prestvicii*, a trigonotarbid of the now extinct subclass Soluta from the Devonian Rhynie Chert of Scotland, which was only 30 mm *1·18 in* long (S F Morris, pers. comm.). Some of the scorpions of prehistory, however, were much more impressive and the aquatic *Brontoscorpio anglicus* from the Lower Paleozoic of Central England dwarfed even the biggest species living today. It measured an incredible 80 cm *31·5 in* in length and must have been a truly formidable sight. The type specimen, now in the British Museum was collected by W W King in Trimpley, Worcestershire in 1933 (Kjellesuig-Waering, 1972). Mention should also be made of the gigantic millipede *Arthropleura* of the Upper Carboniferous, which attained a length of nearly 6 ft *183 cm* and is the largest known terrestrial arthropod (Rolfe and Ingham, 1967; Morris, 1979).

The largest prehistoric bird was the flightless *Dromornis stirtoni*, a huge emu-like creature which lived in central Australia some 10–11 million years ago. No complete skeletons of this species are known, but fossil leg bones belonging to 2–5 individuals found by the Ray E Lemley Expedition in late Miocene lake deposits near Alice Springs in 1974 indicate that this massive-limbed creature must have stood about 10 ft *3·0 m* tall in life and weighed in the region of 1100 lb *500 kg* (Pat V Rich, pers. comm.). It thus surpassed the recently extinct elephant bird (*Aepyornis maximus*) of southern Madagascar, which measured 9–10 ft *2·7–3·0 m* in height and tipped the scales at a computed 965 lb *438 kg* (Amadon, 1947).

Both these giant forms were exceeded in height by the biggest moa, *Dinornis maximus*, of New Zealand, but this enormously tall bird, which may have survived until *c* 1850, was built on more slender lines and probably did not exceed 520 lb *236 kg*. During the period 1937–49 a total of 44 fairly complete skeletons of *D. maximus* ranging from 10 ft *3·0 m* to 12 ft *3·7 m* tall were discovered in Pyramid Valley, Moa Swamp, North Canterbury on South Island (Feduccia, 1980).

The largest known flying bird was the giant teratorn *Argentavis magnificens*, a new genus from the Huayquerian (late Miocene) of Argentina, which had a calculated wingspan of 7·0–7·6 m *23–25 ft* and weighed about 120 kg *265 lb*. Other measurements included a standing height of 1·5 m *4 ft 11 in* and an overall length of 3·35 m *11 ft*. A fragmented partial skeleton of this huge vulture was discovered at a site 100 miles *160 km* west of Buenos Aires in 1979 by two palaeontologists from the La Plata Museum, where the bones were later deposited (Campbell and Tonni, 1980). Because of its tremendous weight, which is equivalent to that of a large hen ostrich, this outsized raptor was probably incapable of flapping flight and must have lived in areas where there were permanent soaring conditions. All it had to do then to get lift-off was simply spread its wings into the wind.

The huge egg of the elephant bird.

Baluchitherium – *the largest land mammal ever recorded. A procession marching six abreast could have walked under its belly with room to spare.*

The only other flying bird of comparable size was possibly *Gigantornis eaglesomei* from the Eocene deposits in Nigeria. It is only known from a breast-bone, but the enormous size of this fossil – and its close similarity to the breastbone of an albatross – suggest that this creature had long, narrow wings spanning as much as 20 ft *6·1 m* (Fisher and Peterson, 1964). Another giant teratorn, *Teratornis incredibilis*, from the Pleistocene of Nevada and California, and the stork-like *Osteodontornis orri* from the Miocene of California had wingspans of 4·9–5·2 m *16 ft 1 in–17 ft 0¾ in* and 5 m *16 ft 5 in* respectively.

The largest eggs laid by any known animal were those of the elephant bird (*Aepyornis maximus*) of southern Madagascar. One huge example preserved in the British Museum measures 856 mm *33·7 in* round the long axis with a circumference of 723 mm *28·5 in*, giving a capacity of 8·88 litres *2·35 gal* (=7 ostrich eggs, 40 goose eggs, 110 duck eggs, 180 hen eggs, 470 pigeon eggs or 12 000 hummingbird eggs). Another one collected in 1841 and now in the Academie des Sciences, Paris, France measures 326×390 mm *12·8×15·4 in* (Heuvelmans, 1958), and probably weighed about 27 lb *12·2 kg* with its contents.

Dr Bjorn Kurten (1968), the Finnish palaeontologist, believes these cells were probably close to the maximum possible. 'In a still larger egg', he says, 'the pressure of the internal fluid would be so great that the shell would have to be excessively thick, and as a result the young would find it difficult to get out.'

Not surprisingly, these eggs are much sought after by collectors, and one American enthusiast paid $10 000 for a specimen measuring 305×254 mm *12×10 in* (Augusta, 1966).

The largest land mammal ever recorded was *Baluchitherium*, a long-necked hornless rhinoceros which roamed over western Asia and Europe (Yugoslavia) about 35 million years ago. The bones of this gigantic browser were first discovered in the Bugti Hills, East Baluchistan in 1907–08 and described by G Pilgrim, who, after examining some teeth, thought they belonged to a giant pig (*sic*). *Baluchitherium* is also represented in *Indricotherium* and *Pristinotherium* of Kazakhstan and *Benaratherium* of Georgia, USSR. In 1922 the Central Asiatic Expedition of the American Museum of Natural History excavated an incomplete skull – together with part of the lower jaw – measuring over 4 ft 6 in *137 cm* in length and other bones at Irden Manha in the Gobi Desert, Mongolia which Prof Henry Fairfield Osborn, the great authority on fossil vertebrates, calculated must have come from a mammal measuring 17 ft 9 in *5·41 m* to the top of the shoulder hump (27 ft *8·2 m* to the crown of the raised head) and 37 ft *11·3 m* in total length. This specimen, named *Baluchitherium grangeri* after its discoverer, Walter Granger, assistant leader of the Expedition, was so huge that a human procession marching six abreast could have walked under its belly with plenty of room to spare. According to Schmidt-Nielsen (1977) *Baluchitherium* weighed about 30 tonnes in the flesh (*cf* 32 tonnes for *Apatosaurus*) and had bones strong enough to support a static load of 280 tonnes.

The only other prehistoric land mammals that approached *Baluchitherium* in size (height) were some of the giant proboscideans.

The tallest of them all was the steppe mammoth *Mammuthus (Parelephas) trogontherii* of the middle Pleistocene of central Europe. A fragmentary skeleton found at Mosbach, Germany indicates a shoulder height of at least 4·5 m *14 ft 9 in*, and De Camp (1965) gives the estimated weight of this mountain of flesh as 40 000 lb *18·14 tonnes* when alive. Fraas's mammoth (*Mammuthus primigenius frassi*) from the Steinheim gravels, Germany, which may have been closely related to *M. trogontherii*, attained a height of 4·3 m *14 ft 1 in* (16 ft *4·9 m* to the top of the hump) and the imperial mammoth (*Mammuthus imperator*) of the late Pleistocene of North America and the straight-tusked elephant *Palaeoloxodon antiquus* of the middle Pleistocene of Europe and England both reached 4 m *13 ft 1½ in*. The mastodons were even more heavily built, but their limb bones were shorter and thicker and the largest known skeleton of *Mastodon americanus* had an estimated shoulder height in life of 3·1 m *10 ft 2 in*.

At the other end of the range, the pygmy elephant *Palaeoloxodon falconeri* of the late Pleistocene of the Mediterranean islands only measured 90 cm *35·4 in* at the shoulder when fully adult, and Burian (1979) says the nasal opening in the middle of the skull may have given rise to the ancient Greek legend of the Cyclops, a fallen race of giants with one central eye.

The longest proboscidean tusks were found in *Palaeoloxodon antiquus germanicus*, which lived in

The exceptionally long tusks of a prehistoric mammoth.

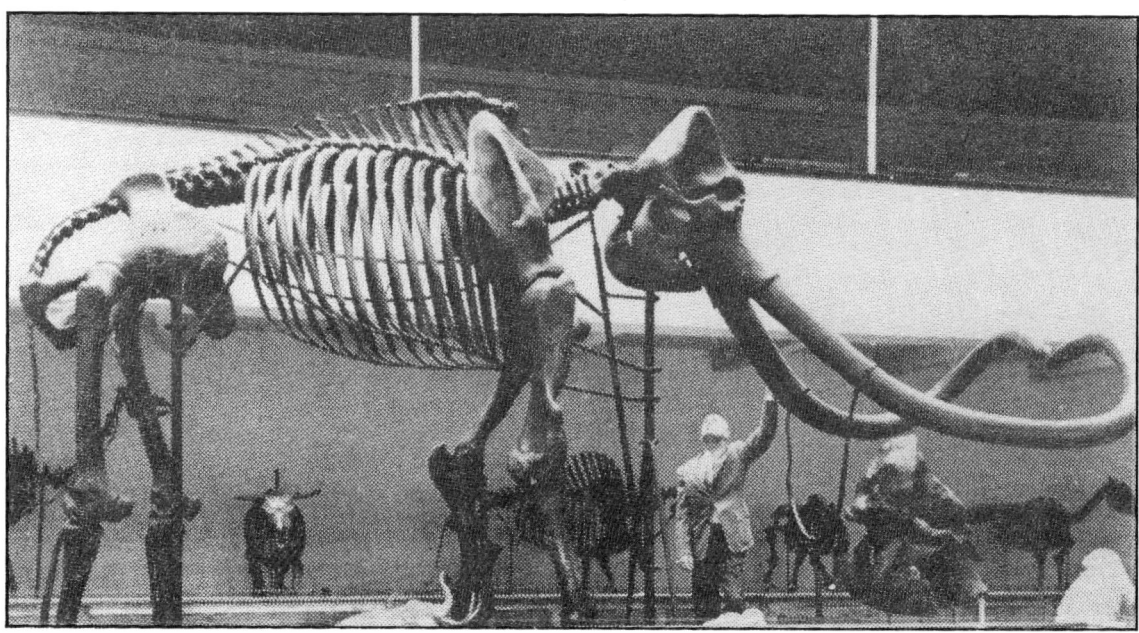

Earliest of their types

a, =Scientific name and year of discovery
b, =Location **c,** =Estimated years before present

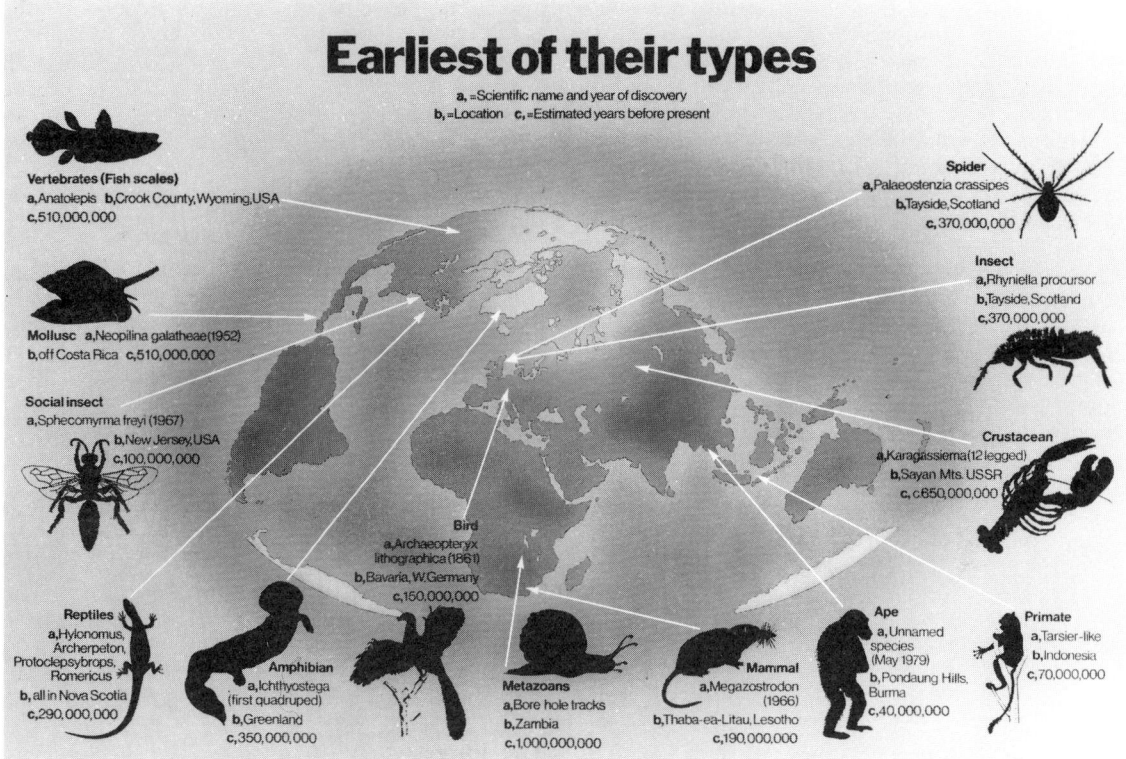

Vertebrates (Fish scales)
a,Anatolepis b,Crook County,Wyoming,USA
c,510,000,000

Mollusc a,Neopilina galatheae(1952)
b,off Costa Rica c,510,000,000

Social insect
a,Sphecomyrma freyi (1967)
b,New Jersey,USA
c,100,000,000

Spider
a,Palaeostenzia crassipes
b,Tayside,Scotland
c,370,000,000

Insect
a,Rhyniella procursor
b,Tayside,Scotland
c,370,000,000

Crustacean
a,Karagassiema(12 legged)
b,Sayan Mts.USSR
c, c650,000,000

Bird
a,Archaeopteryx
lithographica(1861)
b,Bavaria,W.Germany
c,150,000,000

Reptiles
a,Hylonomus,
Archerpeton,
Protoclepsybrops,
Romericus
b,all in Nova Scotia
c,290,000,000

Amphibian
a,Ichthyostega
(first quadruped)
b,Greenland
c,350,000,000

Metazoans
a,Bore hole tracks
b,Zambia
c,1,000,000,000

Mammal
a,Megazostrodon
(1966)
b,Thaba-ea-Litau, Lesotho
c,190,000,000

Ape
a,Unnamed
species
(May 1979)
b,Pondaung Hills,
Burma
c,40,000,000

Primate
a,Tarsier-like
b,Indonesia
c,70,000,000

northern Germany about 300000 years ago. The average length in adult bulls was 5 m *16 ft 5 in*. The spiral tusks of *P. trogontherii* were also very long when measured along the outside curve, and Kurten (1968) mentions a broken ivory from Sussenborn, Germany, which was probably 5 m *16 ft 5 in* when intact. The tusks of the famous woolly mammoth (*Mammuthus primigenius*) of the middle and late Pleistocene of the Northern Hemisphere were equally as impressive, and one example in the Franzens Museum at Brno, Czechoslovakia measures 5·02 m *16 ft 5½ in* along the outside curve (Osborne, 1936–42). In August 1933 a single tusk of an imperial mammoth measuring 16+ ft *4·9+ m* in length (the anterior end is missing), was discovered in Gorzo County near Post, Texas, USA. It was later presented to the American Museum of Natural History (Gerald E Holsinger, pers. comm.).

The heaviest fossil tusks on record are a pair belonging to a 13 ft 4 in *4·06 m* tall Columbian mammoth (*Elephas maibeni*) currently on display in the State Museum at Lincoln, Nebraska, USA which have a combined weight of 498 lb *226 kg* and measure 13 ft 9 in *4·19 m* and 13 ft 7 in *4·14 m* respectively.

They were discovered in April 1915 during an excavation for a new school in Campbell, Nebraska (Barbour, 1925).

The heaviest single tusk is one in the Museo Civico di Storia Naturale, Milan, Italy which weighs 150 kg *331 lb*. The ivory – in two pieces – measures approximately 3·58 m *11 ft 9 in* along the outside curve and has a maximum circumference of 89 cm *35 in* (Giovanni Pinna, pers. comm.).

The largest prehistoric whale was *Basilosaurus (Zeuglodon) cetoides*, which swam in the Late Eocene seas over what are now the American states of Arkansas and Alabama. In July 1961 a farmer ploughing a field near Millry in Washington County, Alabama uncovered an almost complete skeleton which was later presented to the University of Alabama in Tuscaloosa. This specimen measures 60 ft *18·3 m* in length and has a 6 ft *1·8 m* long skull. Other bones have since been found in the same state which must have come from an individual measuring 70 ft *21·3 m* in length.

One man closely associated with the discovery of this primordial whale – although not for the very best of reasons – was Dr Albert C Koch, a profit-minded German immigrant who was a talented collector of fossil bones. In 1845 he excavated a great number of *Basilosaurus* bones in various parts of Alabama and from them constructed a skeleton 114 ft *34·8 m* long which he claimed was the 'behemoth of the Bible'. It was an immediate success, and Dr Koch made a lot of money out of the credulity of the public before he took the skeleton to Europe and presented it to Frederick William IV of Prussia. The King, in turn, gave Dr Koch an annual pension of 1000 thalers, which was a very sizeable sum in those days. Later the sea–serpent, which Dr Koch named *Hydrarchos sillimani* in honour of Prof Benjamin Silliman, an American scientist, was donated to the Berlin Museum of Natural History where palaeontologists quickly discovered the fraud.

Bibliography

Agassiz, Alexander (1865). *Illustrated catalogue of the Museum of Comparative Zoology at Harvard College.* Cambridge, Mass.

Ahuja, M L & Singh, Gurkirpal (1954). Snake Bite in India. India J. Med. Res. 42:661–680.

Akeley, Carl E (1923). Gorillas – real and mythical. Nat. Hist. (N.Y.), 23(5):29–47.

Akimushkin, I I (1965). *Cephalopods of the seas of the U.S.S.R.* (Israel Program for Scientific Translations). Jerusalem.

Aldrich, Frederick A (1967). *Architeuthis* – the giant squid. Ann. Repts. 1967 American Malacol. Union, pp. 24–25.

Aldrich, F A (1968). The distribution of giant squids in N. Atlantic and particularly about the shores of Newfoundland. Sarsia, 34:393–398.

Alexander, W B (1954). Notes on *Pterodroma aterrima.* Ibis. pp. 489–491.

Allen, Glover Morrill (1938–40). *The Mammals of China and Mongolia* (Nat. Hist.) of Central Asia (XI). 2 vols. New York.

Allen, G M (1939). *Bats.* Cambridge, Massachusetts.

Amadon, D (1947). An estimated weight of the largest known bird. Condor 49: 159–164.

Amaral, Afranio do (1948). Serpentes Gigantes Boletim, Museu Paraense E. Goeldi, 10:211–37.

Amaral, A do (1976). *Brazilian snakes.* São Paulo.

Anderson, Sidney & Knox Jones, Jr (eds.) (1967). *Recent mammals of the world: a synopsis of families.* New York.

Andrews, Roy Chapman (1916). *Whale hunting with gun and camera.* London.

Anonymous (1954). 152-year-old sturgeon caught in Ontario. Comm. Fish. Rev. 16(9):28.

Anthony, H E (ed.) (1937). *Animals of America.* Garden City, N.Y.

Appleby, Leonard F (1971). *British Snakes.* London.

Arrow, Gilbert J (1951). *Horned beetles. A study of the fantastic in nature.* The Hague.

Ashley, C W (1926). *The Yankee Whaler.* New York.

Audubon, J (1840). *The Birds of America.* Edinburgh.

Augusta, J & Burian, Z (1966). *The age of monsters.* London.

Averin, Yu V (1948). Nazemnye pozuonochnye Vostochnoi Kamchatki (*Terrestrial Vertebrates of Eastern Kamchatka*). Trudy Kronotskogo Gosudarstvennogo Zapovednika. Moscow.

Azzaroli, Maria L (1968). Second specimen of *Mesoplodon pacificus*, the rarest living Beaked Whale. Monitore Zool. Ital. (N.S.) 2 (Suppl.:67–69).

Bacon, Francis (1645). *Historia Vitae et Mortis.* Dillingen.

Baerg, William J (1958). *The Tarantula.* Lawrence, Kansas.

Baikov, N A (1936). *Big game hunting in Manchuria.* London.

Baker, Samuel W (1874). *Eight years in Ceylon.* London.

Bakker, R T (1971). Ecology of the brontosaurs. Nature, 229:172–174.

Baldridge, H David (1974). *Shark Attack.* Anderson, S. Carolina.

Banziger, H (1968). Bull. Ent. Res., 58:i:159.

Barbour, Erwin H (1925). Skeletal parts of the Columbian mammoth *Elephas maibeni.* Bull. Nebraska State Museum, 10(1):96–118.

Barbour, Thomas (1924). An historic crocodile skull. Copeia 126:16.

Barclay, Ford (1915). 'The Manchurian Tiger'. In: *The Gun at Home and Abroad: The Big Game of Asia and North America.* London.

Barnes, J H (1967). Extraction of Cnidarian Venom from Living Tentacle. In: *Animal Toxins*, (eds. Russell, F. E. & Saunders, P. R.). Oxford-New York.

Barnes, T Alexander (1923). *Across the great craterland to the Congo.* London.

Barrett, Charles (1931). *Megascolides*, the world's biggest earthworm. Aus. Mus. Mag. (Sydney). 4(7):227–230.

Barrows, W B (1912). *Michigan bird life.* Mich. Agric. College, Lansing, p.103.

Bartlett, A D (1899). *Wild animals in captivity.* London.

Barton, A J & Allen, W B (1961). Observations on the feeding, shedding and growth rates of captive snakes (Boidea). Zoologica (N.Y. Zool Soc.). 46(2):83–87.

Bartsch, P (1917). Pirates of the deep, stories of the squid and octopus. Rept. Smithson Instn. (Washington, D.C.), pp. 347–375.

Baughman, J L C (1955). The oviparity of the whale shark, *Rhineodon typus*, etc. Copeia, 1:54–55.

Baumgartel, M W (1965). The Gorillas of Virunga. African Wild Life. 19(1):17–22. Johannesburg.

Baze, William (1957). *Tiger, Tiger.* London.

Beale, Thomas (1839). *The natural history of the sperm whale, to which is added a sketch of a South-Sea Whaling voyage.* London.

Beebe, William (1923). The leisurely sloth. Bull. New York Zool. Soc. 26(1):12–16.

Beebe, W (1938). *Zaca venture.* London.

Beebe, W (1947). Notes on the Hercules Beetle, *Dynastes hercules* (Linn.) at Rancho Grande, Venezuela, etc. Zoologica, New York, 32:109–116.

Bellairs, A (1969). *The life of Reptiles.* 2 vols. London.

Bellrose, F C & Sieh, J G (1960). Massed water-fowl flights in the Mississippi flyway, 1956 and 1957. Wilson Bull. 72:29–59.

Belyaev, G M (1969). New seastars from the abyssal and ultra-abyssal of the Pacific Ocean. Byull. mosk. Obsch. Ispyt. Prir. 74(3):11.

Belyaev, G M (1970). Fauna of the Kurile-Kamchatka Trench. Ultra-abyssal holothurians of the genus *Myriotrochus.* Trudy Inst. Okeanol. 86.

Belyaev, G M (1972). *Hadal bottom fauna of the world ocean.* Inst. Oceanol. Moscow (Israel Program for Scientific Translations). Jerusalem.

Belyaev, G M & Litvinova, N (1972). New Genera and species of deep-sea *Ophiuroidea.* Byulletin 'mosk. obshch. Ispyt. Prir. (Otd. Biol.) 3:5–20.

Belyaev, G M & Mironov, A N (1977). *Holothuroidea* of genus *Myriotrochus* from the deep-sea trenches of the Pacific ocean. Trudy Inst. Okeanol., 108:165–172.

Benchley, Belle J (1930). Experiences with elephant seals. Parks and Recreation, 13(5):317–320.

Benchley, B J (1940). Mountain gorillas in San Diego Zoo. Parks and Recreation, 24(1):19–27.

Benchley, B J (1942). Mbongo–1926–42. Parks and Recreation, 25(9):377–380.

Benedict, Francis G (1936). *The physiology of the elephant.* Carnegie Instit. of Washington.

Benedict, Francis G & Lee, Robert C (1938). Further

observations on the physiology of the elephant. J. Mamm. 19(2):175–194.

Bennet, D B (1974). Growth of the edible crab (*Cancer pagurus* L.) off South-West England. J. mar. biol. Ass. UK. 54:803–23.

Bennett, F D (1840). *Narrative of a Whaling Voyage around the Globe, from the year 1833 to 1836*. London.

Bennett, George (1860). *Gatherings of a naturalist in Australasia*. London.

Bere, Rennie (1966). *The African elephant*. London-New York.

Berg, Leo S (1962). *Freshwater fishes of the USSR and adjacent countries*. Vol. 1. (Israel Program for Scientific Translations). Jerusalem.

Bergman, Sten (1936). Observations on the Kamchatkan bear. J. of Mamm. 17(2).

Berzin, A, Tikhomirov I & Troinin, V (1963). Has Steller's sea-cow disappeared? (in Russian). Piroda, 8:73–75. Moscow.

Berzin, A (1972). *The Sperm Whale* (Israel Program for Scientific Translations). Jerusalem.

Bettini, S (1964). Toxicon. 2, p. 93.

Bigelow, Henry B & Schroeder, William C (1948). Fishes of the Western North Atlantic. Mem. Sears Foundn. Mar. Res. Yale Univ. (New Haven, Conn.). Part 1:1–576.

Bishri, R M (1981). Age, growth and maturity of the Nile Perch. *Lates niloticus* (L). in Jebel Aulyia Reservoir (Sudan). Zool. Soc. Egypt Bull. 30:15–28.

Bisset (1875). *Sport and War*. London.

Blainville, H de (1812). Memoire sur le squale pelerin. Ann. Mus. His. Nat. Paris, 10:88.

Blandford, N (1895–98). *Avifauna of British India*. London.

Blond, Georges (1954). *The Great Whale Game*. London.

Bogert, Charles M & Del Camp, R (1956). The Gila monster and its allies. Bull. Amer. Mus. Nat. His., 109:151–154.

Bonner, W N (1971). An aged Gray Seal (*Halichoeris grypus*). J. Zool. 164:261–262.

Boschma, H (1938). On the teeth and some other particulars of the sperm whale (*Physeter macrocephalus* L.). Temminckia, 111:151–278. Leiden.

Boulenger, G A (1889). *Catalogue of the chelonians, rhynchocephalians and crocodiles in the British Museum* (N.H.). London.

Boulenger, G A (1893). Specimens of *Rana temporia* from Scotland. Ann. Scot. Nat. Hist. 202–204.

Boulenger, G A (1907). *The Fishes of the Nile*. London.

Bourliere, Francois (1955). *The natural history of mammals*. London.

Boyd, Hugh (1972). In: *The Swans*. (Peter Scott and the Wildlife Trust). pp. 17–28. London.

Brander, A Dunbar (1923). *Wild Animals in Central India*. London.

Breland, Osmond P (1963). *Animal life and lore*. New York-London.

Brink, F H van den (1967). *A field guide to the mammals of Britain and Europe*. London.

Bristowe, W S (1947). *Spiders*. Harmondsworth.

Bristowe, W S (1958). *The world of spiders*. London.

Bristowe, W S (1971). *The world of spiders*. (revised edition). London.

Brock, Stanley E (1967). *More about Leemo*. London.

Brockmeier, H (1896). Beitrage zur Biologie unsere Susswassmollusken. Nachrbl. deutsch. malak. Ges., 57.

Brongersma, L D (1972). European Atlantic turtles. Zoologische Verhandelingen Nr. 121. Leiden.

Brown, Barnum (1931). The largest known land tortoise. Nat. Hist. 31(2):186–188.

Brown, B (1938). The mystery dinosaur. Nat. Hist. 41:190–202, 235.

Brown, Joe D (1962). The monster fish of American rivers. Sports Illustrated 17(12):64–78.

Brown, Leslie & Amadon, Dean (1968). *Eagles, hawks and falcons of the world*. 2 vols. London.

Brown, L (1970). *Eagles*. London–New York.

Brown, L (1976). *Birds of prey, their biology and ecology*. London.

Brown, Robert (1973). Has the Thylacine really vanished? Animals Mag. Sept. pp. 416–419.

Brunn, Anton F *et al* (1956). The Galathea deep sea expedition. 1950–52.

Bruyns, W F (1971). *Field Guide of Whales and Dolphins*. Amsterdam.

Bryden, Henry (1936). *Wild life in South Africa*. London.

Buchanan, J B (1964). A comparative study of some features of the biology of *Amphiura filiformis* and *Amphiura chiajei* (Ophiuroidea) considered in relation to their distribution. J. Mar. Biol. Ass. U.K., 44:565–576.

Buchanan, J B (1967). Dispersion and demography of some infaudal echinoderm populations. In: *Echinoderm Biology* (ed. n. Millot). Symp. Zool. Soc. Lond., 20:1–11.

Bucherl, Wolfgang (1971). Classification, Biology and Venom extractions of Scorpions. In: *Venomous Animals and their Venoms. 3. Venomous invertebrates* (eds. Bucherl, W. & Buckley, E. E.), pp. 317–347. New York–London.

Buckland, Frank (1877). *Reports on the crab and lobster fisheries of England and Wales, of Scotland and Ireland*. London.

Buckland, William (1824). Notice on the *Megalosaurus* or great fossil lizard of Stonesfield. Trans. Geol. Soc. London, 2(1):390–396.

Budker, Paul (1971). *The Life of Sharks*. London.

Buffon, Georges Louis (1778). *Epoques de la Nature*, Paris.

Bull, H O (1934). Aquarium observations on the rate of growth and enemies of the common starfish (*Asterias rubens* L.). Rep. Dove Marine Lab., 3(2):60.

Bull, H O (1938). The growth of *Psammechinus miliaris* (Gml) under aquarium conditions. Rep. Dove Marine Lab., 6:39.

Buller, Fred (1979). *The Domesday Book of Mammoth Pike*. London.

Burbridge, Ben (1928). *Gorilla. Tracking and capturing the ape-man of Africa*. London.

Burden, Douglas (1927). *Dragon lizards of Komodo*. New York–London.

Buresch, I & Beron, P (1962). Izv. Zool. Inst. s. Muz., Bulgar. Akad. Nauk.

Burgess, S G (1941). A large black rock scorpion. Field, 12 April, p. 35.

Burian, Zdenek (1979). *Prehistoric Animals and Plants*. London.

Burne, E C (1943). A record of gestation periods and growth of trained elephant calves in the Southern Shan

States, Burma. Proc. Zool. Soc. London, 133:27.

Burr, Malcolm (1939). *The Insect Legion*. London.

Burton, Maurice (1965). *Systematic dictionary of mammals of the world*. London.

Burton, R G (1928). *Sport and Wild Life in the Deccan*. London.

Bussman, J (1946). Beitrag zur Kenntnis der Brutbiologie und des Wachstums des Grosses Buntspechts, *Dryobates major* (L.). Ornith. Beob. 43:137–156.

Bustard, H R & Limpus, C (1970). First international recapture of an Australian tagged loggerhead turtle. Herpetologica. 26:358–359.

Butler, Amos W (1898). *The birds of Indiana*. 22nd Ann. Rept. Dept. Geol. Nat. Res. Indiana. p. 626, Indianapolis.

Butt, Khan Saheb Jamshed (1963). *Shikar*. London.

Cairncross, B L (1956). Size of bull frogs (letter). African Wildl. 10(4). Dec.

Caldwell, Norman (1937). *Fangs of the Sea*. London.

Camp, Sprague L de (1965). Mammoths and Mastodons. Fantasy and Science Fiction, New York. May:35–44.

Camp, S L de & De Camp, Catherine Crook (1968). *The Day of the Dinosaur*. New York.

Campbell, Bruce & Ferguson-Lees, James (1972). *A fieldguide to birds' nests*. London.

Campbell, George (1877). *Long-letters from 'The Challenger'*. London.

Campbell, Kenneth J & Tonni, Eduardo P (1980). A New Genus of Teratorn from the Huayquerian of Argentine (Aves:Teratornithidae). Contribs. in Science. Nat. His. Mus. Los Angeles County. 330:59–68.

Campbell, William A (1937). (letter). African Wildl. (13 Feb.). Johannesburg.

Caras, Roger (1964). *Dangerous to man*. Philadelphia. (1976) 2nd edit.

Carpenter, Nelson (1906). A small egg. Condor, 8(March):57.

Carr, A & Hirth, A (1962). The ecology and migration of sea turtles. 5. Comparative features of isolated green turtle colonies. Am. Mus. Nov. 2091:1–42.

Carr, Carlyle (1927). The speed of pronghorn antelope. J. Mamm. 8(33):249–250.

Carrington, Richard (1958). *Elephants. A short account of their natural history, evolution and influence on mankind*. London.

Catala, R L (1964). *Carnival under the Sea*. Paris.

Cavendish, A E T (1894). *Korea and the Sacred White Mountain*. London.

Chaillu, Paul B (1861). *Exploration and adventures in Equatorial Africa*. New York.

Chamberlain, R V & Ivie, Wilton (1935). The Black Widow Spider and its Varieties in the United States. Bull. Univ. of Utah Vol. XXV, Salt Lake City.

Chandrasekhara, Rao G (1968). On *Psammothuria ganapatii n.ge., n.sp.*, an interstitial holothurian from the beach sands of Waltair coast and its autecology. Proc. Indian Acad. Sci. 67B:202.

Chapman, R F (1971). *The Insects. Structure and function*. London.

Charig, Alan (1979). *A new look at the Dinosaurs*. London.

Chasen, Frederick N (1940). A handlist of Malaysian animals. A systematic list of the Malay Peninsula, Sumatra, Borneo and Java, including the adjacent small islands. Bull. Raffles Mus. (Singapore), 15:1–209.

Cherfas, Jeremy (1978). A tale of Two Turtles. New Scientist (25 May):514–516.

Chisholm, Alec H (1948). *Bird Wonders of Australia*. Sydney–London.

Clapham (1922). *The Book of the Otter*. London.

Clark, Ailsa M (1962). Starfishes and their relations. Pub. Brit. Mus. (N.H.) London.

Clark, H L (1925). A Catalogue of the recent sea-urchins (Echinoidea) in the collection of the British Museum (N.H.). Trustees Brit. Mus.:1–28.

Clark, J T (1966). The Distribution of *Lucanus cervus* (L.) in Britain. Entomol. Monthly Mag. 102:199–204.

Clark, Leonard (1954). *The Rivers ran East*. New York.

Clarke, James (1969). *Man is the Prey*. London.

Clarke, Malcolm R (1966). A review of the systematics and ecology of oceanic squids. Adv. Mar. Biol. 4:93–300 (ed. Frederick S. Russell). London–New York.

Clarke, Robert (1955). A giant squid swallowed by a sperm whale. Norsk. Hvalfangst-Tidende, 44(10):589–593.

Clay, Lesley (1962). Feather fashions. Africana (Dec.), p.41.

Cloudsley-Thompson, J L (1955). Some aspects of the biology of centipedes and scorpions. Naturalist, pp. 147–53.

Cloudsley-Thompson, J L (1958). *Spiders, Scorpions, Centipedes and Mites*. London.

Coates, C W *et al* (1937). The electric discharge of the electric eel *Electrophorus electricus* (L.). Zoologica (N.Y.), 22(1),1–31.

Cochran, Doris M (1943). Poisonous reptiles of the world. War Background Stud. Smithson. Instit. 10, Washington D.C.

Cochran, D M (1967). *Living Amphibians of the World*. New York.

Coffey, D J (1977). *The Encyclopaedia of Sea Mammals*. London.

Colbert, Edwin H (1962a). *Dinosaurs. Their Discovery and their World*. London.

Colbert, E H (1962b). The weights of dinosaurs. Amer. Mus. Novitates, 2076:1–16.

Collett, R (1905). Norges Fiske III. Slutning. Forh. Vidensk. Selsk. Krist. (7):1–173.

Comfort, Alex (1964). *Ageing – The Biology of Senescence*. London.

Conant, Roger & Hudson, Robert (1949). Longevity records for reptiles and amphibians in the Philadelphia Zoological Garden. Herpetologica, 5:1–8.

Constant, P & Cannonge, B (1957). Evaluation de la vitesse de vol des *Miniopteres*. Mammalia, 21:310–312.

Cooch, G (1955). Observations on the autumn migration of Blue Geese. Wilson Bulletin, 67:171–174.

Coolidge, Harold J (1936). Zoological results of the George Vanderbilt African Expedition of 1932. Part 4. Notes on four gorillas from the Sanga River region. Proc. Acad. Nat. Sci. Phila., 88:479–501.

Corbet, G B & Southern, H N (eds.) (1977). *The Handbook of British Mammals*. 2nd edit. Oxford–London–Edinburgh–Melbourne.

Corbett, Jim (1946). *Man-eaters of Kumaon*. London.

Corbett, J (1948). *The man-eating leopard of Rudraprayag*. New York–Bombay.

Corbin, G B (1873). Large otter. Zoologist, 7:3304.

Cott, Hugh B (1954). The palatability of the eggs of birds: mainly based upon observations of an Egg Panel Proc. Zool. Soc. Lond. 124:335–463.

Cott, H B (1961). Scientific results of an inquiry into the ecology and economic status of the Nile crocodile (*Crocodylus niloticus*) in Uganda and Northern Rhodesia. Trans. Zool. Soc. Lond., 29:211–337.

Cottam, Clarence *et al* (1942). Flight and running speeds of birds. Wilson Bull., 54(2):121–131.

Cousins, Don (1972a). Body measurements and weights of wild and captive gorillas. *Gorilla gorilla.* Zool. Garten N.F., Leipzig, 41(6):261–277.

Cousins, D (1972b). Gorillas in captivity past and present. Zool. Garten N.F., Leipzig, 42(5/6):251–281.

Cousins, D (1979). External measurements and weights of captive gorillas. Int. Zoo. News (Nov.) pp. 12–17.

Cousteau, Jacques-Yves & Diole, Philippe (1973). *Octopus and Squid. The Soft Intelligence.* New York.

Covacevich, J & Wombey, J (1976). Recognition of *Parademansia microlepidotus* (McCoy) (Elapidae), a dangerous Australian snake. Proc. Roy. Soc. Qd. 87:29.

Cramp, Bourne & Saunders (1974). *The Seabirds of Britain and Ireland.* London.

Crandall, Lee S (1964). *Management of wild mammals in captivity.* Chicago–London.

Crile, George (1941). *Intelligence, power and personality.* New York.

Cronwright-Schreiner, S C (1925). *The migrating spring-bucks of South Africa.* London.

Cross, H & Fischer, P (1862). Nouveaux documents sur les cephalopodes J. Conch (Paris), 10:124–140.

Crowcroft, Peter (1954). An Ecological Study of British Shrews. D. Phil. unpubl. thesis. Univ. of Oxford.

Crowcroft, P (1956). On the life span of the Common shrew (*Sorex araneus* L.). Proc. Zool. Soc. London, 127:285–292.

Curran, C H (1945). *Insects of the Pacific world.* New York.

D'Abrera, Bernard (1975). The largest butterfly in the world. Wildlife, 17(12).

Dales, R Phillips (1963). *Annelids.* London.

Dall, William H (1885). The arms of the octopus, or devil fish. Science 6:432.

Dalyell, J G (1848). *Rare and remarkable animals of Scotland.* London.

D'Amour, F E, Becker, F E & Van Riper, W (1936). The Black Widow Spider. Quart. Rev. of Biol. XI.

Dance, S Peter (1966). *Shell collection: an illustrated history.* London.

Dance, S P (1969). *Rare shells.* London.

Daniel, R J (1925). *Animal life in the sea.* London.

Davies, David H (1964). *About Sharks and Shark attacks.* Pietermaritzburg, South Africa.

Davies, G (1936). Distribution of the Badger in Denbigh, and Notes on Breeding and other habits. J. Anim. Ecol. 5:97–104.

Davis, R B, Herreid, C F & Short, H L (1962). Mexican free-tailed bats in Texas. Ecological Monographs, 323:11–46.

Dawson, T J & Taylor, C R (1973). Energy cost of locomotion in Kangaroos. Nature. Lond. 246:313–314.

Day, Francis (1880–84). *The fishes of Great Britain and Ireland.* London–Edinburgh. Vol. II.

Dean, S (1954). Length of Python. North Queensland Nat. 22(1):13–14.

Deane, R (1908). The passenger pigeon (*Ectopistes, migratorius*) in confinement. Auk, 25:181–183.

Debenham, F (1955). *Nyasaland.* H.M.S.O. London.

De Jong (1927). Anatomische Notizen uber *Varanus Komodoensis, Ouwens.* Zool. Anz. 70:65.

Dell, R K (1970). A specimen of the giant squid *Architeuthis* from New Zealand. Records Dominion Mus., 7(4):25–36.

Dement'ev, J & Gladkov, P (1966). *The birds of the Soviet Union.* Vol. 1. (Israel Program for Scientific Translations). Jerusalem.

Demoll, R (1918). *Der Flug der Insekten under der Vogel.* Jena.

Deraniyagala, P (1939). *The tetrapod reptiles of Ceylon.* Vol. 1. *Testudinates and crocodilians.* Colombo Nat. Mus., Ceylon.

Deraniyagala, P (1955). *Some extinct elephants, their relatives and the two living species.* Colombo Nat. Mus., Ceylon.

Desmond, Adrian J (1975). *The Hot-Blooded Dinosaurs.* London.

Dice, L R (1945). Minimum intensities of illumination under which owls can find dead prey by sight. American Naturalist, 79:385–416.

Dinsdale, Tim (1966). *The Leviathans.* London.

Ditmars, Raymond L (1933). *Snakes of the World.* New York.

Ditmars, R L (1936). *Reptiles of the World.* New York.

Dobie, J Frank (1943). *The Long-Horns.* London.

Donisthorpe, H (1927). *British ants: their life-history and classification.* London.

Donisthorpe, H (1936). The oldest insect on record. Mammalia (Paris), 18:231–236.

Dowling, Herndon G (1961). How old are they and how big do they grow? Animal Kingdom, 64(6) Nov–Dec.

Downey, M E (1972). *Midgardia xandaros,* new genus, new species a large brisingid starfish from the Gulf of Mexico. Proc. Biol. Soc. Washington, 84(48):421–426.

Downey, M & Wellington T (1978). Bull. Marine Sci. 28(2):375.

Dresner, Simon (1973). King Cobra's Longevity Record. Intl. Zoo News No. 13 (31 May).

Duerden, R (1919). Breeding Experiments with North African and South African Ostriches. 1, 2 and 3 of series. Govt. Dept. of Agriculture.

Dugay, R (1968). Note sur la frequence de la tortue luth *Dermochelys coriacea* L. pres des cotes de la Charente Maritime. Ann. Soc. Nat. Char. Maritime 4(8):8–16.

Dunn, Emmett, R (1944). Los Generos de Anfibios y Reptiles de Colombia, Ill'Caldasia, 3:155–224.

Dunson, William (ed.) (1975). *The biology of sea snakes.* Baltimore–London–Tokyo.

Duron, Michele (1978). Contribution a l'etude de la Biologie de *Dermochelys coriacea* (Linn.) dans les Pertuis Charentais. Bordeaux.

Eason, E H (1964). *Centipedes of the British Isles.* London.

Eaton, Randall L (1974). *The Cheetah: the biology, ecology and behaviour of an endangered species.* London–Toronto–Melbourne.

Edgerton, H, Niedrach, R and Riper, W (1951). Freezing the flight of hummingbirds. Nat. Geogr. Mag., 100(2):245–261.

Edmondston, L (1838). Observations on the distinctions, history and hunting of seals in the Shetland Islands. Wernerian Nat. His. Soc. Mem. 7:1–48.

Edwards, Eric (1979). *The Edible Crab and its fishery in British waters.* Farnham, Surrey.

Einarsen, Arthur S (1948). *The pronghorn antelope and its management.* Wildl. Management Instit. Washington, D.C.

Eisentraut, M (1936). Ergebnisse der Fledermausberingung nach dreijahhriger Versvchzeit. Z. Morphol. Oekol. Tiere 31:1–26.

Elkins, N (1979). Thermal soaring of raptors. British Birds. 72(1):40.

Ellerman, J R & Morrison-Scott, T C (1951). *Checklist of Palaearctic and Indian mammals, 1758–1946.* Brit. Mus. (N.H.), London.

Evans, Glyn (1972). The prodigious jump of the click beetle. New Scientist, 21 Sept. pp. 490–493.

Evans, G & Blower, J G (1973). A Jumping Millipede. Nature 246:427–428.

Evans, W (1894). On the reptiles and batrachians of the Edinburgh district. Proc. Phys. Soc. Edinb. 12:490–526.

Falconer, H & Cautley, P T (1844). On the osteological characters and palaeontological history of the *Colossochelys atlas*, a fossil tortoise of enormous size from the Tertiary strata of the Siwalik Hills in the north of India. Proc. Zool. Soc. London, 12:54–55.

Fawcett, Percy H (1953). *Exploration Fawcett.* London.

Feder, Howard M & Christensen, Aage Moller (1966). Aspects of asteroid biology. In: *Physiology of Echinodermata* (ed. Richard A. Boolootian). pp. 87–128. New York–London–Sydney.

Feduccia, Alan (1980). *The Age of Birds.* Harvard University Press. Cambridge, Massachusetts–London.

Fell, H Barraclough (1966). The ecology of Ophiuroids In: *Physiology of Echinodermata* (ed. Richard A. Boolootian), pp. 129–144. New York–London–Sydney.

Figurier, Louis (1894). *Reptiles and Birds.* London.

Filipek, Karl (1934). Aus der wildschatzkammer des fernen ostens. In: *Deutsches weidwerk und jagd in uberseeischen landern* (ed. Kaiser-Verlag B. Leipa). Prague–Vienna–Leipzig.

Firth, Frank E (1939). Giant lobsters. New Eng. Nat., 9:84–87.

Fish, C J & Cobb, M C (1954). Noxious marine animals of the central and western Pacific Ocean. U.S. Fish Wildlife Serv. 36:17–20.

Fisher, H I (1946). Adaptations and comparative anatomy of the locomotor apparatus of New World vultures. Amer. Midland Nat., 35:545–727.

Fisher, J & Lockley, R M (1954). *Sea-Birds.* Boston.

Fisher, J & Peterson, R T (1964). *The world of birds: a comprehensive guide to general ornithology.* London.

Fisher, James *et al* (1969). *The Red Book. Wildlife in Danger.* London.

Fisher, W K (1928). Asteroidea of the N. Pacific and adjacent waters. II Forcipulata (pt. 1). U.S. Nat. Mus. Bull. 76:1–245.

Fitter, Richard (1968). *Vanishing wild animals of the world.* London.

Fitter, Richard & Scott, Peter (1978). *The Penitent Butchers.* The Fauna Preservation Society 1903–1978. London.

Fleay, David (1952). With a wedge-tailed eagle at the nest. The Emu, 52(1):1–16.

Flecker, H (1936). Cone shell mollusc poisoning with report of a fatal case. Med. J. Aust. 1:464.

Flecker, H & Cotton, B C (1955). Fatal bite from octopus. Med. J. Aust., 2:89.

Flerov, K K (1960). *Musk deer and deer (Fauna of the USSR: Mammals,* Vol. 1, no. 2). Washington. (Israel Program for Scientific Translations).

Fletcher, H O (1959). A giant marine reptile from the Cretaceous rocks of Queensland, Aust. Mus. Mag. (Sydney), 13(2):47–49.

Flinders, M (1798). *A voyage to Terra Australis.* 2 vols. London.

Flower, Stanley S (1906). The span of large birds. J. Bomb. Nat. Hist. Soc. Vol. XXV:752–753.

(1925). Contributions to our knowledge of the duration of life in vertebrate animals. Part I, Fishes, p. 247. Part II, Batrachians, p. 269. Part III, Reptiles, p. 911. Part IV, Birds, p. 1365. Proc. Zool. Soc. London.

(1931). Part V, Mammals, p. 145.

(1935). Further notes on the duration of life in animals. Part I, Fishes.

(1936). Part II, Amphibians, p. 369.

(1937). Part III, Reptiles.

(1947–48). Part V. The alleged and actual ages to which elephants live, p. 680.

Flower, Sir William Henry (1884). *Catalogue of the specimens illustrating the osteology and dentition of vertebrate animals, recent and extinct, contained in the Museum of the Royal College of Surgeons in England.* Pt. 2. Mammalia. London.

Forster, R R (1958). The Spiders of the Family Symphytognathidae. Trans. Roy. Soc. N.Z. 86 (3–4):269–329.

Fountain, P (1914). *The River Amazon.* London.

Francois, Donald D. (1960). Freshwater crayfishes. Aust. Mus. Mag. 13(7):217–221.

Fraser, F C (1974). *Report on Cetacea stranded on the British coasts from 1948 to 1966.* No. 14, Trustees Brit. Mus. (N.H.), London.

Freiheit, Clayton F (1979). A visit to four Chinese Zoos. Intl. Zoo News, 160:9–17.

Friedel, E (1880). Die lebenden Wasserthiere auf der Internationalen Fischerei-Ausstellung zu Berlin im Jahre 1880. Zool. Gart. 21:323.

Frisch, Karl von (1975). *Animal Architecture.* London.

Frith, H J (1962). *The Mallee fowl.* Sydney.

Frith, H J & Calaby, J H (1969). *Kangaroos.* London.

Frost, Nancy (1934). Notes on a giant squid (*Architeuthis* sp.) captured at Dildo, Newfoundland in December 1933. Rept. Newfoundland Fish Comm., 22:100–114.

Frost, W E & Kipling, C (1949). The determination of the age and growth of the pike (*Esox lucius* L.) from scales and opercular bones. J. Cons. Exp. Mer. 24:314–41.

Furlong, M & Pill, V (1970). *Starfish methods of preserving and guides to identification.* Ellison Industries, Edmonds, Washington. pp. 1–104.

Gaetke, Heinrich (1895). *Heligoland as an ornithological observatory: the results of fifty years' experience.* Edinburgh.

Gale, U Toke (1974). *Burmese timber elephants.* Rangoon.

Gambaryan, P P (1974). *How mammals run.* (Israel Program for Scientific Translations). Jerusalem–London.

Gambell, Ray (1968). Aerial observations of Sperm whale behaviour. Norsk Hvalfangst-Tidende, Nr. 6, Nov/Dec.

Gander-Dower, K C (1938). Racing cheetahs: the greyhounds of the East. Indian Wildl. (Lucknow), 3(2):62–65.

Gatti, Attilio (1932). *The King of the Gorillas*. New York.

Gawn, R W (1948). Aspects of the locomotion of whales. Nature. 161 (4080): 44–46. London.

George, J C (1970). *Animals can do anything*. London.

Gertsch, W J (1979). *American spiders*. New York–Toronto–London.

Gewalt, W. (1979). The Commerson's dolphin (*Cephalorhynchus commersonii*) – capture and first experiences. Aquatic Mammals, 7(2):37–40.

Gibson, J D & Sefton, A R (May 1960). Second report of the New South Wales albatross study group. The Emu, 60:125–130.

Gibson-Hill, C A (1947). Field notes on terrestrial crabs. Bull. Raffles. Mus. 18:43–52.

Gibson-Hill, C A (1948). Giant King Cobra. Field (23 Oct.).

Giglioli and Salvadori (1868). Atti. Soc. Ital. Sci. Nat. 11, p. 451.

Gilbert, Perry W (ed.) (1963). *Sharks and survival*. Boston.

Gilliard, E T (1958). *Living birds of the World*. Garden City, N.Y.

Gironiere, Paul de la (1854). *Twenty years in the Philippine Islands*. London.

Goodden, Robert (1978). *British Butterflies*. Newton Abbot.

Gordon, Clyde (1947). The queen is dead – long live the queen! Parks and Recreation, 30(12):591–92.

Gordon, Hugh (1969). Something about Nile perch. Africana (Sept.), pp. 27–30.

Gordon, Seton (1955). *The Golden Eagle*. London.

Graham, Alistair and Beard, Peter (1973). *Eyelids of Morning*. Greenwich. Conn.

Grant, E M (1972). *Guide to Fishes*. Brisbane.

Grasset, E (1946). 'La Vipere du Gabon'. Acta Tropica, III:101.

Gray, James (1968). *Animal Locomotion*. London.

Gray, John Edward (1861). On the Height of the Gorilla. Ann. Mag. Nat. Hist. 8(3):349–50.

Green, Lawrence (1958). *South African beachcomber*. Cape Town.

Greenewalt, Crawford H (1960). *Hummingbirds*. Pub. Amer. Mus. Nat. Hist. New York.

Greenewalt, C H (1962). Dimensional relationships for flying animals. Smithson. Misc. Coll. 144(2):1–46.

Greer, A E (1974). On the maximum total length of the salt-water crocodile (*Crocodylus porosus*). J. Herpetology 8(4):381–384.

Gregor, Paul (1962). *Amazon Fortune Hunter*. London.

Greig, J A (1921). Echinodermata. Rep. Sci. Res. Michael Sars N. Atlant. Deep-sea Exped. 1910, 3(2):1–47.

Griffin, D R & Hitchcock, H B (1965). Probable 24-year longevity records for *Myotis lucifugus*. J. of Mammal. 46:332.

Groves, Colin P (1967). Ecology and Taxonomy of the Gorilla. Nature 213:890–93.

Grzimek, Bernhard (1963). *Twenty animals, one man*. London.

Grzimek, B (1970). *Among animals of Africa*. London.

Gudger, E W (1915). On the occurrence in the southern hemisphere of the basking or bone shark, *Cetorhinus maximus*. Science, 42(1088):653–56.

—— (1934). The largest freshwater fishes – the giant sturgeons of the world. Nat. Hist. (N.Y.), 34:282–286.

—— (1936). From atom to colossus. Nat. Hist. (N.Y.), 36:27–30.

—— (1940). Whale Sharks rammed by Ocean vessels. New Eng. Nat. vol. 7.

—— (1941). The quest for the smallest fish. Nat. Hist. (N.Y.), 48:216–223.

—— (1942). The giant fishes of North America. Sci. Monthly, 49:115–121.

—— (1943). The giant freshwater fishes of South America. Sci. Monthly, 57:500–513.

—— (1944). The giant freshwater perch of Africa. Sci. Monthly, 58:269–272.

—— (1945a). Giant freshwater fish of Europe. Field (Aug.).

—— (1945b). Is the giant catfish, *Silurus glanis*, a predator on man? Sci. Monthly, 61:451–454.

—— (1945c). The giant freshwater fishes of Asia. J. Bomb. Nat. Hist. Soc., 45(3):1–17.

Guggisberg, C A W (1964). The bird that wooed my Landrover. Animals Mag. 4(7):179–183. (7 July).

Guggisberg, C A W (1972). *Crocodiles: their natural history, folklore and conservation*. Newton Abbot.

Guggisberg, C A W (1975). *Wild cats of the world*. London.

Guiler, Eric R (1966). In pursuit of the Thylacine. Oryx, 8(5):307–310.

Guitart, Dario & Milera, Jose (1975). El Monstruo Marino de Cojimar. Mar y Pesca 104:10–11. Havana.

Gunter, Gordon (1941). Occurrence of the manatee in the United States with records from Texas. J. of Mamm., 22(1).

Gunther, A (1870). Cat. Fish. Brit. Mus. (N.H.), 8:392. London.

Gunther, A (1875). Notes on some mammals from Madagascar. *Chirogaleus trichotis*, Proc. Zool. Soc. London. pp. 78–79.

Guppy, Nicholas (1963). The dreaded Piranha. Animals Mag. 2(1):16–19 (25 June).

Guppy, N (1963). The Largest Snake in the World. Animals Mag. (30 July).

Gurney, J H (1899). Comparative ages to which birds live. Ibis, pp. 19–42.

Gurney, Robert (1950). The lobster. Illus. Lond. News (30 Sept.) p. 14.

Haeckel, Ernst (1883). *India and Ceylon*. London.

Hafeli, Hans-Peter (1971). Zur Fortpflanzungsbiologie des Alpensalamanders. Revue suisse de Zoologie 78(2):235–293.

Hagenbeck, Carl (1909). *Beasts and men*. London.

Hall, E R (1951). American weasels. Univ. Kansas Publ., Mus. Nat. Hist., 4:1–466.

Hall, Henry & Smith, Hobart (1947). Selected records of reptiles and amphibians from southeastern Kansas. Trans. Kansas Acad. Sci., 49:447–454.

Halliday, Tim (1978). *Vanishing Birds*. London.

Halstead, B W (1949). Octopus bites in human beings. Leafl. Malacol. 1(5):17–22.

Halstead, B W (1957). Weever stings and their medical management. US Armed Forces Med. J. 8:1441–51.

Halstead, B W (1959). *Dangerous Marine Animals*. Cambridge, Md.

Halstead, B W (1971). Venomous echinoderms and annelids: starfishes, sea urchins, sea cucumbers and segmented worms, pp. 419–441. In: *Venomous animals and their venoms.* Vol. 3. *Venomous invertebrates.* (eds. Bucherl, W. & Buckley, E). New York–London.

Hamilton, H E (1949). Weight, etc. of elephant seal. Nature, 163(4144):536. London.

Hamlet, Sybil E (1968). Oldest zoo resident. Intl. Zoo News, 15(3):83.

Haneveld, G T (1958). Eye lesions caused by the exudate of tropical millipedes. Report of a case. Trop. Geograph. Med. 10:165.

Hanney, Peter W (1975). *Rodents – their lives and habits.* Newton Abbot.

Hantge, E (1968). Zum Beuteerwerb unserer Wanderfalcen. Orn. Mitt. 20:211–217.

Harmer, Sidney (1923). Giant whale of Panama. Proc. Zool. Soc., 55:1085–9.

Harmer, S (1927). Report on cetacea stranded on the British coasts from 1913 to 1926. Pub. Brit. Mus. (N.H.). London. no. 10.

Harper, P & Kinsky, F C (1978). *Southern albatrosses and petrels.* Wellington.

Harrison, R J & Brownell, R L (1971). The gonads of the South American dolphin *Inia geoffrensis, Pontoporia blainvillei* and *Sotalia fluviatilis.* J. Mammal., 52:413–419.

Harting, J E (1906). *Recreations of a naturalist.* London.

Hartman, Daniel S (1979). *Ecology and behaviour of the manatee (Trichechus manatus) in Florida.* Pittsburgh. (Spec. Publ. No. 5. Amer. Soc. of Mammalogists).

Harvey, M (1874). Gigantic cuttlefishes in Newfoundland. Ann. Mag. Nat. Hist., 13:67–70.

Haugum, J & Lowe, A M (1978–79). *A monograph of the Birdwing butterflies.* Vol. 1. *The genus Ornithoptera.* Klampenborg, Denmark.

Hayward, Bruce & Davis, Russell (1964). Flight speeds in Western bats. J. of Mammal., 45(2):236–241.

Hedges, F A Mitchell (1923). *Battles with giant fishes.* London.

Heerden Van (1937). Erdwurms die allerbeste tuiniers. Knewels van 22 voet aangetref in Transvaal. Die Costerlig, after 1937. Port Elizabeth. (Earthworms the very best gardeners – Giants of 22 feet found in the Transvaal).

Heezen, Bruce C (1957). Whales entangled in deep-sea cables. Deep-Sea Res. 4:105–115. London.

Heffner, R & Heffner, H C (1980). Science (May 2)., 208:518.

Helm, Thomas (1961). *Shark! Killer of the Sea.* London.

Henshaw, H W (1920). Autobiographical notes. Condor, 22:3–10.

Herrick, F H (1911). Natural history of the American lobster. Bull. Bur. Fish 29:149–408. (Washington, D.C.).

Herter, Konrad (1938). Die Biologie der Europaischen Igel. (Monogr. Wildsaugetiere vol. 5).

Heuvelmans, Bernard (1958). *On the track of unknown animals.* London.

Heuvelmans, B (1968). *In the wake of the sea-serpents.* New York.

Heuvelmans, B (1981). *Betes Humaines d'Afrique.* Paris.

Hickling, Grace (1962). *Grey seals and the Farne Islands.* London.

Hildebrand, Milton (1959). Motions of the running cheetah and horse. J. Mamm. 40:481–495.

Hildebrand, M (1961). Locomotion of Cheetah. J. Mamm, 42.

Hill, J E (1957). Record ivory in the collection of the British Museum (N.H.). Tanganyika Notes and Records, 46:29–31.

Hill, J E (1974). A new family, genus and species of bat (Mammalia:Chiroptera) from Thailand, Bull. Brit. Mus. (N.H.), 27:301–336.

Hingston, R W G (1936). Earth's highest animals. Zoo Mag. 1(1):90–91.

Hittell, T H (1860). *The adventures of James Capen Adams, mountaineer and grizzly bear hunter of California.* Boston.

Hocking, Brian (1953). The intrinsic range and speed of flight of insects. Trans. Roy. Entomol. Soc. London, 104:225–345.

Hoffman, E C (1929). Cowbirds – decoys – incubation period. Bull. northeast Birdband Assoc. 5:118.

Holder, Charles Frederick (1886). *Marvels of animal life.* London.

Home, Everard (1809). An Anatomical Account of the *Squalus maximus,* etc. Phil. Trans. Roy. Soc. London 98:206–220.

Hooley, R W (1913). Quarterly Journal of the Geological Society. Vol. IXIX.

Hooper, J H D & Hooper, W M (1967). Longevity of *Rhinolophid* bats in Britain. Nature, 216:1135–6. London.

Hornaday, William T (1875). Note on the Florida Crocodile. Amer. Nat., 9:504.

Hornaday, W T (1911). The real height of Jumbo. Bull. New York Zool. Soc., 48:821–22.

Hornaday, W T (1923). Our second pygmy elephant. Bull. New York Zool. Soc. 26(1):3–4.

Hornaday, W T (1926). *Two years in the jungle.* New York.

Housse, Emile (1948). *Les oiseaux du Chili.* Paris.

Howarth, T G (1967). Expensive butterflies. Animal Mag., 10(3):141.

Howell, A (1930). *Aquatic Mammals.* Chicago.

Howse, P E (1970). *Termites – study in social behaviour.* London.

Hoyt, J S Y (1941). High speed attained by *Cnemidophorus sexlineatus.* Copeia, 3:280

Hubbard, W (1927). Crocodiles. Copeia. pp. 115–16.

Huber, Klaus (1954). *25 Jahre Zoologischer Garten, Zurich.* Zurich.

Humboldt, A von (1852). *Personal narrative of travels to the equinoctial regions of America during the years 1799–1804.* Vol. II, London.

Hume, Alan O (1879–80). *The game birds of India, Burmah and Ceylon.* 3 vols.

Hutton, F W (1865). Notes on some of the birds inhabiting the southern oceans. Ibis, 1:276–298.

Ichihara, T (1961). Blue whales in the waters around Kerguelen Island. Norwegian Whal. Gaz., 50(1):1–22. Oslo.

Idyll, C P (1964). *Abyss.* London.

Ingram, Collingwood (1919). Notes on the height at which birds migrate. Ibis. 61:321–325.

Innes, William T (1945). *Exotic aquarium Fishes.* Philadelphia.

Israel, W (1913). *Biologie der Susswassmuscheln.* Stuttgart.

Jacks, Anthony (1953). *Feathered wings: a study of the flight* *of birds*. London.

Jenkins, J T (1925). *The fishes of the British Isles*. London.

Johannessen & Harder (1960). Sustained swimming speeds of Dolphins. Sci. 132:1550–1551.

Johnston, C Scott (1978). Sea creatures and the problem of equipment damage. U.S. Naval Instit. Proc. Aug.

Johnston, Sir Harry (1886). *The Kilimanjaro Expedition*. London.

Jones, E C (1963). *Tremoctopus violaceus* uses *Physalia* tentacles as weapons. Science, 139:764.

Jones, Frederick Wood (1923–24). *The Mammals of South Australia*. Pts 1, 2. Adelaide.

Jones, Marvin L (1972). Longevity of mammals in captivity. Int. Zoo News (30 June) p. 107.

Jordan, David Starr & Evermann, Barton W (1896). The Fishes of North and Middle America. U.S. Nat. Mus. 58 (1240).

Jourdain, F C F (1913). In: *The British Bird Book* (ed. F B Kirkman *et al*), 4:444–446. London.

Kaestner, Alfred (1968). *Invertebrate Zoology*. New York–London–Sydney.

Keegan, H L, Whittlemore, F W & Hedeen, R A (1960). Seasonal variation in venom of black widow spiders. Am. J. Trop. Med. & Hyg., 10:477.

Keegan, H L, Weaver, R E, Toshioka, S & Matsui, T (1964). *Some Venomous and Noxious Animals of East and South East Asia*. 406th Medical Laboratory Special Report. United States Army Medical Command, Japan: 1–43.

Kempf, Walter W (1971). A Preliminary review of the Ponerine Ant Genus *Dinoponera Roger (Rymenoptera: Formicidae)*. Studia Entomologica, 14, (1–4). Rio de Janiero, Brazil.

Kermack, K A (1951). A note on the habits of the sauropods. Ann. Mag. Nat. Hist. 12(4):830–832.

Kessler, K (1956). Zur Ichthyologie des Sudwestlichen Russlands. Bull. Soc. Nat. Moscou, 29:350.

Kielan-Jaworowska, Zofia (1976). *Hunting for dinosaurs*. New York.

Kiff, Lloyd F (1979). Bird egg collections in North America. Auk, 96(4):746–755.

King, James E (1973). Learning and generalization of a two-dimensional sameness–difference concept by chimpanzees and orang utans, J Comp. and Physiol. Psychology, 84(1):140–148.

King, Judith (1964). *Seals of the world*. Pub. British Natural History Museum, London.

Kinghorn, J R (1930). What is the life span of a bird? Aus. Mus. Mag. 4,(2):43–6. Sydney.

Kinghorn, J R (1964). *The Snakes of Australia*. Sydney.

Kinnear, N B (1922). On the birds collected by Mr. A. F. R. Wollaston during the first Mt. Everest expedition. With notes by Mr. A. F. R. Wollaston. Ibis, pp. 495–526.

Kirk, T W (1888). Brief description of a new species of large decapod (*Architeuthis longimanus*). Trans. N.Z. Inst., 20:34–39.

Kirkpatrick, T H (1965). Studies of Macropodidae in Queensland. 2. Age estimation in the grey Kangaroo, the red Kangaroo, the eastern wallaroo and the red-necked wallaby with notes on dental abnormalities. Queensland J. Agri. and Animal Sci. 2:301–317.

Kjellesuig-Waering, Erik N (1972). *Brontoscorpio anglicus*: a gigantic Lower Palaeozoic Scorpion from Central England. J. of Palaeontology. 46:39–42.

Klots, A B & Klots, E B (1961). *Living insects of the world*. London.

Klumov, S K (1962). Right whale (Japanese) of the Pacific Ocean. Trudy Inst. Okeanol., 58:202–97.

Knobel, Peter (1962). Blombergkroten im terrarium Die Aquarien-und-Terrarien-Zeitschrift (Stuttgart), 15(8): 247–49.

Knudson, P M (1977). The Case of the missing Monk Seal. Nat. His. (N.Y.)., Oct.

Koch, C (1952). Von Meinen altesten Urodelen Aquar. Terrav. 2,5:9.

Koford, Carl B (1953). *The California Condor*. New York–Toronto–London.

Kohn, Alan J (1963). Venomous marine snails of the genus Conus. In: *Venomous and poisonous animals and noxious plants of the Pacific region* (ed. H. L. Keegan and W. V. MacFarlane). pp. 83–98. London.

Kojima, Tokuzo (1951). On the brain of the sperm whale (*Physeter catodon*). Sci. Repts. Whales. Res. Inst. (Tokyo). 6:49–72.

Kolb, A (1955). Wie schnell fliegt eine Fledermaus? Saugetierk. Mitteil. 3:176–177.

Kooyman, G L (1969). The Weddell Seal. Sci. Amer. 221:101–106.

Kooyman, G & Andersen, H (1969). Deep diving: In: *The Biology of Marine Mammals* (ed. H Andersen). New York.

Kooyman, G L *et al* (1971). Diving behaviour of the Emperor penguin, *Aptenodytes forsteri*. The Auk, pp. 775–795.

Kooyman, G L (1975). Behaviour and Physiology of Diving. In: *The Biology of Penguins*. (ed. Bernard Stonehouse). London–Basingstoke.

Kopstein, Felix (1927). Over het verslinden van menschen door *Python reticulatus*. Tropische Natuur, 4:65–67.

Kopstein, F (1932). *Bungarus javanicus*, een nieuwe Javaansche Giftsland. Mededelling over een doodelijke Bungarusbeet. Gneeskunde Tijdschrift Nederland-Indies, 72:136–140.

Korschelt, E (1914). Uber Transplantationsversuche, Ruhezustande und Lebensdauer der Lumbriciden. Zool. Anz. 43:537.

Kropach, Chaim (1975). The Yellow-bellied sea snake, *Pelamis*, in the Eastern Pacific. In: *The Biology of Sea Snakes* (ed. W H Dunson), pp. 185–213. Baltimore–London–Tokyo.

Kruuk, H & Turner, M (1967). *Comparative Notes on Predation by Lion, Leopard, Cheetah and Wild Dog in the Serengeti Area, East Africa*. Mammalia, tome 31.

Krzanowski, A (1964). Three long flights by bats. J. Mammal, 45:152.

Kunkel, K (1916). *Zur Biologie der Lungenschnecken*. Heidelberg.

Kunkel, K (1928). Zur Biologie von *Eulota fruticum* Muller. Zool. Jb. (Zool.) 45:317–42.

Kurten, Bjorn (1968). *The age of dinosaurs*. London.

Labitte, A (1916). Longevite de quelques insectes en captivite. Bull. Mus. Nat. Hist. Paris, 22:105.

Lack, D (1960). The height of bird migration. Brit. Birds, 53:5–10.

Lack, D (1976). *Island Biology. Illustrated by the land birds of*

Jamaica. Oxford–London–Edinburgh–Melbourne.

Lane, Frank W (1955). *Nature Parade.* London.

Lane, F W (1957). *Kingdom of the Octopus.* London.

Lang, A (1904). Über Vorversuche zu Untersuchungen über die Varietaten-bildung von *Helix hortensis* und *Helix nemoralis.* Denkschr. d. Med. Naturwiss. Ges. Jena, 2:437·505.

Lang, E M (1967). The birth of an African elephant, *Loxodonta a. africana,* at Basle Zoo. Int. Zoo. Year Book, 7:154–7.

Langmuir, J (1938). The speed of the deer fly. Science, 87:233–234.

Langston, Wann (1981). Pterosaurs. Sci. American, 244(2):92–102.

Laurie, A H (1933). Some aspects of respiration in blue and fin whales. Disc. Repts., 7:363–406.

Lawrence, R (1965). Sun-spiders. Animals Mag., 6(9)(22 April), pp. 232–235.

Laws, R M (1953). Elephant seal (*Mirounga leonina lin.*) 1. Growth and age. Sci. Repts. Falkland Is. Dep. Survey (London). No. 8,62 pp.

Laws, R M (1966). Age criteria for the African elephant. *Loxodonta a. africana.* E. Afr. Wildl. J. 4:1–37.

Laws, R M *et al* (1967). Estimating live weights of elephants from hind-leg weights. E. Afr. Wildl. J. 5:105–106.

Lawson, D A (1975). Pterosaur from the latest Cretaceous of West Texas: discovery of the largest flying creature. Science, 187:947–948.

Laycock, George (1966). *The Alien Animals.* New York.

Lederer, Gustav (1944). Nahrungserwerb, Entwicklung Paarung und Britfursorge von *Python reticulatus* (Schneider). Zool. Jahrbucher (Anatomie) (Jena). 68:363–98.

Legendre, R (1923). Sur des squales pelerins (*Cetorhinus maximus Gunner*) observes a Concarneau. Bull. zool. Paris, 48:257–280.

Lehane, Brendan (1969). *The compleat flea.* London.

Leighton, G (1901). *The life history of British serpents and their local distribution in the British Isles.* London.

Lekagul, B & McNeely, J A (1977). *Mammals of Thailand.* Bangkok.

Lever, Christopher (1977). *The Naturalized Animals of the British Isles.* London.

Lewis, George (1955). *Elephant tramp.* New York.

Liu, C C (1950). *Amphibians of Western China. Fieldiana: Zoology Memoirs,* vol. 2. Chicago Nat Hist. Mus.

Ljungstrom, P O & Reinecke, A J (1969). Ecology and natural history of the microchaetid earthworms of South Africa. Pedobiologia, 9:152–157.

Locket, G H & Millidge, A G (1951–53). *British spiders.* 2 vols. London. (Ryl. Socty.).

Locket, G H, Millidge, A G & Merrett, P (1974). *British spiders.* 3 vols. (Ryl. Socty.).

Lockhart, J G (1895). *Habits.* p. 307.

Lockyer, C (1976). Body weights of some species of large whales. J. Cons. Int. Explor. Mer., 36(3):259–273.

Longman, H A (1926). New records of Cetacea, with a list of Queensland species. Mem. Qu. Mus., 8:266–78.

Loomis, H F (1964). The Millipedes of Panama. Fieldiana: Zoology 47:1–136.

Lord, F A (1948). How Big is the biggest. Nat. Hist. (Dec.). pp. 450–451.

Love, J A, Ball, M E & Newton, I (1978). White-tailed Eagles in Britain and Norway. British Birds, 71(11): 475–481.

Loveridge, Arthur (1929). Blind snakes and pythons of East Africa. Bull. Antivenin Inst. America, 3:14–19.

Loveridge, A (1932). Eight new toads of the genus *Bufo* from East and Central Africa. Occasional papers Boston Soc. Nat. Hist., 8:43–53.

Lowe, Willoughby (1932). *The trail that is always new.* London.

Lubbock, Sir John (1892). *The beauties of nature and the wonders of the world we live in.* London.

Lucas, Robert (1894). *Die Pompiliden-Gattung Pepsis.* Berliner.

Lydekker, R (1901). *The great and small game of Europe, Western and Northern Asia and America, their distribution, habits & structure.* London.

Lydekker, R (1907). The ears as a race character in the African elephant. Proc. Zool. Soc. London, pp. 380–403.

Lydekker, R (1907). *Game animals of India, etc.* London.

Lydekker, R (1911). *The ox and its kindred.* London.

Lyon, George Francis (1825). The private journal of Capt G. F. Lyon of H.M.S. "Hecla" during the recent voyage of discovery under Capt. Parry. London.

MacGinitie, G E & MacGinitie, N (1949). *Natural history of marine animals.* New York–London–Toronto.

MacGinitie, G E & MacGinitie, N (1968). *Natural history of marine animals.* 2nd edition. New York–London–Toronto.

Mackal, Roy P (1976). *The monsters of Loch Ness.* London.

Mackintosh, N A (1942). The southern stocks of whale-bone whales. Disc. Reports, (London), 22:197–300.

Magnan, A & Sainte-Lague (1928). Sur l'equilibre statique des poissons. C. R. Acad. Sci. Paris, 187:388–90.

Magnan, A (1934). *Le vol des insects.* Paris.

Magnin, E (1966). Quelques donnees biologiques sur la reproduction des esturgeons *Acipenser fulvescens.* Can. J. Zool. 44(2):257–263.

Magnus, Olaus (1555). *Historia de gentibus septentrionalibus earum diversis statibus, conditionibus, etc.* Rome.

Mani, S B (1960). Occurrence of the sea cow *Halicore dugong (erxl)* off the Saurashtra coast. J. Bomb. Nat. Hist. Soc., 57:216–217.

Mann, William M (1953). Report on the National Zoological Park for the year ended June 30 1952. Smithson. Inst. Rept. pp. 94–129.

Mantell, G (1825). Notice on the Iguanodon, a newly discovered fossil reptile, from the sandstone of Tilgate forest, in Sussex. Phil. Trans. Roy. Soc., 115:179–186.

Manton, S W (1952). The evolution of Arthropodan locomotory mechanisms – Part 3. The locomotion of the *Chilopoda* and *Pauropoda.* J. Linn. Soc. (Zool.) 42:118–67.

Marais, Eugene N (1971). *The Soul of the White Ant.* London.

Marki, F & Witkop, B (1963). The venom of the Colombian arrow poison frog *Phyllobates bicolor.* Separatum Experientia (Basel), 19:1–10.

Marshall, N B (1954). *Aspects of deep sea biology.* London.

Marshall, N B (1979). *The life of fishes.* London.

Martin, Richard M (1977). *Mammals of the Sea.* London.

Mather, F J (1962). Transatlantic migration of two large bluefin tuna. J. Cons. Int. Explor. Mer., 27:325–327.

Matthews, Harrison & Parker, H W (1950). Notes on the Anatomy and Biology of the Basking shark. Proc. Zool. Soc. London. 120(3):535–576.

Maxwell, Gavin (1952). *Harpoon at a venture*. London.

Mazzotti, L & Bravo-Becherelle, M A (1963). Scorpionism in the Mexican Republic. In: *Venomous and Poisonous Animals and Noxious Plants of the Pacific Region.* (eds. Keegan, H. L. & Macfarlane, W. V.). London.

McCormick, L J (1949). The Pirarucu, or Arapaima of the South American tropics. In: *Game Fish of the World* (eds. Vesey-Fitzgerald, B. & Lamonte, F.). pp. 225–233. London–Brussels.

McCoy, Sir Frederick (1878–90). Prodromus of the zoology of Victoria, etc. Decades I–XX. Melbourne.

McIlhenny, Edward A (1935). *The alligator's life history.* Boston.

McKeown, K C (1952). *Spider wonders of Australia.* Sydney.

McLaren, I A (1958). The biology of the Ringed seal (*Phoca hispida schreber*) in the Eastern Canadian Arctic. Bull. Fish. Res. Bd. Can. 118:1–97.

McMillan, Nora F (1968). *British Shells.* London.

McNabb, D (1953). Field (22 Feb).

Mead, Tom (1962). *Killers of Eden.* London–Sydney.

Meinertzhagen, Richard (1938). Some weights and measurements of large mammals. Proc. Zool. Soc. London, 108:433–439.

Meinertzhagen, R (1954). *Birds of Arabia.* London.

Meinertzhagen, R (1955). The speed and altitude of bird flight (with notes on other animals). Ibis, 97:81–117.

Melacon, Claude (1958). *Les poissons de nos eaux.* 3rd ed. La Société Zool. de Quebec.

Menaker, M (1964). Frequency of spontaneous arousal from hibernation in bats. Nature, 203:540–541. London.

Menard, Wilmon (1947). Hunting the giant octopus. Wide World Mag. 99:203–207.

Menzies, R J, George, R Y & Rowe, G T (1973). *Abyssal Environment and Ecology of the World Oceans.* New York–London.

Merfield, Fred G (1956). *Gorillas were my neighbours.* London.

Merriam, C Hart (1918). Review of the grizzly and big brown bears of North America (genus Ursus) with description of a new genus Vetularctos. N. Amer. Fauna, 41:1–36. Bur. Biol. Survey, U.S. Dept. Agric. (Washington, D.C.).

Meyer-Rochow, V B (1977). Comparison Between 15 *Carapus mourlani* in a Single Holothurian and 19 *C. mourlani* from Starfish. Copeia No. 3 pp. 583–4.

Millais, J (1904–6). *The Mammals of Great Britain and Ireland.* 3 vols. London.

Milligan, R R (1924). Rep. Aus. Assoc. Adv. Soc. vol. 16. Sydney–Wellington.

Millot, J & Vachon, M (1949). Ordre des scorpions. In: *Traite de Zoologie.* (ed. Grasse, P. P.). 6:386–436. Paris.

Minton, Sherman A & Minton, Madge R (1971). *Venomous reptiles.* London.

Minton, S A (1974). *Venom diseases.* Springfield, Illinois.

M'Intosh, William (1875). *The marine invertebrates and fishes of St. Andrews.* Edinburgh–London.

Mitsukuri, K (1903). Notes on the habits and life history of *Stichopus japonicus Selenka.* Annon. Zool. Jap. 5:1–21.

Mitzmain, M B (1910). General observations on the bionomics of the rodent and human flea. U.S. Pub. Health Ser. Bull. 38:1–34.

Mole, R R (1924). The Trinidad Snakes. Proc. Zool. Soc. London. 235–78.

Moore, Hilary B (1935). A comparison of the biology of *Echinus esculentus* in different habitats. J. Mar. Biol. Ass. U.K. 20:109.

Moore, H B (1966). Ecology of Echinoids. In: *Physiology of Echinodermata* (ed. Boolootian, Richard A.): 73–86. New York–London–Sydney.

Morden, J William (1930). Saiga, antelope and Long--haired tiger. Nat. Hist. 30:539–551.

Moriarty, Christopher (1978). *Eels: A natural and unnatural history.* Newton Abbot–London–Vancouver.

Morris, S F (1979). In: *The Encyclopaedia of Prehistoric Life* (eds: Rodney Steel & Anthony P. Harvey). London.

Mortensen, T (1927). *Handbook of the Echinoderms of the British Isles.* London.

Mortensen, T (1936). Echinoidea and Ophiuroidea. Discovery Rep. 12:199–348.

Mosauer, Walter (1935). How Fast can Snakes Travel? Copeia, 1:6–9.

Mouquet, A (1924). Rec. med. vet. loo: 181–185.

Mullenhoff, Karl (1885). Die Grosse der Flugflachen. Pflueger's Arch. Gesamte Physiologie, 35:407–453.

Murie, Claus J (1951). *The Elk of North America.* Harrisburg & Washington.

Murphy, Richard Cushman (1914). Notes on the sea elephant, *Mirounga leonina* (L.) Bull. Amer. Mus. Nat. Hist. 33:63–79.

Murphy, R C (1925). *Bird Islands of Peru.* New York–London.

Murphy, R C (1936). *Oceanic Birds of South America.* New York.

Murphy, R C (1953). *Land Birds of America.* New York.

Murray, Alexander (1874). Capture of a gigantic squid at Newfoundland. Am. Nat. Salem. 8, no. 2. p. 140.

Muus, Bent J & Dahlstrøm, Preben (1974). *Collins Guide to the Sea Fishes of Britain and North Western Europe.* London.

Myers, G & Funkhousar, J (1951). Zoologica, 36:279–281.

Napier, John (1972). *Bigfoot – The Yeti and Sasquatch in myth and reality.* London.

Nappe, Leontine (1974). Desert Fish in hot water. Animals Mag. pp. 556–559.

Neale, Ernest (1977). *Badgers.* Poole, England.

Neill, Wilfred T (1971). *The last of the ruling reptiles.* New York–London.

Nelson, Bryan (1980). *Seabirds: their biology and ecology.* New York–London–Sydney–Toronto.

Neumann, A H (1898). *Elephant-hunting in east equatorial Africa.* London.

Newman, B & Tarlo, B (1967). A giant marine reptile from Bedfordshire. Animals. (June). pp. 61–63.

Newman, B (1970). Stance and gait in the flesh-eating dinosaur *Tyrannosaurus.* Biol. J. Linn. Soc., pp. 119–123.

Nice, M (1953). The question of ten-day incubation periods. Wilson Bull., 65:81–93.

Nigrelli, R (1959). Longevity of fishes in captivity with special reference to those kept in the New York

Aquarium. In: C.I.B.A. Foundn. Colloquia on Ageing. Vol. 5:212–226. London.

Nishiwaki, Masaharu (1950). On the body weight of whales. Sci. Repts. Whales Res. Inst., 4:184–209. Tokyo.

Nishiwaki, M (1972). General Biology. In: *Mammals of the sea* (ed. Sam. H. Ridgeway). pp. 3–204. Springfield, Illinois.

Nixon, M (1969). The lifespan of *Octopus vulgaris*. Lamarck. Proc. Malac. Soc. London. 38:529–540.

Noack, T (1906). Eine Zwergform des afrikanischen Elefanten. Zool. Anz., Leipzig 29:631–33.

Norman, J R & Fraser, F C (1948). *Giant Fishes, Whales and Dolphins*. London.

Norwood, V G (1964). *Jungle Life in Guiana*. London.

Nott, John Fortune (1886). *Wild animals photographed and described*. London.

Novikov, Georgii A (1962). *Carnivorous mammals of the fauna of the USSR*. (Israel Program for Scientific Translations). Jerusalem.

Offerman, P P (1953). The Elephant in the Belgian Congo. In: *The Elephant in East Central Africa*. A monograph. London–Nairobi.

Ogasawara, Frank (1972). Scientist Studies Japan's fantastic long-tailed fowl. Nat. Geogr. Mag. pp. 845–855.

Ognev, S I (1962). *Mammals of the U.S.S.R. and adjacent countries*. Vol. III. Carnivora. (Israel Program for Scientific Translations). Jerusalem.

O'Gorman, Fergus (1963). Observations on terrestrial locomotion in Antarctic Seals. Proc. Zool. Soc., 141:837.

Oldham, C (1942). Notes on *Geomalacus maculosus*. Proc. Malac. Soc. London., vol. 25:10.

Oliver, James A (1955). *The Natural History of North American Amphibians and Reptiles*. New York.

Oliver, J A (1958). *Snakes in Fact and Fiction*. London.

Ommanney, F D (1971). *Lost Leviathan*. London.

Omura, H *et al* (1969). Black right whales in the North Pacific. Sci. Repts. Whales Res. Instit. 1:1–78.

Orr, R T (1938). A new rodent of the genus *Nesoryzomys* from the Galapagos Islands. Proc. Calif. Acad. Sci., 23(21):303–306.

Orton, D A (1975). The speed of a Peregrine's dive. The Field (25 Sept), pp. 588–90.

Osborn, Henry Fairfield (1936–42), *Proboscidea. A monograph of the discovery, evolution, migration and extinction of the mastodons and elephants of the world*. Amer. Mus. Nat. Hist., New York, 2 vols.

Ostrom, John H (1978). New ideas about dinosaurs. Nat. Geogr. Mag. 154(2):152–176.

Oswell, W Cotton (1894). *South Africa fifty years ago*. Badminton Library of Sports and Pastimes, (Big Game Shooting), London.

Ouwens, H (1912). On a large *Varanus* species from the island of Komodo. Bull. Jardin. Botan. Buitenzorg 2,(6):1–3.

Owen, R (1841). Report on British Fossil Reptiles. Report of the Eleventh Meeting of the British Association for the Advancement of Science, pp. 60–204.

Packard, A (1961). Sucker display of Octopus. Nature, London. 190:736–737.

Palmen, F & Rantala, M (1954). On the life-history and ecology of *Pachymerium ferrugineum* (C. L. Koch) (Chilopoda, Geophilidae). Ann. Soc. Zool. Fenn.

Vanamo 16(3):1–44.

Parker, G H (1921). The power of adhesion in the suckers of *Octopus brimaculatus Verrill*. J. Exp. Zool. 33:391–394.

Parkinson, C (1900). The great birds of the Southern Seas. Cornhill Magazine (May). London.

Parrish, H M (1963). Analysis of 460 fatalities from venomous animals. Am. J. Med. Sci., 245:129.

Patten, Robert A (1940). Jessie joins her ancestors. Parks and Recreations, 23(5):200–202.

Patterson, A & Hardin, J (1969). Flight speeds of five species of vespertilionid bats. J. of Mammal. 50:152–3.

Patterson, J (1939). Tuna, how big – how fast. New Engl. Nat., Boston 2:8–10.

Pellegrin, Jacques (1931). Le Silure d'Europe. La Terre et la Vie, Paris. 8:500–501.

Pemberton, J R (1910). Some bird notes from Ventura County. Condor, 12:18–19.

Pennant, Thomas (1776). *The British Zoology*. 4th edit. 4 vols. London.

Perley, M H (1852). *Reports on the sea and river fisheries of New Brunswick*, Fredericton.

Perry, Richard (1964). *The World of the Tiger*. London.

Perry, R (1966). *The World of the Polar Bear*. London.

Perry, R (1970). *The World of the Jaguar*. Newton Abbot.

Peterson, Randolph L (1955). *North American Moose*. Toronto.

Peterson, Roger Tory (1963). *The Birds*. New York.

Peterson, Russell (1964). *Silent by night*. London.

Petrov, V (1927). Izvestiya otdela prikladnoi ikhtiologii, 6(2):213.

Petrunkevitch, A (1955). In: *Treatise on Invertebrate Palaeontology*. Kansas.

Phelps, T (1980). *Poisonous Snakes*. Poole.

Phillipps-Wolley, Clive (1894). *Big game hunting* (Badminton Library). 2 vols. London.

Pi, Jorge Sabater (1965). La mayor rana del mundo vive en nuestra provincia Africana de Rio Muni. Iber. Rev. Sci. News.

Piccard, Jacques (1960). Man's deepest dive. Nat. Geogr. Mag. (Washington, D.C.), 118(2),224–239.

Piers, Harry (1934). Accidental occurrence of the man-eater or Great White shark *Carcharodon carcharias* (L.). in Nova Scotian waters. Proc. Nova Scotian Inst. Sci., 18(3):192–203.

Pilleri, G & Gihr, M (1971). The Central Nervous System of the *Mysticete* and *Odontocete* Whales. In: *Investigations on Cetacea*, Vol. 11: 89–128. Berne.

Pilleri, G (1972). Zoologisch-Cetologische Expedition nach West Pakistan und Reise nach Indien im Jahre 1971. Hiranatomisches Institut, Waldau-Bern.

Pinney, Peter (1976). *To catch a crocodile*. London.

Pitman, Charles R S (1925). The length attained by and the habits of the Gahrial (*G. gangeticus*). J. Bomb. Nat. Hist. Soc., 30:703.

Pitman, C R S (1974). *A Guide to the Snakes of Uganda*. Rev. Ed. Glasgow.

Plowden, Gene (1972). *Gargantua*. New York.

Pocock, R I K (1951). *Catalogue of the Genus Felis*. British Museum (N.H.).

Pollock, F T (1903). *Sporting Days in Southern India*. London.

Pontoppidan, Erik Ludvigsen (1753). *Det forste Forsog paa Norges naturlige Historie*. Copenhagen.

Pope, C H (1956). *The reptile world, etc.* New York.

Pope, C H (1961). *The Giant Snakes.* London.

Pope, Elizabeth C (1953). Sea lice or jellyfish? Aus. Mus. Mag., 11(1):16–21.

Pope, E C (1958). Giant earthworms. Aus. Mus. Mag. (Sydney) 12(10):309–311.

Pope, E C & Rowe, F W (1977). A new Genus and two new species in the Family Mithrodiidae (Echinodermata: Asteroidea) with comments on the status of the species of Mithrodia Gray 1840. Australian Zool. 19(2):201–216.

Powell, A N (1958). *Call of the tiger.* New York.

Poynton, J C (1964). Amphibia of Southern Africa. Ann. Natal Mus. vol. 17:1–334.

Prashad, B (1930) (letter). Giant Estuarine Crocodile. J. Bomb. Nat. Hist. Soc., 34:584–585.

Prater, S H (1929). The dugong or sea cow. J. Bomb. Nat. Hist. Soc., 33:84.

Prater, S H (1965). *The book of Indian animals.* Bomb. Nat. Hist. Soc. Bombay.

Pretorius, P J (1947). *Jungle Man.* London.

Pritchard, Peter (1967). *Living turtles of the world.* N.J.

Pritchard, P. (1971). The leatherback or leathery turtle *Dermochelys coriacea.* IUCN. Monograph 1:1–39.

Probst, R T & Cooper, E L (1954). Age, growth and productions of the Lake Sturgeon (*Acipenser fulvescens*) in the Lake Winnebago region, Wisconsin. Trans. Amer. Fish. Soc. 84:207–227.

Rabes, O (1901). Uber Transplantations-Versuche an Lumbriciden. Biol. Zbl. 21:633.

Rand, Stanley A (1952). Jumping ability of certain anurans, with notes on endurance. Copeia, 1:15–20.

Randall, John E (1973). Size of the Great white shark, Science, 181:169–170.

Ratcliffe, D (1980). *The Peregrine Falcon.* Galton, Staffs.

Raven, Henry C (1931). Gorilla: the greatest of all apes. Nat. Hist. (New York), 31(3):231–242.

Raven, H C (1946). Adventures in Python Country. Nat. Hist., 55:38–41.

Ray, G E (1941). Big for his day. Nat. Hist., 48:36–39.

Reed, Theodore H (1961). Report on the National Zoological Park for the year ended June 30, 1960. Smithson. Inst. Rept. for 1960, pp. 131–171.

Rees, W J & Maul, G E (1956). The Cephalopoda of Madeira. Bull. Brit. Mus. (N.H.) (Zool). 3:259–81.

Regan, C T (1911). *The freshwater fishes of the British Isles.* London.

Reid, H Alistair (1956). *Three Fatal Cases of Sea Snakebite Venoms.* A.A.A.S. Publication No. 44.

Reid, H A (1975). Epidemiology and clinical aspects of sea snake bites. In: *The Biology of Sea Snakes* (ed. Dunson, W. H.), pp. 385–415. Baltimore–London–Tokyo.

Remington, C L (1950). The bite and habits of a giant centipede (*Scolopendra subspinipes*) in the Philippine Islands. Am. J. trop. Med. 30:453–455.

Rensch, Bernhard & Harde, K W (1955). Growth-gradient of Indian elephants, J. Bomb. Nat. Hist. Soc., 52:841–851.

Rice, W (1857). *Tiger Shooting in India.* London.

Rich, P V & Tets, G F Van (1976). Birds from Australia's past. Aus. Nat. His. 18:338–341.

Richards, Aola M (1973). A comparative study of the biology of the Giant wetas *Deinacrida heteracantha* and *D. fallai* (Orthoptera: Henicidae) from New Zealand. J.

Zool. Lond., 169:195–236.

Riess, B H *et al* (1949). The behaviour of two captive specimens of the lowland gorilla (*Gorilla gorilla gorilla*) Zoologica (N.Y.) 34(13):111–117.

Riley, W A & Johannsen, O A (1932). *Medical entomology.* New York.

Risting, Sigurd (1922). Av. Hvalfangstens Historie. Publikatio Nr. 2. Fra Kommander Chr. Christensens Hvalfangstmuseum, 1. Sandefjord, p. 1.

Risting, S (1928). Whales and whale foetuses. Statistics of catch and measurements collected from the Norwegian Whalers' Association 1922–1925. Rapp. Cons. Explor. Mer., 50:1–122.

Roberts, Austin (1951). *The mammals of South Africa.* Cape Town.

Roberts, T J (1977). *The Mammals of Pakistan.* London.

Roberts, T S (1932). *The Birds of Minnesota.* Univ. Press, Minneapolis, vol. 1.

Robson, C W (1887). On a new species of giant cuttlefish stranded at Cape Campbell, June 30th 1886 (*Architeuthis kirkii*). Trans. Proc. N.Z. Int., 19:155–157.

Roche, W Gubbins (1914). Strange Feathers. The Emu. 13:214.

Rockstein, M (1959). The biology of ageing in insects. In: C.I.B.A. Found. colloquia on Ageing. Vol. 5: *The life-span of animals* (ed. Wolstenholme, G. E. & O'Connor, M.). London.

Roe, H S J (1967). Seasonal formation of laminae in the ear plug of the Fin Whale. Discovery Rept. 35:1–30.

Rogers, Michael J and the Rarities Committee (1978). Report on rare birds in Great Britain in 1977. Brit. Birds, 71(11). November.

Rogers, M J *et al* (1980). Report on rare birds in Great Britain in 1979. Brit. Birds 73(11):491–534.

Rolfe, W D & Ingham, J K (1967). Limb structure, affinity and diet of the Carboniferous "centipede" *Arthropleura.* Scottish J. of Geology. 3:118–124.

Rollinat, R (1934). *La Vie des Reptiles de la France Centrale.* Paris.

Rooij, Nelly de (1915). The reptiles of the Indo-Australian Archipelago. 1–150.

Roosevelt, Theodore (1914). *Through the Brazilian wilderness.* London.

Rose, Walter (1950). *The reptiles and amphibians of southern Africa.* Cape Town. 1st ed.

Rose, W (1962). *The reptiles and amphibians of southern Africa.* Cape Town. 2nd ed.

Rosevear, D R (1965). *The Bats of West Africa.* Brit. Mus. (N.H.). London.

Ross, J C (1847). *A voyage of discovery and research in the Southern and Antarctic regions during the years 1839–1843.* London.

Rothschild, M and Clay, T (1952). *Fleas, Flukes and Cuckoos.* London.

Rothschild, M, Schlein, Y, Parker, K, Neville, C and Sternberg, S (1973). The flying leap of the flea. Sci. Amer. (Nov.). pp. 92–100.

Rozhdestvensky, A K (1970). On the gigantic claws of some enigmatic Mesozoic reptiles. Palaeontological Mag. (1): 131–141. Moscow.

Rumbaugh, Duane (1970). Learning skills of anthropoids. In: L. A. Rosenblum (ed.) *Primate Behaviour,* vol. 1:1–70. New York.

Rushby, G G (1965). *No more the tusker*. London.

Russell, D A & Beland, P (1976). Running Dinosaurs. Nature. 264:486.

Russell, F S (1970). *The Medusae of the British Isles*. 2 vols. London.

Rutledge, A (1946). Milstead Repes One. In: *Field and Stream Reader*, pp. 224–238. Garden City, N.Y.

Sanden, W von (1935). Beobachtungen an dem Schwanenbestand des Nordenburger Sees in Ostpreussen seit seiner Besiedlung mit Cygnus olor. Orn. Mber. 43:82–85.

Sanderson, Ivan T (1937). *Animal Treasure*. London.

Sanderson, I T (1940). The Mammals of the North Cameroons Forest Area. Trans. Zool. Soc., 24(7):623–725.

Sanderson, I T (1956). *Follow the Whale*. New York.

Sarich, Vincent M (1973). Nature. London. Sept. 28.

Savory, Theodore H (1928). *Biology of Spiders*. London.

Savory, T H (1945). *The spiders and allied orders of the British Isle*. London.

Savory, T H (1964). *Arachnida*. New York.

Savory, T H (1966). Britain's most elusive spider. Animals 13(1):500–501.

Sawai, Y et al (1969). Studies on the improvement in the treatment of habu (*Trimeresurus flavoridis*) bites. VIII. Jap. J. Exp. Med. 39:197.

Scammon, Charles M (1874). *The marine mammals of the north-western coast of North America*, etc. San Francisco–New York.

Schaller, George B (1967). *The deer and the tiger*. Chicago–London.

Scheffer, Victor B (1969). Super flea. Nat. Hist. New York (May).

Scheffer, V B (1970). Cliche of the Killer. Nat. Hist. New York (Oct).

Scheffer, V B (1974). The Largest Whale. Defenders of Wildlife Intl. 49(4):272–4.

Scheithauer, Walter (1967). *Hummingbirds, flying jewels*. London.

Schmidt, Karl & Inger, R (1957). *Reptiles of the World*. New York–London.

Schmidt, K P (1944). Crocodiles. Fauna 6:67–72.

Schmidt-Nielsen Knut (1977). Problems of Scaling: Locomotion and Physiological Correlates. In: *Scale Effects in Animal Locomotion* (ed. T. J. Pedley): 122. London–New York–San Francisco.

Schmitt, Waldo L (1973). *Crustaceans*. Newton Abbot.

Scholander, P F (1940). Experimental investigations on the Respiratory Function in diving Mammals and Birds. Hvalrad. Skr., 22:1–131.

Schomburgk, Robert H (1841). *Fishes of British Guiana* – Pt. 1. London.

Schomburgk, R H (1847–48). *Travels in British Guiana*. London.

Schonwetter, M (1960–61). *Handbuch der Oologie* (ed. Meiss, W). Akademie-Verlag. Berlin.

Schorger, A W (1947). The deep diving of the Loon and the Old Squaw and its mechanism. Wilson Bulletin, 59:151–159.

Schorger, A W (1955). *The Passenger Pigeon: its natural history and extinction*. Madison, Wisconsin.

Schottler, Wener H (1952). Problems of Antivenin Standardization: Bull. World Health Organisation: 293–320.

Schroeder, William C (1940). The Provincetown 'sea serpent'. New Eng. Nat., 7(2):1–2.

Schubart, O (1966). South African Animal Life. 12:199.

Schultz. Adolph H (1930). The Skeleton of the Trunk and Limbs of Higher Primates. Human Biology, 11(3):303–438.

Schultz, A H (1941). Growth and Development of the Orang-Utan. Contributions to Embryology, 182 (545):57–110. Carnegie Instit. of Washington.

Schultz, Harold (1963). Voracious fish of the Amazon. Animals mag. (29 Oct): 526–529.

Schultz, L P & Stern, Edith (1948). *The Way of Fishes*. New York.

Schwartz & Ogren (1956). Herpetologica 12(2):91–110.

Scoresby, William (1820). *An Account of the Arctic regions with a history and description of the northern whale-fishery*. Edinburgh.

Scouler, J (1826). Accounts of a voyage to Madeira, Brazil, Juan Fernandez and the Gallapagos Islands, performed in 1824 and 1825, etc. Edinburgh J. of Sci., 5:195–214.

Seeley, Harry G (1886). *The freshwater fishes of Europe*. London.

Semakula, S N & Larkin, P A (1968). Age, growth, food and yield of the white sturgeon (*Acipenser transmontanus*) of the Fraser River, British Columbia. J. Fish. Fes. Bd. Canada 2542:2589–2602.

Semper, C (1868). *Ophiocrinus*, eine neue Comatuliden-Gattung. Archiv. F. Naturg., 34:68–69.

Serventy, D L & Whittell, H J (1950). *A handbook of the Birds of Western Australia*. 2nd edit. Perth, W. Australia.

Seshadri, Balakrishna (1969). *The Twilight of India's Wild Life*. London.

Seton, Ernest Thompson (1925–27). *Lives of Game Animals*. 4 vols. New York.

Sharrock, J T R (1974). *Scarce Migrant Birds in Britain and Ireland*. Tring, England.

Sharrock, J T R (1976). *The atlas of breeding birds in Britain and Ireland*. Tring, England.

Shaw, Charles E (1969). Longevity of snakes in North American collections as of 1 January 1968. Zoolog. Garten (N.F.). Leipzig, 37(4–5).

Sheals, J G & Rice, A L (1973). Other Arthropoda. In: *Insects and other Arthropods of Medical importance* (ed. Kenneth G. V. Smith). Trustees Brit. Mus. (N.H.): 474–476.

Shields, G O (ed.) (1890). *The big game of North America*. Chicago.

Shortridge, G C (1934). *The mammals of South West Africa*. 2 vols. London.

Shufeldt, Robert W (1915). Anatomical and other notes on the passenger pigeon (*Ectopistes migratorius*) lately living in the Cincinnati Zoological Gardens. Auk, 32:29–41.

Siemel, Sasha (1954). *Jungle fury*. London.

Sikes, Sylvia (1971). *The Natural History of the African Elephant*. London.

Sikes, S (1972). *Lake Chad*. London.

Simpson, George Gaylord (1933). A New Fossil snake from the Notostylops Beds of Patagonia. Bull. Amer. Mus. Nat. His., 67:1–22.

Singh, Gyan (1961). The Eastern Steppe Eagle (*Aquila n. Hodgsoni*) on the South Col of Everest. J. Bomb. Nat. Hist. Soc., 58(1).

Slijper, E J (1962). *Whales*. London.

Small, George L (1971). *The Blue Whale*. New York–London.

Smith, Andrew (1829). Contributions to the Natural History of South Africa, etc. Zool. J. 4:442–48. London.

Smith, Hugh M (1902). The smallest known vertebrate. Science, Jan 3; also Bull. U.S. Fish Comm. xxxi:167.

Smith, H M & Radcliffe, Lewis (1912). Proc. U.S. Nat. Mus.

Smith, H M (1925). The Whale Shark *Rhineodon* in the Gulf of Siam. Science, N.S. 62:438.

Smith, Jerome van C (1833). *Natural history of the fishes of Massachusetts, etc.* Boston.

Smith, Malcolm (1951). *The British Amphibians and Reptiles*. London.

Smitt, F A (1893). *A history of Scandinavian fishes*. Rev. edit. Stockholm–London.

Smythies, F A (1942). *Big Game Shooting in Nepal*. Calcutta.

Soskin, Mark & Clark, John (1976). *Through the fish's eye*. London.

Sotavalta, Olavi (1947a). The essential factor regulating the wing-stroke frequency of insects in wing mutilation and loading experiments and in experiments at sub-atmospheric pressure (Conts. to the problem of insect flight II) Ann. Zool. Soc. Zool-bot, fenn Vanamo 15:1–67).

Sotavalta, O (1947b). *The flight tone of insects*. Helsinki.

Soule, Gardner (1974). *Wide ocean – discoveries at sea*. Folkestone, England.

Southcott, R V (1973). *Survey of injuries to man by Australian terrestrial arthropods*. Mitcham, S. Australia.

Sowerby, Arthur (1925). *A naturalist's note-book in China*. Shanghai.

Spencer, B & Gillen, T J (1912). *Across Australia*. Vol. 1. London.

Spencer, O R (1943). Nesting habits of the Black-billed Cuckoo. Wilson Bull. 55:11–22.

Spencer, T, Fairfax, R & Loach, I (1979). The Western Australian swamp tortoise (*Pseudemydura umbrina*) in captivity. Intl. Zoo Year Book, 19:58–60.

Spotte, S, Radcliffe, W & Dunn, L (Dec. 31 1979). Notes on Commerson's Dolphin (*Cephalorhynchus commersonii*) in captivity. Cetology, No. 35, pp. 1–9.

Spry, W J J (1877). *The cruise of Her Majesty's ship Challenger*. Toronto.

Stahnke, Herbert L (1950). The Arizona scorpion problem. Ariz. Med., 7:23.

Stahnke, H L (1956). Scorpions. Tempe, Ariz. Arizona State University, 35.

Stahnke, H L (1963). Some pharmacological and biochemical characteristics of *Centruroides sculpturatus* Ewing Scorpion venom. Proc. Int. Pharmac. Meet., Prague, 63–70.

Stead, David G (1963). *Sharks and rays of Australian seas*. London–Toronto–Melbourne–Sydney.

Stebbings, R E (1970). A comparative study of *Plecotus austriacus (Chiroptera Vespertilionidae)* inhabiting one roost. Bijdragen tot de Dierkunde, 40:91–4.

Stedman, J G (1796). *Narrative of a five year's expedition against the revolted negroes of Surinam in Guiana, etc.* 2 vols. London.

Steenstrup, J (1857). Oplysniger om Atlanterhavets colossale Blaeks – prutter. Forh. skand. naturf. 7. mote 1857:182–185.

Steinbach, M A & Money, K E (1973). Eye movement of the owl (letter). Vision Res., 13:889–891.

Steinmetz, H C (1954). Beitraege zur Geschichte unserer Kenntnisse vom see-Elefanten, Zoo. Gart. (Leipzig). N.F. 21:24–43.

Steller, Georg Wilhelm (1749–51). *De Bestis Marinis*. Nova Acta Ptropolitana, Petrograd.

Step, Edward (1924). *Go to the ant, etc.* London.

Stephen, A C (1950). Giant squid *Architeuthis* in Shetland. Scot. Nat., 62:52–53.

Stephen, A C, Rae, B B & Wilson, E (1957). Rare marine invertebrates recently found in the Scottish area. Scot. Nat., 69(3):1–4.

Stephens, F (1895). Notes on the California vulture. Auk, 12:81–82.

Stephens, M (1957). The Otter Report. London. Univ. Fed. Anim. Welfare.

Stephenson, J (1930). *The Oligochaeta*. Oxford.

Stephenson, T A (1935). *The British Sea Anemones*. Vol. 2. (Ray Soc.).

Sterndale, Robert A (1884). *Natural History of the mammalia of India and Ceylon*. Calcutta.

Stewart, A G (1978). Swans flying at 8,000 metres. British Birds, 71(10):459.

Stokes, C W (1953). *Sanctuary*. Cape Town.

Stolpe, M & Zimmer, K (1939). Der Schwirrflug des Kolubri in Zeitlupenfilm. J. Orn., 87:136–155.

Stonehouse, Bernard (1967). The general biology and thermal balances of penguins. In: *Advances in Ecological Research* (ed. Cragg, J. B.). London. 131–96.

Stonehouse, B (ed.) (1975). *The Biology of Penguins*. London–Basingstoke.

Storer, Douglas (1963). *Amazing but true animals*. Greenwich, Conn.

Stracey, P D (1941). The size of Indian elephants. J. Bomb. Nat. His. Soc., 46(4):717–718.

Stracey, P D (1963). *Elephant Gold*. London.

Stresemann, E & Zimmer, K (1932). Ueber die Frequenz des Flugelschlages beim Schwirrflug der Kolibris. Orn. Monatsb., Jarrg. 40(2):129–33.

Stresemann, Erwin (1934). Aves. In: W. Kukenthal & T. Krumbach. Handbuch der Zoologie. Berlin, 7(2).

Summers-Smith, D (1980). House sparrow down coal mines. British Birds. 73(8):325–327.

Sutherland, Struan K (1974). Venomous Australian creatures: the action of their toxins and the care of the envenomated patient. Anaesthesia and Intensive care, 2(4).

Sutherland, S K *et al* (1978). Australia's potentially most venomous snake: *Parademansia microlepidotus*. Med. J. Aust. 1:288–289.

Swaroop, S & Grab, B (1954). Snakebite mortality in the world. Bull. World Health Org., League of Nations, 10(1):35–76.

Swayne, R A (1908). *The Victoria History of the County of Hereford*. London.

Sysoev, V (1960). *Hunting in the Far Eastern Taiga*. Khabarovsk.

Sylva de, Donald P (1975). Attacks by Bluefish (*Pomatomus saltatrix*) on humans in South Florida. Copeia, 1:196–198.

Szuman, J G (1926). Compt. Red. Soc. Biol., 95:1314–1315.

Talbot, Lee M (1960). *A look at a threatened species. A Report on some animals of the Middle East and Southern Asia which are threatened with extinction.* London. Fauna Preservation Society.

Tamiya, N & Puffer, H (1974). Toxicon 12:85–87.

Tao, L (1930). Notes on the ecology and the physiology of *Caudina chilensis* (Muller) in Mutsu Bay. Proc. 4th Pacific Sci. Cong., 3:7–11.

Tarrant, W P (1883). Fishing and catching ducks. Ornith. and Ool., 8:3.

Tate, G H (1947). *Mammals of Eastern Asia.* New York.

Taylor, Leighton R (1977). Megamouth. Oceans, pp. 46–47. Nov.

Taylor, M L (1956). *The Tiger's Claw.* London.

Terres, John (1969). *Flashing Wings.* London.

Thiele, J (1921). Die Cephalopoden der Deutsch Sudpolar-Expedition 1901–1903. Dt. Sudpol. Exped. 16(8):433–465.

Thomas, Gareth (1978). Roseate Future? Birds (RSPB) Summer 1978.

Thomas, Jeremy (1980). Why the large blue became extinct in Britain? Oryx (April).

Thomas, Richard (1965). A new gecko from the Virgin Islands. Quart. J. Florida Acad. Sci.

Thomas, R (1965). The genus *Leptotyphlops* in the West Indies with description of a new species from Hispaniola (*Serpentes, Leptotyphlopidae*). Brevoria (Mus. of Comp. Zoology, Cambridge, Mass). 222:1–12.

Thompson, M C (1961). The flight speed of a Red-breasted merganser. Condor, 63:265.

Thompson, T E & Bennett, I (1969). *Physalia nematocysts* utilized by mollusks for defence. Science, 166:1532.

Thorp, Raymond W & Woodson, Weldon D (1945). *Black Widow – America's Most Poisonous Spider.* The University of North Carolina Press, Chapel Hill.

Tickell, W L N (1968). The biology of the great albatrosses, *Diomedea exulans* and *Diomedea epomophora*, in *Antarctic bird studies.* (ed. Oliver Austin), pp. 1–54. Baltimore.

Tillyard, R J (1917). *The biology of dragonflies.* Cambridge.

Timbs, John (1868). *Strange stories of the animal world.* London.

Tomilin, A G (1967). *Mammals of the USSR and adjacent countries* Vol. 9: *Cetacea.* (Israel Program for Scientific Translations). Jerusalem.

Townsend, C H (1909). West Indian seal at the aquarium. Science (Lancaster). 30(763):212.

Townsend, C H (1923). The West Indian Seal. J. Mammal., 4:55.

Travis, William (1961). *Shark for Sale.* London.

Trinca, G F (1963). Med. J. Australia 1:275–280.

Troughton, E (1965). *The furred animals of Australia.* Sydney–London.

Tuck & Squires (1955). Guillemot trapped in fishing gear set at 40 fathoms off Newfoundland. J. Fish. Res. Bd. Can., 12:781–792.

Tuck, Gerald & Heinzel, Hermann (1978). *A field guide to the Seabirds of Britain and the World.* London.

Tucker, Vance A (1977). Scaling and Avian Flight. In: *Scale effects in animal locomotion* (ed. Pedley, T. J.). London–New York–San Francisco.

Turekian, K *et al* (1975). Proc. Nat. Acad. Sci., 72:28–29.

Tyne, Josselyn van & Berger, A J (1971). *Fundamentals of ornithology.* New York.

Van Musschenbroek, S C (1877). Cachelot-Visscherij in den Nederlandsch Indischen Archipel. Tijdschr. Bev. Nijverheit, vol. 18.

Velain, C (1877). Remarques generales au sujet de la faune des iles St. Paul et Amsterdam, suivies d'une description de la faune malacologique des deux iles. Archs. Zool. exp. gen. 6:1–44.

Vellard, J (1936). *La venin des Araignees.* Paris.

Verany, J B (1851). *Mollusques Mediterraneens. 1. Cephalopodes.* Geneva.

Verrill, A E (1879–81). The cephalopods of the north-eastern coast of America. Trans. Conn. Acad. Arts. Sci. 5:177–446.

Verrill, A E (1895). On some birds and eggs collected . . . at Gough Island, Kerguelen 1sland and the Island of South Georgia. Trans. Conn. Acad. Arts. Sci. 9:430–478.

Verrill, A E (1897a). A gigantic cephalopod on the Florida coast. Am. J. Sci., 4:3, 79, 162–3 and 355–6.

Verrill, A E (1897b). The Florida monster. Science, 5:393 & 476. New York.

Verrill, A H (1929). *Thirty years in the jungle.* New York.

Vesey-Fitzgerald, Brian (1967). *Enquire within about animals.* London.

Vignal, L (1919). Observations sur les Rumina decollata. Bull. Soc. Zool. Fr., 44:115.

Vignal, L (1923). De la duree de la vie chez l'*Helix spiraplana Olivi.* J. Conchyl. 67:262.

Vladykov, V D & McKenzie (1935). The marine fishes of Nova Scotia. Proc. Nova Scotian Inst. Sci., 19(1):17–113.

Wagner, H O (1945). Notes on the Life History of the Mexican Violet-ear. Wilson Bull., 57:165–187.

Walker, Ernest P *et al* (1968). *Mammals of the world.* 3 vols. 2nd ed. Baltimore.

Wallace, Alfred R (1853). *Travels on the Amazon.* London.

Wallace, F W (1923). The Red Snapper Fishery in the Gulf of Mexico. Fishing Gaz. Ann. Rev., New York.

Walters, V & Fierstine, T (1964). Swimming speeds of Yellowfin Tuna and Wahoo. Nature, Lond. 202:209–9.

Wanless, F R (1974). On the occurrence of the scorpion *Euscorpius flavicaudis (De Geer)* at Sheerness Port, Isle of Sheppey, Kent. Bull. Br. arachnol. Soc., 4(2):74–6.

Ward, Rowland (1907). *Records of Big Game (Africa and Asia).* London.
  (1910). *Records of Big Game (Africa and Asia).* London.
  (1928). *Records of Big Game (Africa and Asia).* London.

Ward, R (1962). *Records of Big Game (Africa).* London.
  (1969). *Records of Big Game (Africa).* London.
  (1971). *Records of Big Game (Africa).* London.
  (1975). *Records of Big Game (Africa).* London.

Wardle, C S (1975). Limit of fish swimming speed. Nature, Lond. 255:725–727.

Warner, G F (1977). *The Biology of Crabs.* London.

Warner, S H (1957). Etnografiska museet Goteborg, Arstryck 1955–1956, p. 73.

Watts, C H S & Aslin, H J (1981). *The Rodents of Australia.* London.

Wesse, Dall de (1898). Recreation Mag. Feb. 1898., p. 151.

Wetmore, A (1931). *Warm-blooded vertebrates.* Smithsonian Scientific Series, Vol. 9, Smithsonian Institution Series, New York.

Wetmore, A (1936). The number of contour feathers in Passeriform and related birds. Auk, 53:159–169.

Wheeler, Alwynne (1969). *The fishes of the British Isles and North-West Europe.* London.

Wheeler, Alwynne. (1978). *Key to the Fishes of Northern Europe.* London.

Whitehead, G Kenneth (1964). *The Deer of Great Britain and Ireland.* London.

Whitehead, G K (1972). *Deer of the World.* London.

Whitley, Gilbert P (1940). *The Fishes of Australia.* Pt. I. The sharks, rays, devil-fish and other primitive fishes of Australia and New Zealand. Sydney.

Whitlock, F L (1931). Further notes on ocean derelicts. Emu, 30:263–267.

Whymper, Edward (1892). *Travels amongst the Great Andes of the Equator.* 2 vols. London.

Wieland, G R (1909). Revision of the Protostegidae. Amer. Journ. Sci., 27:101–130.

Williams, C B (1958). *Insect migration.* London.

Williams, W (1952). A giant starfish. Nat. Hist. (N.Y.). 61:397–398.

Willoughby, David P (1950). The gorilla – largest living primate. Sci. Monthly, pp. 48–57. April.

Willoughby, D P (1978). *All about Gorillas.* New Jersey.

Wilson, D P (1949). Notes from the Plymouth aquarium. J. Mar. Biol. Ass. U.K. 28:345.

Wilson, E A (1907). Aves. Brit. Nat. Antarct. Exped. 1901–1904. 2, Zool. pt. 2:1–121.

Wing, Leonard W (1956). *Natural history of birds, a guide to ornithology.* New York.

Wood, F G & Gennaro, J F (1971). An octopus trilogy. Nat. Hist. New York, March, pp. 14–23, 24, 84–97.

Wood, Gerald L (1972). *The Guinness Book of Animal Facts and Feats.* (1976) 2nd edit.

Wood, Roger Conant (1976). *Stupendemys geographicus,* the world's largest turtle. Breviora. Mus. Comp. Zool., 436:1–31.

Woodson, Jack (1911). My Arctic Holiday. Wide World Mag., vol. xxvii (April–Sept.), pp. 426–435.

Wright, Allen (1970). *Valley of the Ironwoods.* Cape Town.

Wright, E P (1870). Six months in the Seychelles. Specibegia Zoologica. pp. 64–5. Dublin.

Wright, William H (1909). *The Grizzly bear.* New York.

Wrogemann, Nan (1975). *Cheetah under the Sun.* Johannesburg.

Yablokov, A V (1958). O stroenii zubnoi i tipakh zubov u kitoobraznykh (Dentition and Types of Teeth in Whales). Byulleten MO1P. Otdel biologicheskii, No. 2.

Yalden, B W & Morris, P A (1975). *The lives of bats.* London–Vancouver.

Yerkes, Robert M (1927). The mind of a gorilla. Genetic Psychol. Monog. 2:1–193, 375–551.

Zahl, Paul A (1959). Giant Insects of the Amazon. Nat. Geogr. Mag. (May). Washington, D.C.

Zahl, P A (1967). The Giant Goliath Frog. Nat. Geogr. Mag. (July). Washington, D.C.

Zara, John L (1972). Breeding and husbandry of the capybara at Evansville Zoo, Indiana. Int. Zoo Year Book. 13:137.

Zemsky, V A & Boronin, V A (1964). Norsky Hvalfangsttid., 53 Arg. (11), pp. 306–11.

Zenkevich, L A *et al* (1955). Issledovaniya donnoi fauny Kurilo-Kamchatskoi vpadiny. (Investigations on the Bottom Fauna of the Kuril-Kamchatka Trench). Trudy Institute Okeanografi Akademii Nauk, vol. 12.

Zervos, S G (1934). La maladie des pecherus d'eponges nus. Paris Med., 93:89.

Index